DICTIONARY OF 1,000 BEST FILMS

DICTIONARY
OF
1,000 BEST FILMS

R. A. E. PICKARD

**Illustrated with photographs
from the archives**

ASSOCIATION PRESS / NEW YORK

DICTIONARY OF 1,000 BEST FILMS

Copyright © 1971 by Association Press
291 Broadway, New York, N. Y. 10007

Grateful acknowledgment is made to the following individuals and organizations: British Lion; Charlton Heston; Contemporary Films/McGraw-Hill; Donald L. Velde Co.; Embassy Pictures Corporation (Donald L. Velde Co.); French Film Office; Janus Films (Donald L. Velde Co.); Katharine Hepburn; London Films; Museum of Modern Art Film Stills Archive; Rank Overseas Film Distributors, Ltd.; Rizzoli Film Distributors, Inc. (Donald L. Velde Co.); Twentieth Century-Fox Film Corporation; United Artists Corporation; Universal Pictures; Warner-Pathé Film Corporation.

International Standard Book Number: 0-8096-1805-2
Library of Congress Catalog Card Number: 70-129433

Printed in the United States of America

INTRODUCTION

Although most dictionaries are self-explanatory and need little in the way of introduction, there are certain aspects of this book that I would like to touch upon.

First, this book, as the title suggests, is meant to be a guide to a thousand of the most famous films produced since 1903, the year of release of *The Great Train Robbery*. Although the selection is obviously a personal one I have tried to include as many of the generally accepted masterpieces as possible, hence the frequent appearance of such names as Eisenstein, Griffith, Pudovkin, Renoir, Dreyer, Bergman and Fellini. All the films are listed in alphabetical order for ease of reference. The brief story synopses and highlights are accompanied by comprehensive production credits, i.e., producer, director, screenwriter and story source, cameraman, composer, art director, editor and leading players. These credits are a most important part of the dictionary, for although many of today's film books are admirable in their critical appraisals few, if any, have accompanied these criticisms with detailed credits. Therefore this particular volume will fill a long-standing need.

Reference is also made to many of the most popular entertainment films such as *The Greatest Show on Earth, The Adventures of Robin Hood, The Magnificent Seven, The Mark of Zorro, The Sea Hawk* and all of the Astaire-Rogers musicals. Several excellent minor films (mostly of American origin and made during the Forties) are also included—among them *I Wake Up Screaming, The Lodger, Sunday Dinner for a Soldier, The Big Clock, Mr. Blandings Builds His Dream House, The Moon and Sixpence, Kiss of Death, Kitty, The Boy With Green Hair,* and *The Actress.*

Although the book deals predominantly with American films it is genuinely international in its scope and covers films from such countries as Britain, France, Italy, Germany, Sweden, Spain, India and Denmark.

5

Films, like so many other things in life, are all a matter of taste, but the selection in this book will give the reader a comprehensive view of the great films of our time and also present, indirectly, a wider picture of the development of the cinematic art over the past seventy years.

My own early recollections of the big screen are of Bambi and Thumper in Disney's magical forest, Jon Hall swashbuckling with the Forty Thieves, and Ray Milland and John Wayne battling it out with the giant squid in DeMille's *Reap the Wild Wind*. Since those early years I have seen more movies than I can count and bought as many film books as I could possibly afford.

There is, however, one space on my bookshelf that has yet to be filled and it is this space that I have tried to fill with this *Dictionary of 1,000 Best Films*. My sincere hope is that it will fill a similar space on your bookshelf also.

A BOUT DE SOUFFLE   France (1959)

Jean-Luc Godard's first movie, a spontaneous account of the last hours of a lonely Bogart-styled criminal (Jean Paul Belmondo) and of his brief relationship with an equally lonely American girl (Jean Seberg) who eventually destroys him. An unremarkable story and, as seen in retrospect, an unremarkable film, but of immense importance in marking the emergence of a considerable new film talent and also the beginning of the French New Wave. The most rewarding things about the film are its improvised style (it was shot on location without a script and with off-the-cuff dialogue), its over-all technical dexterity, and the honesty with which it observes human relationships.

S.N.C. (GEORGES DE BEAUREGARD)

Direction, screenplay & dialogue   *Photography*—Raoul Coutard
  (*from idea by François Truf-*   *Music*—Martial Solal
  faut)—Jean-Luc Godard   *Editing*—Cécile Decugis

PLAYERS: Jean-Paul Belmondo, Jean Seberg, Daniel Boulanger, Jean-Pierre Melville, Liliane David, Henri-Jacques Huet, Van Doude, Claude Mansard

A NOUS LA LIBERTE   France (1931)

After Chaplin's *Modern Times* the most famous satire on factory life, centering on the activities of a couple of ex-prisoners—one of whom, an ambitious crook, becomes the boss of a large factory while the other, a sentimental old tramp, becomes a worker there. Eventually both discover that happiness and peace of mind cannot be bought with money and revert to their former life as vagabonds. One of the best of René Clair's early films; a musical comedy that is full of wit and expert slapstick and which, like Clair's other early sound films, combines images with sound to great effect.

FILMS SONORES TOBIS

Direction, screenplay & dialogue   *Art direction*—Lazare Meerson
  —René Clair   *Music*—Georges Auric
Photography—Georges Perinal   *Sound editing*—René Le Henaff

PLAYERS: Raymond Cordy, Henri Marchand, Rolla France, Germaine Aussey, Paul Olivier, Jacques Shelly, André Michaut, Alexandre d'Arcy

A PROPOS DE NICE   France (1930)

Twenty-minute documentary that contrasts the glittering and wealthy façade of France's famous Riviera resort with the squalor of its back streets. Filmed between 1927 and 1930 while Vigo was living in Nice and photographed by Boris Kaufman, who later worked on Vigo's only two feature films, *Zéro de Conduite* and *L'Atalante.*

Screenplay & direction—   Photography—Boris Kaufman
  Jean Vigo   Assistant—Gyula Zilzer
Editing—Jean Vigo

ABE LINCOLN IN ILLINOIS   U.S.A. (1940)
Raymond Massey's most accomplished screen performance and one of the most sincere and authentic biographical pictures of the period. Based on Robert E. Sherwood's Pulitzer prize-winning stage play and produced at the RKO studio, an unusual event because most of the biographical pictures at this time were made at Warner Bros. Mary Howard appears as Ann Rutledge and Ruth Gordon as Lincoln's wife. Excellent period atmosphere.

RKO RADIO

Production—Max Gordon   Art direction—Van Nest Polglase
Direction—John Cromwell   Photography—
Screenplay—Robert E. Sherwood   James Wong Howe
Adaptation—Grover Jones   Music—Roy Webb
                        Editing—George Hively

PLAYERS: Raymond Massey, Ruth Gordon, Mary Howard, Gene Lockhart, Harvey Stephens, Elizabeth Risdon, Charles Middleton, Dorothy Tree

ACCIDENT   Gt. Britain (1967)
Bitingly funny study of the underlying emotional tensions brought to the surface when a young Austrian student (Jacqueline Sassard) disrupts the lives of a small group of people living in a middle-aged academic community. A brilliantly directed and written (Pinter) film that observes the complexities of human relationships with an irony and truth that is rare in the film medium. Stanley Baker and Dirk Bogarde (two of Losey's favorite actors but appearing together for the first time in a Losey film) play the Oxford dons who become emotionally involved with the student, Vivien Merchant appears as Bogarde's wife, Delphine Seyrig as his ex-lover, and Michael York as a young student whose death in a car accident begins and ends the film.

Production—Joseph Losey &
  Norman Priggen
Direction—Joseph Losey
Screenplay (*based on novel by*
  Nicholas Mosley)—
  Harold Pinter

Photography (*Eastmancolor*)—
  Gerry Fisher
Art direction—Carmen Dillon
Music—John Dankworth
Editing—Reginald Beck

PLAYERS: Dirk Bogarde, Stanley Baker, Jacqueline Sassard, Michael York, Vivien Merchant, Delphine Seyrig, Alexander Knox, Ann Firbank

ACE IN THE HOLE (Also titled *The Big Carnival*)   U.S.A. (1951)
Billy Wilder's bleakest work, a cynical story of a down-and-out newspaper reporter who discovers a man trapped in a remote desert cave and then exploits the situation by delaying rescue operations to keep the story in the national headlines. The most effective indictment of gutter journalism ever put on screen and memorable for its biting screenplay (an original that closely parallels the Floyd Collins case of the 1920's), Wilder's shrewd direction, and the New Mexico photography. The film was the first made by Wilder after his break with producer and co-writer Charles Brackett.

PARAMOUNT

Production & direction—
  Billy Wilder
Screenplay—Billy Wilder, Lesser
  Samuels, Walter Newman
Photography—Charles Lang

Art direction—Hal Pereira, Earl
  Hedrick
Music—Hugo Friedhofer
Editing—Doane Harrison, Arthur
  Schmidt

PLAYERS: Kirk Douglas, Jan Sterling, Bob Arthur, Porter Hall, Frank Cady, Richard Benedict, Ray Teal, Lewis Martin

ACT OF VIOLENCE   U.S.A. (1949)
Little-known Fred Zinnemann suspense movie about an American POW (Van Heflin) who betrays his fellow prisoners to the Germans and is then pursued in peacetime by a vengeful ex-comrade (Robert Ryan). A taut, well-observed, skillfully directed thriller of the kind rarely made these days. Mary Astor appears as an aging small-town floozie.

METRO–GOLDWYN–MAYER

Production—William H. Wright
Direction—Fred Zinnemann

Screenplay (*from story by Collier*
  Young)—Robert L. Richards

9

Photography—Robert Surtees   *Music*—Bronislau Kaper
Art direction—Cedric Gibbons &   *Editing*—Conrad A. Nervig
  Hans Peters
PLAYERS: Van Heflin, Robert Ryan, Janet Leigh, Mary Astor, Phyllis
Thaxter

ACTRESS, THE   U.S.A. (1953)
Tender account of the lives and troubles of a poor hard-working family
living in a small town near Boston in the early 1900's. Spencer Tracy
plays a retired longshoreman, Teresa Wright plays his wife, and Jean
Simmons appears as their 17-year-old daughter who astonishes them
with her announcement that she intends to go on the stage. A minor
work but ranking with Cukor's best and perfectly capturing the charm
and leisure of life in a now forgotten age. Scripted by Ruth Gordon
from her own autobiographical stage play *Years Ago*.

METRO–GOLDWYN–MAYER

Production—   *Photography*—Harold Rosson
  Lawrence Weingarten   *Art direction*—Cedric Gibbons &
Direction—George Cukor   Arthur Lonergan
Assistant director—   *Musical direction*—
  Jack Greenwood   Bronislau Kaper
Screenplay—Ruth Gordon   *Editing*—George Boemler
PLAYERS: Spencer Tracy, Jean Simmons, Teresa Wright, Anthony Perkins,
Ian Wolfe, Kay Williams, Mary Wickes, Norma Jean Nilsson, Dawn
Bender

ADAM'S RIB   U.S.A. (1949)
A lively, witty comedy with Spencer Tracy and Katharine Hepburn as
pair of married lawyers who carry their marriage differences into the
courtroom where they appear on opposite sides in an attempted murder
case. Beautifully played by both the principals—their sixth film together
—and by Judy Holliday (a gem of a performance as a dumb wife),
Tom Ewell and Jean Hagen in supporting roles. Expertly directed by
George Cukor.

METRO–GOLDWYN–MAYER

Production—   *Photography*—George J. Folsey
  Lawrence Weingarten   *Art direction*—Cedric Gibbons,
Direction—George Cukor   William Ferrari
Screenplay & original story—   *Music*—Miklos Rozsa
  Garson Kanin, Ruth Gordon   *Editing*—George Boemler

10

PLAYERS: Spencer Tracy, Katharine Hepburn, Judy Holliday, Tom Ewell, David Wayne, Jean Hagen, Hope Emerson, Eve March, Clarence Kolb, Emerson Treacy

ADVENTURER, THE   U.S.A. (1917)
Charlie Chaplin as an escaped convict on the run from the police. His last film for Mutual and a return to the more basic form of slapstick comedy that made him famous. Best scenes: Charlie being chased by the police around cliff paths and across beaches, emerging from the sand and looking straight into the barrel of a guard's rifle, and dropping ice cream down a woman's bare back.

A MUTUAL COMEDY

Direction—Charles Chaplin   Photography—R. H. Totheroh,
Screenplay—Charles Chaplin   W. C. Foster
PLAYERS: Charlie Chaplin, Albert Austin, Monta Bell, Henry Bergman, Eric Campbell, Frank J. Coleman, Toraichi Kono, Edna Purviance

ADVENTURES OF A YOUNG MAN   U.S.A. (1962)
Another attempt by Hollywood to do justice to the works of Ernest Hemingway. The film is far from being a success, but in the early scenes around the Michigan lakes and through the minor performances of Paul Newman as a punch-drunk ex-prize fighter and Dan Dailey as a dope-addicted publicity agent, traces of the real Hemingway occasionally show through. The film also serves as a notable example of Lee Garmes' skill as a color cameraman.

TWENTIETH CENTURY–FOX

Production—Jerry Wald   Photography (Deluxecolor/
Direction—Martin Ritt   CinemaScope)—Lee Garmes
Screenplay (based on Ernest   Art direction—Jack Martin Smith
   Hemingway's "Nick Adams"   & Paul Groesse
   stories)—A. E. Hotchner   Music—Franz Waxman
                                    Editing—Hugh S. Fowler
PLAYERS: Diane Baker, Richard Beymer, Corinne Calvet, Fred Clark, Dan Dailey, Paul Newman, James Dunn, Juano Hernandez, Arthur Kennedy, Ricardo Montalban, Susan Strasberg, Jessica Tandy

ADVENTURES OF ICHABOD AND MR. TOAD, THE
                                                   U.S.A. (1949)
Perhaps the least known of all Disney's cartoons but marking something of a return to form after several years of the inferior work repre-

sented by *Make Mine Music, Melody Time, Fun and Fancy Free*. The film is made up of two stories, the first (35 minutes) dealing with the adventures of the eccentric Mr. Toad and his river friends Rat, Mole, and the Scottish MacBadger (all derived from Kenneth Grahame's *The Wind in the Willows*), and the second (33 minutes) with the misadventures and chase by the headless horseman of schoolteacher Ichabod Crane, the leading character of Washington Irving's "The Legend of Sleepy Hollow." Basil Rathbone narrates the Mr. Toad episode and Bing Crosby relates and sings some of the songs from *Ichabod*.

WALT DISNEY PRODUCTIONS/RKO RADIO

Production—Walt Disney
Production supervisor—
  Ben Sharpsteen
Direction—Jack Kinney, Clyde
  Geronimi, James Algar
Story—Erdman Penner, Ted
  Sears, Winston Hibler, Homer
  Brightman, Joe Rinaldi, Harry
  Reeves

Musical direction—
  Oliver Wallace
Vocal arrangements—Ken Darby
Orchestration—Joseph Dubin
Ichabod *songs*—Don Raye, Gene
  De Paul
Editor—John O. Young

ADVENTURES OF ROBIN HOOD, THE   U.S.A. (1938)

Vastly enjoyable and easily the best of the many versions of the Robin Hood story, handsomely photographed in Technicolor by Warner's two leading cameramen of the 1930's and climaxed by one of the most exciting sword duels ever put on the screen. Errol Flynn (Robin Hood), Alan Hale (Little John) and Eugene Pallette (Friar Tuck) lead the good guys and Basil Rathbone (Guy of Gisbourne) and Claude Rains (Prince John) the bad guys.

WARNER BROS.

Production—Hal B. Wallis
Direction—Michael Curtiz &
  William Keighley
Screenplay—Norman Reilly Raine
  & Seton I. Miller

Photography (*Technicolor*)—
  Sol Polito & Tony Gaudio
Art direction—Carl Jules Weyl
Music—Erich Wolfgang Korngold
Editing—Ralph Dawson

PLAYERS: Errol Flynn, Olivia de Havilland, Basil Rathbone, Claude Rains, Patric Knowles, Eugene Pallette, Alan Hale, Melville Cooper

ADVENTURES OF ROBINSON CRUSOE, THE   Mexico (1952)

Intelligent version of Daniel Defoe's 17th-century novel about a shipwrecked mariner who spends several years on a tropical island with only a cat and an Alsatian dog for company and later with a savage he names Man Friday. The terrible loneliness that reduces a normal sane man to an eccentric recluse is conveyed with supreme skill by Luis Buñuel who shot this somewhat neglected picture in and around the Manzanillo jungle in Mexico. Remade in 1965 as the ingenious science-fiction thriller *Robinson Crusoe on Mars* (see page 370).

ULTRAMAR FILMS (OSCAR DANCIGERS & HENRY F. EHRLICH)

Direction—Luis Buñuel
Screenplay—Luis Buñuel & Philip Roll
Photography (*Pathécolor*)— Alex Phillips

Art direction— Edward Fitzgerald
Music—Anthony Collins
Editing—Carlos Savage & Alberto Valenzuela

PLAYERS: Dan O'Herlihy, Jaime Fernandez, Felipa da Alba, Chel Lopez, Jose Chavez, Emilio Garibay

ADVENTURES OF TOM SAWYER, THE   U.S.A. (1938)

David Selznick's respectful version of Mark Twain's famous classic. A slow, well-directed film which perfectly catches the leisurely atmosphere of Mississippi village life in the mid-1800's. Some notable Technicolor photography by James Wong Howe and some excellent playing by Walter Brennan (Muff Potter), Victor Jory (Injun Joe), and Tommy Kelly and Jackie Moran as the two boy adventurers Tom Sawyer and Huckleberry Finn.

SELZNICK PRODUCTIONS/UNITED ARTISTS

Production—David Selznick
Direction—Norman Taurog
Screenplay—John V. A. Weaver
Photography (*Technicolor*)— James Wong Howe

Cave sequence design— William Cameron Menzies
Music—Franz Waxman
Editing—Hal C. Kern

PLAYERS: Tommy Kelly, Jackie Moran, May Robson, Walter Brennan, Victor Jory, Victor Killian, Nana Bryant, Ann Gillis, Micky Rentschler, Spring Byington

ADVISE AND CONSENT   U.S.A. (1962)

Fascinating exploration into the workings of the U.S. Senate, which is asked by the President to "advise and consent" to the appointment as Secretary of State of a controversial left-wing intellectual (Henry Fonda). The melodrama, which includes blackmail, homosexuality and suicide, often mars the more serious political aspects of the story, although Sam Leavitt's harsh, documentary-style photography of real Washington backgrounds and the performances of a veteran cast help make the film one of Preminger's most satisfactory and absorbing works. A splendid performance by Charles Laughton as a devious Southern senator, and nostalgic support from Walter Pidgeon as the Senate minority leader, Franchot Tone as the sick President, Lew Ayres as the Vice President, and Gene Tierney, in a minor role, as a Washington socialite.

COLUMBIA

Production & direction—
Otto Preminger
*Screenplay (from novel by Allen Drury)—*Wendell Mayes

Photography (Panavision)—
Sam Leavitt
*Art direction—*Lyle Wheeler
*Music—*Jerry Fielding
*Editing—*Louis R. Loeffler

PLAYERS: Franchot Tone, Lew Ayres, Henry Fonda, Walter Pidgeon Charles Laughton, Don Murray, Peter Lawford, Gene Tierney, Burgess Meredith, Eddie Hodges, Paul Ford

AEROGRAD (Known also as *Frontier*)   U.S.S.R. (1935)
Alexander Dovzhenko's account of the construction of an army aviation post in the Soviet Far East. The miracles of Russian achievement under the revolutionary regime were by this time becoming overfamiliar, but Dovzhenko and Eduard Tissé (Eisenstein's celebrated cameraman) so perfectly capture the feeling and beauty of the Siberian landscape that the film is raised to a poetic level far above the political banalities of its theme.

MOSFILM & UKRAINFILM

Direction & screenplay—
Alexander Dovzhenko
*Assistants—*Yulia Solntseva & S. Kevorkov

*Photography—*Eduard Tissé & Mikhail Gindin
*Art direction—*Alexander Utkin & V. Panteleyev
*Music—*Dmitri Kabalevsky

PLAYERS: Semyon Shagaida, Stepan Shkurat, Boris Dobronravov, Sergei Stolyarov

AFRICAN LION, THE   U.S.A. (1955)
Close-up look at some of the animals living on the high plateau country of Africa, an area dominated by the huge mountain of Kilimanjaro. The husband-and-wife camera team spent some three years observing, much

14

The African Queen

of the time with telephoto lenses, the habits of different animals. The film was the third of Disney's "True-Life Adventures" and although marred, like its predecessors *The Living Desert* and *The Vanishing Prairie,* by an over-cute commentary it is still among the most interesting documentaries about African wild life ever made.

WALT DISNEY PRODUCTIONS

Production—Walt Disney
Associate producer—
Ben Sharpsteen
Direction—James Algar
Screenplay—James Algar, Wiston Hibler, Ted Sears, Jack Moffit

Photography—Alfred & Elina Milotte
Narration—Winston Hibler
Music—Paul Smith
Editing—Norman Palmer
Animation effects—
Joshua Meador & Art Riley

AFRICAN QUEEN, THE   Gt. Britain (1951)

John Huston's most surprising film success is due not so much to his direction, although admirable, as to the astonishing performances of his two stars, Humphrey Bogart and Katharine Hepburn, who as Captain Charlie Allnut and missionary Rose Sayer take an old tugboat down an uncharted African river and blow a World War I German gunboat to smithereens. Bogart and Hepburn are on screen alone for some 90 per cent of the film. Bogart was nominated for and received an Academy Award for his portrayal of the dissipated captain. Hepburn was also nominated for the Award for her missionary spinster but lost, rather undeservedly, to Vivien Leigh's Blanche duBois in *A Streetcar Named Desire.*

HORIZON—ROMULUS

Production—S. P. Eagle (Sam Spiegel)
Direction—John Huston
Screenplay (based on novel by C. S. Forester)—James Agee & John Huston

Photography (Technicolor)—Jack Cardiff
Art direction—Wilfred Shingleton
Music—Alan Gray
Editing—Ralph Kemplen

PLAYERS: Humphrey Bogart, Katharine Hepburn, Robert Morley, Peter Bull, Theodore Bikel, Walter Gotell, Gerald Onn, Peter Swanwick, Richard Marner

ALEXANDER NEVSKY   U.S.S.R. (1938)

Impressive reconstruction of the conflict between the Russian peasants, led by Prince Alexander Nevsky, and the invading Teutonic Knights during the war between Russia and Germany in the 13th century. Prokofiev's music and Tissé's camera work are superb, and the climactic battle on the ice of Lake Peipus is among Eisenstein's most spectacular set pieces. Nikolai Cherkasov, later to play the leading role in Kozintsev's *Don Quixote,* appears as Nevsky.

MOSFILM

Direction—Sergei Eisenstein	*Art direction*—Isaac Shpinel,
Screenplay—Pyotr Pavlenko &	N. Soloviov, K. Yeliseyev
Sergei Eisenstein	*Music*—Sergei Prokofiev
Photography—Eduard Tissé	

PLAYERS: Nikolai Cherkasov, Nikolai Okhlopkov, Andrei Abrikosov, Valentina Ivashova, Dmitri Orlov, Vladimir Yershov, Varvara Massalitinova

ALL ABOUT EVE   U.S.A. (1950)

Sophisticated and very witty picture of New York theater life tells of the meteoric rise of an unscrupulous young actress (Anne Baxter) who blackmails and lies her way to the top in her profession, using everyone she comes in contact with to further her career. Beautifully performed by Miss Baxter, although the film belongs completely to Bette Davis, whose performance as an aging, vain, neurotic and successful New York stage actress (closely modeled on the late Tallulah Bankhead) is perhaps the finest of her career. The film won six Academy Awards, including best picture, best supporting actor—George Sanders as cynical theater columnist—and best writing and direction, both the latter awards going to Mankiewicz who, a year earlier, had also won writing and direction Oscars for his work on *A Letter to Three Wives.*

TWENTIETH CENTURY—FOX

Production—Darryl F. Zanuck	*Art direction*—Lyle Wheeler &
Direction & screenplay (based on	George W. Davis
The Wisdom of Eve *by Mary*	*Music*—Alfred Newman
Orr*)*—Joseph L. Mankiewicz	*Editing*—Barbara McLean
Photography—Milton Krasner	

PLAYERS: Bette Davis, Anne Baxter, George Sanders, Celeste Holm, Gary Merrill, Hugh Marlowe, Thelma Ritter, Marilyn Monroe

ALL QUIET ON THE WESTERN FRONT   U.S.A. (1930)

This bitter cry against war shows the experiences of a group of German youths who volunteer to serve the fatherland during the Great War but are gradually disillusioned by the endless death and misery surround-

17

ing them in the trenches. By the film's close (a famous one in which Lew Ayres is shot by a sniper while reaching for a butterfly) all have been killed and replaced by a new set of young volunteers. A great film and still the most compassionate of all antiwar movies. Academy Awards for best film and best direction. Milestone's other great war film, *A Walk in the Sun,* was devoted to the Second World War and released in 1946.

UNIVERSAL

Production—Carl Laemmle
Direction—Lewis Milestone
Screenplay (based on novel by Erich Maria Remarque)— Dell Andrews, Maxwell Anderson & George Abbott
Dialogue—Maxwell Anderson & George Abbott

Photography—Arthur Edeson
Art direction—Charles D. Hall & W. R. Schmitt
Synchronization & score— David Broekman
Editing—Edgar Adams & Milton Carruth

PLAYERS: Lew Ayres, Louis Wolheim, John Wray, Owen Davis Jr., Raymond Griffith, Slim Summerville, Ben Alexander, Scott Kolk

ALL THAT MONEY CAN BUY   U.S.A. (1941)

A brilliant adaptation of Stephen Vincent Benét's fantasy "The Devil and Daniel Webster" that belongs to the latter years of RKO's greatest period when Welles, Wyler, Dieterle and others were making some of the most interesting movies in Hollywood. Set in New Hampshire in the 1840's the film closely parallels the Faust legend: a young farmer signs a seven-year contract with the devil in exchange for gold. Walter Huston's brilliant performance as the mischievous Mr. Scratch (the devil) is equaled by Edward Arnold's fine portrayal of Daniel Webster, the famous American advocate who, in a memorably acted and directed climax, fights to save the young farmer's soul before a jury of the damned. A now classic movie, handsomely photographed and beautifully scored, and one that stands the test of time almost as well as the masterly *Citizen Kane* made in the same year.

RKO RADIO

Production & direction— William Dieterle
Screenplay—Dan Totheroh, Stephen Benét

Photography—Joseph August
Art direction—Van Nest Polglase
Music—Bernard Herrmann
Editing—Robert Wise

PLAYERS: Edward Arnold, Walter Huston, James Craig, Jane Darwell, Simone Simon, Gene Lockhart, John Qualen, H. B. Warner

18

ALL THE KING'S MEN U.S.A. (1949)
Broderick Crawford in the best role of his career as the idealistic Willie
Stark, a backwater hick politician who rises swiftly to become governor
of his Midwestern state, but is then corrupted by power and destroyed
by the hand of an assassin. Adapted from Robert Penn Warren's Pulitzer
Prize-winning novel which was closely modeled on the career of
Louisiana's Huey "Kingfish" Long, the film was shot largely on location
and won three Academy Awards, including an Oscar for best picture of
the year. Only in Preston Sturges' satirical *The Great McGinty* have
U.S. politics been more honestly examined.

COLUMBIA

Production, direction & screen-   *Art direction*—Sturges Carne
   play—Robert Rossen   *Music*—Louis Gruenberg
Photography—Burnett Guffey   *Editing*—Al Clark
PLAYERS: Broderick Crawford, John Ireland, John Derek, Joanne Dru,
Mercedes McCambridge, Anne Seymour

ALPHAVILLE France (1965)
Jean-Luc Godard looks into the future and sends secret agent Lemmy
Caution into another galaxy where he sets about destroying a com-
puterized antihuman state where love is forbidden and everything con-
trolled by the logic of a giant computer called Alpha 60. A fascinating
marriage of pulp fiction and advanced film technique carried along by
its sheer exuberance and the considerable ingenuity of its director who
uses, with remarkable success, the city of Paris—neon streets, exteriors
and interiors of shiny office blocks, etc.—for his township of the future.

CHAUMIANE (A. MICHELIN)

Direction, screenplay & dialogue   *Music*—Paul Misraki
   —Jean-Luc Godard   *Editing*—Agnès Guillemot
Photography—Raoul Coutard
PLAYERS: Eddie Constantine, Anna Karina, Howard Vernon, Akim
Tamiroff, Laszlo Szabo

AMERICAN IN PARIS, AN U.S.A. (1951)
Oscar-winning musical with Gene Kelly as American painter and
Leslie Caron as young Parisienne singing and dancing their way through
a superb Gershwin score. High spots are: "Our Love Is Here to Stay,"
a Kelly/Caron duet sung on the banks of the Seine; "I Got Rhythm,"
danced by Kelly with some French street urchins, and a 17-minute
ballet designed in different scenes in the styles of Dufy, Renoir, Utrillo,

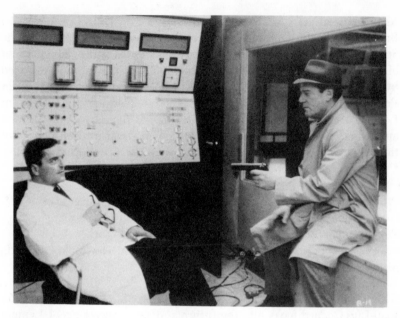

Alphaville

Van Gogh, etc. The first musical since *The Great Ziegfeld* (1936) to win the Academy Award for best picture. Oscars also for best story and screenplay, color photography, art direction, costume design, and music scoring.

METRO–GOLDWYN–MAYER

Production–Arthur Freed
Direction–Vincente Minnelli
Screenplay–Alan Jay Lerner
Photography (*Technicolor*)–
  Alfred Gilks
Photography of ballet–
  John Alton

Art direction–Cedric Gibbons &
  Preston Ames
Music–George Gershwin
Lyrics–Ira Gershwin
Choreography–Gene Kelly
Musical direction–Johnny Green
  & Saul Chaplin
Editing–Adrienne Fazan

PLAYERS: Gene Kelly, Leslie Caron, Oscar Levant, Georges Guetary, Nina Foch

ANATOMY OF A MURDER U.S.A. (1959)

Small-town lawyer (James Stewart) gets his big chance when he is assigned to defend a U.S. Army lieutenant (Ben Gazzara) from a murder charge. The longest (160 minutes) and best of all trial movies, based on the book by Robert Traver (itself based on a real-life incident) and shot on location in the upper peninsula of Michigan. Among the others in the courtroom are: George C. Scott, memorable as the prosecuting counsel; Arthur O'Connell, a boozy old lawyer making a comeback; Lee Remick, the lieutenant's sexy wife, and Joseph N. Welch (a genuine Boston attorney) as the judge. The jazz score is by Duke Ellington, who also appears briefly in one scene.

COLUMBIA

Production & direction—   *Production design—*Boris Leven
  Otto Preminger   *Music—*Duke Ellington
*Screenplay—*Wendell Mayes   *Editing—*Louis Loeffler
*Photography—*Sam Leavitt

PLAYERS: James Stewart, Lee Remick, Ben Gazzara, Arthur O'Connell, Kathryn Grant, Eve Arden, Joseph N. Welch, George C. Scott

ANCHORS AWEIGH   U.S.A. (1945)

A 140-minute Metro·musical about two sailors (Gene Kelly and Frank Sinatra) on shore leave who become involved with a small boy who has run away from home to join the Navy. Not in any way a forerunner of the brilliant *On the Town*, but with some pleasing Sinatra numbers, "I Fall in Love Too Easily" and "The Charm of You," and two inventive dance sequences by Kelly—the first with an enchanting little girl to the music of the "Mexican Hat Dance" and the second with Jerry the cartoon mouse. This last exuberant routine was one of the most successful of the early attempts to combine live action with animation.

METRO–GOLDWYN–MAYER

*Production—*Joe Pasternak   *Art direction—*Cedric Gibbons &
*Direction—*George Sidney   Randall Duell
Screenplay (suggested by story by   *Music direction—*Georgie Stoll
  *Natalie Marcin)—*Isobel Lennart   *Dances created by—*Gene Kelly
Photography (Technicolor)—   *Songs—*Jule Styne & Sammy Cahn
  Robert Planck   *Editing—*Adrienne Fazan

PLAYERS: Frank Sinatra, Kathryn Grayson, Gene Kelly, Jose Iturbi, Dean Stockwell, Pamela Britton, Rags Ragland

AND THEN THERE WERE NONE   U.S.A. (1944)

Minor René Clair movie adapted from a creaky Agatha Christie bestseller and set on a lonely island where ten people are murdered, one by one, for crimes they have committed in their past lives. Made in the

21

United States in wartime and enjoyable mainly for the larger-than-life performances of Barry Fitzgerald as a homicidal judge, Walter Huston as an alcoholic doctor, and Roland Young as an English detective. Among the victims are Mischa Auer as an exiled Russian prince and C. Aubrey Smith as a retired general.

POPULAR PICTURES CORPORATION/TWENTIETH CENTURY–FOX

Production & direction–
René Clair
*Screenplay–*Dudley Nichols
*Photography–*Lucien Andriot
*Art direction–*Ernst Fegte
*Musical direction–*Charles Previn
*Editing–*Harvey Manger

PLAYERS: Barry Fitzgerald, Walter Huston, Louis Hayward, Roland Young, June Duprez, C. Aubrey Smith, Judith Anderson, Mischa Auer, Queenie Leonard, Richard Haydn

ANGELS WITH DIRTY FACES   U.S.A. (1938)
Brilliant gangster film tracing the careers of former slum kids James Cagney (hoodlum) and Pat O'Brien (priest) as they become tragically embroiled in crime and violence on New York's Lower East Side. Humphrey Bogart appears as Cagney's crooked lawyer and the Dead End Kids (later to become the Bowery Boys) are featured as O'Brien's young parishioners. Although more ambitious American films of the period now look jaded, this one remains almost as good as new–a tribute not only to Curtiz's considerable skill as a director but also to the editing of Owen Marks, one of Warner Bros. most talented editors of the period. Marks did equally distinguished work for Curtiz on *Casablanca* and *The Private Lives of Elizabeth and Essex* and also cut *The Treasure of Sierra Madre* for Huston.

FIRST NATIONAL/WARNER BROS.

Associate producer–
Samuel Bischoff
*Direction–*Michael Curtiz
*Photography–*Sol Polito
*Music–*Max Steiner
Screenplay (based on original
story by Rowland Brown)–
Warren Duff
*Editing–*Owen Marks
*Art direction–*Robert Haas

PLAYERS: James Cagney, Pat O'Brien, Humphrey Bogart, Ann Sheridan, George Bancroft, Billy Halop, Bobby Jordan, Leo Gorcey

ANGRY SILENCE, THE   Gt. Britain (1959)
British drama, set in a Midlands industrial town, about a conscientious worker (Richard Attenborough) who is victimized by his colleagues when he refuses to join in their unofficial strike. A solid, straightfor-

ward, realistic tale with a refreshingly honest script. Bernard Lee as shop steward, Geoffrey Keen as works manager, and Alfred Burke as a professional agitator are excellent in supporting roles.

A BEAVER FILM

Production—Richard Attenborough & Bryan Forbes
Direction—Guy Green
Photography—Arthur Ibbetson
Art direction—Ray Sim

Screenplay (from original story by Richard Gregson & Michael Craig)—Bryan Forbes
Music—Malcolm Arnold
Editing—Anthony Harvey

PLAYERS: Richard Attenborough, Pier Angeli, Michael Craig, Bernard Lee, Alfred Burke, Penelope Horner, Michael Wynne, Norman Bird

ANIMAL CRACKERS   U.S.A. (1930)

Wisecracking Groucho Marx (as big-game hunter Jeffrey T. Spaulding) together with Harpo, Chico and Zeppo involved in the theft of an oil painting at a Long Island high-society party given by wealthy socialite Mrs. Rittenhouse (Margaret Dumont). Fast, confused, zany, funny; the Marx Brothers' second film and, like their first, *The Cocoanuts,* based on an earlier Broadway stage success. Songs: "Hooray for Captain Spaulding" and "Why Am I So Romantic?"

PARAMOUNT

Direction—Victor Heerman
Screenplay (based on musical play, book by George S. Kaufman & Morrie Ryskind)— Morrie Ryskind

Continuity—Pierre Collins
Photography—George Folsey
Music & lyrics—Bert Kalmar & Harry Ruby

PLAYERS: Groucho, Harpo, Chico and Zeppo Marx, Margaret Dumont, Lillian Roth, Louis Sorin, Hal Thompson, Margaret Irving, Kathryn Reece

ANIMAL FARM   Gt. Britain (1955)

Animated version of George Orwell's political fable about farm animals who rise up against the cruelty of a drunken farmer and then find themselves living under equally terrible conditions when the ruthless pig Napoleon (who helped lead the revolution) appoints himself as supreme dictator. A witty movie, cleverly translating into cartoon terms Orwell's theme that absolute power corrupts absolutely. The first full-length cartoon made in Britain. Produced and directed by the husband and wife team of John Halas and Joy Batchelor and sponsored by American producer Louis de Rochemont.

23

Production & direction—
John Halas & Joy Batchelor
*Story development—*Lothar
Wolff, Borden Mace, Philip
Stapp, John Halas, Joy
Batchelor

Animation direction (Technicolor)
—John Reed
*Narration—*Gordon Heath
*Music—*Matyas Seiber
Voices of animals—
Maurice Denham

ANNA CHRISTIE   U.S.A. (1930)

Ex-prostitute Anna Christie (Greta Garbo) returns home to her drunken
father's river barge and finds happiness with honest young sailor (Charles
Bickford). Competent Clarence Brown version of Eugene O'Neill's
sordid play is enhanced considerably by its realistic New York river
settings and the camera work of William Daniels. Historically important as Garbo's first sound film and publicized at the time with the words
"Garbo Speaks." Excellent supporting cameo from Marie Dressler as
pub-crawling old waterfront hag. This was the eighth time that William
Daniels had worked with Garbo. (He photographed all but five of the
twenty-four movies she made between 1926 and 1941.) Garbo/Daniels
collaborations: *The Torrent, Flesh and the Devil, Love, The Mysterious Lady, A Woman of Affairs, Wild Orchids, The Kiss, Anna Christie,
Romance, Inspiration, Susan Lennox: Her Fall & Rise, Mata Hari,
Grand Hotel, As You Desire Me, Queen Christina, The Painted Veil,
Anna Karenina, Camille, Ninotchka*

METRO–GOLDWYN–MAYER

*Direction—*Clarence Brown
*Adaptation—*Frances Marion
*Photography—*William Daniels

*Art direction—*Cedric Gibbons
*Editing—*Hugh Wynn

PLAYERS: Greta Garbo, Charles Bickford, George F. Marion, Marie
Dressler, James T. Mack, Lee Phelps

ANNIE GET YOUR GUN   U.S.A. (1950)

Film version of the stage hit with Betty Hutton (in the role originally
intended for Judy Garland) as the sharpshooting backwoods girl Annie
Oakley and Howard Keel as the rival sharpshooter she competes with
in Buffalo Bill's Wild West Show. Lively, exuberant and vastly entertaining; energetically played by Betty Hutton who is at her best with
such raucous songs as "Doin' What Comes Naturally" and "You Can't
Get a Man With a Gun." Louis Calhern and Edward Arnold play the
two rival circus owners, Buffalo Bill and Pawnee Bill.

24

Production–Arthur Freed
Direction–George Sidney
Screenplay (from musical play: book by Dorothy Fields & Herbert Fields, and music and lyrics by Irving Berlin)– Sidney Sheldon
Photography (Technicolor)– Charles Rosher

Art direction–Cedric Gibson & Paul Groesse
Music direction– Adolph Deutsch
Music–Irving Berlin
Editing–James E. Newcom
Musical numbers staged by– Robert Alton

PLAYERS: Betty Hutton, Howard Keel, Louis Calhern, Edward Arnold, Keenan Wynn, J. Carrol Naish, Clinton Sundberg

ANTOINE AND ANTOINETTE France (1946)

Disarming little French comedy about a young married couple struggling to exist in the austerity of postwar Paris and of their happiness and disappointment when they find they have won a lottery but lost the ticket. Very lightweight but enjoyable for its observations of life in a Parisian suburb and for Grunenwald's music score. Directed by Jacques Becker who was assistant to Jean Renoir on several films before the war, including *Les Bas-Fonds* and *La Grande Illusion*.

S.N.E. GAUMONT

Direction–Jacques Becker
Screenplay & dialogue–Maurice Griffe, Francoise Giroud & Jacques Becker
Photography–Pierre Montazel

Art direction–Robert Jules Garnier
Music–Jean-Jacques Grunenwald
Editing–Marguerite Renoir

PLAYERS: Roger Pigaut, Claire Mafféi, Noël Roquevert, Pierre Trabaud, Gérard Oury, Annette Poivre, Gaston Modot

APACHE U.S.A. (1954)

Superior Robert Aldrich Western (his first major feature) finds the last Apache warrior (Burt Lancaster) wandering across Arizona with his squaw (Jean Peters) and waging a one-man war against the U.S. Army. Based on historical fact and containing some pungent comments on the treatment of the Apaches by the white man after the surrender of Geronimo, the film is marred ultimately by an off-key happy ending. Shot in 34 days and photographed by Ernest Laszlo who worked regularly with Aldrich during the 1950's, most notably on *Vera Cruz, Kiss Me Deadly* and *The Big Knife*.

HECHT–LANCASTER PRODUCTIONS/UNITED ARTISTS

Production–Harold Hecht
Direction–Robert Aldrich
Screenplay (*from novel* Broncho
  Apache *by Paul I. Wellmann*)
  –James R. Webb

Photography (*Technicolor*)–
  Ernest Laszlo
Production design–
  Nicolai Remisoff
Music–David Raksin
Editing–Alan Crosland

PLAYERS: Burt Lancaster, Jean Peters, John McIntyre, Charles Buchinsky (later Bronson), John Dehner, Paul Guilfoyle, Ian MacDonald, Walter Sande, Morris Ankrum, Monte Blue

APARAJITO   India (1957)

The continuing struggles of the penniless scholar of *Pather Panchali* who, in this film, leaves his village with the surviving members of his family—his wife and son—and starts a new life in the city of Benares. After the death of the father the film concentrates on the relationship between the growing boy and his mother and of the latter's attempts to earn enough money to send her son to the University of Calcutta. Everyday life, this time in the poorer quarters of a bustling city, is once again observed by Ray with great sensitivity, and the film itself is of the same poetic quality as its predecessor. Awarded a Golden Lion at the Venice Film Festival, 1957.

Production & direction–
  Satyajit Ray
Photography–Subrata Mitra
Music–Ravi Shankar

Screenplay (*from novel by*
  Bidhutibhustan Bandapad-
  haya)–Satyajit Ray
Editing–Dulal Dutta

PLAYERS: Pinaki Sen Gupta, Smaran Ghosal, Karuna Banerjee, Kanu Banerjee, Ramani Sen Gupta, Charu Ghosh

APARTMENT, THE   U.S.A. (1960)

A frustrated young office clerk (Jack Lemmon), stuck in a groove in a big New York insurance company, finds that the quickest way to advance his career is to hire out his apartment to executives for conducting their extramarital affairs. The underlying theme of this brilliant movie is basically a sordid one, but the crackling screenplay, which looks with a jaundiced eye at office politics and modern urban morality, makes it one of the most bitterly funny American films of the period. Five Academy Awards: best film, direction, screenplay, art direction, and editing. The film marks the third time that Billy Wilder collaborated with I. A. L. Diamond. Other movies scripted by this pair: *Love in the After-*

noon; Some Like It Hot; One, Two, Three; Irma La Douce; Kiss Me,
Stupid; The Fortune Cookie, and *The Private Life of Sherlock Holmes.*

MIRISCH COMPANY/UNITED ARTISTS

Production & direction—
  Billy Wilder
*Screenplay—*Billy Wilder &
  I. A. L. Diamond

Photography (Panavision)—
  Joseph I aShelle
*Art direction—*Alexander Trauner
*Editing—*Daniel Mandell

PLAYERS: Jack Lemmon, Shirley MacLaine, Fred MacMurray, Ray
Walston, David Lewis, Jack Kruschen, Joan Shawlee, Edie Adams

APPLAUSE   U.S.A. (1929)

Rouben Mamoulian's ambitious first film about an aging burlesque
queen (brilliantly played by Helen Morgan) and her desperate attempts to prevent her daughter from entering the same sordid world
as a striptease artiste. Distinguished mainly by Mamoulian's revolutionary use of sound, the mobility of the camera work, and for the way
in which it realistically evokes the seedy atmosphere of New York's
twice-a-night burlesque theaters. The film was actually shot in New
York and used, for the first time, two separate channels in recording
sound.

PARAMOUNT

*Direction—*Rouben Mamoulian
*Adaptation—*Garrett Fort
*Story—*Beth Brown

*Photography—*George J. Folsey
*Editing—*John Bassler

PLAYERS: Helen Morgan, Joan Peers, Fuller Mellish, Jr., Jack Cameron,
Henry Wadsworth, Dorothy Cumming

ARSENAL   U.S.S.R. (1929)

Dovzhenko's first major film is a tribute to the workers of the Ukraine,
tracing their struggles for liberty from the days of the First World War,
through the February and October Revolutions, to a revolt in a Kiev
munitions factory in 1918. Scripted in a fortnight and shot in six
months, it ranks as the first important work of the Ukrainian cinema.
Photographed by Danylo Demutsky, who later worked for Dovzhenko
on *Earth* and *Ivan.*

VUFKU

Screenplay & direction—
  Alexander Dovzhenko
*Assistants—*Lazar Bodik,
  A. Kapler
*Photography—*Danylo Demutsky

*Art direction—*Isaac Shpinel,
  Vladimir Muller
Music (for performance)—
  Igor Belza

27

PLAYERS: Semyon Svashenko, Mikola Nademsky, Ambrose Buchma, Pyotr Masokha

ARSENIC AND OLD LACE   U.S.A. (1944)

Frank Capra's version of Joseph Kesselring's Broadway comedy about an amiable young drama critic (Cary Grant) whose honeymoon is suddenly complicated when he discovers that his timid little aunts (Josephine Hull and Jean Adair) are a couple of poisoners and that there are twelve bodies buried in the basement. Also on the scene are Raymond Massey and Peter Lorre as a couple of weird criminals and John Alexander as a crazy cousin who thinks he's Teddy Roosevelt.

WARNER BROS.

Production & direction—   Photography—Sol Polito
  Frank Capra   Art direction—Max Parker
Screenplay—Julius J. & Philip G.   Music—Max Steiner
  Epstein   Editing—Daniel Mandell

PLAYERS: Cary Grant, Priscilla Lane, Raymond Massey, Peter Lorre, Jack Carson, Josephine Hull, Jean Adair, Edward Everett Horton, James Gleason

ASHES AND DIAMONDS   Poland (1958)

Zbigniew Cybulski (dressed in tight jeans and wearing dark glasses to represent contemporary Polish youth) and Adam Pawlikowski as two members of the national underground movement with orders to assassinate a Russian-trained provincial secretary, symbol of the postwar Communist regime in Poland. The most complex and brilliantly observed of Wajda's remarkable wartime trilogy (see also *A Generation* and *Kanal*), capturing all the bitterness and disillusionment of the Polish people during the political struggles that followed the liberation in 1945.

KADR GROUP/FILM POLSKI

Direction—Andrzej Wajda   Art direction—Roman Mann
Screenplay (from novel by   Music—Filip Nowak & the
  Andrzejewski)—Jerzy   Wroclaw Rhythm Quartet
  Andrzejewski & Andrzej Wajda   Editing—Halina Nawrocka
Photography—Jerzy Wojcik

PLAYERS: Zbigniew Cybulski, Ewa Krzyzewska, Waclaw Zastrzezynski, Adam Pawlikowski, Jan Ciecierski, Arthur Mlodnicki

Ashes and Diamonds

ASPHALT JUNGLE, THE   U.S.A. (1950)

W. R. Burnett's story about a group of criminals who plan and execute a million-dollar jewel robbery. A cold, efficient, sometimes brilliant thriller directed by John Huston and containing some of his best work. Excellent city exteriors by cameraman Hal Rosson who worked again with Huston, equally notably, on *The Red Badge of Courage*. There are several fine performances from a little-known but very talented cast —particularly Sam Jaffe (Grand Prize at Venice, best actor, 1950) as the little German doctor who masterminds the robbery, Louis Calhern as a crooked lawyer, and Sterling Hayden as small-time hoodlum.

METRO–GOLDWYN–MAYER

Production—Arthur Hornblow, Jr.
Direction—John Huston
Screenplay—John Huston,
  Ben Maddow
Photography—Harold Rosson

Art direction—Cedric Gibbons,
  Randall Duell
Music—Miklos Rozsa
Editing—George Boemler

PLAYERS: Sterling Hayden, Louis Calhern, Jean Hagen, Sam Jaffe, James Whitmore, John McIntire, Marc Lawrence, Barry Kelley, Anthony Caruso, Marilyn Monroe

29

ATTACK

U.S.A. (1956)

Uncompromising and occasionally hysterical war movie that looks at the cowardice and corruption of some American officers during the fighting in Belgium in the later stages of World War II. Among the best of Robert Aldrich's early films, distinguished by some forceful acting from Eddie Albert, Jack Palance and Lee Marvin (excellent in an early role as a cynical colonel), and by some excitingly handled action scenes, particularly those depicting an infantry platoon's assault on a German-occupied town. Edited, scored, photographed, etc., by Aldrich's regular team of technicians and very definitely made *without* the cooperation of the War Department.

THE ASSOCIATES & ALDRICH/UNITED ARTISTS

Production & direction—
  Robert Aldrich
Screenplay (from play Fragile
  Fox *by Norman Brooks)—*
  James Poe

*Photography—*Joseph Biroc
*Art direction—*William Glasgow
*Music—*Frank de Vol
*Editing—*Michael Luciano

PLAYERS: Jack Palance, Eddie Albert, Lee Marvin, Robert Strauss, Richard Jaeckel, Buddy Ebsen, Strother Martin, Steve Geray, Peter van Eyck

AWFUL TRUTH, THE

U.S.A. (1937)

Lively, if flimsy, comedy featuring Cary Grant and Irene Dunne as happily married couple who during an unimportant quarrel decide on a divorce but then, in the six months between the decree nisi and the final divorce, come together again. A familiar story engagingly played; scripted and directed with a sure touch by McCarey, who won the 1937 Oscar as best director of the year.

COLUMBIA

Production & direction—
  Leo McCarey
Screenplay (from play by Arthur
  *Richman)—*Viña Delmar
*Photography—*Joseph Walker

*Art direction—*Stephen Goosson
  & Lionel Banks
*Music—*Ben Oakland
*Editing—*Al Clark

PLAYERS: Irene Dunne, Cary Grant, Ralph Bellamy, Alexander D'Arcy, Cecil Cunningham, Molly Lamont, Esther Dale

BABES IN ARMS

U.S.A. (1939)

Judy Garland and Mickey Rooney as children of vaudeville put on a show and prove to their disbelieving parents that vaudeville is still alive and kicking. Rooney's impersonation of Clark Gable and Judy Garland's touching version of "I Cried for You" are the main attributes of a film which although brash and oversentimental is fairly typical of the kind of musical produced at Metro before Kelly, Minnelli and Donen got into their stride in the postwar era.

METRO–GOLDWYN–MAYER

Production–Arthur Freed
Direction–Busby Berkeley
Screenplay (from play by Richard Rodgers & Lorenz Hart)– Jack McGowan, Kay Van Riper
Photography–Ray June
Art direction–Cedric Gibbons

Music–Rodgers & Hart, Nacio Herb Brown, Arthur Freed, Harold Arlen, E. Y. Harburg
Orchestral arrangements– Leo Arnaud, George Bassman
Editing–Frank Sullivan

PLAYERS: Mickey Rooney, Judy Garland, Charles Winninger, Guy Kibbee, June Preisser, Grace Hoyes, Betty Jaynes, Douglas MacPhail, Rand Brooks

BABES ON BROADWAY   U.S.A. (1941)
Busby Berkeley musical about the efforts of stage-struck youngsters to conquer Broadway and stage a massive show for charity. Oversentimental and routine for the most part, but enlivened by some bright musical numbers (the "Hoe Down" sequence is Berkeley at his best) and by the performances of Judy Garland and Mickey Rooney. Vincente Minnelli also worked on the film, directing Judy Garland's solo numbers.

METRO–GOLDWYN–MAYER

Production–Arthur Freed
Direction–Busby Berkeley
Screenplay (from story by Fred Finklehoffe)–Fred Finklehoffe & Elaine Ryan
Photography–Lester White

Music direction–Georgie Stoll
Songs–E. Y. Harburg, Burton Lane, Ralph Freed, Roger Edens & Harold Rome
Editing–Frederick Y. Smith

PLAYERS: Judy Garland, Mickey Rooney, Fay Bainter, Ray McDonald, Virginia Weidler, Alexander Woollcott, Richard Quine

BABY DOLL   U.S.A. (1956)
Characteristic Tennessee Williams tale about an ignorant Southern white girl (Carroll Baker) and her relations with her degenerate cotton miller husband (Karl Malden) and a vengeful Sicilian seducer (Eli Wallach). A sordid, basically uninteresting tale, but notable for the

quality of the performances and for the expert observation of life among the poor white community of the Mississippi delta. Based on Williams' plays *An Unsatisfactory Meal* and *Twenty-seven Wagons Full of Cotton* and photographed by Boris Kaufman, Kazan's associate on *On the Waterfront* and *Splendor in the Grass*.

NEWTOWN PRODUCTIONS/WARNER BROS.

Production & direction—
Elia Kazan
*Screenplay—*Elia Kazan
*Photography—*Boris Kaufman

*Art direction—*Richard Sylbert,
Paul Sylbert
*Music—*Kenyon Hopkins
*Editing—*Gene Milford

PLAYERS: Carroll Baker, Karl Malden, Eli Wallach, Mildred Dunnock, Lonny Chapman, Eades Hogue, Noah Williamson

BABY FACE NELSON   U.S.A. (1957)

Gangster thriller, 1958 style, with pint-sized Mickey Rooney (M-G-M's golden boy of the early 1940's) following in the footsteps of Bogart, Cagney, etc., as moronic hoodlum Baby Face Nelson who, after the death of John Dillinger in the early 1930's, became Public Enemy Number One. Notable for Don Siegel's direction, which has style and pace, some convincing period atmosphere, and the supporting performances of assorted heavies Jack Elam, Ted de Corsia and Tony Caruso. Carolyn Jones is Rooney's doomed moll and, more surprisingly, Cedric Hardwicke appears as a drunken surgeon on the side of the gangsters.

UNITED ARTISTS

*Production—*Al Zimbalist
*Direction—*Don Siegel
*Screenplay—*Irving Schulman &
Daniel Mainwaring

*Photography—*Hal Mohr
*Music—*Van Alexander
*Editing—*Leon Barsche

PLAYERS: Mickey Rooney, Carolyn Jones, Cedric Hardwicke, Chris Dark, Ted de Corsia, Jack Elam, Tony Caruso, Emile Meyer, Leo Gordon

BACHELOR PARTY   U.S.A. (1957)

The false gaiety, boredom and loneliness of five office accountants as they go out for a night on the town to celebrate the impending marriage of one of their colleagues. A cleverly observed, realistic piece of everyday life; a writer's film more than anything else (it was adapted by Chayefsky from his own TV play), although the performances of the then little known cast add immeasurably to its success. Don Murray plays a young married accountant studying for examinations, Jack

Warden an office wolf, Philip Abbott the reluctant groom, and Carolyn
Jones the existentialist they encounter at a Greenwich Village party.

NORMA/UNITED ARTISTS

Production—Harold Hecht
Direction—Delbert Mann
Story & screenplay—
  Paddy Chayefsky
Photography—Joseph LeShelle

Art direction—
  Edward S. Haworth
Music direction—
  C. Bakaleinikoff
Editing—William B. Murphy

PLAYERS: Don Murray, E. G. Marshall, Jack Warden, Philip Abbott,
Larry Blyden, Patricia Smith, Carolyn Jones

BAD AND THE BEAUTIFUL, THE   U.S.A. (1952)
The rise and fall of a fanatical movie producer (Kirk Douglas) who
reaches the top by using and then ruthlessly discarding all the people
he becomes associated with. The film has dated more rapidly than
Hollywood's other "anti-Hollywood" movies of the period (*Sunset
Boulevard, A Star Is Born*), although the intelligence and satirical content of its script are still apparent. Dick Powell as the best-selling
author who is lured by Douglas to Hollywood to write a screenplay
emerges with most distinction from the star-studded cast. Vincente
Minnelli directed between such musical assignments as *An American
in Paris* and *The Band Wagon*.

METRO–GOLDWYN–MAYER

Production—John Houseman
Direction—Vincente Minnelli
Screenplay (*from story by*
  George Bradshaw)—Charles
  Schnee

Photography—Robert Surtees
Art direction—Cedric Gibbons &
  Edward Carfagno
Music—David Raksin
Editing—Conrad A. Nervig

PLAYERS: Lana Turner, Kirk Douglas, Walter Pidgeon, Dick Powell,
Barry Sullivan, Gloria Grahame, Gilbert Roland, Leo G. Caroll, Vanessa Brown, Paul Stewart

BAD DAY AT BLACK ROCK   U.S.A. (1955)
Economical, suspenseful little melodrama with Spencer Tracy as one-
armed war veteran avenging a murder in fear-ridden prairie shack
town in California. Remarkable on two counts: first for its sweeping
desert vistas and imaginative use of CinemaScope (together with *A
Star Is Born* and *East of Eden* it was one of the first films to demonstrate the possibilities of the process), and second for the splendid
performances of Tracy and assorted villains Ryan, Borgnine, Marvin.

Production–Dore Schary
Direction–John Sturges
Screenplay (*based on story by
   Howard Breslin*)–Millard
   Kaufman
Music–Andre Previn

Photography (*Eastmancolor/
   CinemaScope*)–William C.
   Mellor
Art direction–Cedric Gibbons &
   Malcolm Brown
Editing–Newell P. Kimlin

PLAYERS: Spencer Tracy, Robert Ryan, Anne Francis, Dean Jagger, Walter Brennan, John Ericson, Ernest Borgnine, Lee Marvin

BALL OF FIRE   U.S.A. (1941)

Sparkling Goldwyn comedy about a burlesque dancer (Barbara Stanwyck) and her gangster boyfriend who become involved with Gary Cooper and a group of learned professors. Fast, faultlessly timed and impeccably directed by Howard Hawks from a Wilder/Brackett screenplay. An inferior musical remake starring Danny Kaye and again directed by Hawks was made seven years later under the title *A Song Is Born.*

GOLDWYN/RKO RADIO

Production–Samuel Goldwyn
Direction–Howard Hawks
Screenplay (*from story "From A
   to Z" by Wilder and Thomas
   Monroe*)–Billy Wilder,
   Charles Brackett

Photography–Gregg Toland
Art direction–Perry Ferguson
Music–Alfred Newman
Editing–Daniel Mandell

PLAYERS: Gary Cooper, Barbara Stanwyck, Oscar Homolka, Dana Andrews, Dan Duryea, Henry Travers, S. Z. Sakall, Tully Marshall

BAMBI   U.S.A. (1942)

A 70-minute Disney adaptation of Felix Salten's story about the life of a forest deer from his early days as a baby fawn to the time when he reigns supreme as king of the forest. Oversentimental and not quite up to the standard of *Pinocchio,* although Disney's cartoon birds and animals—among them the impetuous rabbit Thumper, the skunk Flower and Friend Owl—are among the most inventive of his career. The song "Love Is a Song that Never Ends" earned composer Frank Churchill and lyricist Larry Morey an Academy Award nomination.

WALT DISNEY PRODUCTIONS/RKO RADIO

Production–Walt Disney
Supervising director–David Hand

Story direction–Perce Pearce

Music score—Frank Churchill,
Edward Plumb

Orchestration—Charles Wolcott,
Paul J. Smith

BAND WAGON, THE   U.S.A. (1953)
Fred Astaire as an aging dancer and Jack Buchanan as a highbrow actor-producer involved in putting on a Broadway musical version of *Faust*. Witty, colorful and packed with inventive dance routines, among them "A Shine on Your Shoes," an Astaire solo in an amusement arcade, and "The Girl Hunt Ballet," an imaginative skit on the Mickey Spillane-style thriller, danced by Astaire and Cyd Charisse. Minnelli's best musical of the 1950's.

METRO–GOLDWYN–MAYER

Production—Arthur Freed
Direction—Vincent Minnelli
Screenplay—Betty Comden &
   Adolph Green
Photography (Technicolor)—
   Harry Jackson
Art Direction—Cedric Gibbons,
   & Preston Ames

Musical direction—
   Adolph Deutsch
*Dances & musical numbers
   staged by*—Michael Kidd
Musical numbers designed by—
   Oliver Smith
Editing—Albert Akst

PLAYERS: Fred Astaire, Cyd Charisse, Jack Buchanan, Oscar Levant, Nanette Fabray, James Mitchell, Robert Gist

BANK DICK, THE   U.S.A. (1941)
Lively W. C. Fields comedy about town drunk who is rewarded with the position of bank guard after accidentally capturing a robber. Scripted by Fields himself (under the zany pseudonym of Mahatma Kane Jeeves) and climaxed by a wild car chase over a mountain pass. Amiable and enjoyable, it is among Fields' best.

UNIVERSAL

Direction—Edward Cline
Screenplay—Mahatma Kane Jeeves
Photography—Milton Krasner

Art direction—Jack Otterson
Music direction—Charles Previn
Editing—Arthur Hilton

PLAYERS: W. C. Fields, Cora Witherspoon, Una Merkel, Evelyn Del Rio, Jessie Ralph, Franklin Pangborn, Shemp Howard, Richard Purcell

BANK HOLIDAY   Gt. Britain (1938)
Early Carol Reed film follows the lives of a half dozen people during an August holiday weekend. An uneventful movie pleasantly played by some of the minor performers, especially Wally Patch as the father

35

of a family of squabbling kids and Wilfrid Lawson in a three-minute sketch as a country policeman, but of interest now only for its skillful evocation of a bank holiday atmosphere—noisy stations, uncomfortable trains, overspilling beaches, etc.

GAINSBOROUGH

Direction—Carol Reed
Photography—Arthur Crabtree
Editing—R. E. Dearing

Screenplay (from original story by Hans Wilhelm & Ackland)—Rodney Ackland, Roger Burford

PLAYERS: John Lodge, Margaret Lockwood, Hugh Williams, Rene Ray, Merle Tottenham, Linden Travers, Wally Patch, Kathleen Harrison, Garry Marsh, Wilfrid Lawson

BAREFOOT CONTESSA, THE U.S.A. (1954)

The checkered life and career of a Spanish slum girl from her days as a flamenco dancer in Madrid to the time when she becomes a leading Hollywood film star. Joseph Mankiewicz's polished screenplay has some sharp, amusing things to say about both the Hollywood scene and the Riviera high-society set and there is a splendid performance by Edmond O'Brien (Academy Award, best supporting actor, 1954) as a sweating, fast-talking Hollywood publicity man. Humphrey Bogart appears as cynical, broken-down film director.

FIGARO INC./UNITED ARTISTS

Direction & screenplay—
  Joseph L. Mankiewicz
Photography (Technicolor)—
  Jack Cardiff

Art direction—Arrigo Equini
Music—Mario Nascimbene
Editing—William Hornbeck

PLAYERS: Ava Gardner, Humphrey Bogart, Edmond O'Brien, Marius Goring, Valentina Cortese, Rossano Brazzi, Elizabeth Sellars, Warren Stevens

BARKLEYS OF BROADWAY, THE U.S.A. (1949)

Pleasing musical about a famous Broadway dancing team (Fred Astaire and Ginger Rogers) who split up when the female partner decides to become a great tragic actress. Undeservedly neglected when it first appeared, but full of pleasant song numbers and imaginative dance routines, e.g., "Shoes with Wings On," an Astaire solo; "Manhattan Downbeat," a large-scale production number with Astaire in top hat, white tie and tails, and an Astaire/Rogers thirties-styled dance sequence to Gershwin's evergreen "You Can't Take That Away From

Me." The tenth, and last, occasion that Astaire and Rogers appeared together.

METRO–GOLDWYN–MAYER

Production–Arthur Freed
Direction–Charles Walters
Screenplay & idea–
 Betty Comden & Adolph Green
Photography (Technicolor)–
 Harry Stradling

Art direction–Cedric Gibbons &
 Edward Carfagno
Music–Harry Warren
Lyrics–Ira Gershwin
Choreography–Robert Alton &
 Hermes Pan
Editing–Albert Akst

PLAYERS: Fred Astaire, Ginger Rogers, Oscar Levant, Billie Burke, Gale Robbins, Jacques François, Clinton Sundberg

BATTLEGROUND   U.S.A. (1949)

A vivid reconstruction of the 1944 defense of Bastogne in the Battle of the Bulge during Von Rundstedt's last offensive of the war. One of Hollywood's more interesting war films, not as ambitious as King's *Twelve O'Clock High*, but still of unusual class. William Wellman expertly handles a large M–G–M cast and there is some outstanding monochrome photography from Paul Vogel, who won an Academy Award.

METRO–GOLDWYN–MAYER

Production–Dore Schary
Direction–William A. Wellman
Screenplay (from his own story)–
 Robert Pirosh
Photography–Paul C. Vogel

Art direction–Cedric Gibbons &
 Hans Peters
Music–Lennie Hayton
Editing–John Dunning

PLAYERS: Van Johnson, John Hodiak, Ricardo Montalban, George Murphy, Marshall Thompson, Jerome Courtland, James Whitmore, Denise Darcel

BATTLE OF SAN PIETRO, THE   U.S.A. (1944)

One of the major film documentaries to come out of World War II, an on-the-spot account of Allied attempts to capture a German-fortified Italian mountain village in the winter of 1943. Written and directed by John Huston (who also did the narration) and shot with hand-held cameras, the film concentrates in particular on the experiences of a Texas infantry regiment, showing not only the blood and death of the fighting but also the horrifying aftermath, e.g., the death agonies of American soldiers and the numbed, hollow faces of Italian children

37

when the Allied troops finally enter the village. The film was cut from five reels to three by the War Department because of its strong antiwar attitudes, but even in its shortened 32-minute version it remains one of the most uncompromising protests against war ever put on the screen.

ARMY PICTORIAL SERVICE OF THE U.S. SIGNAL CORPS

Direction & screenplay—
  John Huston
*Commentary—*John Huston

*Photography—*John Huston,
  Jules Buck & photographers
  of the U.S. Signal Corps.
*Music—*Dimitri Tiomkin

BATTLESHIP POTEMKIN   U.S.S.R. (1925)

Sergei Eisenstein's reconstruction of the real-life mutiny which occurred on the Russian battleship *Prince Potemkin* during the abortive revolution of 1905. Famous for its brilliant editing techniques, the film has as its centerpiece the most memorable single sequence in all cinema—the Odessa steps sequence in which hundreds of citizens are systematically murdered by advancing Cossacks. Together with *Birth of a Nation* and *The Cabinet of Dr. Caligari* the picture, shot by Eisenstein in three months, was one of the most influential of all the silent films.

1ST GOSKINO

Director of production—
  Jacob Bliokh
Direction & Editing—
  Sergei M. Eisenstein
Story & first treatment—
  N. Agadjanovoi
*Photography—*Eduard Tissé

Assistant director—
  Grigori Alexandrov
*Assistants—*A. Antonov,
  M. Gomorov, M. Shtaukh,
  A. Levshin
*Camera assistant—*V. Popov
*Art direction—*Vasili Rakhals

PLAYERS: A. Antonov, Vladimir Barski, Grigori Alexandrov, Repnikova, Marusov, I. Bobrov, A. Fait

BAY OF ANGELS   France (1963)

Jacques Demy's second feature, a totally hypnotic study of a compulsive lady gambler and her involvement with a young Parisian bank clerk who becomes attached both to her and to her gambling habits during his holiday on the Riviera. Not a major film, but very stylishly handled and with blond-haired Jeanne Moreau at her dazzling best in the leading role. Bernard Evein's rich casino interiors and Jean Rabier's photography are additional assets.

SUD PACIFIQUE FILMS (PAUL-EDMOND DECHARME)

Bay of Angels

*Direction, screenplay &
   dialogue*—Jacques Demy
Photography—Jean Rabier
PLAYERS: Jeanne Moreau, Claude Mann, Paul Guers, Henri Nassiet

Art direction—Bernard Evien
Music—Michel Legrand
Editing—Anne-Marie Cotret

BEAST WITH FIVE FINGERS, THE   U.S.A. (1947)
Peter Lorre descends slowly into madness as the disembodied hand of a dead pianist returns from the grave to haunt and eventually kill him. Made with some style by Robert Florey—his first horror assignment since his Universal films of the early 1930's. Despite being cut by Warners prior to release, it ranks as perhaps the best of the horror films made in the immediate postwar period. The last scene, in which the hand that appears to have choked Lorre to death fades from sight, reveals the whole sequence of events to have occurred only in his deranged mind.

WARNER BROS.

Executive producer—Jack L. Warner
Direction—Robert Florey
*Screenplay (from story by
   William Fryer Harvey)*—
   Curt Siodmak

Photography—Wesley Anderson
Art Direction—Stanley Fleischer
Music—Max Steiner
Editing—Frank Magee

PLAYERS: Robert Alda, Andrea King, Peter Lorre, Victor Francen, J. Carrol Naish, Charles Dingle, John Alvin, David Hoffman

BEAU GESTE   U.S.A. (1926)
P. C. Wren's famous adventure story about three young English brothers who run off to join the Foreign Legion when one of them is suspected of stealing the family sapphire "Blue Water." A routine tale that was already beginning to date when this film version was made over forty years ago. The famous opening scene of the relief of Fort Zinderneuf, a desert outpost manned only by dead men, is a classic of its kind, however, and still eerily effective. Ronald Colman (in one of the best of his early roles) plays Beau, Neil Hamilton is featured as Digby, and Ralph Forbes is John. Noah Beery is the sadistic Sergeant Lejaune. The film was remade in 1939 by William Wellman with Gary Cooper, Robert Preston and Ray Milland in the leading roles.

PARAMOUNT/FAMOUS PLAYERS LASKY

Direction—Herbert Brenon   Adaptation—John Russell &
Screenplay—Paul Schofield   Herbert Brenon
                                  Photography—J. Roy Hunt
PLAYERS: Ronald Colman, Neil Hamilton, Ralph Forbes, Alice Joyce, Mary Brian, Noah Beery, William Powell

BECKY SHARP   U.S.A. (1935)
Faithful Hollywood version of Thackeray's Victorian novel is historically important as the first all-Technicolor movie and addtionally so for Rouben Mamoulian's inventive and subtle use of color itself, particularly in the famous scenes following the breakup of the Duchess of Richmond's ball in Brussels on the eve of Waterloo when the screen is dominated by the bright scarlet uniforms of the soldiers as they leave for battle. Miriam Hopkins is featured as the unscrupulous gold-digging Becky, Alan Mowbray plays Rawdon Crawley, and Cedric Hardwicke the Marquis of Steyne. One other color movie—*The Trail of the Lonesome Pine*—also was released in 1935.

RKO RADIO

Direction—Rouben Mamoulian   *Screenplay (from novel* Vanity
Photography (Technicolor)—   Fair *by Thackeray and the*
   Ray Rennahan   *play* Becky Sharp *by Langdon*
Editing—Archie Marshek   *Mitchell*)—
                                     Francis Edward Faragoh
PLAYERS: Miriam Hopkins, Frances Dee, Cedric Hardwicke, Billie

Burke, Alison Skipworth, Colin Tapley, G. P. Huntley, Jr., Alan Mowbray

BEDLAM   U.S.A. (1946)
Macabre tale about the infamous 18th-century London asylum has
Boris Karloff in one of his lesser-known roles as the sadistic asylum
director who is bricked up alive by the inmates. Directed by Mark
Robson from a story suggested by the eighth picture of Hogarth's
"Rake's Progress." Good period atmosphere and excellent sets by
D'Agostino and Keller, who designed all eight Val Lewton horror
films made between 1942 and 1946.
                              RKO RADIO
Production—Val Lewton   Art direction—
Direction—Mark Robson   Albert S. D'Agostino
Screenplay—Carlos Keith &   & Walter E. Keller
  Mark Robson   Music—Roy Webb
Photography—Nicholas Musuraca   Editing—Lyle Boyer
PLAYERS: Boris Karloff, Anna Lee, Billy House, Richard Fraser, Glenn
Vernon, Ian Wolfe

BELLE DE JOUR   France/Italy (1967)
Enigmatic, richly colored Luis Buñuel version of Joseph Kessel's novel
about a wealthy young surgeon's wife who indulges her masochistic
fantasies by working as a part-time prostitute in a Paris brothel. A
subtle, erotic, wickedly funny movie that concerns itself with the sexual
problems and perversions of men and women and which tantalizingly
and ingeniously switches from reality to fantasy and from fantasy to
reality. Exquisitely played by Catherine Deneuve as the tormented
wife and brilliantly so by Geneviève Page as the lesbian madam of a
brothel. Awarded a Golden Lion at the Venice Film Festival in 1967.
                PARIS FILM (PARIS)/FIVE FILMS (ROME)
Direction—Luis Buñuel   Photography (Eastmancolor)—
Screenplay—Luis Buñuel &   Sacha Vierny
  Jean-Claude Carrière   Art direction—Robert Clavel
                                     Editing—Walter Spohr
PLAYERS: Catherine Deneuve, Jean Sorel, Michel Piccoli, Geneviève
Page, Francisco Rabal, Pierre Clémenti, Georges Marchal

BELLISSIMA   Italy (1951)
A little known though not unrewarding picture about an ambitious

41

Roman mother who attempts, against all odds, to turn her plain five-year-old daughter into a film star, but then becomes so disillusioned with the film world and the people in it that she eventually refuses a large contract with a major studio. The explosive Anna Magnani completely dominates the film with her performance as the mother. Francesco Rosi, later director of such films as *The Moment of Truth* and *Hands Across the City*, worked on the screenplay.

SALVO D'ANGELO

Direction—Luchino Visconti
Screenplay—Zavattini, Luchino
  Visconti, Suso Cecchi d'Amico
  & Francesco Rosi

Photography—Piero Portalupi &
  Paul Ronald
Art direction—Gianni Polidori
Editing—Mario Serandrei

PLAYERS: Anna Magnani, Walter Chiari, Tina Apicella, Alessandro Blasetti

BEND OF THE RIVER U.S.A. (1952)

This Anthony Mann Western (his first in color) is about the adventures of a wagon train of farmers heading to new farmlands in Oregon and their subsequent struggle to get food supplies through to the settlement. A solid, realistic film well played by James Stewart (hero) and Arthur Kennedy (heavy) as the two Missouri outlaws who lead the trek, Jay C. Flippen as the head farmer, and Rock Hudson in an early co-starring role as a young gambler.

UNIVERSAL–INTERNATIONAL

Production—Aaron Rosenberg
Direction—Anthony Mann
Screenplay—Borden Chase
Photography (*Technicolor*)—
  Irving Glassberg

Art Direction—
  Bernard Herzbrun,
  Nathan Juran
Music—Hans J. Salter
Editing—Russell Schoengarth

PLAYERS: James Stewart, Arthur Kennedy, Julia Adams, Rock Hudson, Jay C. Flippen, Stepin Fetchit, Lori Nelson, Henry Morgan

BEN-HUR U.S.A. (1926)

A spectacular epic of the silent cinema, this adaptation of General Lew Wallace's biblical novel centers on the conflict between paganism, in the form of Roman tribune Messala, and Christianity as represented by Jewish hero Ben-Hur. The film's highlights are a sea battle and a superbly staged chariot race, shot by some 42 cameramen, and supervised by second-unit director Reaves Eason. Production of the film began in Rome in 1923 with Charles Brabin directing George Walsh as Ben-Hur and Francis X. Bushman as Messala. When the Goldwyn company merged with Metro, however, Louis B. Mayer scrapped all that had been filmed and assigned a new director (Fred Niblo) and star (Ramon Novarro), leaving only Francis X. Bushman in his original role. Filming continued in Italy and later in Hollywood where the epic was eventually completed. The picture, which cost M-G-M an estimated $4,000,000 to produce, was released in 1925.

METRO–GOLDWYN–MAYER

Direction—Fred Niblo	*Photography*—Rene Guissart,
Screenplay—Carey Wilson	Percy Hilburn, Karl Struss,
Adaptation—June Mathis	Clyde de Vinna, George
Continuity—Carey Wilson &	Meehan, E. Burton Steene
Bess Meredyth	*Editing*—Lloyd Nosler,
	Basil Wrangell

PLAYERS: Ramon Novarro, Francis X. Bushman, May McAvoy, Betty Bronson, Claire McDowell, Kathleen Key, Carmel Myers, Nigel de Brulier, Mitchell Lewis, Leo White, Frank Currier

BEN-HUR U.S.A. (1959)

William Wyler's impressive remake shot mainly in the giant Cinecitta studios in Rome and featuring Charlton Heston (Ben-Hur) and Stephen Boyd (Messala) in the leading roles. Second-unit men Andrew Marton and Yakima Canutt took three months to film the 11-minute chariot race on a vast 18-acre set packed with some 15,000 extras. Unlike its predecessor the film was relatively free of production troubles, although some controversy arose when Karl Tunberg received the sole writing credit. (It was known that Christopher Fry, Maxwell Anderson, S. N. Behrman, Gore Vidal and several others had contributed to the screenplay.) Statistics: 6½-month shooting schedule, 365 speaking parts, over 300 sets, 78 horses, and, eventually, 11 Oscars including awards to Heston, Wyler, cameraman Robert L. Surtees, and composer Miklos Rozsa.

METRO–GOLDWYN–MAYER

Production—Sam Zimbalist	*Photography* (*Technicolor/MGM*
Direction—William Wyler	*Camera* 65)—Robert L. Surtees
Screenplay (*based on novel by*	*Art direction*—
Lew Wallace)—Karl Tunberg	William A. Horning
Second unit—Andrew Marton	& Edward Carfagno
& Yakima Canutt	*Editing*—Ralph E. Winters,
Music—Miklos Rozsa	John D. Dunning

PLAYERS: Charlton Heston, Jack Hawkins, Stephen Boyd, Hugh Griffith, Martha Scott, Cathy O'Donnell, Haya Hayareet, Sam Jaffe, Finlay Currie, Frank Thring

BESPOKE OVERCOAT, THE   Gt. Britain (1955)
A 33-minute adaptation of Gogol's classic short story about a down-trodden Jewish warehouse clerk who returns from the grave to claim the sheepskin overcoat he longed for during his lifetime. Jack Clayton's first film as a director is marked by a great performance from Alfie Bass as the old clerk and an excellent one from David Kossoff as the poor Jewish tailor he befriends. First prize as best short story film at Venice Film Festival in 1955.

REMUS

Production & direction—
 Jack Clayton
*Screenplay—*Wolf Mankowitz
*Photography—*Wolfgang Suschitzky

*Art direction—*Anthony Masters
*Music—*Georges Auric
*Editing—*Stanley Hawkes

PLAYERS: David Kossoff, Alfie Bass, Alan Tilvern

BEST MAN, THE   U.S.A. (1964)
Adapted by Gore Vidal from his own stage play this little-known film is among the best of America's political movies. It centers on the dirty infighting at a national convention when the outgoing President (Lee Tracy) fails to nominate his successor. The hurly-burly of the political convention is well observed, the acting of Henry Fonda and Cliff Robertson as the two leading contenders is excellent, and the script is among the wittiest of its kind. The most satisfying of Franklin Schaffner's early films.

MILLAR TURMAN PRODS./UNITED ARTISTS

*Production—*Stuart Millar,
 Lawrence Turman
*Direction—*Franklin Schaffner
*Screenplay—*Gore Vidal

*Photography—*Haskell Wexler
*Art direction—*Lyle R. Wheeler
*Music—*Mort Lindsey
*Editing—*Robert E. Swink

PLAYERS: Henry Fonda, Cliff Robertson, Edie Adams, Margaret Leighton, Shelley Berman, Lee Tracy, Ann Sothern, Kevin McCarthy

BEST YEARS OF OUR LIVES, THE   U.S.A. (1946)
William Wyler's famous, if at times oversentimental, film about three American soldiers and the problems they face when readjusting to

civilian life after World War II. Belonging very much to its time although Robert Sherwood's script is still a model of its kind; the sheer professional skill with which the film was made stands it in good stead even after some 25 years. The three veterans are played by Fredric March, Dana Andrews and nonprofessional Harold Russell (an actual handless veteran of the war), and the photography is by Gregg Toland whose last film for Wyler this was. Seven Academy Awards including best picture of the year, best actor (March), best director, and best screenplay.

A SAMUEL GOLDWYN PRODUCTION RELEASED BY RKO RADIO

Production—Samuel Goldwyn
Direction—William Wyler
Screenplay (based on novel by
  Mackinlay Kantor)—
  Robert E. Sherwood
Photography—Gregg Toland

Art direction—Perry Ferguson
  & George Jenkins
Music score—Hugo Friedhofer
Music direction—Emil Newman
Editing—Daniel Mandell

PLAYERS: Fredric March, Dana Andrews, Harold Russell, Myrna Loy, Teresa Wright, Virginia Mayo, Steve Cochran, Hoagy Carmichael, Gladys George, Cathy O'Donnell, Roman Bohnen, Ray Collins

BICYCLE THIEF, THE (Ladri di biciclette)   Italy (1948)
The desperate attempts of an Italian workingman and his small son to locate the stolen bicycle that is so essential to the father in his newly obtained job as a billposter—a job which is his first of many months and on which the future livelihood of his family depends. The film records nothing more than this ultimately useless one-day search, but its observations of the relationship between father and son (two non-professional actors) and its realistic portrait of the poverty-stricken streets, back alleys, brothels and black markets of Rome make it per-haps the most rewarding of all the Italian films of the postwar era. The final shot when the man and his son, having themselves been driven to attempt to steal a bicycle, disappear dejectedly, hand in hand, into a Roman crowd is deeply moving. Directed by Vittorio De Sica shortly after his brilliant *Shoeshine*.

PDS (ENIC) UMBERTO SCARPELLI

Direction—Vittorio De Sica
Assistant directors—
  Gerardo Guerrieri,
  Luisa Alessandri
Photography—Carlo Montuori

Screenplay (from story by Luigi
  Batolini)—Cesare Zavattini
Music—Alessandro Cicognini
Sound—Gino Fiorelli

PLAYERS: Lamberto Maggiorani, Enzo Staiola, Lianella Carell, Gino Saltamerenda, Vittorio Antonucci

BIG BUSINESS U.S.A. (1929)

Brilliant silent two-reeler with Laurel and Hardy as pair of Christmas-tree salesmen trying to persuade obstinate customer (James Finlayson) to purchase one of their trees in mid-July. Ingenious, wonderfully timed, perpetually funny, it ends in an orgy of tit-for-tat destruction with Stan and Ollie tearing down Finlayson's house as he, in ever-increasing rage, methodically dismantles their car.

HAL ROACH/METRO–GOLDWYN–MAYER

Direction—James Horne

PLAYERS: Stan Laurel & Oliver Hardy, James Finlayson, Tiny Sanford

BIG CLOCK, THE U.S.A. (1948)

Crime-magazine editor (Ray Milland) finds himself framed and on the run for a murder committed by his tycoon boss (Charles Laughton). A brisk, efficient, skillfully written thriller that improves with the years and which stands high among underrated John Farrow's best work. Superb monochrome camera work by John Seitz, at his peak in the 1940's when he worked with distinction for Billy Wilder and Preston Sturges.

PARAMOUNT

Production—Richard Maibaum
Direction—John Farrow
Screenplay (from novel by
  Kenneth Fearing)—
  Jonathan Latimer
Photography—John Seitz

Art direction—Hans Dreier,
  Roland Anderson,
  Albert Nozaki
Music—Victor Young
Editorial supervision—
  Eda Warren

PLAYERS: Ray Milland, Charles Laughton, Maureen O'Sullivan, George Macready, Rita Johnson, Elsa Lanchester, Harold Vermilyea, Dan Tobin

BIG COUNTRY, THE U.S.A. (1958)

William Wyler's only postwar Western is pictorially magnificent through Franz Planer's beautiful color photography and contains one of the most famous music scores ever composed for a Western film. The story, about an ex-sea captain (Gregory Peck) who goes west to marry a rancher's daughter (Carroll Baker) and becomes involved in

46

a cattlemen's feud, is less than distinguished, however. Jean Simmons plays a ranch owner, Charlton Heston a ranch foreman, and Charles Bickford and Burl Ives are featured as feuding cattlemen.

UNITED ARTISTS

Production—William Wyler, Gregory Peck
Direction—William Wyler
Screenplay (from novel by David Hamilton)—James R. Webb, Sy Bartlett & Robert Wilder

Photography (Technicolor/Technirama)—Franz Planer
Art direction—Frank Hotaling
Music—Jerome Moross
Editing—Robert Belcher & John Faure

PLAYERS: Gregory Peck, Jean Simmons, Carroll Baker, Charlton Heston, Burl Ives, Charles Bickford, Chuck Connors

BIG HEAT, THE
U.S.A. (1953)

Top-drawer gangster picture revolving around determined young cop (Glenn Ford) and his vigorous efforts to track down the racketeers who have murdered his wife. Fritz Lang's best postwar movie, intelligently scripted by Sidney Boehm from a William McGivern novel. Lee Marvin, then at the start of his career, appears as a sadistic thug, Gloria Grahame is his moll, and Alexander Scourby an underworld boss.

COLUMBIA

Production—Robert Arthur
Direction—Fritz Lang
Screenplay—Sidney Boehm
Photography—Charles Lang

Art direction—Robert Peterson
Music—Daniele Amfitheatrof
Editing—Charles Nelson

PLAYERS: Glenn Ford, Gloria Grahame, Jocelyn Brando, Alexander Scourby, Lee Marvin, Jeanette Nolan, Peter Whitney, Willis Bouchey

BIG KNIFE, THE
U.S.A. (1955)

Star-studded version of Clifford Odets' anti-Hollywood play about a disillusioned film star (Jack Palance) who wants to give up his acting career but is threatened, blackmailed and eventually driven to suicide by the ruthless studio head. Melodrama takes control of the film long before the end of its 111 minutes although there are enough sharply etched scenes about Hollywood morals to make it an interesting work. Palance is uneasy in the title role, but Rod Steiger's film tycoon is an arresting performance. Wendell Corey as the studio hatchet man, Everett Sloane as Palance's press agent, and Shelley Winters as a studio call girl are splendid in supporting roles.

Production & direction—
  Robert Aldrich
*Screenplay—*James Poe
*Photography—*Ernest Laszlo

*Art direction—*William Glasgow
*Music—*Frank de Vol
*Editing—*Michael Luciano

PLAYERS: Jack Palance, Ida Lupino, Wendell Corey, Rod Steiger, Shelley Winters, Jean Hagen, Ilka Chase, Everett Sloane, Wesley Addy

BIG PARADE, THE   U.S.A. (1925)

Large-scale American war movie, told from the viewpoint of the ordinary soldier, traces the experiences of three men—a rich young American (John Gilbert), a barman (Tom O'Brien), and a riveter (Karl Dane)—during the war in France. Overromantic at times but strongly antiwar in its attitudes, it contains one memorable sequence in which American troops leave their billets in a French village and set off in a fleet of trucks for the front line. The film was a big commercial hit and established John Gilbert as a leading star and M-G-M as a major production company. Renée Adoree was featured in the cast as a French farm girl.

METRO–GOLDWYN–MAYER

*Direction—*King Vidor
Screenplay (from play by
  Laurence Stallings)—
  Harry Behn

*Photography—*John Arnold
*Music—*David Mendoza &
  William Axt
*Editing—*Hugh Wynn

PLAYERS: John Gilbert, Renée Adoree, Karl Dane, Tom O'Brien, Hobart Bosworth, Claire McDonald, George K. Arthur

BIG SKY, THE   U.S.A. (1952)

Ambitious, sometimes slow-moving Western concerns the adventures of early fur traders on a 1000-mile keelboat trip up the Missouri River in the 1830's. Vigorously played by Kirk Douglas and Dewey Martin as a pair of Kentucky mountaineers and Arthur Hunnicutt (excellent) as a grizzled old-timer. Impressively photographed by Russell Harlan who won an Academy Award nomination for this film and who also worked with Hawks on two of his other Westerns: *Red River* and *Rio Bravo*.

WINCHESTER/RKO RADIO

Production & direction—
  Howard Hawks
Screenplay (from novel by A. B.
  *Guthrie)—*Dudley Nichols
*Photography—*Russell Harlan

*Art direction—*Albert S.
  D'Agostino, Perry Ferguson
*Music—*Dimitri Tiomkin
*Editing—*Christian Nyby

PLAYERS: Kirk Douglas, Dewey Martin, Elizabeth Threatt, Arthur Hunnicutt, Buddy Baer, Steven Geray, Hank Worden, Jim Davis

BIG SLEEP, THE U.S.A. (1946)

The most complicated of all Raymond Chandler's thrillers with Humphrey Bogart as private-eye Philip Marlowe investigating some eight killings and becoming involved with, among others, Lauren Bacall as a smart-talking rich girl, Martha Vickers as her nymphomaniac sister, and Elisha Cook as a small-time hoodlum. Witty, sharp, confused, now almost a classic of its kind. Directed by Hawks from a script written in just eight days.

WARNER BROS.

Production & direction— Howard Hawks

Screenplay—William Faulkner, Leigh Brackett, Jules Furthman

Photography—Sidney Hickox
Art direction—Carl Jules Weyl
Music—Max Steiner
Editing—Christian Nyby

PLAYERS: Humphrey Bogart, Lauren Bacall, John Ridgely, Martha Vickers, Dorothy Malone, Peggy Knudsen, Regis Toomey, Charles Waldren, Elisha Cook, Jr.

BILLY LIAR Gt. Britain (1963)

Screen version of the popular stage success about an undertaker's young clerk who lives with his parents in an industrial suburb. In order to escape from the reality of his dreary existence, he imagines himself in all kinds of Walter Mitty-type situations, i.e., a dictator, a soldier, a cripple, a novelist, etc. Basically a tragedy—when Billy does at last get the chance to start a new life in London, he loses his nerve and returns to the world of his dreams—the film is carried along briskly by the comedy of its hero's imaginary situations and by his real-life involvement with two fiancées. John Schlesinger's observations of suburban life are often wickedly funny. Tom Courtenay plays Billy and Julie Christie makes a late but memorable appearance as the young beatnik girl who almost persuades him to break free of his chains.

A JOSEPH JANNI PRODUCTION/ANGLO AMALGAMATED

Production—Joseph Janni
Direction—John Schlesinger
Screenplay—Keith Waterhouse & Willis Hall

Photography ('Scope)— Denys Coop
Art direction—Ray Simm
Music—Richard Rodney Bennett
Editing—Roger Cherrill

PLAYERS: Tom Courtenay, Julie Christie, Wilfred Pickles, Mona Washbourne, Ethel Griffies, Finlay Currie, Rodney Bewes, Helen Fraser

BIRDS, THE   U.S.A. (1963)

For 120 engrossing minutes Alfred Hitchcock is at his ingenious best as he relates a horrifying story (based loosely on a tale by Daphne du Maurier) about thousands of birds who, for no apparent reason, suddenly attack and terrorize a small community on the Pacific Coast. Slow-moving for the first hour and marred by some inferior playing but technically superb, it contains several of Hitchcock's most fiendish set pieces, such as heroine Tippi Hedren being savagely attacked by birds while trapped in a telephone booth and the ominous buildup of hundreds of crows in a playground as they wait for the children to leave school. The use of sound—the screeching and flapping of the birds and the noise of beaks splintering wood—is outstanding.

UNIVERSAL

Production & direction—
Alfred Hitchcock
*Screenplay—*Evan Hunter
Photography (Technicolor)—
Robert Burks
Production design—
Norman Deming

*Art direction—*Robert Boyle &
George Milo
Sound consultant—
Bernard Herrmann
*Editing—*George Tomasini

PLAYERS: Rod Taylor, Tippi Hedren, Jessica Tandy, Suzanne Pleshette, Veronica Cartwright, Ethel Griffies, Charles McGraw, Ruth McDevitt

BIRTH OF A NATION, THE   U.S.A. (1915)

D. W. Griffith's classic 165-minute movie traces the experiences of two pairs of lovers during the turbulent years of the Civil War. The film covers the period immediately before the war, the long years of the war itself, and the aftermath when Negro factions rose to power and the Ku Klux Klan was formed in the South. Griffith carefully reconstructed all the major events of the war including the assassination of Abraham Lincoln, but was accused of anti-Negro bias because he told his story from the Southern viewpoint and looked sympathetically on the activities of the Klan. The movie, which considerably developed editing and other film techniques, was shot between July and October of 1914, and previewed in New York in March of the following year. Lillian Gish, Mae Marsh and Henry Walthall appeared in the leading roles and minor parts were played by Donald Crisp (as General Grant), Raoul Walsh (John Wilkes Booth), and Joseph Henabery (Abraham Lincoln). Erich von Stroheim also appeared in a bit part.

The Birth of a Nation

EPOCH PRODUCING CORPORATION (D. W. GRIFFITH)

Direction—D. W. Griffith

Photography—G. W. Bitzer, assisted by Karl Brown

Music arranged by—Joseph Carl Breil & D. W. Griffith

Screenplay (based on novel and play The Clansman, *with additional material from* The Leopard's Spots, *all by Thomas Dixon)*—D. W. Griffith, assisted by Frank Woods

PLAYERS: Lillian Gish, Mae Marsh, Henry Walthall, Miriam Cooper, Mary Alden, Ralph Lewis, George Seigmann, Walter Long, Robert Harron

BLACK CAT, THE   U.S.A. (1934)

Eccentric scientist (Bela Lugosi) revenges himself on crazy architect (Boris Karloff), a devil worshipper who has stolen his wife and daughter and who uses human life for sacrifice. Little-known horror movie, somewhat overshadowed by Universal's more famous horror tales (*Frankenstein, Dracula*) of this period, is as grisly as they come and contains one of Boris Karloff's best performances.

UNIVERSAL

Direction—Edgar G. Ulmer	*Photography*—John Mescall
Screenplay (from story by Edgar	*Art direction*—Charles D. Hall
Allan Poe)—Peter Ruric	

PLAYERS: Boris Karloff, Bela Lugosi, David Manners, Jacqueline Wells (later Julie Bishop), Lucille Lund, Egon Brecher, Anna Duncan, Henry Armetta

BLACK SWAN, THE   U.S.A. (1942)

An exuberant version of the Rafael Sabatini novel notable on many counts, but especially for the period sets of Richard Day and James Basevi and for the excellence of Shamroy's color photography (this was the first of his four Academy Award films). Tyrone Power appears as a 17th-century swashbuckler, Maureen O'Hara as the heroine, Laird Cregar as Sir Henry Morgan, and George Sanders as a villainous privateer.

TWENTIETH CENTURY–FOX

Production—Robert Bassler	*Art direction*—Richard Day &
Direction—Henry King	James Basevi
Screenplay—Ben Hecht &	*Photography (Technicolor)*—
Seton I. Miller	Leon Shamroy
Music—Alfred Newman	*Editing*—Barbara McLean

PLAYERS: Tyrone Power, Maureen O'Hara, Laird Cregar, Thomas Mitchell, George Sanders, Anthony Quinn, George Zucco

BLACKBOARD JUNGLE, THE   U.S.A. (1955)

Juvenile delinquency in a slum high school in New York City examined boldly, if a little hysterically, by writer-director Richard Brooks in a tough story about an idealistic young English teacher (Glenn Ford) and his attempts to communicate with a class of 35 terrifying adolescents. The ending is overly glib, but the film still manages to disturb and shock even after some 15 years. The ear-shattering music is by Bill Haley and his Comets who introduced the song "Rock Around the Clock" which began the rock craze of the mid 1950's.

METRO–GOLDWYN–MAYER

Production—Pandro S. Berman	*Art direction*—Cedric Gibbons
Direction—Richard Brooks	& Randall Duell
Screenplay (based on novel by	*Music*—Bill Haley & his Comets
Evan Hunter)—Richard Brooks	*Music adaptation*—
Photography—Russell Harlan	Charles Wolcott
	Editing—Ferris Webster

PLAYERS: Glenn Ford, Anne Francis, Louis Calhern, Margaret Hayes, John Hoyt, Richard Kiley, Emile Meyer, Warner Anderson, Sidney Poitier, Vic Morrow

BLACKMAIL   Gt. Britain (1929)
Straightforward thriller with Anny Ondra as the girlfriend of detective (John Longden) becoming involved in murder and with blackmailer (Donald Calthrop). Of interest primarily for Hitchcock's imaginative use of sound (this was his first sound film) and for the spectacular climactic chase across the dome of the British Museum. The film was shot originally as a silent production, but was later revamped with sound. Hitchcock makes his customary brief appearance as a man on a train. Other famous names associated with the film are Ronald Neame who was clapper boy and Michael Powell, stills photographer.

BRITISH INTERNATIONAL PICTURES

Executive producer—   Photography—John Cox
  John Maxwell   Art direction—Norman Arnold &
Direction—Alfred Hitchcock   Wilfred Arnold
Screenplay (from play by Charles   Music—Hubert Bath &
  Bennett)—Alfred Hitchcock,   Henry Stafford
  Benn W. Levy & Bennett   Editing—Emile de Ruelle
PLAYERS: Anny Ondra, John Longden, Sara Allgood, Charles Paton, Donald Calthrop, Cyril Ritchard, Hannah Jones, Harvey Braban, Phyllis Monkman

BLIND DATE   Gt. Britain (1959)
Modest but well-constructed and often quite sexy whodunit with Hardy Kruger as a young Dutch painter framed by his mistress on a murder charge and Stanley Baker as the tough milk-drinking police detective who interrogates him. Well performed but distinguished mainly by its script, which contains some hints of corruption in high places and which takes a cynical and often disquieting view of the workings of the London police force. This was Stanley Baker's first performance for Losey. He later appeared again for the director in *The Criminal, Eve* and *Accident.*

INDEPENDENT ARTISTS/A JULIAN WINTLE—LESLIE PARKYN PRODUCTION

Production—David Deutsch   Screenplay (based on novel by
Direction—Joseph Losey   Leigh Howard)—Ben Barzman
                                  & Millard Lampell

Photography—Christopher Challis   *Musical direction*—
Art direction—Harry Pottle   Malcolm Arnold
Music—Richard Bennett   *Editing*—Reginald Mills
PLAYERS: Hardy Kruger, Stanley Baker, Micheline Presle, Robert
Flemyng, Gordon Jackson, John Van Eyssen, Jack MacGowran, George
Roubicek

BLIND HUSBANDS   U.S.A. (1918)
Triangular sex melodrama about a neglected American wife (Francilla
Billington) who is seduced by an unscrupulous military officer (Erich
von Stroheim) while holidaying with her surgeon husband (Sam de
Grasse) in the Austrian Tyrol. This uneven movie was von Stroheim's
first film as a director and, although not so ambitious as his later works,
the characters are shrewdly drawn and the playing, especially of von
Stroheim, assured. Von Stroheim later repeated his role of callous
seducer in several of his subsequent silent films.
UNIVERSAL

Direction—Eric von Stroheim   *Photography*—Ben Reynolds
Screenplay (from his story The   *Art direction*—Eric von Stroheim
   Pinnacle)—Eric von Stroheim
PLAYERS: Erich von Stroheim, Gibson Gowland, Sam de Grasse, Fran-
cilla Billington, Fay Holderness

BLITHE SPIRIT   Gt. Britain (1945)
An elegant, straightforward film version of Noel Coward's London
stage success about novelist (Rex Harrison) who finds married life to
second wife (Constance Cummings) seriously complicated by the appearance of his first wife's ghost (Kay Hammond). Witty, sophisticated,
skillfully directed and quite beautifully played, especially by Margaret
Rutherford as Madame Acate, the eccentric medium who starts all the
trouble. The least important but most entertaining of the four films
made by the Lean/Coward combination.
NOEL COWARD PRODUCTIONS—CINEGUILD

Production—Noel Coward   *Art direction*—C. P. Norman
Direction—David Lean   *Musical direction*—
Screenplay—Noel Coward   Muir Mathieson
Photography (Technicolor)—   *Editing*—Jack Harris
   Ronald Neame   *Music*—Richard Addinsell
PLAYERS: Rex Harrison, Constance Cummings, Kay Hammond, Margaret
Rutherford, Hugh Wakefield, Joyce Carey, Jacqueline Clarke

BLONDE IN LOVE (Lásky Jedné Plavovlásky) Czechoslovakia (1965)
Czech factory girl (Hana Brejchová), desperately bored with the drab
provincial town in which she lives, falls in love with a young jazz
pianist and follows him ecstatically to Prague where he lives with his
parents. A week later she tearfully returns home again when she realizes that he has already forgotten her. A fresh, simple little comedy
that honestly reflects the problems of adolescence and looks with an
amused eye at the Czech provincial scene. Directed by Miloš Forman
who also made the delightful *Fireman's Ball*.

SEBOR–BOR, BARRANDOV STUDIO

Direction—Miloš Forman
Screenplay—Miloš Forman,
  Jaroslav Papousek, Ivan Passer
Photography—Miroslav Ondricek
Art direction—Karel Cerný
Music—Evcen Hilin

PLAYERS: Hana Brejchová, Vladimír Pucholt, Vladimir Mensík, Antonin
Blazejovsky, Milada Jezková, Josef Sebanek

BLOOD AND SAND   U.S.A. (1941)
Elaborate remake of Vincent Blasco Ibanez's romantic novel about the
life and loves of Spanish bullfighter (Tyrone Power) who becomes involved with two women—Madrid aristocrat (Rita Hayworth) and
childhood sweetheart (Linda Darnell)—before meeting his death in
the bull ring. Mostly trite, often tedious, but with an occasional scene
to remember (a boy playing his first bull alone in the moonlight) and
some absolutely magnificent Technicolor which deservedly won Academy Awards for cameramen Ray Rennahan and Ernest Palmer and for
which sole reason the film is mentioned here.

TWENTIETH CENTURY–FOX

Production—Darryl F. Zanuck
Direction—Rouben Mamoulian
Screenplay—Jo Swerling
Photography (*Technicolor*)—
  Ray Rennahan & Ernest Palmer
Art direction—Richard Day &
  Joseph C. Wright
Music direction—Alfred Newman
Editing—Robert Bischoff

PLAYERS: Tyrone Power, Linda Darnell, Rita Hayworth, Alla Nazim-
ova, Anthony Quinn, J. Carroll Naish, John Carradine, Lynn Bari,
Laird Cregar

BLOW-UP   Gt. Britain (1966)
Antonioni film that mixes an abstract, intellectual view of swinging
London with an intriguing mystery story in which a young fashion
photographer (David Hemmings) finds that he has accidentally taken

a photograph of a crime being committed in a London park. The thriller aspects of the story have an almost Hitchcockian intensity, but the remaining scenes (those revolving around the photographer's empty way of life) are obscure and full of pretentious symbolism. Beautiful color work by Carlo Di Palma.

BRIDGE FILMS/METRO–GOLDWYN–MAYER

Production—Carlo Ponti

Direction—
Michelangelo Antonioni

Screenplay (based on short story by Julio Cortazar)—
Michelangelo Antonioni &
Tonino Guerra

Photography (Eastmancolor Print by Metrocolor)—
Carlo Di Palma

Art direction—Assheton Gorton

Music—Herbert Hancock

Editing—Frank Clarke

PLAYERS: David Hemmings, Vanessa Redgrave, Peter Bowles, Sarah Miles, John Castle, Jane Birkin and Gillian Hills, Harry Hutchinson

BLUE ANGEL, THE   Germany (1930)

Deeply depressing German melodrama about a respectable middle-aged schoolmaster's tragic infatuation with a cheap night-club singer. One of von Sternberg's finest achievements, superbly acted by Emil Jannings as the schoolmaster, but still remembered mainly as the film that brought the legendary, black-stockinged Marlene Dietrich to the screen. Her seductive rendering of the song "Falling in Love Again" remains a famous moment in German cinema.

UFA–PARAMOUNT

Production—Erich Pommer

Direction—Josef von Sternberg

Screenplay (based on novel Professor Unrath by Heinrich Mann)—Josef von Sternberg

Adaptation—Carl Zuckmayer,
Karl Vollmoeller, Robert
Liebmann

Photography—Günther Rittau,
Hans Schneeberger

Set design—Otto Hunte,
Emil Hasler

Editing—Sam Winston

Music—Friedrich Hollander

Lyrics—Robert Liebmann

PLAYERS: Emil Jannings, Marlene Dietrich, Kurt Gerron, Rosa Valetti, Hans Albers, Eduard von Winterstein, Reinhold Bernt, Hans Roth

BLUE DAHLIA, THE   U.S.A. (1946)

Raymond Chandler scripted toughie about war veteran (Alan Ladd) involved once again with "peek-a-boo" actress Veronica Lake (they appeared together four times during the forties) and tracking down the murderer of Ladd's unfaithful wife (Doris Dowling). A slick, professional entertainment notable for its observation of the seamier aspects of urban life, the laconic wit of Chandler's dialogue, and the performances of the supporting players—especially William Bendix as an ex-soldier suffering from an old head wound and Howard da Silva as the owner of a night club on Sunset Strip. The film was George Marshall's best of the decade and one of the first with which John Houseman (one of Hollywood's most distinguished producers) was associated. Other Houseman productions include *Letter from an Unknown Woman, They Live by Night, Executive Suite* and *All Fall Down.*

PARAMOUNT

Production—John Houseman	*Art direction*—Hans Dreier &
Direction—George Marshall	Walter Tyler
Screenplay—Raymond Chandler	*Music direction*—Victor Young
Photography—Lionel Lindon	*Editing*—Arthur Schmidt

PLAYERS: Alan Ladd, Veronica Lake, William Bendix, Howard da Silva, Doris Dowling, Tom Powers, Hugh Beaumont

BLUE LAMP, THE   Gt. Britain (1949)

Intermittently impressive Ealing film about the London police force, tracing in particular the efforts of the man on the beat and the flying squad to track down a desperate young hooligan who has committed a murder outside a London movie house. Solid performances, well-observed London backgrounds, and an excitingly staged climactic car chase; at its best in the documentary scenes of police routine.

EALING STUDIOS

Production—Michael Balcon	*Photography*—Gordon Dines
Direction—Basil Dearden	*Art direction*—Jim Morahan
Associate producer—	*Music direction*—Ernest Irving
Michael Relph	*Editing*—Peter Tanner
Screenplay—T. E. B. Clarke	

PLAYERS: Jack Warner, Jimmy Hanley, Dirk Bogarde, Robert Flemying, Bernard Lee, Peggy Evans, Gladys Henson

BLUEBEARD'S EIGHTH WIFE   U.S.A. (1938)

Ernst Lubitsch's first association with scriptwriters Brackett and Wilder. A gay, fast-moving sex comedy about the extraordinary love affair between a much-married multimillionaire (Gary Cooper) who suffers from insomnia and Claudette Colbert, whose cure for sleeplessness is

57

to spell "Czechoslovakia" backwards. Excellent performances, brilliant dialogue; Lubitsch's last for Paramount.

PARAMOUNT

Production & direction—
Ernst Lubitsch
*Screenplay (from play by Alfred Savoir, adapted by Charlton Andrews)—*Charles Brackett & Billy Wilder

*Photography—*Leo Tover
*Art direction—*Hans Dreier & Robert Usher
*Music—*Werner Heymann & Frederick Hollander
*Editing—*William Shea

PLAYERS: Claudette Colbert, Gary Cooper, Edward Everett Horton, David Niven, Elizabeth Patterson, Herman Bing, Warren Hymer

BODY AND SOUL   U.S.A. (1947)

Boxing movie tracing the career of a Jewish boy (John Garfield) from New York's Lower East Side who enters the fight game to make money and becomes corrupted on his way to the middleweight championship. The rather conventional story is helped by the intelligence of Abraham Polonsky's screenplay which exposes the murkier aspects of the box- ing racket and also by the realism of the fight scenes. Although the film is not the best of the three boxing pictures produced in America in the late forties (see *Champion* and *The Set Up*), it is nonetheless of inter- est as one of the most important works in Rossen's early career as a director. Hazel Brooks as a gold-digging night-club floozie stands out from a strong supporting cast.

ENTERPRISE—UNITED ARTISTS CORP.

*Production—*Bob Roberts
*Direction—*Robert Rossen
*Assistant director—*Robert Aldrich
*Art direction—*Nathan Juran & Edward J. Boyle

*Screenplay—*Abraham Polonsky
*Photography—*James Wong Howe
*Music—*Rudolph Polk & Hugo Friedhofer
*Editing—*Francis Lyon

PLAYERS: John Garfield, Lilli Palmer, Hazel Brooks, Anne Revere, William Conrad, Joseph Pevney, Canada Lee, Lloyd Goff

BODY SNATCHER, THE   U.S.A. (1945)

Robert Louis Stevenson's story of body snatching in 19th-century Edin- burgh, skillfully adapted and played to the hilt by Boris Karloff, Henry Daniell and Bela Lugosi. One of Lewton's most famous horror films, rich in period detail and strikingly photographed by Robert de Grasse.

RKO RADIO

Production—Val Lewton
Direction—Robert Wise
Screenplay—Philip MacDonald,
  Carlos Keith
Photography—Robert de Grasse

Art direction—
  Albert S. D'Agostino,
  Walter Keller
Music—Roy Webb
Editing—J. R. Whittredge

PLAYERS: Boris Karloff, Bela Lugosi, Henry Daniell, Edith Atwater, Russell Wade, Rita Corday, Sharyn Moffett, Donna Lee

BONNIE AND CLYDE   U.S.A. (1967)

Extraordinary gangster movie, tender, funny and violent by turns, follows the activities of Clyde Barrow (Warren Beatty) and Bonnie Parker (Faye Dunaway) in the early depression years when they robbed and murdered some eighteen people in a three-year killing spree in the Midwest. Stylishly made, frequently brilliant, it is a director's film if ever there was one, though Burnett Guffey's extraordinary color photography deserves and received (Academy Award, 1967) the highest praise. The gunfight outside a motel at night and the final slow-motion murder of the young gangsters are now classic scenes, the latter being imitated by Sam Peckinpah in the opening and closing sequences of his Western *The Wild Bunch*. Other members of the Barrow gang are Michael J. Pollard as the driver-mechanic recruited at a gas station, Gene Hackman as Clyde's brother, and Estelle Parsons as his sister-in-law.

TATIRA/HILLER/WARNER BROS.

Production—Warren Beatty
Direction—Arthur Penn
Screenplay—David Newman &
  Robert Benton

Photography (*Technicolor*)—
  Burnett Guffey
Art direction—Dean Tavoularis
Music—Charles Strouse
Editing—Dede Allen

PLAYERS: Warren Beatty, Faye Dunaway, Michael J. Pollard, Gene Hackman, Estelle Parsons, Denver Pyle, Dub Taylor, Evans Evans, Gene Wilder

BOOMERANG   U.S.A. (1947)

Classic semidocumentary about the murder of an old priest in a New England town. Beautifully played by Dana Andrews as the honest district attorney and Lee J. Cobb as the overworked police chief. Screenplay was based on an actual unsolved murder case and the film was shot completely outside the studio in the streets of Stamford, Conn.

TWENTIETH CENTURY–FOX

Production—Louis de Rochemont
Direction—Elia Kazan
Screenplay (from article by
  Fulton Oursler writing under
  pen name of Anthony Abbott)
  —Richard Murphy

Photography—Norbert Brodine
Art direction—James Basevi,
  Chester Gore
Music—David Buttolph
Editing—Harmon Jones

PLAYERS: Dana Andrews, Jane Wyatt, Lee J. Cobb, Cara Williams, Arthur Kennedy, Sam Levene, Robert Keith, Taylor Holmes, Lester Lonergan, Lewis Leverett, Philip Coolidge, Barry Kelley, Ed Begley, Karl Malden

BORN YESTERDAY   U.S.A. (1950)

The film version of Garson Kanin's long-running Broadway play about a tough junk tycoon who employs a young journalist to give his dumb mistress an education. A very amusing movie, expertly handled by George Cukor, with excellent performances from Broderick Crawford as the tycoon and William Holden as the journalist, plus a hilarious Academy Award-winning one from Judy Holliday as the bird-brained, mink-coated blonde, Billie Dawn.

COLUMBIA

Production—S. Sylvan Simons
Direction—George Cukor
Screenplay—Albert Mannheimer
Photography—Joseph Walker

Art direction—Harry Horner
Music—Frederick Hollander
Editing—Charles Nelson

PLAYERS: Judy Holliday, William Holden, Broderick Crawford, Howard St. John, Frank Otto, Larry Oliver, Barbara Brown, Grandon Rhodes

BOY WITH GREEN HAIR, THE   U.S.A. (1948)

Dean Stockwell as a solemn young orphan boy who is singled out by the starving orphans of Europe to represent them in the United States. To draw attention to him and to their own desperate plight, they turn his hair green overnight. A minor but well-intentioned Losey fantasy (his first feature), much, much too whimsical although the message comes across strongly. The script contains some caustic comments about man's resentment of anything or anyone different in his society—even such a minor thing as green hair.

RKO RADIO

Executive producer—Dore Schary
Production—Adrian Scott,
  replaced by Stephen Ames
Direction—Joseph Losey

Screenplay (based on story by
  Betsy Beaton)—Ben Barzman,
  Alfred Lewis Levitt

Photography (Technicolor)— *Art direction—*
  George Barnes   Albert S. D'Agostino
Music—Leigh Harline   & Ralph Berger
                 Editing—Frank Doyle
PLAYERS: Dean Stockwell, Pat O'Brien, Robert Ryan, Barbara Hale, Samuel S. Hinds, Walter Catlett, Richard Lyon, Charles Meredith, Regis Toomey

BREAKFAST AT TIFFANY'S   U.S.A. (1961)

Cleaned up but nonetheless endearing version of Truman Capote's novella concerning the wild escapades of New York "super tramp" Holly Golightly and her relationship with the struggling short-story writer living in the upstairs apartment. Full of good things—handsome color photography, a fine Mancini score, delightful performances from Miss Hepburn, Martin Balsam as a Hollywood agent, and John Mc-Giver as a Tiffany's jewelry salesman—and belonging with Hollywood's most assured romantic films of the 1960's. In fact, a unique and stylish success for director Blake Edwards. Henry Mancini received Oscars for his song "Moon River" and for his complete musical score.

JUROW–SHEPHERD/PARAMOUNT

Production—Martin Jurow & *Photography (Technicolor)—*
  Richard Shepherd   Franz Planer
Direction—Blake Edwards *Art direction*—Roland Anderson
Screenplay—George Axelrod *Music*—Henry Mancini
                 Editing—Howard Smith
PLAYERS: Audrey Hepburn, George Peppard, Patricia Neal, Mickey Rooney, Buddy Ebson, Jose-Luis de Villa Longa, Martin Balsam, John McGiver

BREAKING POINT, THE   U.S.A. (1950)

Tough, disillusioned Harry Morgan, weary of hiring out his motorboat for unprofitable fishing trips, turns instead to crime and becomes involved with smugglers and racetrack racketeers. A much underrated version of Hemingway's *To Have and Have Not*, beautifully directed by Michael Curtiz (the film ranks with *Angels with Dirty Faces* and *Casablanca* as one of his best works), and well played by John Garfield as Morgan, Patricia Neal as a smart-talking tart on the make, and Wallace Ford as a shady lawyer. A far superior adaptation of the story than was the more famous Bogart-Bacall version made six years earlier.

WARNER BROTHERS

61

Production—Jerry Wald
Direction—Michael Curtiz
Screenplay—Ranald MacDougall
Photography—Ted McCord
Art direction—Edward Carrere
Music direction—Ray Heindorf
Editing—Alan Crosland Jr.

PLAYERS: John Garfield, Patricia Neal, Phyllis Thaxter, Juano Hernandez, Wallace Ford, Edmon Ryan, Ralph Dumke

BRIDE OF FRANKENSTEIN, THE   U.S.A. (1935)

Satirical sequel to James Whale's *Frankenstein* has monster Boris Karloff escaping from the burning windmill and being given a female companion by Frankenstein (played again by Colin Clive) and new associate Dr. Praetorious (Ernest Thesiger) who includes among his hobbies miniaturizing and preserving people in large jars. A brilliant parody, full of wit and dry humor and containing also a number of genuinely horrific scenes, particularly those in which the screeching, white-shrouded Elsa Lanchester first appears as the she monster. Franz Waxman contributed an imaginative musical score and John Mescall (*The Invisible Man, The Black Cat*) was on camera.

UNIVERSAL

Direction—James Whale
Photography—John D. Mescall
Music—Franz Waxman
Editing—Ted Kent
Screenplay (*based on characters created by Mary Shelley*)—
John L. Balderston &
William Hurlbut

PLAYERS: Boris Karloff, Colin Clive, Valerie Hobson, Elsa Lanchester, Ernest Thesiger, O. P. Heggie, Dwight Frye, E. E. Clive

BRIDGE ON THE RIVER KWAI, THE   Gt. Britain (1957)

Alec Guinness, William Holden and Jack Hawkins in one of Britain's most ambitious war movies of the 1950's; a long (2-hour 41-minute) tale about the construction by British prisoners of a railway bridge in the Siamese jungle and its eventual destruction by a British commando unit. The essence of the film lies in the conflict between the fanatical Japanese commandant (Sessue Hayakawa) in charge of the bridge building and the British colonel (Alec Guinness) who fails to see that by instructing his men to build the bridge to the best of their ability (as a morale booster) he is, in fact, collaborating with the Japanese. The movie has strong antiwar attitudes, but the "war is madness" undertones are often lost among the more routine adventure aspects of the story and it is on this level that the film works best. Jack Hildyard, Lean's associate on *The Sound Barrier, Hobson's Choice*

62

Brief Encounter

and *Summertime,* was on camera and Malcolm Arnold made ingenious use of the "Colonel Bogey" march in his music score. The film won Lean his first Oscar and also several other Academy Awards including best film, actor (Guinness), screenplay, music and photography.

A HORIZON PRODUCTION/COLUMBIA

Production—Sam Spiegel
Direction—David Lean
Screenplay (based on his novel)—Pierre Boulle

Photography (Technicolor)— Jack Hildyard
Art direction—Donald M. Ashton
Music—Malcolm Arnold
Editing—Peter Taylor

PLAYERS: Alec Guinness, William Holden, Jack Hawkins, Sessue Hayakawa, Geoffrey Horne, James Donald, Andre Morell, Peter Williams

BRIEF ENCOUNTER   Gt. Britain (1946)

he story of a love affair between a middle-aged married doctor and ordinary suburban housewife who spend a few furtive afternoons gether before agreeing to part. The misery of two adult people caught p in a hopeless affair is reflected with infinite skill by director David Lean and by Noel Coward who helped develop the script from his own one-act play. Celia Johnson, through whose eyes the story is told, plays the woman and Trevor Howard the doctor. The last and best of Lean's four films with Coward.

CINEGUILD

Production—Noel Coward, Anthony Havelock-Allan & Ronald Neame
Direction—David Lean
Photography—Robert Krasker

Screenplay—Noel Coward, David Lean & Anthony Havelock-Allan
Art direction—L. P. Williams
Editing—Jack Harris

PLAYERS: Celia Johnson, Trevor Howard, Stanley Holloway, Joyce Carey, Cyril Raymond, Everley Gregg, Margaret Barton

BRINGING UP BABY — U.S.A. (1938)

A staid professor (Cary Grant) and a madcap heiress (Katharine Hepburn) are involved in chase of tame leopard across the Connecticut countryside and in search for a missing bone from reconstructed dinosaur. One of the zaniest and, along with Hawks' own *His Girl Friday* and Preston Sturges' *The Palm Beach Story,* one of the fastest-moving comedies ever made. Also in the cast are Charles Ruggles as an eccentric big-game hunter and Barry Fitzgerald as his drunken gardener.

RKO RADIO

Production & direction— Howard Hawks
Screenplay (*from story by Wilde*)—Dudley Nichols, Hager Wilde
Photography—Russell Metty

Art direction— Van Nest Polglase, Perry Ferguson
Music—Roy Webb
Editing—George Hively

PLAYERS: Cary Grant, Katharine Hepburn, Charles Ruggles, Walter Catlett, Barry Fitzgerald, May Robson, Fritz Feld, Leona Roberts, George Irving, Tala Birrell

BROADWAY MELODY, THE — U.S.A. (1929)

First really big screen musical built around the then original plot of two stage-struck country girls (Bessie Love and Anita Page) tryin to carve out careers on the Broadway stage—a plot that was to beco a familiar Hollywood standby in the years ahead. The Nacio H Brown and Arthur Freed (later an M-G-M producer) score inclu the title tune, "You Were Meant for Me" and "The Wedding of t Painted Doll." Vaudeville star Charles King appeared as the romanti lead. It won the Academy Award for best picture in 1929.

Direction—Harry Beaumont
Screenplay—Sarah Y. Mason
Dialogue—Norman Houston,
  James Gleason
Story—Edmund Goulding
Photography (*Technicolor*
  sequences)—John Arnold
Art direction—Cedric Gibbons

Lyrics & Music—Arthur Freed &
  Nacio Herb Brown
Editing:
  Sound version—
  Sam S. Zimbalist
  Silent version—
  William LeVanway

PLAYERS: Bessie Love, Anita Page, Charles King, Jed Prouty, Kenneth Thompson, Edward Dillon, Mary Doran, Eddie Kane

BROADWAY MELODY OF 1938   U.S.A. (1937)
Routine, undistinguished addition to the series of *Broadway Melody* musicals made by M-G-M during the 1930's. This is the one, however, in which 15-year-old Judy Garland sang "Dear Mr. Gable. . . . You made me love you" to a portrait of Clark Gable and for this scene alone it will always be remembered. The *Broadway Melody* musicals were used by M-G-M to exploit new talent. Warner Bros. (*Gold Diggers of . . .*) and Paramount (*The Big Broadcast of . . .*) produced similar series.

Production—Jack Cummings
Direction—Roy Del Ruth
Screenplay—Jack McGowan
Story—Jack McGowan,
  Sid Silvers
Music & Lyrics—
  Nacio Herb Brown,
  Arthur Freed

Music direction—George Stoll
Music arrangements—
  Roger Edens
Dance ensembles—Dave Gould
Photography—William Daniels
Art direction—Cedric Gibbons
Editing—Blanche Sewell

PLAYERS: Robert Taylor, Eleanor Powell, George Murphy, Buddy Ebsen, Sophie Tucker, Judy Garland, Charles Igor Gorin, Raymond Walburn, Robert Benchley, Charles Grapewin

THE BROKEN ARROW   U.S.A. (1950)
Sincere, well-made, altogether outstanding Western about the efforts of frontier scout Tom Jeffords to bring to an end the Apache wars that ravaged Arizona in 1870. Among the best in the genre, and the first of the postwar cycle to attempt a serious portrayal of the American Indian. Excellent performances from James Stewart as Jeffords,

Debra Paget as his Indian bride, and Jeff Chandler as the dignified Cochise. Ernest Palmer's lovely Technicolor photography won him a well-deserved Academy Award nomination.

TWENTIETH CENTURY–FOX

Production—Julian Blaustein
Direction—Delmer Daves
Screenplay (from novel Blood
  Brother by Elliott Arnold)—
  Michael Blankfort

Photography (Technicolor)—
  Ernest Palmer
Art direction—Lyle Wheeler,
  Albert Hogsett
Music—Hugo Friedhofer
Editing—J. Watson Webb

PLAYERS: James Stewart, Jeff Chandler, Debra Paget, Basil Ruysdael, Will Geer, Arthur Hunnicutt, Raymond Bramley, Jay Silverheels

BROKEN BLOSSOMS   U.S.A. (1919)

Moving, beautifully acted love story of London's Limehouse area where Chinaman Richard Barthelmess ("the yellow man") silently and tragically worships innocent young street waif (Lillian Gish). Directed by the great D. W. Griffith and photographed by G. W. Bitzer and Hendrick Sartov who used blue, orange and gold tints to reflect the film's varying moods. The picture was released in May 1919 and was the first to be produced by United Artists, the company formed by Chaplin, Pickford, Fairbanks and Griffith in January of that year. Donald Crisp was the third star of the movie, appearing as Miss Gish's sadistic boxer father.

UNITED ARTISTS

Direction—D. W. Griffith
Screenplay (based on "The Chink
  and the Child" in Thomas
  Burke's Limehouse Nights)—
  D. W. Griffith

Photography—G. W. Bitzer
Special effects—Hendrick Sartov
Music arranged by—Louis F.
  Gottschalk & D. W. Griffith
Technical advisor—Moon Kwan

PLAYERS: Lillian Gish, Richard Barthelmess, Donald Crisp, Arthur Howard, Edward Peil, George Beranger, Norman Selby (Kid McCoy)

BROWNING VERSION, THE   Gt. Britain (1951)

Strongly etched portrayal of a lonely middle-aged schoolmaster (Michael Redgrave) whose life both as teacher and as husband has been a failure and whose ill health has caused his premature retirement from the school in which he has taught for twenty years. Quietly and compassionately directed by Anthony Asquith from Terence Rattigan's adaptation of his own play and made notable by the acting of Michael

Redgrave whose portrayal of schoolmaster "Crocker" Harris is perhaps the most accomplished of his screen career. Redgrave was named best actor at the 1951 Cannes Film Festival.

A JAVELIN PRODUCTION

Production—Teddy Baird
Direction—Anthony Asquith
Screenplay—Terence Rattigan

Photography—
  Desmond Dickinson
Art direction—Carmen Dillon
Editing—John D. Guthridge

PLAYERS: Michael Redgrave, Jean Kent, Nigel Patrick, Wilfred Hyde White, Brian Smith, Bill Travers, Ronald Howard, Paul Medland, Ivan Samson

BULLITT   U.S.A. (1968)

Ruthless assistant district attorney (Robert Vaughn) hires conscientious cop (Steve McQueen) to guard a vital witness whose testimony will help smash a crime syndicate. The witness is murdered and, as the hunt for the killer begins, the tension between the two men grows. This expertly directed police thriller (British director Peter Yates' first U.S. movie) makes great use of San Francisco locations and is famous for two exhilarating chases: the first a car chase through San Francisco's hilly streets, the second a pursuit on foot across a busy airport.

SOLAR/WARNER–PATHÉ

Production—Philip D'Antoni
Direction—Peter Yates
Screenplay (*based on novel*
  Mute Witness *by Robert L.*
  Pike)—Alan R. Trustman,
  Harry Kleiner

Photography (*Technicolor*)—
  William A. Fraker
Art direction—Albert Brenner
Music—Lalo Schifrin
Editing—Frank P. Keller

PLAYERS: Steve McQueen, Robert Vaughn, Jacqueline Bisset, Don Gordon, Robert Duvall, Simon Oakland, Norman Fell, Carl Reindel

BURMESE HARP, THE   Japan (1956)

Haunting war movie set in Burma is an account of a young Japanese soldier's spiritual conversion at the end of hostilities when, disguised in a priest's robes, he remains behind on Burmese soil dedicating his life to burying his dead comrades and becoming a companion and peace bringer to the dead of all nations. A unique film quieter in tone than the majority of pacifist movies, but in its own way equally effective. Directed by Kon Ichikawa whose later work includes the memorable *Tokyo Olympiad*.

Direction—Kon Ichikawa
Screenplay (*from story by*
   Michio Takeyama)—
   Natto Wada

Photography—
   Minoru Yokoyama
Music—Akira Ifukibe
Art direction—
   Takashi Matsuyama

PLAYERS: Rentaro Mikuni, Shoji Yasui, Tatsuya Mihashi, Taniye Kitabayashi, Yunosuke Ito

BUSY BODIES   U.S.A. (1933)
Carpenters Laurel and Hardy are involved in a variety of slapstick accidents in a sawmill. A perfectly timed two-reeler, by far the best of the six Laurel and Hardy shorts that Lloyd French directed. Among the funniest gags: Ollie being sucked into an air vent, becoming painfully caught up in a window frame, and the pair's car being cut in two by a huge saw.

HAL ROACH/METRO–GOLDWYN–MAYER

Direction—Lloyd French
PLAYERS: Stan Laurel and Oliver Hardy, Tiny Sanford, Charlie Hall

BUTCH CASSIDY AND THE SUNDANCE KID   U.S.A. (1969)
The best of three magnificent Westerns (see *True Grit* and *The Wild Bunch*) produced in 1969. This film traces the last months in the lives of two outlaws (Paul Newman and Robert Redford) who, in the turn-of-the-century West, robbed trains and banks and finished their careers violently in the jungles of Bolivia. As in *The Wild Bunch* the predicament of men living on borrowed time in an increasingly law-abiding society is sympathetically explored although, unlike Peckinpah's film, the violence is kept to the minimum and the treatment is gentle, indeed often lighthearted. Conrad Hall makes intelligent use of sepia tints in his Technicolor photography (Academy Award, 1969) and Burt Bacharach's music is among the most charming of Western scores.

CAMPANILE PRODUCTIONS/TWENTIETH CENTURY–FOX
A NEWMAN–FOREMAN PRESENTATION

Executive producer—
   Paul Monash
Production—John Foreman
Direction—George Roy Hill
Screenplay—William Goldman

Photography (*DeLuxe*/
   Panavision)—Conrad Hall
Art direction—Jack Martin Smith
   & Philip Jefferies

Butch Cassidy and the Sundance Kid

Music & musical direction—
  Burt Bacharach
*Editing—*John C. Howard &
  Richard C. Meyer

Song "Raindrops Keep Fallin'
  on My Head" by—
  Burt Bacharach & Hal David

PLAYERS: Paul Newman, Robert Redford, Katharine Ross, Strother Martin, Henry Jones, Jeff Corey, George Furth, Cloris Leachman

BUTCHER BOY, THE   U.S.A. (1917)
Two-reel Roscoe Arbuckle short involving a series of comic incidents in a village store. Routine for the most part with all the usual vaudeville slapstick scenes, but important because it marks the first appearance of Buster Keaton before the movie cameras. Keaton appeared in some 15 Arbuckle shorts between 1917 and 1919.

COMICQUE FILM CORPORATION/PARAMOUNT FAMOUS PLAYERS–LASKY
*Production—*Joseph M. Schenck   *Direction & screenplay—*
*Photography—*Elgin Lessley (?)   Roscoe Arbuckle
PLAYERS: Roscoe Arbuckle, Buster Keaton, Al St. John, Josephine Stevens, Arthur Earle, Agnes Neilson

CABIN IN THE SKY   U.S.A. (1943)
A witty, stylish all-Negro musical based on the fantasies of a wounded

gambler (Eddie "Rochester" Anderson) as he hovers between life and death while the forces of good (represented by his wife) and evil (the devil) battle for possession of his soul. Vincente Minnelli's first film; among the best sequences: Ethel Water's rendering of "Happiness Is Just a Thing Called Joe" and the Lena Horne/Eddie Anderson duet "Life's Full o' Consequence."

METRO–GOLDWYN–MAYER

Production—Arthur Freed
Direction—Vincente Minnelli
Photography—Sidney Wagner
Art direction—Cedric Gibbons &
  Leonid Vasian
Musical direction—Georgie Stoll

Screenplay [based on the 1930's
  musical play by Lynn Root
  (book), John Latouche
  (lyrics) and Vernon Duke
  (music)]—Joseph Schrank
Editing—Harold F. Kress

PLAYERS: Ethel Waters, Eddie "Rochester" Anderson, Lena Horne, Louis Armstrong, Rex Ingram, Kenneth Spencer, John W. Bublett, Oscar Polk, Mantan Moreland

CABINET OF DR. CALIGARI, THE   Germany (1919)
Horror fantasy examining, through the eyes of a madman, the activities of a mysterious doctor (Werner Krauss) who creates a reign of terror in a small German town by hypnotizing a somnambulist (Conrad Veidt) into committing a series of terrible crimes. The distorted sets, with their uneven shapes and weird shadows, were designed by three architects who borrowed from expressionist and cubist painting in order to translate the madman's vision into cinema terms. Krauss and Veidt made their debuts in the film which was the most experimental of all those made in the period after the First World War.

DECLA–BIOSKOP/ERICH POMMER

Direction—Robert Wiene
Screenplay—Carl Mayer &
  Hans Janowitz

Photography—Willi Hameister
Art direction—Walter Reimann,
  Hermann Warm &
  Walter Röhrig

PLAYERS: Werner Krauss, Conrad Veidt, Lil Dagover, Friedrich Feher, H. H. von Twardowski

CABIRIA   Italy (1914)
Early superproduction from Italy concerning the escapades of a young woman during the Punic wars. Some excitingly staged spectacles—the eruption of Mount Etna, Hannibal's crossing of the Alps, the siege

of Syracuse, etc.—and some fine camera work. The film took seven months to shoot, included several impressive full-sized sets, and was one of the most influential of the early Italian films.

Direction/script/theme—Piero Fosco (Giovanni Pastrone)

Photography—Segundo de Chomon, Giovanni Tomatis, Auguste Batagliotti & Natale Chiusano

Literary & dramatic adviser & captions—Gabriele D'Annunzio

Music—Idebrando Pizzetti

PLAYERS: Italia Almirante Manzini, Umberto Mazzato, Lydia Quaranta, Bartolomeo Pagano

CAGED   U.S.A. (1950)

The story of a 19-year-old first offender (Eleanor Parker) who is corrupted and turned into a hardened criminal by her experiences inside a women's prison. A sordid, pitiless but impressive movie that shows the talents of underrated director John Cromwell. Others in the all-female cast include Hope Emerson as a sadistic matron and Agnes Moorehead as the sympathetic superintendent. The entire movie is set inside the prison walls.

WARNER BROS.

Production—Jerry Wald
Direction—John Cromwell
Screenplay—Virginia Kellogg & Bernard Schoenfeld

Photography—Carl Guthrie
Art direction—Charles Clarke
Music—Max Steiner
Editing—Owen Marks

PLAYERS: Eleanor Parker, Agnes Moorehead, Hope Emerson, Ellen Corby, Betty Garde, Jan Sterling, Lee Patrick, Olive Deering, Jane Darwell, Getrude Michael

CAINE MUTINY, THE   U.S.A. (1954)

A straightforward adaptation of Herman Wouk's novel and stage play about a combat-weary commander in the U.S. Navy who loses his nerve when his minesweeper runs into a typhoon and is relieved of command by his first officer. Slow, somewhat unimaginative film is partly redeemed by Humphrey Bogart's superb performance as the tragic, demoralized Captain Queeg and by beautifully written court-martial climax. Jose Ferrer is the defense counsel, Van Johnson and Fred McMurray the two mutinous officers, and Tom Tully (an outstanding cameo) an old sea dog.

STANLEY KRAMER PRODUCTIONS/COLUMBIA

Production—Stanley Kramer
Direction—Edward Dmytryk
Screenplay—Stanley Roberts
Additional dialogue—
   Michael Blankfort
Photography (Technicolor)—
   Franz Planer

Art direction—Cary Odell
Production design—
   Rudolph Sternad
Music—Max Steiner
Editing—William Lyon,
   Henry Batista

PLAYERS: Humphrey Bogart, Jose Ferrer, Van Johnson, Fred Mac-Murray, Robert Francis, May Wynn, Tom Tully, E. G. Marshall, Arthur Franz, Lee Marvin, Warner Anderson, Claude Akins

CALABUCH   Spain/Italy (1956)
Satirical little Spanish fantasy about an American rocket scientist who, in order to escape from the pressures of the atomic age, disappears into the seclusion of a small fishing community where he becomes friends with everybody and spends his time making a gigantic firework for the forthcoming fiesta. Gay, charming, and with a richly humorous climax (as villagers prepare to declare war on the U.S. fleet in order to hold on to their guest). British-born character actor Edmund Gwenn appears as the scientist.

AGUILA FILMS—FILM COSTELLAZIONE

Production—Jose Luis Jerez
Direction—Luis G. Berlanga
Screenplay—Leonardo Martin,
   Florentino Soria,
   Ennio Flaianno &
   Luis G. Berlanga

Story—Leonardo Martin
Photography—
   Francisco Sempere
Art direction—Ramon Calatayud
Music—Francesco A. Lavagnino
Editing—Pepita Orduxa

PLAYERS: Edmund Gwenn, Valentina Cortese, Franco Fabrizi, Juan Calvo, Jose Isbert

CALL NORTHSIDE 777   U.S.A. (1948)
Vigorous, well-observed crime thriller of same genus as *The House on 92nd Street* and *Kiss of Death* centers on the efforts of newspaper reporter (James Stewart) to establish the innocence of convict (Richard Conte), a Polish-American serving a 13-year sentence for murder. Efficiently directed by Henry Hathaway and admirably photographed by Joe MacDonald, who shot a large part of the picture in state penitentiaries and in the dingier streets and back alleys of Chicago.

TWENTIETH CENTURY—FOX

Production—Otto Lang
Direction—Henry Hathaway

Photography—Joe MacDonald

Art direction—Lyle Wheeler, Mark-Lee Kirk
Screenplay—Jerome Cady, Jay Dratler
Music direction—Alfred Newman
Adaptation (based on articles by James P. McGuire)—Leonard Hoffman, Quentin Reynolds
Editing—J. Watson Webb, Jr
PLAYERS: James Stewart, Richard Conte, Lee J. Cobb, Helen Walker, Betty Garde, Kasia Orazewski, Joanne de Bergh, Howard Smith, Moroni Olsen, John McIntire, Paul Harvey

CAMERAMAN, THE U.S.A. (1928)

Buster Keaton, loose in New York with a vintage Pathé movie camera, outscoops master cameraman (Harold Goodwin) and wins the affections of his adoring girl (Marceline Day). The first of his two films at M-G-M and the last of the great comedies he made between 1923 and 1928. After his next film—the little known *Spite Marriage*—Keaton's career as a great comedian ended and he was reduced to playing in minor vehicles and making guest appearances.

METRO–GOLDWYN–MAYER

Production—Buster Keaton
Direction—Edward Sedgwick
Screenplay—Clyde Bruckman, Lew Lipton
Photography—Elgin Lessley, Reggie Lanning
Editing—Hugh Wynn
Technical direction—Fred Gabourie (?)
PLAYERS: Buster Keaton, Marceline Day, Harry Gribbon, Harold Goodwin, Sidney Bracy

CAMILLE U.S.A. (1937)

Greta Garbo in perhaps her best role of the 1930's, with George Cukor directing her to a New York Critics Award as the doomed "La Dame aux camélias," Dumas' tragic young courtesan dying of tuberculosis in 19th-century Paris. Garbo's exquisite performance and Cukor's stylish direction turned an otherwise absurd tale into a distinguished piece of filmcraft. Robert Taylor, then at the start of his career, played the young lover Armand.

METRO–GOLDWYN–MAYER

Production—Irving G. Thalberg
Direction—George Cukor
Screenplay (from novel and play by Alexandre Dumas)—Zoe Akins, Frances Marion & James Hilton
Photography—William Daniels & Karl Freund
Art direction—Cedric Gibbons
Music—Herbert Stothart
Editing—Margaret Booth

PLAYERS: Greta Garbo, Robert Taylor, Lionel Barrymore, Jessie Ralph, Henry Daniell, Laura Hope Crews

CAPTAIN BLOOD U.S.A. (1935)

The first of the vigorous Flynn-Curtiz swashbucklers made at Warner's between 1935 and 1940. Errol Flynn portrays a 17th-century physician turned pirate and the set piece is an excitingly staged duel to the death with French buccaneer Basil Rathbone. The film, first of Flynn's eight with leading lady Olivia de Havilland, is based on the 1922 novel by Rafael Sabatini.

A COSMOPOLITAN PRODUCTION: A FIRST NATIONAL PICTURE (WARNER BROS.)

Executive producer—
Hal B. Wallis
*Direction—*Michael Curtiz
*Screenplay—*Casey Robinson
*Photography—*Hal Mohr

Additional photography—
Ernest Haller
*Art direction—*Anton Grot
Music—
Erich Wolfgang Korngold
*Editing—*George Amy

PLAYERS: Errol Flynn, Olivia de Havilland, Lionel Atwill, Basil Rathbone, Ross Alexander, Guy Kibbee, Henry Stephenson, Robert Barrat

CAPTAIN HORATIO HORNBLOWER Gt. Britain (1951)

C. S. Forester's naval hero brought to the screen in the person of handsome Gregory Peck who, in between sinking a Spanish galleon and destroying four French ships of the line, finds time to love, lose and love again the sister of the Duke of Wellington, played somewhat improbably by Virginia Mayo. Robust, perfectly in period, in fact splendidly done all around though nothing quite matches up to the vigorously staged sea battles of Raoul Walsh who made a number of sea yarns—*The World in His Arms, Blackbeard the Pirate, Sea Devils*, etc.

WARNER BROS.

Production & direction—
Raoul Walsh
*Screenplay—*Ivan Goff, Ben
Roberts & Aeneas MacKenzi
Photography (Technicolor)—
Guy Green

*Art direction—*Tom Morahan
*Music—*Robert Farnon
*Musical direction—*Louis Levy
*Editing—*Jack Harris

PLAYERS: Gregory Peck, Virginia Mayo, Robert Beatty, James Robertson Justice, Denis O'Dea, Moultrie Kelsall, Terence Morgan, Richard Hearne

74

CAPTAINS COURAGEOUS   U.S.A. (1937)
A millionaire's spoiled son learns humility and respect for his fellow
men when circumstances force him to live among some poor fishermen.
Strikingly played by Freddie Bartholomew as the egotistical child,
Spencer Tracy (Academy Award, best actor, 1937) as Manuel, the
simple Portuguese fisherman, and Lionel Barrymore as a salty old sea
captain.

METRO–GOLDWYN–MAYER

Production–Louis D. Lighton
Direction–Victor Fleming
Screenplay (from novel by Rudyard Kipling)–John Lee Mahin, Marc Connelly, Dale Van Every

Photography–Harold Rosson
Art direction–Cedric Gibbons
Music–Franz Waxman
Editing–Elmo Vernon

PLAYERS: Spencer Tracy, Freddie Bartholomew, Lionel Barrymore,
Melvyn Douglas, Charles Grapewin, Mickey Rooney, John Carradine

CAREFREE   U.S.A. (1938)
Fred Astaire and Ginger Rogers' contribution to the musical scene of
1938. An uneven film showing a further decline from the standards of
Top Hat and *The Gay Divorcee,* but redeemed by impeccable dancing
and by such tuneful Berlin numbers as "Change Partners," "The Yam,"
and "The Night Is Filled with Music." Sandrich's fifth and last film in
the series.

RKO RADIO

Production–Pandro S. Berman
Direction–Mark Sandrich
Screenplay–Allan Scott & Ernest Pagano

Story & adaptation–Dudley Nichols & Hagar Wilde
Photography–Robert deGrasse
Art direction–Van Nest Polglase
Music & lyrics–Irving Berlin

PLAYERS: Fred Astaire, Ginger Rogers, Ralph Bellamy, Luella Grear,
Jack Carson, Clarence Kolb, Franklin Pangborn

CARRIE   U.S.A. (1952)
The rise of a Chicago factory girl (Jennifer Jones) to leading stage
actress and the decline and degradation of the wealthy restaurateur
(Laurence Olivier) who is infatuated with her. Directed by William
Wyler from Theodore Dreiser's classic novel *Sister Carrie* and some-
what overshadowed by an earlier Dreiser adaptation–George Stevens'

A Place in the Sun—but with superb period décor and capturing the full feel of life in turn-of-the-century Chicago. Olivier's portrayal of the broken restaurateur is among his best.

PARAMOUNT

Production & direction—
William Wyler
Screenplay—Ruth & Augustus
Goetz
Photography—Victor Milner

Art direction—Hal Pereira &
Roland Anderson
Music—David Raksin
Editing—Robert Swink

PLAYERS: Laurence Olivier, Jennifer Jones, Miriam Hopkins, Eddie Albert, Basil Ruysdael, Ray Teal, Barry Kelley, Sara Berner

CASABLANCA   U.S.A. (1943)
One of the greatest romantic melodramas ever made in Hollywood, set in Vichy Morocco in 1941 and featuring Humphrey Bogart as the tough disillusioned owner of Rick's Bar, a rendezvous for every crook and refugee in Casablanca. Directed by Michael Curtiz (Academy Award, best director, 1943) and beautifully acted by one of the best casts ever assembled on the Warner lot with Claude Rains eventually coming out on top with his witty portrait of a corrupt police official. Ingrid Bergman's famous request "Play it again, Sam," and Dooley Wilson's subsequent rendering of "As Time Goes By" belong to Hollywood folklore.

WARNER BROS.

Production—Hal B. Wallis
Direction—Michael Curtiz
Screenplay (from play Every-
body Comes to Ricks *by*
Murray Burnett & Joan Alison)
—Julius J. & Philip G. Epstein,
Howard Koch

Photography—Arthur Edeson
Art direction—Carl Jules Weyl
Music—Max Steiner
Editing—Owen Marks
Montages—Don Siegel,
James Leicester

PLAYERS: Humphrey Bogart, Ingrid Bergman, Paul Henreid, Claude Rains, Conrad Veidt, Sydney Greenstreet, Peter Lorre, S. Z. Sakall

CASQUE D'OR (Golden Marie)   France (1952)
The tragic love affair between an alluring underworld courtesan (Simone Signoret) and a young carpenter's assistant (Serge Reggiani) in turn-of-the-century Paris. Jacques Becker's detailed re-creation of the life and background of the period combines with the quality of the acting, particularly of Miss Signoret who here gives one of the finest performances of her career, to make this one of the great French films.

Direction—Jacques Becker
Screenplay—Jacques Becker &
  Jacques Companeez
Dialogue—Jacques Becker
Photography—Robert Le Febvre

Art direction—J. A. D'Eaubonne
Music—Georges Van Parys
Editing—Marguerite Renoir &
  Jacques Becker

PLAYERS: Simone Signoret, Serge Reggiani, Claude Dauphin, Raymond Bussières, Gaston Modot, Dominique Davray

CAT AND THE CANARY, THE   U.S.A. (1927)

One of the best American horror films of the 1920's with Laura La Plante, Creighton Hale, Tully Marshall and others involved in mysterious happenings in a castle at midnight during the reading of an eccentric millionaire's will. Based on John Willard's Broadway play and directed with considerable style by German-born Paul Leni who made full use of such standard haunted house ingredients as billowing curtains, sliding doors, and long, darkly lit corridors. Remade in 1930 as *The Cat Creeps* (Rupert Julian) and in 1939 as *The Cat and the Canary* (Elliott Nugent).

UNIVERSAL

Direction—Paul Leni
Screenplay—Robert F. Hill &
  Alfreda Cohn

Photography—Gilbert Warrenton
Art direction—Charles D. Hall

PLAYERS: Laura La Plante, Creighton Hale, Forest Stanley, Gertrude Astor, Tully Marshall, Flora Finch, Arthur Edmund Carewe, Martha Mattox

CAT BALLOU   U.S.A. (1965)

A pretty young schoolteacher (Jane Fonda), forced to become an outlaw when her father is murdered by crooked industrialists, hires a drunken has-been gunfighter (Lee Marvin) to help her gain revenge. This is one of Hollywood's relatively few Western spoofs, and although not entirely successful the script does have some genuinely witty moments, with Marvin's Kid Shelleen a classic.

COLUMBIA

Production—Harold Hecht
Direction—Elliot Silverstein
*Screenplay (from novel by Roy
  Chanslor)*—Walter Newman,
  Frank R. Pierson

Photography (Technicolor)—
  Jack Marta
Art direction—Malcolm Brown
Music—Frank De Vol
Editing—Charles Nelson

PLAYERS: Jane Fonda, Lee Marvin, Michael Callan, Dwayne Hickman, Nat King Cole, Stubby Kaye, Tom Nardini, John Marley, Reginald Denny, Jay C. Flippen, Arthur Hunnicutt

CAT PEOPLE, THE   U.S.A. (1942)

This is the film that began Val Lewton's five-year cycle of horror B movies at RKO, an understated, cleverly directed fantasy about a tormented Balkan-born girl who discovers that she is descended from a race of panther women and has the power to change into an outsized homicidal cat. This bizarre theme is treated with unusual restraint by director Jacques Tourneur and the film's most effective scenes are those in which the stalking cat is sensed and heard but never seen; e.g., a young girl being pursued by something unknown through Central Park at night and being trapped in a dark, deserted swimming pool where the only sounds are those of lapping water and the breathing of the cat. Photographed by Nicholas Musuraca who also worked on a number of other Lewton horror pictures and edited by Mark Robson who later graduated to director on *The Seventh Victim* and *Isle of the Dead*.

RKO RADIO

Production—Val Lewton
Direction—Jacques Tourneur
Screenplay—DeWitt Bodeen
Photography—
  Nicholas Musuraca

Art direction—
  Albert S. D'Agostino &
  Walter E. Keller
Music—Roy Webb
Editing—Mark Robson

PLAYERS: Simone Simon, Kent Smith, Tom Conway, Jane Randolph, Jack Holt, Alan Napier

CESAR   France (1933)

The last film in Marcel Pagnol's trilogy brings to a conclusion his long saga about the people who live in the old port of Marseilles and unites at last Fanny, widowed by the death of Panisse, and her wandering lover Marius. The film is set some twenty years after the events described in *Fanny* (see page 131) and is the only part of the trilogy to be directed by Pagnol himself. Raimu (César), Pierre Fresnay (Marius), Orane Demazis (Fanny) and Charpin (Panisse) appeared in all three films over a period of four years. See also *Marius* (page 283).

LES FILMS MARCEL PAGNOL

Direction—Marcel Pagnol
Screenplay (from his own play)
  —Marcel Pagnol

Photography—Willy, assisted by
  Gricha & Ledru
Art direction—Marius Brouquier
Music—Vincent Scotto

PLAYERS: Raimu, Orane Demazis, Pierre Fresnay, André Fouché, Charpin, Edouard Delmont, Milly Mathis

CHAMPION U.S.A. (1949)

The life and times of Midge Kelly (Kirk Douglas), an arrogant young boxer who fights his way up from poverty to the middleweight championship, trampling on his manager, crippled brother, and assorted girlfriends in the process. The film has realistic fight scenes and impressive playing, especially from Paul Stewart as the long-suffering manager, but is saddled with a cliché-ridden script. It is somewhat overshadowed by *The Set-Up*, released a month earlier.

UNITED ARTISTS

Production—Stanley Kramer
Direction—Mark Robson
Screenplay (from Ring Lardner
  story "Champion")—
  Carl Foreman

Photography—Franz Planer
Production design—
  Rudolph Sternad
Music—Dimitri Tiomkin
Editing—Harry Gerstad

PLAYERS: Kirk Douglas, Marilyn Maxwell, Ruth Roman, Lola Albright, Arthur Kennedy, Paul Stewart

CHARGE OF THE LIGHT BRIGADE, THE U.S.A. (1936)

Errol Flynn in his element as a gallant British major who leads the 27th Lancers in their disastrous charge against the Russian artillery during the war in the Crimea. The story is a fictitious one set largely in India and is nothing more than romantic nonsense, but the charge itself, filmed by both Michael Curtiz and second-unit director B. Reeves Eason and brilliantly edited by George Amy, is a tour de force. C. Henry Gordon plays the Indian heavy who eventually sides with the Russians against the British.

WARNER BROS.

Executive producer—
  Hal B. Wallis
Associate producer—
  Samuel Bischoff
Direction—Michael Curtiz
Photography—Sol Polito
Art direction—John Hughes

Screenplay (based on original
  story by Michel Jacoby)—
  Michel Jacoby &
  Rowland Leigh
Music—Max Steiner
Editing—George Amy

PLAYERS: Errol Flynn, Olivia de Havilland, Patric Knowles, Henry Stephenson, Nigel Bruce, Donald Crisp, David Niven, C. Henry Gordon, G. P. Huntley, Jr.

CHARGE OF THE LIGHT BRIGADE, THE   Gt. Britain (1968)

This Tony Richardson movie has little in common with the Curtiz version and concentrates on examining the sordidness of life in mid-nineteenth century England and the political events (often linked by witty Richard Williams cartoons) that led to the disastrous cavalry charge in the Crimea. It is a long, muddled, sometimes slow film although the charge itself is realistically handled and there is a superb performance from Trevor Howard as the fiery Lord Cardigan. Others in the cast are John Gielgud (Lord Raglan), Harry Andrews (Lord Lucan), and Howard Marion Crawford (Sir George Brown).

WOODFALL/UNITED ARTISTS

Production—Neil Hartley
Direction—Tony Richardson
Screenplay—Charles Wood
Photography (Panavision/
    Deluxecolor)—David Watkin

Art direction—Edward Marshall
Music—John Addison
Titles & animation sequences—
    Richard Williams
Editing—Kevin Brownlow

PLAYERS: Trevor Howard, Vanessa Redgrave, John Gielgud, Harry Andrews, Jill Bennett, David Hemmings, Peter Bowles, Howard Marion Crawford

CHEYENNE AUTUMN   U.S.A. (1964)

The last epic Western by Ford, this fine film displays his visual style at its most striking in telling the tragic story of the last of the Cheyenne Indians (some 286 men, women and children) who are pursued by the U.S. Cavalry from a barren Oklahoma reservation to their native Yellowstone 1,500 miles away. Richard Widmark plays a cavalry commander, Carroll Baker a Quaker schoolteacher, and Sal Mineo, Ricardo Montalban and Gilbert Roland are featured as Indians. James Stewart (Wyatt Earp) and Arthur Kennedy (Doc Holliday) appear in a lighthearted interlude, the Battle of Dodge City.

FORD–SMITH PRODUCTIONS/WARNER BROS.

Production—Bernard Smith
Direction—John Ford
Screenplay (from book by Mari
    Sandoz)—James R. Webb
Art direction—Richard Day

Photography (Technicolor/
    Super Panavision 70)—
    William Clothier
Music—Alex North
Editing—Otho Lovering

PLAYERS: Richard Widmark, Carroll Baker, James Stewart, Edward G. Robinson, Karl Malden, Sal Mineo, Dolores Del Rio, Ricardo Montalban, Gilbert Roland, Arthur Kennedy

CHILDHOOD OF MAXIM GORKY, THE   U.S.S.R. (1938)

The first part in Mark Donskoi's distinguished trilogy about the early life of Russian writer Maxim Gorky centers on his childhood with his mother and grandparents in late-19th-century provincial Russia. Honestly and compassionately observed and reflecting all the hardship and misery suffered by the peasant community under Tsarist rule. Alexei Lyarsky plays the child, Mikhail Troyanovsky his irascible grandfather, and Massalitinova is unforgettable as the wise old grandmother who keeps her courage and zest for life despite the poverty and terrible conditions around her. (See also *My Childhood* and *My Universities.*)

SOYUZDETFILM

Direction—Mark Donskoi
Screenplay (from Gorky's memoirs)—I. Gruzdev & Mark Donskoi
Photography—Pyotr Yermolov
Art direction—I. Stepanov
Music—Lev Schwartz

PLAYERS: Alexei Lyarsky, Varvara Massalitinova, Mikhail Troyanovsky, Daniel Sagal

CHIMES AT MIDNIGHT   Spain/Switzerland (1966)

After his award-winning *Othello,* this is Orson Welles' most successful Shakespearean film, centering on Falstaff's friendship with young Prince Hal and his rejection when the Prince becomes King of England. Some of Welles' most memorable scenes are in this film, particularly the boisterous sequences in the tavern of Mistress Quickly (Margaret Rutherford) and the Battle of Shrewsbury. Heading the cast are Welles as Falstaff, Keith Baxter as Prince Hal, John Gielgud as Henry IV, and Norman Rodway as Hotspur.

INTERNACIONAL FILMS ESPANOLA (MADRID)/ALPINE (BASLE)

Executive producer— Alessandro Tasca
Production—Emiliano Piedra, Angel Escolano
Direction—Orson Welles
Screenplay (adapted from Richard II, Henry IV Parts I & II, Henry V, The Merry Wives of Windsor by William Shakespeare)—Orson Welles
Photography—Edmond Richard
Art direction—Jose Antonio de la Guerra, Mariano Erdorza
Music— Angelo Francesco Lavagnino
Editing—Fritz Mueller
Narration—Ralph Richardson

PLAYERS: Orson Welles, Keith Baxter, John Gielgud, Margaret Rutherford, Jeanne Moreau, Norman Rodway, Marina Vlady, Alan Webb

CINDERELLA
U.S.A. (1950)

One of Disney's ambitious attempts to transfer an established children's classic into an animated cartoon, a practice he was to continue with ever-decreasing success (*Alice in Wonderland, Peter Pan, The Sleeping Beauty*) throughout the 1950's. This one, however, is charming and easily the best of the series mainly because of the addition of several animal characters to the established Cinderella story line. Most endearing of these are Gus and Jaq, a couple of domestic mice; Bruno, an affable dog, and an arrogant, pampered black cat named Lucifer. Oversugary but fresh and enjoyable. Best songs: "A Dream Is a Wish Your Heart Makes" and "Bibbidi-Bobbidi-Boo."

WALT DISNEY PRODUCTIONS/RKO RADIO

Production—Walt Disney
Production supervisor—
  Ben Sharpsteen
Direction—Wilfred Jackson,
  Hamilton Luske,
  Clyde Geronimi

*Script from story by Charles
  Perrault*
Music direction—Oliver Wallace,
  Paul Smith
Songs—Mack David, Jerry
  Livingston, Al Hoffman

CIRCUS, THE
U.S.A. (1928)

Charlie Chaplin's optimistic little tramp finds a job in a circus where he becomes a top clown and also, in one superb scene, a stand-in tight-rope walker. Not Chaplin's best known or most accomplished work; although, as always, the pathos and slapstick are perfectly blended and the gags impeccably timed. Won Chaplin a special Oscar—his only Academy Award—for "his versatility and genius in writing, acting, directing and producing *The Circus*."

UNITED ARTISTS

Production & direction—
  Charles Chaplin
Assistant director—
  Harry Crocker

Screenplay—Charles Chaplin
Photography—R. H. Totheroh
Cameramen—Jack Wilson,
  Mark Marklatt

PLAYERS: Charles Chaplin, Myrna Kennedy, Betty Morrissey, Harry Crocker, Allan Garcia, Henry Bergman, Stanley J. Sanford, George Davis

CITIZEN KANE
U.S.A. (1941)

The life and death of an American newspaper tycoon pieced together by a newsreel reporter as he endeavors to find the truth about the man behind the legend by interviewing those people most closely connected with him during his lifetime. Closely modeled on the career of William Randolph Hearst, this technically superb film is frequently quoted as being one of the best pictures, if not *the* best picture, of all time. It marked the film debut (both as actor and director) of Orson Welles, then only 25 years old, who, together with his gifted cameraman Gregg Toland, made striking use of wide-angle photography and dramatic lighting. The distinguished cast was made up entirely from Welles' own Mercury Company.

A MERCURY PRODUCTION/RKO RADIO

Production & direction— Orson Welles

*Screenplay—*Herman J. Mankiewicz & Orson Welles

*Photography—*Gregg Toland

*Art direction—*Van Nest Polglase & Perry Ferguson

*Music—*Bernard Herrmann

*Editing—*Robert Wise & Mark Robson

PLAYERS: Orson Welles, Joseph Cotten, Dorothy Comingore, Everett Sloane, Ruth Warrick, Agnes Moorhead, Ray Collins

CITY LIGHTS   U.S.A. (1931)

Melancholy Chaplin masterpiece which traces the efforts of the little tramp to restore the sight of a pretty young flower seller. In many ways Chaplin's best film, at once excruciatingly funny and terribly sad, and containing several quite memorable scenes, e.g. the boxing match with Hank Mann, the street-cleaning sequences, and the final almost unbearably poignant moments when Chaplin meets the girl for the first time after her sight has been restored. The film was released as a silent (Chaplin halted production halfway through to consider switching to sound) even though sound pictures had then been in existence for some four years. Jean Harlow, who by the time the film was released was a star, appears as an extra in a night-club sequence.

UNITED ARTISTS

*Production, direction & screenplay—*Charles Chaplin

*Assistant directors—*Harry Crocker, Henry Bergman & Albert Austin

*Music—*Charles Chaplin

*Photography—*R. H. Totheroh, Gordon Pollock & Mark Marklatt

Musical direction— Alfred Newman

*Settings—*Charles D. Hall

PLAYERS: Charles Chaplin, Virginia Cherrill, Harry Myers, Hank Mann, Florence Lee, Allan Garcia, Eddie Baker, Henry Bergman, Albert Austin

Cleo Between 5 and 7

CITY STREETS   U.S.A. (1931)
Gangster movie, 1931 vintage, with hero (Gary Cooper) involved with
gang girl (Sylvia Sydney) and in the liquor rackets of hoodlums Guy
Kibbee, Paul Lukas and William Boyd (later of Hopalong Cassidy
fame). Not the most distinguished film in the genre but important because of the direction of Rouben Mamoulian, who treated the subject
with great style, experimenting boldly with sound and camera movement. Based on a novel by Dashiell Hammett who later wrote *The
Thin Man* and *The Maltese Falcon*.

PARAMOUNT

Direction—Rouben Mamoulian   *Adaptation*—Max Marcin
Screenplay—Oliver Garrett   *Photography*—Lee Garmes
PLAYERS: Sylvia Sydney, Gary Cooper, Guy Kibbee, Paul Lukas, Wil-
liam Boyd, Stanley Fields

CLEO BETWEEN 5 AND 7 (Cleo, de 5 à 7)   France/Italy (1962)
Agnes Varda examines the restlessness and melancholy mood of a feck-
less young pop singer (Corinne Marchand) as she wanders aimlessly
across Paris while waiting for the medical report that will tell her
whether or not she is suffering from cancer. A slight film, made satisfy-

ing by the way Varda captures the mood, atmosphere and loneliness of life in a great city. Shot among the boulevards and bistros of Paris by Jean Rabier who also worked on, among others, *Le Bonheur* for Varda and *La Bai des Anges* and *Les Parapluies de Cherbourg* for husband Jacques Demy.

ROME–PARIS FILMS

Direction, screenplay & dialogue   *Art direction*—Bernard Evein
—Agnes Varda   *Music*—Michel Legrand
Photography—Jean Rabier   *Editing*—Janine Verneau
PLAYERS: Corinne Marchand, Antoine Bourseiller, Dorothée Blank, Michel Legrand, Dominique Davray

CLEOPATRA   U.S.A. (1963)

Notorious and disastrously expensive historical epic that almost brought Twentieth Century-Fox to its knees, with Elizabeth Taylor as the politically ambitious Egyptian queen and Rex Harrison (Caesar) and Richard Burton (Antony) as her two Roman lovers. Out of some 243 minutes of screen time Cleopatra's spectacular entry into Rome, Harrison's performance as the aging Caesar, and Joseph Mankiewicz's literate and often witty screenplay are worth remembering. Excellent second-unit work by Ray Kellogg and Andrew Marton, the latter of whom also staged the chariot race in *Ben-Hur*.

TWENTIETH CENTURY–FOX

Production—Walter Wanger   *Photography* (*DeLuxecolor/
Direction—   Todd AO*)—Leon Shamroy
  Joseph L. Mankiewicz   *Second unit crew*—Andrew
Screenplay (*from works of*   Marton & Ray Kellogg
  Plutarch, Suetonius, Appian,   *Art direction*—John DeCuir, Jack
  The Life of Cleopatra *by Carlo   Martin Smith, Hilyard Brown,
  Maria Franzero,* Antony &   Herman A. Blumenthal, Elven
  Cleopatra *and* Julius Caesar   Webb, Maurice Pelling & Boris
  by William Shakespeare,   Juraga
  Caesar and Cleopatra *by*   *Music*—Alex North
  George Bernard Shaw*)*—   *Editing*—Dorothy Spencer &
  Joseph L. Mankiewicz,   Elmo Williams
  Ranald MacDougall &
  Sidney Buchman
PLAYERS: Elizabeth Taylor, Rex Harrison, Richard Burton, Pamela Brown, George Cole, Hume Cronyn, Cesare Danova, Kenneth Haigh, Andrew Keir, Martin Landau, Roddy McDowall

COCOANUTS, THE   U.S.A. (1929)

The Marx Brothers' first film, shot at Paramount's Long Island studios in New York. Groucho appears as the owner-manager of a 600-room Florida hotel and wealthy widow Margaret Dumont (in the first of her seven Marx Brothers films) is the butt for most of his wisecracks. Mary Eaton and Oscar Shaw share top billing. The film was pruned to some 96 minutes after running to 140 at a preview. Songs by Irving Berlin.

PARAMOUNT

Production—Walter Wanger
Direction—Robert Florey &
  Joseph Santley
Photography—George Folsey
Music & lyrics—Irving Berlin
Musical direction—Frank Tours

Adaptation (*based on musical play, book by George S. Kaufman & Morrie Ryskind*)
  —Morrie Ryskind
Editing—Barney Rogan

PLAYERS: Groucho, Harpo, Chico & Zeppo Marx, Margaret Dumont, Mary Eaton, Oscar Shaw, Kay Francis, Cyril Ring, Basil Ruysdael, Sylvan Lee

COLLEGE   U.S.A. (1927)

Buster Keaton working his way through college and vying with bone-head athlete (Harold Goodwin) for the favors of girlfriend (Ann Cornwall). Outstanding sequences: Keaton coxing a boat with the rudder tied to his behind, and trying to emulate—with disastrous results—the college champion in all the major sporting events. Co-directed by James W. Horne who was later responsible for many of the Laurel and Hardy pictures.

BUSTER KEATON PRODUCTIONS INC./UNITED ARTISTS

Production—Joseph M. Schenck
Direction—Buster Keaton,
  James W. Horne
Screenplay—Carl Harbaugh,
  Bryan Foy

Photography—J. Devereux
  Jennings, Bert Haines
Editing—J. S. Kell
Technical direction—
  Fred Gabourie

PLAYERS: Buster Keaton, Ann Cornwall, Harold Goodwin, Snitz Edwards, Florence Turner, Flora Bramley, Buddy Mason, Grant Withers

COME BACK, LITTLE SHEBA   U.S.A. (1952)

Based on a play by William Inge this powerful piece of cinema is held together mainly by the extraordinarily fine acting of Shirley Booth (Academy Award, best actress, 1952) and Burt Lancaster. The story is about the gradually disintegrating marriage of two mismatched middle-aged people—the woman a fat, slovenly housewife, the man a reformed alcoholic whose medical career was ruined years before when he was forced into a loveless marriage. The film marked the directorial debut of Daniel Mann.

PARAMOUNT

Production—Hal B. Wallis
Direction—Daniel Mann
Screenplay—Ketti Frings
Photography—
  James Wong Howe

Art direction—Hal Pereira &
  Henry Bumstead
Music—Franz Waxman
Editing—Warren Low

PLAYERS: Shirley Booth, Burt Lancaster, Terry Moore, Richard Jaeckel, Philip Ober, Edwin Max, Lisa Golm

COMPULSION U.S.A. (1959)

Intelligently scripted version of Meyer Levin's novel about two rich Chicago youths who murder a 14-year-old schoolboy in order to prove their distorted theory that their "intellectual superiority" exempts them from moral law. Based on the true-life Leopold and Loeb case of the 1920's and rising to great heights in the later sequences when Orson Welles, thinly disguised as lawyer Clarence Darrow, makes a passionate plea for the lives of the murderers and for the abolition of capital punishment. Welles, Dean Stockwell and Bradford Dillman (who played the boys) were the joint winners of the best actor award at the 1959 Cannes Film Festival.

TWENTIETH CENTURY—FOX

Production—Richard D. Zanuck
Direction—Richard Fleischer
Screenplay—Richard Murphy
Photography (CinemaScope)—
  William C. Mellor

Art direction—Lyle Wheeler &
  Mark Lee-Kirk
Music—Lionel Newman
Editing—William Reynolds

PLAYERS: Dean Stockwell, Bradford Dillman, Orson Welles, E. G. Marshall, Diane Varsi, Martin Milner, Richard Anderson

CONFESSIONS OF A NAZI SPY U.S.A. (1938)

Fast-moving piece of anti-Nazi propaganda with Edward G. Robinson in sympathetic role as an FBI agent who helps smash a Nazi spy ring operating in the United States. Paul Lukas and George Sanders lead the Nazi heavies and Francis Lederer appears as the German-American they use to obtain Government secrets. Based on the revelations of an ex-G-man and on spy trials held in the United States just before the war.

Executive producer—
  Hal B. Wallis
*Associate producer—*Robert Lord
*Direction—*Anatole Litvak
*Photography—*Sol Polito
*Art direction—*Carl Jules Weyl

Screenplay (based on articles by
  *Leon G. Turrou)—*Milton
  Krims & John Wexley
Musical direction—
  Leo F. Forbstein
*Editing—*Owen Marks

PLAYERS: Edward G. Robinson, Francis Lederer, George Sanders, Paul Lukas, Henry O'Neill, Dorothy Tree, Lya Lys, Grace Stafford

CONFIDENTIAL REPORT   Spain (1955)

Bizarre thriller by Orson Welles about a wealthy financier who systematically eliminates all the criminals he was associated with in his early life so as to hide the truth about his shady past from his daughter. Some isolated moments of brilliance, e.g. the murder of an old criminal in Zurich on Christmas Eve, and cameo performances by Michael Redgrave as a Dutch antique dealer, Mischa Auer as the owner of a flea circus, and Katina Paxinou as the retired madam of a brothel. Shot in eight months in France, Spain, Germany and Italy, and known also as *Mr. Arkadin,* which was the title of Welles' novel from which the film was made.

A MERCURY PRODUCTION/WARNER BROS.

*Direction—*Orson Welles
*Screenplay—*Orson Welles
*Photography—*Jean Bourgoin

*Art direction—*Orson Welles
*Music—*Paul Misraki
*Editing—*Renzo Lucidi

PLAYERS: Orson Welles, Paolo Mori, Robert Arden, Michael Redgrave, Patricia Medina, Akim Tamiroff, Mischa Auer, Katina Paxinou, Jack Watling, Peter Van Eyck

COUNTY HOSPITAL   U.S.A. (1932)

One of Laurel and Hardy's established classics; an early sound two-reeler in which Stan, bearing gifts of nuts and hard-boiled eggs, visits Ollie who is recovering in hospital from a broken leg. The ensuing chaos includes an unfortunate hospital doctor (Billy Gilbert) being catapulted out of a window, Ollie dangling upside down by his injured leg, and Stan sitting on a hypodermic needle that will put him to sleep for a week.

HAL ROACH/METRO–GOLDWYN–MAYER

*Direction—*James Parrott
PLAYERS: Stan Laurel & Oliver Hardy, Billy Gilbert

COVERED WAGON, THE   U.S.A. (1923)

Large-scale reconstruction (this was the first epic Western) by James Cruze of the 1849 pioneer trek to California and Oregon, notable for its realistic presentation of the hardship and loneliness endured by the pioneers and for its spectacular action. J. Warren Kerrigan, Lois Wilson and Alan Hale play hero, heroine and villain, while Ernest Torrence and Tully Marshall appear as a couple of drunken old frontier scouts. The photography is by Karl Brown who earlier worked as a Griffith cameraman.

PARAMOUNT–FAMOUS PLAYERS LASKY

Direction–James Cruze
Photography–Karl Brown
Editing–Dorothy Arzner
Screenplay (*adapted from novel by Emerson Hough*)– Jack Cunningham

PLAYERS: J. Warren Kerrigan, Lois Wilson, Alan Hale, Charles Ogle, Ethel Wales, Ernest Torrence, Tully Marshall

COVER GIRL   U.S.A. (1944)

Columbia musical set against a show-business and fashion-magazine background and featuring Rita Hayworth, then at the height of her popularity, as a Brooklyn career girl who rises from obscure singer and dancer to cover girl on the Golden Wedding issue of *Vanity* Magazine. Hayworth and Gene Kelly provide the dancing, wiscracking Eve Arden and Phil Silvers the comedy, and Ira Gershwin and Jerome Kern ("Put Me to the Test," "Long Ago and Far Away" and "Make Way for To-morrow") the songs. Zippy, colorful; directed by erratic Charles Vidor who, two years later, directed the classic black thriller *Gilda*.

COLUMBIA

Production–Arthur Schwartz
Direction–Charles Vidor
Screenplay–Virginia Van Upp
Photography (*Technicolor*)– Rudolph Mate & Allen M. Davey
Art direction–Lionel Banks & Cary Odell
Music & lyrics–Jerome Kern & Ira Gershwin
Musical direction– Morris W. Stoloff
Dance direction–Val Raset & Seymour Felix
Editing–Viola Lawrence

PLAYERS: Rita Hayworth, Gene Kelly, Lee Bowman, Phil Silvers, Jinx Falkenburg, Leslie Brooks, Eve Arden, Otto Kruger

THE CRANES ARE FLYING (Letyat Zhuravli)   U.S.S.R. (1958)

The tragic wartime experiences of a young Russian girl from the time of her love affair with a young student who is killed at the front to her bitter marriage to his cousin and subsequent life in Siberia nursing wounded Soviet soldiers. A technically striking Russian picture; Tatiana Samoilova's unforgettable performance as the girl won her the acting Grand Prix at the 1958 Cannes Film Festival.

MOSFILM

Direction—Mikhail Kalatozov
Screenplay—V. Rosov
Photography—S. Urusevsky

Art direction—E. Svidetelev
Music—M. Vainberg

PLAYERS: Tatiana Samoilova, Alexei Batalov, A. Shvorin, Vasily Merkuryev, S. Kharitonova, V. Zubkov

CRIMINAL, THE   Gt. Britain (1960)
Highly regarded crime melodrama about the last few weeks in the life (in and out of prison) of tough independent crook (Stanley Baker). The scenes of the intrigues and brutalities of English prison life show director Joseph Losey near peak form. The rest of the story and the climactic gang battle over a stolen racetrack haul is only routine. Nicely played by Baker and brilliantly so by Patrick Magee as sadistic prison warden.

MERTON PARK STUDIOS

Production—Jack Greenwood
Direction—Joseph Losey
Screenplay (based on original
   story by Jimmy Sangster)—
   Alun Owen

Photography—Robert Krasker
Art direction—Scott Macgregor
Music—Johnny Dankworth
Editing—Reginald Mills

PLAYERS: Stanley Baker, San Wanamaker, Margit Saad, Patrick Magee, Gregoire Aslan, Jill Bennett, Rupert Davies, Laurence Naismith

CRIMINAL LIFE OF ARCHIBALDO DE LA CRUZ, THE
   (Ensayo de un Crimen)   Mexico (1955)
A superb example of black humor by Luis Buñuel. A perverted though outwardly respectable young aristocrat (Ernesto Alonso) finds that whenever he decides to kill someone the intended victim dies from other causes before he has a chance to carry out his plans. Wickedly funny and one of Buñuel's best films, intended basically as a satire on the psychological horror film.

ALIANZA CINEMATOGRAFICA (ALFONSO PATINO GOMEZ)

Direction—Luis Buñuel
Screenplay (from story by

Rodolfo Usigli)—Luis Buñuel
   & Eduardo Ugarte

Photography—Agustin Jiménez   *Music*—Jesús Bracho &
Editing—Pablo Gomez   José Pérez
PLAYERS: Ernesto Alonso, Miroslava Stern, Rita Macedo, Ariadna Walter, Rodolfo Landa, Andres Palma, Carlos Riquelme, J. Maria Linares Rivas, Leonor Llansas

CRIN BLANC   France (1953)
Poetic 37-minute movie about a small fisher-boy and his determined efforts to conquer the beautiful white stallion that roams the salt marshes near Marseilles. Two memorable sequences—the first when a group of horses fight in the corral, the second when the boy is dragged by the horse for miles through the reeds of the marshlands—and some lyrical monochrome photography. Directed by Albert Lamorisse who, three years later, made the equally successful *The Red Balloon*.

LES FILMS MONTSOURIS

Direction—Albert Lamorisse   *Music*—Maurice Le Roux
Photography—Edmond Sechan   *Editing*—Alepee
PLAYERS: Alain Emery, Pascal Lamorisse

CRISIS   U.S.A. (1950)
Slickly made melodrama, similar in theme to Britain's *State Secret* released the same year, about an American surgeon (Cary Grant) who is forced against his will to perform a dangerous brain operation on a South American dictator (Jose Ferrer). Basically a well-made thriller but sometimes raised to a higher level by the script's perceptive observations of the extremist mentality of a dictator. In smaller parts, Gilbert Roland is a revolutionary leader and Ramon Novarro a police colonel. Richard Brooks' first film as a director

METRO—GOLDWYN—MAYER

Production—Arthur Freed   *Art direction*—Cedric Gibbons
Direction & screenplay (from   & Preston Ames
   story by George Tabori)—   *Music*—Miklos Rosza
   Richard Brooks   *Editing*—Robert J. Kern
Photography—Ray June
PLAYERS: Cary Grant, Jose Ferrer, Signe Hasso, Paula Raymond, Ramon Novarro, Gilbert Roland, Antonio Moreno, Teresa Celli, Leon Ames

CROSSFIRE   U.S.A. (1947)
A taut, well-written thriller about the murder of a Jew by a drunken G.I. Based on Richard Brooks' novel *The Brick Foxhole* the film was

the first to raise the question of anti-Semitism in the United States and was an important milestone in Hollywood's attempt to bring serious subjects to the screen. An interesting performance by Robert Ryan as the bigoted killer and some expert direction from Edward Dmytryk, who, during the forties, was one of the brightest young talents on the Hollywood scene.

RKO RADIO

Production—Adrian Scott
Direction—Edward Dmytryk
Screenplay—John Paxton
Photography—J. Roy Hunt

Art direction—Albert S.
    D'Agostino, Alfred Herman
Music—Roy Webb
Editing—Harry Gerstad

PLAYERS: Robert Young, Robert Mitchum, Robert Ryan, Gloria Grahame, Paul Kelly, Richard Benedict, Sam Levene, Steve Brodie, Jacqueline White, George Cooper, Richard Powers

CROWD, THE   U.S.A. (1928)
The problems and tragedies of an ordinary young clerk and his family as they live out a humdrum existence in a cheap apartment in New York City. One of Hollywood's earliest attempts at social realism, studying for the first time on the screen the plight of the average man in the soulless world of modern urban society. Long (14 reels), uncompromising and as big a failure at the box office as *The Big Parade* (another Vidor vehicle) was a success. Without doubt, however, this is Vidor's finest film. Little known actor James Murray, who played the leading role, went into an alcoholic decline shortly after the film was made and met an early death in the Hudson River.

METRO—GOLDWYN—MAYER

Direction—King Vidor
Screenplay (from story by
    King Vidor)—King Vidor,
    John V. A. Weaver &
    Harry Behn

Photography—Henry Sharp
Art direction—Cedric Gibbons
    & Arnold Gillespie
Editing—Hugh Wynn
Titles—Joe Farnum

PLAYERS: James Murray, Eleanor Boardman, Bert Roach, Estelle Clark

CRY THE BELOVED COUNTRY   Gt. Britain (1951)
An elderly black priest searches Johannesburg for his criminal son who has murdered the son of a neighboring white farmer. A melodramatic story, but raised well out of the normal rut by Alan Paton's sincere screenplay and by the film's realistic depiction of the poverty of the native districts in the city and the degradation of the African in a

Cry the Beloved Country

hostile white society. Canada Lee plays the old priest, Charles Carson the white farmer, and 26-year-old Sidney Poitier appears in an early role as a young African priest.

LONDON FILMS

Production & direction—
  Zoltan Korda
Screenplay (adapted from his
  *novel)—*Alan Paton

*Photography—*Robert Krasker
Art direction—
  Wilfrid Shingleton
*Editing—*David Eady

PLAYERS: Canada Lee, Charles Carson, Sidney Poitier, Joyce Carey, Geoffrey Keen, Michael Goodliffe, Edric Connor

CURE, THE   U.S.A. (1917)

Boisterous and perhaps the funniest of Chaplin's Mutual comedies. Charlie (unusually clad in light coat and straw hat) becomes involved in a series of slapstick adventures at a spa. Several memorable scenes, including those in which Charlie suffers on a masseur's table and Eric Campbell's foot gets caught in a revolving door.

A MUTUAL COMEDY

*Direction—*Charles Chaplin
*Screenplay—*Charles Chaplin

*Photography—*R. H. Totheroh &
  W. C. Foster

PLAYERS: Charles Chaplin, Albert Austin, Henry Bergman (the masseur), Eric Campbell, Frank J. Coleman, James T. Kelly, Edna Purviance, John Rand

CURSE OF THE CAT PEOPLE, THE   U.S.A. (1944)
Eerie little thriller that works equally well as a ghost story (a 6-year-old girl communicates with the spirit of the insane woman of *The Cat People*) and as a subtle study of the sensitive and lonely days of childhood. Directed by former editor Robert Wise, photographed by Musuraca, and designed by RKO's regular art directors D'Agostino and Keller who worked on all eight of the Val Lewton horror movies made at RKO between 1942 and 1947.

RKO RADIO

Production—Val Lewton	*Art direction*—
Direction—Robert Wise	Albert S. D'Agostino
Screenplay—DeWitt Bodeen	& Walter E. Keller
Photography—	*Music*—Roy Webb
Nicholas Musuraca	*Editing*—J. R. Whittredge

PLAYERS: Simone Simon, Kent Smith, Jane Randolph, Ann Carter, Elizabeth Russell, Eve March

DAMNED, THE   Gt. Britain (1962)
Top government research scientist (Alexander Knox) experiments on a group of radioactive children he keeps secretly in an underground cave, schooling them by TV and immunizing them against nuclear fallout so that they will survive the inevitable Third World War. Some poor acting mars on otherwise intriguing science-fiction thriller, although the ultimate effect is fatalistic and depressing. Shot by Losey against the background of a Dorset coast resort.

HAMMER/SWALLOW

Executive producer—	*Screenplay (based on novel*
Michael Carreras	The Children of Light *by*
Production—Anthony Hinds	H. L. Lawrence)—
Direction—Joseph Losey	Evan Jones
Photography (Hammerscope)—	*Music*—James Bernard
Arthur Grant	*Editing*—Reginald Mills
Art direction—Don Mingave	

PLAYERS: Macdonald Carey, Shirley Ann Field, Viveca Lindfors, Alexander Knox, Oliver Reed, Walter Gotell, James Villiers, Thomas Kempinski

DARK PASSAGE   U.S.A. (1947)
Escaped convict (Humphrey Bogart) undergoes plastic surgery and
becomes involved with sulky rich girl (Lauren Bacall) as he endeavors
to prove himself innocent of the murder of his wife. Highly competent
but neglected 1940's thriller, among the first films to be directed by
former writer Delmer Daves whose directorial skill was never more
in evidence than in the opening sequence depicting an escape from
San Quentin. Gains much from the slick production values of Jerry
Wald, who worked regularly at Warner's during the 1940's. Other Wald
productions for Warner Bros. include *Objective Burma* (Walsh),
Mildred Pierce, The Breaking Point (Curtiz), *Humoresque, Johnny
Belinda* (Negulesco), *Possessed* (Curtis Bernhardt), *Key Largo* (Huston) and *Storm Warning* (Heisler).

WARNER BROS.–FIRST NATIONAL

Production–Jerry Wald   *Photography*–Sid Hickox
Direction–Delmer Daves   *Art direction*–
Screenplay (based on novel   Charles H. Clarke
  by David Goodis)–   *Music*–Franz Waxman
  Delmer Daves   *Editing*–David Weisbart
PLAYERS: Humphrey Bogart, Lauren Bacall, Bruce Bennett, Agnes
Moorehead, Tom D'Andrea, Clifton Young, Douglas Kennedy, Rory
Mallinson, Houseley Stevenson

DARK VICTORY   U.S.A. (1939)
Superior melodrama with Bette Davis in superb form (Academy
Award nomination; she lost to Vivien Leigh's Scarlett O'Hara) as a
wealthy society girl who, after an operation, discovers that she is dying
from a brain tumor and has only a few months to live. Made with all
the expertise and craftsmanship at Warner's disposal and photographed
by Davis' favorite cameraman Ernest Haller who, over three decades,
worked with her on no less than 14 occasions.

WARNER BROS.–FIRST NATIONAL

Production–Hal B. Wallis in   *Screenplay (based on play*
  association with David Lewis   *by George Emerson Brewer,*
Direction–Edmund Goulding   *Jr. and Bertram Block)*–
Photography–Ernest Haller   Casey Robinson
Art direction–Robert Haas   *Music*–Max Steiner
          Editing–William Holmes
PLAYERS: Bette Davis, George Brent, Geraldine Fitzgerald, Humphrey
Bogart, Ronald Reagan, Henry Travers, Cora Witherspoon

Darling

DARLING   Gt. Britain (1965)
John Schlesinger's portrait of an arrogant little opportunist who whores
her way up the social scale by using, first, an idealistic young TV
interviewer (Dirk Bogarde) who helps her career as an actress, then
a business executive (Laurence Harvey) who introduces her to the
decadent pleasures of Parisian and London society, and finally an
Italian prince who imprisons and frustrates her in a loveless marriage.
The film hits out, often savagely, at the "smart life" and the moneyed
classes, but is at its most impressive when concentrating on the frustrations and loneliness of a young girl caught up in the empty glamour of
the jet-set life. Julie Christie won an Oscar for her excellent portrayal,
although Bogarde's performance is far and away the best in the film.

                A JOSEPH JANNI PRODUCTION/ANGLO AMALGAMATED

Production—Joseph Janni   *Photography*—Ken Higgins
Direction—John Schlesinger   *Art direction*—Ray Simm
Screenplay (based on idea by   *Music*—John Dankworth
  Frederic Raphael, Joseph   *Editing*—James Clark
  Janni and John Schlesinger)—
  Frederic Raphael

PLAYERS: Dirk Bogarde, Laurence Harvey, Julie Christie, Roland Cur-
ram, Alex Scott, Basil Henson, Helen Lindsay, Tyler Butterworth

DAVID AND LISA   U.S.A. (1962)
Sensitive study of two emotionally disturbed adolescents, one a 17-year-
old neurotic boy, the other a 15-year-old schizophrenic girl, and of their
relationship with each other as they are guided slowly back to normal
life by the psychiatrist of a mental institution. The first movie of Frank
Perry, shot in Philadelphia, and based on a real-life case. Keir Dullea
and Janet Margolin play the adolescents and Howard da Silva the
psychiatrist.

ASSOCIATE PRODUCERS–VISION ASSOCIATES INC.

Production–Paul M. Heller   Photography–
Direction–Frank Perry   Leonard Hirschfield
Screenplay (based on book by   Art direction–Paul M. Heller
  Theodore Isaac Rubin, M.D.)   Music–Mark Lawrence
  –Eleanor Perry   Editing–Irving Oshman
PLAYERS: Keir Dullea, Janet Margolin, Howard da Silva, Neva Patter-
son, Clifton James, Richard MacMurray

DAVID COPPERFIELD   U.S.A. (1935)
The most successful of Hollywood's attempts to translate Charles
Dickens to the screen, not as poetic or visually rewarding as the postwar Lean adaptations, but capturing the full flavor of the novel and
with some memorable playing from one of the most talented casts ever
assembled on a Metro stage: Lionel Barrymore (Peggotty), Edna
May Oliver (Betsy Trotwood), Roland Young (Uriah Heep), Basil
Rathbone (Mr. Murdstone), Freddie Bartholomew (David), and,
above all, W. C. Fields who completely stole the show with an amusing
vaudevillian portrait of Mr. Micawber. George Cukor directed with
taste and an unerring sense of period.

METRO–GOLDWYN–MAYER

Production–David O. Selznick   Photography–Oliver T. Marsh
Direction–George Cukor   Art direction–Cedric Gibbons
Screenplay (from adaptation   & Merrill Pye
  by Hugh Walpole)–   Music–Herbert Stothart
  Howard Estabrook   Editing–Robert J. Kern
PLAYERS: W. C. Fields, Lionel Barrymore, Edna May Oliver, Roland
Young, Basil Rathbone, Freddie Bartholomew, Maureen O'Sullivan,
Madge Evans, Lewis Stone, Frank Lawton, Elizabeth Allan, Elsa
Lanchester

DAY AT THE RACES, A   U.S.A. (1937)
Screwball Marx Brothers comedy with Groucho as horse doctor in

charge of a sanatorium, the incomparable Margaret Dumont as a wealthy patient, Chico as ice-cream seller at racetrack, and Harpo as jockey who wins a steeplechase by showing his horse a picture of the man they both hate. The romantic interludes between Allan Jones and Maureen O'Sullivan slacken the pace, but whenever the zany trio are on screen the film is superb. Directed by Sam Wood (*A Night at the Opera*) and co-scripted by George Seaton, later a writer-director at Fox and Paramount.

METRO–GOLDWYN–MAYER

Production—Irving G. Thalberg & Sam Wood

Direction—Sam Wood

Screenplay—George Seaton, Robert Pirosh & Robert Oppenheimer

Story—George Seaton & Robert Pirosh

Photography— Joseph Ruttenberg

Art direction—Cedric Gibbons, Stan Rogers & Edwin B. Willis

Music direction—Franz Waxman

Editing—Frank E. Hull

PLAYERS: Groucho, Harpo & Chico Marx, Margaret Dumont, Siegfried Rumann, Allan Jones, Maureen O'Sullivan, Douglas Dumbrille, Leonard Ceeley

DAY OF WRATH (Dies Irae *or* Vredens Dag)   Denmark (1943)
Carl Dreyer's austere, exceedingly powerful picture of witch-hunting and religious persecution in a small Puritan community in 17th-century Denmark. A slow, deeply depressing, often harrowing film—it begins and ends at the stake—which relentlessly emphasizes man's incredible cruelty to his fellow man. A great film, strikingly photographed, as powerful today as when it was first made. Ranks with Dreyer's earlier masterpieces *Le Passion de Jeanne d'Arc* and *Vampyr*.

PALLADIUM FILM

Production & direction— Carl Dreyer

Screenplay (based on novel Anne Pedersdotter *by Wiers Jenssens)*—Carl Dreyer, Poul Knudsen, Mogens Skot-Hansen

Photography—Carl Andersson

Sets—Erik Aes & Lis Fribert

Music—Poul Schierbeck

PLAYERS: Thorkild Roose, Lisbeth Movin, Sigrid Neeiendam, Preben Lerdorff, Olaf Ussing, Anna Svierkier

DAY THE EARTH STOOD STILL, THE   U.S.A. (1951)
A refined, thoughtful, sometimes amusing piece of science fiction, short

on horror but full of intelligent comment about the dangers of international aggression in a nuclear age. Crisply written and directed (one
of Robert Wise's best films of his Fox period) and well played by
Michael Rennie as the visitor from outer space who warns that unless
Earth abolishes war the more advanced planets of the universe will
destroy it.

TWENTIETH CENTURY–FOX

Production–Julian Blaustein
Direction–Robert Wise
Screenplay (from story by
  Harry Bates)–
  Edmund H. North

Photography–Leo Tover
Art direction–Lyle Wheeler,
  Addison Hehr
Music–Bernard Herrmann
Editing–William Reynolds

PLAYERS: Michael Rennie, Patricia Neal, Hugh Marlowe, Sam Jaffe,
Billy Gray, Frances Bavier, Lock Martin

DEAD END   U.S.A. (1937)

Hackneyed, slow, now badly dated version of Sidney Kingsley's play
about the youngsters who during the 1930's fought for survival in the
slums of New York's Lower East Side. Famous now only for the fact
that it introduced the Dead End Kids to the screen and gave Humphrey Bogart one of his best gangster roles of the prewar period.
Photographed on one gigantic set by Gregg Toland.

GOLDWYN/UNITED ARTISTS

Production–Samuel Goldwyn
Direction–William Wyler
Screenplay–Lillian Hellman
Photography–Gregg Toland

Art direction–Richard Day
Music–Alfred Newman
Editing–Daniel Mandell

PLAYERS: Sylvia Sidney, Joel McCrea, Humphrey Bogart, Wendy
Barrie, Claire Trevor, Allen Jenkins, Marjorie Main, Billy Halop,
Huntz Hall, Leo Gorcey

DEAD OF NIGHT   Gt. Britain (1945)

Ambitious portmanteau movie consisting of five separate stories and a
prologue about the macabre and supernatural. Naunton Wayne and
Basil Radford are amusing as a pair of ghost golfers and Michael Redgrave brilliant in "The Ventriloquist's Dummy" (director Cavalcanti),
a terrifying little tale of a mentally disturbed ventriloquist who gradually becomes dominated by the vicious personality of his dummy.

EALING STUDIOS

99

Production—Michael Balcon
Direction—Cavalcanti, Charles
  Crichton, Basil Dearden &
  Robert Hamer
Screenplay—John V. Baines &
  Angus MacPhail
Photography—Stan Pavey &
  Douglas Slocombe

Additional dialogue (based on
  original stories by H. G. Wells,
  E. F. Benson, John V. Baines
  & Angus MacPhail)—
  T. E. B. Clarke
Art direction—Michael Relph
Music—Georges Auric
Editing—Charles Hassey

PLAYERS: Michael Redgrave, Mervyn Johns, Googie Withers, Basil Radford, Naunton Wayne, Sally Ann Howes, Roland Culver, Frederick Valk

DEADLINE U.S.A.   U.S.A. (1950)

Crusading editor (Humphrey Bogart) successfully exposes a big-time racketeer while trying less successfully to stop his newspaper from being absorbed by a rival. A fast-moving, professional little thriller made when running times were edited to their proper lengths—in this case 87 minutes—and of interest as an early example of Richard Brooks' work as a director. The newspaper background is convincingly caught and, as always in this type of Hollywood film, the supporting parts are outstandingly well played. Ed Begley and Paul Stewart are particularly effective as a couple of newspapermen and Martin Gabel equally so as the racketeer. Ethel Barrymore made one of her rare screen appearances as the widow of the paper's founder.

TWENTIETH CENTURY–FOX

Production—Sol C. Siegel
Direction—Richard Brooks
Screenplay—Richard Brooks
Photography—Milton Krasner

Art direction—Lyle Wheeler &
  George Patrick
Music—Cyril Mockridge &
  Sol Kaplan
Editing—William B. Murphy

PLAYERS: Humphrey Bogart, Ethel Barrymore, Kim Hunter, Ed Begley, Warren Stevens, Paul Stewart, Martin Gabel, Joe De Santis

DEATH OF A CYCLIST (Muerte di un Ciclista) Spain/Italy (1955)

The story of a pair of doomed lovers—he a university lecturer, she the spoiled young wife of a rich industrialist—whose affair begins to disintegrate when the consequences of a road accident in which they kill a cyclist undermine their relationship and result in their own destruction. Made with great style and technical brilliance by Juan Bardem. It is his social criticism of the corruption of the privileged classes of

Spain that makes the film so interesting, coming as it does from a country with strict political censorship rules.

GUION/SUEVIA/GONZALEZ (MADRID) /TRIONFALCINE (ROME)

Direction & screenplay (from   *Music*—Isidro Maiztegui
story by Luis F. de Igoa)—   *Art direction*—Enrique Alarcôn
Juan Antonio Bardem   *Editing*—Margarita Ochoa
Photography—Alfredo Fraile
PLAYERS: Lucia Bosé, Alberto Closas, Otello Toso, Carlos Casarvilla, Bruna Corra, Julia Delgado Caro

DEATH OF A SALESMAN   U.S.A. (1951)
Straightforward film version of Arthur Miller's great play about the last days of Willy Loman, an aging traveling salesman who comes home to die with his family after a lifetime of failure and self-delusion. Through this tragic story of a man who invents a world of phony success to hide his own inadequacies, Miller ruthlessly indicts American get-rich-quick philosophy and worship of success. The movie is basically nothing more than a filmed stage play, but is carried by the sheer brilliance of its acting. Fredric March (best actor, Venice, 1952) plays Loman, Mildred Dunnock is his quiet, long-suffering wife, and Kevin McCarthy and Cameron Mitchell his two sons.

COLUMBIA

Production—Stanley Kramer   *Production design*—
Direction—Laslo Benedek   Rudolph Sternad
Screenplay—Stanley Roberts   *Art direction*—Cary Odell
Photography—Franz Planer   *Music*—Alex North
                Editing—William Lyon
PLAYERS: Fredric March, Mildred Dunnock, Kevin McCarthy, Cameron Mitchell, Howard Smith, Royal Beal

DEFIANT ONES, THE   U.S.A. (1958)
Two convicts—one white (Tony Curtis), the other black (Sidney Poitier)—make their escape from a police van in the South, but have to spend their short-lived freedom together chained by the wrist. Their growing respect for each other as they are pursued by the police forms the basis of perhaps the most effective—and optimistic—of all Hollywood's films about racial prejudice. Directed by Stanley Kramer who earlier tackled the subject as a producer in *Home of the Brave* and who returned to it in the 1960's with *Guess Who's Coming to Dinner*. New York Critics Award for best film, best direction (Kramer); Academy

Award for best screenplay (Nathan E. Douglas and Harold Jacob Smith).

STANLEY KRAMER CO./UNITED ARTISTS

Production & direction—   *Photography—*Sam Leavitt
  Stanley Kramer   *Art direction—*Fernando Carrere
*Screenplay—*Nathan E. Douglas   *Music—*Ernest Gold
  & Harold Jacob Smith   *Editing—*Frederic Knudtson
PLAYERS: Tony Curtis, Sidney Poitier, Theodore Bikel, Charles McGraw, Lon Chaney, Cara Williams

DESIGN FOR LIVING   U.S.A. (1933)

An attempt to transfer Noel Coward's risqué stage comedy into film terms. Not the best Lubitsch, but Hecht's efforts to guide an awkward subject past the Hays Office are ingenious, and the playing, as always in a Lubitsch film, is immensely assured. Miriam Hopkins is the adventurous heroine who loves both dramatist Fredric March and painter Gary Cooper simultaneously and lives with each in turn in her Paris apartment.

PARAMOUNT

*Direction—*Ernst Lubitsch   *Art direction—*Hans Dreier
*Screenplay—*Ben Hecht   *Music direction—*Nat Finston
*Photography—*Victor Milner   *Editing—*Francis Marsh
PLAYERS: Gary Cooper, Miriam Hopkins, Fredric March, Edward Everett Horton, Franklin Pangborn, Isabel Jewell, Harry Dunkinson

DESIRE   U.S.A. (1936)

Frank Borzage comedy styled after Lubitsch (who acted as producer) about a Continental jewel thief (Marlene Dietrich) and an unsuspecting tourist (Gary Cooper) who helps her smuggle a pearl necklace out of Spain. Witty, polished, deliciously entertaining but, considering the wealth of talent behind the camera (Charles Lang's soft photography is an additional asset), surprisingly underrated.

PARAMOUNT

*Production—*Ernst Lubitsch   *Photography—*Charles Lang &
*Direction—*Frank Borzage   Victor Milner
Screenplay (from play by Hans   *Art direction—*Hans Dreier &
  Szekeley & R. A. Stemmle)—   Robert Usher
  Edwin Justus Mayer,   *Music & lyrics—*
  Waldemar Young &   Frederick Hollander &
  Samuel Hoffenstein   Leo Robin
                  *Editing—*William Shea

PLAYERS: Marlene Dietrich, Gary Cooper, John Halliday, William Frawley, Ernest Cossart, Akim Tamiroff, Alan Mowbray

DESTINATION MOON U.S.A. (1950)
The first film in the postwar science-fiction cycle. A sober, straightforward account, based on scientific knowledge of the time, of four men's journey to the moon and back in an atomic rocket. Striking Technicolor photography and some ingenious, fairly accurate moonscapes. The picture won an Academy Award for best special effects of 1950.

EAGLE LION

Production—George Pal
Direction—Irving Pichel
Screenplay (from novel by
  Robert Heinlein)—Rip Van
  Ronkel, Robert Heinlein,
  James O'Hanlon

Photography (Technicolor)—
  Lionel Lindon
Production design—Ernst Fegte
Music—Leith Stevens
Editing—Duke Goldstone

PLAYERS: John Archer, Warner Anderson, Tom Powers, Dick Wesson, Erin O'Brien Moore

DESTINY (Der Mude Tod) Germany (1921)
(Known also as The Tired Death, The Three Lights, and Between Worlds). Symbolic German fantasy about a young girl (Lil Dagover) who, distressed at the death of her lover, seeks out Death (Bernhard Goetzke). He tells her that if she can save a life in any one of three periods of history—Old Baghdad, 17th-century Venice or ancient China—her lover will be returned to her. Fritz Lang's first silent masterpiece is conceived and executed on the grand scale, enhanced considerably by the remarkable trick camera work of Fritz Arno Wagner whose first film for Lang this was and who subsequently worked with him on Spione, M and The Last Will of Dr. Mabuse.

DECLA—BIOSCOP

Direction—Fritz Lang
Screenplay—Fritz Lang,
  Thea von Harbou
Art direction—Hermann Warm,
  Robert Herth, Walter Röhrig

Lighting—Robert Hegerwald
Photography—
  Erich Nilzschmann, Fritz Arno
  Wagner, Hermann Saalfrank

PLAYERS: Bernhard Goetzke, Lil Dagover, Walter Janssen, Rudolph Klein-Rogge, Georg John, Eduard von Winterstein, Max Adalbert, Paul Biensfeldt

DESTINY OF A MAN (Sudba Chelvieka) U.S.S.R. (1959)
Tragic tale of a Russian carpenter who survives the horrors of a Ger-

man concentration camp only to find that his wife and daughter have been killed in an air raid and his son killed at the front. An unashamedly sentimental and at times quite overwhelming film which ends on a more hopeful note when the carpenter adopts a homeless orphan boy and starts life anew. Sergei Bondarchuk, who also directed, plays the carpenter.

MOSFILM

Direction—Sergei Bondarchuk
Art direction—I. Novoderezhkin, S. Voronkov
Photography— Vladimir Monakhov

Screenplay (based on story by Mikhail Sholokhov)—Y. Lukin, F. Shakhmagonov
Music—V. Basner
Editing—V. Leonov

PLAYERS: Sergei Bondarchuk, Pavlik Boriskin, Z. Kirienko, P. Volkov, Y. Averin, K. Alekseyev

DESTRY RIDES AGAIN   U.S.A. (1939)
Spoof Western which has earned a false reputation over the years, but which is justly famous for Marlene Dietrich's flamboyant performance as Frenchie the dance-hall girl and for her husky rendering of the song "The Boys in the Back Room." Also in the cast are James Stewart as the sheriff who refuses to carry a gun, Mischa Auer as a comic cowboy from Russia, and Brian Donlevy in his familiar role as the heavy who runs a crooked gambling joint.

UNIVERSAL

Production—Joe Pasternak
Direction—George Marshall
Photography—Hal Mohr

Screenplay (from story by Max Brand)—Felix Jackson, Gertrude Purcell, Henry Myers
Editing—Milton Carruth

PLAYERS: James Stewart, Marlene Dietrich, Charles Winninger, Brian Donlevy, Una Merkel, Irene Hervey, Jack Carson

DETECTIVE STORY   U.S.A. (1951)
This grimly realistic movie looks at the lives of some of the cops and criminals who inhabit a New York police station during one typical afternoon. Police routine is well observed and the seedy atmosphere of the station is captured with great skill, but the acting is the film's strongest asset. The most notable performances come from Kirk Douglas as a vengeful detective and George Macready as a shady abortionist. Other cops: William Bendix and Horace MacMahon. Other crooks: Lee Grant as a shoplifter and Joseph Wiseman as an hysterical killer.

104

Production & direction—   Photography—Lee Garmes
    William Wyler   Art direction—Hal Pereira &
Screenplay (based on play by   Earl Hedrick
    Sidney Kingsley)—Philip   Editing—Robert Swink
    Yordan & Robert Wyler
PLAYERS: Kirk Douglas, Eleanor Parker, William Bendix, Lee Grant, Bert Freed, Joseph Wiseman, Frank Faylen, George Macready, Horace MacMahon

DEVIL AND MISS JONES, THE   U.S.A. (1941)
Millionaire department store owner (Charles Coburn), aghast at being burnt in effigy outside one of his own stores, takes a job as an assistant in the shoe department in order to observe the grievances of the workers at first hand. This expertly directed, beautifully acted but neglected little comedy is one of the best produced in Hollywood during the war period. Jean Arthur (superb), Robert Cummings and Spring Byington lead the workers and Edmund Gwenn is featured as an unpleasant department manager.

Direction—Sam Wood   Production design—
Story & screenplay—   William Cameron Menzies
    Norman Krasna   Music direction—Roy Webb
Photography—Harry Stradling   Editing—Sherman Todd
Art direction—Van Nest Polglase
PLAYERS: Jean Arthur, Robert Cummings, Edmund Gwenn, Charles Coburn, Spring Byington, S. Z. Sakall, William Demarest, Walter Kingsford

DEVIL DOLL, THE   U.S.A. (1936)
Wrongly convicted scientist (Lionel Barrymore) learns the secret of miniaturization from a fellow prisoner at Devil's Island. On his escape from prison he poses as the female owner of a toy shop and uses dolls (in actuality two miniaturized people) to carry out his murderous revenge on the men responsible for his imprisonment. Fantasy director Tod Browning's last major work in the horror genre; superior outsize sets by Cedric Gibbons.

Direction—Tod Browning   Art direction—Cedric Gibbons
Photography—Leonard Smith   Music—Franz Waxman

Screenplay (based on novel   Garrett Fort, Guy Endore,
  Burn, Witch Burn *by A. A.*   Erich von Stroheim
  Merritt)—Tod Browning,
PLAYERS: Lionel Barrymore, Maureen O'Sullivan, Frank Lawton, Henry
B. Walthall, Rafaela Ottiano, Grace Ford, Arthur Hohl, Juanita Quigley

DEVIL'S EYE, THE (Djävulens Öga)   Sweden (1960)
Elegant Ingmar Bergman morality play derived from the saying "A
woman's chastity is a sty in the eye of the Devil." Stig Järrel plays the
Devil, Bibi Andersson the charming young virgin who causes him so
much pain, and Jarl Kulle the haggard Don Juan who is released from
hell and sent up to earth to seduce her. Minor Bergman but consistently
amusing and enjoyable; belongs, along with *A Lesson in Love* and
Smiles of a Summer Night, to his small group of lighter works.
SVENSK FILMINDUSTRI

Direction & screenplay—   *Art direction*—P. A. Lundgren
  Ingmar Bergman   *Music*—Domenico Scarlatti
Photography—Gunnar Fischer   *Editing*—Oscar Rosander
PLAYERS: Jarl Kulle, Bibi Andersson, Stig Järrel, Nils Poppe, Gertrud
Fridh, Sture Lagerwall, Gunnar Björnstrand, Georg Funkquist

DIARY OF A CHAMBERMAID, THE   U.S.A. (1946)
Half-comic, half-tragic story of a young chambermaid's experiences in
a wealthy provincial household in 19th-century France. An unusual,
brilliantly directed study in decadence with fine performances from
Paulette Goddard as Celestine the chambermaid, Burgess Meredith as
a crazy old captain, and Francis Lederer as a homicidal butler. Jean
Renoir's penultimate film in America. Remade in 1964 by Luis Buñuel
with Jeanne Moreau in the leading role.
UNITED ARTISTS

Production—Benedict Bogeaus   *Photography*—Lucien Andriot
Direction—Jean Renoir   *Art direction*—Eugène Lourie
Screenplay (from novel by   *Music*—Michel Michelet
  Octave Mirbeau)—Jean Renoir   *Editing*—James Smith
  & Burgess Meredith
PLAYERS: Paulette Goddard, Burgess Meredith, Francis Lederer, Hurd
Hatfield, Judith Anderson, Reginald Owen, Florence Bates, Irene Ryan

DIARY OF A COUNTRY PRIEST, THE
  (Le Journal d'un Curé de Campagne)   France (1951)
Somber account of the life of a mortally sick young priest as he at-

tempts to administer his first parish, a small, suspicious community in a remote part of Northern France. A slow, complex picture conceding nothing to popular taste in its attempts to frame on film the priest's solitude and his inner struggles to hold on to his faith during his unhappiness. Among the best of Bresson's limited output and one of the few truly religious films the cinema has produced.

U.G.C.

Direction, screenplay & dialogue (*from novel by Georges Bernanos*)—Robert Bresson	*Art direction*— Pierre Charbonnier
Photography—Léonce-Henry Burel	*Music*— Jean-Jacques Grunenwald
	Editing—Paulette Robert

PLAYERS: Claude Laydu, Armand Guibert, Marie-Monique Arkell, Nicole Ladmiral, Jean Riveyre, Nicole Maurey, Jean Danet, Antoine Balpêtre, Martine Lemaire

DIE NIBELUNGEN   Germany (1924)

Released in two parts—*Siegfried* and *Kriemhilds Revenge*—and originally shown on consecutive evenings. Massive two-part medieval epic derived from the Norse sagas and the great early 13th-century poem *Die Nibelungenlied*. As was fashionable in Germany in the twenties the film was released in two parts, the first and best known under the title *Siegfried* and the second and more superior work as *Kriemhilds Revenge*. Fritz Lang directed with great style and visual flair and the sequence in the former film in which Siegfried battles and eventually slays a fire-breathing dragon is a most brilliantly staged piece of film work.

DECLA—BIOSCOP—UFA

Direction—Fritz Lang	*Art direction*—Otto Hunte,
Screenplay—Fritz Lang, Thea von Harbou	Erich Kettelhut, Karl Vollbrecht
Photography—Carl Hoffmann, Günther Rittau	*Costumes*—Paul Gerd Guderian
Animation—Walter Ruttmann	*Music*—Gottfried Huppertz
	Production—Erich Pommer

PLAYERS: Paul Richter, Margarete Schön, Rudolph Klein-Rogge, Georg August Koch, Theodor Loos, Bernhard Goetzke, Hans Adalbert von Schlettow, Georg John, Gertrude Arnold

DILLINGER   U.S.A. (1945)

This miniature (70-minute) gangster feature from the Monogram studio stands isolated from most films in the genre in that it was one of the few of its kind produced in the war period. It is basically a study of the criminal career of Public Enemy Number One, John Dillinger (Lawrence Tierney), and his association with a rival American gang leader (played by Edmund Lowe). Its most celebrated sequence is the final one in which Dillinger, betrayed by girlfriend Anne Jeffreys, is shot while leaving a movie theater. The taut screenplay is by Philip Yordan, who was later responsible for the scripts of such films as *House of Strangers* (Mankiewicz), *Detective Story* (Wyler), and *The Harder They Fall* (Robson).

MONOGRAM

Production—Franklin King, Maurice King
Direction—Max Nosseck

Screenplay—Philip Yordan
Photography—Jackson Rose
Editing—Otho Lovering

PLAYERS: Edmund Lowe, Anne Jeffreys, Lawrence Tierney, Eduardo Ciannelli, Marc Lawrence, Elisha Cook, Jr., Ralph Lewis, Ludwig Stössell

DINNER AT EIGHT U.S.A. (1933)

Polished all-star Metro vehicle in the *Grand Hotel* tradition looks at the lives of some wealthy guests who attend a dinner party thrown by a social climber (Billie Burke). The lavish production is expertly handled by Cukor and flamboyantly performed by, among others, Marie Dressler as an aging actress, Wallace Beery as a vulgar industrialist, and Jean Harlow as his sluttish wife. Based on the stage success by George S. Kaufman and Edna Ferber.

METRO–GOLDWYN–MAYER

Production—David O. Selznick
Direction—George Cukor
Screenplay—
  Herman J. Mankiewicz
  & Frances Marion

Photography—William Daniels
Art direction—Cedric Gibbons
Music—D. R. William Axt
Editing—Ben Lewis

PLAYERS: Marie Dressler, John Barrymore, Wallace Beery, Jean Harlow, Lionel Barrymore, Lee Tracy, Edmund Lowe, Billie Burke

DISHONORED U.S.A. (1931)

Espionage tale based on an original idea by von Sternberg about a Viennese whore (Marlene Dietrich) who becomes spy X27 for the Austrian Government and then falls in love with the Russian spy she has been ordered to trap. Extravagant nonsense but very well made. Photographed by Lee Garmes who, together with Harold Rosson and Bert Glennon, was one of the three major cameramen to work regularly with von Sternberg during his most creative period (1927–1937). Other von Sternberg/Garmes films: *Morocco, An American Tragedy, Shanghai Express.*

PARAMOUNT

Direction—Josef von Sternberg   *Photography*—Lee Garmes
Screenplay—Daniel N. Rubin   *Set designer*—Hans Dreier
PLAYERS: Marlene Dietrich, Victor McLaglen, Lew Cody, Gustav von Seyffertitz, Warner Oland, Barry Norton, Davison Clark, Wilfred Lucas, Bill Powell

DIVORCE—ITALIAN STYLE (Divorzio all'Italiana)   Italy (1961)
The superb performance of Marcello Mastroianni dominates this amusing little film about an impoverished Sicilian nobleman who, because divorce is not allowed in Italy, finds that the only way he can court his attractive young cousin is by murdering his amiable but demanding wife. A stylish, wickedly funny black comedy directed by Pietro Germi and containing some delightful satire on the vanishing Sicilian aristocracy.

LUX/VIDES/GALATEA

Production—Franco Cristaldi   *Photography*—Leonida Barboni
Direction—Pietro Germi   *Art direction*—Carlo Egidi
Screenplay—Ennio De Concini,   *Music*—Carlo Rustichelli
   Alfredo Giannetti, Pietro Germi   *Montage*—Robert Cinquini
PLAYERS: Marcello Mastroianni, Daniella Rocca, Stefania Sandrelli, Leopoldo Trieste, Odoardo Spadaro, Angela Cardile

DR. EHRLICH'S MAGIC BULLET   U.S.A. (1940)
The story of Dr. Paul Ehrlich, the German research chemist who first discovered a cure for syphilis. Not the best known of Dieterle's biographical pictures but equally as good as either *The Life of Emile Zola* or *Juarez* and far bolder in its choice of subject. Edward G. Robinson's performance is one of the best of his long career.

WARNER BROS.

Direction—William Dieterle   *Photography*—
Screenplay (from idea by   James Wong Howe
   Norman Burnside)—Herald &   *Art direction*—Carl Jules Weyl
   Norman Burnside   *Music*—Max Steiner
                      Editing—Warren Low
PLAYERS: Edward G. Robinson, Ruth Gordon, Otto Kruger, Donald Crisp, Maria Ouspenskaya, Montague Love, Sig Rumann, Donald Meek

DR. JEKYLL AND MR. HYDE U.S.A. (1932)

Technically exciting and by far the most successful of Hollywood's attempts to translate Robert Louis Stevenson's macabre tale to the screen, with Fredric March giving a brilliant performance and winning an Academy Award for his portrayal of the doomed doctor. Director Rouben Mamoulian (this was his third film and his only venture into the horror genre) brought style and great visual imagination to the story, helped considerably by two of Paramount's ablest technicians—cameraman Karl Struss and German-born art director Hans Dreier who, between them, created a gothic and misty portrait of late Victorian London. The highlight—the transformation of Jekyll into the bestial Hyde—was done without cuts or opticals and is still the most convincing interpretation of this scene yet put on film.

PARAMOUNT

Production & direction— Rouben Mamoulian
*Screenplay—*Samuel Hoffenstein & Percy Heath

*Photography—*Karl Struss
*Art direction—*Hans Dreier
*Editing—*William Shea

PLAYERS: Fredric March, Miriam Hopkins, Rose Hobart, Halliwell Hobbes, Holmes Herbert, Edgar Morton, Tempe Pigott

DR. MABUSE THE GAMBLER (Dr. Mabuse der Spieler)
Germany (1922)

Part I—*Dr. Mabuse the Gambler*; Part II—*Inferno*. Fast-moving Fritz Lang thriller about a power-mad master criminal (Rudolph Klein-Rogge) who uses his secret organization of murderers and thieves, and also his hypnotic powers, to create his own personal criminal empire. Although basically a thriller the film works equally well on a higher level and contains some penetrating observations on the decadence of German society in the 1920's. Like Lang's earlier *The Spiders* which it resembles, it was released in two parts. The combined running time of the two films amounted to almost $4\frac{1}{2}$ hours.

ULLSTEIN—UCO FILM—DECLA–BIOSCOP—UFA

*Direction—*Fritz Lang
*Screenplay (from novel by Norbert Jacques)—*Fritz Lang, Thea von Harbou

*Photography—*Carl Hoffmann
*Art direction—*Otto Hunte, Stahl-Urach

PLAYERS: Rudolph Klein-Rogge, Alfred Abel, Aud Egede Nissen, Gertrude Welcker, Bernhard Goetzke, Forster Larringa, Paul Richter, Hans Adalbert von Schlettow

DOCTOR STRANGELOVE, Or How I Learned to Stop Worrying
and Love the Bomb   Gt. Britain (1964)
Stanley Kubrick's brilliant satire on nuclear war centers on the predicament of American President Mirkin Muffley when one of his Air Force
commanders goes berserk and sends his B-52's to H-bomb Russia,
triggering off the Soviet Union's Doomsday Weapon which will destroy
all life on earth for a hundred years. The ultimate in black comedies
and, prior to *2001*, Kubrick's most ambitious project. Peter Sellers appeared in three roles—as the President, as America's top atom scientist
(the German Doctor Strangelove of the title), and as an R.A.F. officer.
A brilliantly designed, imaginary Pentagon war room by Ken Adam
and crisp editing by Anthony Harvey who later directed *Dutchman*
and *A Lion in Winter*.

HAWKS FILMS/COLUMBIA

Direction—Stanley Kubrick

*Screenplay (from Peter George's
  novel* Red Alert)—Stanley
  Kubrick, Terry Southern &
  Peter George

Photography—Gilbert Taylor

Art direction—Ken Adam

Music—Laurie Johnson

Editing—Anthony Harvey

PLAYERS: Peter Sellers, George C. Scott, Sterling Hayden, Keenan
Wynn, Slim Pickens, Peter Bull

DOCTOR ZHIVAGO   U.S.A. (1965)
An idealistic Russian doctor-poet (Omar Sharif) finds himself in sym-
pathy with the ideals of the revolutionaries but unable to adjust to the
new society when the revolution finally occurs. Although sometimes
obscured by spectacle and trivial romance, this important basic theme
of Pasternak's complex novel still shows through in David Lean's honor-
able film version which, like his earlier *Lawrence of Arabia,* is distinguished principally by Freddie Young's thrilling color landscapes
(an old train crossing the snow-covered plains toward the Urals is an
astonishingly beautiful sight) and by Maurice Jarre's music score.

METRO–GOLDWYN–MAYER

Production—Carlo Ponti

Direction—David Lean

*Screenplay (from novel by Boris
  Pasternak)*—Robert Bolt

Production design—John Box

*Photography (Metrocolor/
  Panavision)*—F. A. Young

Art direction—Terence Marsh

Music—Maurice Jarre

Editing—Norman Savage

111

PLAYERS: Omar Sharif, Julie Christie, Tom Courtenay, Rod Steiger, Ralph Richardson, Geraldine Chaplin, Alec Guinness, Siobhan McKenna, Rita Tushingham

DOG'S LIFE, A   U.S.A. (1918)
Bittersweet three-reel comedy in which desperate beggar (Charlie Chaplin) teams up with a mongrel dog called Scraps and becomes involved with crooks and stolen money. Some brilliantly timed comedy but distinguished mainly by its pathos and realistic emphasis on the little tramp's desperate struggle for survival. The film was Chaplin's first acknowledged masterpiece and was also the first of nine movies made under a million-dollar contract for First National. Edna Purviance appeared as cabaret girl.
                          FIRST NATIONAL
Direction—Charles Chaplin   *Photography*—R. H. Totheroh
Screenplay—Charles Chaplin
PLAYERS: Charles Chaplin, Albert Austin, Henry Bergman, Sydney Chaplin, Bud Jamison, Park Jones, James T. Kelly, Edna Purviance

DON QUIXOTE   U.S.S.R. (1957)
Respectful, richly colored Russian version of Cervantes' story with Nikolai Cherkasov (Alexander Nevsky in Eisenstein's prewar film) as the melancholy knight who tilts at windmills and Yuri Tolubeyev as his plump traveling companion Sancho Panza. Among the few really successful film adaptations of a classic novel ever made. Solid direction by Grigori Kozintsev, a veteran film-maker who began his career in the 1920's, and impeccably shot by Moskvin and Dudko, whose Russian exteriors served remarkably well for the landscapes of Spain.
                             LENFILM
Direction—Grigori Kozintsev   *Screenplay*—Yevgeni Schwartz
Photography (*Sovcolor/*   *Art direction*—Yevgeni Enei
  SovScope)—Andrei Moskvin,   *Music*—Kar-Karayev
  Apollinari Dudko
PLAYERS: Nikolai Cherkasov, Yuri Tolubeyev, Serafima Birman

DOUBLE INDEMNITY   U.S.A. (1944)
Billy Wilder's first major film is a cold, pitiless drama, acidly scripted by Raymond Chandler from a James M. Cain novel, about an insurance salesman who murders his mistress' husband so that they can collect on the insurance. Tense, uncompromising and frequently brilliant, it is

admirably played by Fred MacMurray as the insurance man, Barbara Stanwyck as the sleazy *femme fatale*, and Edward G. Robinson as the insurance agent who investigates the crime. Photographed by veteran John Seitz who worked on several of Wilder's Paramount pictures.

PARAMOUNT

Production—Joseph Sistrom
Direction—Billy Wilder
Screenplay—Raymond Chandler,
  Billy Wilder
Photography—John Seitz
Art direction—Hans Dreier,
  Hal Pereira
Music—Miklos Rozsa
Editing—Doane Harrison

PLAYERS: Fred MacMurray, Barbara Stanwyck, Edward G. Robinson, Porter Hall, Jean Heather, Tom Powers, Byron Barr, Richard Gaines

DOUBLE LIFE, A   U.S.A. (1947)

Farfetched but well-acted tale of a schizophrenic actor who finds himself becoming so identified with the role of Othello he is playing on the Broadway stage that he begins to live the part in real life even to the point where he commits murder. Strikingly well played by Ronald Colman (Academy Award, best actor, 1947) and by Millard Mitchell, Edmond O'Brien and Shelley Winters in supporting roles. The film was the first in which director George Cukor was associated with Garson Kanin. They later worked together on such films as *Adam's Rib, The Marrying Kind* and *Pat and Mike.*

UNIVERSAL–INTERNATIONAL

Production—Michael Kanin
Direction—George Cukor
Screenplay—Ruth Gordon &
  Garson Kanin
Photography—Milton Krasner
Art direction—
  Bernard Herzbrun
  & Harvey Gillett
Music—Miklos Rozsa
Editing—Robert Parrish

PLAYERS: Ronald Colman, Signe Hasso, Edmond O'Brien, Shelley Winters, Ray Collins, Millard Mitchell, Philip Loeb, Joe Sawyer

DRACULA   U.S.A. (1931)

Bela Lugosi as the terrifying vampire count in the best known of all the many versions of Bram Stoker's bloodthirsty tale. The film was based more on the stage adaptation than the original novel and as a result lost something of the mystery and horror of the original, but there are some effective gothic scenes of vampires leaving coffins in cobwebbed crypts and Lugosi's performance is a triumph. Several sequels and remakes, among them *Dracula's Daughter, Son of Dracula* and the Hammer version with Christopher Lee, were filmed during the 1940's and '50's.

UNIVERSAL

Direction—Tod Browning
Dialogue—Dudley Murphy
Photography—Karl Freund
Art direction—Charles D. Hall

Screenplay (from novel by Bram Stoker and play by Hamilton Deane & John L. Balderston)—Garrett Fort

PLAYERS: Bela Lugosi, Helen Chandler, David Manners, Dwight Frye, Edward Van Sloan, Frances Dade, Herbert Bunston, Charles Gerrard

DRÔLE DE DRAME   France (1937)

Marcel Carné's engaging burlesque of the English Edwardian detective story played with a splendid sense of fun by Michel Simon as a timid botanist who writes crime novels. Françoise Rosay is his wife, Louis Jouvet an Anglican bishop, and Jean Louis Barrault is a goose-necked murderer who kills butchers because he loves animals. Scripted by Jacques Prévert, who was associated with the majority of Carné's films of the 1930's.

CORNIGLION—MOLINIER

Direction—Marcel Carné
Screenplay, adaptation &
  dialogue (from novel His
  First Offence *by Storer-*
  Clouston)—Jacques Prévert

Photography—Eugen Schüfftan
Art direction—
  Alexander Trauner
Music—Maurice Jaubert
Editing—Marthe Poncin

PLAYERS: Michel Simon, Françoise Rosay, Louis Jouvet, Annie Cariel, Jean-Louis Barrault

DRUMS ALONG THE MOHAWK   U.S.A. (1939)

Dogged young pioneer (Henry Fonda) and his aristocratic New York wife (Claudette Colbert) help defeat both the Indians and the British in the Mohawk Valley during the last months of the American War of Independence. Not one of Ford's most serious works, but his initial use of color, especially in the sequence when Fonda is pursued by Indians through forests and moorland at sunrise, makes it one of the most significant color films of the late 1930's.

TWENTIETH CENTURY—FOX

Executive producer—
  Darryl F. Zanuck
Production—Raymond Griffith
Direction—John Ford

Screenplay (from novel by Walter D. Edmonds)—
  Lamar Trotti &
  Sonya Levien

Photography (Technicolor)—
Bert Glennon,
Ray Rennahan

Art direction—Richard Day,
Mark Lee Kirk
Music—Alfred Newman
Editing—Robert Simpson

PLAYERS: Claudette Colbert, Henry Fonda, Edna May Oliver, Eddie Collins, John Carradine, Dorris Bowdon, Jessie Ralph, Arthur Shields

DUCK SOUP   U.S.A. (1933)

Superb Marx Brothers movie, directed by Leo McCarey (this was the only occasion that the team worked with a major comedy director), is set in the mythical Balkan kingdom of Freedonia where the preposterous Groucho (Rufus T. Firefly) is dictator and Harpo and Chico are spies from the neighboring state of Sylvania. Beautifully put together and containing not only all the usual visual gags and wisecracks but also a large element of satire. Others in the cast are Louis Calhern as a conniving villain and the inimitable Margaret Dumont as a wealthy widow whose limitless supply of funds alone keeps the country's economy in a healthy condition.

PARAMOUNT

Direction—Leo McCarey
Screenplay—Bert Kalmar &
Harry Ruby
Additional dialogue—
Arthur Sheekman &
Nat Perrin
Photography—Henry Sharp

Art direction—Hans Dreier &
Wiard B. Ihnen
Music & lyrics—Bert Kalmar &
Harry Ruby
Musical direction—
Arthur Johnston
Editing—LeRoy Stone

PLAYERS: Groucho, Harpo, Chico & Zeppo Marx, Margaret Dumont, Louis Calhern, Raquel Torres, Edgar Kennedy, Edmund Breese, William Worthington

DUEL IN THE SUN   U.S.A. (1946)

An expensive, sexy, hugely enjoyable Selznick Western set in Texas during the 1880's and centering on the feud between two brothers—one good (Joseph Cotten), one bad (Gregory Peck)—for the affections of a half-breed Indian girl (Jennifer Jones). An outrageous film, pretentious and vulgar most of the time, but occasionally rising to the heights, especially in the brilliant opening dance sequence with Tilly Losch. Directed mainly by King Vidor and also occasionally by William Dieterle (the opening sequence), Otto Brower (most of the spectacu-

115

lar scenes), and Reaves Eason (the train wreck). Lionel Barrymore as a hard-bitten old cattle baron, Lillian Gish as his wife, and Walter Huston as a prairie revivalist lead the supporting cast. Orson Welles served as narrator.

DAVID SELZNICK PRODS./UNITED ARTISTS

Production—David O. Selznick
Direction—King Vidor
Screenplay (adapted by Oliver
  H. P. Garrett from novel
  by Niven Busch)—
  David O. Selznick
Production design—
  J. McMillan Johnson

Photography (Technicolor)—
  Lee Garmes, Harold Rosson,
  Ray Rennahan
Art direction—
  James Basevi
Music—Dimitri Tiomkin
Supervising editor—
  Hal C. Kern

PLAYERS: Jennifer Jones, Gregory Peck, Joseph Cotten, Lionel Barrymore, Herbert Marshall, Lillian Gish, Walter Huston, Charles Bickford

DUMBO
U.S.A. (1941)

Cartoon story of a baby circus elephant who learns to fly by using his enormous ears as wings. Delightful Disney movie; his animal creations, among them Dumbo himself and his morale booster and business advisor Timothy Q. Mouse, are superior even to those invented for *Bambi*. High spots: a parade of pink elephants and the rendering of the song "Casey Junior" by the railway engine that pulls the circus train. Other songs include "Baby Mine" and "When I See an Elephant Fly." Disney's fifth full-length feature and, after *Fantasia* and *Pinocchio*, his most delightful cartoon.

WALT DISNEY PRODUCTIONS/RKO RADIO

Production—Walt Disney
Supervising director—
  Ben Sharpsteen
Screenplay (from book by
  Helen Aberson &

  Harold Pearl)—
  Joe Grant & Dick Huemer
Music—Oliver Wallace,
  Frank Churchill
Lyrics—Ned Washington

EARTH
U.S.S.R. (1930)

Lyrical, slow-moving masterpiece about the clash between the land-owning kulaks and the collective farmers of the New Order during Russia's first Five-Year Plan—a time when the social system of the country was being changed and the new revolutionary ideas were beginning to affect the lives of the peasant population. Full of unforgettable images of Ukrainian peasant life, it belongs not only with the

116

most beautiful of Russia's silent pictures but also with the most visually rewarding films of all time. The film was Alexander Dovzhenko's fourth picture and also his last silent production. It was photographed by Danylo Demutsky, Dovzhenko's regular cameraman at that time.

VUFKU

Direction & screenplay—
Alexander Dovzhenko
Photography—Danylo Demutsky

Art direction—Vasili Krichevsky
Music (for performance)—
L. Revutsky

PLAYERS: Semyon Svashenko, Stepan Shkurat, Mikola Nademsky, Yelena Maximova, Pyotr Masokha

EAST OF EDEN   U.S.A. (1955)
Twentieth-century allegory of the Cain and Abel story is set in California in 1917 and features James Dean and Richard Davalos as the two contrasted sons competing for the love of their patriarchal father. Remembered mainly for Dean's performance (this was the first of his three films) and for Kazan's skillful use of color and CinemaScope, e.g., the opening sequences in the seashore town where Dean searches for his mother, and the later, visually beautiful scenes set against the background of green Californian meadows. Of interest additionally are the minor portrayals of Jo Van Fleet (Academy Award, best supporting actress, 1955) as the proprietress of a fancy brothel and Burl Ives as local sheriff.

WARNER BROS.

Production & direction—
Elia Kazan
Screenplay (from novel by
John Steinbeck)—
Paul Osborn

Photography (Warnercolor/
CinemaScope)—Ted McCord
Art direction—James Basevi,
Malcolm Bert
Music—Leonard Rosenman
Editing—Owen Marks

PLAYERS: James Dean, Julie Harris, Raymond Massey, Burl Ives, Richard Davalos, Jo Van Fleet, Albert Dekker, Lois Smith, Harold Gordon

EASTER PARADE   U.S.A. (1948)
Formula musical set in the early 1920's with chorus girl (Judy Garland) taking over from ambitious Ann Miller as Astaire's new dancing partner. The story line is hackneyed, the direction of Charles Walters only so-so, but the film does come alive occasionally during some of the more vigorous Berlin numbers, particularly Astaire's "Drum Crazy" and hoofer Ann Miller's scintillating "Shakin' the Blues Away." The most

117

famous number (although not the best) is "We're a Couple of Swells" with Astaire and Garland in tramp costume.

METRO–GOLDWYN–MAYER

Production—Arthur Freed
Direction—Charles Walters
Screenplay (from their story)—
  Frances Goodrich &
  Albert Hackett
Photography (Technicolor)—
  Harry Stradling

Art direction—Cedric Gibbons
  & Jack Martin Smith
Lyrics & music—Irving Berlin
Musical direction—
  Johnny Green
Editing—A. Akst

PLAYERS: Judy Garland, Fred Astaire, Peter Lawford, Ann Miller, Jules Munshin, Clinton Sundburg, Jeni LeGon

EASY LIVING   U.S.A. (1937)

This lighthearted vehicle is a mixture of witty comedy, slapstick and farce. It revolves around the lives of four people—a rich banker (Edward Arnold), his argumentative wife (Mary Nash), a young working girl (Jean Arthur) who accidentally inherits the wife's fur coat, and the banker's son (Ray Milland) who spends his time working as a waiter in a restaurant.

PARAMOUNT

Production—
  Arthur Hornblow Jr.
Direction—Mitchell Leisen
Screenplay (from story by
  Vera Caspary)—
  Preston Sturges

Photography—Ted Tetzlaff
Art direction—Hans Dreier &
  Ernest Fegte
Music direction—Boris Morros
Editing—Doane Harrison

PLAYERS: Jean Arthur, Edward Arnold, Ray Milland, Luis Alberni, Mary Nash, Franklin Pangborn, Barlowe Borland, William Demarest

EASY RIDER   U.S.A. (1969)

The story of two long-haired hippies who set off on a motorcycle odyssey across the United States, discovering on their travels the immense beauty of the countryside and encountering also the bigoted, small-minded conformist society around them. Dennis Hopper (who also directed) and Peter Fonda (who produced) play the hippies and Jack Nicholson gives a brilliant portrayal of an alcoholic civil-rights lawyer. The sleeper of recent years and a unique success.

PANDO COMPANY IN ASSOCIATION WITH RAYBERT PRODUCTIONS/COLUMBIA

Production—Peter Fonda   *Photography* (*Technicolor*)—
Direction—Dennis Hopper   Laszlo Kovaks
Screenplay—Dennis Hopper,   *Art direction*—Jerry Kay
   Peter Fonda & Terry Southern   *Editing*—Donn Cambren
PLAYERS: Peter Fonda, Dennis Hopper, Antonio Mendoza, Phil Spector, Mac Mashourian, Warren Finnerty, Tita Colorado, Luke Askew, Luana Anders, Sabrina Scharf, Sandy Wyeth, Robert Walker, Jack Nicholson

EASY STREET   U.S.A. (1917)
The most famous of Chaplin's films for Mutual finds Charlie in the role of a reformed derelict who becomes a policeman and cleans up a tough city street. Very funny although, like *The Vagabond,* containing several moments of genuine pathos and emphasizing the struggle for life in the slum areas of a big city. High spot: Charlie overcoming head bully Eric Campbell by pushing his head through the top of a street gas lamp. Other Chaplin regulars in the cast are Edna Purviance as mission worker, Albert Austin as a minister, and Henry Bergman as a tough.

A MUTUAL COMEDY

Direction—Charles Chaplin   *Photography*—R. H. Totheroh
Screenplay—Charles Chaplin   & W. C. Foster
PLAYERS: Charles Chaplin, Albert Austin, Henry Bergman, Eric Campbell, Frank J. Coleman, James T. Kelly, Charlotte Mineau, Edna Purviance

EDOUARD ET CAROLINE   France (1951)
Minor but immensely likable Jacques Becker comedy tracing a few quarrelsome hours in the lives of a young married couple (Daniel Gélin and Anne Vernon) as they prepare to attend the snob party that will launch the husband on a successful career as a concert pianist. A thin and very simple story, but enchantingly played and containing, in the later sequences, some often shrewd observations of high-society life.

U.G.C.

Direction—Jacques Becker   *Photography*—Robert le Febvre
Screenplay—Annette Wademant   *Art direction*—Jacques Colombier
   & Jacques Becker   *Music*—Jean-Jacques Grunenwald
Dialogue—Annette Wademant   *Editing*—Marguerite Renoir
PLAYERS: Daniel Gélin, Anne Vernon, Jacques François, Jean Galland, Elisa Labourdette

119

8½

8½   Italy (1963)
The memories, fantasies and desires of an artistically exhausted Italian
film director as he rests his mind and body at a spa and searches desperately for a story for his new film. An extraordinary and almost certainly
partly autobiographical Fellini picture that constantly mixes reality
with dream sequences and which, during its 138 minutes, gives a revealing self-portrait of the director himself and of the friends that
inhabit his professional and private worlds. Beautifully performed by
Marcello Mastroianni (the director), Anouk Aimée (his wife), and
Sandra Milo (his mistress). It is enriched by the dazzling monochome
photography of Gianni Di Venanzo who was also Fellini's cameraman
on *Juliet of the Spirits*. This was the eighth full-length feature that
Fellini made, the ½ referring to the episodes he directed in *Boccaccio
70* and *Amore in Citta*.

ANGELO RIZZOLI

Production—Angelo Rizzoli   *Photography*—
Direction—Federico Fellini   Gianni Di Venanzo
Screenplay (*based on story by*   *Art direction*—Piero Gherardi
  Fellini and Flaiano)—   *Music*—Nino Rota
  Federico Fellini, Ennio Flaiano,   *Editing*—Leo Cattozzo
  Tullio Pinelli & Brunello Rondi

PLAYERS: Marcello Mastroianni, Claudia Cardinale, Anouk Aimée, Sandra Milo, Rossella Falk, Barbara Steele, Guido Alberti, Madeleine Lebeau, Jean Rougeul

EL CID   U.S.A. (1961)
A 160-minute epic by Anthony Mann about the adventures of the half-legendary Castilian warrier El Cid (Charlton Heston) who, in the 11th century, united the Moors and Christians under one king. The script is no more than adequate and the acting uneven, but the camera work is superb. British photographer Robert Krasker (*Henry V, Odd Man Out, The Third Man*) achieves some of the finest Technicolor images of his distinguished career, particularly during the final battle for Valencia when the dead El Cid, dressed in full armor and strapped to his white horse, rides out along the misty seashore and is lit suddenly by the first rays of the morning sun. Scored by Miklos Rozsa whose other epic music scores include *Quo Vadis, Ben-Hur* and *King of Kings*.

SAMUEL BRONSTON/DEAR FILMS

Production—Samuel Bronston
Direction—Anthony Mann
Screenplay—Philip Yordan & Frederic M. Frank
Designers—Veniero Colasanti & John Moore

Photography (*Technicolor/ Super Technirama 70*)— Robert Krasker
Music—Miklos Rozsa
Editing—Robert Lawrence

PLAYERS: Charlton Heston, Sophia Loren, Genevieve Page, Raf Vallone, John Fraser, Gary Raymond, Hurd Hatfield, Douglas Wilmer, Frank Thring

EL DORADO   U.S.A. (1967)
Enjoyable Howard Hawks Western that is virtually a remake of his earlier success *Rio Bravo*. John Wayne again stars as a gunfighter who, together with drunken sheriff (Robert Mitchum), young riverboat gambler (James Caan) and old-timer (Arthur Hunnicutt), defies a gang of killers in a small Western town. There is some broad comedy, superbly staged scenes of violent action, and handsome Technicolor photography. Not a classic Western in the accepted sense but put together with great professional skill.

PARAMOUNT/LAUREL

Production & direction— Howard Hawks
Photography (*Technicolor*) Harold Rosson

Screenplay (*based on novel* The Stars in Their Courses *by Harry Brown*)—Leigh Brackett

121

Art direction—Hal Pereira,   *Music & musical direction*—
   Carl Anderson   Nelson Riddle
                                  Editing—John Woodcock
PLAYERS: John Wayne, Robert Mitchum, James Caan, Charlene Holt, Michele Carey, Arthur Hunnicutt, R. G. Armstrong, Edward Asner

ELMER GANTRY   U.S.A. (1960)
Long (145 minutes) version of Sinclair Lewis's 1920's novel about a whoring, whisky-drinking salesman (Burt Lancaster) who joins up with a tent-pitching revivalist group in the Midwest and through his talent for rabble-rousing turns the enterprise into big business. Skillful direction from Brooks, much excellent period detail, and some intelligent and frequently penetrating observations on the danger of inducing mass hysteria. It is Lancaster's film without a doubt, but also has excellent playing from Jean Simmons as the priestess of the cult, Dean Jagger as her business manager, and Arthur Kennedy as a skeptical reporter. Academy Awards went to Lancaster (best actor), Brooks (screenplay), and Shirley Jones (best supporting actress).
                ELMER GANTRY PRODS./UNITED ARTISTS
Production—Bernard Smith   *Photography* (*Eastmancolor*)—
Direction—Richard Brooks   John Alton
Screenplay—Richard Brooks   *Music*—Andre Previn
Art direction—Edward Carrere   *Editing*—Marjorie Fowler
PLAYERS: Burt Lancaster, Jean Simmons, Arthur Kennedy, Shirley Jones, Dean Jagger, Patti Page, Edward Andrews, John McIntyre

ELVIRA MADIGAN   Sweden (1967)
The story of an idyllic but doomed love affair between a young tightrope dancer and a Swedish army officer in pastoral, late-19th-century Denmark. A Mozart piano concerto accompanies the lovers' enchantment, but the exquisite color camera work lingers longest in the mind. The color and beauty of the summer landscape of trees, lakes and green meadows is so breathtakingly photographed that the film frequently resembles a Renoir painting.
                          EUROPA FILM
Direction & screenplay—   *Music*—Mozart's Piano
   Bo Widerberg   Concerto no. 21
Photography (*Eastmancolor*)—   *Musical direction*—Ulf Bjorlin
   Jörgen Persson   *Editing*—Bo Widerberg
PLAYERS: Pia Degermark, Thommy Berggren, Lennart Malmer, Nina Widerberg, Cleo Jensen

                              122

EMIL AND THE DETECTIVES   Germany (1932)
Engaging version of Erich Kästner's famous children's story about a
12-year-old German boy (Rolf Wenkhaus) who enlists the help of
Gustav-with-the-motor-horn (Hans Joachim Schaufuss) and his gang
of boy detectives to track down an international bank robber loose in
Berlin. Exciting and amusing script by Billy Wilder. Fritz Rasp appeared as the villain, known throughout the film as "the man in the
bowler hat."

UFA

Production—Gunther Stapenhorst   *Photography*—Werner Brandes
Direction—Gerhard Lamprecht   *Music*—Allan Gray
Screenplay—Billy Wilder
PLAYERS: Fritz Rasp, Käthe Haack, Rolf Wenkhaus, Rudolf Biebrach,
Olga Engl, Martin Baumann, Hans-Joachim Schaufuss, Hans Richter,
Hubert Schmitz, Hans Albrecht Löhr

ENCHANTED COTTAGE, THE   U.S.A. (1945)
Tearjerker, set in a New England cottage in wartime, about the romance
between a badly disfigured pilot (Robert Young) and an unattractive
girl (Dorothy McGuire), whose deep and mutual love makes them
appear beautiful in each other's eyes. Sugary, sentimental and belonging very much to its time, although the performances of the two principals are nicely judged and the film's painful theme is treated with
great delicacy by underrated director John Cromwell. Adapted from a
play by Sir Arthur Wing Pinero.

RKO RADIO

Production—Harriet Parsons   *Art direction*—Albert S.
Direction—John Cromwell   D'Agostino, Carroll Clark
Screenplay—DeWitt Bodeen,   *Music*—Roy Webb
   Herman J. Mankiewicz   *Editing*—Joseph Noriega
Photography—Ted Tetzlaff
PLAYERS: Dorothy McGuire, Robert Young, Herbert Marshall, Mildred
Natwick, Spring Byington, Richard Gaines

END OF ST. PETERSBURG, THE (Konyets Sankt-Peterburga)
                                          U.S.S.R. (1927)
Classic Russian silent film tracing, through the eyes of a young peasant
worker, the events that led to a St. Petersburg strike, the country's
involvement in the First World War, the overthrow of the Tsar in the
October Revolution, and the replacement of old St. Petersburg with

123

the new revolutionary city of Leningrad. Pudovkin's mastery of film technique, particularly his brilliant cutting, and his emotional involvement with the historic events he describes makes this film almost as impressive as Eisenstein's more famous *October* which deals basically with the same series of events.

MEZHRABPOM–RUSS

Direction—Vsevolod Pudovkin	*Assistants*—A. Gendelstein,
Co-director—Mikhail Doller	A. Ledashov, Alexander
Screenplay—Nathan Zarkhi	Feinzimmer & V. Strauss
Photography—Anatoli Golovnya	*Art direction*—Sergei Kozlovsky

PLAYERS: A. Chistyakov, Vera Baranovskaya, Ivan Chuvelyov, V. Obolensky

ENFORCER, THE   U.S.A. (1951)

Humphrey Bogart as a tough assistant district attorney working his way through countless murders and smashing the powerful gangster syndicate that organizes murder as a business. Based substantially on fact (Murder Incorporated was uncovered in New York in 1940) and vigorously, sometimes brilliantly, directed by Bretaigne Windust, although veteran Raoul Walsh is reported to have directed many of the film's key scenes. Everett Sloane is impressive as the crime syndicate overlord and Zero Mostel enjoys several effective moments in the minor role of stool pigeon.

WARNER BROS.

Production—Milton Sperling	*Photography*—Robert Burks
Direction—Bretaigne Windust	*Art direction*—Charles H. Clarke
Original screenplay—	*Music*—David Buttolph
Martin Rackin	*Editing*—Fred Allen

PLAYERS: Humphrey Bogart, Zero Mostel, Ted De Corsia, Everett Sloane, Roy Roberts, Lawrence Tolan, King Donovan, Bob Steele

ENTERTAINER, THE   Gt. Britain (1960)

Tony Richardson turns again to a John Osborne play for his second film. In it he follows the sordid decline of drunken music-hall entertainer Archie Rice as he works out his last engagement in a British seaside town. Most of the film's action takes place within the confines of the resort, and it is the skillful way in which director Richardson and cameraman Oswald Morris evoke the atmosphere of the town—with its raucous amusements, beauty parlors, and shabby, half-empty theaters—and also the superb quality of the acting that gives the film its

124

distinction. Laurence Olivier's Archie Rice, a third-rate broken-down variety artist who has spent most of his life as a failure in the provinces, is a repeat of the tour de force he created on the London stage.

A WOODFALL PRODUCTION

Production—Harry Saltzman
Direction—Tony Richardson
Screenplay—John Osborne &
  Nigel Kneale

Photography—Oswald Morris
Art direction—Ralph Brinton
Music—John Addison
Editing—Alan Osbiston

PLAYERS: Laurence Olivier, Brenda de Banzie, Joan Plowright, Roger Livesey, Alan Bates, Daniel Massey, Albert Finney, Miriam Karlin, Shirley Ann Field, Thora Hird

ENTR'ACTE   France (1924)

A two-reel avant-garde short by René Clair prepared especially for showing between the two acts of the ballet *Relache*. The film has no story line and is made up of a succession of more or less unrelated images, including repeated shots of a ballet dancer's legs and a chase of a funeral carriage.

ROLF DE MARÉ (BALLETS SUEDOIS)

Direction—René Clair
Screenplay & sets—
  Francis Picabia

Photography—Jimmy Berliet
Original music—Erik Satie

PLAYERS: Jean Borlin, Inge Friess, Francis Picabia, Man Ray & Marcel Duchamp, Marcel Achard, Touchagues, Rolf de Maré

EROICA   Poland (1957)

The romantic ideal of individual heroism is satirized by Andrzej Munk in two contrasting stories about the Warsaw Rising: the first is a humorous tale about a young opportunist who succeeds, in spite of himself, in becoming a Resistance hero, and the second a tragedy centering on some Polish occupants of a German prison camp who pathetically attempt to keep their hopes alive by remembering the legend (a false one) of the man who once escaped from the camp. Beautifully put together, this is among the most ironic films to be made about World War II.

KADR FILM UNIT

Direction—Andrzej Munk
Screenplay—
  Jerzy Stefan Stawinski
Photography—Jerzy Wojcik

Art direction—Jan Grandys
Music—Jan Krenz
Editing—Jadwiga Zaicek,
  Miroslawa Garlicka

125

PLAYERS: Edward Dziewonski, Barbara Polomska, Leon Niemczyk, Ignacy Machowski, Kazimierz Opalinski, Jozef Nowak, Roman Klosowski

EVE   France/Italy (1962)
Losey's stylish study in sexual obsession and sado-masochism with Jeanne Moreau in brilliant form as the malicious, luxury-loving femme fatale of the title and Stanley Baker as the phony Welsh writer she loves and then coolly destroys. An ambitious, much mutilated film raised to a considerably higher level than the superficial James Hadley Chase novel from which it originated, and acted to within an inch of its life by the two principals. Splendid winter backgrounds of Rome and Venice by the late Gianni Di Venanzo.

PARIS FILM (PARIS)/INTEROPA FILM (ROME)

Production—Robert & Raymond
  Hakim
Direction—Joseph Losey
Screenplay—Hugo Butler &
  Evan Jones
Editing—Reginald Beck &
  Franca Silvi

Photography (Venice Festival
  sequence shot by Henri Decae)
  —Gianni Di Venanzo
Art direction—
  Richard MacDonald &
  Luigi Scaccianoce
Music—Michel Legrand

PLAYERS: Jeanne Moreau, Stanley Baker, Virna Lisi, Giorgio Albertazzi, James Villiers, Riccardo Garrone, Lisa Gastoni, Checco Rissone

EXECUTIVE SUITE   U.S.A. (1954)
The scramble for power by top-level executives when the president of a vast furniture organization dies suddenly without nominating his successor. An adult movie, efficiently directed by Robert Wise, among the best of 1954. In an all-star cast Fredric March's ruthless company accountant stands out. Excellent cameos from Louis Calhern as a Wall Street gambler and Nina Foch as the late president's confidential secretary. A shrewd screenplay by Ernest Lehman, who later contributed to such films as The Sweet Smell of Success (co-scripted with Clifford Odets), North by Northwest, and Who's Afraid of Virginia Woolf.

METRO—GOLDWYN—MAYER

Production—John Houseman
Direction—Robert Wise
Screenplay (from novel by
  Cameron Hawley)—
  Ernest Lehman

Photography—George Folsey
Art direction—Cedric Gibbons &
  Edward Carfagno
Editing—Ralph Winters

PLAYERS: William Holden, June Allyson, Barbara Stanwyck, Fredric March, Walter Pidgeon, Shelley Winters, Paul Douglas, Louis Calhern, Dean Jagger, Nina Foch

EXODUS   U.S.A. (1960)
Film of Leon Uris's 600-page best-seller about the founding of the state of Israel and the subsequent conflict between Jews and Arabs. A much underrated Otto Preminger movie that skillfully combines fact, e.g., the dynamiting of the King David Hotel in Jerusalem, with fiction and which carries its length better than most 3½-hour epics. Notable for Sam Leavitt's splendid color work (the film was shot in Cyprus and Israel) and Ernest Gold's heroic score, the film is marred only by some uneven and often ragged playing from the international cast.

UNITED ARTISTS

Production & direction—   Photography (Technicolor/
  Otto Preminger   Super Panavision 70)—
Screenplay—Dalton Trumbo   Sam Leavitt
Art direction—Richard Day   Music—Ernest Gold
                                       Editing—Louis Loeffler

PLAYERS: Paul Newman, Eva Marie Saint, Sal Mineo, Jill Haworth, Ralph Richardson, Peter Lawford, Lee J. Cobb, John Derek, Hugh Griffith

EXTERMINATING ANGEL, THE (El Angel Exterminador)
                                                      Mexico (1962)
A group of Mexican aristocrats prepare to return home after attending a formal dinner party, but find that a mystic force prevents them from leaving the room. As the hours and days go by and the wrappings of civilized society are stripped away, the people begin to break down. Greed, lust and superstition all rise to the surface as they revert to their basic instincts. A hypnotic, startlingly original film that shows director Luis Buñuel at his most surrealist—and brilliant. Wickedly funny, marred only by the "B-picture" quality of the playing.

GUSTAVO ALATRISTE

Direction—Luis Buñuel   Photography—Gabriel Figueroa
Screenplay (adapted from play   Music—extracts from Paradisi,
  Los Náufragos de la Calle de   Scarlatti & Gregorian chants
  la Providencia by José   Art direction—Jesús Bracho
  Bergamín—Luis Buñuel &   Editing—Carlos Savage Jr.
  Luis Alcoriza

127

PLAYERS: Jacqueline Andere, José Baviera, Silvia Pinal, Augusto Benedico, Luis Beristein, Antonio Bravo, Claudio Brook, Enrique Rambal

EYES WITHOUT A FACE (Les Yeux Sans Visage)   France (1959)
Grisly, and to many people repulsive, French horror movie about a mad surgeon (Pierre Brasseur) who kidnaps a number of pretty young women, removes their facial tissue, and then attempts, unsuccessfully, to graft a new face onto the daughter he has so hideously disfigured in a car accident. A much censored film and, in its scenes of face surgery and its climax when the surgeon is himself disfigured by a pack of killer dogs, undeniably disturbing, but Eugen Shuftan's camera work is a thing of beauty and Franju's direction often inspired. Alida Valli played the surgeon's assistant and Edith Scob his daughter.

CHAMPS ELYSÉES–LUX

Production–Jules Borkon
Direction–Georges Franju
Dialogue–Pierre Gascar
Photography–Eugen Shuftan
Art direction–Auguste Capelier
Music–Maurice Jarre

Screenplay (from novel)–
     Jean Redon
Adaptation–Franju, Jean
     Redon, Claude Sautet, Pierre
     Boileau, Thomas Narcejac
Editing–Gilbert Natot

PLAYERS: Pierre Brasseur, Alida Valli, Edith Scob, François Guérin, Juliette Mayniel, Beatrice Altariba, Alexandre Rignault, René Génin, Claude Brasseur

FACE, THE (Ansiktet)   Sweden (1958)
After The Seventh Seal and Wild Strawberries this is the most ambitious of all Ingmar Bergman's films of the fifties. It is set in mid-19th-century Sweden and tells of a traveling magician (Max Von Sydow) and his troupe who are challenged by a mocking, sceptical medical officer (Gunnar Björnstrand) to prove their supernatural powers. The film turns on the central theme of reason versus the irrational and allows Bergman to voice once again his thoughts on faith and doubt and good and evil. Brilliant playing from Von Sydow, Björnstrand and the rest of the Bergman entourage, and a stunningly photographed sequence of genuine horror when the magician, supposedly dead, methodically revenges himself on the doctor by tormenting him with a series of phony tricks.

SVENSK FILMINDUSTRI

Direction & screenplay–
     Ingmar Bergman
Photography–Gunnar Fischer

Art direction–P. A. Lundgren
Music–Erik Nordgren
Editing–Oscar Rosander

128

PLAYERS: Max Von Sydow, Ingrid Thulin, Ake Fridell, Naima Wifstrand, Lars Ekborg, Gunnar Björnstrand, Erland Josephson, Gertrud Fridh

FACE IN THE CROWD, A   U.S.A. (1957)
The rise from obscurity to nationwide TV fame of guitar-playing hillbilly Lonesome Rhodes (Andy Griffith) beloved for his wholesome humor and cracker-barrel philosophy but in reality corrupt and rotten to the core. Overhysterical at times, but Budd Schulberg's sharp script is consistently on target and ruthlessly attacks TV values and public gullibility. Directed by Elia Kazan from Schulberg's story. "Your Arkansas Traveler."

NEWTOWN PRODUCTIONS/WARNER BROS.

Production & direction—   *Art direction*— Richard & Paul
  Elia Kazan   Sylbert
Screenplay—Budd Schulberg   *Music*—Tom Glazer
Photography—Harry Stradling   *Editing*—Gene Milford
  & Gayne Rescher

PLAYERS: Andy Griffith, Patricia Neal, Anthony Franciosa, Walter Matthau, Lee Remick, Percy Waram, Rod Brasfield

FAHRENHEIT 451   Gt. Britain (1966)
Truffaut's version of Ray Bradbury's science-fiction novel about a futuristic zombie society in which books are banned because they make people antisocial and in which firemen are employed not to put out fires (the buildings are fireproof), but to burn whatever books are still in existence. An intelligent though depressing little movie with some startlingly beautiful color by Nicolas Roeg and an intriguing score by Bernard Herrmann. It is flawed ultimately, however, by the performances of Oskar Werner (as a fireman) and Julie Christie (as the book-reading girl who converts him), both of whom are considerably below form. The opening credits are spoken against colored shots of television aerials.

ANGLO–ENTERPRISE/VINEYARD

Production—Lewis M. Allen   *Additional dialogue*—David
Associate producer—   Rudkin & Helen Scott
  Michael Delamar   *Photography (Technicolor)*—
Direction—François Truffaut   Nicolas Roeg
Screenplay—François Truffaut &   *Art direction*—Syd Cain
  Jean-Louis Richard   *Music*—Bernard Herrmann
                                   Editing—Thom Noble

PLAYERS: Oskar Werner, Julie Christie, Cyril Susack, Anton Diffring, Jeremy Spenser, Bee Duffell, Gillian Lewis, Ann Bell

FALLEN ANGEL   U.S.A. (1945)
Realistic, smartly tailored whodunit by Otto Preminger about a tough-talking drifter (Dana Andrews) who becomes mixed up in the murder of a sultry cafe waitress (Linda Darnell) but is eventually saved and shown the error of his ways by organ-playing good girl (Alice Faye). Rich in sleazy small-town detail—flashing neon, dark streets, wayside cafes, etc.—and with some moments of brilliance, still it is something of a letdown after Preminger's classic *Laura* a year earlier. John Carradine appears in a supporting role as a bogus spiritualist.

TWENTIETH CENTURY—FOX

Production & direction—   *Art direction—*Lyle Wheeler &
  Otto Preminger   Leland Fuller
Screenplay (from novel by   *Music—*Emil Newman
  *Marty Holland)—*Harry Kleiner   *Editing—*Harry Reynolds
*Photography—*Joseph LaShelle
PLAYERS: Alice Faye, Dana Andrews, Linda Darnell, Charles Bickford, Anne Revere, Bruce Cabot, John Carradine

FALLEN IDOL, THE   Gt. Britain (1948)
An 8-year-old boy (Bobby Henrey), left in the charge of butler (Ralph Richardson) and his wife (Sonia Dresdel) in a foreign embassy in London, becomes a witness to the wife's accidental death and almost involves the butler (whom he hero-worships) in a murder charge. A quiet, subtle look into the mind of a young boy adapted by Graham Greene from his short story "The Basement Room" and directed with great skill by Carol Reed, who made this one between his two masterworks *Odd Man Out* and *The Third Man.*

LONDON FILMS

Production & direction—   *Photography—*Georges Perinal
  Carol Reed   *Art direction—*Vincent Korda
*Screenplay—*Graham Greene   with James Sawyer
*Additional dialogue—*Lesley   *Music—*William Alwyn
  Storm & William Templeton   *Editing—*Oswald Hafenrichter
PLAYERS: Ralph Richardson, Sonia Dresdel, Michele Morgan, Jack Hawkins, Denis O'Dea, Dora Bryan, Walter Fitzgerald, Bobby Henrey

FALLEN SPARROW, THE   U.S.A. (1943)
Bizarre, sometimes extraordinary, but now almost forgotten little thriller

130

focusing on a young American who returns from fighting in the Spanish Civil War only to become involved with pursuing Nazis in New York City. The excellent John Garfield is well supported by Walter Slezak as the crippled heavy. Nicholas Musuraca (his camerawork here is as good as anything he did for Lewton) proves once again that he was one of the most talented and underrated cameramen of the 1940's.

RKO RADIO

Production—Robert Fellows
Direction—Richard Wallace
Screenplay (from novel by Dorothy B. Hughes)—Warren Duff

Photography—Nicholas Musuraca
Art direction—Albert S. D'Agostino, William Keller
Editing—Robert Wise

PLAYERS: John Garfield, Maureen O'Hara, Walter Slezak, Martha O'Driscoll, Patricia Morison, John Miljan, Miles Mander, Rosina Galli

FANFAN LA TULIPE   France (1951)
Engaging historical burlesque built around the romantic exploits of dashing Gérard Philipe who, in true Fairbanks tradition, duels, loves, and escapes from death a thousand times before eventually winning the hand of shapely princess (Gina Lollobrigida). A witty script spoofs almost every kind of historical romance and Christian Jaque's direction has considerable style. Marcel Herrand appears in a supporting role as Louis XV.

FILMSONOR—ARIANE—AMATO

Direction—Christian Jaque
Screenplay—Rene Wheeler & Rene Fallet
Adaptation—Christian Jaque, Henri Jeanson & Rene Wheeler

Dialogue—Henri Jeanson
Photography—Christian Matras
Art direction—Robert Gys
Music—Georges Van Parys & Maurice Thiriet

PLAYERS: Gérard Philipe, Gina Lollobrigida, Noël Roquevert, Olivier Hussenot, Marcel Herrand, Jean-Marc Tennberg

FANNY   France (1932)
The continuing story of the people who inhabit César's quayside Bar de la Marine in Old Marseilles, centering on the young fish-seller Fanny who, having been deserted by her seafaring lover Marius, marries the elderly widower Panisse in order to give her unborn child a name. Rich in atmosphere, brilliantly played, especially by Raimu as César and even more successful than the first part in the trilogy, thanks to the guiding hand of director Marc Allégret. See also *César* (page 78) and *Marius* (page 283).

131

Fantasia

LES FILMS MARCEL PAGNOL–LES ETABLISSEMENTS RICHEBÉ

Direction–Marc Allégret

Screenplay (from his own play)
–Marcel Pagnol

Art direction–Scognamillo

Photography–Toporkoff,
assisted by Dantan, Hubert &
Georges Benoit

Music–Vincent Scotto

PLAYERS: Raimu, Orane Demazis, Pierre Fresnay, Alida Rouffe, Charpin, Robert Vattier, Milly Mathis, Paul Dulac

FANTASIA   U.S.A. (1940)

Pictorial interpretation by Walt Disney of eight widely differing pieces of classical music ranging from abstract visuals for a Bach fugue and Mickey Mouse as the Sorcerer's Apprentice to the triumphant pre-historic visions of Stravinsky's "Rite of Spring." A remarkably bold experiment and still, some thirty years later, the most ambitious ani-mated cartoon ever made. Main highlights: the dancing hippopota-muses in "The Dance of the Hours" and the equally energetic mush-rooms in "The Nutcracker Suite," the arrival of the dinosaurs in "The Rite of Spring" and the charming landscapes of Greek mythology in Beethoven's Pastoral Symphony.

Production (Technicolor)—
  Walt Disney
Production supervisor—
  Ben Sharpsteen
Commentary—Deems Taylor
Story direction—Joe Grant,
  Dick Huemer
Musical direction—
  Edward H. Plumb
Musical film editor—
  Stephen Csillag
Directors—Samuel Armstrong,
  James Algar, Bill Roberts,
  Hamilton Luske, Jim Handley,
  Ford Beebe, T. Hee, Norm.
  Ferguson, Wilfred Jackson

Recording—William E. Garity,
  C. O. Slyfield, J. N. A.
  Hawkins
Music—Toccata & Fugue in D
  Minor by Bach, The Nut-
  cracker Suite by Tchaikovsky,
  The Sorcerer's Apprentice by
  Dukas, The Rite of Spring by
  Stravinsky, The Pastoral Sym-
  phony by Beethoven, Dance
  of the Hours by Ponchielli,
  Night on the Bare Mountain
  by Moussorgsky, Ave Maria
  by Schubert. All played by the
  Philadelphia Orchestra con-
  ducted by Leopold Stokowski

FAR COUNTRY, THE   U.S.A. (1954)

Cattle-drive movie with rancher (James Stewart) and partner (Walter Brennan) driving a large herd of cattle from Wyoming to the Klondike and becoming involved in the famous Gold Rush of 1896. Competent, well-performed Western with stunning Technicolor exteriors by William Daniels who also photographed *Winchester 73, Thunder Bay, The Glenn Miller Story* and *Strategic Air Command* for Mann.

UNIVERSAL/INTERNATIONAL

Production—Aaron Rosenberg
Direction—Anthony Mann
Screenplay—Borden Chase
Photography (Technicolor)—
  William Daniels

Art direction—Bernard Herzbrun
  & Alex Golitzen
Music—Joseph Gershenson
Editing—Russell Schoengarth

PLAYERS: James Stewart, Ruth Roman, Corinne Calvet, Walter Brennan, John McIntyre, Jay C. Flippen, Henry Morgan, Steve Brodie

FAR FROM THE MADDING CROWD   Gt. Britain (1967)

John Schlesinger's faithful, visually brilliant version of Thomas Hardy's 19th-century Wessex novel about a tempestuous young Dorset girl and her passionate involvement with three men—a young cavalry officer, a wealthy landowner, and a herdsman—when she inherits a prosperous farm from her uncle. Lovely West Country locations and some fine

133

performances, although Julie Christie is miscast and too modern as the heroine Bathsheba. The men, however—Terence Stamp as the swaggering Serjeant Troy, Peter Finch as William Boldwood, and Alan Bates as the devoted Gabriel Oak—are exactly right. Schlesinger's first in color and one of the most underrated films of the 1960's.

WARNER–PATHÉ/VIC-APPIA

Production—Joseph Janni
Direction—John Schlesinger
Screenplay—Frederic Raphael
Music—Richard Rodney Bennett
Musical direction—Marcus Dods

Photography (Panavision/
  Technicolor)—
  Nicolas Roeg
Art direction—Roy Smith
Editing—Malcolm Cooke

PLAYERS: Julie Christie, Terence Stamp, Peter Finch, Alan Bates, Fiona Walker, Prunella Ransome, Alison Leggatt, Paul Dawkins

FAREWELL MY LOVELY   U.S.A. (1944)
A neat, well-made version of Raymond Chandler's detective story with Dick Powell as the tough, laconic private eye Philip Marlowe. Tense, confused, often violent, and with some well-observed big-city backgrounds. Among the best of its kind, helped enormously by John Paxton's intelligent adaptation of Chandler's dialogue. Claire Trevor is the bad girl, Anne Shirley the good girl, and Esther Howard (superb) a drunken old floozy.

RKO RADIO

Production—Adrian Scott
Direction—Edward Dmytryk
Screenplay—John Paxton
Photography—Harry J. Wild

Art direction—Albert S.
  D'Agostino, Carroll Clark
Music—Roy Webb
Editing—Joseph Noriega

PLAYERS: Dick Powell, Claire Trevor, Anne Shirley, Otto Kruger, Mike Mazurki, Dougas Walton, Don Douglas, Miles Mander, Esther Howard

FATHER OF THE BRIDE   U.S.A. (1950)
Spencer Tracy in one of his finest comedy roles as the harassed, often bewildered father who has to pay for his daughter's large and over-expensive wedding. A crisp, likable, shrewdly observed domestic comedy that ranks with *Mr. Blandings Builds His Dream House* as one of the best of its kind produced in the postwar years. Joan Bennett plays the mother, Elizabeth Taylor the daughter, and Leo G. Carroll a haughty caterer.

METRO–GOLDWYN–MAYER

Production—Pandro S. Berman   Direction—Vincente Minnelli

*Screenplay (from novel by
Edward Streeter)*—Frances
Goodrich & Albert Hackett
Photography—John Alton
PLAYERS: Spencer Tracy, Joan Bennett, Elizabeth Taylor, Don Taylor,
Billie Burke, Leo G. Carroll, Moroni Olsen, Melville Cooper

Art direction—Cedric Gibbons
& Leonid Vasian
Music—Adolph Deutsch
Editing—Ferris Webster

FATHER'S LITTLE DIVIDEND   U.S.A. (1950)

A sequel to *Father of the Bride* and featuring the same set of characters focusing this time on the domestic upheaval caused by the expectation and arrival of a baby. Not (perhaps inevitably) as witty as its predecessor, but amusing nonetheless and for a sequel remarkably accomplished. Directed again by Minnelli from a Goodrich/Hackett script.

METRO–GOLDWYN–MAYER

Production—Pandro S. Berman
Direction—Vincent Minnelli
*Screenplay (based on characters
created by Edward Streeter)*—
Albert Hackett &
Frances Goodrich

Photography—John Alton
Art direction—Cedric Gibbons
& Leonid Vasian
Music—Albert Sendrey
Editing—Ferris Webster

PLAYERS: Spencer Tracy, Joan Bennett, Elizabeth Taylor, Don Taylor,
Billie Burke, Moroni Olsen, Richard Rober, Marietta Canty

FIENDS, THE (Les Diaboliques)   France (1955)

The headmaster of a Paris boarding school is murdered by his wife
(Véra Clouzot) and mistress (Simone Signoret), but keeps mysteriously reappearing at windows and in darkened rooms, driving his already ailing wife to a fatal breakdown. An ingeniously developed, cleverly plotted Clouzot thriller. The scene in which Véra Clouzot finally dies of a heart attack as she watches her husband's "corpse" come alive is Grand Guignol at its best. Charles Vanel also appears in the film as the ambiguous private detective investigating the case.

FILMSONOR

Direction—Henri-Georges Clouzot
*Screenplay, adaptation &
dialogue (from novel* Celle qui
n'était plus *by Boileau &
Narcejac)*—Henri-Georges
Clouzot, Jérôme Géronimi,

René Masson & Frédéric
Grendel
Photography—Armand Thirard
Art direction—Léon Barsacq
Music—Georges Van Parys
Editing—Madeleine Gug

135

PLAYERS: Simone Signoret, Véra Clouzot, Paul Meurisse, Charles Vanel, Pierre Larquey

FIREMAN, THE   U.S.A. (1916)
Chaplin as a blundering fireman does all the wrong things at the wrong time, but still manages to rescue lovely Edna Purviance from a burning house. An early two-reel Mutual farce with Eric Campbell as the fire chief being once again the butt for many of Chaplin's jokes. This was Campbell's second appearance as a Chaplin heavy and he was featured in all but one (*One A.M.*) of the twelve Mutual comedies before his untimely death in a car accident in 1917.

A MUTUAL COMEDY

Direction—Charles Chaplin   *Photography*—R. H. Totheroh &
Screenplay—Charles Chaplin   W. C. Foster
PLAYERS: Charles Chaplin, Albert Austin, Lloyd Bacon, Eric Campbell, Frank J. Coleman, James T. Kelly, Edna Purviance, John Rand, Leo White

FIVE BOYS FROM BARSKA STREET   Poland (1953)
Polish film about a gang of juvenile delinquents who, after being put on probation by a sympathetic judge, gradually adjust themselves to the new postwar society. Overly melodramatic and heavy with propaganda but, like *Shoeshine*, uncommonly honest in its approach to the problems of children whose homes and education suffered from the war.

FILM POLANSKI, WARSAW

Direction—Aleksander Ford   *Photography* (*Agfacolor*)—
Screenplay (*from Kozniewski's*   Jaroslaw Tuzar &
own novel)—   Karol Chodura
  Kazimierz Kozniewski & Ford   *Camerawork*—Jerzy Lipman
Art direction—   *Music*—Kazimierz Serocki
  Anatol Radzinowicz   *Editing*—W. Otocka & H. Kubik
PLAYERS: Aleksandra Śląska, Tadeusz Janczar, Andrzej Kozak, Tadeusz Lomnicki, Marian Rulka, Wlodzimierz Skoczylas

FIVE FINGERS   U.S.A. (1952)
Joseph L. Mankiewicz's outstanding spy film about an Albanian valet, known as Cicero, who photographs top-secret British war documents and sells them to the Germans for £300,000. Polished, witty, expertly made, and with a fine suave performance from James Mason as Cicero

and a minor gem from John Wengraf as Von Papen. One of the best of spy films and almost a masterpiece of its kind.

TWENTIETH CENTURY–FOX

Production—Otto Lang

Direction—Joseph L. Mankiewicz

Screenplay (*from book* Operation Cicero *by L. C. Moyzisch*)— Michael Wilson

Photography—Norbert Brodine

Art direction—Lyle Wheeler, George W. Davis

Music—Bernard Herrmann

Editing—James B. Clark

PLAYERS: James Mason, Danielle Darrieux, Michael Rennie, Walter Hampden, Oscar Karlweis, Herbert Berghof, John Wengraf, A. Ben Astar, Roger Plowden, Michael Pate, Ivan Triesault

FLESH AND THE DEVIL   U.S.A. (1927)

Glossy emotional drama about two Austrian army comrades (John Gilbert and Lars Hanson) who are almost destroyed by their infatuation with a wealthy married temptress (Greta Garbo). Noted for its somewhat torrid love scenes the film marked the first occasion that the great Swedish actress played opposite Gilbert and was also her first association with Clarence Brown, who directed several of her films during the 1930's. Garbo/Brown movies: *Flesh and the Devil, Love, A Woman of Affairs, Anna Christie, Romance, Inspiration, Anna Karenina* and *Marie Walewska*.

METRO–GOLDWYN–MAYER

Direction—Clarence Brown

Photography—William Daniels

Editing—Lloyd Nosler

Adaptation (*from novel* The Undying Past *by Hermann Sudermann*)— Benjamin F. Glazer

PLAYERS: John Gilbert, Greta Garbo, Lars Hanson, Barbara Kent, William Orlamund, George Fawcett, Eugene Besserer

FLOORWALKER, THE   U.S.A. (1916)

Charlie Chaplin's first for Mutual has Charlie loose in a large department store and becoming a hero when he prevents villainous store manager (Eric Campbell) and accomplice floorwalker (Lloyd Bacon) from robbing the safe. High spot: a wild chase up and down a moving staircase. Shot at the Lone Star Studio by Chaplin who, at the age of 26, was earning $10,000 a week.

A MUTUAL COMEDY

Direction—Charles Chaplin

Screenplay—Charles Chaplin

Photography—R. H. Totheroh & W. C. Foster

137

PLAYERS: Charlie Chaplin, Albert Austin, Lloyd Bacon, Henry Bergman, Eric Campbell, Frank J. Coleman, Bud Jamison, James T. Kelly

FLYING DOWN TO RIO   U.S.A. (1933)
Routine, rather dull Dolores Del Rio musical but historically important as the first film in which Fred Astaire and Ginger Rogers, on this occasion in supporting roles, played opposite each other. The brightest sequences in the film are the Astaire-Rogers dance routines, with the "Carioca" number being particularly effective.

RKO RADIO

Direction–Thornton Freeland
Associate producer–Lou Brock
Screenplay (from play by
  Ann Caldwell and Lou Brock
  based on original story by
  Louis Brock)–
Cyril Hume, H. W. Hanemann,
Erwin Gelsey

Photography–J. J. Faulkner
Music direction–Max Steiner
Editing–Jack Kitchin
Music–Vincent Youmans
Lyrics–Edward Eliscu,
  Gus Kahn, Dave Gould

PLAYERS: Dolores Del Rio, Gene Raymond, Raoul Roulien, Ginger Rogers, Fred Astaire, Blanche Frederics, Walter Walker

FOLLOW THE FLEET   U.S.A. (1936)
The usual Fred Astaire–Ginger Rogers musical love affair set this time against a naval background and helped along by such excellent Irving Berlin numbers as "Let Yourself Go," "All My Eggs in One Basket," and "Let's Face the Music and Dance." Light, engaging and directed again by Mark Sandrich although not up to the standard of his two previous Astaire–Rogers musicals *The Gay Divorcee* and *Top Hat*.

RKO RADIO

Production–Pandro S. Berman
Direction–Mark Sandrich
Screenplay (from play Shore Leave
  by Hubert Osborne *&* Allen
  Scott)–Dwight Taylor

Photography–David Abel
Music & lyrics–Irving Berlin
Music direction–Max Steiner
Editing–Henry Berman

PLAYERS: Fred Astaire, Ginger Rogers, Randolph Scott, Harriet Hilliard, Astrid Allwyn, Harry Beresford

FOOLISH WIVES   U.S.A. (1921)
Early von Stroheim movie about a bogus Russian nobleman (Stroheim) who, together with two Russian "princesses" earns a not unprofitable

living by seducing and then blackmailing the rich women living on the Riviera. Originally planned for showing in two parts, but later cut from 21 reels to 14. The movie took over a year to shoot and cost over a million dollars to produce. Although not a financial success it nonetheless established Universal as a major studio. This was the first time that von Stroheim had used two cameramen on one of his pictures and both Ben Reynolds and William Daniels (Garbo's cameraman of the 1930's) worked with him again on *The Merry-Go-Round, Greed* and *The Merry Widow.*

UNIVERSAL

Direction & screenplay—
  Erich von Stroheim
*Photography—*Ben Reynolds &
  William Daniels

Art direction & costumes—
  Erich von Stroheim
  & Richard Day
*Music—*Sigmund Romberg

PLAYERS: Erich von Stroheim, Maude George, Mae Busch, George Christians, Miss Dupont, Cesare Gravina, Malvine Polo, Dale Fuller

---

FOOTLIGHT PARADE   U.S.A. (1933)

Warner musical of the early 1930's with James Cagney as a hoofing stage producer and Joan Blondell as his secretary. The inconsequential plot is bolstered by some smart lines and several of Busby Berkeley's most engaging production numbers, among them "Honeymoon Hotel," "Shanghai Lil" (with Cagney and Ruby Keeler), and the stunning aqua ballet "By a Waterfall," perhaps the most impressive of all Berkeley's geometric creations.

WARNER BROS.

*Direction—*Lloyd Bacon
*Screenplay—*Manuel Seff,
  James Seymour
*Photography—*George Barnes
*Editing—*George Amy

*Choreography—*Busby Berkeley
*Songs—*Sammy Fain,
  Irving Kahal, Al Dubin,
  Harry Warren

PLAYERS: James Cagney, Joan Blondell, Dick Powell, Ruby Keeler

---

FOR ME AND MY GAL   U.S.A. (1942)

Brash, vigorous M-G-M musical about the ups and downs of an American vaudeville team during World War I. Well below Metro's usual standard despite such pleasing old-time songs as "After You've Gone" and "When You Wore a Tulip," but significant because it marked the first film appearance of brilliant New York dancing star Gene Kelly. Keenan Wynn, one of M-G-M's most reliable character

139

actors of the 1940's and '50's also made his debut in this picture as a vaudeville agent.

METRO–GOLDWYN–MAYER

Production—Arthur Freed

Direction—Busby Berkeley

Screenplay (from story by
  Howard Emmett Rogers)—
  Richard Sherwood,
  Fred Finklehoffe & Sid Silvers

Photography—William Daniels

Art direction—Cedric Gibbons

Music—Roger Edens &
  Georgie Stoll

Editing—Ben Lewis

PLAYERS: Judy Garland, Gene Kelly, George Murphy, Martha Eggerth, Ben Blue, Richard Quine, Lucille Norman

FOR WHOM THE BELL TOLLS   U.S.A. (1943)

Ernest Hemingway's violent story of the Spanish Civil War with Gary Cooper as an American schoolteacher and Ingrid Bergman as a tortured orphan girl joining up with a band of peasant guerrillas to fight for democracy. Uneven and overlong but with some occasional moments of brilliance (the savage mob beatings outside the city hall, the blowing up of the bridges), some distinguished Technicolor photography, and a towering performance by Katina Paxinou as the passionate and fiery woman guerrilla leader Pilar.

PARAMOUNT

Production & direction—
  Sam Wood

Screenplay—Dudley Nichols

Production design—
  William Cameron Menzies

Music—Victor Young

Photography (Technicolor)—
  Ray Rennahan

Art direction—Hans Dreier &
  Haldane Douglas

Editing—Sherman Todd &
  John Link

PLAYERS: Gary Cooper, Ingrid Bergman, Akim Tamiroff, Arturo de Cordova, Joseph Calleia, Katina Paxinou

FORBIDDEN PARADISE   U.S.A. (1924)

Witty Lubitsch satire dealing with the amorous affairs of Catherine the Great of Russia. Adapted loosely from the play Czarina and set in the 18th century although Lubitsch permitted such modern updatings as bobbed hair and the use of automobiles in order that the events in the film should be seen to apply not only to Imperial Russia but to any period of history. German-born Pola Negri, then one of Hollywood's major stars, played Catherine.

PARAMOUNT

Direction—Ernst Lubitsch   *Screenplay (from play* Czarina
Photography—   *by Lajos Biro & Melchior*
  Charles Van Enger   *Lengyel)*—Hans Kraly &
Art direction—Hans Dreier   Agnes Christine Johnston
PLAYERS: Pola Negri, Rod La Rocque, Adolphe Menjou, Pauline
Starke, Fred Malatesta, Nick de Ruiz

FORCE OF EVIL   U.S.A. (1949)
An exposure of New York's numbers racket hinging on the relationship
between two brothers—one a smart-talking, get-rich-quick lawyer
(John Garfield), the other an honest man (Thomas Gomez) struggling
to free himself from a dishonest business. The script is the film's main
strength although there are several sequences of great visual power,
especially the murder of a bookkeeper in a New York basement. Based
on the novel *Tucker's People* by Ira Wolfert.

AN ENTERPRISE PICTURE/METRO–GOLDWYN–MAYER

Production—Bob Roberts   *Photography*—George Barnes
Direction—Abraham Polonsky   *Art direction*—Richard Day
Screenplay—Abraham Polonsky &   *Music*—David Raksin
  Ira Wolfert   *Editing*—Art Seid
PLAYERS: John Garfield, Beatrice Pearson, Thomas Gomez, Roy Roberts,
Marie Windsor, Howland Chamberlin, Paul McVey, Jack Overman

FOREIGN AFFAIR, A   U.S.A. (1948)
Caustic humor among the ruins of postwar Berlin with a U.S. Army
captain (John Lund) involved with a night-club singer (Marlene
Dietrich) who is also the ex-girl friend of a top-ranking Nazi, and with
a staid Congresswoman (Jean Arthur) sent to Germany to investigate
the morale of American troops. One of Billy Wilder's forgotten and
consequently most underrated pictures. Superb cameo of a wisecracking colonel by Millard Mitchell.

PARAMOUNT

Production—Charles Brackett   *Photography*—
Direction—Billy Wilder   Charles B. Lang, Jr.
Screenplay (based on original   *Art direction*—Hans Dreier &
  story by David Shaw)—   Walter Tyler
  Charles Brackett, Billy Wilder   *Music & musical direction*—
  & Richard L. Breen   Frederick Hollander
Adaptation—Robert Harari   *Editing*—Doane Harrison
PLAYERS: Marlene Dietrich, Jean Arthur, John Lund, Millard Mitchell,
Bill Murphy, Stanley Prager, Peter von Zerneck, Raymond Bond

FOREIGN CORRESPONDENT   U.S.A. (1940)
The story of an American journalist (Joel McCrea) who is sent to
Europe in 1939 to cover the political situation and who becomes involved with fifth columnists and Nazi spies. A splendid Hitchcock
movie (his second in Hollywood), fast, exciting, very imaginative and
strongly reminiscent of his British thrillers. Among the highlights: an
attempted murder on the top of Westminster Cathedral, a brilliant
sequence in an isolated Dutch windmill, and, above all, a magnificently
handled assassination scene in pouring rain. Edmund Gwenn in a minor
role as a gentlemanly little murderer out-acted everyone in the picture.

UNITED ARTISTS

Production—Walter Wanger
Direction—Alfred Hitchcock
Screenplay—Charles Bennett,
    Joan Harrison
Dialogue—James Hilton
    Robert Benchley

Photography—Rudolph Mate
Art direction—William Cameron
    Menzies, Alexander Golitzen
Music—Alfred Newman
Editing—Otto Lovering,
    Dorothy Spencer

PLAYERS: Joel McCrea, Laraine Day, Herbert Marshall, George Sanders,
Albert Bassermann, Robert Benchley, Eduardo Cianelli, Edmund
Gwenn, Harry Davenport, Martin Kosleck

FORT APACHE   U.S.A. (1948)
John Ford's first film about the U.S. Cavalry (recalling Custer's last
stand) features Henry Fonda as the West Point colonel and ex-Civil
War general whose arrogance and stupidity leads to the massacre of
his entire regiment by the Indians. Not in the front rank of Ford films,
but competently played by Fonda, Wayne, McLaglen and company
and with some fine Arizona locations.

ARGOSY PICTURES—RKO RADIO

Production—Merian C. Cooper
    John Ford
Direction—John Ford
Photography—Archie Stout

Screenplay (from story "Mas-
    sacre" by James Warner Bellah)
    —Frank S. Nugent
Art direction—James Basevi
    Music—Richard Hageman

PLAYERS: John Wayne, Henry Fonda, Shirley Temple, John Agar, Ward
Bond, George O'Brien, Victor McLaglen, Pedro Armandariz, Anna Lee,
Irene Rich

42ND STREET   U.S.A. (1933)
Early musical with Warner Baxter as a chain-smoking stage director

142

struggling against heavy odds to put on a Broadway show. Among those helping and hindering him—Bebe Daniels as a temperamental star, Ruby Keeler as the chorus girl who steps into Bebe's shoes, and Ginger Rogers as tough gold-digging hoofer "Any-Time Annie." Top songs: "You're Getting to Be a Habit With Me," "Shuffle Off to Buffalo," "Young and Healthy," and the climactic "42nd Street." The choreography was by Busby Berkeley who, during the thirties, became famous for his large-scale geometrically designed dance routines.

WARNER BROS.

Direction—Lloyd Bacon
Screenplay (based on novel by
  Bradford Ropes)—James
  Seymour & Rian James
Photography—Sol Polito

Art direction—Jack Okey
Costumes—Orry-Kelly
Songs—Al Dubin & Harry Warren
Editing—Thomas Pratt

PLAYERS: Warner Baxter, Bebe Daniels, George Brent, Ruby Keeler, Guy Kibbee, Ned Sparks, Dick Powell, Ginger Rogers, Lyle Talbot, Una Merkel

FOUR FEATHERS, THE   Gt. Britain (1939)

Harry Faversham (John Clements), branded a coward by his fiancée, sets out for Egypt and performs fantastic feats of endurance in order to prove his courage. A terribly silly story, of the variety usually known as "boy's classics," that unashamedly glorifies war as a romantic adventure. The film is marked, however, by some fine location (Sudan) photography by Osmond Borrodaile and is worthy of mention here because of one memorable scene in which Ralph Richardson goes blind through sunstroke and finds himself alone in the desert with only his dead comrades and vultures for company.

LONDON FILMS PRODUCTIONS

Production—Alexander Korda
Associate producer—
  Irving Asher
Direction—Zoltan Korda
Screenplay (from novel by
  A. E. W. Mason)—R. C. Sherriff
Additional dialogue—Lajos Biro,
  Arthur Wimperis
Art direction—Vincent Korda

Photography (Technicolor)—
  Georges Perinal
Sudan photography—
  Osmond Borrodaile
Music—Miklos Rozsa
Supervising editor—
  William Hornbeck
Editing—Henry Cornelius,
  Godfrey Brennan

PLAYERS: John Clements, Ralph Richardson, C. Aubrey Smith, June Duprez, Allan Jeayes, Jack Allen, Donald Gray, Frederick Culler

FOUR HORSEMEN OF THE APOCALYPSE, THE   U.S.A. (1921)

The movie that launched Rudolph Valentino into stardom; a long, sprawling, exotic affair based on a Spanish novel by Vicente Blasco Ibanez and centering on two European families living in South America who ultimately, and tragically, become embroiled in the First World War. The film's most famous scene is the one in which Valentino dances the tango, but more impressive technically are the war passages in the latter part of the picture and the visions of the four horsemen—Conquest, Slaughter, Famine and Death—riding across a turbulent sky. Photographed by John Seitz, who was associated with Ingram on all his major productions of the 1920's—*The Prisoner of Zenda, Scaramouche, Where the Pavement Ends,* etc.

METRO PICTURES

Direction—Rex Ingram   *Photography*—John Seitz
Screenplay—June Mathis   *Editing*—Grant Whytock

PLAYERS: Rudolph Valentino, Alice Terry, Pomeroy Cannon, Joseph Swickard, Alan Hale, Nigel de Brulier, John Sainpolis, Stuart Holmes, Jean Hersholt, Wallace Beery

FOURTEEN HOURS   U.S.A. (1951)

Henry Hathaway's excellent little thriller about a young man threatening suicide from the fifteenth-story ledge of a New York hotel. A perfect example of Hollywood craftsmanship at its best, the film is packed with tension and superbly acted by Richard Basehart as the would-be suicide, Paul Douglas as the traffic cop who helps him, and Agnes Moorehead as Basehart's hysterical mother. Not the least of the film's many assets is Joe MacDonald's stunning location photography of New York.

TWENTIETH CENTURY—FOX

Production—Sol C. Siegel   *Art direction*—Lyle Wheeler,
Direction—Henry Hathaway   Leland Fuller
Screenplay (*from story by Joel*   *Music*—Alfred Newman
   Sayre)—John Paxton   *Editing*—Dorothy Spencer
Photography—Joe MacDonald

PLAYERS: Richard Basehart, Paul Douglas, Barbara Bel Geddes, Debra Paget, Agnes Moorehead, Robert Keith, Howard da Silva, Jeffrey Hunter, Martin Gabel, Jeff Corey

FRANKENSTEIN   U.S.A. (1931)

James Whale's film adaptation of the horror classic about a brilliant

Frankenstein

scientist (Colin Clive) who assembles a living monster from the organs of dead bodies. There is some creaky dialogue and heavy overplaying by Clive, but a remarkably sympathetic performance from Boris Karloff as the monster and any number of brilliantly cinematic scenes, e.g., the monster being brought to life for the first time in the midst of a raging thunderstorm and his later tragic lakeside encounter with

a little girl. Co-scripted by Robert Florey and photographed by Arthur
Edeson who, along with John Mescall and Karl Freund, worked on the
majority of the Universal horror films made between 1930 and 1935.

UNIVERSAL

Direction—James Whale   Screenplay (after play by Peggy
Photography—Arthur Edeson   Webling based on the romance
Editing—Clarence Kolster   by Mary Shelley)—F. E.
                               Faragoh & Robert Florey
PLAYERS: Colin Clive, Boris Karloff, Mae Clarke, John Boles, Edward
van Sloan, Dwight Frye, Lionel Belmore, Marilyn Harris

FREAKS   U.S.A. (1932)
Beautiful trapeze artiste (Olga Baclanova) marries circus dwarf (Harry
Earles) for his money; then, with the help of her strong-man boyfriend
(Henry Victor), attempts to murder him. After discovering the plot the
rest of the circus freaks band together and wreak a terrible revenge
on the guilty pair—killing the strong man and transforming the girl,
through hideous surgery, into a mutilated sideshow attraction. A grotesque little tale based on the novel Spurs by Tod Robbins and directed
by Tod Browning shortly after he had completed Dracula at Universal.

METRO—GOLDWYN—MAYER

Direction—Tod Browning   Photography—
Screenplay—Willis Goldbeck,   Merritt B. Gerstad
   Leon Gordon   Art direction—Cedric Gibbons
Dialogue—Al Boasberg   Editing—Basil Wrangell
PLAYERS: Olga Baclanova, Henry Victor, Leila Hyams, Wallace Ford,
Harry Earles, Daisy Earles

FRENCH CANCAN   France (1954)
Jean Renoir's tribute to the French music hall; a gay, lightweight movie
set in the Paris of the 1880's and featuring Jean Gabin as an amorous
impresario who founds the famous Moulin Rouge in Montmartre. One
of Renoir's most joyous films, magnificently photographed in Technicolor and climaxed by a 20-minute cancan sequence. The film was the
first made by Renoir in a French studio since his prewar masterpiece
La Regle du Jeu.

FRANCO—LONDON FILMS/JOLLY FILMS

Direction—Jean Renoir   Photography (Technicolor)—
Screenplay (from idea by André   Michel Kelber
  -Paul Antoine)—Jean Renoir   Music—Georges Van Parys
Art direction—Max Douy   Editing—Boris Lewin

PLAYERS: Jean Gabin, Françoise Arnoul, Maria Félix, Jean-Roger Caussimon, Gianni Esposito, Franco Pastorino, Dora Doll

FRENCHMAN'S CREEK   U.S.A. (1945)
Set in 17th-century England this stylish Mitchell Leisen film is a trite tale about the romance between an English lady (Joan Fontaine) and a handsome French pirate (Arturo de Cordova), but the costumes of Raoul Pene du Bois plus the rich décor and Technicolor make it as exciting visually as any American movie of the early 1940's. Hans Dreier and Ernst Fegte won Academy Awards for the best color art direction of 1945.

PARAMOUNT

Production & direction—   *Art direction—*Hans Dreier &
Mitchell Leisen   Ernst Fegte
Screenplay (from novel by   *Costumes—*
Daphne du Maurier)—   Raoul Pene du Bois
Talbot Jennings   *Music—*Victor Young
Photography (Technicolor)—   *Editing—*Alma Macrorie
George Barnes

PLAYERS: Joan Fontaine, Arturo de Cordova, Basil Rathbone, Nigel Bruce, Cecil Kellaway, Ralph Forbes, Harald Ramond, Billy Daniels

FRENZY   Sweden (1944)
The film that signaled the rebirth of Swedish cinema: a cold, sordid study in perversion, set mainly in a boys' school and focusing on sadistic schoolmaster who brutally terrorizes an adolescent schoolboy. Stylishly made (helped considerably by Martin Bodin's dramatic photography) and brilliantly played by Stig Järrel (made up not unintentionally to resemble Himmler) as the schoolmaster. Also historically important as the first film to be scripted by Ingmar Bergman.

SVENSK FILMINDUSTRI

*Production—*C. A. Dymling   *Art direction—*Arne Akermark
*Direction—*Alf Sjöberg   *Music—*Hilding Rosenberg
*Screenplay—*Ingmar Bergman   *Editing—*Oscar Rosander
*Photography—*Martin Bodin

PLAYERS: Alf Kjellin, Stig Järrel, Mai Zetterling, Stig Olin, Jan Molander, Olof Winnerstrand, Gösta Cederlund, Gunnar Björnstrand

FRESHMAN, THE   U.S.A. (1925)
An enthusiastic and very determined young college student (Harold Lloyd) finds that the quickest way to college popularity is by joining

147

the football team. After being ridiculed, knocked about, and humiliated during practice games he eventually becomes the hero of the hour by scoring the winning touchdown in the big game. After *Safety Last* this is the funniest of all Lloyd's gag comedies. Others in the cast included Brooks Benedict as the college cad and Hazel Keener as the college belle.

PATHÉ–HAROLD LLOYD CORPORATION

Direction–Samuel Taylor,
  Fred Newmeyer
Photography–Walter Lundin

Screenplay–Samuel Taylor,
  John Grey, Ted Wilde, Tim
  Whelan

PLAYERS: Harold Lloyd, Jobyna Ralston, Brooks Benedict, James Anderson, Hazel Keener

FRIENDLY PERSUASION   U.S.A. (1956)

Leisurely tale of a Quaker family living in southern Indiana during the Civil War and of their spiritual struggles to reconcile their nonviolent beliefs when the fighting threatens the peace of their home. Gary Cooper plays the Quaker farmer, Dorothy McGuire his preacher wife, and Anthony Perkins their tortured son. Much underrated when first shown, but now ranking with William Wyler's most distinguished work. Excellent music score by Dimitri Tiomkin.

ALLIED ARTISTS

Production & direction–
  William Wyler
*Screenplay (from book by
  Jessamyn West)*–Michael
  Wilson (uncredited)
Photography (Deluxecolor)–
  Ellsworth Fredericks

Art direction–
  Edward S. Haworth
Music–Dimitri Tiomkin
Editing–Robert Swink, E. A.
  Biery & R. A. Belcher

PLAYERS: Gary Cooper, Dorothy McGuire, Marjorie Main, Anthony Perkins, Mary Carr, Richard Eyer, Robert Middleton

FROM HERE TO ETERNITY   U.S.A. (1953)

Expert, cleaned-up adaptation of James Jones' Army novel (yet another of the "books they couldn't film") about the day-to-day experiences of American soldiers serving in an infantry outfit in Hawaii just before the attack on Pearl Harbor. A brutal, very professional piece of film-making, somewhat uncharacteristic of Zinnemann but skillfully reduced by Daniel Taradash from 750 pages of text to two hours of screen time. Memorable mainly for the playing of its talented cast: Montgomery

Clift and Frank Sinatra appearing as GI's, Burt Lancaster as a tough sergeant, Deborah Kerr as the disillusioned wife of the company commander, and Donna Reed as a professional hostess "just two steps up from the pavement." Eight Academy Awards, including best picture, direction and screenplay.

COLUMBIA

Production—Buddy Adler
Direction—Fred Zinnemann
Screenplay—Daniel Taradash
Photography—Burnett Guffey

Art direction—Cary Odell
Music—George Duning
Editing—William Lyon

PLAYERS: Burt Lancaster, Montgomery Clift, Frank Sinatra, Deborah Kerr, Donna Reed, Philip Ober, Mickey Shaughnessy, Harry Bellaver, Ernest Borgnine

FRONT PAGE, THE   U.S.A. (1931)
Brilliantly written movie based on the stage play by Ben Hecht and Charles MacArthur about a group of newspapermen as they wait in the reporters' room of a prison to cover an execution. The newspaper scene is portrayed with unusual frankness and the satire of the unscrupulous methods used by some newspapermen to get a good story is biting and sustained. Good performances from Pat O'Brien as the reporter who shields a criminal when he breaks jail, and from Adolphe Menjou as his thick-skinned managing editor. Remade by Howard Hawks as *His Girl Friday* (1940).

UNITED ARTISTS

Direction—Lewis Milestone
Photography—Glenn
    MacWilliams, Bert Camm

Screenplay—Bartlett Cormack
Art direction—Richard Day
Editing—W. Duncan Mansfield

PLAYERS: Adolphe Menjou, Pat O'Brien, Mary Brian, Edward Everett Horton, Matt Moore, Frank McHugh, Spencer Charters

FUNNY FACE   U.S.A. (1957)
Fashion magazine editor (Kay Thompson), ace photographer (Fred Astaire), and Greenwich Village salesgirl (Audrey Hepburn) at large in Paris in a sophisticated Stanley Donen musical that includes several delightful evergreen numbers ("How Long Has This Been Going On" and "I Love Your Funny Face") as well as a number of Roger Edens originals ("Think Pink," "Bonjour Paris" and "On How to Be Lonely"). Visually one of Donen's most delightful films and the last major original screen musical of the decade.

Production—Roger Edens
Direction—Stanley Donen
Screenplay—Leonard Gershe
Photography (Technicolor/
VistaVision)—Ray June
Art direction—Hal Pereira &
George W. Davis

Music & lyrics—George & Ira
Gershwin
Additional music & lyrics—
Roger Edens &
Leonard Gershe
Music adaptation—
Adolph Deutsch
Editing—Frank Bracht

PLAYERS: Audrey Hepburn, Fred Astaire, Kay Thompson, Michel Auclair, Robert Flemyng

FUNNY GIRL   U.S.A. (1968)
The story of Fanny Brice (Barbra Streisand), the legendary East Side chorus girl who rose, via the music hall and the Ziegfeld Follies, to become one of the biggest stars on Broadway. William Wyler's first musical is an unqualified triumph, although the film is Streisand's from first to last—and never more so than in the exhilarating "Don't Rain on My Parade" number when she rushes impetuously by train to marry her gambler lover (Omar Sharif), and in the final unforgettable fade-out (shot in close-up against a darkened stage) when she sings "My Man." Other numbers include "People" and "Second Hand Rose." Walter Pidgeon appears as Florenz Ziegfeld.

RASTAR PRODUCTIONS/COLUMBIA

Production—Ray Stark
Direction—William Wyler
Screenplay (based on musical
play by Isobel Lennart
(book), Jule Styne (music)
& Bob Merrill (lyrics), from
story by Isobel Lennart)—
Isobel Lennart
Art direction—Robert Luthardt

Photography (Technicolor/
Panavision 70)—
Harry Stradling
Production design—
Gene Callahan
Musical supervision/Musical
direction—Walter Scharf
Editing—Maury Winetrobe,
William Sands

PLAYERS: Barbra Streisand, Omar Sharif, Kay Medford, Anne Francis, Walter Pidgeon, Lee Allen, Mae Questel, Gerald Mohr, Frank Faylen

FURY   U.S.A. (1936)
Disturbing tale of innocent young small-town American (Spencer Tracy) who is arrested and nearly lynched for a kidnapping he did

not commit and who later wreaks a bitter revenge on his persecutors. A powerful picture that ranks with LeRoy's *They Won't Forget*, made a year later, as one of Hollywood's most uncompromising studies of mass hysteria and mob rule. Fritz Lang's first American movie and still among his best.

METRO–GOLDWYN–MAYER

Production—
Joseph L. Mankiewicz
Direction—Fritz Lang
Screenplay (based on original story by Norman Krasna)—
Bartlett Cormack &
Fritz Lang

Photography—
Joseph Ruttenberg
Music—Franz Waxman
Art direction—Cedric Gibbons
Associate art directors—
William A. Horning &
Edwin B. Willis
Editing—Frank Sullivan

PLAYERS: Spencer Tracy, Sylvia Sydney, Walter Abel, Bruce Cabot, Edward Ellis, Walter Brennan, George Walcott, Frank Albertson

GASLIGHT   Gt. Britain (1939)

Unscrupulous murderer (Anton Walbrook) marries his victim's niece (Diana Wynyard), then tries to acquire her inheritance by slowly and methodically driving her insane. A skillful adaptation of Patrick Hamilton's stage thriller set for the most part within the confines of a large house in Victorian London and directed with some style by Thorold Dickinson. Remade four years later in Hollywood after the negative of this version had been bought and destroyed by M-G-M.

BRITISH NATIONAL

Production—John Corfield
Direction—Thorold Dickinson
Screenplay—A. R. Rawlinson,
Bridget Boland
Photography—Bernard Knowles

Art direction—
Duncan Sutherland
Music—Richard Addinsell
Editing—Sydney Cole

PLAYERS: Anton Walbrook, Diana Wynyard, Cathleen Cordell, Robert Newton, Frank Pettingell, Jimmy Hanley

GASLIGHT   U.S.A. (1944)

George Cukor's equally stylish but more polished remake with Ingrid Bergman taking over from Diana Wynyard as the terrified wife and winning the first of her two Hollywood Oscars. French actor Charles Boyer appears in the original Walbrook role. This film was renamed

The Murder in Thornton Square in Britain so as not to confuse audiences with the British Dickinson version. Some prints of the English film did actually survive and were later shown in the United States as *Angel Street,* the title of the original play.

METRO–GOLDWYN–MAYER

Direction–George Cukor
Screenplay (from play by Patrick Hamilton)–Walter Reisch & John L. Balderston
Photography–Joseph Ruttenberg

Art direction–Cedric Gibbons & William Ferrari
Music–Bronislau Kaper
Editing–Ralph E. Winters

PLAYERS: Charles Boyer, Ingrid Bergman, Joseph Cotten, Angela Lansbury, Dame May Whitty, Barbara Everest

GAY DIVORCEE, THE   U.S.A. (1934)
The second and, after *Top Hat,* the best of the nine Astaire-Rogers musicals of the 1930's is full of superb numbers: "Night and Day," "Looking for a Needle in a Haystack" (an Astaire solo), "Don't Let It Bother You," and climaxed by a brilliantly edited ten-minute dance routine around "The Continental" (Academy Award, best song, 1934). The usual supporting players—Edward Everett Horton, Eric Blore, Erik Rhodes—are featured in the cast, and Mark Sandrich, who made five of the prewar musicals, served as director.

RKO RADIO

Production–Pandro S. Berman
Direction–Mark Sandrich
Screenplay (from novel by Dwight Taylor)–George Marion, Jr., Dorothy Yost & Edward Kaufman

Photography–David Abel
Music & lyrics–Cole Porter, Mack Gordon, Harry Revel, Con Conrad & Herb Magidson
Music direction–Max Steiner
Editing–William Hamilton

PLAYERS: Fred Astaire, Ginger Rogers, Alice Brady, Edward Everett Horton, Erik Rhodes, Eric Blore

GENERAL, THE   U.S.A. (1926)
Buster Keaton as a Southern locomotive engineer chasing and being chased by Yankees along miles of railway track during the Civil War. The best train film ever made, with seven of the eight reels devoted to the train chase. The film is fast, ingenious and packed with impeccably timed visual gags. It was co-directed by Clyde Bruckman, an old associate of Keaton's who had earlier contributed to the scripts of *Seven Chances, The Navigator, Sherlock Junior,* etc.

BUSTER KEATON PRODUCTIONS INC./UNITED ARTISTS CORPORATION

Production—Joseph M. Schenck
Direction & screenplay—Buster
  Keaton, Clyde Bruckman
Adaptation—Al Boasberg,
  Charles Smith
Photography—J. Devereux
  Jennings, Bert Haines
Technical direction—
  Fred Gabourie

PLAYERS: Buster Keaton, Marian Mack, Glen Cavender, Jim Farley, Frederick Vroom, Charles Smith, Frank Barnes, Joe Keaton

GENERATION, A   Poland (1954)

This film, the first in Wajda's trilogy about wartime Poland, is set in Warsaw during the German Occupation and deals with a young Polish boy who is hardened and forced prematurely into manhood by his experiences as a member of the Communist Resistance. A compassionate, deeply felt film which is among the most moving of all those made about World War II. Other films in the trilogy are *Kanal* (page 214) and *Ashes and Diamonds* (page 28).

W. F. F. WROCLAW

Direction—Andrzej Wajda
Screenplay (from his novel)—
  Bohdan Czeszko
Photography—Jerzy Lipman
Art direction—Roman Mann
Music—Andrzej Markowski
Editing—Czeslaw Raniszewski

PLAYERS: Urzula Modrzynska, Tadeusz Lomnicki, Januz Palusziewicz, Roman Polanski

GENEVIEVE   Gt. Britain (1953)

British comedy about two motorcar enthusiasts (John Gregson and Kenneth More) and their experiences with their vintage cars and female traveling companions (who give them just as much trouble as the vehicles) during the annual London to Brighton run. Amusingly played, the honors go to Kenneth More as the young driver always hoping to combine the car run with "a really beautiful emotional experience" and Kay Kendall as his delicious trumpet-playing girlfriend. An unusual harmonica music score composed and played by Larry Adler.

SIRIUS

Production & direction—
  Henry Cornelius
Screenplay—William Rose
Photography (Technicolor)—
  Christopher Challis
Art direction—Michael Stringer
Music—Larry Adler
Editing—Clive Donner

PLAYERS: John Gregson, Dinah Sheridan, Kenneth More, Kay Kendall, Geoffrey Keen, Harold Siddons, Joyce Grenfell

Gentleman's Agreement

GENTLEMAN'S AGREEMENT U.S.A. (1947)
Glossy example of the Hollywood postwar "message" movie focusing on the problems of a magazine journalist (Gregory Peck) when he poses as a Jew in order to write a series of articles about anti-Semitism in the United States. Despite a clever and sometimes courageous script by Moss Hart and an excellent performance by John Garfield in a minor role as a returning Jewish ex-serviceman, this is not as good a film as *Crossfire* (also 1947), which tackled the same subject more successfully within the framework of the thriller.

TWENTIETH CENTURY–FOX

Production–Darryl F. Zanuck
Direction–Elia Kazan
Screenplay (from novel by Laura Z. Hobson)–Moss Hart
Photography–Arthur Miller

Art direction–Lyle R. Wheeler & Mark Lee Kirk
Music–Alfred Newman
Editing–Harmon Jones

PLAYERS: Gregory Peck, Dorothy McGuire, John Garfield, Celeste Holm, Anne Revere, June Havoc, Albert Dekker, Jane Wyatt, Dean Stockwell

GERMANY–YEAR ZERO Italy/Germany (1948)
Bleak Rossellini picture set in the ruins of postwar Berlin where the

young son of a starving German family gets caught up in the wretched-
ness and corruption around him and is driven to murder and eventual
suicide. A neglected, part documentary, work somewhat overshadowed
by Rossellini's earlier and more highly praised *Paisan* and *Open City*,
but realistically reflecting the tragic aftermath of the war in Germany.
Fine playing from Edmund Meschke as the boy.

TEVERFILM

Direction–Roberto Rossellini   *Photography*–Robert Juillard
Screenplay–Roberto Rossellini,   *Art direction*–Roberto Filippone
   Carlo Lizzani & Max Kolpet   *Music*–Renzo Rossellini
PLAYERS: Edmund Meschke, Ernest Pittschau, Ingetraud Hinze, Franz
Grüger, Erich Guhne

GIANT   U.S.A. (1956)
Based on Edna Ferber's epic novel this 3-hour 18-minute movie spans
three generations of a Texas landowning family, concerning itself primarily with the conflict between land-proud cattle boss (Rock Hudson)
and hired ranch hand (James Dean) who discovers oil on his patch of
land and rapidly becomes the richest man in Texas. One of George
Stevens' finest films, examining all aspects of Texas life and concentrating for much of its length on the racial discrimination between
Texan and Mexican. Dean's pacing out of his small plot of land and his
subsequent discovery of oil are among the most celebrated scenes.

WARNER BROS.

Production–George Stevens &   *Photography* (*Warnercolor*)–
   Henry Ginsberg   William C. Mellor
Direction–George Stevens   *Production design*–Boris Leven
Screenplay–Fred Guiol &   *Music*–Dimitri Tiomkin
   Ivan Moffat   *Editing*–William Hornbeck
PLAYERS: Elizabeth Taylor, Rock Hudson, James Dean, Jane Withers,
Chill Wills, Mercedes McCambridge, Carroll Baker, Dennis Hopper

GIGI   U.S.A. (1958)
Elegant, beautifully designed turn-of-the-century musical based on the
Colette story about an innocent young Paris schoolgirl (Leslie Caron)
who is trained by her grandmother (Hermione Gingold) and aunt
(Isabel Jeans) for the role of *grande cocotte*. The more tuneful Lerner
& Loewe songs–"Thank Heaven for Little Girls," "The Night They
Invented Champagne"–are surpassed by the bittersweet "I Remember
It Well," a Chevalier/Gingold duet, and by Chevalier's solo "I'm Glad
I'm Not Young Anymore." Minnelli received an Oscar for this one, al-

though his earlier and more inventive musical work (*Meet Me in St. Louis, The Pirate, The Band Wagon,* etc.) had been ignored by the Academy. The film received eight additional awards including best picture, color photography (Ruttenberg's fourth Oscar), art direction, and music scoring.

METRO–GOLDWYN–MAYER

Production–Arthur Freed
Direction–Vincente Minnelli
Screenplay & lyrics–
  Alan Jay Lerner
Photography (CinemaScope/ Metrocolor)–
  Joseph Ruttenberg

Costumes, scenery & production design–Cecil Beaton
Art direction–William A. Horning & Preston Ames
Music–Frederick Loewe
Musical direction–Andre Previn
Editing–Adrienne Fazan

PLAYERS: Leslie Caron, Maurice Chevalier, Louis Jourdan, Hermione Gingold, Eva Gabor, Jacques Bergerac, Isabel Jeans, John Abbott

GILDA
U.S.A. (1946)

Bleak thriller set in Latin America where a sultry torch singer (Rita Hayworth) becomes involved with an ex-lover (Glenn Ford) and, more dangerously, with smooth-talking villain (George Macready) a rich casino owner with plans for world power. A classic of its kind, not the least of its attributes are Rudolph Mate's glittering black-and-white camera work and the rendering by Rita Hayworth (clad in elbow-length gloves and clinging Jean Louis gown) of "Put the Blame on Mame, Boys." Directed by Charles Vidor who also did *Cover Girl* but little else of note.

COLUMBIA

Production–Virginia Van Upp
Direction–Charles Vidor
Screenplay–Marion Parsonnett
Story–E. A. Ellington
Adaptation–Jo Eisinger
Photography–Rudolph Mate

Art direction–Stephen Goosson, Van Nest Polglase
Musical direction–Morris Stoloff, Marlin Skiles
Editing–Charles Nelson

PLAYERS: Rita Hayworth, Glenn Ford, George Macready, Joseph Calleia, Steven Geray, Joe Sawyer, Ludwig Donath, Lionel Royce

GIRL IN BLACK, A
Greece (1956)

Michael Cacoyannis' drama about the passions and hatreds aroused on a small Greek island when a village widow has a passionate love affair with a young novelist from Athens. British cameraman Walter Lassally captures the atmosphere of life in a sun-drenched Greek harbor town in this, his first film for Cacoyannis. Others now include *A Matter of Dignity, Our Last Spring, Electra,* and *Zorba the Greek.*

HERMES FILM

Direction—Michael Cacoyannis   *Music*—Argyris Kounadis
Photography—Walter Lassally   *Editing*—Emile Provelengios
PLAYERS: Ellie Lambetti, Dimitri Horn, Georges Foundas, Eleni Zafiriou, Stefanos Stratigos, Notis Pergialis

GIRL ROSEMARIE, THE (Das Mädchen Rosemarie)
West Germany (1958)
Stylish West German production based on the unsolved murder of Rosemarie Nitribitt, a Frankfurt call girl who, in 1957, numbered among her clients several of West Germany's leading industrialists. Shrewd, cynical, well played, and with some persistently sharp comments about the German economic miracle. Satirical Brecht-style songs, sung by a pair of street musicians, link the action and serve as a commentary.

ROXY

Direction—Rolf Thiele   *Photography*—
Screenplay—Erich Kuby &   Klaus von Rautenfeld
    Rolf Thiele   *Music*—Norbert Schultze
    Lyrics—Jo Herbst & Rolf Ulrich
PLAYERS: Nadja Tiller, Peter Van Eyck, Carl Raddatz, Gert Frobe, Horst Frank, Mario Adorf, Jo Herbst

GLENN MILLER STORY, THE   U.S.A. (1954)
Popular rags-to-riches musical biography of bandleader Glenn Miller (James Stewart) is routine and cliché-ridden for the most part, but notable for one superb sequence in which Louis Armstrong and Gene Krupa lead an impromptu jam session at Basin Street. "Tuxedo Junction," "In the Mood," "Chattanooga Choo Choo" and many other Miller song hits are featured on the sound track.

UNIVERSAL–INTERNATIONAL

Production—Aaron Rosenberg   *Art direction*—Bernard
Direction—Anthony Mann   Herzbrun, Alexander Golitzen
Screenplay—Valentine Davies,   *Musical adaptation*—
    Oscar Brodney   Henry Mancini
Photography (*Technicolor*)—   *Editing*—Russell Schoengarth
    William Daniels

PLAYERS: James Stewart, June Allyson, Henry Morgan, Charles Drake, Marion Ross, Irving Bacon, George Tobias

GODDESS, THE   U.S.A. (1958)
Merciless examination of the life of a Hollywood film star, beginning with her unhappy childhood in a squalid Maryland town, continuing through two failed marriages, and ending with her at the age of thirty, a lonely and neurotic woman taken to drink and drugs and living in a state of moral collapse. Most anti-Hollywood films have attacked Hollywood itself. This one concentrates on the mental make-up of an actress, and bears, in retrospect at least, certain uncomfortable resemblances to the tragic career of Marilyn Monroe. Kim Stanley's performance in the leading role is outstanding.

COLUMBIA

Production—Milton Perlman   *Art direction*—Edward Haworth
Direction—John Cromwell   *Music*—Virgil Thompson
Screenplay—Paddy Chayefsky   *Editing*—Carl Lerner
Photography—Arthur J. Ornitz
PLAYERS: Kim Stanley, Lloyd Bridges, Steve Hill, Betty Lou Holland, Joan Copeland, Patty Duke

GOING MY WAY   U.S.A. (1944)
Bing Crosby, in holy orders for the first time, sorting out, together with older, irascible priest Barry Fitzgerald, the problems of the poor community of St. Dominic's and writing a song to help raise funds for the church. Some pleasant numbers—"Swinging on a Star," "The Day After Forever," and the title song—fail to save the film from mawkishness and vulgarity, although director Leo McCarey held the thing expertly together and earned Academy Awards for himself and his two leading actors. The film was the biggest box-office success of the war period, and its current gross stands at over 6½-million dollars.

PARAMOUNT

Production & direction—   *Art direction*—Hans Dreier &
   Leo McCarey   William Flannery
Screenplay (from original story   *Musical direction*—
   by Leo McCarey)—Frank   Robert Emmett Dolan
   Butler & Frank Cavett   *Editing*—Leroy Stone
Photography—Lionel Lindon
PLAYERS: Bing Crosby, Barry Fitzgerald, Risë Stevens, James Brown, Jean Heather, Frank McHugh, Gene Lockhart

GOLD DIGGERS OF 1933   U.S.A. (1933)

This classic example of the Warner musical of the early 1930's is of interest today mainly because of Busby Berkeley's lavish, geometrically designed dance routines, and for such evergreen songs as "We're in the Money," "Shadow Waltz" and "Pettin' in the Park." Ruby Keeler, Ginger Rogers, Joan Blondell and Aline MacMahon play tough show girls, Dick Powell a songwriter, and character actor Ned Sparks a hard-up producer.

WARNER BROS.

Direction—Mervyn LeRoy
Screenplay (*from play* Gold
  Diggers of Broadway *by Avery*
  Hopwood)—Erwin Gelsey &
  James Seymour
Photography—Sol Polito

Dialogue—David Boehn &
  Ben Markson
Choreography—Busby Berkeley
Lyrics—Al Dubin &
  Harry Warren
Editing—George Amy

PLAYERS: Warren William, Joan Blondell, Aline MacMahon, Ruby Keeler, Ginger Rogers, Dick Powell, Guy Kibbee, Ned Sparks

GOLD RUSH, THE   U.S.A. (1925)

Chaplin's greatest silent film, a masterly combination of pathos, humor and tragedy revolving around an amateur prospector and his attempts to find gold in Alaska at the turn of the century. After *City Lights* this is the funniest and saddest of all Chaplin's comedies. Most famous scenes: a starving Charlie reduced to cooking one of his shoes, and fighting Mack Swain in a small cabin which has been blown to the edge of a precipice and which totters backward and forward as the fight progresses. The film took some 14 months to make, the snow scenes being filmed in Nevada, and was one of the biggest commercial successes of the 1920's.

UNITED ARTISTS

Production, direction &
  screenplay—Charles Chaplin
Associate director—
  Charles Riesner

Assistant director—
  H. d'Abbadie d'Arrast
Photography—R. H. Totheroh
Cameraman—Jack Wilson

PLAYERS: Charles Chaplin, Mack Swain, Georgia Hale, Tom Murray, Henry Bergman, Malcolm Waite, Betty Morrissey

GONE WITH THE WIND   U.S.A. (1939)

Perhaps the best-loved film of all time, a 3-hour 40-minute adaptation of Margaret Mitchell's Civil War novel about the loves of tempestuous

Southern belle Scarlett O'Hara (Vivien Leigh). Not a great film in the true sense of the word, but undeniably a great piece of *film-making* and a monument to the skill of the technicians and actors associated with its production. Most celebrated sequence: the great pull-back shot which starts with a close-up of Scarlett and finishes by revealing hundreds of wounded and dying soldiers at the railroad station in Atlanta. Clark Gable played Rhett Butler, Leslie Howard played Ashley Wilkes, and Olivia de Havilland was featured as Melanie Hamilton.

Statistics: Although the unknown Vivien Leigh eventually got the role of Scarlett, several well-known Hollywood actresses, including Joan Crawford, Bette Davis, Claudette Colbert and Katharine Hepburn, were rumored to be in the running for the part. Paulette Goddard, who did a most satisfying test for Selznick, apparently came closest to landing the role. George Cukor worked on the film for a few weeks (the birth of Melanie's baby and the shooting of the Union deserter are two of the scenes he directed), but was replaced, reputedly at Gable's request, by Victor Fleming, who shot the greater part of the film. Toward the end of shooting Fleming collapsed, and both Sam Wood and Sidney Franklin worked on the final scenes. Shooting took 22 weeks starting on January 26, 1939 and ending on July 1. The film was premiered in Atlanta on December 15 and received nine Oscars, including awards for best film, direction, actress, and photography.

A SELZNICK–INTERNATIONAL PICTURE/M–G–M

Production—David O. Selznick
Direction—Victor Fleming
Screenplay—Sidney Howard
Photography (Technicolor)—
  Ernest Haller & Ray Rennahan
Art direction—Lyle Wheeler

Designer—
  William Cameron Menzies
Technicolor associates—Ray
  Rennahan & Wilfred Cline
Musical score—Max Steiner
Editing—Hal C. Kern &
  James E. Newcom

PLAYERS: Clark Gable, Vivien Leigh, Olivia de Havilland, Leslie Howard, Hattie McDaniel, Thomas Mitchell, Ona Munson, Victor Jory, Jane Darwell, Evelyn Keyes, Ann Rutherford, Butterfly McQueen, Laura Hope Crews, Harry Davenport, Eric Linden, Ward Bond, Roscoe Ates, George Reeves

GOOD NEWS U.S.A. (1947)

Delightful M-G-M version of the 1920's musical stage hit with Peter Lawford as young football hero and June Allyson as his devoted co-ed admirer working her way through college. Some pleasant old songs ("Lucky in Love," "The Best Things in Life Are Free"), a brilliant new song ("The French Lesson") by Betty Comden, Adolph Green and Roger Edens, and some neat direction by Charles Walters, whose first full directorial assignment this was.

METRO–GOLDWYN–MAYER

Production–Arthur Freed
Direction–Charles Walters
Screenplay (from musical by
  Lawrence Schwab, Lew Brown,
  Frank Mandel, B. G. de
  Sylva & Ray Henderson)–
  Betty Comden & Adolph Green
Photography (Technicolor)–
  Charles Schoenbaum

Art direction–Cedric Gibbons &
  Edward Carfagno
Music & lyrics–De Sylva,
  Brown, Henderson, Comden,
  Green, Edens, Martin, Blane,
  Rodgers & Hart
Editing–Albert Akst

PLAYERS: June Allyson, Peter Lawford, Patricia Marshall, Joan McCracken, Ray McDonald, Mel Torme

GOSPEL ACCORDING TO ST. MATTHEW   Italy/France (1964)
The story of Christ from his birth to Resurrection. Filmed against the background of the impoverished villages and dusty landscapes of Southern Italy the picture uses dialogue directly from the Book of St. Matthew and is the most realistic and rewarding of all the films made about Christ. Directed by Italian novelist and poet Pier Pasolini and performed entirely by nonprofessionals, among them Enrique Irazoqui, a Spanish student who plays Christ, and Pasolini's own mother, who appears as the Virgin Mary in her later years.

ARCO FILM (ROME)/LUX (PARIS)

Direction & screenplay (from
  Gospel according to St.
  Matthew [Assisi text])–
  Pier Paolo Pasolini
Photography–Tonino Delli Colli
Art direction–Luigi Scaccianoce

Music–Bach, Mozart, Prokofiev,
  Webern & the Congolese Mass
  "Missa Luba"
Original music–Luis E. Bacalov
Editing–Nino Baragli

PLAYERS: Enrique Irazoqui, Margherita Caruso, Susanna Pasolini, Marcello Morante, Mario Socrate, Settimio Di Porto, Otello Sestili

GRADUATE, THE   U.S.A. (1967)
American college student (Dustin Hoffman) returns home to Los Angeles where he finds himself unable to communicate with his smug

suburban parents and where he is rapidly initiated into the pleasures of sex by the neurotic wife (played by Anne Bancroft) of one of his father's business associates. A witty, often very funny film reflecting a wide range of attitudes, but saving most of its satirical comment for the social habits of the American middle class. Slick Academy Award-winning direction by Mike Nichols, memorable music score by Simon and Garfunkel.

EMBASSY/LAWRENCE TURMAN/UNITED ARTISTS

Production—Lawrence Turman
Direction—Mike Nichols
Screenplay (*based on novel by Charles Webb*)—Calder Willingham, Buck Henry
Photography (*Panavision/ Technicolor*)—Robert Surtees

Production design—Richard Sylbert
Music—David Grusin
Songs—Paul Simon, sung by Simon & Garfunkel
Editing—Sam O'Steen

PLAYERS: Dustin Hoffman, Anne Bancroft, Katharine Ross, William Daniels, Murray Hamilton, Elizabeth Wilson, Brian Avery, Walter Brooke

GRAND HOTEL   U.S.A. (1932)

The most famous portmanteau movie of all time, based on Vicki Baum's novel of life in a large luxury hotel and featuring almost every major star on the M-G-M lot during the early 1930's. A glossy, manufactured entertainment but beautifully acted. Heading the cast are Lionel Barrymore as a clerk dying from a fatal disease and spending his last days in luxury, Wallace Berry as a Prussian business tycoon, John Barrymore as an impoverished baron, and Greta Garbo as a great ballerina who, in this film, actually speaks the immortal words "I want to be alone."

METRO–GOLDWYN–MAYER

Direction—Edmund Goulding
Adaptation—Hans Kraly
Photography—William Daniels

Art direction—Cedric Gibbons
Editing—Blanche Sewell

PLAYERS: Greta Garbo, John Barrymore, Joan Crawford, Wallace Beery, Lionel Barrymore, Lewis Stone, Jean Hersholt, Frank Conroy

GRAPES OF WRATH, THE   U.S.A. (1940)

One of the few great films of the forties (*Citizen Kane* and *All That Money Can Buy* are others) that look as good today as when they were shown thirty years ago. The story tells how the impoverished Joad family, forced off their land in the Oklahoma Dust Bowl during the depression, head westward in an old Ford to California where they struggle to begin a new life as fruit pickers. Faithfully adapted by Nunnally Johnson from John Steinbeck's compassionate novel and directed by John Ford, the film reflects all the bitterness, hardship and social injustice of the depression years and is one of the most outspoken and perhaps only truly socialistic film of the American cinema. Memorable photography by Gregg Toland especially in the opening sequences which perfectly evoke the "feel" of the dusty, drought-ridden Oklahoma landscapes, and excellent performances from Henry Fonda as Tom Joad and Jane Darwell as Ma who, as she quietly destroys her letters and souvenirs in front of the fire before quitting her home for good, participates in one of the most moving scenes in all cinema.

TWENTIETH CENTURY–FOX

Production–Darryl F. Zanuck	Photography–Gregg Toland
Direction–John Ford	Art direction–Richard Day,
Associate producer–	Mark Lee Kirk
Nunnally Johnson	Music–Alfred Newman
Screenplay–Nunnally Johnson	Editing–Robert Simpson

PLAYERS: Henry Fonda, Jane Darwell, John Carradine, Charley Grapewin, Dorris Bowdon, Russell Simpson, O. Z. Whitehead, John Qualen

GREAT ADVENTURE, THE   Sweden (1952)
Charming tale of two Swedish boys who rescue a tiny otter from a hunter's trap, adopt it as a pet, and keep it secretly on their father's farm throughout the snowbound winter. This slight story line holds together what is in many ways the most accomplished film about wild life ever made. Director Arne Sucksdorff observed the animals and birds of central Sweden for some 2½ years before editing down his 250,000 feet of film into a 75-minute outdoor masterpiece.

SANDREWS

Production, direction,	Assistant production & sound
photography & editing–	director–Nils Gustav Orn
Arne Sucksdorff	Assistants–Sigvard Kihlgren,
Music–Lars Erik Larsson	Ake Backlund

PLAYERS: The animals, wild and farmyard and especially "Otty," the children and the grown-ups around a farm in central Sweden

GREAT DICTATOR, THE   U.S.A. (1940)
Uneven but frequently penetrating satire on the evils of Fascism with

Chaplin playing the dual role of a little Jewish barber and the dictator of a mythical European country. The final scenes in which Chaplin expresses his views on war and intolerance were thought by some critics to be pompous and unnecessary, but the sequences in the ghetto are very moving. The visual satire, particularly the scene in which Chaplin as the dictator does a ballet with the globe of the world, is brilliantly handled. Paulette Goddard, appearing in her second consecutive Chaplin film, plays an impoverished girl of the ghetto and Jack Oakie a Mussolini-style tyrant called Napaloni.

UNITED ARTISTS

Production, direction &	*Photography*—R. H. Totheroh,
screenplay—Charles Chaplin	Karl Struss
Assistant directors—Dan James,	*Musical direction*—
Wheeler Dryden &	Meredith Willson
Bob Meltzer	*Art direction*—J. Russell Spencer
Music—Charles Chaplin	*Editing*—Willard Nico

PLAYERS: Charles Chaplin, Jack Oakie, Paulette Goddard, Reginald Gardiner, Henry Daniell, Billy Gilbert, Grace Hayle, Carter De Havem, Maurice Moscovich, Emma Dunn

GREAT EXPECTATIONS   Gt. Britain (1947)
Poetic version of Charles Dickens' novel about a young country blacksmith who becomes a gentleman in London society through the generosity of an unknown benefactor. Still the best Dickens film ever made (there have been over fifty) and containing perhaps the most famous opening scene in all British cinema, i.e., the meeting of the boy Pip with the convict in the churchyard. John Mills as the young hero is supported by, among others, Bernard Miles (Joe Gargery), Francis L. Sullivan (lawyer Jaggers), Martita Hunt (Miss Havisham) and Finlay Currie (Magwitch). American Oscars (an unusual honor for British films in those days) went to Guy Green (monochrome photography) and John Bryan (art direction).

CINEGUILD

Production—Ronald Neame	*Production design*—John Bryan
Direction—David Lean	*Art direction*—
Screenplay—David Lean,	Wilfrid Shingleton
Ronald Neame	*Music*—Walter Goehr
Photography—Guy Green	*Editing*—Jack Harris

PLAYERS: John Mills, Valerie Hobson, Bernard Miles, Francis L. Sullivan, Finlay Currie, Martita Hunt, Anthony Wager, Jean Simmons, Alec Guinness, Ivor Barnard, Freda Jackson

GREAT McGINTY, THE   U.S.A. (1940)
Down-and-outer (Brian Donlevy) gains the favor of crooked political
boss (Akim Tamiroff) by voting 37 times in one day and rises swiftly
to become governor of the state. Only when he becomes involved in
romance and attempts to go straight does he fall from power. Still the
most celebrated of all American political satires, wickedly funny and
completely uncompromising for most of its length. It marked the direc-
torial debut of writer Preston Sturges who won the 1940 Academy
Award for the best original screenplay of the year.
                            PARAMOUNT
Direction—Preston Sturges   *Art direction*—Hans Dreier &
Original screenplay—   Earl Hedrick
   Preston Sturges   *Music*—Frederick Hollander
Photography—William C. Mellor   *Editing*—Hugh Bennett
PLAYERS: Brian Donlevy, Muriel Angelus, Akim Tamiroff, Allyn Joslyn,
William Demarest, Louis Jean Heydt, Harry Rosenthal

GREAT MAN, THE   U.S.A. (1957)
Acid attack on American television industry centering on reporter (Jose
Ferrer) who discovers, through a series of interviews for a memorial
program, that a recently deceased TV personality was both a fake and
a voluptuary and not the homespun idol ("loved by 150 million") the
network made him out to be. Directed and part-scripted by Ferrer;
excellent supporting cameos from Julie London as an alcoholic singer,
Keenan Wynn as a TV executive, and father Ed Wynn as the little man
who gave the celebrity his start in show business.
                      UNIVERSAL–INTERNATIONAL
Production—Aaron Rosenberg   *Art direction*—Richard H. Riedel
Direction—Jose Ferrer   & Eric Orbom
Screenplay—Jose Ferrer &   *Music*—Herman Stein
   Al Morgan   *Editing*—Sherman Todd &
Photography—Harold Lipstein   Al Joseph
PLAYERS: Jose Ferrer, Dean Jagger, Keenan Wynn, Julie London, Joanne
Gilbert, Ed Wynn, Jim Backus

GREAT TRAIN ROBBERY, THE   U.S.A. (1903)
The robbery of a train by outlaws, their pursuit by the law and their
final capture in an 11-minute Western drama in 14 scenes. The most
famous of the early films and the first to tell a coherent story through
moving pictures. This film established the reputation of Edwin S.
Porter and also marked the first appearance of Max Aaronson (the out-

law leader) who as "Broncho Billy" Anderson later became one of the most popular of the early Western stars.

EDISON

Direction & script—   *Photography—*Edwin S. Porter
  Edwin S. Porter

PLAYERS: Max Aaronson, Marie Murray, George Barnes, Frank Hanaway

GREAT ZIEGFELD, THE   U.S.A. (1936)

Large-scale musical biography of Florenz Ziegfeld made in the mid 1930's when the M-G-M studio was at the height of its power. The film contains some of the most lavish production numbers ever put on the screen, particularly the "A Pretty Girl Is Like a Melody" sequence which earned Seymour Felix an Oscar for best dance direction of 1936. Oscars were also awarded to the film itself as best production of the year and to Luise Rainer (best actress) as Ziegfeld's first wife Anna Held. Others in the cast are Myrna Loy as Billie Burke and Fanny Brice who played herself and sang "My Man" and "Yiddle on Your Fiddle."

METRO—GOLDWYN—MAYER

*Production—*Hunt Stromberg   *Musical director—*Arthur Lange
*Direction—*Robert Z. Leonard   *Musical numbers—*Walter
Story & screenplay—   Donaldson & Harold Adamson
  William Anthony McGuire   *Dance direction—*Seymour Felix
*Photography—*Oliver T. Marsh   *Editing—*William S. Gray
*Art direction—*Cedric Gibbons

PLAYERS: William Powell, Myrna Loy, Luise Rainer, Frank Morgan, Fanny Brice, Ray Bolger, Virginia Bruce, Nat Pendleton, Reginald Owen, Herman Bing, Dennis Morgan

GREATEST SHOW ON EARTH, THE   U.S.A. (1952)

Betty Hutton as a trapeze artiste, Cornel Wilde as a rival aerialist, Charlton Heston as a tough circus manager and James Stewart (hidden throughout the film behind a clown's make-up) as a doctor wanted by the police for murder. One of the most agreeable of all DeMille movies, it is long, vulgar and full of the usual hokum, but also marked on this occasion by some skillful observation of life behind the glamour of the sawdust ring. High spot: a spectacular train crash in which the animals of the circus train are set free. Named best film of the year by the Academy of Motion Pictures Arts & Sciences, it is the only one of DeMille's seventy films to be so honored.

Production & direction—
Cecil B. DeMille
Screenplay (from story by
Fredric M. Frank and Frank
Cavett)—Barre Lyndon &
Theodore St. John

Photography—George Barnes,
J. Peverell Marley &
Wallace Kelley
Art direction—Hal Pereira &
Walter Tyler
Music—Victor Young
Editing—Anne Bauchens

PLAYERS: Betty Hutton, Cornel Wilde, Charlton Heston, Dorothy Lamour, Gloria Grahame, James Stewart, Lyle Bettger, Henry Wilcoxon

GREED   U.S.A. (1923)

A savage, very sordid movie tracing the slow decline, degradation and death of a San Francisco dentist (Gibson Gowland) and his wife (Zasu Pitts)—a woman whose obsession with gold turns her into a crazed miser and her husband into a drunkard and a murderer. The climax—in which Gowland and his wife's former suitor (Jean Hersholt) die, handcuffed by the wrist, in the terrible sun of Death Valley—is one of the most powerful in the history of the cinema. Erich von Stroheim adapted Frank Norris's book almost page for page, finishing with 42 reels of film—some 10 hours' screen time. He reduced this to 20 reels, but Metro, wanting a still shorter film, handed the picture to Rex Ingram and June Mathis who cut it to a running time of just over two hours. Even in its final, mutilated version the film is a landmark.

GOLDWYN COMPANY/M–G–M

Direction—Erich von Stroheim
Screenplay (based on novel
  McTeague *by Frank Norris)*—
  Erich von Stroheim

Photography—Ben Reynolds &
  Billy Daniels
Art direction—Cedric Gibbons
Editing (released version)—
  Rex Ingram & June Mathis

PLAYERS: Gibson Gowland, Zasu Pitts, Jean Hersholt, Cesare Gravina, Dale Fuller, Chester Conklin, Sylvia Ashton, Hughie Mack

GROUP, THE   U.S.A. (1966)

The hopes, loves and disappointments of eight young Vassar College girls as they experience the frequently harsh realities of life in America during the depression years. A convincing, finely acted Lumet film adapted from Mary McCarthy's best-selling novel and capturing, through Anna Hill Johnstone's costumes and Boris Kaufman's soft muted colorwork, the essence of the period. Joanna Pettet as Kay, the girl hopelessly caught up in a tragic marriage, Candice Bergen as the lesbian Lakey, and Shirley Knight as the young hospital worker Polly are the three actresses best served by Sidney Buchman's intelligent screenplay.

FAMOUS ARTISTS/FAMARTISTS/UNITED ARTISTS

Production—Sidney Buchman
Direction—Sidney Lumet
Screenplay—Sidney Buchman
Photography (DeLuxecolor)—
  Boris Kaufman
Production design—Gene Callahan

Musical supervision—
  Charles Gross
Musical direction—
  Robert de Cormier
Editing—Ralph Rosenbloom

PLAYERS: Candice Bergen, Joan Hackett, Elizabeth Hartman, Shirley Knight, Joanna Pettet, Mary-Robin Redd, Jessica Walter, Kathleen Widdoes, James Broderick, Larry Hagman

GUESS WHO'S COMING TO DINNER   U.S.A. (1967)
Spencer Tracy and Katharine Hepburn as liberal parents brought face to face with their principles when their only daughter (Katharine Houghton) brings home a young Negro doctor (Sidney Poitier) and requests immediate permission to marry him. The problems of inter-racial marriage are examined seriously enough by screenwriter William Rose and director Stanley Kramer, but it is for its performances that this lush, romantic film will best be remembered, particularly those of Tracy and Hepburn who appeared here together for the last time (Tracy was ill throughout the shooting and died just ten days after shooting finished). The Tracy/Hepburn partnership lasted 25 years, during which time they made nine films together under seven directors.

Tracy/Hepburn movies: *Woman of the Year* (George Stevens); *Keeper of the Flame, Adam's Rib* and *Pat and Mike* (all George Cukor); *Without Love* (Harold S. Bucquet); *Sea of Grass* (Elia Kazan); *State of the Union* (Frank Capra); *The Desk Set* (Walter Lang), and *Guess Who's Coming to Dinner* (Stanley Kramer).

STANLEY KRAMER PRODS./COLUMBIA

Production & direction—
  Stanley Kramer
Screenplay—William Rose
Photography (Technicolor)—
  Sam Leavitt

Production design—
  Robert Clatworthy
Music—DeVol
Editing—Robert C. Jones

PLAYERS: Spencer Tracy, Katharine Hepburn, Sidney Poitier, Katharine Houghton, Cecil Kellaway, Beah Richards, Roy E. Glenn, Sr., Isabell Sanford

GUNFIGHT AT THE O.K. CORRAL   U.S.A. (1957)

King-size Technicolor Western with Burt Lancaster as Wyatt Earp cleaning up Tombstone with the help of his three brothers and the poker-playing consumptive dentist, Doc Holliday (Kirk Douglas). Routine and cliché-ridden for the most part, but notable for John Sturges' vivid restaging of the famous gunfight and for Dimitri Tiomkin's rousing score. Also in the cast are Jo Van Fleet as Kate Fisher and Lyle Bettger as Ike Clanton.

PARAMOUNT

Production—Hal B. Wallis
Direction—John Sturges
Screenplay (from magazine
    article by George Scullin)—
    Leon Uris

Photography (Technicolor/
    VistaVision)—Charles Lang
Art direction—Hal Pereira &
    Walter Tyler
Music—Dimitri Tiomkin
Editing—Warren Low

PLAYERS: Burt Lancaster, Kirk Douglas, Rhonda Fleming, Jo Van Fleet, John Ireland, Frank Faylen, George Matthews

GUNFIGHTER, THE   U.S.A. (1950)

The last tragic hours of a tired gunfighter who wants to settle down quietly with his wife and leave his past behind. Taut, suspenseful, set entirely in a small Southwestern town, this adult, antiromantic Western was the first breakaway from the traditional concepts of the genre and was the first classic of the fifties. Solidly directed by Henry King (one of his best films) and finely acted by Gregory Peck, complete with authentic drooping moustache, as the gunman, and Millard Mitchell as his old outlaw friend turned sheriff.

TWENTIETH CENTURY–FOX

Production—Nunnally Johnson
Direction—Henry King
Screenplay (from story by
    William Bowers & Andre de
    Toth)—William Bowers,
    William Sellers

Photography—Arthur Miller
Art direction—Lyle Wheeler,
    Richard Irvine
Music—Alfred Newman
Editing—Barbara McLean

PLAYERS: Gregory Peck, Helen Westcott, Millard Mitchell, Jean Parker, Karl Malden, Skip Homeier, Anthony Ross, Verna Felton, Ellen Corby, Richard Jaeckel

GUNGA DIN   U.S.A. (1939)

Well-staged piece of Hollywood hokum based on Rudyard Kipling's poem about an Indian water boy who sacrifices his life to save a British regiment. Plenty of rousing action and some enjoyable tongue-in-cheek performances from Cary Grant, Douglas Fairbanks, Jr. and Victor McLaglen as a trio of British officers and Eduardo Ciannelli (the leading heavy) as the chief of the Thuggees. An uncharacteristic George Stevens film but very efficiently directed.

RKO RADIO

In charge of production—	*Story—*Ben Hecht &
Pandro S. Berman	Charles MacArthur
Production & direction—	*Photography—*Joseph August
George Stevens	*Art direction—*Van Nest Polglase
*Screenplay—*Joel Sayre,	*Music—*Alfred Newman
Fred Guiol	*Editing—*Henry Berman,
	John Lockert

PLAYERS: Cary Grant, Victor McLaglen, Douglas Fairbanks, Jr., Sam Jaffe, Eduardo Ciannelli, Joan Fontaine, Montague Love, Robert Coote

HAIL THE CONQUERING HERO   U.S.A. (1944)

Timid Marine Woodrow Truesmith, afraid to tell his mother that he has been discharged because of hay fever, is carried home in triumph by six sympathetic Marines and given a hero's welcome. This witty, bitterly ironic comedy hits out at such things as mother love, heroism, the U.S. Marines, and small-town politics, and is the most sustained of all Sturges' satires. The riotous sequence showing the reception at the railway station is one of the most cleverly staged set pieces in all of his films.

PARAMOUNT

Direction & screenplay—	*Art direction—*Hans Dreier,
Preston Sturges	Haldane Douglas
*Photography—*John Seitz	*Music—*Werner Heymann
	*Editing—*Stuart Gilmore

PLAYERS: Eddie Bracken, Ella Raines, Bill Edwards, Raymond Walburn, William Demarest, Jimmy Dundee, Georgia Caine, Alan Bridge, James Damore, Freddy Steele, Stephen Gregory

HAMLET   Gt. Britain (1948)

Laurence Olivier's second Shakespearean production, not so well-known as its predecessor *Henry V*—mainly because there is nothing to equal the splendid Agincourt sequence—but, like all Olivier's films, brilliantly played and of sufficient stature to become the first British production ever to win the Hollywood Oscar as best picture of the

Hamlet

year. A blond Laurence Olivier also won an Academy Award for his portrayal of the doomed Danish prince, as did Roger Furse for his costume design and bleak interiors of Elsinore Castle. The film was criticized, however, on two counts, firstly for its extensive use of tracking and dolly shots which slowed the pace considerably and secondly for its large-scale text omissions which reduced a 4½-hour play to a 155-minute film. Eighteen-year-old Jean Simmons played Ophelia, Felix Aylmer played Polonius, and Basil Sydney and Eileen Herlie were the King and Queen.

A TWO CITIES FILM

Production & direction—
Laurence Olivier
*Text advisor—*Alan Dent
Associate producer—
Reginald Beck

Photography—
Desmond Dickinson
*Design & costumes—*Roger Furse
*Art direction—*Carmen Dillon
*Music—*William Walton
*Editing—*Helga Cranston

PLAYERS: Laurence Olivier, Eileen Herlie, Basil Sydney, Jean Simmons, Felix Aylmer, Norman Wooland, Terence Morgan, Harcourt Williams, Patrick Troughton, Peter Cushing, Stanley Holloway

HANGMEN ALSO DIE   U.S.A. (1943)

Fritz Lang movie that fictionalizes the assassination of *Reichsprotektor* Heydrich (Hitler's hangman) in Prague in 1942. Uneven but intermittently impressive and, within the limitations of the thriller, presenting an accurate and disturbing picture of a Nazi-occupied country in wartime. Some fine photography by James Wong Howe (the only time he ever worked for Lang) and interesting minor performances from Gene Lockhart as a Nazi informer and Alexander Granach as a Gestapo inspector.

ARNOLD PRODUCTIONS–UNITED ARTISTS

Direction & production—
Fritz Lang
Screenplay (from story by
Fritz Lang & Bertolt Brecht)—
Fritz Lang, Bertolt Brecht,
John Wexley

Photography—
James Wong Howe
*Art direction—*William Darling
*Music—*Hanns Eisler
*Editing—*Gene Fowler, Jr.

PLAYERS: Brian Donlevy, Walter Brennan, Anna Lee, Gene Lockhart, Dennis O'Keefe, Alexander Granach, Margaret Wycherly, Nana Bryant

HARDER THEY FALL, THE   U.S.A. (1956)

An attempt by director Mark Robson and writer Philip Yordan (via Budd Schulberg's novel) to expose the corruption in American boxing circles. The film examines the efforts of boxing racketeer (Rod Steiger) and ex-sports writer (Humphrey Bogart) to make a fortune out of a 7-ft. Argentinian with a "powder puff punch and a glass jaw" by fixing some twenty-five fights and then betting against him before he takes a savage beating at the hands of the champion. Fine performances, expertly evoked boxing atmosphere and realistic fight scenes, but marred by the basic improbabilities of its story line. Boxing personalities Jersey Joe Walcott and Max Baer appear in the film, which was director Robson's second shot at a boxing story, his first being *Champion* made some seven years earlier for Stanley Kramer.

COLUMBIA

*Production—*Philip Yordan
*Direction—*Mark Robson
*Screenplay—*Philip Yordan
*Photography—*Burnett Guffey

*Art direction—*William Flannery
*Music—*Hugo Friedhofer
*Editing—*Jerome Thoms

PLAYERS: Humphrey Bogart, Rod Steiger, Jan Sterling, Mike Lane, Max Baer, Jersey Joe Walcott, Edward Andrews, Harold J. Stone, Carlos Montalban, Nehemiah Persoff

172

HÄXAN (Witchcraft Through the Ages)   Sweden (1921)
Witchcraft, sorcery and man's cruelty over the centuries examined by
Danish director Benjamin Christensen in a bizarre part-documentary,
part-fantasy Swedish film that is at its most chilling when examining
the persecution and hysteria that existed in the Middle Ages. There is
also a prologue made up of images from early civilizations and a final
section set in modern times (1920). The cast is made up of both professional and nonprofessional actors and includes Christensen himself
who appeared as the Devil.

SVENSK FILMINDUSTRI

Direction & screenplay—   *Art direction*—Richard Louw
   Benjamin Christensen   *Music*—Daniel Humair
Photography—Johan Ankerstjerne   *Narrator*—William Burroughs
PLAYERS: Maren Pedersen, Clara Pontoppidan, Tora Teje, Elith Pio,
Benjamin Christensen, Oscar Stribolt, Johs Andersen, Karen Winther

HEIRESS, THE   U.S.A. (1949)
William Wyler's dignified beautifully mounted version of Henry James's
Washington Square with Olivia de Havilland as the shy, unfortunate
Catherine, Ralph Richardson as her arrogant father (a masterly performance), and Montgomery Clift as her fortune-hunting suitor. An
impressive, cleverly directed film with impeccable sets and costumes
and a notable Academy Award-winning score by Aaron Copland.

PARAMOUNT

Production & direction—   *Photography*—Leo Tover
   William Wyler   . *Art direction*—John Meehan,
Screenplay (based on their own   Harry Horner
   dramatization)—Ruth &   *Music*—Aaron Copland
   Augustus Goetz   *Editing*—William Hornbeck
PLAYERS: Olivia de Havilland, Ralph Richardson, Montgomery Clift,
Miriam Hopkins, Vanessa Brown, Betty Linley, Ray Collins, Mona
Freeman, Selena Royle

HELLZAPOPPIN   U.S.A. (1942)
The plot of this crazy film within a film is almost nonexistent, but what
story line there is hinges on the attempts of the movie producers filming
Hellzapoppin (the long-running Broadway stage hit) to include a love
story with the zany humor. Everything goes in this cleverly directed
movie, including split screen, double exposure, film-upon-film, and sev-

eral other ingenious technical devices. Ole Olsen and Chic Johnson repeat their stage performances supported by the magnificent Martha Raye.

UNIVERSAL

Direction–H. C. Potter
Screenplay (based on original story by Nat Perrin suggested by the stage play "Olsen and Johnson's Hellzapoppin")–
Nat Perrin & Warren Wilson

Photography–Woody Bredell
Special photographic effects–
John Fulton
Art direction–Jack Otterson
Musical direction–
Charles Previn
Editing–Milton Carruth

PLAYERS: Ole Olsen, Chic Johnson, Martha Raye, Hugh Herbert, Jane Frazee, Robert Paige, Mischa Auer

HENRY V   Gt. Britain (1945)

Imaginative, though occasionally gimmicky, film version of Shakespeare's play which starts on stage at the Globe Theatre during the first London performance, then expands and flashes back in time to a realistic 15th century before returning again to the Theatre and finishing as it began as a photographed play. The opening and closing sequences are not altogether successful, though once the film broadens out it comes magnificently alive, particularly in the scenes before and during the Battle of Agincourt in which the charge of the French cavalry against the English bowmen is thrillingly accompanied by William Walton's music. Olivier makes a youthful and heroic King and he is admirably supported by Robert Newton as Ancient Pistol, Rene Asherson as the French princess Katharine, and Leslie Banks as the Chorus.

A TWO CITIES FILM

Production & direction–
Laurence Olivier, in close association with the editor
Reginald Beck
Photography (Technicolor)–
Robert Krasker
Operating cameraman–
Jack Hildyard

Text advisor–Alan Dent
Art direction–Paul Sheriff
Assistant art direction–
Carmen Dillon
Costumes–Roger Furse
Assistant costume designer–
Margaret Furse
Music–William Walton

PLAYERS: Laurence Olivier, Robert Newton, Leslie Banks, Rene Asherson, Esmond Knight, Leo Genn, Felix Aylmer, Ralph Truman, Nicholas Hannen, Harcourt Williams

174

HIGH NOON
U.S.A. (1952)

Tension Western by Fred Zinnemann with Gary Cooper as a retiring small-town mashal who is abandoned by the townspeople he has defended for so long and left alone at noon to face a vengeful killer and his gang of outlaws. A key work in the development of the genre and one that continues to exert its influence. Outstanding in a strong supporting cast are Lloyd Bridges as Cooper's ambitious deputy and Grace Kelly, in an early role, as his young Quaker bride. Dimitri Tiomkin won Academy Awards for his music score and his song "Do Not Forsake Me, Oh, My Darlin'." He has been regularly associated with the Western genre since composing the music for *Duel in the Sun* in 1946. His other major Western scores include *Red River*, *The Big Sky*, *Rio Bravo* (all for Hawks), *Gunfight at OK Corral* (Sturges) and *The Alamo* (Wayne).

STANLEY KRAMER PRODS./UNITED ARTISTS

Production—Stanley Kramer
Direction—Fred Zinnemann
Screenplay—Carl Foreman
Photography—Floyd Crosby

Art direction—
  Rudolph Sternad
Music—Dimitri Tiomkin
Editing—Elmo Williams

PLAYERS: Gary Cooper, Thomas Mitchell, Lloyd Bridges, Katy Jurado, Grace Kelly, Otto Kruger, Lon Chaney, Henry Morgan

HIGH SIERRA
U.S.A. (1941)

The last days of big-time racketeer Roy Earle (Humphrey Bogart) who is sprung from jail to lead a holdup of a California resort hotel, but becomes emotionally involved with a crippled girl (Joan Leslie) and finishes up in the mountains shooting it out with the cops. Ranks with *The Roaring Twenties* and *White Heat* as the best of Walsh's gangster movies. Bogie in perhaps the most developed of his hoodlum roles is well supported by Ida Lupino as a hard-bitten cabaret girl; Arthur Kennedy as a hood and Cornel Wilde as a hotel clerk also appear in minor roles.

WARNER BROS.—FIRST NATIONAL

Executive producer—
  Hal B. Wallis
Associate producer—
  Mark Hellinger
Direction—Raoul Walsh
Photography—Tony Gaudio

Screenplay (based on novel by
  W. R. Burnett)—John Huston
  & W. R. Burnett
Art direction—Ted Smith
Music—Adolph Deutsch
Editing—Jack Killifer

175

PLAYERS: Humphrey Bogart, Ida Lupino, Alan Curtis, Arthur Kennedy, Joan Leslie, Henry Hull, Henry Travers, Jerome Cowan, Cornel Wilde

HIROSHIMA MON AMOUR   France/Japan (1959)

Love and death and the complexities of memory are explored by Alain Resnais against the background of modern Hiroshima where a young French actress and a Japanese architect have a brief love affair. They remember back, as they spend their last night together, to the dropping of the atomic bomb on Hiroshima and to the girl's tragic love affair with a young German soldier in Nevers during the Occupation. The way in which Resnais cuts back and forth in time, illogically just as memory itself is illogical, made the film initially difficult to understand, but the passing of the years and Resnais' own later, even more complex, works have made it easier to comprehend. A landmark in film history as important technically as Orson Welles' classic *Citizen Kane*.

ARGOS FILMS/COMO FILMS/DAIEI MOTION PICTURES/PATHÉ OVERSEAS

Direction—Alain Resnais
Screenplay—Marguerite Duras
Photography—Sacha Vierny &
  Michio Takahashi
Art direction—Esaka, Mayo & Petri

Music—Giovanni Fusco &
  Georges Delerue
Editing—Henri Colpi &
  Jasmine Chasney

PLAYERS: Emmanuelle Riva, Eiji Okada, Bernard Fresson, Stella Dassas, Pierre Barbaud

HIS GIRL FRIDAY   U.S.A. (1940)

Fast-paced, continuously funny Howard Hawks remake of *The Front Page* in which the journalist (played originally by Pat O'Brien) becomes smart-talking female reporter Rosalind Russell and the managing editor (who in this version is her ex-husband) charming Cary Grant. The last word in American wisecracking comedies and, together with *Bringing Up Baby*, Hawks' funniest film. Ralph Bellamy also featured to good effect as Miss Russell's dim-witted insurance salesman suitor.

COLUMBIA

Production & direction—
  Howard Hawks
Photography—Joseph Walker
Music—Morris W. Stoloff
Editor—Gene Havlick

Screenplay (from play The
  Front Page *by Ben Hecht &
  Charles MacArthur)*—
  Charles Lederer

PLAYERS: Cary Grant, Rosalind Russell, Ralph Bellamy, Gene Lockhart, Porter Hall, Ernest Truex, Cliff Edwards, Clarence Kolb, Roscoe Karns

HOBSON'S CHOICE   Gt. Britain (1953)

Film version of Harold Brighouse's play about the strong-willed daughter (Brenda de Banzie) of a tyrannical Lancashire bootmaker (Charles Laughton) who defies her father by marrying his simple boot hand (John Mills) and turning him into a successful businessman. The film is a minor Lean work, but enjoyable for the way in which it captures the flavor of life at the end of the last century and for the extravagant performance of Laughton who is here in full flow, particularly during his drunken chase of the moon's reflection through a series of street puddles.

LONDON FILMS

Production & direction—
   David Lean
*Screenplay—*David Lean,
   Norman Spencer,
   Wynyard Browne

*Photography—*Jack Hildyard
Art direction—
   Wilfrid Shingleton
   *Music—*Malcolm Arnold
   *Editing—*Peter Taylor

PLAYERS: Charles Laughton, John Mills, Brenda de Banzie, Daphne Anderson, Prunella Scales, Richard Wattis, Derek Blomfield, Helen Haye, Joseph Tomelty

HOLD BACK THE DAWN   U.S.A. (1941)

Mitchell Leisen directed many of the most accomplished Paramount comedies and melodramas before the rise of writers Preston Sturges and Billy Wilder. This movie (scripted by Wilder and Charles Brackett) is one of his best in the melodrama category and centers on a European gigolo (Charles Boyer) who finds himself stranded in a Mexican border town and decides to marry a naive schoolteacher (Olivia de Havilland) in order to gain entrance into the United States. Told in flashbacks as Boyer recounts his life to a film director (played by Leisen himself) the film is marked by its literate dialogue, excellent performances, and the sheer style that Leisen gives to the novelettish story. Paulette Goddard also appears in the film as Charles Boyer's ex-mistress.

PARAMOUNT

*Production—*Arthur Hornblow, Jr.
*Direction—*Mitchell Leisen
Screenplay (from story by
   *Ketti Fring)—*Charles Brackett
   & Billy Wilder

*Photography—*Leo Tover
*Art direction—*Hans Dreier &
   Robert Usher
   *Music—*Victor Young
   *Editing—*Doane Harrison

PLAYERS: Charles Boyer, Olivia de Havilland, Paulette Goddard, Victor Francen, Walter Abel, Curt Bois, Rosemary DeCamp

HOLIDAY U.S.A. (1938)

Another in Cukor's long line of filmed stage plays of the 1930's (others include *The Royal Family of Broadway, A Bill of Divorcement, Dinner at Eight*), adapted this time from Philip Barry's play *Holiday* and featuring Katharine Hepburn as the rebellious daughter of a wealthy New York family who scandalizes her snobbish relatives by falling in love with middle-class Cary Grant. A breezy script, impeccably delivered by the two principals, and some Capra-style social philosophy thrown in for good measure. One of the least-known but most rewarding of Cukor's comedies.

COLUMBIA

Production—Everett Riskin
Direction—George Cukor
Screenplay—Donald Ogden Stewart
& Sidney Buchman
Photography—Franz Planer

Art direction—Stephen Goosson
& Lionel Banks
Music—Morris Stoloff
Editing—Otto Meyer &
Al Clark

PLAYERS: Katharine Hepburn, Cary Grant, Doris Nolan, Edward Everett Horton, Jean Dixon, Lew Ayres

HOMBRE U.S.A. (1966)

Slow-moving Martin Ritt Western set in Arizona where a white man (Paul Newman) brought up by the Apaches is forced reluctantly into aiding a group of stagecoach travelers in their fight against Richard Boone and his gang of bandits. The dialogue is on a higher level than that found in most Westerns, the landscapes are stunningly photographed, and there is an excitingly staged shoot-out in an abandoned mining shack on the edge of the desert. Strongly reminiscent at times of Ford's prewar *Stagecoach*. Fredric March steals the film with his performance of a dishonest Indian agent who has embezzled money supplied to the Indian reservations.

HOMBRE PRODUCTIONS/TWENTIETH CENTURY–FOX

Production—Martin Ritt &
Irving Ravetch
Direction—Martin Ritt
Screenplay (*based on novel
by Elmore Leonard*)—
Irving Ravetch &
Harriet Frank, Jr.

Photography (*DeLuxecolor/
Panavision*)—
James Wong Howe
Art direction—Jack Martin Smith
& Robert E. Smith
Music & musical direction—
David Rose
Editing—Frank Bracht

PLAYERS: Paul Newman, Fredric March, Richard Boone, Diane Cilento, Martin Balsam, Barbara Rush, Cameron Mitchell, Peter Lazer

HOME OF THE BRAVE U.S.A. (1949)

An honest, Stanley Kramer-produced study of racial antagonism among GIs in wartime. Based on the play by Arthur Laurents (in which the problem was anti-Semitism) the film was the first to openly discuss color prejudice and was, in turn, followed by a long line of imitators including Kazan's *Pinky* and Kramer's own *The Defiant Ones*.

UNITED ARTISTS

Production—Stanley Kramer	*Production design*—
Direction—Mark Robson	Rudolph Sternad
Screenplay—Carl Foreman	*Music*—Dimitri Tiomkin
Photography—Robert DeGrasse	*Editing*—Harry Gerstad

PLAYERS: Lloyd Bridges, Frank Lovejoy, Douglas Dick, Steve Brodie, James Edwards, Jeff Corey, Cliff Clark

HORSE FEATHERS U.S.A. (1932)

The hilarious Marx Brothers Paramount comedy with Groucho as Professor Quincey Adams Wagstaff who becomes the new president of Darwin College and signs up speakeasy assistant Chico and dog-catcher Harpo to help out with the college football team. Some uneven passages but superior to most of the team's later M-G-M vehicles and with a highly inventive football match for a climax. Thelma Todd appears as college widow who receives the amorous attentions of all four brothers, particularly Zeppo.

PARAMOUNT

Direction—Norman Z. McLeod	*Photography*—Ray June
Screenplay—Bert Kalmar,	*Music & lyrics*—Bert Kalmar
Harry Ruby, S. J. Perelman &	& Harry Ruby
Will B. Johnstone	

PLAYERS: Groucho, Harpo, Chico & Zeppo Marx, Thelma Todd, David Landau, Robert Greig, James Pierce, Nat Pendleton, Reginald Barlow, Florine McKinney

HÔTEL DU NORD France (1938)

The loneliness and despair of the people living in a shabby canal-side hotel in a poorer quarter of prewar Paris. Arletty plays a whore, Louis Jouvet is her fancy man, and Annabella and Jean-Pierre Aumont are a

179

suicidal pair of lovers. Memorable acting but the film depends more on Alexandre Trauner's dingy hotel interiors and Thirard's lensing of back-street bars and waterways to put its pessimistic mood across. A minor classic directed by Marcel Carné just a year before *Le Jour se Lève*.

SEDIF

Direction—Marcel Carné
Screenplay & adaptation (from novel by Eugène Dabit)— Henri Jeanson, Jean Aurenche

Dialogue—Henri Jeanson
Photography—Armand Thirard
Art direction— Alexandre Trauner
Music—Maurice Jaubert

PLAYERS: Annabella, Jean-Pierre Aumont, Arletty, Louis Jouvet, André Brunot, Jane Marken

HOUSE ON 92ND STREET, THE   U.S.A. (1945)

A fast-moving, exciting semidocumentary about the efforts of the FBI to smash a Nazi spy-ring attempt to steal the secrets of the atomic bomb. Produced by Louis de Rochemont (of "March of Time" fame), cleverly directed by Henry Hathaway, and shot with the co-operation of the FBI and on the actual locations where the story occurred. The film was the first in Hollywood's long postwar cycle of documentary thrillers and was a considerable influence on such later works as *Boomerang, Naked City* and Hathaway's own *Call Northside 777*.

TWENTIETH CENTURY–FOX

Production—Louis de Rochemont
Direction—Henry Hathaway
Screenplay (from story by Charles G. Booth)—Barre Lyndon, Charles G. Booth, John Monks, Jr.

Photography—Norbert Brodine
Art direction—Lyle Wheeler, Lewis Creber
Music—David Buttolph
Editing—Harmon Jones

PLAYERS: William Eythe, Lloyd Nolan, Signe Hasso, Gene Lockhart, Leo G. Carroll, Lydia St. Clair, William Post Jr., Harry Bellaver, Bruno Wick

HOW GREEN WAS MY VALLEY   U.S.A. (1941)

Richard Llewellyn's sentimental but moving story of a coal-mining family living in Wales at the end of the last century. Of interest primarily for its visual qualities, i.e., Arthur Miller's monochrome photography and the impressive studio set of a Welsh mining town, and also for the performances of Donald Crisp and Sara Allgood as family elders. The film was somewhat surprisingly awarded five Oscars in a year that also saw the release of *Citizen Kane* and *The Maltese Falcon.* It was the first John Ford production to feature Maureen O'Hara, one of the director's favorite heroines. Miss O'Hara was later featured in Ford's *Rio Grande, The Quiet Man, The Long Gray Line* and *The Wings of Eagles.*

TWENTIETH CENTURY—FOX

Production—Darryl F. Zanuck
Direction—John Ford
Screenplay—Philip Dunne
Photography—Arthur Miller

Art direction—Richard Day & Nathan Juran
Music—Alfred Newman
Editing—James B. Clark

PLAYERS: Walter Pidgeon, Maureen O'Hara, Donald Crisp, Anna Lee, Roddy McDowall, John Loder, Sara Allgood, Barry Fitzgerald

HOW THE WEST WAS WON U.S.A. (1963)

Huge (155 minutes) Cinerama Western with three different directors telling the story of the taming of the West between the years 1839 and 1889. A surprisingly effective movie which despite some routine passages also includes a brilliant 20-minute Civil War episode by John Ford and a breathtakingly staged gunfight on a runaway train by Henry Hathaway. An impressive cast (thirteen stars and eleven co-stars), fine scenery and a memorable music score by veteran composer Alfred Newman. Henry Hathaway directed the sequences on the rivers, the plains and the outlaws, George Marshall the coming of the railroad, and John Ford the Civil War episode.

METRO—GOLDWYN—MAYER

Producer—Bernard Smith
Direction—Henry Hathaway,
   John Ford & George Marshall
Screenplay (*suggested by series
   of articles in* Life *Magazine*)—
   James R. Webb
Photography (*Technicolor/
   Cinerama*)—William H. Daniels,

Milton Krasner, Charles Lang
   & Joseph LaShelle
Art direction—George W. Davis,
   William Ferrari &
   Addison Hehr
Music—Alfred Newman
Editing—Harold F. Kress

PLAYERS: Gregory Peck, James Stewart, Henry Fonda, Richard Widmark, Debbie Reynolds, Karl Malden, Carroll Baker, George Peppard, Robert Preston, Lee J. Cobb, Eli Wallach, John Wayne

HUD U.S.A. (1963)

Martin Ritt movie about the changing face of the American West contrasts the mythical pioneer values of the older generation, as represented by aging cattleman Melvyn Douglas, with those of his arrogant, Cadillac-owning son Paul Newman. The film's strength lies in its screenplay and powerful acting (Douglas and Patricia Neal as the ranch housekeeper both won deserved Oscars), but James Wong Howe's sharp monochrome photography of the Texas locations is an additional asset. Howe also worked with Martin Ritt on *The Outrage*, *Hombre* and *The Molly Maguires*.

SALEM-DOVER/PARAMOUNT

Production—Irving Ravetch, Martin Ritt
Direction—Martin Ritt
Screenplay (*based on novel* Horseman, Pass By *by Larry McMurty*)—Irving Ravetch & Harriet Frank Jr.

Photography (*Panavision*)— James Wong Howe
Art direction—Hal Pereira & Tambi Larsen
Music—Elmer Bernstein
Editing—Frank Bracht

PLAYERS: Paul Newman, Patricia Neal, Melvyn Douglas, Brandon de Wilde, John Ashley, Whit Bissell

HUE AND CRY   Gt. Britain (1947)
The first of Ealing's successful postwar comedies, set among the bombed ruins of London East End, concerns a group of boys who track down and capture a gang of fur thieves. Lively, amusing, reminiscent at times of the prewar German production *Emil and the Detectives*, with some authentic London backgrounds and two expert performances from Jack Warner as the chief villain and Alastair Sim as an eccentric author of "blood and thunder" stories.

EALING STUDIOS

Production—Michael Balcon
Direction—Charles Crichton
Screenplay—T. E. B. Clarke
Photography—Douglas Slocombe

Art direction—Norman G. Arnold
Music—Georges Auric
Editing—Charles Hasse

PLAYERS: Alastair Sim, Jack Warner, Valerie White, Harry Fowler, Frederick Piper, Heather Delaine, Douglas Barr

HUMORESQUE   U.S.A. (1947)
Outrageous melodrama about the anguished love affair between a wealthy married woman (Joan Crawford) and the ill-mannered but talented slum violinist (John Garfield) she helps to the top. Warners dressed up this ridiculous Fannie Hurst story into a very glossy piece

of entertainment with everyone behind the cameras—particularly Jean Negulesco whose stylish direction was the best of his career, and cameraman Ernest Haller—excelling themselves far beyond the call of the material. The film's greatest claim to fame, however, is its climax, which topped everything that had gone before and in which Miss Crawford, clad in a black sequin dress and with the strains of Wagner's love music from "Tristan and Isolde" coming over the radio, walks magnificently into the Pacific Ocean to her death.

WARNER BROS.

Production—Jerry Wald   Photography—Ernest Haller
Direction—Jean Negulesco   Art direction—Hugh Reticker
Screenplay (based on story by   Music—Franz Waxman
   Fannie Hurst)—Clifford Odets   Editing—Rudi Fehr
   & Zachary Gold
PLAYERS: Joan Crawford, John Garfield, Oscar Levant, J. Carrol Naish, Joan Chandler, Tom D'Andrea, Peggy Knudsen, Ruth Nelson

HUNCHBACK OF NOTRE DAME, THE   U.S.A. (1923)
Victor Hugo's great tragedy about a hunchback's unrequited love for a beautiful gypsy girl adapted by Universal into a 1½-million-dollar superproduction. Skillfully made, with some gigantic sets of 15th-century Paris and some spectacular crowd scenes, but dominated entirely by Lon Chaney's sympathetic portrait of the grotesque Quasimodo, a performance that made him world-famous.

UNIVERSAL

Direction—Wallace Worsley   Adaptation (from novel by
Screenplay—Edward T. Lowe Jr.   Victor Hugo)—
Art direction—E. E. Sheeley,   Perley Poore Sheehan
   Sydney Ullman   Photography—Robert Newhard
PLAYERS: Lon Chaney, Patsy Ruth Miller, Ernest Torrence, Norman Kerry, Raymond Hatton, Tully Marshall, Brandon Hurst, Nigel de Brulier

HUNCHBACK OF NOTRE DAME, THE   U.S.A. (1939)
RKO's extraordinary remake, equally as lavish as its predecessor but more imaginative in treatment and laying more emphasis on the grim social conditions of the period. Well played by Charles Laughton, then at the height of his powers, as Quasimodo, Thomas Mitchell as the King of the Beggars, and Maureen O'Hara (in her pre-Ford days) as the gypsy girl, and magnificently designed by Van Nest Polglase whose

set of Notre Dame cathedral dominated the entire production. A superior example of Dieterle's work and nearly a masterpiece.

RKO RADIO

Production—Pandro S. Berman
Direction—William Dieterle
Screenplay (from novel by
   Victor Hugo)—Sonya Levien,
   Bruno Frank
Photography—Joseph August

Art direction—Van Nest Polglase
Music adaptation—
   Alfred Newman
Editing—William Hamilton,
   Robert Wise

PLAYERS: Charles Laughton, Cedric Hardwicke, Thomas Mitchell, Maureen O'Hara, Edmond O'Brien, Alan Marshall, Walter Hampden

HUSTLER, THE   U.S.A. (1961)

Distinguished Robert Rossen film tracing career of a young pool shark (Paul Newman) who cons a living in cheap poolrooms while preparing for a big game in New York with champ Minnesota Fats (Jackie Gleason). The opening sequence depicting a marathon 24-hour pool game is superbly done and, despite falling somewhat below this high standard for the rest of its length, the film nevertheless succeeds in capturing the seedy atmosphere of airless billiard halls. It belongs with the most accomplished American films made about professional sport. Piper Laurie is Newman's crippled girlfriend and George C. Scott his cynical manager.

TWENTIETH CENTURY—FOX

Production & direction—
   Robert Rossen
Screenplay (from novel by
   Walter S. Tevis)—
   Robert Rossen &
   Sidney Carrol

Photography (CinemaScope)—
   Eugen Shuftan
Art direction—Harry Horner &
   Gene Callahan
Music—Kenyon Hopkins
Editing—Dedee Allan

PLAYERS: Paul Newman, Jackie Gleason, Piper Laurie, George C. Scott, Myron McCormick, Murray Hamilton, Michael Constantine, Stefan Gierasch

I AM A FUGITIVE FROM A CHAIN GANG   U.S.A. (1932)

One of Hollywood's earliest social protest films, it concerns the cruelty and misery suffered by an ex-soldier (Paul Muni) wrongly condemned to hard labor on a Georgia chain gang. The brutalities of the chain gang were so emphatically exposed that there was a public outcry when it was first shown, resulting in drastic reforms of the system. Directed by Mervyn LeRoy, who also made the classic gangster movie *Little Caesar* and the anti-lynching picture *They Won't Forget*. The film was adapted from a novel by Robert Elliott Burns who in real life was sentenced to a chain gang after taking part in a minor robbery.

WARNER BROS.

Production—Hal B. Wallis
Direction—Mervyn LeRoy
Photography—Sol Polito
Art direction—Jack Okey
Editing—William Holmes

Screenplay (*from novel* I Am a Fugitive from a Georgia Chain Gang *by Robert E. Burns*)—Howard J. Green & Brown Holmes

PLAYERS: Paul Muni, Glenda Farrell, Preston Foster, Helen Vinson, David Landau, Sally Blane

I BAMBINI CI GUARDANO (The Children Are Watching Us)

Italy (1943)

Early De Sica film looks at the life of a small child when his world collapses suddenly due to the estrangement of his parents. Mawkish at times but with some shrewd observations of human behavior, and a remarkable performance from 4-year-old Luciano de Ambrosis as the little boy. This was De Sica's first serious film (his earliest pictures had been adaptations of stage comedies) and also the first in which he directed a child actor.

SCALERA

Direction—Vittorio De Sica
Screenplay (*based on novel* Prico *by C. G. Viola*)— Gherardo Gherardi, Cesare Giulio Viola, Adolfo Franci,

Margherita Maglione & Vittorio De Sica
Photography— Giuseppe Caracciolo
Art direction—Vittorio Valentini
Music—Renzo Rossellini

PLAYERS: Emilio Cigoli, Isa Pola, Adriano Rimoldi, Luciano de Ambrosis

I CONFESS   U.S.A. (1953)

Complex, slow-moving Hitchcock thriller not originally thought to be among his best work but now ranking as one of his most rewarding movies. The story concerns a young Quebec priest (Montgomery Clift) who hears a confession from a murderer and is then himself accused of the crime. The moral dilemma of the priest is fully explored by Hitchcock who screws up the tension to a riveting climax in a deserted dance hall. Shot on location in the City of Quebec.

Production & direction—
Alfred Hitchcock
Screenplay (from play by Paul
Anthelme)—George Tabori
& William Archibald

Photography—Robert Burks
Art direction—
Edward S. Haworth
Music—Dmitri Tiomkin
Editing—Rudi Fehr

PLAYERS: Montgomery Clift, Anne Baxter, Karl Malden, Brian Aherne, O. E. Hasse, Dolly Haas, Roger Dann, Charles André

I MARRIED A WITCH   U.S.A. (1942)
Vengeful witch (Veronica Lake) returns to earth to disrupt the life of political candidate (Fredric March) whose ancestors burned her at the stake for practising sorcery. This amusing and quite witty little fantasy is the best of Clair's limited American output and contains one of March's best comedy performances along with some amusing trick camera work. Cecil Kellaway appears as Miss Lake's sorcerer father.

PARAMOUNT

Production & direction—
René Clair
Screenplay (based on novel by
Thorne Smith & Norman
Matson)—Robert Pirosh &
Marc Connelly

Photography—Ted Tetzlaff
Art direction—Hans Dreier &
Ernst Fegte
Musical direction—Roy Webb
Editing—Eda Warren

PLAYERS: Veronica Lake, Fredric March, Susan Hayward, Cecil Kellaway, Robert Benchley, Elizabeth Patterson, Robert Warrick, Eily Malyon

I REMEMBER MAMA   U.S.A. (1948)
A nostalgic picture on the everyday life of a poor Norwegian family living in San Francisco at the turn of the century. Some strikingly photographed San Francisco exteriors and some distinguished playing by Irene Dunne, outstanding as the self-sacrificing mother. Oscar Homolka as the warmhearted uncle, and Barbara Bel Geddes as the eldest daughter who relates the story. An affectionate work but one that stands somewhat isolated from Stevens' sparkling comedies of the earlier war period and his famous trilogy (*A Place in the Sun, Shane* and *Giant*) of the fifties.

RKO RADIO

Production—Harriet Parsons
Executive producer—
George Stevens

Direction—George Stevens
Photography—
Nicholas Musuraca

Screenplay (based on play by
John Van Druten based on
novel Mama's Bank Account
by Kathryn Forbes)—
DeWitt Bodeen

Art direction—
Albert S. D'Agostino,
Carroll Clark
Music—Roy Webb
Editing—Robert Swink

PLAYERS: Irene Dunne, Barbara Bel Geddes, Oscar Homolka, Philip Dorn, Cedric Hardwicke, Edgar Bergen, Rudy Vallee, Barbara O'Neil, Florence Bates

I VITELLONI
Italy (1953)

A bleak, honest look at the boredom and restlessness of a group of middle-class young men as they fritter away their lives aimlessly in the bars and streets of a small north Italian seaside town. Sympathetically directed by Federico Fellini (his debut) who made this a year before he established his international reputation with *La Strada*. Realistic observations of a seaside resort out of season—empty cafes, desolate seashores, third-rate touring shows, etc.

PEG FILM/CITÉ FILM

Production—Lorenzo Pegoraro
Direction—Federico Fellini
Screenplay—Federico Fellini,
Ennio Flaiano, Tullio Pinelli

Photography—Otello Martelli,
Luciano Trasatti, Carlo Carlini
Art direction—Mario Chiari
Music—Nino Rota
Editing—Rolando Benedetti

PLAYERS: Franco Interlenghi, Alberto Sordi, Franco Fabrizi, Eleonora Ruffo, Leopoldo Trieste, Riccardo Fellini, Lida Baarowa, Carlo Romano

I WAKE UP SCREAMING
U.S.A. (1942)

Unpretentious, very enjoyable Bruce Humberstone thriller (the only quality movie he directed) concerns a sinister psychopathic cop (Laird Cregar) and his search for the killer of a blond glamour girl. Victor Mature and Betty Grable (in a rare straight appearance) play the leads but, Cregar's performance apart, the most distinguished thing about the film is the quality of the supporting cast—Allyn Joslyn as a newspaper columnist, Alan Mowbray as a well-known stage actor, and Elisha Cook, Jr. as a night switchboard operator.

TWENTIETH CENTURY—FOX

Production—Milton Sperling
Direction—Bruce Humberstone
Screenplay (from novel by
Steve Fisher)—Dwight Taylor

Photography—Edward Cronjager
Art direction—Richard Day,
Nathan Juran

Music—Cyril Mockridge,   *Editing*—Robert Simpson
    Emil Newman
PLAYERS: Betty Grable, Victor Mature, Carole Landis, Laird Cregar, William Gargan, Alan Mowbray, Allyn Joslyn, Elisha Cook, Jr., Morris Ankrum

I WALKED WITH A ZOMBIE   U.S.A. (1943)
The best of the three horror films that Jacques Tourneur made for Val Lewton. Similar in theme to *Jane Eyre* (a young nurse is hired by a wealthy West Indies planter to care for his sick wife), the film is memorable for its visual qualities (J. Roy Hunt was Tourneur's cameraman) and for its terrifying climax when the nurse and the insane wife journey through the sugar plantations to the sinister voodoo ceremony. This last sequence stands as one of the most poetic passages in all of Lewton's horror films.

RKO RADIO

Production—Val Lewton   *Photography*—J. Roy Hunt
Direction—Jacques Tourneur   *Art direction*—Albert S.
Screenplay (from original story   D'Agostino, Walter E. Keller
    by Inez Wallace)—   *Music*—Roy Webb
    Curt Siodmak, Ardel Wray   *Editing*—Mark Robson
PLAYERS: James Ellison, Frances Dee, Tom Conway, Edith Barrett, James Bell, Christine Gordon

I WANT TO LIVE   U.S.A. (1958)
The life, times and death of bad-girl Barbara Graham who was executed in the gas chamber at San Quentin for a murder the film strongly implies she did not commit. The movie does not attempt to whitewash the character of "Bloody Babs" as she became known during her trial, but presents her as an habitual criminal who is both immoral and irresponsible. The film's importance lies in its strong indictment of capital punishment and in its harrowing, clinical presentation of the prelude to an execution. The execution itself is shown in full. This caused the film to be cut in some countries, among them Britain where approximately three minutes were deleted. Scored with jazz music by John Mandel and strongly played by Susan Hayward who won an Academy Award for her performance.

FIGARO INC./UNITED ARTISTS

Production—Walter Wanger   *Photography*—Lionel Lindon
Direction—Robert Wise   *Art direction*—Edward Haworth

188

Screenplay (*from newspaper*
articles by Ed Montgomery)—
Nelson Gidding &
Don Mankiewicz

Music—John Mandel
Editing—William Hornbeck

PLAYERS: Susan Hayward, Simon Oakland, Virginia Vincent, Theodore
Bikel, Wesley Lau, Philip Coolidge, Lou Krugman

I WAS A MALE WAR BRIDE U.S.A. (1949)

Amusing, well-timed little movie set in the ruins of postwar Germany
and focusing on the marital problems of French Intelligence officer
(Cary Grant) and American lieutenant (Ann Sheridan) when Army
red tape prevents them from sleeping together. Not up to the standard
of Hawks' earlier comedies *Bringing Up Baby* and *His Girl Friday* but
still better than most. Known also under title *You Can't Sleep Here*.

TWENTIETH CENTURY–FOX

Production—Sol C. Siegel
Direction—Howard Hawks
Screenplay (*from novel by Henri
Rochard*)—Charles Lederer,
Leonard Spigelgass, Hagar
Wilde

Photography—Norbert Brodine,
O. H. Borrodaile
Art direction—Lyle Wheeler,
Albert Hogsett
Music—Cyril Mockridge
Editing—James B. Clark

PLAYERS: Cary Grant, Ann Sheridan, William Neff, Eugene Gericke,
Marion Marshall, Randy Stuart, Ruben Wendorff, Lester Sharpe

IF . . . Gt. Britain (1968)

Lindsay Anderson looks at everyday life and archaic rituals in an imaginary English public school and offers, in a surrealist climax when the
boys revolt against the masters and governors on Speech Day, an anarchistic attack on the outmoded ideas that the school and authoritarian
society as a whole represent. One of the most brilliant British films of
the 1960's, bearing a close resemblance, especially in its surrealist attitudes, to Jean Vigo's masterpiece *Zéro de Conduite*.

MEMORIAL ENTERPRISES/PARAMOUNT

Production—Michael Medwin &
Lindsay Anderson
Direction—Lindsay Anderson
Screenplay (*based on scenario
Crusaders by David Sherwin
& John Howlett*)—David
Sherwin

Photography (*Eastmancolor*)—
Miroslav Ondricek
Production design—
Jocelyn Herbert
Music & musical direction—
Marc Wilkinson: Sanctus from
"Missa Luba"
Editing—David Gladwell

PLAYERS: Malcolm McDowell, David Wood, Richard Warwick, Robert Swann, Christine Noonan, Hugh Thomas, Rupert Webster, Peter Jeffrey, Arthur Lowe, Mona Washbourne

IF I HAD A MILLION   U.S.A. (1932)

Paramount portmanteau comedy about eight assorted people who suddenly find themselves worth a million dollars when an eccentric multimillionaire chooses them at random to inherit his fortune. Uneven but with some amusing moments—especially the scenes in which downtrodden clerk Charles Laughton hands in his notice, and a raspberry, to his employers (a Lubitsch episode), and old-time actors W. C. Fields and Alison Skipworth buy a fleet of second-hand cars and go about wrecking all the road hogs they can find. Eighteen writers, seven directors, fourteen stars.

PARAMOUNT

Direction—Ernst Lubitsch, Norman Taurog, Stephen Roberts, Norman McLeod, James Cruze, William A. Seiter, H. Bruce Humberstone
Screenplay (from story by Robert D. Andrews)—Claude Binyon, Whitney Bolton, Malcolm Stuart Boyland, John Bright, Sidney Buchman, Lester Cole, Isabel Dawn, Boyce DeGaw, Walter DeLeon, Oliver H. P. Garrett, Harvey Gates, Grover Jones, Ernst Lubitsch, Lawton Mackaill, Joseph L. Mankiewicz, William Slavens McNutt, Seton I. Miller, & Tiffany Thayer

PLAYERS: Gary Cooper, Wynne Gibson, George Raft, Charles Laughton, Richard Bennett, Jack Oakie, Frances Dee, Charlie Ruggles, Alison Skipworth, W. C. Fields, Mary Boland, Roscoe Karns, May Robson, Gene Raymond, Lucien Littlefield, Joyce Compton

IL BIDONE   Italy (1955)

Searching study of the crooked activities and personal lives of a trio of tricksters who earn a meager living by disguising themselves as priests and swindling the simple peasants of Italy. Fellini concentrates, not so much on the effects of the criminals' activities on the poor, as on the loneliness and seediness of the criminals themselves and draws sharp performances from his three leading actors—Franco Fabrizi and Americans Richard Basehart and Broderick Crawford whose portrayal of the oldest and loneliest member of the gang belongs with his finest acting performances.

A TITANUS FILM

Production manager–   Photography–Otello Martelli
    Giuseppe Colizzi   Art direction–Dario Cecchi
Direction–Federico Fellini   Music–Nino Rota
Screenplay–Federico Fellini,   Editing–Mario Serandrei &
    Ennio Flaiano & Tullio Pinelli   Giuseppe Vari
PLAYERS: Broderick Crawford, Richard Basehart, Franco Fabrizi,
Giulietta Masina, Giacomo Gabrielli, Alberto De Amicis, Lorella De
Luca, Irene Cefaro, Sue Ellen Blake

IL GRIDO (The Cry)   Italy (1957)
Penetrating Antonioni study of spiritual desolation centers on a young
engineer (Steve Cochran) who, deserted by his mistress (Valli), wanders aimlessly with his little daughter through the bleak Po Valley in
search of peace of mind and a new start in life. Underrated when it
first appeared but now regarded as one of the finest of Antonioni's
early works. Of interest also because it studies the environment of the
working class and not the upper and middle classes portrayed in such
later Antonioni films as *L'Avventura* and *La Notte*.

SPA CINEMATOGRAFICA

Production–Danilo Marciani   Photography–Gianni di Venanzo
Direction–   Art direction–Franco Fontana
    Michelangelo Antonioni   Music–Giovanni Fusco
Story–Antonioni   Editing–Eraldo da Roma
Script–Antonioni, Elio
    Bartolini, Ennio De Concini
PLAYERS: Steve Cochran, Alida Valli, Betsy Blair, Gabriella Pallotti,
Dorian Gray, Lynn Shaw, Mirna Girardi

IL TETTO (The Roof)   Italy (1956)
Part-comic, part-tragic De Sica picture about an impoverished young
Italian couple who, after struggling unsuccessfully to find a home of
their own, finally erect their own "house"–a one-room brick shack–
on a disused piece of municipal ground in Rome. Not as moving as
De Sica's earlier neo-realist movies but, like all his films, full of compassion and humor and containing some brilliant observations of everyday life. Performed as usual by a mostly nonprofessional cast.

A TITANUS FILM

Direction–Vittorio De Sica   Set design–Gastone Medin
Screenplay–Cesare Zavattini   Music–Alessandro Cicognini
Photography–Carlo Montuori   Editing–Eraldo Da Roma

191

PLAYERS: Gabriella Pallotta, Giorgio Listuzzi, Gastone Renezelli, Maria Di Rollo, Giuseppe Martini, Emilia Martini

ILLUSTRATED MAN, THE   U.S.A. (1968)
This dazzling episodic movie, based on three short stories from a Ray Bradbury collection, is stylistically one of the most interesting of con- temporary science-fiction films and is perhaps director Jack Smight's most successful film to date. The first story is of two children who can conjure up on their nursery wall any scene of their chosing (in this case an African plateau on which their parents are eaten by lions), the second concerns the experiences of a rocket-ship crew on a rain-drenched planet, and the third deals with the last night of the world. The illus- trated man of the title—a man who has been covered from head to toe with tattoos, each of which depicts a different story—is played by Rod Steiger.

WARNER BROS./AN SKM PRODUCTION

Production—Howard B. Kreitsek, Ted Mann	*Photography* (*Technicolor/ Panavision*)—Philip Lathrop
Direction—Jack Smight	*Art direction*—Joel Schiller
Screenplay—Howard B. Kreitsek	*Music*—Jerry Goldsmith
	Editing—Archie Marshek

PLAYERS: Rod Steiger, Claire Bloom, Robert Drivas, Don Dubbins, Jason Evers, Tim Weldon, Christie Matchett

IMMIGRANT, THE   U.S.A. (1917)
Chaplin's penultimate Mutual comedy with Charlie and fellow immi- grant Edna Purviance sharing hardship and happiness as they make a new life together in America. Slower paced than most of the other comedies, but containing some acute observations of the difficulties and loneliness experienced by outsiders in a foreign country. Almost the entire last half of the film revolves around a single comic incident— Chaplin and waiter Eric Campbell continually finding and losing a coin in a restaurant.

A MUTUAL COMEDY

Direction—Charles Chaplin	*Photography*—R. H. Totheroh,
Screenplay—Charles Chaplin	W. C. Foster

PLAYERS: Charles Chaplin, Albert Austin, Henry Bergman (in two roles), Eric Campbell, Frank J. Coleman, James T. Kelly, Edna Purvi- ance, John Rand

The Immigrant

IN THE HEAT OF THE NIGHT   U.S.A. (1967)
Neat thriller that works well as a straightforward whodunit but which
is also constantly working away on a much higher level, telling, as it
does, of the antagonism between a slow-thinking white police chief
(Rod Steiger) and a Negro "homicide" expert (Sidney Poitier) from
Philadelphia as they search for a killer in a small backwater town in
Mississippi. Ranks in the same category as Edward Dmytryk's *Crossfire*
which also examined an important racial problem within the framework
of a thriller. The film was rather surprisingly awarded an Oscar as best
of the year when more favored films such as *Bonnie and Clyde* and
The Graduate were also up for the award. An Oscar also went to
Steiger as best actor.

MIRISCH/UNITED ARTISTS

Production—Walter Mirisch   *Photography (DeLuxecolor)*—
Direction—Norman Jewison   Haskell Wexler
Screenplay (based on novel by   *Art direction*—Paul Groesse
   John Ball)—Stirling Silliphant   *Music*—Quincy Jones
                                        Editing—Hal Ashby
PLAYERS: Rod Steiger, Sidney Poitier, Warren Oates, Quentin Dean,
James Patterson, William Schallert, Lee Grant, Scott Wilson

193

IN WHICH WE SERVE   Gt. Britain (1942)
The story of British destroyer HMS *Torrin* and of the men who served
on her during the early days of the Second World War. Told in flashbacks from the *Torrin's* sinking in the Battle of Crete, the film concentrates on the thoughts of three survivors—captain (Noel Coward), chief
petty officer (Bernard Miles) and ordinary seaman (John Mills)—as
they remember their lives on board ship and ashore with their wives
in Plymouth. A museum piece now although some of its integrity and
feeling for men in war still shows through. Historically important in any
case as the first film which David Lean had a hand in directing.

A TWO CITIES FILM

Production—Noel Coward	*Screenplay*—Noel Coward
Associate producer—	*Photography*—Ronald Neame
Anthony Havelock-Allan	*Art direction*—David Rawnsley
Direction—Noel Coward &	*Music*—Noel Coward
David Lean	*Editing*—Thelma Myers

PLAYERS: Noel Coward, John Mills, Bernard Miles, Celia Johnson,
Joyce Carey, Kay Walsh, Derek Elphinstone, Michael Wilding

INCIDENT AT OWL CREEK   France (1961)
Director Robert Enrico captures on film the last thoughts of a Confederate soldier about to be hanged on a bridge in Alabama during the
Civil War. As the soldier awaits his execution he imagines that he
escapes from his captors and reaches the safety of his home and his
wife's waiting arms. When he feels her arms around him, however, he
is brought back to reality and realizes that in effect they represent the
hangman's rope around his neck. The film then ends with his execution.
Absorbing to watch, finely acted and deeply moving; one of the best
short films (27 minutes) of recent years.

FILM ARTIC/MARCEL ICHAC/FILMS DU CENTAURE/PAUL DE ROUBAIX

Production—René Aulois	*Screenplay* (*based on Ambrose*
Direction—Robert Enrico	*Bierce's short story "An*
Photography—Jean Boffety	*Occurrence at Owl Creek*
Music—Henri Lanoé	*Bridge"*)—Robert Enrico
Editing—Denise de Casabianca	

PLAYERS: Roger Jacquet, Anne Cornaly, Anker Larsen, Stéphane Fey,
Jean-Francois Zeller, Pierre Dany, Louis Adelin

INCREDIBLE SHRINKING MAN, THE   U.S.A. (1957)
Little-known science-fiction thriller of the 1950's belonging, like *Them*,
to the "effects of radiation" category, although in this case instead of

194

ants being turned into giants because of atomic testing, the theme is reversed and a healthy young man (accidentally infected by a radio-active cloud) finds himself diminishing at the rate of an inch a week until he is no larger than an atom. An uneven little film, at its best in the trick photography sequences when the miniature hero is required to escape from a giant-sized cat and to fight to the death with a huge spider.

UNIVERSAL–INTERNATIONAL

Production—Albert Zugsmith
Direction—Jack Arnold
Screenplay (from novel)— Richard Matheson
Photography—Ellis W. Carter
Art direction—Alexander Golitzen & Robert Clatworthy
Music—Joseph Gershenson
Editing—Al Joseph

PLAYERS: Grant Williams, Randy Stuart, April Kent, Paul Langton, Raymond Bailey, William Schallert, Diana Darrin

INDISCRETION (Terminal Station)   Italy (1954)

Much maligned film that fused several major screen talents—producer David Selznick, director Vittorio De Sica, writers Cesare Zavattini and Truman Capote—in telling a simple story of two lovers parting at a large Italian railway station. The film is set entirely amid the noise and bustle of the station and concentrates on the two lovers—he an Italian college professor, she a Philadelphia housewife—during the hour before the woman's train is to leave. Something of a screen oddity the film is nevertheless an interesting work and deserves more critical attention than it received when first shown. Montgomery Clift (superb) and Jennifer Jones play the lovers, and the photography is by G. R. Aldo who uses the close-up more effectively than perhaps any cameraman since William Mellor photographed George Stevens' *A Place in the Sun*.

SELZNICK ORGANIZATION

Production & direction— Vittorio De Sica
Screenplay (from story by Zavattini)—Cesare Zavattini, Luigi Chiarini & Giorgio Prosperi
Dialogue—Truman Capote
Photography—G. R. Aldo
Art direction—Virgilio Marchi
Music—Alessandro Cicognini
Editing—Eraldo Da Roma & Jean Barker

PLAYERS: Jennifer Jones, Montgomery Clift, Richard Beymer

INFORMER, THE   U.S.A. (1935)

John Ford's classic version of Liam O'Flaherty's story of betrayal and murder in Dublin during the troubles. A deeply moving performance from Victor McLaglen as the slow-witted informer Gypo Nolan and some inspired direction from Ford, although Van Nest Polglase (sets), Joseph August (camera work) and Max Steiner (music) all contribute equally to the film's success. Shot in three weeks at RKO on a low budget; Oscars to Ford, McLaglen, Nichols and Steiner, and New York Critics Awards for best film and best direction.

RKO RADIO

Associate producer—Cliff Reid
Direction—John Ford
Screenplay—Dudley Nichols
Photography—Joseph H. August

Art direction—Van Nest Polglase, Charles Kirk
Music—Max Steiner
Editing—George Hively

PLAYERS: Victor McLaglen, Heather Angel, Preston Foster, Margot Grahame, Wallace Ford, Una O'Connor, J. M. Kerrigan, Joseph Sawyer

INHERIT THE WIND   U.S.A. (1960)

Courtroom drama based on the Tennessee monkey trial of the 1920's with Spencer Tracy as Henry Drummond (Clarence Darrow) defending, and Fredric March as Matthew Harrison Brady (William Jennings Bryan) prosecuting, a young schoolteacher on trial for teaching the Darwinian theory of evolution in a Southern school. Superb performances from the two stars, but the film is important primarily for its condemnation of bigotry and intolerance and for the fine screenplay by Nathan Douglas and Harold Smith who also authored *The Defiant Ones* for Kramer. Edited by Frederic Knudtson who cut Kramer's subsequent trial movie *Judgment at Nuremberg* as well as, among others, *The Defiant Ones, On the Beach* and *It's a Mad, Mad, Mad, Mad World*.

UNITED ARTISTS

Production & direction—
  Stanley Kramer
Screenplay (*based on play by Jerome Lawrence & Robert E. Lee*)—Nathan Douglas & Harold Smith

Photography—Ernest Laszlo
Music—Ernest Gold
Production design—
  Rudolph Sternad
Editing—Frederic Knudtson

PLAYERS: Spencer Tracy, Fredric March, Gene Kelly, Florence Eldridge, Dick York, Donna Anderson, Harry Morgan

INNOCENTS, THE   Gt. Britain (1961)

Subtle ghost story about an English governess who finds that the personalities of the two children in her charge have been taken over by the spirits of two dead lovers who, through the innocent bodies of the children, carry on the evil relationship they enjoyed while they were alive. Some critics regard the film as nothing more than a straightforward ghost story, others see it as something essentially Freudian and regard the happenings in the story as taking place entirely in the frustrated governess's mind. Whichever view is correct, the ghost aspects of the tale—mysterious figures on top of towers, faces at windows, etc.—are skillfully handled by Jack Clayton. The playing of Deborah Kerr as the governess is immensely assured.

TWENTIETH CENTURY–FOX

Production & direction—
Jack Clayton
Screenplay (based on The Turn of the Screw *by Henry James)*
—William Archibald & Truman Capote

Additional scenes—
John Mortimer
*Photography—*Freddie Francis
Art direction—
Wilfred Shingleton
*Music—*Georges Auric
*Editing—*James Clark

PLAYERS: Deborah Kerr, Michael Redgrave, Peter Wyngarde, Megs Jenkins, Martin Stephens, Pamela Franklin, Clytie Jessop

INTOLERANCE   U.S.A. (1916)

D. W. Griffith's epic made up of four separate stories about man's continuing struggle against intolerance. The stories, which are told simultaneously in parallel action, are set in different periods of history and deal with the conflict of Christ with the Pharisees, the war between Catholics and Huguenots in 16th-century France, the destruction of the Babylonian empire, and the struggle between capitalism and socialism in America during the 1920's. Griffith supervised every part of the film's production and built several vast sets, the most famous being the colossal full-sized replica of the city of Babylon which is still one of the most famous film sets of all time. The film cost almost two million dollars to make (a fantastic sum in those days), but proved a disappointment at the box office, its receipts falling far below those of Griffith's masterpiece *The Birth of a Nation,* released a year earlier.

WARK PRODUCING CORPORATION (D. W. GRIFFITH)

Direction & screenplay (modern story based on "The Mother and the Law" & records of the Stielow murder case)—
D. W. Griffith
*Photography—*G. W. Bitzer & Karl Brown

Construction supervisor—
Frank Wortman
*Assistant direction—*George Siegmann, W. S. Van Dyke, Joseph Henaberry, Erich von Stroheim, Edward Dillon & Tod Browning

197

PLAYERS: *All Ages:* Lillian Gish; *Modern Story:* Mae Marsh, Fred Turner, Robert Harron, Sam de Grasse, Vera Lewis, Monte Blue, Tod Browning, Edward Dillon; *Judean Story:* Howard Gaye, Lillian Langdon, Olga Grey, Erich von Stroheim, Gunther von Ritzau, Bessie Love; *Medieval French Story:* Margery Wilson, Eugene Pallette, Frank Bennett, Josephine Crowell, Constance Talmadge, Maxfield Stanley; *Babylonian Story:* Constance Talmadge, Elmer Clifton, Alfred Paget, Seena Owen, Carl Stockdale, Tully Marshall, George Siegmann, Elmo Lincoln, Ted Duncan

INTRUDER IN THE DUST   U.S.A. (1949)

The least known but most convincing of Hollywood's attempts to deal with the question of color prejudice in the deep South centers on the efforts of three white people—a young boy, his lawyer uncle, and an 80-year-old spinster—to prove the innocence of an elderly Negro who has been accused of murdering a white man. The quiet and dangerous pre-lynching mood of a small Southern town obsessed with hate is cleverly observed by Clarence Brown whose direction, particularly of the scene in which a lynch mob gathers in the square outside the jailhouse, ranks with the best of his career. Scripted by Ben Maddow from the novel by William Faulkner and shot mostly on location in Faulkner's home town of Oxford, Mississippi.

METRO–GOLDWYN–MAYER

Production & direction—   *Art direction—*Cedric Gibbons &
  Clarence Brown   Randall Duell
*Screenplay—*Ben Maddow   *Music score—*Adolph Deutsch
*Photography—*Robert L. Surtees   *Editing—*Robert J. Kern

PLAYERS: David Brian, Claude Jarman Jr., Juano Hernandez, Porter Hall, Elizabeth Patterson, Charles Kemper, Will Geer

INVASION OF THE BODY SNATCHERS   U.S.A. (1956)

Subtle science-fiction drama full of menacing undercurrents (the horror is suggested, never shown) which starts quietly in a small town and ends on a note of high terror as beings from outer space, having taken over the minds and bodies of people living in one state, begin to move across the United States to take over the entire country. Directed by Don Siegel (his best film) and, despite the atrocious title, one of the most accomplished films in the genre.

ALLIED ARTISTS

*Production—*Walter Wanger   *Direction—*Don Siegel

Screenplay (*based on* Collier's   *Photography* (*Superscope*)—
  Magazine serial by Jack   Ellsworth Fredericks
  Finney)—Daniel Mainwaring   *Music*—Carmen Dragon
                                Editing—Robert Eisen
PLAYERS: Kevin McCarthy, Dana Wynter, Larry Gates, King Donovan,
Carolyn Jones, Jean Willes, Ralph Dumke

INVISIBLE MAN, THE   U.S.A. (1933)
Convincing adaptation of H. G. Wells' classic novel with Claude Rains
(not seen until the last few minutes) making perhaps the most unusual
debut in screen history as the megalomaniac Dr. Griffin who succeeds
in rendering himself invisible while experimenting with an Indian drug
called monocaine. An excellent radio performance by Rains—his superb
speaking voice was never heard to better advantage—and some remarkable trick camera work by John Mescall and Arthur Edeson, particularly in the scene when Rains, for the first time, unwraps the bandages
around his face and reveals . . . nothing. Directed by Universal's
"horror king," James Whale, who, during the 1930's, made the most
memorable of the studio's horror productions—*The Old Dark House,
Frankenstein, Bride of Frankenstein,* etc.
                            UNIVERSAL
Direction—James Whale   *Photography*—John Mescall &
Screenplay—R. C. Sherriff (with   Arthur Edeson
  Philip Wylie)   *Special Effects*—John P. Fulton
PLAYERS: Claude Rains, Gloria Stuart, William Harrigan, Henry Travers,
Una O'Connor, Forrester Harvey, Holmes Herbert, E. E. Clive

IRON HORSE, THE   U.S.A. (1924)
The film that established John Ford (then 29) as a major director; a
long (160-minute) epic about the building of the first transcontinental
railroad, distinguished mainly by its splendidly staged action sequences:
Indians attacking the passengers of a train with a derailed locomotive,
a buffalo charge, etc., and by Ford's imaginative use of natural scenery.
The film—superior to the better-known *The Covered Wagon* made by
James Cruze a year earlier—earned Fox some two million dollars.
                              FOX
Direction—John Ford   *Photography*—George
Screenplay (*from story by*   Schneiderman, Burnett Guffey
  Kenyon & John Russell)—   *Titles*—Charles Darnton
  Charles Kenyon   *Music score*—Erno Rapee

                              199

PLAYERS: George O'Brien, Madge Bellamy, Judge Charles Edward Bull, William Walling, Fred Kohler, Cyril Chadwick, Gladys Hulette, James Marcus

ISLAND OF LOST SOULS   U.S.A. (1932)
Minor, frequently tasteless but at times oddly effective horror film directed by little-known Erle Kenton and containing a bravura performance from Charles Laughton as a grotesque scientist who, after being outlawed from society because of his experiments, spends his time cross-breeding animal species on a remote desert island. Adapted from H. G. Wells' novel *The Island of Dr. Moreau* and photographed by Karl Struss who the same year shot *Dr. Jekyll and Mr. Hyde* for Rouben Mamoulian.

PARAMOUNT

Direction—Erle C. Kenton   *Screenplay*—Waldemar Young &
Photography—Karl Struss   Philip Wylie
PLAYERS: Charles Laughton, Bela Lugosi, Richard Arlen, Leila Hyams, Kathleen Burke, Arthur Hohl, Stanley Fields, Tetsu Komai

ISLE OF THE DEAD   U.S.A. (1945)
Slow-moving horror thriller about a group of people marooned on a Greek island during a plague. Not the best of Lewton's RKO horror movies; although the last thirty minutes, in which a cataleptic woman who has been buried alive escapes from her coffin completely insane, are filmed with great skill by Mark Robson who, like Jacques Tourneur and Robert Wise before him, employed sound with great subtlety to register horror.

RKO RADIO

Production—Val Lewton   *Art direction*—Albert S.
Direction—Mark Robson   D'Agostino & Walter E. Keller
Screenplay—Ardel Wray &   *Music*—Leigh Harline
    Josef Mischel   *Editing*—Lyle Boyer
Photography—Jack Mackenzie
PLAYERS: Boris Karloff, Ellen Drew, Mare Cramer, Katherine Emery, Helen Thimig, Alan Napier

IT ALWAYS RAINS ON SUNDAY   Gt. Britain (1947)
London's East End again portrayed by Ealing, but this time in more dramatic form with John McCallum as an escaped criminal and Googie Withers as his married ex-girlfriend who hides him from the police

for one wet, dismal Sunday. Sordid, intelligent, made almost memorable by Robert Hamer's brilliant observation of working-class life and by Douglas Slocombe's inspired photography of London's streets, pubs, railyards, etc.

EALING STUDIOS

Production—Michael Balcon
Direction—Robert Hamer
Associate producer—
  Henry Cornelius
Screenplay (from novel by
  Arthur la Bern)—Angus
  Macphail, Robert Hamer,
  Henry Cornelius

Photography—
  Douglas Slocombe
Art direction—
  Duncan Sutherland
Music—Georges Auric
Editing—Michael Truman

PLAYERS: John McCallum, Googie Withers, Jack Warner, Edward Chapman, John Slater, Susan Shaw, Patricia Plunkett, David Lines, Sidney Tafler, Betty Ann Davies, Jane Hylton

IT HAPPENED ONE NIGHT   U.S.A. (1934)

Typical 1930's screwball comedy featuring Claudette Colbert as runaway heiress and Clark Gable as cynical, hard-boiled newspaperman who pursues and woos her across America. Some amusing Robert Riskin dialogue and two famous scenes: Colbert hoisting her skirt and showing a leg to hitch a lift, and sharing a room with Gable with only a wall-to-wall blanket ("the walls of Jericho") between them. The film remains the only picture ever to win all four major Academy Awards— best production, best actor (Gable), best actress (Colbert), and best director (Capra). A fifth Oscar went to Riskin for his screenplay.

COLUMBIA

Production—Harry Cohn
Direction—Frank Capra
Screenplay (based on Night Bus
  by Samuel Hopkins Adams)—
  Robert Riskin

Photography—Joseph Walker
Art direction—Stephen Goosson
Music direction—Louis Silvers
Editing—Gene Havlick

PLAYERS: Claudette Colbert, Clark Gable, Walter Connolly, Roscoe Karns, Alan Hale, Ward Bond, Jameson Thomas, Eddie Chandler

IT SHOULD HAPPEN TO YOU   U.S.A. (1954)

Judy Holliday giving another variation on her dumb blonde characterization (it was her fourth such role since her debut in Born Yesterday) as Gladys Glover, a young unemployed model who spends her life sav-

201

ings advertising her name on a large New York billboard and succeeds in complicating the mechanics of American big business. Not the best of the Cukor/Kanin comedies but containing the usual irresistible Holliday performance and some sharp satire on advertising techniques.

COLUMBIA

Production—Fred Kohlmar
Direction—George Cukor
Screenplay (from story by Garson
  Kanin)—Garson Kanin

Photography—Charles Lang
Art direction—John Meehan
Music—Frederick Hollander
Editing—Charles Nelson

PLAYERS: Judy Holliday, Peter Lawford, Jack Lemmon, Michael O'Shea, Vaughn Taylor, Connie Gilchrist, Walter Klavun, Whit Bissell

ITALIAN STRAW HAT, THE (Un Chapeau de Paille d'Italie)
France (1927)

Classic silent comedy by René Clair with Albert Préjean as a young man who, on his wedding day, becomes entangled with a married lady and her lover, and has to find an exact replica of a special kind of straw hat, the recovery of which is essential to the saving of the lady's honor. A fresh, witty, satirical comedy of manners derived from a mid-19th-century stage farce by Eugene Labiche and Marc Michel. Designed by Lazare Meerson whose subsequent Clair films include *Les Deux Timides, Sous les Toits de Paris, Le Million, A Nous la Liberté* and *Quatorze Juillet.*

FILMS ALBATROS

Direction & screenplay—
  René Clair
Photography—Maurice
  Desfassiaux, Nicolas Roudakov

Art direction—
  Alexandre Kamenka
Sets—Lazare Meerson
Editing—Henri Dobb

PLAYERS: Albert Préjean, Olga Tschekowa, Marise Maia, Yvonneck, Alice Tissot, Alex Bondi, Vital Geymond, Paul Olivier

IT'S A GIFT   U.S.A. (1934)

Early W. C. Fields comedy belonging to his Paramount period tells the adventures of the proprietor of a small-town general store when he attempts to buy an orange grove in California. Sometimes crude, often clumsy, but always funny when Fields is around which, luckily, is for most of the time. Directed by Norman McLeod who earlier guided the Marx Brothers through *Monkey Business* and *Horse Feathers,* and scripted from a story by J. P. McEvoy and Charles Bogle, the latter name being one of the many pseudonyms used by Fields when accepting writing credit.

Production—William LeBaron   *Photography*—Henry Sharp
Direction—Norman McLeod   *Art direction*—Hans Dreier,
Screenplay—Jack Cunningham   John B. Goodman
PLAYERS: W. C. Fields, Jean Rouverol, Julian Madison, Kathleen
Howard, Tom Bupp, Tammany Young

IT'S A MAD, MAD, MAD, MAD WORLD   U.S.A. (1963)

Massive, all-star Cinerama comedy that looks at the effects of greed
on an assorted group of people as they chase wildly across the United
States in search of 350,000 dollars' worth of buried loot. Too much of a
good thing really, but out of 193 minutes there are inevitably some
good things, notably a number of skillfully staged car stunts, Phil
Silvers in a sinking motorcar, Terry Thomas as a retired English
colonel, and Spencer Tracy as an honest cop who is himself eventually
caught up in the fever of the hunt. Buster Keaton and Zasu Pitts appear
in bit parts. This ultra-expensive film (unusual for Kramer) cost over
$9 million to produce but to date has grossed nearly $20 million.

UNITED ARTISTS/STANLEY KRAMER PRODUCTION

Direction—Stanley Kramer   *Art direction*—Rudolph Sternad
Screenplay—William & Tania   *Music*—Ernest Gold
  Rose   *Editing*—Frederic Knudtson,
Photography (Technicolor)—   Robert C. Jones & Gene Fowler
  Ernest Laszlo
PLAYERS: Spencer Tracy, Milton Berle, Sid Caesar, Buddy Hackett,
Ethel Merman, Mickey Rooney, Dick Shawn, Phil Silvers, Terry Thomas,
Jonathan Winters, Edie Adams, Jimmy Durante

IT'S A WONDERFUL LIFE   U.S.A. (1946)

A 1930's-styled piece of whimsy about a young man (James Stewart)
who longs to make his name in the big city but who, for family and
business reasons, never leaves his home town. When, facing bank-
ruptcy, he attempts to take his own life, an angel (Henry Travers)
comes to save him and shows him what the town would have been like
had he not been born. A warm, human, sentimental film with a wealth
of lovingly drawn small-town detail and fine supporting performances
from Lionel Barrymore, Thomas Mitchell and H. B. Warner. The last
"quality" film that the great Frank Capra directed.

RKO RADIO

Production & direction—   *Photography*—Joseph Walker,
  Frank Capra   Joseph Biroc

Screenplay (from story by Philip Van Doren Stern)—Frances Goodrich, Albert Hackett & Capra

Art direction—Jack Okey
Music—Dimitri Tiomkin
Editing—William Hornbeck

PLAYERS: James Stewart, Donna Reed, Lionel Barrymore, Henry Travers, Beulah Bondi, Thomas Mitchell, Gloria Grahame, Ward Bond, Frank Faylen, H. B. Warner, Samuel S. Hinds, Frank Albertson

IVAN   U.S.S.R. (1932)
Dovzhenko's first sound film, not so well-known as his two silent masterpieces *Arsenal* and *Earth*, but no less visually rewarding. The story of a young Ukrainian peasant who becomes involved in the building of the great hydroelectric project on the Dneiper River.

UKRAINFILM

Direction & screenplay—
    Alexander Dovzhenko
Photography—Danylo Demutsky,
    Yuri Yekelchik & Mikhail
    Glider

Art direction—Yuri Khomaza
Music—Igor Belza, Yuli Meitus
    & Boris Lyatoshinsky

PLAYERS: Pyotr Masokha, Stepan Shkurat, Semyon Shagaida

IVAN THE TERRIBLE   U.S.S.R. (1944–1946)
Part I—*Ivan the Terrible*
Part II—*The Boyars Plot*
Sergei Eisenstein's two-part film (the work was originally intended as a trilogy but Eisenstein died before the third part could be put into production) about the life of the first Tsar traces Ivan's struggles with his enemies both inside and outside Russia and his attempts to found a strong, united state. The huge close-ups, rich décor and Prokofiev's choral music help make the film one of the great achievements of the Russian cinema although it is a slow-moving and often oppressive work far removed from its director's dynamically edited silent masterpieces *Strike* and *Battleship Potemkin*.

MOSFILM/ALMA—ATA FILM STUDIOS

Direction & screenplay—
    Sergei M. Eisenstein
Photography—Andrei Moskvin &
    Eduard Tissé

Art direction—Yosip Spinel
Music—Sergei Prokofiev
Editing—E. Tobak

PLAYERS: Nikolai Cherkassov, Ludmila Tselikovskaya, Serafima Birman, Pavel Kadochinkow, Mikhail Nazvanov, Andrei Abrikosov

Ivan the Terrible

JANE EYRE   U.S.A. (1944)
The brooding, melancholy atmosphere of Charlotte Brontë's romantic novel is surprisingly well transposed to the screen in this skillful adaptation. Orson Welles as Edward Rochester, the moody young squire with a mad wife locked away in his mansion, gives one of the best of his early Hollywood performances, and Joan Fontaine is more than competent as the orphaned governess Jane. A stylish, highly individual work superbly photographed by George Barnes.

TWENTIETH CENTURY–FOX

Production—William Goetz   *Photography*—George Barnes
Direction—Robert Stevenson   *Art direction*—James Basevi &
Screenplay—Aldous Huxley, Jack   Wiard B. Ihnen
    Houseman, & Robert Stevenson   *Editing*—Walter Thompson
PLAYERS: Orson Welles, Joan Fontaine, Margaret O'Brien, Peggy Ann Garner, John Sutton, Sara Allgood, Henry Daniell, Agnes Moorhead

JAZZ SINGER, THE   U.S.A. (1927)
The first talking (one scene) movie, a corny second-rate story about a young Jewish boy (Al Jolson) who sings ragtime against his father's wishes. Important though because it *was* the first and because it sig-

naled the beginning of the end for silent pictures. The songs include "Dirty Hands, Dirty Face," "My Mammy," "Toot, Toot, Tootsie Goodbye" and Irving Berlin's "Blue Skies." May McAvoy played the romantic female lead.

WARNER BROS.

Direction—Alan Crosland
Screenplay (from play by
Samson Raphaelson)—
Alfred A. Cohn
Photography—Hal Mohr

Music by various hands, including "Blue Skies" by Irving Berlin
Editing—Harold McCord

PLAYERS: Al Jolson, May McAvoy, Warner Oland, Eugenie Besserer, Cantor Josef Rosenblatt, Otto Lederer

JESSE JAMES   U.S.A. (1939)
Over-romanticized, but still the most famous film dealing with the exploits of Jesse James who together with his brother Frank and their gang of outlaws committed bank and train robberies across the West during the 1870's. Tyrone Power is featured as Jesse, Henry Fonda as Frank, and John Carradine appears as the notorious Bob Ford who murdered Jesse at his home in 1882. Photographed in early Technicolor, the film was given a sequel in 1940 when Fritz Lang made *The Return of Frank James* starring Fonda.

TWENTIETH CENTURY—FOX

Production—Darryl F. Zanuck
Executive producer—
Nunnally Johnson
Direction—Henry King
Screenplay—Nunnally Johnson
Historical Research—
Rosalind Schaeffer &
Jo Frances

Photography (Technicolor)—
George Barnes &
W. Howard Greene
Art direction—
William S. Darling &
George Dudley
Music direction—Louis Silvers
Editing—Barbara McLean

PLAYERS: Tyrone Power, Henry Fonda, Nancy Kelly, Randolph Scott, Henry Hull, Slim Summerville, J. Edward Bromberg, Brian Donlevy, John Carradine

JEUX INTERDITS (Forbidden Games)   France (1952)
Remarkable film about two French children—one a five-year-old girl whose parents have been killed in a German air attack, the other a small peasant boy—who, influenced by the death and destruction around them, build a cemetery for dead animals and become obsessed

like their elders with the ritual of death. A major work (unquestionably Clément's best) showing the effects of war and violence on the minds of children. Brigitte Fossey appeared as the girl and Georges Poujouly as the boy. The sensitive guitar score is by Narciso Yepes.

ROBERT DORFMAN/SILVER FILM

Direction—René Clément
Screenplay (from novel by
François Boyer)—
Pierre Bost, René Clément,
Jean Aurenche & Boyer
Photography—Robert Juilliard
Art direction—Paul Bertrand
Music—Narciso Yepes
Editing—Roger Dwyre

PLAYERS: Brigitte Fossey, Georges Poujouly, Lucien Hubert, Suzanne Courtal, Jacques Marin, Laurence Badie, André Wasley

JEZEBEL   U.S.A. (1938)
Elegantly designed romantic melodrama set in New Orleans in the 1850's and featuring Bette Davis in one of her best roles as the wealthy, spoiled Southern belle Julie Marston. Stylishly directed by William Wyler, enjoying his first break from a series of Goldwyn stage adaptations—*These Three, Dodsworth, Dead End*—and well photographed by Ernest Haller who between 1932 and 1964 worked with Bette Davis on no less than 14 occasions.

WARNER BROS.

Production & direction—
William Wyler
Associate producer—
Henry Blanke
Photography—Ernest Haller
Art direction—Robert Haas
Screenplay (based on play by
Owen Davis)—Clements Ripley,
Abem Finkel, John Huston
Music—Max Steiner
Editing—Warren Low

PLAYERS: Bette Davis, Henry Fonda, George Brent, Donald Crisp, Fay Bainter, Margaret Lindsay, Richard Cromwell, Henry O'Neill, Spring Byington

JOHNNY BELINDA   U.S.A. (1948)
The famous weepie about a deaf-mute farm girl living in a remote Nova Scotia community who is befriended and tutored by young sympathetic doctor. A poignant performance by Jane Wyman and some sensitive direction from Jean Negulesco fail to save the film from an overmelodramatic second half with its ugly scenes of rape and murder. Lew Ayres, in one of his rare appearances, is admirable as the doctor, and Charles Bickford gives splendid support as the girl's father.

WARNER BROS.

Production—Jerry Wald
Direction—Jean Negulesco
Screenplay (*from play by*
   Elmer Harris)—Irmgard von
   Cube & Allen Vincent

Photography—Ted McCord
Art direction—Robert Haas
Music—Max Steiner
Editing—David Weisbart

PLAYERS: Jane Wyman, Lew Ayres, Charles Bickford, Agnes Moorehead, Jan Sterling, Stephen McNally, Dan Seymour

JOHNNY GUITAR   U.S.A. (1954)

Bizarre, wildly extravagant Western with Joan Crawford (in high boots, tight black breeches and dark blue shirt) as a saloonkeeper cashing in on the coming of the railroad to Arizona. Among the supporting players are Sterling Hayden and Scott Brady as a couple of gunfighters, Ward Bond as a cattle baron, and Mercedes McCambridge as a half-crazy girl banker who, in a startling climax, fights it out to the death with Miss Crawford. Highly regarded by European critics although not so in Britain or the United States.

REPUBLIC (A HERBERT J. YATES PRESENTATION)

Production—Herbert J. Yates
Direction—Nicholas Ray
Screenplay (*from novel by*
   Roy Chanslor)—
   Philip Yordan

Photography (*Trucolor*)—
   Harry Stradling
Art direction—
   James W. Sullivan
Music—Victor Young
Editing—Richard L. Van Enger

PLAYERS: Joan Crawford, Sterling Hayden, Scott Brady, Mercedes McCambridge, Ben Cooper, Ernest Borgnine, Royal Dano, Ward Bond

JOHNNY O'CLOCK   U.S.A. (1947)

Small-scale crime melodrama has professional gambler (Dick Powell) involved in murder and blackmail and at odds with crooked gambling partner (Thomas Gomez) and laconic police inspector (Lee J. Cobb) who, during this period, was one of Hollywood's most regular cops. Unpretentious but smartly done; Robert Rossen's first attempt at directing one of his own screenplays.

COLUMBIA

Production—Edward G. Nealis
Direction—Robert Rossen
Screenplay (*from story by*
   Milton Holmes)—
   Robert Rossen
Photography—Burnett Guffey

Art direction—Stephen Goosson,
   Cary Odell & James Crowe
Music—George Duning
Editing—Warren Low &
   Al Clark

PLAYERS: Dick Powell, Evelyn Keyes, Ellen Drew, Lee J. Cobb, Nina Foch, Thomas Gomez, John Kellogg, Jeff Chandler

JOUR DE FÊTE (The Big Day)   France (1949)
Jacques Tati film (his first feature) about a village postman influenced by an advertising film at a visiting fair who decides that he can deliver his mail just as fast as the streamlined New York Postal Services. Full of simple humor and brilliant mime and containing some of the finest slapstick since the heyday of Chaplin and Keaton. The atmosphere of French village life on a lazy summer's day is beautifully evoked.

CADY FILMS (FRED ORAIN)

Direction—Jacques Tati   Photography—
Screenplay & dialogue—   Jacques Mercanton
    Jacques Tati & Henri Marquet   Art direction—René Moulaert
    with the collaboration of   Music—Jean Yatove
    René Wheeler   Editing—Marcel Moreau
PLAYERS: Jacques Tati, Guy Decombe, Paul Frankeur, Santa Relli, Maine Vallée, Roger Rafal, Beauvais, Delcassan

JOURNEY INTO AUTUMN (Kvinnodrom)   Sweden (1955)
An essay in sexual frustration about two women—one a middle-aged fashion photographer (Eva Dahlbeck), the other her young model (Harriet Andersson)—who snatch briefly at love during a day's business trip to Goteborg. Skilfully played with Gunnar Björnstrand in particularly good form as the younger girl's would-be sugar daddy. Among the last of Bergman's films dealing with the battle of the sexes theme.

SANDREWS

Direction & screenplay—   Art direction—Gittan Gustafsson
    Ingmar Bergman   Editing—Carl-Olov Skeppstedt
Photography—Hilding Bladh
PLAYERS: Eva Dahlbeck, Harriet Andersson, Gunnar Björnstrand, Ulf Palme, Inga Landgré, Sven Lindberg, Naima Wilfstrand, Bengt-Ake Benktsson

THE JOYLESS STREET (Die Freudlose Gasse)   Germany (1925)
The bitter experiences of a group of people living in a small street in Vienna during the early 1920's when the inflationary effects of the First World War were causing the economic and moral decay of the middle class. Although deeply depressing this uncompromising film is a key work in Pabst's career and one of the most distinguished of the

entire German silent cinema. Greta Garbo, appearing in her third film, plays the daughter of a destitute ex-councillor, and Asta Nielsen is a working-class girl forced by unemployment into prostitution.

HIRSCHAL SOFAR

Direction—G. W. Pabst

Screenplay (from novel by
  Hugo Bettauer)—Willi Haas

Photography—Guido Seeber &
  Kurt Oertel

Art direction—Söhnle & Erdmann

PLAYERS: Asta Neilsen, Valeska Gert, Greta Garbo, Agnes Esterhazy, Tamara Tolstoy, Werner Krauss

JUAREZ   U.S.A. (1939)

Dignified historical biography set in mid-19th-century Mexico and depicting the struggle of Emperor Maximilian von Habsburg and his wife Carlotta with Indian democrat Juarez, who rose from humble beginnings to become President of Mexico. Filmed with restraint by William Dieterle and ranking with his best biographies of the 1930's even though it is his least well-known. Paul Muni followed his previous portrayals of Pasteur and Zola with another fine performance as Juarez, and Brian Aherne and Bette Davis were featured as Maximilian and Carlotta. Also in the cast is Claude Rains as Napoleon III.

WARNER BROS.

Production—Hal B. Wallis in
  association with Henry Blanke

Direction—William Dieterle

Photography—Tony Gaudio

Art direction—Anton Grot

Music score—
  Erich Wolfgang Korngold

Musical direction—
  Leo F. Forbstein

Screenplay (based in part on play
  Juarez and Maximilian by Franz
  Werfel and book The
  Phantom Crown by Bertita
  Harding)—John Huston,
  Aeneas MacKenzie &
  Wolfgang Reinhardt

Editing—Warren Low

PLAYERS: Bette Davis, Paul Muni, Brian Aherne, Claude Rains, John Garfield, Donald Crisp, Joseph Calleia, Gale Sondergaard

JUDEX   France (1963)

Stylish and immensely entertaining tribute to Louis Feuillade, the pioneer French film director who made hundreds of popular films and serials during the silent period including a 12-part 1917 serial dealing with the escapades of a masked, black-cloaked avenger named Judex. Full of roof-top fights, thrilling escapes, last-minute rescues, and so on, the film is graced by some lovely photography and glittering décor.

Franju's Judex is played by dove conjurer Channing Pollock and the cat-suited villainess by Francine Bergé.

C.F.F.P./FILMES (ROME)

Direction—Georges Franju
Adaptation & dialogue (from 1916 screenplay by Arthur Bernède & Louis Feuillade)— Jacques Champreux & Francis Lacassin

Photography—Marcel Fradetal
Art direction—Robert Giordani
Music—Maurice Jarre
Editing—Gilbert Natot

PLAYERS: Channing Pollock, Francine Bergé, Sylva Koscina, Edith Scob, Théo Sarapo, Jacques Jouanneau, Michel Vitold, René Génin, Roger Fradet

JUDGMENT AT NUREMBERG   U.S.A. (1961)

Three hours of courtroom drama with elderly small-town American judge Spencer Tracy presiding over the Nuremberg trial of four former Hitler judges and attempting to appraise the guilt and responsibility of the German people for Hitler's Third Reich. The film suffers from excessive length and less-than-subtle direction, but is notably well acted by an all-star cast, particularly Maximilian Schell as the fiercely nationalistic German defense lawyer, Montgomery Clift and Judy Garland as two Jewish witnesses, and Tracy himself. Scripted by Abby Mann from his television play.

UNITED ARTISTS

Production & direction— Stanley Kramer
Screenplay—Abby Mann
Photography—Ernest Laszlo

Production design— Rudolph Sternad
Music—Ernest Gold
Editing—Frederic Knudtson

PLAYERS: Spencer Tracy, Burt Lancaster, Richard Widmark, Marlene Dietrich, Maximilian Schell, Judy Garland, Montgomery Clift

JULES ET JIM   France (1961)

Nostalgic study of deep and lasting friendship between two students— German Jules (Oskar Werner) and French Jim (Henry Serre)—and of their complex relationship with an inscrutable woman (Jeanne Moreau) who loves each in turn but whose varying moods, unconventional morality, and views on love eventually defeat them both. A stylish, dazzlingly conceived picture set before, during, and after the Great War and containing some of Truffaut's most triumphant scenes, e.g. the kaleidoscope of opening shots establishing the relationship of

211

Juliet of the Spirits

the two students, the foot race across a railway bridge and the later charming bicycle ride in the country, a scene strongly reminiscent of Renoir. Hauntingly scored by Georges Delerue who also did *La Peau Douce* for Truffaut.

FILMS DU CARROSSE/S.E.D.I.F.

Direction—François Truffaut
Photography—Raoul Coutard
Music—Georges Delerue
Editing—Claudine Bouché

Screenplay, adaptation & dialogue (from novel by Henri-Pierre Roché)— François Truffaut & Jean Gruault

PLAYERS: Jeanne Moreau, Oskar Werner, Henri Serre, Marie Dubois, Vanna Urbino, Sabine Haudepin

JULIET OF THE SPIRITS (Giulietta Degli Spiriti)

France/Italy (1965)

Upper-class middle-aged Italian wife (Giulietta Masina) is shattered by the fact that her unfaithful husband has a mistress and, afraid of the loneliness that will ensue if he leaves her, takes refuge from reality by living in a world of subconscious fantasies conjured up during spiritual séances. An overlong (145 minutes), tedious, frequently trivial Fellini film far below the standard of such earlier works as *La Strada,* and *The Nights of Cabiria,* but of interest for the stunningly beautiful Technicolor fantasy images of Gianni Di Venanzo.

FEDERIZ (ROME)/FRANCORIZ (PARIS)

Production—Angelo Rizzoli
Direction—Federico Fellini
Screenplay—Federico Fellini,
  Tullio Pinelli, Brunello Rondi
  & Ennio Flaiano

Photography (Technicolor)—
  Gianni Di Venanzo
Art direction—Piero Gherardi
Music—Nino Rota
Editing—Ruggero Mastroianno

PLAYERS: Giulietta Masina, Mario Pisu, Sandra Milo, Valentina Cortese, Caterina Boratto, Sylva Koscina, Lucia della Noce, Lou Gilbert

JULIUS CAESAR   U.S.A. (1953)

An engrossing 121 minutes in the company of a superlative British/ American cast as they interpret into screen terms Shakespeare's great political melodrama about the assassination of Julius Caesar in 44 B.C. Producer John Houseman and director Joe Mankiewicz resisted the temptation to expand the story into a spectacular (the climactic Battle of Philippi for instance is not overstressed), shooting the film in monochrome against austere but authentically designed backgrounds and relying on the skill of their actors to put the drama across, which they do with splendid effect, particularly John Gielgud as the intellectual archplotter Cassius, Marlon Brando as an unconventional Mark Antony, and James Mason as the tragic Brutus. A film of great dramatic power, far superior to Olivier's three Shakespearean adaptations (themselves distinguished pictures) and arguably the greatest Shakespearean film ever made.

METRO–GOLDWYN–MAYER

Production—John Houseman
Direction—Joseph L. Mankiewicz
Adaptation—Joseph L. Mankiewicz
Photography—Joseph Ruttenberg

Art direction—Cedric Gibbons
  & Edward Carfagno
Music—Miklos Rozsa
Costumes—Herschel McCoy
Editing—John Dunning

PLAYERS: Marlon Brando, James Mason, John Gielgud, Louis Calhern, Edmond O'Brien, Greer Garson, Deborah Kerr, George Macready

KAMERADSCHAFT   Germany (1931)

G. W. Pabst's best-known sound film, a reconstruction of an actual mining disaster which took place on the frontier between Germany and France at the beginning of the century and in which German miners went to the aid of their trapped French comrades. The film was used by Pabst as a plea for international co-operation and is distinguished both by its observations of men under stress and for the documentary-style realism of its mining sequences.

NERO–FILM

Direction–G. W. Pabst
Screenplay–Ladislaus Vayda,
  Karl Otten,
  Peter Martin Lampel

Photography–
  Fritz Arno Wagner,
  Robert Baberske
Art direction–Ernö Metzner,
  Karl Vollbrecht

PLAYERS: Alexander Granach, Fritz Kampers, Ernst Busch, Elisabeth Wendt, Gustav Püttjer, Oskar Höcker, Daniel Mendaille, Georges Charlia, Andrée Ducret

KANAL   Poland (1957)

Terrifyingly graphic account of the last tragic days of the Warsaw uprising when the remnants of the doomed Polish Resistance Fighters were driven into the sewers beneath the ruined city. A film of tremendous power that relentlessly re-creates the sweat, agony and bitterness of one of the grimmest episodes of World War II. Harsh, unforgettable, almost a masterpiece of its kind.

THE KADR UNIT OF FILM POLSKI

Production–Stanislaw Adler
Direction–Andrzej Wajda
Screenplay–Jerzy Stawinski
Photography–Jerzy Lipman

Art direction–Roman Mann
Music–Jan Krenz
Editing–Halina Nawrocka

PLAYERS: Teresa Izewska, Tadeusz Janczar, Wienczyslaw Gunski, Emil Karewicz, Wladyslaw Sheybal, Tadeusz Gwiazdowski

KEY LARGO   U.S.A. (1948)

Set almost entirely within the confines of a resort hotel on the Florida Keys where a deported racketeer (Edward G. Robinson) and his hoods hold Bogart, Bacall and company as hostages, this moody gangster movie remains a static dialogue piece for most of its running time, but builds to a spectacular To Have and Have Not–style climax when Bogie disposes of Edward G. and his gang in a motorboat gun battle. Not vintage Huston but made with typical Warners professionalism and containing a notable Academy Award-winning cameo from Claire Trevor as a faded torch singer. Edward G. Robinson's henchmen were played by Thomas Gomez, Harry Lewis, Dan Seymour and William Haade.

Production—Jerry Wald
Direction—John Huston
Photography—Karl Freund
Art direction—Leo K. Kuter
Music—Max Steiner

Screenplay (based on play by Maxwell Anderson)—
Richard Brooks &
John Huston
Editing—Rudi Fehr

PLAYERS: Humphrey Bogart, Edward G. Robinson, Lauren Bacall, Lionel Barrymore, Claire Trevor, Thomas Gomez, Harry Lewis, Dan Seymour, William Haade

KID, THE   U.S.A. (1921)

Charlie Chaplin comedy in which the little tramp adopts an abandoned baby boy and rears him as his own son before returning him eventually to his real mother. The film shows Chaplin in a more serious vein than ever before and combines humorous incident with scenes of almost straight drama. A huge commercial success, it launched five-year-old Jackie Coogan on a remarkable screen career.

Direction—Charles Chaplin
Screenplay—Charles Chaplin
Photography—R. H. Totheroh

PLAYERS: Charles Chaplin, Jackie Coogan, Carl Miller, Edna Purviance, Chuck Riesner, Tom Wilson, Albert Austin, Nellie Bly Baker

KID AUTO RACES AT VENICE   U.S.A. (1914)

Chaplin's second film but the first in which he appeared in the world-famous tramp costume. Reputedly shot in only 45 minutes during the last week of 1913 the picture consists of nothing more than a single man (Chaplin) making a nuisance of himself by constantly getting in the way of cameras filming a children's auto race at Venice, the Los Angeles seaside resort. The film was released on a split reel (500 feet or less) with a factual educational short *Olives and their Oil*.

Production—Mack Sennett   *Direction*—Henry Lehrman
PLAYERS: Charles Chaplin, Henry Lehrman, The Keystone Kids (Bill Jacob, Thelma Salter, Gordon Griffith, Charlotte Fitzpatrick)

KID GALAHAD   U.S.A. (1937)

An early examination of professional boxing with Edward G. Robinson (honest) and Humphrey Bogart (crooked) as a pair of rival fight managers at odds over the rise of former bellhop Wayne Morris to the world championship. The commendably grubby atmosphere, ferocious boxing scenes, and Michael Curtiz's skillful direction raise this piece well above most movies of its kind. Bette Davis is also on hand as Robinson's mistress.

WARNER BROS./FIRST NATIONAL

Executive producer—
  Hal B. Wallis
*Direction—*Michael Curtiz
Screenplay (based on novel by
  Francis Wallace)—
  Seton I. Miller

*Photography—*Tony Gaudio
*Art direction—*Carl Jules Weyl
*Music score—*Heinz Roemheld
  & Max Steiner
*Editing—*George Amy

PLAYERS: Edward G. Robinson, Bette Davis, Humphrey Bogart, Wayne Morris, William Haade, Jane Bryan, Harry Carey, Soledad Jiminez

KILLERS, THE   U.S.A. (1946)

Stylish adaptation of Hemingway's short story with Burt Lancaster (debut) as the "Swede" and William Conrad and Charles McGraw as the two gangsters who come to kill him. An uneven, confused, very tough film that, although failing to maintain the quality of its first ten minutes, is still considerably superior to most of its kind. A notable script by Anthony Veiller and (uncredited) John Huston, and some early Dragnet-type music.

UNIVERSAL

*Production—*Mark Hellinger
*Direction—*Robert Siodmak
*Screenplay—*Anthony Veiller
*Photography—*Woody Bredell

*Art direction—*Jack Otterson,
  Martin Obzina
*Music—*Miklos Rozsa
*Editing—*Arthur Hilton

PLAYERS: Burt Lancaster, Ava Gardner, Edmond O'Brien, Albert Dekker, Sam Levene, William Conrad, Charles McGraw, Donald McBride, Phil Brown, John Miljan

KILLING, THE   U.S.A. (1956)

Cheaply made crime movie about a shabby gang of tired thugs who, led by ex-convict Sterling Hayden, clean out a racetrack of some two million dollars and are then betrayed and ultimately destroyed by traitors and fate. A rather familiar story, but turned into a minor classic by the young Stanley Kubrick (then 27) whose imaginative use of flashbacks and sharp editing put the film almost into *The Asphalt Jungle* class, a movie which it often closely resembles. Elisha Cook Jr. as a downtrodden little racetrack cashier and Marie Windsor as his luxury-loving wife are the best of an excellent supporting cast which also includes Joe Sawyer as a bartender, Jay C. Flippen as a reformed alcoholic, and Ted de Corsia in his by now familiar role as a crooked cop.

HARRIS–KUBRICK PRODS./UNITED ARTISTS

Production–James B. Harris
Direction–Stanley Kubrick
Screenplay (based on novel
  Clean Break *by Lionel*
  White)–Stanley Kubrick

Photography–Lucien Ballard
Art direction–
  Ruth Sobotka Kubrick
Music–Gerald Fried
Editing–Betty Steinberg

PLAYERS: Sterling Hayden, Jay C. Flippen, Marie Windsor, Elisha Cook Jr., Coleen Gray, Vince Edwards, Ted de Corsia, Joe Sawyer

KIND HEARTS AND CORONETS   Gt. Britain (1949)
Black Ealing comedy, set in Edwardian England, about a vengeful young draper's assistant (Dennis Price) who kills off, one by one, the dozen relatives standing between him and a dukedom. The most ambitious of Ealing's comedies, witty, consistently amusing and forever famous as the film in which Alec Guinness plays eight of Price's ill-fated cousins, among them an admiral, a general, an amateur photographer, a clergyman (the most developed role), and a suffragette. A delicious cameo also from Miles Malleson as a snobbish public hangman.

EALING STUDIOS

Production–Michael Balcon
Associate producer–
  Michael Relph
Direction–Robert Hamer
Screenplay–Robert Hamer,
  John Dighton

Photography–
  Douglas Slocombe
Art direction–William Kellner
Editing–Peter Tanner
Music–Mozart's *Don Giovanni*

PLAYERS: Alec Guinness, Dennis Price, Joan Greenwood, Valerie Hobson, Audrey Fildes, Miles Malleson

KIND OF LOVING, A   Gt. Britain (1962)
Kitchen-sink drama of the early 1960's set against the familiar background of industrial Britain and revolving around the unhappy experiences of two young people—a draftsman (Alan Bates) and a typist (June Ritchie)—who decide to wed when the girl becomes pregnant and make the best of the resulting unfortunate marriage. What lifts a dated film clear of the rut is the playing of Bates and John Schlesinger's perceptive observations of working-class life.

Production—Joseph Janni
Direction—John Schlesinger
Screenplay (adapted from novel
  by Stan Barstow)—Willis Hall &
  Keith Waterhouse
Photography—Denys Coop
Art direction—Ray Simm
Music—Ron Grainer
Editing—Roger Cherrill

PLAYERS: Alan Bates, June Ritchie, Thora Hird, Bert Palmer, Gwen Nelson, Malcolm Patton, Pat Keen

KING AND COUNTRY   Gt. Britain (1964)

The horrors of trench warfare and the futility of individual protest against war itself are examined by Joseph Losey in his film version of John Wilson's television play about a young soldier's desertion from the trenches in World War I and the last few hours before his execution. Tom Courtenay appears as the deserter and Dirk Bogarde is the sympathetic defending officer who fails to save him from the firing squad—the only scene in the film in which shots are fired. This was Bogarde's third film with Losey.

Production—Norman Priggen &
  Joseph Losey
Direction—Joseph Losey
Screenplay (from play Hamp
  by John Wilson, based on
  story by James Landsdale
  Hodson)—Evan Jones
Photography—Denys Coop
Art direction—Peter Mullins
Music & musical direction—
  Larry Adler
Editing—Reginald Mills

PLAYERS: Dirk Bogarde, Tom Courtenay, Leo McKern, Barry Foster, James Villiers, Peter Copley, Barry Justice, Vivian Matalon, Jeremy Spenser

KING KONG   U.S.A. (1933)

Giant ape King Kong, captured on an unexplored island off the coast of Africa, is taken to New York where he runs amok in the city streets before meeting his death on top of the Empire State Building. Directed with style by Ernest B. Schoedsack who later made several other less noteworthy horror entertainments (*Son of Kong, Dr. Cyclops,* etc.), but most notable for Max Steiner's primeval music score and the technical effects of Willis O'Brien. Bruce Cabot plays the leader of the explorers and Fay Wray is the terrified heroine who spends much of her time sitting precariously in Kong's giant hand.

Production & direction—Ernest
 B. Schoedsack & Merian C.
 Cooper
*Screenplay (from story by Merian
 C. Cooper & Edgar Wallace)*—
 James Creelman & Ruth Rose

Photography—Edward Lindon,
 Verne Walker & J. O. Taylor
Special effects—Willis O'Brien
Art direction—Carroll Clark &
 Al Herman
Music—Max Steiner
Editing—Ted Cheesman

PLAYERS: Fay Wray, Robert Armstrong, Bruce Cabot, Frank Reicher, Sam Hardy, Noble Johnson, James Flavin, Steve Clemento, Victor Wong

KING OF KINGS U.S.A. (1927)

DeMille's life of Christ is not nearly so vulgar as one would imagine, due mainly to H. B. Warner's sensitive performance as the Savior and DeMille's tasteful handling of the Crucifixion and Last Supper sequences. Ernest Torrence appears as Peter, Dorothy Cumming as Mary, and Joseph Schildkraut as Judas. Among the others in the huge cast: Jacqueline Logan (Mary Magdalene), Victor Varconi (Pontius Pilate), and George Seigmann (Barabbas).

PATHÉ EXCHANGE, INC.

Production & direction—
 Cecil B. DeMille
*Screenplay (adapted from the
 Four Gospels in the Holy
 Bible)*—Jeanie Macpherson

Photography—J. Peverell Marley
Musical setting—
 Hugh Riesenfeld
Editing—Anne Bauchens &
 Harold McLernon

PLAYERS: H. B. Warner, Dorothy Cumming, Ernest Torrence, Joseph Schildkraut, Jacqueline Logan, Victor Varconi, George Seigmann

KING'S ROW U.S.A. (1941)

Accomplished though often quite ugly melodrama about life in a small town at the turn of the century. Based on the novel by Henry Bellamann, the film is remembered for the sequence in which a sadistic doctor (Charles Coburn) unnecessarily amputates Ronald Reagan's legs and for Reagan's famous line of dialogue: "Where's the rest of me?" Claude Rains, a poisoner with a mad wife who murders his daughter because she too is tainted with madness, plays the town's other doctor. Ann Sheridan and Robert Cummings appear as more normal members of the community.

Production—Hal B. Wallis
Direction—Sam Wood
Screenplay—Casey Robinson
Photography—
    James Wong Howe

Art direction—
    Carl Jules Weyl
Music—
    Erich Wolfgang Korngold
Editing—Ralph Dawson

PLAYERS: Ann Sheridan, Robert Cummings, Ronald Reagan, Betty Field, Charles Coburn, Claude Rains, Judith Anderson, Nancy Coleman

KISS ME DEADLY
U.S.A. (1955)

Ralph Meeker as fascist-styled private-eye Mike Hammer pitted against mobster (Paul Stewart) and atomic heavy (Albert Dekker). A stylish, much censored and extraordinarily effective Robert Aldrich movie that was unjustly neglected when first shown. It has proved to be of direct influence on several French New Wave directors, among them Truffaut and Godard when they began their careers in the late 1950's. Photographed by Ernest Laszlo, Aldrich's associate on *Apache, Vera Cruz* and *The Big Knife.*

PARKLANE PICTURES/UNITED ARTISTS

Production & direction—
    Robert Aldrich
Screenplay (from novel by
    Mickey Spillane)—
    A. I. Bezzerides

Photography—Ernest Laszlo
Art direction—William Glasgow
Music—Frank de Vol
Editing—Michael Luciano

PLAYERS: Ralph Meeker, Albert Dekker, Paul Stewart, Juano Hernandez, Wesley Addy, Marian Carr, Maxine Cooper

KISS ME KATE
U.S.A. (1953)

Third and best of George Sidney's filmed stage musicals with Howard Keel and Kathryn Grayson as temperamental stage couple starring in a musical version of *Taming of the Shrew* and finding themselves acting out their parts in real life. A talented cast interprets Cole Porter's score with verve and gusto, particularly long-legged Ann Miller who steals the film with such scintillating numbers as "Tom, Dick or Harry," "Always True to You in My Fashion," and most memorably "Too Darn Hot." Comic thugs James Whitmore and Keenan Wynn very nearly steal it back with their rendering of "Brush Up Your Shakespeare."

METRO—GOLDWYN—MAYER

Production—Jack Cummings
Direction—George Sidney

Photography (Anscocolor/3-D)
    —Charles Rosher

Screenplay (from play by Samuel & Bella Spewack)—Dorothy Kingsley
Art direction—Cedric Gibbons & Urie McCleary

Musical direction—Andre Previn & Saul Chaplin
Choreography—Hermes Pan
Editing—Ralph E. Winters

PLAYERS: Kathryn Grayson, Howard Keel, Ann Miller, Bobby Van, Keenan Wynn, Tommy Rall, Kurt Kasznar, Bob Fosse

KISS OF DEATH
U.S.A. (1947)

Ex-crook (Victor Mature) serving time for robbery with violence is persuaded by district attorney (Brian Donlevy) to inform on and help trap his former accomplices. A very effective gangster picture filmed almost completely in the streets of New York by Henry Hathaway, whose films of this period (*The House on 92nd Street, Call Northside 777*) were among the best of his career. The film is now regarded as something of a minor classic, notable for its opening robbery sequence and for the performances of Richard Widmark (debut) as the giggling, sadistic gangster and Taylor Holmes as a crooked lawyer. Brilliantly photographed by Norbert Brodine who, together with Joe MacDonald, was responsible for the camera work on many of Fox's semidocumentary thrillers of the late forties.

TWENTIETH CENTURY—FOX

Production—Fred Kohlmar
Direction—Henry Hathaway
Screenplay (from story by Eleazar Lipsky)—Ben Hecht, Charles Lederer

Photography—Norbert Brodine
Art direction—Lyle Wheeler, Leland Fuller,
Music—David Buttolph
Editing—J. Watson Webb

PLAYERS: Victor Mature, Brian Donlevy, Coleen Gray, Richard Widmark, Taylor Holmes, Howard Smith, Karl Malden

KITTY
U.S.A. (1945)

Historical movie, set in 18th-century London, tracing the rags-to-riches career of cockney slut (Paulette Goddard) who becomes an heiress and finally a duchess through two appropriate marriages and with the help of caddish Ray Milland. The script has wit and the playing is extraordinarily good, but what distinguishes the film most are the superb period sets and costumes—something of a rarity in Hollywood films of the time. Much of the picture's accuracy can be attributed to Mitchell Leisen, a former art director who spent some twelve years as DeMille designer before becoming Paramount director in the 1930's.

Production—Darrell Ware, Karl Tunberg
Direction—Mitchell Leisen
Screenplay (*from novel by Rosamond Marshall*)—Karl Tunberg

Photography—Daniel L. Fapp
Art direction—Hans Dreier & Walter Tyler
Music—Victor Young
Editing—Alma Macrorie

PLAYERS: Ray Milland, Paulette Goddard, Patric Knowles, Cecil Kellaway, Reginald Owen, Constance Collier, Dennis Hoey, Sara Allgood

KNIFE IN THE WATER, THE (Noz W. Wodzie)   Poland (1962)
A young beatnik hitches a lift from a middle-aged journalist and his wife who casually invite him to spend the weekend with them on their holiday yacht. During the day and night that they are all together the boy intrudes uncomfortably on the couple's private lives and tests their marriage relationship to the full. A polished, deceptively simple surface hides a complex film full of underlying tensions. The first picture of Polish director Roman Polanski.

ZRF "CAMERA," WARSAW/FILM POLSKI

Direction—Roman Polanski
Screenplay—Jerzy Skolimowski, Jakub Goldberg & Roman Polanski

Photography—Jerzy Lipman
Music—Krzysztof Komeda
Editing—Halina Prugar

PLAYERS: Leon Niemczyk, Jolanta Umecka, Zygmunt Malanowicz

KNIGHTS OF THE TEUTONIC ORDER, THE   Poland (1960)
A 3-hour Polish epic revolving round the 14th-century conflict between the Polish state and the warlike order of the Teutonic Knights. Some spectacular battles, a great deal of violence, and more surprisingly, some penetrating glimpses into the ordinary way of life of the monarchy, feudal lords and serfs during the Middle Ages.

Direction—Aleksander Ford
Screenplay (*based on novel by Henryk Sienkiewicz*)—Jerzy Stefan Stawinski & Aleksander Ford
Art direction—Roman Mann

Photography (*Eastmancolor/ Dyaliscope*)—Mieczyslaw Jahoda
Music—Kazimierz Serocki
Editing—Miroslawa Garlicka, Alina Faflik

PLAYERS: Urszula Modrzynska, Grazyna Staniszewska, Andrzej Szalawski, Henryk Borowski, Aleksander Fogiel, Mieczyslaw Kalenik, Emil Karewicz

LA BATAILLE DU RAIL   France (1946)

Among the best of Europe's postwar semidocumentaries this excitingly staged film concentrates on the role played in the Resistance by French railwaymen, particularly their efforts to prevent a 12-train German convoy from reaching its destination. Acted by both professionals and the railwaymen themselves and awarded the Grand Prix International at the 1946 Cannes Film Festival.

COOPÉRATIVE GÉNÉRALE DU CINÉMA FRANÇAIS

Direction—René Clément
Screenplay—René Clément, in collaboration with Colette Audry & Jean Daurand

Photography—Henri Alekan
Music—Yves Baudrier
Editing—Jacques Désagneaux

PLAYERS: Jean Daurand, Clarieux, Désagneaux, Laurent and railway workers

LA BELLE EQUIPE (They Were Five)   France (1936)

Part-comic, part-tragic story of five unemployed men who decide to build a riverside cafe with the 100,000 francs they win in a lottery but who, for varying reasons, drift apart before the venture is completed. An idealistic film that carries the moral that comradeship outweighs everything else in life. Not Duvivier's best work but like nearly all French films of this period quite brilliantly acted, especially by Gabin as the leader of the group.

CINÉ ARYS

Direction—Julien Duvivier
Screenplay—Charles Spaak, Julien Duvivier
Art direction—J. Krauss

Photography—J. Kruger & M. Fossard
Music—Maurice Yvain
Editing—Marthe Poncin

PLAYERS: Jean Gabin, Charles Vanel, Viviane Romance, Micheline Cheirel, Raphaël Medina, Charles Dorat, Aimos

LA BELLE ET LA BÊTE (Beauty and the Beast)   France (1946)

Beautiful and very faithful version of Mme. Leprince de Beaumont's famous 18th-century fairy story about a young woman's love for an agonized and pathetic beast that lives in a fearful castle lit by a thousand torches. Marked by richness of décor and costumes and also by trick camera work particularly effective in the scenes inside the magical castle with its disembodied arms and legs catering to every physical need. An exquisite music score. The leading roles were played by Josette Day and Jean Marais respectively.

Direction, screenplay & dialogue   *Art direction*—Christian Bérard
—Jean Cocteau   *Music*—Georges Auric
Photography—Henri Alekan   *Editing*—Claude Ibéria
PLAYERS: Josette Day, Jean Marais, Mila Parély, Nane Germon, Michel
Auclair, Marcel André

LA BÊTE HUMAINE   France (1938)
Powerful, absorbing film version of Emile Zola's novel about a locomotive engineer (Jean Gabin) who suffers from hereditary fits of
homicidal mania and who is eventually driven to murder by his amoral
mistress (Simone Simon). Grim, deeply depressing, made notable by
the quality of Gabin's performance and by Renoir's realistic observation
of railways and railway life. Especially memorable is the opening
sequence, shot from the floor of the locomotive cab, of the Paris–Le
Havre run. The film was remade by Fritz Lang as *Human Desire*
(U.S.A. 1954).

PARIS FILMS PRODUCTION
Direction—Jean Renoir   *Art direction*—Eugène Lourié
Screenplay—Jean Renoir   *Music*—Joseph Kosma
Photography—Curt Courant   *Editing*—Marguerite Renoir
PLAYERS: Jean Gabin, Simone Simon, Fernand Ledoux, Carette, Blanch-
ette Brunoy

LA DOLCE VITA (The Sweet Life)   Italy (1960)
Fellini's famous exposure of the more decadent aspects of Roman cafe
society revolving around the activities of a gutter journalist (Marcello
Mastroianni) as he searches for material for his scandal sheet while
on an endless round of parties and orgies. A long (173 minutes) episodic
film that created something of a sensation when it first appeared, but
which is, in fact, extremely moral in its attitudes and vigorously condemns the corruption it sets out to expose. Stunningly played by an
international cast who excelled themselves in a variety of plum acting
roles—particularly impressive are Yvonne Furneaux as the reporter's
neurotic mistress, Anita Ekberg as a visiting film star, and Anouk Aimée
(the best performance in the film) as a millionaire's daughter who gets
her kicks from sleeping in a whore's bed. A melancholy Nino Rota score
adds substantially to the mood of the film.

La Dolce Vita

RIAMA FILM/PATHÉ CONSORTIUM CINEMA/CINERIZ

Production—Giuseppe Amato
Direction—Federico Fellini
Screenplay (*based on story by Fellini, Flaiano & Pinelli*)— Federico Fellini, Ennio Flaiano, Tullio Pinelli & Brunello Rondi

Photography (*Totalscope*)— Otello Martelli
Art direction—Piero Gherardi
Music—Nino Rota
Editing—Leo Cattozzo

PLAYERS: Marcello Mastroianni, Yvonne Furneaux, Anouk Aimée, Anita Ekberg, Alain Cuny, Annibale Ninchi, Magali Noël, Lex Barker, Nadia Gray

LA FEMME DU BOULANGER (The Baker's Wife)   France (1938) The problems and confusion caused in a Provençal village when the baker's wife runs off with a shepherd and the baker in his sorrow refuses to bake any more bread until she is found. Director Marcel Pagnol skillfully re-creates all the charm and lazy atmosphere of French country life, although the film undeniably belongs to Raimu whose portrait of the unhappy baker is almost as memorable a creation as his César in Pagnol's trilogy (*César, Fanny, Marius*).

FILMS MARCEL PAGNOL

Direction & screenplay (from story by Jean Giono)—Marcel Pagnol	*Production manager*—Charles Pons
Music—Vincent Scotto	*Photography*—G. Benoit, R. Ledru, N. Daries

PLAYERS: Raimu, Ginette Leclerc, Charles Moulin, Robert Vattier, Charpin, Robert Barsac

LA FIN DU JOUR   France (1939)

Touching story of a group of retired stage performers living out the final years of their lives in an old actors' home in the South of France. One of the most moving of all films about old age; the acting, particularly of Victor Francen as a tragedian, Michel Simon as an old comedian, and Louis Jouvet as a former matinee idol still trying to exert his influence over women, is of the very highest class. Julien Duvivier's last prewar film.

REGINA

Direction & screenplay—Julien Duvivier	*Photography*—Christian Matras
Adaptation—Julien Duvivier & Charles Spaak	*Art direction*—J. Krauss
	Music—Maurice Jaubert
Dialogue—Charles Spaak	*Editing*—Marthe Poncin

PLAYERS: Louis Jouvet, Michel Simon, Victor Francen, Madeleine Ozeray, Gabrielle Dorziat, Gaston Modot

LA GRANDE ILLUSION   France (1937)

A powerful attack on the stupidity and spiritual waste of war, set in 1917, depicts the strange comradeship that develops between the maimed commander (Erich von Stroheim) of a German prison camp and a French aristocrat prisoner (Pierre Fresnay). A profound, almost great film dominated by the intellectual arguments of its script. It stands with Milestone's *All Quiet on the Western Front* and Kubrick's *Paths of Glory* as one of the most important antiwar films ever made.

R.A.C.

Direction—Jean Renoir	*Art direction*—Eugène Lourié
Screenplay & dialogue—Charles Spaak, Jean Renoir	*Music*—Joseph Kosma
	Editing—Marguerite Renoir
Photography—Christian Matras	

PLAYERS: Jean Gabin, Pierre Fresnay, Erich von Stroheim, Dalio, Carette, Gaston Modot, Jean Dasté

LA KERMESSE HEROÏQUE (Carnival in Flanders)   France (1935)
Stylish French comedy, set in the early 17th century, about the women of a small Flemish town who give their menfolk a lesson in diplomacy by using their charm and sex appeal to disarm an army of Spanish invaders. A triumphant satire, witty, polished and perfectly in period, justly famous for its visual qualities (Lazare Meerson's sets are especially memorable) and for the performances of Françoise Rosay as the burgomaster's wife and Louis Jouvet as a Dominican friar.

A TOBIS PRODUCTION

Direction—Jacques Feyder	*Décors*—Lazare Meerson
Dialogue (adapted from story	*Costumes designed by*—
by Charles Spaak)—Bernard	G. K. Benda
Zimmer	*and executed by*—J. Muelle
Photography—Harry Stradling	*Music*—Louis Beydts
	Sound—Herman Storr

PLAYERS: Françoise Rosay, Louis Jouvet, Jean Murat, Alerme, Lyne Clevers, Micheline Cheirel, Maryse Wendling

LA NOTTE (The Night)   Italy/France (1961)
Antonioni's masterpiece: a bleak, despairing look at a young and rich Milanese couple who have long since fallen out of love and who are observed in the film in the final stages of their disintegrating marriage. The entire action is concentrated into 24 hours and, like several of Antonioni's works, is more literary than cinematic; but the problems of love and marriage and of loneliness and the inability to communicate in modern society have never been better examined. A superior film to the highly praised *L'Avventura* and more accomplished than anything Antonioni has achieved since.

NEPI–FILM, SILVA–FILM (ROME), SOFITEDIP (PARIS)

Production—Paolo Frasca	*Photography*—Gianni di Venanzo
Direction—	*Music*—Giorgio Gaslini
Michelangelo Antonioni	*Art direction*—Piero Zuffi
Story & script—Antonioni, Ennio	*Editing*—Eraldo Da Roma
Flaiano, Tonino Guerra	

PLAYERS: Jeanne Moreau, Marcello Mastroianni, Monica Vitti, Bernhard Wicki, Maria Pia Luzi, Rosy Mazzacurati, Vincenzo Corbella

LA PASSION DE JEANNE D'ARC
(The Passion of Joan of Arc)   France (1928)
Austere Carl Dreyer masterpiece shows the anguish of the French

peasant girl during the last day of her trial and her execution. Remarkable both for the starkness of the décor and for Dreyer's frequent use of enormous close-ups, and also for the intensity of Falconetti's performance which was a tour de force and one of the greatest of all silent screen portrayals. The cameraman was Polish-born Rudolph Maté who worked again with Dreyer on *Vampyr* and later, in Hollywood, with Wyler (*Dodsworth*), Hitchcock (*Foreign Correspondent*), and Charles Vidor (*Cover Girl, Gilda*).

SOCIÉTÉ GÉNÉRAL DE FILMS, PARIS

Direction—Carl Dreyer

Screenplay—Carl Dreyer & Joseph Delteil

Photography—Rudolph Maté

Art direction—Jean Hugo & Hermann Warm

PLAYERS: Falconetti, Silvain, Maurice Schutz, Antonin Artaud, Michel Simon

LA RÈGLE DU JEU (The Rules of the Game)   France (1939)

The decaying prewar French aristocracy is satirized in a tragicomedy about the guests at a country house party who involve themselves in amorous intrigues with each other's wives and husbands, and are responsible for the destruction of two lovers (the only principled people among them) who don't understand the rules of the game. Made just prior to the outbreak of World War II the film was banned in France and was also refused release by Vichy and German authorities. Beneath its farcical surface it is the most penetrating of all Renoir's works and is frequently voted by world critics as one of the best films of all time.

LA NOUVELLE EDITION FRANÇAISE (CLAUDE RENOIR)

Direction—Jean Renoir

Screenplay—Jean Renoir & Carl Koch

Photography—Jean Bachelet

Art direction—Eugène Lourié, Max Douy

Music—Mozart, Chopin, Monsigny, Saint-Saëns, Johann Strauss

Editing—Marguerite Renoir, Madame Huguet

PLAYERS: Marcel Dalio, Nora Grégor, Jean Renoir, Roland Toutain, Mila Parély, Paulette Dubost, Julien Carette, Gaston Modot

LA RONDE   France (1950)

Dazzling Max Ophuls film consists of a series of episodes about the nature of physical love. The episodes are linked by Anton Walbrook as the cynical figure of Destiny who presides over a roundabout of love in turn-of-the-century Vienna and introduces the amours of first a soldier and a streetwalker, then the same soldier and a housemaid, then the housemaid and the son of the house, and so on until, having ranged from top to bottom of Viennese society, the circle is completed and the film ends with the same soldier hurrying quickly in the direction of the original streetwalker. A near-perfect film of its kind, amoral and witty, elegant and sophisticated, and by far the most distinguished work of Ophuls' career. Oscar Strauss's unforgettable little waltz became one of the most famous theme tunes of the postwar cinema.

SACHA GORDINE

Direction—Max Ophuls
Screenplay (adapted from play
  Reigen *by Arthur Schnitzler*)
  —Jacques Natanson & Max
  Ophuls

Dialogue—Jacques Natanson
Photography—Christian Matras
Art direction—Jean d'Eaubonne
Music—Oscar Strauss
Editing—Leonide Azar

PLAYERS: Anton Walbrook, Simone Signoret, Serge Reggiani, Simone Simon, Daniel Gélin, Danielle Darrieux, Fernand Gravey, Odette Joyeux, Jean-Louis Barrault, Isa Miranda, Gérard Philipe

LA STRADA   Italy (1954)

Fellini's award-winning but nonetheless neglected second film about a simple Italian waif (Giulietta Masina) and her relationships with her traveling strongman lover (Anthony Quinn) and the unbalanced acrobat (Richard Basehart) who almost rescues her from her slavelike existence. A moody, sad little tale, beautifully played. Otello Martelli's lensing of rainy desolate towns and bleak Italian landscapes adds considerably to the film's mood as does Nina Rota's melancholy theme "Stars Shine in Your Eyes" which became one of the big international song hits of the 1950's.

PONTI/DE LAURENTIIS

Direction—Federico Fellini
Screenplay (based on story by
  Fellini and Pinelli)—Fellini,
  Ennio Flaiano, Tullio Pinelli

Photography—Otello Martelli
Art direction—Mario Ravasco
Music—Nino Rota
Editing—Leo Cattozzo

PLAYERS: Giulietta Masina, Anthony Quinn, Richard Basehart, Aldo Silvani, Marcella Rovena, Lidia Venturina

LA TERRA TREMA   Italy (1948)

Visconti's 2-hour 40-minute film about the poverty-stricken fishermen of Sicily and their struggle for better working conditions. The ultimate

La Strada

in Italian neo-realism, shot entirely in the village of Aci Trezzia and acted by real fishermen who played their parts without a written screenplay and with dialogue suggested by themselves. The film was intended to be the first part of a Sicilian trilogy, but the commercial failure of the first part (cut for commercial showing) caused the rest of the project to be abandoned. Photographed by G. R. Aldo the distinguished Italian cameraman who was later killed while working for Visconti on *Senso*.

UNIVERSALIA

Production–Salvo D'Angelo   *Music*–Luchino Visconti,
Direction–Luchino Visconti   W. Ferrero
Photography–G. R. Aldo   *Editing*–Mario Serandrei
Cameraman–Gianni Di Venanzo
PLAYERS: Sicilian fishermen and their families

LA TRAVERSEE DE PARIS   France (1956)
Simple story, set in Paris under the German Occupation, about a small-

230

time black marketeer (Bourvil) who, together with an adventurous painter (Jean Gabin), undertakes to carry four suitcases of pork across the capital at night to a dealer on the far side of the city. The oddly matched couple's experiences with stray dogs, gendarmes, greedy civilians and German patrols make up the hard core of the film and allow Claude Autant-Lara to make some penetrating observations of life under the Occupation. A cynical and for the most part amusing film although beneath the surface the mood is often bitter.

FRANCO–LONDON FILMS/CONTINENTALE PRODUZIONE

Direction—Claude Autant-Lara
Screenplay, adaptation & dialogue
  (from story by Marcel Aymé)
  —Jean Aurenche & Pierre Bost

Photography—Jacques Natteau
Art direction—Max Douy
Music—René Cloërec
Editing—Madeleine Gug

PLAYERS: Jean Gabin, Bourvil, Louis de Funès, Jeanette Batti, Bernard Lajarrige

LADY EVE, THE   U.S.A. (1941)

Typical Sturges comedy featuring Barbara Stanwyck as card-sharp adventuress and Henry Fonda as dumb, accident-prone brewery heir she sets out to con. One of the funniest American films of the decade, sharp, witty, mischievous, with fine performances from both principals and equally from Charles Coburn as "Handsome Harry" Harrington (Barbara Stanwyck's crooked father), Eugene Pallette as millionaire, and Eric Blore as fake lord.

PARAMOUNT

Production—Paul Jones
Direction & screenplay (from story by Monckton Hoffe)—
  Preston Sturges
Photography—Victor Milner

Art direction—Hans Dreier,
  Ernst Fegte
Musical direction—
  Sigmund Krumgold
Editing—Stuart Gilmore

PLAYERS: Barbara Stanwyck, Henry Fonda, Charles Coburn, Eugene Pallette, William Demarest, Eric Blore, Melville Cooper, Martha O'Driscoll, Janet Beecher, Robert Greig, Dora Clement

LADY FOR A DAY   U.S.A. (1933)

Wretched Times Square peddler Apple Annie (May Robson) dismayed at the thought of impending visit of her daughter, to whom she has pretended to be a rich society woman, is installed in a luxurious apartment and made respectable for the day by her racket and gambling friends on Broadway. Sentimental little New York fairy tale directed by Capra (his first big success) from a short story by Damon Runyon. May Robson won an Academy Award nomination for her performance and Warren William as "Dave the Dude," Glenda Farrell as night-club hostess "Missouri," and Guy Kibbee as a pool shark head the hard-boiled Runyon types in the supporting cast.

COLUMBIA

Direction—Frank Capra	*Photography*—Joseph Walker
Screenplay & dialogue—	*Art direction*—Stephen Goosson
Robert Riskin	*Editing*—Gene Havlick

PLAYERS: Warren William, May Robson, Glenda Farrell, Guy Kibbee, Ned Sparks, Jean Parker, Barry Norton, Walter Connolly

LADY FROM SHANGHAI, THE   U.S.A. (1947)
Uneven, very confused Orson Welles thriller revolving around an Irish sailor who becomes an unsuspecting pawn in a murder plot. The most unimaginative but also the most frequently overrated of Welles' earlier films, of interest today mainly for its stunning climax in which the blond *femme fatale* (Rita Hayworth) and her crippled lawyer husband (Everett Sloane) shoot each other to death in a hall of mirrors.

COLUMBIA

Production & direction—	*Photography*—
Orson Welles	Charles Lawton, Jr.
Screenplay (from novel by	*Art direction*—Sturges Carne &
Sherwood King)—Orson	Stephen Goosson
Welles	*Music*—Heinz Roemheld
	Editing—Viola Lawrence

PLAYERS: Orson Welles, Rita Hayworth, Everett Sloane, Glenn Anders, Ted de Corsia, Gus Schilling, Erskine Sanford

LADYKILLERS, THE   Gt. Britain (1956)
Typical piece of Ealing nonsense with weird "music" professor Alec Guinness and his assorted gang of crooks descending on 70-year-old Katie Johnson and renting her house as a headquarters for their planned £60,000 robbery. Very amusing and only slightly below the peak standard of such earlier Ealing comedies as *The Lavender Hill Mob* and *The Man in the White Suit*. Guinness's gang is made up of Cecil Parker (a phony major), Herbert Lom (a gangster), Peter Sellers (a flashy dresser who lives by his wits), and Danny Green (a bonehead muscleman).

232

Production—Michael Balcon
Direction—
  Alexander Mackendrick
Associate producer—Seth Holt
Story & screenplay—
  William Rose

Photography (Technicolor)—
  Otto Heller
Art direction—Jim Morahan
Music—Tristram Cary
Editing—Jack Harris

PLAYERS: Alec Guinness, Cecil Parker, Herbert Lom, Peter Sellers, Danny Green, Katie Johnson, Jack Warner, Frankie Howerd, Philip Stainton

LADY VANISHES, THE   Gt. Britain (1938)
Margaret Lockwood as a vacationing debutante and Michael Redgrave as a young folksong collector become involved in European espionage when an elderly English governess (Dame May Whitty) disappears from the transcontinental train on which they are passengers. Ingenious, lightweight, fast-moving; set for all but the opening twenty minutes on board the train and ranking with *The Man Who Knew Too Much* and *The Thirty-nine Steps* as one of the best of Alfred Hitchcock's prewar thrillers. Basil Radford and Naunton Wayne add considerably to the film's entertainment value with their amusing portraits of cricket-mad Englishmen desperately trying to get the latest Test Match score from England.

GAINSBOROUGH PICTURES

Production—Edward Black
Direction—Alfred Hitchcock
Screenplay (from novel by Ethel
  Lina White)—Sidney Gilliat
  & Frank Launder
Additional dialogue—
  Alma Reville

Photography—Jack Cox
Art direction—Alec Vetchinsky,
  Maurice Carter & Albert
  Jullion
Music—Louis Levy
Editing—Alfred Roome &
  R. E. Dearing

PLAYERS: Margaret Lockwood, Michael Redgrave, Paul Lukas, Dame May Whitty, Googie Withers, Cecil Parker, Linden Travers, Naunton Wayne, Basil Radford, Mary Clare

LADY WITH A LITTLE DOG, THE (Dama s Sobachko)
                                            U.S.S.R. (1959)
Film version of Anton Chekhov's short story about the love affair between two lonely married people—a bank official and a bored young

wife who meet while on holiday in Yalta and then attempt to carry on the affair after they return to their respective partners. The film brilliantly evokes life in prerevolutionary Russia and is one of the best examples of a classic literary work being adapted successfully into cinema terms.

LENFILM STUDIOS

Direction & screenplay—
Josif Heifitz
Photography—Andrei Moskvin &
D. Meschiev

Art direction—B. Manevitch &
I. Kaplan
Music—N. Simonian
Editing—S. Derevimsky

PLAYERS: Ya Savvina, Alexei Batalov, Ala Chostakova, N. Alisova, D. Zebrov

LAST COMMAND, THE   U.S.A. (1928)

Intriguing melodrama about a Russian general who flees from his country during the October Revolution and ends up as a film extra in Hollywood. Von Sternberg clashed regularly with Emil Jannings during the shooting of the picture, but despite the difficulties Jannings still gave a remarkable performance and was named best actor of the year by the Academy of Motion Picture Arts and Sciences. Director and star were reunited two years later when von Sternberg went to Germany to direct the classic *The Blue Angel.*

FAMOUS PLAYERS–LASKY/PARAMOUNT

Direction—Josef von Sternberg
Screenplay (based on idea by
Ernst Lubitsch)—Josef von
Sternberg
Adaptation—John F. Goodrich

Photography—Bert Glennon
Set designer—Hans Dreier
Editing—William Shea
Titles—Herman J. Mankiewicz

PLAYERS: Emil Jannings, Evelyn Brent, William Powell, Nicholas Soussanin, Michael Visaroff

LAST FRONTIER, THE   U.S.A. (1955)

Army scout (Victor Mature) and U.S. Cavalry captain (Guy Madison) versus ambitious Indian-hating colonel (Robert Preston) in Wyoming during the Civil War. The theme of this little-known Anthony Mann Western is not an original one, but the dialogue is unusually distinguished and enables the actors, particularly Mature and Preston, to function well above the normal standard of performance required by the genre. Among Mann's most rewarding films of the period.

COLUMBIA

234

Production—William Fadiman
Direction—Anthony Mann
Screenplay (*based on novel by Richard Emery Roberts*)—Philip Yordan & Russell S. Hughes

Photography (*Technicolor/CinemaScope*)—William Mellor
Art direction—Robert Peterson
Music—Leigh Harline
Editing—Al Clark

PLAYERS: Victor Mature, James Whitmore, Robert Preston, Guy Madison, Anne Bancroft, Peter Whitney, Pat Hogan

LAST HURRAH, THE   U.S.A. (1958)

Sentimental account of an aging Irish-American mayor's last election campaign. Spencer Tracy is in superb form as the mayor and there's wonderful support from the veteran supporting cast of Pat O'Brien, James Gleason and Ricardo Cortez as Tracy's loyal henchmen, banker Basil Rathbone and newspaper publisher John Carradine as his opponents, Donald Crisp as a cardinal, and such old Ford regulars as Wallace Ford, Ken Curtis and Jane Darwell.

COLUMBIA

Production & direction—John Ford
Screenplay (*from novel by Edwin O'Connor*)—Frank Nugent

Photography—Charles Lawton, Jr.
Art direction—Robert Peterson
Editing—Jack Murray

PLAYERS: Spencer Tracy, Jeffrey Hunter, Dianne Foster, Pat O'Brien, Basil Rathbone, Donald Crisp, James Gleason, Edward Brophy, John Carradine, Willis Bouchey, Ricardo Cortez, Basil Ruysdael, Wallace Ford

LAST LAUGH, THE   Germany (1924)

The tragedy of an elderly hotel porter (Emil Jannings) who is suddenly relieved of his job and the uniform he prizes so highly and demoted by his employers to the humiliating position of lavatory attendant. Told without the use of a single subtitle the film was one of the most influential of German silent films and is notable both for Jannings' brilliant performance and for director Murnau's revolutionary use of camera movement.

UFA

Direction—F. W. Murnau
Screenplay—Carl Mayer
Photography—Karl Freund

Art direction—Robert Herlth, Walter Röhrig

235

PLAYERS: Emil Jannings, Mady Delschaft, Max Hiller, Emile Kurz, Hans Unterkirchen, Olaf Storm

LAST TRAIN FROM GUN HILL   U.S.A. (1958)

John Sturges' tension Western with determined marshal (Kirk Douglas) tracking down the killers of his wife and finding that one of them is the son of old friend Anthony Quinn, now a cattle baron and uncrowned king of the territory. Built in the *High Noon* and *3:10 to Yuma* mold and ranking above *Gunfight at the O.K. Corral* as Sturges' best Western of the 1950's. One of the first large-scale Paramount Westerns produced by Hal Wallis during the last two decades.

BYRNA/PARAMOUNT

Production—Hal B. Wallis
Direction—John Sturges
Screenplay—James Poe
Photography (*Technicolor/*
    VistaVision)—Charles Lang

Story—Les Crutchfield
Art direction—Hal Pereira,
    Walter Tyler
Music—Dimitri Tiomkin
Editing—Warren Low

PLAYERS: Kirk Douglas, Anthony Quinn, Carolyn Jones, Earl Holliman, Brian Hutton, Ziva Rodann, Lars Henderson

LAST WILL OF DR. MABUSE, THE

(Das Testament des Dr. Mabuse)   Germany (1932)

Fritz Lang's sequel to his own *Dr. Mabuse* (played again by Rudolph Klein-Rogge) in which the sinister master criminal, now insane and confined to an asylum, hypnotizes the hospital director into carrying on his criminal activities from the outside. The film was blatantly anti-Nazi (Lang put many of the Nazi slogans into the mouth of the madman) and was banned by Goebbels early in 1933. Lang and his scriptwriter wife Thea von Harbou, who was then a member of the Nazi party, were divorced the same year.

NERO FILM—CONSTANTIN—DEUTSCHE UNIVERSAL

Production & direction—
    Fritz Lang
Screenplay (*based on characters
    from a novel by Norbert
    Jacques*)—Fritz Lang,
    Thea von Harbou
Art direction—Karl Vollbrecht,
    Emil Hasler

Photography—
    Fritz Arno Wagner,
    Karl Vash
*Adaptation for the French
    version* (*shot simultaneously*)—
    A. René-Sti
Music—Dr. Hans Erdmann

PLAYERS: Rudolph Klein-Rogge, Oskar Beregi, Karl Meixner, Theodor Loos, Otto Wernicke, Klaus Pohl, Wera Liessem, Gustav Diesel

LAST YEAR IN MARIENBAD

(L'Année Dernière à Marienbad)   France/Italy (1961)
One of the most ambiguous and fashionable movies of the 1960's, an
Alain Resnais puzzle about the complex relationships of three people
staying in an immense baroque hotel in Bavaria. The three people
involved are a young man (Giorgio Albertazzi) who is trying to re-
new a love affair with a beautiful married woman, the woman (Delphine Seyrig) herself who remembers nothing of the affair, and a
second, older man (Sacha Pitoëff) who is possibly the woman's husband. All three are referred to only by letters of the alphabet—X, A and
M respectively. As in *Hiroshima Mon Amour* Resnais is obsessed with
the complexities of memory and flashes back and forth in time, as
well as into the future, even more ambitiously than he did in his previous film. Despite its technical brilliance and visual splendour the
picture is so complex that it quickly becomes a bore. Ultimately it
seems nothing more than a rather hollow experience in film technique.

TERRA–FILM/FILMS TAMARA/FILMS CORMORAN/PRÉCITEL/
COMO–FILMS/ARGOS–FILMS/CINÉTEL/SILVER–FILMS/CINERIZ (ROME)

Direction—Alain Resnais
Screenplay—Alain Robbe-Grillet
Photography—Sacha Vierny
Art direction—Jacques Saulnier

Music—Francis Seyrig
Editing—Henri Colpi,
    Jasmine Chasney

PLAYERS: Delphine Seyrig, Giorgio Albertazzi, Sacha Pitoëff, Pierre
Barbaud, Francoise Bertin, Luce Garcia-Ville, Héléna Kornel, Jean
Lanier

L'ATALANTE   France (1934)
Straightforward little tale about a newly-married village girl (Dita
Parlo) who travels with her bargeman husband (Jean Dasté) and a
drunken old sailor (Michel Simon) on a slow canal voyage to Paris.
The simple undramatic incidents of their daily lives make up this
minor masterpiece which, although beautifully performed, especially
by Simon, relies on its earthy lyricism, the visual power of Kaufman's
camera work and, above all, on Jean Vigo's direction for its effective-
ness. Vigo died (aged 29) shortly before the film's premiere in Paris
in 1934.

J. L. NOUNEZ-GAUMONT

Direction—Jean Vigo
Screenplay—Jean Guinée,
    Jean Vigo and
    Albert Riera

Photography—Boris Kaufman,
    Louis Berger
Art direction—Francis Jourdain
Music—Maurice Jaubert

237

LAUGHING GRAVY   U.S.A. (1931)
One of the most enjoyable and aggressive of the Laurel and Hardy sound two-reelers revolving around the unfortunate pair's attempts to conceal a dog in their bedroom against their landlord's wishes and then, when the dog is eventually discovered and thrown out into the snow, trying desperately to get him back again. Ollie suffers more than usual in this one, slipping on a bar of soap, tumbling down a chimney, and sliding off a snow-covered roof into a barrel of freezing water. Charlie Hall is the enraged landlord and the film was directed by James Horne who directed a dozen Laurel and Hardy films including *Big Business* and *Way Out West*.

HAL ROACH/METRO–GOLDWYN–MAYER
Direction—James Horne
PLAYERS: Stan Laurel and Oliver Hardy, Charles Hall

LAURA   U.S.A. (1944)
Polished mystery thriller that revolves around a beautiful and supposedly dead advertising girl (Gene Tierney) and the men suspected by a detective (Dana Andrews) of murdering her. A classic of its kind, the film runs just 88 minutes (the perfect length for this type) and is of interest for Clifton Webb's brilliant performance as an acid-tongued gossip columnist and for David Raksin's lush theme tune which became one of the most widely played standards of the 1940's.

TWENTIETH CENTURY–FOX

Production & direction— Otto Preminger	*Photography*—Joseph LaShelle
Screenplay (from novel by Vera Caspary)—Jay Dratler & Samuel Hoffenstein	*Art direction*—Lyle Wheeler & Leland Fuller
	Music—David Raksin
	Editing—Louis R. Loeffler

PLAYERS: Gene Tierney, Dana Andrews, Clifton Webb, Vincent Price, Judith Anderson

LAVENDER HILL MOB, THE   Great Britain (1951)
A bright, amusing little Ealing comedy about a meek, bowler-hatted bank clerk (Alec Guinness) who, together with artist friend Stanley Holloway and professional burglars Sidney James and Alfie Bass, robs his employers of a million pounds' worth of gold bullion. Witty, imaginative, very British and completely original. Especially memorable

L'Avventura

is the inspired climax in which Alec Guinness broadcasts misleading instructions to pursuing police cars.

EALING STUDIOS

Production—Michael Balcon   *Art direction*—William Kellner
Direction—Charles Crichton   *Music*—Georges Auric
Screenplay—T. E. B. Clarke   *Editing*—Seth Holt
Photography—Douglas Slocombe
PLAYERS: Alec Guinness, Stanley Holloway, Sidney James, Alfie Bass, Marjorie Fielding, Edie Martin, John Gregson, Arthur Hambling, Gibb McLaughlin, Sidney Tafler

L'AVVENTURA (The Adventure)   Italy/France (1960)
Masterly Antonioni film that starts with a girl's disappearance on a yachting weekend and then concentrates on the relationship that develops between the missing girl's lover (Gabriele Ferzetti) and her best girlfriend (Monica Vitti) as they continue the search across Italy. A long (145 minutes), very slow, beautifully photographed film which has the dimensions and complexities of a novel and which contains some penetrating observations on spiritual loneliness and some meanings of love. The film was booed when first shown at the Cannes Film

Festival in 1960 but brought world fame to Antonioni and is now regarded by many as a masterpiece.

CINO DEL DUCA, PRODUZIONI CINEMATOGRAFICHE EUROPEE (ROME),
SOCIETE CINEMATOGRAPHIQUE LYRE (PARIS)

Production—Luciano Perugia *Photography*—Aldo Scavarda
Direction—Michelangelo Antonioni *Art direction*—Piero Poletto
Story—Antonioni *Music*—Giovanni Fusco
Script—Antonioni, Elio Bartolini, *Editing*—Eraldo Da Roma
Tonino Guerra

PLAYERS: Gabriele Ferzetti, Monica Vitti, Lea Massari, Dominique Blanchar, Renzo Ricci, James Addams, Dorothy de Poliolo, Lelio Lutazzi

LAWLESS, THE U.S.A. (1949)

Unpretentious Losey film about the prejudices and bigotry aroused in a small California town when a young Spanish-American from the wrong side of the tracks is accused of having killed a policeman. The movie, shot on location in only 23 days, admirably captures the mood of violence and fear lurking beneath the outwardly civilized exterior of a small American community. It was produced, somewhat surprisingly, by William H. Pine and William C. Thomas, who both before and after this film were associated almost exclusively with double-feature hokum, usually starring John Payne, Rhonda Fleming and Forrest Tucker.

PARAMOUNT—A PINE–THOMAS PRODUCTION

Production—William H. Pine & *Screenplay (based on novel*
William C. Thomas *The Voice of Stephen*
Direction—Joseph Losey *Wilder)*—Geoffrey Homes (i.e.
Photography—Roy Hunt Daniel Mainwaring)
Art direction—Lewis H. Creber *Music*—Mahlon Merrick
Editing—Howard Smith

PLAYERS: Macdonald Carey, Gail Russell, Lalo Rios, John Sands, Lee Patrick, John Hoyt, Maurice Jara, Walter Reed

LAWRENCE OF ARABIA Gt. Britain (1962)

Long (221 minutes) ambitious attempt to unravel the complex and enigmatic character of T. E. Lawrence who, during his two years in Arabia in the First World War, succeeded in uniting the Arab tribes against the Turks and became known as the legendary "El Aurens." The most distinguished things about the film are the glorious desert landscapes of Freddie Young and the music score of Maurice Jarre.

240

But the film also contains splendid performances from then unknown
Peter O'Toole as Lawrence, Jack Hawkins as Allenby, Alec Guinness
as Prince Feisel, and Jose Ferrer in a minor role as the Turkish bey.
Impeccable direction by David Lean; seven Academy Awards including best film, direction, photography, music, etc.

HORIZON PICTURES/COLUMBIA

Production—Sam Spiegel
Direction—David Lean
Screenplay—Robert Bolt
Photography (*Technicolor/*
  Super Panavision)—
  F. A. Young
Production design—John Box

2nd unit photography—
  Skeets Kelly, Nicolas Roeg,
  Peter Newbrook
Art direction—John Stoll
Costumes—Phyllis Dalton
Music—Maurice Jarre
Editing—Anne V. Coates

PLAYERS: Peter O'Toole, Alec Guinness, Anthony Quinn, Jack Hawkins,
Omar Sharif, Jose Ferrer, Anthony Quayle, Claude Rains, Arthur Kennedy, Donald Wolfit

LE AMICHE (The Girl Friends)   Italy (1955)
Pre-*L'Avventura* film by Antonioni (his fifth) that explores the intricate
emotional relationships of five young women living in the rich social
circle of Turin. A slight film compared with his later work, but with
some brilliant passages and made with much of the stylish precision
that was later to make him world-famous. Photographed by Gianni
di Venanzo (the second of his five films with Antonioni) and awarded
a Silver Lion at Venice in 1955.

TRIONFALCINE

Production—Pietro Notarianni
Direction—Michelangelo Antonioni
Story (*from* Tra Donne Sole
  by Cesare Pavese)—Antonioni
Photography—Gianni di Venanzo
Art direction—Gianni Polidori

Script—Antonioni,
  Suso Cecchi D'Amico,
  Alba De Cespedes
Music—Giovanni Fusco
Editing—Eraldo Da Roma

PLAYERS: Eleanora Rossi Drago, Yvonne Furneaux, Madeleine Fischer,
Valentina Cortese, Annamaria Pancani, Gabriele Ferzetti, Franco
Fabrizi, Ettore Manni

LE BEAU SERGE   France (1958)
A young student (Jean-Claude Brialy) returns to his native village to
convalesce after illness and tries to rehabilitate his boyhood friend
(Gérard Blain) who has degenerated into a drunkard after his unhappy
marriage and the birth of his still-born mongoloid child. Former critic

Claude Chabrol's first film and the one that began the French New Wave movement of the 1960's. Bleak, well-observed rural settings; shot on location in a village near Limoges and financed with money inherited by Chabrol's wife.

AJYM

Direction, screenplay &
  dialogue—Claude Chabrol
Photography—Henri Decaë

Music—Emile Delpierre
Editing—Jacques Gaillard

PLAYERS: Gérard Blain, Jean-Claude Brialy, Michèle Meritz, Bernadette Lafont

LE BONHEUR   France (1965)

Agnès Varda's third film and among her best; a disturbing, melancholy little story of a young French carpenter (Jean-Claude Drouot) and his relationships with the two women who simultaneously bring him total happiness—his lovely wife (Claire Drouot) who has borne him two children and the mistress (Marie-France Boyer) who eventually replaces her. Beautifully done with some exquisite color work particularly in the scenes in the French countryside which are strongly reminiscent of those in Renoir's *Le Déjeuner sur l'Herbe.*

PARC FILM (MAG BODARD)

Direction, screenplay &
  dialogue—Agnès Varda
Photography (Eastmancolor)—
  Jean Rabier & Claude Beausoleil

Art direction—Hubert Montloup
Music—Mozart
Editing—Janine Verneau

PLAYERS: Jean-Claude Drouot, Claire Drouot, Marie-France Boyer, Sandrine Drouot, Olivier Drouot, Paul Vecchiali

LE CORBEAU (The Crow)   France (1943)

Henri-Georges Clouzot's first big success. A cold, sordid but frequently brilliant film about the explosive effect of a series of poison pen letters on a small French town. Very tense, often extremely unpleasant, and full of acute observation of French provincial life. Shot in 1943 during the German Occupation and remade less successfully, as *The Thirteenth Letter* by Otto Preminger in 1951.

CONTINENTAL FILMS

Direction—Henri-Georges Clouzot
Screenplay—Louis Chavance
Adaptation & dialogue—
  Clouzot & Chavance

Photography—Nicolas Hayer
Art direction—André Andreyew
Music—Tony Aubin
Editing—Marguerite Beaugé

PLAYERS: Pierre Fresnay, Pierre Larquey, Noël Roquevert, Ginette Leclerc, Micheline Francey

LE CRIME DE MONSIEUR LANGE   France (1936)

One of the most unusual and, until recently, one of the least known of Renoir's films, based on a script by Prevert (the only time that he and Renoir collaborated) and centering on a group of printing workers who take over a publishing firm when the dishonest proprietor absconds with the capital. A bold, original, realistic film, among the most socially optimistic works to come out of France in the thirties.

OBÉRON

Direction—Jean Renoir
Screenplay & dialogue (from
  idea by Renoir & Jean
  Castanier)—Jacques Prévert
Photography—Jean Bachelet

Art direction—Jean Castanier,
  Robert Gys
Music—Jean Wiener
Editing—Marguerite Renoir

PLAYERS: René Lefèvre, Jules Berry, Florelle, Nadia Sibirskaia, Sylvia Bataille, Marcel Levesque, Henri Guisol, Maurice Bacquet, Odette Talazac

LE DIABLE AU CORPS (Devil in the Flesh)   France (1947)

About an illicit and ultimately tragic love affair between a 17-year-old student and a young married woman during the absence of her husband at the front in the First World War. A basically immoral but refreshingly unsentimental work, faithfully adapted from Raymond Radiguet's novel and exceptionally well played especially by Gérard Philipe who brilliantly conveys all the agony and despair of a young boy physically in love.

TRANSCONTINENTAL FILMS

Direction—Claude Autant-Lara
Screenplay—Jean Aurenche,
  Pierre Bost
Photography—Michel Kelber

Art direction—Max Douy
Music—René Cloërec
Editing—Madeleine Gug

PLAYERS: Micheline Presle, Gérard Philipe, Denise Grey, Jean Debucourt

LE FEU FOLLET (Will o' the Wisp)   France/Italy (1963)

The last 48 hours in the life of a disillusioned ex-alcoholic intellectual (Maurice Ronet) who wanders across Paris visiting his former friends, drinking companions and mistresses in a vain attempt to find a reason for living, but finds instead that the lives they lead only emphasize his own desolation. Malle's direction is the best of his career and Ghislain Cloquet's suitably gray photography adds substantially to the mood of a film which, although deeply depressing, ranks with the very best produced in France during the 1960's. Jeanne Moreau makes a memorable ten-minute appearance as an ex-mistress who has taken to drugs.

N.E.F./ARCO FILMS (ALAIN QUEFFELEAN)

Direction, screenplay &
  dialogue (from novel by
  Drieu la Rochelle)—Louis Malle
Photography—Ghislain Cloquet
Art direction—Bernard Evein
Music—Erik Satie
Editing—Suzanne Baron

PLAYERS: Maurice Ronet, Léna Skerla, Hubert Deschamps, Jeanne Moreau, Yvonne Clech, Jean-Paul Moulinot, Ursula Kubler, Henri Serre

LE GRAND JEU   France (1933)
Lonely young Frenchman (Pierre Richard-Wilm), ruined by his love for a Paris playgirl, joins the Foreign Legion and finds in a Moroccan whore a substitute for the worthless woman who deserted him. A morbid, fatalistic, essentially novelettish picture made remarkable by its sleazy Moroccan atmosphere and the performance of Françoise Rosay as an aging trollop who spends her time telling fortunes with cards.

FILMS DE FRANCE

Production & direction—
  Jacques Feyder
Assistant director—Marcel Carné
Screenplay—Jacques Feyder &
  Charles Spaak
Photography—Harry Stradling &
  Maurice Forster
Art direction—Lazare Meerson
Music—Hans Eisler
Editing—Jacques Brillouin

PLAYERS: Françoise Rosay, Pierre Richard-Wilm, Marie Bell, Charles Vanel, Georges Pitoeff, Pierre Larquey, Pierre Labry, Camille Bert

LE JOUR SE LÈVE   France (1939)
The last of Marcel Carné's prewar masterpieces, this melancholy film presented Jean Gabin with perhaps the finest role of his career as the doomed French factory worker who barricades himself in an attic room against the police and thinks back over the events that have led him to murder and finally to suicide. Jacqueline Laurent plays the workman's sweetheart, Jules Berry is the dissipated showman who dies for seducing her, and Arletty is the showman's mistress. The despair and pessimism so prevalent in the French cinema of the 1930's was

never more in evidence than in this bleak story of human tragedy in a drab French industrial town.

VOG/SIGMA

Direction—Marcel Carné
Screenplay—Jacques Viot
Adaptation & dialogue—
  Jacques Prévert
Photography—Curt Courant

Art direction—
  Alexandre Trauner
Music—Maurice Jaubert
Editing—René Le Hénaff

PLAYERS: Jean Gabin, Arletty, Jacqueline Laurent, Jules Berry, Mady Berry, Jacques Baumer

LE MILLION   France (1931)

One of René Clair's greatest achievements, a slight, romantic musical comedy, full of wit and high spirits, about a pair of young lovers who lose a lottery ticket worth a million francs and then chase it frantically across Paris. The film is especially notable for the way in which musical use of sound is integrated with the action. It was the first of Clair's works to receive immediate and universal success.

FILMS SONORES TOBIS

Direction, screenplay &
  dialogue (based on musical
  comedy by Georges Berr and
  Guillemaud)—René Clair
Photography—Georges Perinal

Sets—Lazare Meerson
Music—Georges Van Parys,
  Armand Bernard,
  Philippe Parès
Sound editor—René Le Hénaff

PLAYERS: René Lefevre, Annabella, Louis Allibert, Wanda Greville, Paul Olivier, Odette Talazac, Constantin Stroesco, Raymond Cordy

LE MYSTERE PICASSO   France (1956)

Pablo Picasso is observed on film and in color by Henri-Georges Clouzot as he creates, with a special ink, some 15 original pictures—drawings, water colors, oil paintings—on a semitransparent canvas that is photographed in close-up from the reverse side so that the audience can follow, stroke by stroke, the growth of each picture. For the greater part of the film's 75-minute running time the screen is filled with nothing more than Picasso's images, although on two occasions Clouzot does allow the camera to observe Picasso discussing his work with the film crew. Clouzot expanded the screen into CinemaScope size to accommodate the more ambitious oil paintings and Georges Auric scored his music for each canvas individually.

FILMSONOR

Direction & screenplay—
  Henri-Georges Clouzot
*Music—*Georges Auric
PLAYER: Pablo Picasso

Photography (Eastmancolor)—
  Claude Renoir
*Editing—*Henri Colpi

LE PASSAGE DU RHIN   France (1960)
Slow, complicated and somewhat unusual war film that follows more
or less simultaneously the fortunes of two French prisoners of war—
one of whom, a journalist (Georges Rivière), escapes and makes his
way back to France where he becomes a Resistance hero, while the
other, a simple baker (Charles Aznavour), is content to serve out his
time in prison, remaining in Germany after the war where he settles
down happily with a German girl. Director Cayatte skillfully contrasts
the characters of the two men and raises some important questions
about the principles and motives of people during wartime. The film
was awarded the Grand Prix at the 1960 Cannes Film Festival.
              FRANCO LONDON FILM/LES FILMS GIBÉ (PARIS)—
              JONIA FILM (ROME)–UFA (BERLIN)

*Production manager—*Ralph Baum
*Direction—*André Cayatte
*Screenplay—*André Cayatte &
  Armand Jammot
*Adaptation—*André Cayatte &
  Pascal Jardin

*Dialogue—*Maurice Aubergé
*Photography—*Roger Fellous
*Art direction—*Robert Clavel
*Music—*Louiguy
*Editing—*Borys Lewin &
  Alix Paturel

PLAYERS: Charles Aznavour, Nicole Courcel, Georges Rivière, Cordula
Trantow, Betty Schneider, Georges Chamarat, Alfred Schieske

LE PLAISIR   France (1952)
Three Guy de Maupassant stories collected in one film by Max Ophuls.
Le Masque, a story of an old man who wears a young man's mask so
that he can dance with girls, and *Le Modèle,* the love affair between a
painter and his model, are strictly minor episodes. *La Maison Tellier,*
however, which takes up the major part of the film is a delightfully
amusing piece and tells of the awful boredom suffered by the males of
a small provincial town when Madame Tellier temporarily closes her
brothel and takes her ladies to a communion in the country. A polished,
sophisticated, very witty film beautifully performed by, among others,
Jean Gabin, Simone Simon, Daniel Gélin, Madeleine Renaud (as
Madame Tellier), and lovely Danielle Darrieux as her main attraction.
                    C.C.F.C.–STERA FILMS

Direction—Max Ophuls
Screenplay—Jacques Natanson &
    Max Ophuls
Dialogue—Jacques Natanson
Sets—Jean d'Eaubonne

Photography—Christian Matras
    & Philippe Agostini
Music—Joë Hajos &
    Maurice Yvain
Editing—Léonide Azar

PLAYERS: Claude Dauphin, Gaby Morlay, Jean Galland, Madeleine Renaud, Danielle Darrieux, Ginette Leclerc, Jean Gabin, Pierre Brasseur, Daniel Gélin, Simone Simon

LE SANG DES BÊTES   France (1949)

French documentary looks at the day-to-day workings of a Paris slaughterhouse, and observes not only the routine slaughter of animals but also the quietness and melancholy of the district in which the abbattoir is set and the surprisingly genial people who work there. Magnificent monochrome camera work; Franju's first film and one of the most impressive documentaries of the period.

FORCES ET VOIX DE FRANCE

Direction & screenplay—
    Georges Franju
Photography—Marcel Fradetal
Music—Joseph Kosma

Commentary (spoken by Nicole
    Ladmiral & Georges
    Hubert)—Jean Painlevé
Editing—André Joseph

LE SILENCE EST D'OR   France (1947)

René Clair's affectionate tribute to the makers of silent films in France is set in Paris of the early 1900's, and shows the sometimes sad, sometimes amusing love affair between an elderly French film producer and his attractive young film-struck ward. Slight, ironic, beautifully acted, it is among the best of Clair's postwar comedies. The picture was the first made by Clair in a French studio since Le Dernier Milliardaire in 1934.

PATHÉ–RKO

Direction—René Clair
Screenplay—René Clair
Photography—Armand Thirard

Sets—Léon Barsacq
Music—Georges Van Parys
Editing—Louisette Hautecoeur

PLAYERS: Maurice Chevalier, François Périer, Marcelle Derrien, Dany Robin, Robert Pizani, Raymond Cordy, Paul Oliver, Roland Armontel

LE TROU   France/Italy (1960)

Engrossing study of five prisoners and their attempts to break out of the Sante prison in Paris by tunneling through the unused basement and sewers that run beneath their cells. Directed with a quiet realism by Jacques Becker (his last film), the tension is sustained from beginning to end. Becker shot most of the film in an actual prison using several nonprofessional actors, including Raymond Meunier who was involved in some 15 escapes or attempted escapes during his 12 years in prison. A major work and, along with Robert Bresson's *Un Condamné à Morte S'Est Échappé*, the best prison film ever made.

PLAY ART/FILMSONOR (PARIS)/TITANUS (ROME)

Direction—Jacques Becker
Adaptation (*from novel by Giovanni*)— Jacques Becker, José Giovanni & Jean Aurel

Dialogue—Jacques Becker & José Giovanni
Photography—Ghislain Cloquet
Art direction—Rino Mondellini
Editing—Marguerite Renoir

PLAYERS: Michel Constantin, Jean Keraudy, Philippe Leroy, Raymond Meunier, Marc Michel

L'ECLISSE (The Eclipse)   Italy/France (1962)
Accomplished Antonioni film about the boredom and mental despair of a young woman living in an expensive suburb of Rome who drifts into an affair with a young stockbroker (Alain Delon) while searching for the elusive love that will give meaning to her life. A complex, exhausting study in desolation, not as good a film as *L'Avventura* or *La Notte* but with some finely observed Roman backgrounds and a remarkable performance from Monica Vitti in the central role.

INTEROPA FILM, CINERIZ (ROME), PARIS FILM PRODUCTIONS—
ROBERT & RAYMOND HAKIM (PARIS)

Production—Danilo Marciani
Direction—Michelangelo Antonioni
Story—Antonioni & Tonino Guerra
Script—Antonioni, Guerra, Elio Bartolini & Ottiero Ottieri

Photography—Gianni di Venanzo
Art direction—Piero Poletto
Music—Giovanni Fusco
Editing—Eraldo Da Roma

PLAYERS: Alain Delon, Monica Vitti, Francisco Rabal, Lilla Brignone, Rossana Rory, Mirella Ricciardi, Louis Seignier

LEFT-HANDED GUN, THE   U.S.A. (1958)
The life of Billy the Kid (Paul Newman) from the time he becomes involved in the Lincoln County war to his death at the hands of Marshal Pat Garrett. Directed with style by Arthur Penn (directorial debut) from a play by Gore Vidal, but despite some effective moments, usually the violent ones, too bizarre and uneven to rank with the great

Westerns. On the credit side, however, there is some fine monochrome photography by veteran cameraman J. Peverell Marley and a beautifully realized performance from John Dehner as Garrett.

WARNER BROS./A HARROLL PRODUCTION

Production—Fred Coe
Direction—Arthur Penn
Screenplay—Leslie Stevens
Photography—J. Peverell Marley

Art direction—Art Joel
Sets—William L. Kuehl
Music—Alexander Courage
Editing—Folmar Blangsted

PLAYERS: Paul Newman, Lita Milan, John Dehner, Hurd Hatfield, James Congdon, James Best, Colin Keith-Johnston, John Dierkes

LEOPARD MAN, THE   U.S.A. (1943)
Well-staged little thriller about a series of brutal murders committed by a psychopath in a small New Mexico town. Tourneur's third and last horror movie for Val Lewton is marked, like his two previous films *The Cat People* and *I Walked with a Zombie,* by ingenious use of sound and excellent photography. Based on a novel *Black Alibi* by Cornell Woolrich.

RKO RADIO

Production—Val Lewton
Direction—Jacques Tourneur
Screenplay—Ardel Wray
Additional dialogue—
        Edward Dein

Photography—Robert deGrasse
Art direction—Albert S.
        D'Agostino & Walter E. Keller
Music—Roy Webb
Editing—Mark Robson

PLAYERS: Dennis O'Keefe, Margo, Jean Brooks, Isabel Jewell, James Bell, Margaret Landry

LES AMANTS   France (1958)
Louis Malle's elegant, extremely erotic account of a love affair between a dissatisfied married woman (Jeanne Moreau) and the young man (Jean-Marc Bory) she invites to a house party, and with whom, after a single night of love, she leaves, abandoning her home, child and wealthy husband The film was updated from an 18th-century story and basically is nothing more than a study of a mature woman's gradual awakening to love, although it also contains some quite penetrating satire on the aristocratic circles in which she moves. Impeccably shot and acted and with a musical score made up entirely from Brahm's Sextet for Strings.

N.E.F.

Direction—Louis Malle
Screenplay & adaptation (from
  "*Point de Lendemain*" *by*
  Dominique Vivant)—
  Louis Malle &
  Louise de Vilmorin
Dialogue—Louise de Vilmorin
Photography—Henri Decaë
Art direction—Bernard Evein &
  Jacques Saulnier
Music—Brahms
Editing—Léonide Azar

PLAYERS: Jeanne Moreau, Alain Cuny, Jean-Marc Bory, Judith Magre, José-Luis Villalonga, Gaston Modot, Claude Mansart, Georgette Lobbe, Patricia Garcin

LES BAS-FONDS   France (1936)

Grim, somber Gorki tale about à group of derelict human beings living out a wretched existence in a cheap rooming house in prerevolutionary Russia. An undeservedly neglected Renoir movie, made during his greatest period and brilliantly acted by Jean Gabin (the first of his four pictures with Renoir) as the thief struggling to free himself from his environment and Louis Jouvet as the penniless aristocrat resigned to his degradation.

ALBATROS

Direction—Jean Renoir
Screenplay—E. Zamiatine,
  Jacques Companeez
Adaptation & dialogue—Charles
  Spaak, Jean Renoir
Photography—Fedote Bourgassof
Art direction—Eugène Lourié,
  Hugues Laurent
Music—Jean Wiener
Editing—Marguerite Renoir

PLAYERS: Jean Gabin, Louis Jouvet, Suzy Prim, Vladimir Sokolov, Robert le Vigan, Junie Astor, René Génin, Gabriello

LES BELLES-DE-NUIT   France/Italy (1952)

Gay, lighthearted frolic featuring Gerard Philipe as a discontented provincial music teacher who, in order to escape from his dreary existence, daydreams that he is performing heroic deeds in French history. Light, engaging, beautifully scored; it is reminiscent at times of Clair's silent comedies, especially in its hilarious slapstick climax in which the hero is chased back to the present from the dangers of the Stone Age.

FRANCO–LONDON FILM–RIZZOLI

Producer—Leon Carre
Direction, screenplay &
  dialogue—René Clair
Photography—Armand Thirard
Sets—Leon Barsacq
Music—Georges Van Parys
Editing—Louisette Hautecoeur,
  Denise Natot

PLAYERS: Gérard Philipe, Martine Carol, Gina Lollobrigida, Magali Vendeuil, Marylin Bufferd, Paolo Stoppa, Raymond Bussieres

Les Biches

LES BICHES   France/Italy (1968)
Triangular story set in St. Tropez and centering on the complex relationships between a wealthy lesbian photographer (Stéphane Audran), a young girl artist (Jacqueline Sassard), and the architect (Jean-Louis Trintignant) who disrupts their apparently contented affair by seducing them both. An elegant, subtle, impeccably acted film that mixes wry humor with the more dramatic and psychological aspects of its themes and which marked something of a return to form for Chabrol after a number of undistinguished potboilers. Photographed by Jean Rabier who has worked on the majority of Chabrol's films including the first four on which he operated the camera under Henri Decaë.

FILMS LA BOÉTIE (PARIS)/ALEXANDRA (ROME)

Production—André Génovès

Direction—Claude Chabrol

Screenplay—Paul Gégauff & Claude Chabrol

Photography (Eastmancolor)— Jean Rabier

Art direction—Marc Berthier

Music—Pierre Jansen

Editing—Jacques Gaillard

PLAYERS: Jean-Louis Trintignant, Jacqueline Sassard, Stéphane Audran, Nane Germon, Serge Bento, Dominique Verdi, Pierre Attal, Claude Chabrol

LES BONNES FEMMES   France/Italy (1959)
Intriguing picture about four romantic young shopgirls and their widely differing experiences as they search for love and happiness in the city of Paris. Cold and immensely assured, it is among Chabrol's best. There is much excellent observation of Parisian life along with impressive performances from Bernadette Lafont, Lucile Saint-Simon, Clothilde Joano and Stéphane Audran as the four girls. Henri Decaë was again Chabrol's cameraman, this being their fourth film together. Earlier Decaë/Chabrol collaborations: *Le Beau Serge, Les Cousins* and *A Double Tour.*

PARIS FILM PRODUCTION/PANITALIA (ROBERT & RAYMOND HAKIM)

Direction—Claude Chabrol
Screenplay & dialogue—Paul
   Gégauff & Claude Chabrol
Photography—Henri Decaë
Art direction—Jacques Mély
Music—Paul Misraki &
   Pierre Jansen
Editing—Jacques Gaillard

PLAYERS: Bernadette Lafont, Lucile Saint-Simon, Clothilde Joano, Stéphane Audran, Mario David, Ave Ninchi

LES COUSINS   France (1959)
Movie about the corruptive and also destructive influence of an amoral young Parisian student upon his innocent, hard-working young cousin from the provinces. Original and at times quite brilliant in the way it captures the atmosphere of an amoral, semi-intellectual young Parisian society, though the mood it ultimately engenders is one of melancholy.

AJYM

Direction & screenplay—
   Claude Chabrol
Dialogue—Paul Gégauff
Photography—Henri Decaë
Art direction—Jacques Saulnier
   & Bernard Evein
Music—Paul Misraki
Editing—Jacques Gaillard

PLAYERS: Jean-Claude Brialy, Gérard Blain, Claude Cerval, Juliette Mayniel

LES DISPARUS DE SAINT AGIL   France (1938)
Peculiar goings-on in a seedy French boarding school where masters disappear without trace and a group of adventurous boys become involved with a dastardly gang of counterfeiters. Expert little comedy thriller marked by the performances of Erich von Stroheim, cast against type as a kindly schoolteacher, and Michel Simon as the drunken art master. Ranks with *Emil and the Detectives* and *Hue and Cry* among the best school stories ever filmed.

Direction—Christian-Jaque   *Settings*—P. Schold
Adaptation & dialogue (from   *Music*—Henri Verdun
  novel by Pierre Véry)—   *Editors*—William Barache,
  Jean-Henri Blanchon   Claude Nicole
Photography—Marcel Lucien
PLAYERS: Aimé Clariond, Erich von Stroheim, Michel Simon, Pierre
Labry, Rene Genin, J. Derives, Armand Bernard

LES ENFANTS DU PARADIS (Children of Paradise)

France (1945)

Ambitious, 3-hour Marcel Carné masterpiece tracing the lives of the actors and thieves who inhabited the Boulevard du Temple (Paris's famous theater street) during the 1830's. Stylish flamboyant, sumptuously mounted. Perhaps no film has ever re-created a past era so convincingly or been so enriched by such a gallery of outstanding performances. Arletty plays the beautiful actress Garance around whom the story unfolds, Pierre Brasseur (as the actor Lemâitre), Louis Salou (as Count de Monteray), and Jean-Louis Barrault (as the mime Baptiste), play her lovers, and Marcel Herrand the anarchistic criminal Lacenaire. Scripted by Jacques Prévert (his last film with Carné) and filmed during the German Occupation.

S.N. PATHÉ CINÉMA

Direction—Marcel Carné   *Music*—Maurice Thiriet in col-
Screenplay—Jacques Prévert   laboration with Joseph Kosma
Photography—Roger Hubert   *Editing*—Henri Rust &
Art direction—Alexandre Trauner   Madeleine Bonin
PLAYERS: Arletty, Jean-Louis Barrault, Pierre Brasseur, Marcel Herrand,
Maria Casarès, Pierre Renoir, Etienne Decroux, Louis Salou

LES MISTONS

France (1957)

Tender movie about the lives of five French schoolboys during one summer when they leave the innocence of their childhood behind them and stumble uncertainly into adolescence. Fresh, uninhibited, shot almost entirely in the open air. The picture runs only 26 minutes and was originally intended to be the first part of a trilogy about youth, but the remaining episodes were never filmed. Truffaut went on to direct his first feature—*Les Quatre Cents Coups*—some two years later.

LES FILMS DU CARROSSE

Direction—François Truffaut
Photography—Jean Malige
Music—Maurice LeRoux
Editing—Cécile Decugis
PLAYERS: Gérard Blain, Bernadette Lafont

*Screenplay, adaptation &
dialogue (from story by
Maurice Pons)*—François
Truffaut & Maurice Pons

LES QUATRE CENTS COUPS (The 400 Blows)   France (1959)

François Truffaut's first feature movie, derived in part from memories of his own childhood, traces the sometimes amusing but mostly heartbreaking experiences of a 12-year-old boy (Jean-Pierre Léaud) as he wanders across Paris to escape from his preoccupied parents and the dismal school that represses him. A marvelously observed film, shot in the streets of Paris by Henri Decaë, that probes deeply into the heart and mind of a child and truthfully reflects all the agonies, boredom and confusion of early adolescence. Jean Constantin's music score helps make the film perhaps the only enduring masterpiece of the French New Wave movement.

LES FILMS DU CARROSSE/S.E.D.I.F.

Direction & screenplay—
François Truffaut
Adaptation—François Truffaut &
Marcel Moussy
Dialogue—Marcel Moussy

Photography—Henri Decaë
Art direction—Bernard Evein
Music—Jean Constantin
Editing—Marie-Josephe Yoyotte

PLAYERS: Jean-Pierre Léaud, Claire Maurier, Albert Rémy, Patrick Auffray, Robert Beauvais, Bouchon

LES VISITEURS DU SOIR   France (1942)

Two emissaries of the Devil—a troubadour (Alain Cuny) and his beautiful traveling companion (Arletty)—become so enmeshed in earthly love affairs that the Devil (Jules Berry) eventually turns them into stone. Beneath the stone, however, their hearts continue to beat. Through this stylish and richly designed version of a 15th-century legend, Marcel Carné paralleled the predicament of France under the German Occupation and in his final message of good triumphing over evil offered encouragement to moral resistance against the Nazis.

ANDRÉ PAULVÉ

Direction—Marcel Carné
Screenplay—Jacques Prévert &
Pierre Laroche
Photography—Roger Hubert

Art direction—Georges Wakhévitch &
Alexander Trauner
Music—Maurice Thiriet, with
Joseph Kosma
Editing—Henri Rust

PLAYERS: Alain Cuny, Arletty, Marie Déa, Jules Berry, Fernand Ledoux, Marcel Herrand

LESSON IN LOVE, A (En Lektion i Kärlek) Sweden (1954)
Adult little Swedish comedy about the marital problems of a middle-aged gynecologist (Gunnar Björnstrand) and his attractive wife (Eva Dahlbeck) who, after 16 years of marriage and two children, find themselves turning to other partners for amusement. The lightest of all Ingmar Bergman's films, witty, sophisticated, uninhibited; a comedy of morals as well as manners.

SVENSK FILMINDUSTRI

Screenplay & direction—   Art direction—P. A. Lundgren
  Ingmar Bergman   Music—Dag Wirén
Photography—Martin Bodin   Editing—Oscar Rosander

PLAYERS: Eva Dahlbeck, Gunnar Björnstrand, Yvonne Lombard, Harriet Andersson, Ake Grönberg, Olof Winnerstrand, Renée Björling, Birgitte Reimer

LETTER, THE U.S.A. (1940)
Bette Davis in one of her most accomplished roles as the disturbed, calculating planter's wife who murders her lover and then lies and schemes her way to acquittal at the ensuing trial. Stylishly directed by William Wyler (the second of his three films with Davis) and intelligently adapted by Howard Koch from Somerset Maughan's original story. A very superior example of the type of melodrama produced by Warner Bros. during the forties.

WARNER BROS.

Production—Jack L. Warner,   Photography—Tony Gaudio
  Hal B. Wallis   Art direction—Carl Jules Weyl
Direction—William Wyler   Music—Max Steiner
Screenplay—Howard Koch   Editing—George Amy

PLAYERS: Bette Davis, Herbert Marshall, James Stephenson, Frieda Inescourt, Gale Sondergaard, Bruce Lister, Cecil Kellaway

LETTER FROM AN UNKNOWN WOMAN U.S.A. (1948)
Max Ophuls' best American film: a sad, characteristic little story of the brief love affair between a 16-year-old girl (Joan Fontaine) and a philandering concert pianist (Louis Jourdan) in turn-of-the-century Vienna. The story is told in flashbacks and remembered years later by the dying woman as she writes a last letter to the pianist who has long since for-

255

gotten her. Slight and naive, but beautifully rendered; exquisite photography by German-born Franz Planer.

UNIVERSAL–INTERNATIONAL/A RAMPART PRODUCTION

Production—John Houseman
Direction—Max Ophuls
Screenplay (based on story by
  Stefan Zweig)—Howard Koch
Photography—Franz Planer

Art direction—
  Alexander Golitzen
Music—Daniele Amfitheatrof
Editing—Ted J. Kent

PLAYERS: Joan Fontaine, Louis Jourdan, Mady Christians, Marcel Journet, Art Smith, Howard Freeman, John Good, Leo P. Pessin

LETTER TO THREE WIVES, A   U.S.A. (1949)

Three small-town wives receive a joint message from a local vamp telling them that she has run off with one of their husbands. Each has sudden reason to suspect that it is her husband who is the culprit. One of the best American comedies of the late 1940's, witty, shrewd, consistently funny, with splendid work from the entire cast, but particularly from Paul Douglas as a small-time tycoon, Linda Darnell (her best role), as his calculating wife, and Ann Sothern as the wife making a name for herself by writing for commercial radio. Joe Mankiewicz's razor-sharp script, which won him an Academy Award, contains some often biting satire on American institutions and illusions.

TWENTIETH CENTURY–FOX

Production—Sol C. Siegel
Direction & screenplay (from the
  Cosmopolitan Magazine story
  by John Klemper, adapted by
  Vera Caspary)—
  Joe Mankiewicz

Photography—Arthur Miller
Art direction—Lyle Wheeler,
  J. Russell Spencer
Music—Alfred Newman
Editing—J. Watson Webb, Jr.

PLAYERS: Jeanne Crain, Linda Darnell, Ann Sothern, Kirk Douglas, Paul Douglas, Barbara Lawrence, Jeffrey Lynn, Connie Gilchrist, Thelma Ritter

LIBELED LADY   U.S.A. (1936)

Brisk, wittily scripted Jack Conway movie with newspaper editor Spencer Tracy, fiancée Jean Harlow, millionairess Myrna Loy, and lawyer William Powell involved in a $5 million libel suit. One of the most amiable American comedies of the 1930's. The playing of the star quartet, particularly wisecracking Jean Harlow, is a revelation.

METRO–GOLDWYN–MAYER

Production—
Lawrence Weingarten
*Direction—*Jack Conway
*Photography—*Norbert Brodine
*Art direction—*Cedric Gibbons
*Music—*William Axt

*Screenplay (based on story by
Wallace Sullivan)—*Howard
Emmett Rogers & George
Oppenheimer
*Editing—*Frederick Y. Smith

PLAYERS: Spencer Tracy, Jean Harlow, William Powell, Myrna Loy, Walter Connolly, Charley Grapewin, Cora Witherspoon

LIFE OF EMILE ZOLA, THE   U.S.A. (1937)
The Warner Bros. lengthy Oscar-winning tribute to Emile Zola (Paul Muni) is based mainly on the crusading novelist's connection with Captain Alfred Dreyfus, a French Army officer who, largely because of anti-Semitic feeling, was unjustly accused of treason and condemned to imprisonment on Devil's Island. A superb performance from Muni, and Joseph Schildkraut as Dreyfus received an Academy Award as best supporting actor of the year. The film was the second in the series of distinguished biographies made by William Dieterle during the thirties and early forties. Others: *The Story of Louis Pasteur, Juarez, Dr. Ehrlich's Magic Bullet, This Man Reuter.*
WARNER BROS.

*Production—*Hal B. Wallis
*Direction—*William Dieterle
*Screenplay—*Heinz Herald, Geza
Herczeg & Norman Reilly
Raine

*Story—*Heinz Herald &
Geza Herczeg
*Photography—*Tony Gaudio
*Art direction—*Anton Grot
*Music—*Max Steiner
*Editing—*Warren Low

PLAYERS: Paul Muni, Gloria Holden, Joseph Schildkraut, Gale Sondergaard, Dickie Moore, Rolla Gourvitch, Donald Crisp, Grant Mitchell

LILI   U.S.A. (1953)
Appealing movie derived from a Paul Gallico tale about a little orphan girl (Leslie Caron) who attaches herself to a traveling carnival where she falls in love with a conjuror and is herself loved by a crippled puppeteer (Mel Ferrer) who speaks to her through his marionettes. The fantasy dream ballet in which Miss Caron dances with life-sized puppets is delightful. Bronislau Kaper won an Academy Award for his music score which included the song "Hi-Lili, Hi-Lo."
METRO–GOLDWYN–MAYER

*Production—*Edwin H. Knopf   *Direction—*Charles Walters

Screenplay—Helen Deutsch
Photography (Technicolor)—
  Robert Planck
Music—Bronislau Kaper
Art direction—Cedric Gibbons,
  Paul Groesse
Choreography—Charles Walters
Editing—Ferris Webster
PLAYERS: Leslie Caron, Mel Ferrer, Jean Pierre Aumont, Zsa Zsa Gabor,
Kurt Kasznar, Amanda Blake

LIMELIGHT   U.S.A. (1952)

Chaplin's last American film is a tender, nostalgic story of an elderly music-hall comedian who saves a young dancer from suicide, nurses her back to health and later helps her to become a successful ballerina. A major work of art, not quite a masterpiece but full of pathos and deep insight into human character, and containing superb performances from Chaplin himself as the faded comic and newcomer Claire Bloom as the young dancer. The film brilliantly captures the atmosphere of London's music halls at the turn of the century and reaches the heights in the last fifteen minutes when Chaplin and Buster Keaton combine in a brilliant knockabout duet.

UNITED ARTISTS

Production, direction, original
  story & screenplay—
  Charles Chaplin
Photography—Karl Struss
Art direction—Eugene Lourie
Music—Charles Chaplin
Editing—Joe Inge
Assistant director—
  Robert Aldrich

PLAYERS: Charles Chaplin, Claire Bloom, Sydney Chaplin, Nigel Bruce,
Norman Lloyd, Buster Keaton, Marjorie Bennett

LINEUP, THE   U.S.A. (1958)

Minor thriller with Eli Wallach and Robert Keith as a couple of criminals involved in a dope-smuggling racket in San Francisco. The film is generally undistinguished, but the final car chase is a real hair-raiser and every bit as good as the more famous Steve McQueen chase in *Bullitt* ten years later. Warner Anderson and Emile Meyer lead the cops and the script is by Stirling Silliphant who later wrote the Academy Award-winning *In the Heat of the Night*.

COLUMBIA/A FRANK COOPER PRODUCTION

Production—Jaime Del Valle
Direction—Don Siegel
Screenplay (based on TV series
  "The Lineup" by Lawrence L.
  Klee)—Stirling Silliphant
Photography—Hal Mohr
Art direction—Ross Bellah
Musical direction—
  Mischa Bakaleinikoff
Editing—Al Clark

PLAYERS: Eli Wallach, Robert Keith, Warner Anderson, Richard Jaeckel, Mary LaRoche, William Leslie, Emile Meyer, Marshall Reed, Cheryl Callaway

LITTLE CAESAR   U.S.A. (1930)
Tough gangster melodrama traces the rise and fall of East Side Italian racketeer Rico Bandello (Edward G. Robinson). Although not the first of the gangster pictures (Von Sternberg's *Underworld* and other lesser-known pictures had appeared in the late 1920's), the film was the first to become a financial success and was succeeded by literally hundreds of imitators during the 1930's. Scripted by Francis Faragoh from a novel by W. R. Burnett, whose later books *High Sierra* (Raoul Walsh, 1941) and *The Asphalt Jungle* (John Huston, 1950) were also filmed with distinction by Hollywood.

WARNER BROS.

Production—Hal B. Wallis   Photography—Tony Gaudio
Direction—Mervyn LeRoy   Art direction—Anton Grot
Screenplay—Francis Faragoh
PLAYERS: Edward G. Robinson, Douglas Fairbanks Jr., William Collier Jr., Ralph Ince, Glenda Farrell, George Stone, Thomas Jackson

LITTLE FOXES, THE   U.S.A. (1941)
Based on the Broadway stage success by Lillian Hellman (who adapted her play into screen terms), this stylish William Wyler film traces the breakdown of a decadent family living in the deep South at the turn of the century. Bette Davis is at the top of her form as the scheming vixen Regina Giddens, and never more so than in the famous scene when she deliberately leaves husband Herbert Marshall to die of a heart attack. Excellent period atmosphere and fine lensing by Gregg Toland (this was the sixth of his seven films with William Wyler). Wyler/Toland movies: *These Three, Come and Get It, Dead End, Wuthering Heights, The Westerner, The Little Foxes, The Best Years of Our Lives.*

SAMUEL GOLDWYN/RKO RADIO

Production—Samuel Goldwyn   Additional scenes and dialogue—
Direction—William Wyler   Dorothy Parker, Arthur Kober
Screenplay—Lillian Hellman   & Alan Campbell
Photography—Gregg Toland   Art direction—Stephen Goosson
Music—Meredith Willson   Editing—Daniel Mandell
PLAYERS: Bette Davis, Herbert Marshall, Teresa Wright, Richard Carlson, Patricia Collinge, Dan Duryea, Charles Dingle, Carl Benton Reid

LITTLE FUGITIVE, THE U.S.A. (1953)

Engaging low-budget, 75-minute movie made independently by three young Americans—Ray Ashley, Morris Engel and Ruth Orkin. The film is about the adventures of a 6-year-old boy who, believing that he has killed his brother in an accident, runs away from home and spends 24 hours at the gaudy fun fair of Coney Island. Richie Andrusco appeared as the boy.

UNITED ARTISTS

Production—Morris Engel, Ray Ashley
Direction & screenplay—Ray Ashley, Morris Engel, Ruth Orkin

Photography—Morris Engel
Music—Eddy Manson
Editing—Ruth Orkin, Lester Troob

PLAYERS: Richie Andrusco, Ricky Brewster, Winifred Cushing, Jay Williams, Will Lee, Charlie Moss, Tommy de Canio

LITTLE WOMEN U.S.A. (1933)

Katharine Hepburn as the .tomboyish Jo and Joan Bennett (Amy), Frances Dee (Meg) and Jean Parker (Beth) as her three sisters in George Cukor's faithful and highly satisfying transcription of Louisa May Alcott's sentimental tale of family life in rural America during the 1860's. A good script, commendable period atmosphere, and delightful playing particularly from Hepburn. Remade by Mervyn LeRoy in 1949 with June Allyson, Elizabeth Taylor, Janet Leigh and Margaret O'Brien in the leading roles.

RKO RADIO

Executive producer—Merian C. Cooper
Associate producer—Kenneth MacGowan
Direction—George Cukor

Screenplay—Sarah Y. Mason & Victor Heerman
Photography—Henry Gerrard
Art direction—Van Nest Polglase
Music direction—Max Steiner
Editing—Jack Kitchin

PLAYERS: Katharine Hepburn, Frances Dee, Jean Parker, Joan Bennett, Edna May Oliver, Paul Lukas, Douglass Montgomery

LIVES OF A BENGAL LANCER U.S.A. (1935)

Gary Cooper, Franchot Tone and Richard Cromwell as three officers in the 41st Bengal Lancers involved in heroic adventure on India's North-West Frontier. Notable Indian location work and several impressive action sequences by Henry Hathaway. Sir Guy Standing and C. Aubrey Smith are two hard-bitten colonels and Douglas Dumbrille is a treacherous border chieftain. One of the most enjoyable spectaculars ever made in Hollywood.

PARAMOUNT

Production—Louis D. Lighton
Direction—Henry Hathaway
Screenplay—Waldemar Young, John L. Balderston, Achmed Abdullah
Photography—Charles Lang

Adaptation (from book by Francis Yeats-Brown)—Grover Jones, William Slavens McNutt
Art direction—Hans Dreier, Roland Anderson
Editing—Ellsworth Hoagland

PLAYERS: Gary Cooper, Franchot Tone, Richard Cromwell, Sir Guy Standing, Kathleen Burke, C. Aubrey Smith, Colin Tapley, Monte Blue, Akim Tamiroff, Douglas Dumbrille

LIVING (Ikiru)   Japan (1952)
Akira Kurosawa film about the last days of an elderly Tokyo businessman who, after learning that he is dying of cancer, attempts to make up for the waste of his earlier life by persuading the city authorities to transform a slum area into a children's playground. Very long (nearly 2½ hours), sometimes slow, but impeccably directed and acted especially by Takashi Shimura who captures all of the dying man's loneliness and nostalgia in his remarkable performance. After *Rashomon* and *Seven Samurai*, Kurosawa's greatest film.

TOHO

Production—Shojiro Motoki
Direction—Akira Kurosawa
Screenplay—Shinobu Hashimoto, Hideo Oguni, Akira Kurosawa

Photography—Asakazu Nakai
Music—Fumio Hayasaka
Art direction—So Matsuyama

PLAYERS: Takashi Shimura, Nobuo Kaneko, Kyoko Seki, Makoto Kabori, Kumeko Urabe, Yoshie Minami

LIVING DESERT, THE   U.S.A. (1953)
The first of Walt Disney's full-length "True Life Adventures" was photographed in different areas of the Great American Desert and shows, often in revealing close-up, the innumerable animals and insects which live there. A vulgar music score and commentary mar an otherwise absorbing documentary. Among the highlights: a mating battle between two male tortoises for a female, the courtship of a tarantula, and a battle between a red-tailed hawk and a rattlesnake.

WALT DISNEY PRODUCTIONS

261

Production—Walt Disney
Direction—James Algar
Script—James Algar, Winston
  Hibler, Ted Sears
Narration—Winston Hibler

Photography (*print by Techni-
  color*)—N. Paul Kenworthy, Jr.,
  Robert H. Crandall
Musical direction—Paul Smith
Editing—Norman Palmer

LODGER, THE   Great Britain (1926)
Hitchcock's first major film, adapted from Marie Belloc Lowndes' fam-
ous novel, and featuring Ivor Novello as the young lodger suspected by
his landlady of being the notorious Jack the Ripper. A tense, imag-
inative, occasionally overextravagant piece of work, historically im-
portant as Hitchcock's first film in the thriller genre.
                            GAINSBOROUGH
Production—Michael Balcon
Direction—Alfred Hitchcock
Screenplay—Alfred Hitchcock,
  Eliot Stannard
Photography—Baron Ventimiglia

Art direction—C. Wilfred Arnold,
  Bertram Evans
Editing & subtitles—
  Ivor Montague

PLAYERS: Ivor Novello, June, Malcolm Keen, Arthur Chesney, Marie
Ault

LODGER, THE   U.S.A. (1944)
Gothic remake with Laird Cregar giving perhaps the best performance
of his tragically short career as the mass murderer and Cedric Hard-
wicke and Sara Allgood playing the old couple who unknowingly har-
bor him in their London boardinghouse. Excellent re-creation of a
Victorian East End by designers James Basevi and John Ewing and
atmospheric camera work by Lucien Ballard. Superior in every way to
its predecessor and continues to improve with age.
                      TWENTIETH CENTURY–FOX
Production—Robert Bassler
Direction—John Brahm
Screenplay (*from novel by Marie
  Belloc-Lowndes*)—Barre
  Lyndon

Photography—Lucien Ballard
Art direction—James Basevi &
  John Ewing
Music—Hugo Friedhofer
Editing—J. Watson Webb

PLAYERS: Laird Cregar, Merle Oberon, George Sanders, Cedric Hardwicke, Sara Allgood, Aubrey Mather, Queenie Leonard, Doris Lloyd

LOLA   France/Italy (1960)
Light, bittersweet little fantasy revolving around the life of a young
cabaret dancer (Anouk Aimée) as she waits for the return of the lover

Lola

who seven years earlier had left her with a child. The film concentrates
on revealing the character of the dancer through the people who continually cross and recross her path—a former lover, an American sailor,
a widow and her young daughter, etc.—and depends more on its evocation of mood and atmosphere than its story. Directed with great style
by Jacques Demy whose first feature this was and who shot most of the
film in his home town of Nantes. A complex work despite its fairy-tale
quality and beautifully photographed by Raoul Coutard.

ROME–PARIS FILMS (CARLO PONTI & GEORGES BEAUREGARD)

Direction, screenplay & dialogue —Jacques Demy	*Art direction*—Bernard Evein
	Music—Michel Legrand
Photography—Raoul Coutard	*Editing*—Anne-Marie Cotret

PLAYERS: Anouk Aimée, Marc Michel, Jacques Harden, Alan Scott,
Elina Labourdette

LOLA MONTÈS   France/Germany (1955)
The rise and fall of a notorious 19th-century adventuress (Martine
Carol) from the time of her love affairs with Franz Liszt and the King
of Bavaria to her final degradation as a circus sideshow attraction. Told
in flashback by the circus ringmaster (Peter Ustinov), the film was Max
Ophuls' last and most ambitious work and demonstrates to the full his

technical virtuosity and taste for lavish costumes and décor. It was, however, a commercial disaster (it cost over 650-million francs to produce) and suffered from excessive cutting, being reduced from its original 140 minutes to a mere 110.

GAMMA FILMS–FLORIDA (PARIS)AND OSKA FILMS (MUNICH)

Direction—Max Ophuls
Screenplay (based on La Vie
    Extraordinaire de Lola Montes
    by Cecil St. Laurent)—Max
    Ophuls, Annette Wademant &
    Franz Geiger
Dialogue—Jacques Natanson

Photography (Eastmancolor/
    CinemaScope)—Christian
    Matras
Art direction—Jean d'Eaubonne,
    Willy Schatz
Music—Georges Auric
Editing—Madeleine Gug

PLAYERS: Martine Carol, Peter Ustinov, Anton Walbrook, Ivan Desny, Will Quadflieg, Oscar Werner, Lise Delamare, Henri Guisol

LONELINESS OF THE LONG DISTANCE RUNNER, THE
Gt. Britain (1962)

Flashback examination of the unhappy life of a rebellious borstal boy who recollects his past experiences while training for a cross-country race with the champion of a neighboring public school. Despite the overfamiliar industrial backgrounds (in this case the poorer quarters of Nottingham) and the equally familiar "anger against society" theme, the film is technically an exciting one and comes closest of all Britain's realistic pictures of the early 1960's to the productions of the French New Wave. Michael Redgrave plays the smug, pipe-smoking borstal governor and Tom Courtenay appears as the hero who makes his ultimate defiant gesture against society by deliberately throwing away the race he has won so easily. John Addison's ironic music score continually emphasizes the hymn "Jerusalem."

A WOODFALL FILM

Production & direction—
    Tony Richardson
*Screenplay (adapted from his
    short story)*—Alan Sillitoe
Photography—Walter Lassally

Production design—Alan Kaplan
Art direction—Ted Marshall
Music—John Addison
Editing—Anthony Gibbs

PLAYERS: Tom Courtenay, Michael Redgrave, Avis Bunnage, James Bolam, Dervis Ward, Topsy Jane, Alec McCowen, James Cairncross

LONG PANTS
U.S.A. (1927)

Shy small-town boy Harry Langdon becomes involved with some crooks and a beautiful lady gangster (Alma Bennett) before returning home to the safer and more relaxing arms of the girl next door. Langdon was at his peak here although shortly afterwards his career began a tragic decline, due partly to his splitting with writer/director Frank Capra who was associated with Langdon on both of his earlier feature comedies—*Tramp, Tramp, Tramp* (as writer only) and *The Strong Man* (as writer and director).

HARRY LANGDON CORPORATION/FIRST NATIONAL

Direction—Frank Capra   *Screenplay*—Arthur Ripley
PLAYERS: Harry Langdon, Alan Roscoe, Gladys Brockwell, Priscilla Bonner, Alma Bennett, Betty Francisco

LONG VOYAGE HOME, THE   U.S.A. (1940)
Somber, somewhat neglected John Ford film about the lives of the crew of a British tramp steamer carrying munitions across the Atlantic in wartime. Positively played by the Ford regulars—Wayne, Mitchell, Fitzgerald, etc.—but distinguished mainly by the deep focus images of Gregg Toland who was at his peak during this period and who was unlucky not to win the 1940 Academy Award for his work both on this film and on Ford's *The Grapes of Wrath* which was released the same year.

WANGER—UNITED ARTISTS

Production—Walter Wanger   *Screenplay* (*from "The Moon of*
Direction—John Ford   *the Caribbees," "In the Zone,"*
Photography—Gregg Toland   *"Bound East for Cardiff," &*
Art direction—James Basevi   *"The Long Voyage Home,"*
Music—Richard Hageman   *four one-act plays by Eugene*
Editing—Sherman Todd   *O'Neill*)—Dudley Nichols
PLAYERS: Thomas Mitchell, John Wayne, Ian Hunter, Barry Fitzgerald, Wilfrid Lawson, Mildred Natwick, John Qualen, Ward Bond

LOOK BACK IN ANGER   Gt. Britain (1959)
Tony Richardson's first feature, an adaptation by Nigel Kneale and John Osborne of Osborne's famous stage play about the protesting Jimmy Porter (Richard Burton) who rebels loudly against the injustices of the world, taking out much of his anger on his long-suffering wife (Mary Ure) whose upper-middle-class background drives him into a frenzy. Not as effective on screen as it was on the stage and, in retrospect, much ado about nothing really, but important because, along with *Room at the Top*, it represented the first of Britain's new realism

of the late 1950's and because it undoubtedly reflected the mood of its generation. The one improvement it did make on the original was in its introduction of Ma Tanner (beautifully played by Edith Evans), an old lady who sets Jimmy up with his candy stall in a London market and a character who is only mentioned in the play and never seen.

A WOODFALL PRODUCTION

Production—Gordon L. T. Scott
Executive producer—
  Harry Saltzman
Direction—Tony Richardson
Screenplay—Nigel Kneale

Additional dialogue—
  John Osborne
Photography—Oswald Morris
Art direction—Peter Glazier
Music—Chris Barber & his band
Editing—Richard Best

PLAYERS: Richard Burton, Claire Bloom, Mary Ure, Edith Evans, Gary Raymond, Glen Byam Shaw, Phyllis Neilson-Terry, Donald Pleasance

LOS OLVIDADOS (The Young and the Damned)   Mexico (1950)
The film that marked the return of Luis Buñuel to the screen after twenty years of obscurity; a sordid, realistic story about two delinquent boys who are corrupted and then destroyed by the Mexican slums in which they live. The film is compassionate, deeply felt and uncompromising, and ends bleakly on a note of utter despair. Shot on location in four weeks by Gabriel Figueroa whose sharp photography perfectly evokes the feeling of the hot, dusty slums of Mexico City.

ULTRAMAR FILMS (OSCAR DANCIGERS)

Direction—Luis Buñuel
Screenplay—Luis Buñuel & Luis
  Alcoriza
Photography—Gabriel Figueroa

Art direction—Edward Fitzgerald
Music (*on themes by Gustova
  Pitaluga*)—Rodolfo Halffter
Editing—Carlos Savage

PLAYERS: Estela Inda, Miguel Inclán, Alfonso Mejía, Roberto Cobo, Hector López Portillo, Salvador Quiros

LOST HORIZON   U.S.A. (1937)
Expensive film version of James Hilton's fantasy novel about a young Englishman (Ronald Colman) who discovers an idyllic Utopian community hidden away in the Himalayas in Tibet. Uneven and often pretentious, although Stephen Goosson's Shangri-La set designs are still impressive and Sam Jaffe's ancient High Lama remains an interesting portrayal. Directed by Frank Capra as a break from his successful social comedies of the 1930's.

COLUMBIA

Production & direction—   *Art direction—*Stephen Goosson
   Frank Capra   *Music—*Dimitri Tiomkin
*Screenplay—*Robert Riskin   *Editing—*Gene Havlick &
*Photography—*Joseph Walker   Gene Milford
PLAYERS: Ronald Colman, Edward Everett Horton, H. B. Warner, Jane
Wyatt, Sam Jaffe, Margo, John Howard, Thomas Mitchell, Isabel
Jewell

LOST WEEKEND, THE   U.S.A. (1945)
Three agonizing days in the life of a dipsomaniac novelist as he pours
out his shattered dreams to a New York bartender and drinks himself
into a horrifying bout of the DTs. Despite his unlikely redemption in
the last reel, a courageous and hard-hitting picture that was the first
to treat the subject of alcoholism seriously and which drew from Ray
Milland (Academy Award) the most efficient performance of his act-
ing career. Oscars also went to Billy Wilder for his direction and to
Wilder and Charles Brackett for their screenplay. Realistic, drab New
York exteriors by John Seitz (his third film for Wilder) and skillful
supporting cameos from Howard da Silva as the bartender and Frank
Faylen as a sinister male nurse.
                        PARAMOUNT
*Production—*Charles Brackett   *Photography—*John F. Seitz
*Direction—*Billy Wilder   *Art direction—*Hans Dreier &
Screenplay (based on novel   Earl Hedrick
   by Charles R. Jackson)—   *Music—*Miklos Rozsa
   Charles Brackett &   *Musical direction—*Victor Young
   Billy Wilder   *Editing—*Doane Harrison
PLAYERS: Ray Milland, Jane Wyman, Howard da Silva, Philip Terry,
Doris Dowling, Frank Faylen, Mary Young, Lillian Fontaine

LOUISIANA STORY   U.S.A. (1948)
Documentary director Robert Flaherty's last film, a slow-moving,
tender account of the experiences of a 13-year-old Cajun boy as he
paddles his canoe through the bayou swamps hunting and fishing and
observing the crew of a huge derrick as they begin drilling for oil. A
quiet little film, shot in its entirety in the bayou country of southern
Louisiana and scored by Virgil Thompson whose lovely music is built
up from the folk tunes of the district. The cameraman was British-born
Richard Leacock, brother of director Philip Leacock.
              ROBERT J. FLAHERTY PRODS. INC.

Production associates—   Screenplay—Robert & Frances
  Richard Leacock &   Flaherty
  Helen Van Dongen   Photography—Richard Leacock
Direction—Robert J. Flaherty   Music—Virgil Thompson
                                  Editing—Helen Van Dongen
PLAYERS: Joseph Boudreaux, Lionel le Blanc, Frank Hardy, Mrs. E. Bienvenu

LOVE ME TONIGHT   U.S.A. (1932)
Advanced Hollywood musical of the early 1930's with Maurice Chevalier as a poor Parisian tailor masquerading as a prince and winning once again the hand of Ruritanian princess Jeanette MacDonald. The director on this occasion, however, was not Lubitsch (*The Love Parade, One Hour with You*, etc.) but Rouben Mamoulian who, although influenced by the wit and gloss of the Lubitsch romances, and also by the work of René Clair, brought his own original style to the film, particularly in his use of sound and rhythmic dialogue. The Rodgers and Hart score included such standards as "Mimi," "Lover," and "Isn't It Romantic."

PARAMOUNT

Production & direction—   Waldemar Young &
  Rouben Mamoulian   George Marion Jr.
Screenplay (based on play   Photography—Victor Milner
  by Leopold Marchand &   Art direction—Hans Dreier
  Paul Armont)—   Songs—Richard Rodgers &
  Samuel Hoffenstein,   Lorenz Hart
PLAYERS: Maurice Chevalier, Jeanette MacDonald, Myrna Loy, Charlie Ruggles, Charles Butterworth, C. Aubrey Smith

LOVE OF JEANNE NEY, THE
  (Die Liebe der Jeanne Ney)   Germany (1927)
German spy melodrama with Brigitte Helm as blind girl involved in a web of crime and political intrigue in revolutionary Russia. Not Pabst's best silent film but of interest historically for its elaborate cutting and Fritz Arno Wagner's camera work. This was the first time that Wagner had worked with Pabst. They later collaborated on such famous pictures as *Westfront 1918, Kameradschaft* and *Die Dreigroschenoper*.

UFA

Direction—G. W. Pabst   Art direction—Otto Hunte

268

Screenplay (from novel by
  Ehrenburg)—Ilya Ehrenburg,
  Ladislaus Vayda
Photography—
  Fritz Arno Wagner,
  Walter Robert Lach
PLAYERS: Edith Jehanne, Brigitte Helm, Hertha von Walther, Uno Henning, Fritz Rasp, Adolf Edgar Licho, Eugen Jensen, Hans Jaray, Wladimir Sokoloff, Siegfried Arno

LOVE PARADE, THE
U.S.A. (1929)

Stylish, witty Hollywood musical with Maurice Chevalier and Jeanette MacDonald teamed for the first time under Lubitsch's direction and performing such Victor Schertzinger songs as "Dream Love," "My Love Parade," and "Let's Be Common." Lubitsch's first talkie, and, because of his imaginative use of the sound track and camera, the most advanced of the early musicals. Lush interiors by Paramount's ace designer Hans Dreier.

PARAMOUNT

Direction—Ernst Lubitsch
Screenplay (from play The
  Prince Consort *by Leon*
  Xanrof & Jules Chancel)—
  Ernest Vajda & Guy Bolton
Photography—Victor Milner
Art direction—Hans Dreier
Music—Victor Schertzinger
Lyrics—Clifford Grey
Editing—Merrill White
PLAYERS: Maurice Chevalier, Jeanette MacDonald, Lupino Lane, Lillian Roth, E. H. Calvert, Eugene Pallette, Andre Cheron

LUST FOR LIFE
U.S.A. (1956)

Imaginative and visually rewarding attempt to adapt Irving Stone's biography of Van Gogh to the screen. The paintings themselves (beautifully reproduced in Metrocolor) inevitably dominate the film, but the performances of Kirk Douglas (Van Gogh) and Anthony Quinn (Gauguin), and the splendid photography of Freddie Young and Russell Harlan are also very much on the credit side.

METRO—GOLDWYN—MAYER

Production—John Houseman
Direction—Vincente Minnelli
Screenplay—Norman Corwin
Photography (Metrocolor/
  CinemaScope)—Frederick A.
  Young & Russell Harlan
Art direction—Cedric Gibbons,
  Preston Ames &
  Hans Peters
Music—Miklos Rozsa
Editing—Adrienne Fazan
PLAYERS: Kirk Douglas, Anthony Quinn, James Donald, Pamela Brown, Everett Sloane, Niall MacGuinnis, Noel Purcell, Henry Daniell

M Germany (1931)

Legendary Fritz Lang crime movie (his first sound film) that gave Peter Lorre the best role of his early career as the mentally disturbed child murderer Hans Beckert who is hunted through the streets of Dusseldorf by police and criminals alike. A brilliantly directed thriller that makes an intelligent and compassionate attempt to examine the inner workings of a deranged mind. The film, based on the real-life Peter Kurten, a child murderer known as "The Vampire of Dusseldorf," was shot in six weeks in a temporary studio outside Berlin. Sound was used with great effect, especially during the murder sequences which were accompanied by the whistling of the opening bars of "In the Hall of the Mountain King" from *Peer Gynt*.

NERO FILM A.–G.–VER. STAR FILM G.M.B.H.

Production—Seymour Nebenzal
Direction—Fritz Lang
Screenplay—Fritz Lang,
 Thea von Harbou
Photography—
 Fritz Arno Wagner,
 Gustav Rathje

Art direction—Karl Vollbrecht,
 Emil Hasler
Music (*excerpts from
 Peer Gynt*)—Edvard Greig

PLAYERS: Peter Lorre, Otto Wernicke, Gustav Gründgens, Theo Lingen, Theodor Loos, Georg John, Ellen Widmann, Inge Landgut

M U.S.A. (1951)

Joseph Losey's unjustly neglected remake, updated and transferred to a modern American city but otherwise closely modeled on Lang's original. David Wayne (an excellent performance) plays the psychopath, Howard da Silva the chief of police, and Luther Adler and Martin Gabel are the underworld leaders. Shot in 20 days, partly on location in Los Angeles. Robert Aldrich also worked on *The Prowler*, again for Losey, and on *Limelight* for Chaplin.

COLUMBIA

Production—Seymour Nebenzal
Direction—Joseph Losey
Screenplay (*based on original
 script by Thea von Harbou
 & Fritz Lang*)—Norman Reilly
 Raine, Leo Katcher

Assistant director—Robert Aldrich
Additional dialogue—Waldo Salt
Photography—Ernest Laszlo
Art direction—Martin Obzina
Music—Michel Michelet
Editing—Edward Mann

PLAYERS: David Wayne, Howard da Silva, Luther Adler, Martin Gabel, Steve Brodie, Raymond Burr, Glenn Anders, Karen Morley

MADAME DE   France/Italy (1953)

Slight, bitter-sweet tale, set in 19th-century Paris, revolving around a pair of earrings that pass from husband to wife, lover to mistress and finally return to their original owner. Elegant, witty, beautifully designed. Danielle Darrieux plays the wife, Charles Boyer the husband, and Vittorio de Sica the lover.

FRANCO–LONDON FILMS–FILM INDUS-RIZZOLI

Director–Max Ophuls
Director of production– Ralph Baum
Screenplay (based on novel Madame de . . . *by Louise de Vilmorin)*–Marcel Achard, Max Ophuls & Annette Wademant

Dialogue–Marcel Achard
Photography–Christian Matras
Sets–Jean d'Eaubonne
Music–Oscar Straus & Georges Van Parys
Editing–Borys Lewin

PLAYERS: Danielle Darrieux, Charles Boyer, Vittorio de Sica, Jean Debucourt, Lia de Lea, Mireille Perrey, Jean Galland, M. Peyret

MADAME DUBARRY   Germany (1919)

Ambitious, large-scale German production about the life of the famous 18th-century French courtesan. The film, which was renamed *Passion* in the United States, established the international reputation of director Ernst Lubitsch and was the first German picture to be shown abroad after the First World War. Pola Negri, later to become one of Hollywood's biggest stars, played DuBarry and Emil Jannings appeared as Louis XV. Scriptwriter Hans Kraly later followed Lubitsch to America where he worked with him on such sophisticated comedies as *Forbidden Paradise* and *Kiss Me Again*.

UNION–UFA

Direction–Ernst Lubitsch
Screenplay–Fred Orbing & Hans Kraly
Photography–Theodor Sparkuhl

Sets–Karl Machus & Kurt Richter
Costumes–Ali Hubert
Technical advisor– Kurt Waschneck

PLAYERS: Pola Negri, Emil Jannings, Harry Liedtke, Eduard von Winterstein, Reinhold Schünzel, Elsa Berna, Frederich Immler, Gustabe Czimeg, Carl Platen

MAGNIFICENT AMBERSONS, THE   U.S.A. (1942)

The slow decline of a wealthy Midwestern family during the early years of the 20th century when the rapidly expanding automobile age was bringing prosperity to a new industrial middle class. Overshadowed by *Citizen Kane,* made a year earlier, but a remarkable film by any standards and containing some of Welles' most imaginative work, e.g. the brilliant scene setting in a small Indianapolis town, the sleigh ride in the snow and the famous ball sequence in the Amberson mansion. The film runs 88 minutes, although the last three reels (some 45 minutes screen time) were deleted by the RKO studio in order to make the film a more commercial length. Stylish low-key photography by Stanley Cortez who more than a decade later did equally distinguished work for Charles Laughton on *Night of the Hunter.*

A MERCURY PRODUCTION (ORSON WELLES)/RKO

Direction & narration—
    Orson Welles
Screenplay (from novel by
    Booth Tarkington)—
    Orson Welles

*Photography—*Stanley Cortez
*Art direction—*Mark Lee Kirk
*Music—*Bernard Herrmann
*Editing—*Robert Wise

PLAYERS: Tim Holt, Joseph Cotten, Dolores Costello, Anne Baxter, Agnes Moorehead, Ray Collins, Erskine Sanford, Richard Bennett, Don Dillaway

MAGNIFICENT SEVEN, THE   U.S.A. (1960)
John Sturges transfers Kurosawa's *Seven Samurai* (see page 391) into Western terms by changing the locale to Mexico, the villagers into Mexican peasants, and the Samurai warriors into Texas gunfighters. Not a screen masterpiece like its Japanese predecessor, although as a Western it has its moments not only in its effectively staged action scenes but also in its quieter periods when it examines the characters and motives of the seven outlaws. Charles Lang's color photography is a joy and Elmer Bernstein's music score is perhaps the most exhilarating ever composed for a Western film. The seven are played by Yul Brynner, Steve McQueen, Charles Bronson, Robert Vaughn, James Coburn, Brad Dexter and Horst Buchholz.

MIRISCH—ALPHA/UNITED ARTISTS

Production & direction—
    John Sturges
Screenplay (based on
    Akira Kurosawa's film The
    Seven Samurai)—
    William Roberts

Photography (DeLuxecolor/
    *Panavision)—*Charles Lang
Art direction—
    Edward Fitzgerald
*Music—*Elmer Bernstein
*Editing—*Ferris Webster

PLAYERS: Yul Brynner, Horst Buchholz, Eli Wallach, Steve McQueen, Charles Bronson, Robert Vaughn, Brad Dexter, James Coburn

MAJOR AND THE MINOR, THE   U.S.A. (1942)
Hard-up, disillusioned New York model (Ginger Rogers) takes a half-fare trip to her home in Iowa by masquerading as a 12-year-old, but finishes up instead at a Midwestern military academy and is romantically attached to major Ray Milland. An amusing, cleverly scripted little picture important as first film Billy Wilder directed.

PARAMOUNT

Production—Arthur Hornblow, Jr.   Charles Brackett,
Direction—Billy Wilder   Billy Wilder
Screenplay (suggested by play   *Photography*—Leo Tover
  Connie Goes Home *by*   *Art direction*—Hans Dreier,
  Edward Childs Carpenter and   Roland Anderson
  story Sunny Goes Home *by*   *Music*—Robert Emmett Dolan
  Fannie Kilbourne)—   *Editing*—Doane Harrison
PLAYERS: Ginger Rogers, Ray Milland, Rita Johnson, Robert Benchley, Diana Lynn, Edward Fielding, Frankie Thomas, Raymond Roe

MAJOR DUNDEE   U.S.A. (1964)
Sam Peckinpah's mutilated Civil War Western is about a fanatical Yankee officer (Charlton Heston) who recruits a private army of misfits, cutthroats and Southern prisoners for a punitive expedition into Mexico against the Apaches who have kidnapped several children. Handsome color landscapes by Sam Leavitt and some well-staged battle scenes, but more a film of parts than a satisfactory whole, inevitable perhaps in view of the fact that some 30 minutes were deleted from the film's running time without Peckinpah's consent. Strongly played by Heston, Richard Harris as his second-in-command, and James Coburn as a one-armed Indian scout.

JERRY BRESLER PRODUCTIONS/COLUMBIA

Production—Jerry Bresler   *Photography* (*Eastmancolor/*
Direction—Sam Peckinpah   *Technicolor Panavision*)—
Screenplay (*from story by*   Sam Leavitt
  Harry Julian Fink)—Fink,   *Music*—Daniele Amfitheatrof
  Oscar Saul & Sam Peckinpah   *Editing*—William Lyon,
Art direction—Al Ybarra   Don Starling, Howard Kunin
PLAYERS: Charlton Heston, Richard Harris, Jim Hutton, James Coburn, Michael Anderson, Jr. Senta Berger, Mario Adorf, Brock Peters

273

MAKING A LIVING
U.S.A. (1914)

Later reissued under the titles: *A Busted Johnny, Troubles,* and *Doing His Best.*

Chaplin's first film, made in three days in December of 1913 by Mack Sennett's second-in-command Henry Lehrman. Chaplin, then 24 years old and on a salary of $150 a week, plays an Englishman down on his luck and appears in the unfamiliar costume of frock coat, high silk hat, walrus mustache and monocle. His famous tramp costume was not used until his second film *Kid Auto Races at Venice* (see page 215).

KEYSTONE FILMS

Production—Mack Sennett

Direction—Henry Lehrman

Reputedly photographed by—
E. J. Vallejo

PLAYERS: Charlie Chaplin, Henry Lehrman, Virginia Kirtely, Alice Davenport, Minta Durfee, Chester Conklin

MALTESE FALCON, THE
U.S.A. (1941)

Tense and cynically humorous 100 minutes in the company of laconic private-eye Sam Spade (Humphrey Bogart) and assorted villains Sydney Greenstreet, Peter Lorre and Elisha Cook Jr. as they search desperately for the priceless jewel-encrusted statuette of the title. John Huston's first film as a director and still regarded by many critics as his best. A classic example of how to adapt an outstanding novel into an equally outstanding film and at the same time retain all the quality and atmosphere of the original. Mary Astor plays the *femme fatale* and Jerome Cowan, one of Hollywood's most reliable character actors of the 1940's, appears in the earlier scenes as Bogart's partner.

WARNER BROS.–FIRST NATIONAL

Executive producer—
Hal B. Wallis

Associate producer—
Henry Blanke

Direction—John Huston

Photography—Arthur Edeson

Screenplay (based on novel by Dashiell Hammett)—
John Huston

Art direction—Robert Haas

Music—Adolph Deutsch

Editing—Thomas Richards

PLAYERS: Humphrey Bogart, Mary Astor, Gladys George, Peter Lorre, Barton MacLane, Sydney Greenstreet, Ward Bond, Lee Patrick, Jerome Cowan, Elisha Cook, Jr.

MAN AND A WOMAN, A (Un Homme et une Femme)
France (1966)

Glossy, souped-up story of the love affair between a widowed racing

274

driver (Jean-Louis Trintignant) and a beautiful young widow (Anouk Aimée) who meet one Sunday while collecting their children from a boarding school at Deauville. One of the most unashamedly romantic films of the 1960's notable for the performance of Miss Aimée, the music, and the dazzling color camera work. The film won the Grand Prix at the 1966 Cannes Film Festival.

LES FILMS 13

Direction–Claude Lelouch	Art direction–Robert Luchaire
Screenplay–Claude Lelouch &	Music & Songs–Francis Lai
Pierre Uytterhoeven	Lyrics–Pierre Barouh
Photography (Eastmancolor)–	Editing–Claude Barrois &
Claude Lelouch	Claude Lelouch

PLAYERS: Anouk Aimée, Jean-Louis Trintignant, Pierre Barouh, Valérie Lagrange, Simone Paris, Paul le Person, Henri Chemin, Antoine Sire, Souad Amidou

MAN FOR ALL SEASONS, A   Gt. Britain (1966)
The battle of wills between Henry VIII and 16th-century statesman Sir Thomas More who refuses, as a matter of private conscience, to sign the Act of Succession which condones the King's divorce from Catherine of Aragon and marriage to Anne Boleyn. After resigning the post of Lord Chancellor More is imprisoned, tried for high treason and executed. Few stage plays have been better adapted to the screen than this one which is directed with a great feeling for period by Fred Zinnemann and played with authority by Paul Scofield who repeats his stage performance as More. Others in the cast—Leo McKern (Cromwell), Robert Shaw (Henry), Orson Welles (Cardinal Wolsey), John Hurt (Rich) and Nigel Davenport (Duke of Norfolk). Academy Award, best picture, 1966.

COLUMBIA

Production & direction–	Photography (Technicolor)–
Fred Zinnemann	Ted Moore
Screenplay–Robert Bolt	Music–Georges Delerue
Production design–John Box	Editing–Ralph Kemplen

PLAYERS: Paul Scofield, Wendy Hiller, Leo McKern, Robert Shaw, Orson Welles, Susannah York, Nigel Davenport, John Hurt, Corin Redgrave, Colin Blakely

MAN FROM LARAMIE, THE   U.S.A. (1955)
In a Western set in New Mexico James Stewart plays a vengeful

stranger searching for the man responsible for his brother's death, Donald Crisp plays an aging cattle baron, Aline MacMahon a rival rancher, and Arthur Kennedy the heavy who sells guns to the Indians. A bleak, brutal work not up to some of Mann's other Westerns. Some fine New Mexico landscapes by Charles Lang and a then fashionable theme tune of the *High Noon* variety from Leslie Lee and Ned Washington.

COLUMBIA

Production–William Goetz
Direction–Anthony Mann
Screenplay (*from* Saturday
 Evening Post *story by*
 Thomas T. Flynn)–
 Philip Yordan & Frank Burt

Photography (*Technicolor/
 CinemaScope*)–Charles Lang
Editing–William Lyon
Art direction–Cary Odell
Music–George Duning

PLAYERS: James Stewart, Arthur Kennedy, Donald Crisp, Cathy O'Donnell, Alex Nicol, Aline MacMahon, Wallace Ford, Jack Elam

MAN HUNT   U.S.A. (1941)

One of the best of Fritz Lang's early American films, adapted from Geoffrey Household's novel *Rogue Male* and set in the period just prior to the outbreak of the Second World War. Walter Pidgeon plays an English big-game hunter who plans to assassinate Hitler, but finishes up being hounded by Nazi spies through a foggy and very German-looking London. Joan Bennett appears as the prostitute who offers him shelter. George Sanders, Ludwig Stössel and John Carradine (as a Fascist assassin with a sword-umbrella) lead Nazi treachery and sadism.

TWENTIETH CENTURY–FOX

Direction–Fritz Lang
Screenplay–Dudley Nichols
Photography–Arthur Miller

Art direction–Richard Day,
 Wiard B. Ihnen
Music–Alfred Newman
Editing–Allen McNeil

PLAYERS: Walter Pidgeon, Joan Bennett, George Sanders, John Carradine, Roddy McDowall, Ludwig Stössel, Heather Thatcher, Frederick Walock

MAN IN THE WHITE SUIT, THE   Gt. Britain (1951)

This most ambitious of all the Ealing comedies is about a young inventor who runs into trouble with management and labor when he tries to put his indestructible, stain-resisting fabric on the market.

The Man in the White Suit

Witty, original, gently satirical, and delightfully played by Alec Guinness as the young research chemist, Cecil Parker, Ernest Thesiger and Michael Gough as a trio of capitalists, and Vida Hope as a vigorous trade unionist.

EALING STUDIOS

Production—Michael Balcon   Alexander Mackendrick
Direction—   *Photography*—Douglas Slocombe
   Alexander Mackendrick   *Art direction*—Jim Morahan
Screenplay—Roger MacDougall,   *Music*—Benjamin Frankel
   John Dighton,
PLAYERS: Alec Guinness, Joan Greenwood, Cecil Parker, Michael Gough, Ernest Thesiger, Howard Marion Crawford, Vida Hope, Patric Doonan, Duncan Lamont

MAN OF ARAN   Gt. Britain (1934)
Restrained, beautifully observed Robert Flaherty documentary (his first sound film) tracing the everyday life of a family—a man and his wife and their young son—and their struggles to earn a livelihood on

the isle of Aran off the west coast of Ireland. Flaherty spent some two years on the project and lived for eighteen months among the islanders themselves, using a cottage for the film's interiors and converting another into a cutting room.

GAINSBOROUGH/GAUMONT BRITISH

Production—Michael Balcon
Direction, screenplay &
  photography—
  Robert & Frances Flaherty

Assistant—David Flaherty
Music—John Greenwood
Editing—John Monck

PLAYERS: Colman Tiger King, Maggie Dirrane, Michael Dillane

MAN OF THE WEST   U.S.A. (1958)
Anthony Mann's last Western of note and the only occasion that he worked with Gary Cooper. The film, set in Arizona during the 1870's, is a brutal one and describes how Cooper, an ex-outlaw who has renounced killing, becomes involved again with his bandit stepfather (Lee J. Cobb) and his gang of outlaws. Julie London appears as a dance-hall singer, Arthur O'Connell as a cardsharp, and John Dehner, Jack Lord and Royal Dano lead Cobb's assorted gang of cutthroats.

ASHTON PRODUCTIONS/UNITED ARTISTS

Production—Walter M. Mirisch
Direction—Anthony Mann
Screenplay (from novel by
  Will C. Brown)—
  Reginald Rose

Photography (DeLuxecolor/
  CinemaScope)—Ernest Haller
Art direction—Hilyard Brown
Music—Leigh Harline
Editing—Richard Heermance

PLAYERS: Gary Cooper, Julie London, Lee J. Cobb, Arthur O'Connell, Jack Lord, John Dehner, Royal Dano, Robert J. Wilke

MAN ON THE FLYING TRAPEZE, THE   U.S.A. (1935)
Bank clerk Ambrose Wolfinger (W. C. Fields) takes his first afternoon off in 25 years to attend a wrestling match and becomes disastrously involved with a tyrannical traffic cop, a truculent chauffeur, and in a chase after a runaway tire. Disjointed but amusing Fields comedy made during his Paramount period. Directed by Clyde Bruckman, scriptwriter of several Buster Keaton comedies of the twenties.

PARAMOUNT

Production—William LeBaron
Direction—Clyde Bruckman
Screenplay (from an original
  story by Charles Bogle
  (W. C. Fields) & Sam

Hardy)—Ray Harris,
  Sam Hardy, Jack Cunningham
  & Bobby Vernon
Photography—Al Gilks
Editing—Richard Currier

PLAYERS: W. C. Fields, Mary Brian, Kathleen Howard, Grady Sutton, Vera Lewis, Lucien Littlefield, Oscar Apfel, Lew Kelly

MAN WHO KNEW TOO MUCH, THE   Gt. Britain (1934)
Wildly improbable but thoroughly entertaining Hitchcock thriller involving a plot to assassinate a foreign political leader in London. Some ingenious set pieces include an attempted murder in Albert Hall and a thrilling cops-and-robbers climax which closely parallels the famous Sidney Street siege of 1911. Lionel Banks and Edna Best play the straight leads and Peter Lorre, in his first English-speaking role, is the leader of the spy ring.

GAUMONT BRITISH

Production—Michael Balcon
Direction—Alfred Hitchcock
*Screenplay (from original
theme by Charles Bennett &
D. B. Wyndham-Lewis)*—
A. R. Rawlinson,
Edwin Greenwood

Photography—Curt Courant
Art direction—Alfred Junge,
Peter Proud
Music—Arthur Benjamin
Editing—H. St. C. Stewart
Additional dialogue—
Emlyn Williams

PLAYERS: Leslie Banks, Edna Best, Peter Lorre, Frank Vosper, Hugh Wakefield, Nova Pilbeam, Pierre Fresnay, Cicely Oates

MAN WHO KNEW TOO MUCH, THE   U.S.A. (1956)
Hitchcock's much longer (2 hours as against 1¼) American remake telling basically the same story with Sidney Street siege omitted and locale of opening scenes changed from Switzerland to Morocco. The assassination attempt is even more exciting and precisely worked out than in the British version of 20 years before. James Stewart and Doris Day replace the original leads, Bernard Miles and Brenda de Banzie lead the heavies, and Reggie Nalder is the Albert Hall assassin.

FILWITE PRODUCTIONS

Production & direction—
Alfred Hitchcock
*Screenplay (from story by
Charles Bennett & D. B.
Wyndham-Lewis)*—
John Michael Hayes
& Angus McPhail

Photography (Technicolor)—
Robert Burks
Art direction—Hal Pereira &
Henry Bumstead
Music—Bernard Herrmann
Editing—George Tomasini

PLAYERS: James Stewart, Doris Day, Daniel Gelin, Brenda de Banzie, Ralph Truman, Mogens Wieth, Alan Mowbray, Reggie Nalder, Bernard Miles

MAN WHO SHOT LIBERTY VALANCE, THE   U.S.A. (1962)

John Ford separates Western fact from Western legend in telling how a greenhorn Eastern lawyer (James Stewart) wins fame and fortune for killing the notorious Liberty Valance, an outlaw who actually meets his death at the hands of sharpshooting rancher (John Wayne). Despite its limited setting—most of the action takes place in bars, shacks and town streets—the film ranks as one of Ford's most ambitious Westerns. In addition to telling the personal story it also traces the attempts of Western pioneers to win statehood and law and order for their territory. In supporting roles: Edmond O'Brien as an alcoholic newspaper editor, Andy Devine as a bumbling sheriff, and Lee Marvin as the whip-carrying Liberty Valance.

FORD PRODUCTIONS/PARAMOUNT

Production—Willis Goldbeck
Direction—John Ford
Screenplay (from story by
   Dorothy M. Johnson)—
   Willis Goldbeck &
   James Warner Bellah

Photography—
   William H. Clothier
Art direction—Hal Pereira &
   Eddie Imazu
Music—Cyril J. Mockridge
Editing—Otho Lovering

PLAYERS: James Stewart, John Wayne, Vera Miles, Lee Marvin, Edmond O'Brien, Andy Devine, Ken Murray, John Carradine

MAN WITH THE GOLDEN ARM, THE   U.S.A. (1955)

Drug-addicted poker dealer (Frank Sinatra) struggling to kick the "monkey on his back" and to live on good terms with his crippled wife (Eleanor Parker) and the general assortment of drunks, cardsharpers, and dope peddlers that inhabit his world. Excellently played (particularly by Sinatra) and with some finely realized backgrounds of the Chicago slums although the things that stay in the memory long after the rest of the film has been forgotten are Elmer Bernstein's strident jazz score (played by Shorty Rogers) and the ingenious credit titles of Saul Bass who designed the titles for a number of Preminger's films including *Carmen Jones* and *Advise and Consent* and also worked on *Walk on the Wild Side* for Dmytryk (credit titles over a stalking black cat), *Around the World in 80 Days* for Mike Todd, and *Vertigo, North by Northwest* and *Psycho* for Hitchcock.

UNITED ARTISTS

Production & direction
   Otto Preminger

Screenplay (from novel by
   Nelson Algren)—Walter
   Newman & Lewis Meltzer

Photography—Sam Leavitt   *Music*—Elmer Bernstein
Production design—Joe Wright   *Editing*—Louis Loeffler
PLAYERS: Frank Sinatra, Eleanor Parker, Kim Novak, Arnold Stang, Darren McGavin, Robert Strauss

MANCHURIAN CANDIDATE, THE   U.S.A. (1962)
Ingenious Frankenheimer movie concerns a brainwashed Korean war hero (Laurence Harvey) who is returned to the United States for the purpose of assassinating a Presidential candidate whose death would enable a Communist to occupy the White House. Brilliant direction, a witty script, especially during the early brainwashing sequences in Manchuria and the climax at a political convention. Expert playing from Frank Sinatra as dedicated army officer, and Angela Lansbury and James Gregory as undercover Communists.
MC PRODUCTIONS/UNITED ARTISTS

Production—George Axelrod &   *Screenplay (based on novel by*
  John Frankenheimer   *Richard Condon)*—
Executive producer—   George Axelrod
  Howard W. Koch   *Art direction*—Richard Sylbert
Direction—John Frankenheimer   *Music*—David Amram
Photography—Lionel Lindon   *Editing*—Ferris Webster
PLAYERS: Frank Sinatra, Laurence Harvey, Janet Leigh, Angela Lansbury, Henry Silva, James Gregory, Leslie Parrish, John McGiver

MANDY   Gt. Britain (1952)
Restrained, intermittently impressive Ealing film about the problems and heartaches of a young middle-class couple (Phyllis Calvert and Terence Morgan) who discover that their only child (Mandy Miller) is deaf and dumb. A curious mixture of trite fiction and absorbing documentary; the conventional plot and stereotyped characters are completely overshadowed by the documentary scenes—shot in Manchester's Royal Residential Schools for the Deaf—showing the long, difficult struggle to teach children to lip-read and formulate sound. Warmly directed by Alexander Mackendrick and with sympathetic performances from Jack Hawkins as the head teacher and Dorothy Alison as a dedicated children's nurse.
EALING STUDIOS (A MICHAEL BALCON PRODUCTION)

Production—Leslie Norman   *Screenplay (adapted from* The
Direction—   Day Is Ours *by Hilda*
  Alexander Mackendrick   Lewis)—Nigel Balchin &
     Jack Whittingham

281

Photography—Douglas Slocombe   *Music*—William Alwyn
Art direction—Jim Morahan   *Editing*—Seth Holt
PLAYERS: Phyllis Calvert, Jack Hawkins, Terence Morgan, Godfrey Tearle, Mandy Miller, Nancy Price, Edward Chapman, Marjorie Fielding, Dorothy Alison

MANON   France (1949)
Updated version of novel with 16-year-old Cécile Aubry as the luxury-craving young wanton and Michel Auclair as the enslaved lover she drags through the brothels and black markets of postwar Paris and eventually entices to murder. A sordid story, told in flashbacks and with considerable skill, although the cuts the film received at the hands of world censors reduced much of its dramatic power. Gabrielle Dorziat contributes a finely realized cameo as the madam of a well-run brothel.

ALCINA (PAUL-EDMOND DECHARME)

Direction—   *Adaptation & dialogue*—
    Henri-Georges Clouzot   Clouzot & Ferry
Screenplay (*from novel*   *Photography*—Armand Thirard
    Manon Lescaut *by the Abbé*   *Art direction*—Max Douy
    Prévost)—Henri-Georges Clouzot   *Music*—Paul Misraki
    & Jean Ferry   *Editing*—Monique Kirsanoff
PLAYERS: Cécile Aubry, Michel Auclair, Serge Reggiani, Gabrielle Dorziat, Henri Gilbert, Raymond Souplex

MARGIE   U.S.A. (1946)
Charming film about American small-town college life during the late 1920's is notable on many counts but especially for the excellence of Charles Clarke's Technicolor and for its skillful evocation of the atmosphere of the period. Jeanne Crain plays the shy young college girl, and the nostalgic songs include "Avalon," "Ain't She Sweet" and "I'll See You in My Dreams." Not the most ambitious film of 1946 but certainly one of the best.

TWENTIETH CENTURY–FOX

Production—Walter Morosco   *Photography* (*Technicolor*)—
Direction—Henry King   Charles C. Clarke
Screenplay (*based on stories*   *Music direction*—
    by Ruth McKenney &   Alfred Newman
    Richard Bransten)—   *Editing*—Barbara McLean
    F. Hugh Herbert

PLAYERS: Jeanne Crain, Glenn Langan, Lynn Bari, Alan Young, Barbara Lawrence, Conrad Janis, Hattie McDaniel

MARIUS   France (1930)
The first part of Marcel Pagnol's delightful trilogy about the people who live on the waterfront in the old port of Marseilles. César (Raimu), the proprietor of the quayside bistro, his son Marius (Pierre Fresnay), and the pretty young fish-seller Fanny (Orane Demazis) all appeared on the screen for the first time in this film as did Panisse (Charpin), the warmhearted master sailmaker. The film tells of the love affair between Marius and Fanny and ends as Marius, torn between his love for Fanny and for the sea, sails away leaving his father and mistress behind him. The story continues in *Fanny* (page 131) and *César* (page 78).

LES FILMS MARCEL PAGNOL

Direction—Alexander Korda   *Photography*—Ted Pahle
Screenplay (from his own   *Editing*—Roger Spiri Mercanton
    play)—Marcel Pagnol   *Music*—Francis Grammon
PLAYERS: Raimu, Orane Demazis, Pierre Fresnay, Alida Rouffe, Charpin, Robert Vattier, Paul Dulac, Milly Mathis

MARK OF ZORRO, THE   U.S.A. (1940)
Tyrone Power as handsome masked avenger, Linda Darnell as his heroine and Basil Rathbone as the suave heavy who is eventually disposed of by Power in an excitingly staged sword duel. The film is based on Johnston McCulley novel *The Curse of Capistrano* set in 19th-century California. Arthur Miller's black-and-white photography, and Richard Day and Joseph Wright's sets are among the best in the swashbuckling genre.

TWENTIETH CENTURY–FOX

Direction—Rouben Mamoulian   *Art direction*—Richard Day &
Screenplay—John Taintor Foote   Joseph C. Wright
Adaptation—Garrett Fort &   *Music*—Alfred Newman
    Bess Meredyth   *Editing*—Robert Bischoff
Photography—Arthur Miller
PLAYERS: Tyrone Power, Linda Darnell, Basil Rathbone, Gale Sondergaard, Eugene Pallette, J. Edward Bromberg, Montagu Love, Janet Beecher

MARNIE   U.S.A. (1964)
Old-style thriller about a sexually frigid kleptomaniac (Tippi Hedren)

whose psychological troubles and hatred of the color *red* stem from her childhood when she clubbed to death one of her prostitute mother's less endearing clients. Not highly regarded when it was first shown but like many of Hitchcock's films it improves with age and now occupies, together with the masterly *Vertigo*, a unique place in the master's work. Sean Connery played the heroine's patient husband and Bernard Herrmann contributed his eighth Hitchcock score.

UNIVERSAL

Production & direction—
Alfred Hitchcock
Screenplay (from novel by Winston Graham)—
Jay Presson Allen

Photography (Technicolor)—
Robert Burks
*Art direction—*Robert Boyle & George Milo
*Music—*Bernard Herrmann
*Editing—*George Tomasini

PLAYERS: Tippi Hedren, Sean Connery, Diane Baker, Martin Gabel, Louise Latham, Bob Sweeney, Alan Napier, S. John Launer

MARRIAGE CIRCLE, THE   U.S.A. (1924)
First of Lubitsch's sophisticated social comedies of the 1920's is about the complicated domestic lives of two married couples—Marie Prevost and Adolphe Menjou, and Florence Vidor and Monte Blue—living in prewar Vienna. Light, subtle and engagingly played especially by the suave Menjou and Marie Prevost who, in this film, proved herself quite a brilliant comedienne. The picture was a huge commercial success and the forerunner of a long series of Hollywood sex comedies, several by Lubitsch himself.

WARNER BROS.

*Direction—*Ernst Lubitsch
Photography—
Charles Van Enger

Screenplay (from play Only a Dream *by Lothar Schmidt)—*
Paul Bern

PLAYERS: Florence Vidor, Monte Blue, Marie Prevost, Creighton Hale, Dale Fuller, Adolphe Menjou

MARRYING KIND, THE   U.S.A. (1952)
Garson Kanin scripted this comedy drama about the gradual breakup of the 7-year marriage of Judy Holliday and Aldo Ray. Told in flashbacks from the chambers of a sympathetic woman judge and full of realistic observation of the domestic ups and downs of married life. An uncomfortably honest little movie that stands as one of Cukor's best.

COLUMBIA

Marty

Production—Bert Granet
Direction—George Cukor
Screenplay—Ruth Gordon &
  Garson Kanin

Photography—Joseph Walker
Art direction—John Meehan
Music—Hugo Friedhofer
Editing—Charles Nelson

PLAYERS: Judy Holliday, Aldo Ray, Madge Kennedy, Sheila Bond, John Alexander, Rex Williams, Phyllis Povah

MARTY   U.S.A. (1955)

Moving little tale of a lonely, unattractive New York butcher (Ernest Borgnine) and his love affair with the shy schoolteacher (Betsy Blair) he meets at a Saturday night dance. Unpretentious, beautifully acted, occasionally oversentimental; notable primarily for the sensitive writing of Chayefsky and for Delbert Mann's realistic depiction of life in the Bronx, New York. Esther Minciotti as Marty's mother and Joe Mantell as his friend head the supporting cast. Grand Prix, Cannes, 1955 and Academy Awards for best film, actor, director and screenplay.

Production—Harold Hecht   *Art direction*—Edward S.
Direction—Delbert Mann   Haworth & Walter Simonds
Screenplay (based on his own   *Music*—Roy Webb
  TV play)—Paddy Chayefsky   *Editing*—Alan Crosland, Jr.
Photography—Joseph LaShelle
PLAYERS: Ernest Borgnine, Betsy Blair, Joe Mantell, Esther Minciotti, Augusta Ciolli, Karen Steele, Jerry Paris, Frank Sutton

MARY OF SCOTLAND   U.S.A. (1936)
Somber Hollywood movie about the love of Mary Queen of Scots for the Earl of Bothwell and her bid to oust Elizabeth from the throne of England. Elaborate Polglase sets and a proud, defiant Mary from Katharine Hepburn. Made by the director (Ford), writer (Nichols) and cameraman (August) responsible for *The Informer*.

Production—Pandro S. Berman   *Photography*—Joseph H. August
Direction—John Ford   *Art direction*—Van Nest Polglase
Screenplay (from play by   & Carroll Clark
  Maxwell Anderson)—Dudley   *Music*—Max Steiner
  Nichols   *Costumes*—Walter Plunkett
                            Editing—Jane Loring
PLAYERS: Katharine Hepburn, Fredric March, Florence Eldridge, Douglas Walton, John Carradine, Monte Blue, Jean Fenwick, Robert Barrat

MATTER OF LIFE AND DEATH, A   Gt. Britain (1946)
The most elaborate of Britain's early postwar films, conceived, produced and directed by the ambitious Powell/Pressburger team. A young RAF airman, after miraculously escaping from a burning plane, undergoes a critical brain operation and imagines himself to be on trial for his life in a heavenly assizes. An intriguing fantasy not, perhaps inevitably, entirely successful. Imaginatively designed by Alfred Junge whose sets included a stratospheric escalator and brilliantly photographed by Jack Cardiff who shot the reality sequences in Technicolor and the hallucinatory scenes in monochrome. David Niven played the airman, Raymond Massey the heavenly prosecutor, and Roger Livesey the defending counsel.

Production, direction & screenplay—Michael Powell & Emeric Pressburger
Photography (Technicolor)—Jack Cardiff

Production design—Alfred Junge
Art direction—Arthur Lawson
Music—Allan Gray
Editing—Reginald Mills

PLAYERS: David Niven, Roger Livesey, Raymond Massey, Kim Hunter, Marius Goring, Abraham Sofaer, Robert Coote, Bonar Colleano

MEET ME IN ST. LOUIS U.S.A. (1944)

Nostalgic musical portrait of a St. Louis family at the turn of the century. A charming, warmhearted picture, among Minnelli's best, with some delightful songs, notably "The Trolley Song" and "The Boy Next Door," and some exquisite sets. Beautifully played by Judy Garland and Margaret O'Brien as the two sisters, Mary Astor and Leon Ames as the parents, and Harry Davenport as the grandfather. One of the best musicals ever made by Metro-Goldwyn-Mayer.

METRO—GOLDWYN—MAYER

Production—Arthur Freed
Direction—Vincente Minnelli
Screenplay (from book by Sally Benson)—Irving Brecher, Fred F. Finklehoffe
Photography (Technicolor)—George Folsey, Henri Jaffa

Art direction—Cedric Gibbons, Lemuel Ayers, Jack Martin Smith
Musical direction—Georgie Stoll
Dance direction—Charles Walters
Editing—Albert Akst

PLAYERS: Judy Garland, Margaret O'Brien, Lucille Bremer, Joan Carroll, Mary Astor, Leon Ames, Tom Drake, Marjorie Main, Harry Davenport, June Lockhart, H. H. Daniels, Jr.

MEMBER OF THE WEDDING U.S.A. (1952)

Quiet, leisurely film version of Carson McCullers' book and play about a lonely 12-year-old girl growing up into adolescence during a lazy summer in a small Southern town. A modest little movie made when producer Stanley Kramer was turning regularly to the stage for film material (this was his seventh filmed play in three years) and of interest primarily for the performances of the then 26-year-old Julie Harris as the girl and Ethel Waters as the old colored housekeeper she confides in. Photographed by veteran cameraman Hal Mohr who was associated with a number of interesting small-scale pictures during the 1950's—The Four Poster, Baby Face Nelson, The Line-Up, etc.

STANLEY KRAMER PRODS./COLUMBIA

Production—Stanley Kramer
Direction—Fred Zinnemann
Screenplay—Edna & Edward
    Anhalt
Photography—Hal Mohr
Art direction—Cary Odell
Music—Alex North
Editing—William Lyon

PLAYERS: Ethel Waters, Julie Harris, Brandon de Wilde, Arthur Franz, Nancy Gates, William Hansen, James Edwards

MEMPHIS BELLE   U.S.A. (1944)
A 4-reel documentary about heavy bomber operations over Germany during World War II. Directed and edited by William Wyler who flew five combat missions in order to get his material and handsomely photographed in Technicolor by Harold Tannenbaum and William H. Clothier (Ford's cameraman on *The Horse Soldiers, The Man Who Shot Liberty Valance* and *Cheyenne Autumn*).
    WAR ACTIVITIES COMMITTEE/PARAMOUNT DISTRIBUTION

Production & direction—
    William Wyler
Screenplay—William Wyler
Photography (Technicolor)—
    Harold Tannenbaum,
    William H. Clothier
Additional photography—
    William Wyler
Music—Gail Kubik
Editor—Lynn Harrison
Narration—Lester Koenig

MEN, THE   U.S.A. (1950)
Dignified, intelligent study of the problems of paraplegics—men whose war injuries left them paralyzed from the waist down. Set in a hospital ward and exceptionally well played by Marlon Brando (debut) as one of the wounded soldiers, Teresa Wright as his girlfriend, and especially Everett Sloane as the tireless hospital doctor who tries to bring back his patients to a physical and social life. One of Stanley Kramer's earliest productions and vastly superior to the majority of his later films.
    UNITED ARTISTS

Production—Stanley Kramer
Direction—Fred Zinnemann
Screenplay—Carl Foreman
Photography—Robert de Grasse
Production design—
    Rudolph Sternad
Music—Dimitri Tiomkin
Editing—Harry Gerstad

PLAYERS: Marlon Brando, Teresa Wright, Everett Sloane, Jack Webb, Richard Erdman, Arthur Jurado

METROPOLIS   Germany (1926)
Ambitious, very expensive film about life in a Utopian city in the year

2000. Heavily symbolic (the workers live underground, their masters on top) and dominated completely by the enormous architectural city designs of Otto Hunte, Erich Kettelhut and Karl Vollbrecht. These breathtaking sets and the film's over-all conception so impressed Goebbels that he later asked Lang to make Nazi pictures, but Lang refused and, after directing *The Last Will of Dr. Mabuse* in 1933, left Germany to work in France and the United States.

UFA

Direction—Fritz Lang

Screenplay—Fritz Lang, Thea von Harbou

Photography—Karl Freund, Günther Rittau

Special photographic effects— Eugene Schufftan

Art direction—Otto Hunte, Erich Kettelhut, Karl Vollbrecht

Sculptures— Walter Schultze-Middendorf

Music—Gottfried Huppertz

PLAYERS: Brigitte Helm, Alfred Abel, Gustave Frölhich, Rudolph Klein-Rogge, Heinrich Georg, Fritz Rasp, Theodor Loos, Erwin Biswanger

MIDNIGHT   U.S.A. (1939)

Claudette Colbert amiably teamed with John Barrymore, Mary Astor and Don Ameche in a smart, artificial 1930's comedy. Miss Colbert plays a young American girl who becomes involved with aristocrat John Barrymore in Paris and agrees to masquerade as his mistress so that his wife, acid-tongued society bitch Mary Astor, will become jealous and drop her current lover Francis Lederer. Don Ameche as a taxi driver in love with Miss Colbert complicates the issue still further. The film has style, a witty screenplay and shows Leisen (a most unappreciated craftsman) at the top of his comedy form.

PARAMOUNT

Production— Arthur Hornblow Jr.

Direction—Mitchell Leisen

Screenplay—Charles Brackett & Billy Wilder

Photography—Charles Lang

Story—Edwin Justus Mayer & Franz Schulz

Art direction—Hans Dreier & Robert Usher

Music—Frederick Hollander

Editing—Doane Harrison

PLAYERS: Claudette Colbert, Don Ameche, John Barrymore, Francis Lederer, Mary Astor, Elaine Harrie

MIDNIGHT COWBOY   U.S.A. (1969)

Deeply moving account of two young drifters—one a Texas hustler

(Jon Voight) in cowboy gear, the other a tubercular down-and-outer (Dustin Hoffman)—as they come to depend on each other during their struggles to exist in the cruel, unfriendly lower stratums of New York. A portrait of loneliness that is given added poignancy by British director John Schlesinger's acute observations of the urban scene. Flawlessly performed, technically exciting; excellent music score.

A JEROME HELLMAN/JOHN SCHLESINGER PRODUCTION—UNITED ARTISTS

Production—Jerome Hellman
Direction—John Schlesinger
Screenplay (from novel by James Leo Herlihy)—Waldo Salt
Music—John Barry

Photography (Deluxecolor)—Adam Holender
Production design—John Robert Lloyd
Editing—Hugh A. Robertson

PLAYERS: Dustin Hoffman, Jon Voight, Sylvia Miles, John McGiver, Brenda Vaccaro, Barnard Hughes, Ruth White, Jennifer Salt

MILDRED PIERCE U.S.A. (1945)

This slick adaptation of James Cain's novel is keyed to the attempts of a self-made woman (Joan Crawford) to give her only daughter (Ann Blyth) all the opportunities and luxuries she herself missed in early life. Not unnaturally the daughter turns into a spoiled, unscrupulous little brat and also, though less predictably, a murderess when she disposes of a wealthy playboy (Zachary Scott). A superior Michael Curtiz thriller, made with all the Warner Studio's expertise; also on hand—Bruce Bennett as Miss Crawford's husband, wisecracking Eve Arden, and vulgar real-estate man Jack Carson.

WARNER BROS.

Production—Jerry Wald
Direction—Michael Curtiz
Screenplay—Ranald MacDougall
Photography—Ernest Haller

Art direction—Anton Grot
Music—Max Steiner
Editing—David Weisbart

PLAYERS: Joan Crawford, Jack Carson, Zachary Scott, Eve Arden, Ann Blyth, Bruce Bennett, Lee Patrick, Moroni Olsen

MILLION DOLLAR LEGS U.S.A. (1932)

Early W. C. Fields vehicle about the problems that befall the mythical, sports-addicted country of Klopstokia when it decides to enter a team for the Olympic Games. Packed with slapstick, old-style chases, smartly-written gags; Fields is Klopstokia's president and silent, slapstick comedian Ben Turpin pops up regularly as a mysterious cross-eyed spy. Adapted from story by Joseph L. Mankiewicz and directed by Edward

Cline who, after Edward Sutherland, made more Fields movies than any other director.

PARAMOUNT

Direction—Edward Cline   *Screenplay*—Henry Myers &
Photography—Arthur Todd   Nick Barrows
PLAYERS: Jack Oakie, W. C. Fields, Andy Clyde, Lyda Roberti, Susan Fleming, Ben Turpin, Hugh Herbert, George Barbier

MIRACLE IN MILAN (Miracolo a Milano)   Italy (1951)
A group of down-and-outers living in a Milan shantytown are threatened with eviction when oil is discovered on their land, but are saved by the young modern saint who lives among them and works miracles on their behalf. The mixture of realism and fantasy doesn't quite work, but the satire on the greed of rich industrialists is sharp and there are moments of great tenderness and pathos. Not up to the standard of *Shoeshine* or *Bicycle Thief* but still a remarkable film.

A "SOCIETA" PRODUZIONA DESICA FILM, IN ASSOCIATION WITH I.E.N.I.C.

Direction—Vittorio DeSica   *Music*—Alessandro Cicognini
Screenplay—Cesare Zavattini,   *Art direction*—Guido Fiorini
  Vittorio DeSica   *Editing*—Eraldo Da Roma
Photography—Aldo Graziati
PLAYERS: Emma Gramatica, Francesco Golisano, Paolo Stoppa, Guglielmo Barnabo, Brunella Bovo, Anna Carena

MIRACLE OF MORGAN'S CREEK, THE   U.S.A. (1944)
Outrageous Preston Sturges comedy about small-town girl seeking a stand-in father for her baby, conceived at a wild "kiss the boys goodbye" party. Satirical, fast-moving film which, though not on same level with *The Lady Eve* and *Sullivan's Travels,* is far ahead of most comedies of the war period. Betty Hutton plays the girl, Eddie Bracken the stuttering "father," and there are delightful supporting performances from William Demarest as the town constable and Porter Hall as a justice of the peace.

PARAMOUNT

Direction & screenplay—   *Photography*—John Seitz
  Preston Sturges   *Music*—Leo Shuken,
Art direction—Hans Dreier,   Charles Bradshaw
  Ernst Fegte   *Editing*—Stuart Gilmore
PLAYERS: Eddie Bracken, Betty Hutton, Diana Lynn, William Demarest, Porter Hall, Emory Parnell, Alan Bridge, Julius Tannen, Victor Portel

MIRACLE ON 34TH STREET   U.S.A. (1947)
An engaging Capra-style comedy about a department-store Santa Claus
in New York who thinks he really is Santa Claus. George Seaton (screenplay) and Edmund Gwenn (supporting actor) both won Oscars for
their work and there are delightful minor performances from William
Frawley as a cigar-chewing politician, Gene Lockhart as a bewildered
judge, Jerome Cowan as a harassed prosecutor, and Porter Hall as a
phony psychiatrist.

TWENTIETH CENTURY–FOX

Production–William Perlberg
Direction & screenplay–
  George Seaton
Story–Valentine Davies
Music–Cyril Mockridge

Photography–Charles G. Clarke
  & Lloyd Ahern
Art direction–Richard Day &
  Richard Irvine
Editing–Robert Simpson

PLAYERS: Maureen O'Hara, John Payne, Edmund Gwenn, Gene Lockhart, Natalie Wood, Porter Hall, William Frawley, Jerome Cowan,
Philip Tonge

MIRACLE WORKER, THE   U.S.A. (1962)
Well acted film version of William Gibson's stage play about the struggles of Boston teacher Annie Sullivan (Anne Bancroft) to communicate
with and then teach the deaf, blind and mute child, Helen Keller (Patty
Duke). Directed with great authority by Arthur Penn who guided both
of his actresses to deserved Academy Awards, and containing at least
one unforgettable scene–that in which the child first realizes that the
word *water* being tapped out on her hand by her teacher refers to the
liquid pouring from the pump in front of her. Victor Jory and Inga
Swenson appear as the two Keller parents.

UNITED ARTISTS (A PLAYFILMS PRODUCTION)

Production–Fred Coe
Direction–Arthur Penn
Screenplay (from his play)–
  William Gibson
Photography–Ernest Caparros

Art direction–George Jenkins &
  Mel Bourne
Music–Laurence Rosenthal
Editing–Aram Avakian

PLAYERS: Anne Bancroft, Patty Duke, Victor Jory, Inga Swenson, Andrew
Prine, Kathleen Comegys, Beah Richards, Jack Hollander

MISS JULIE (Fröken Julie)   Sweden (1950)
Miss Julie (Anita Björk), the repressed daughter of a Swedish nobleman, tempts her father's valet (Ulf Palme) into seducing her, then

Miss Julie

commits suicide rather than face the inevitable consequences of her
act. A bleak, complex film, beautifully photographed and performed,
in which Sjöberg explores the sexual as well as social conflict between
the working class and decadent aristocracy of 19th-century Sweden.
Extended from August Strindberg's long one-act play and, prior to the
advent of Bergman, the most important work of contemporary Swedish
cinema.

SANDREW–BAUMAN (RUNE WALDEKRANZ)

Direction & screenplay–   *Art direction–*Bibi Lindström
  Alf Sjöberg   *Music–*Dag Wirén
*Photography–*Göran Strindberg   *Editing–*Lennart Wallén
PLAYERS: Anita Björk, Ulf Palme, Märta Dorff, Anders Henrikson, Lissie
Alandh, Inger Norberg, Jan Hagerman, Ake Fridell

MR. BLANDINGS BUILDS HIS DREAM HOUSE U.S.A. (1948)
Amusing domestic comedy about the troubles that befall advertising
executive Cary Grant when he decides to give up his cramped New
York apartment and move to a large house in the country. Witty script
by Norman Panama and Melvin Frank and neatly played by all concerned, particularly Cary Grant as the bewildered house buyer and

Reginald Denny as smooth-talking architect. A polished, skillful film, among the best comedies produced in Hollywood during the postwar period.

RKO RADIO

Production & screenplay (from book by Eric Hodgkins)— Norman Panama, Melvin Frank
Direction—H. C. Potter
Photography— James Wong Howe

Art direction—Albert D'Agostino, Carroll Clark
Music—C. Bakaleinikoff
Editing—Harry Marker

PLAYERS: Cary Grant, Myrna Loy, Melvyn Douglas, Reginald Denny, Sharyn Moffett, Connie Marshall, Louise Beavers

MR. DEEDS GOES TO TOWN   U.S.A. (1936)

Naive, tuba-playing country boy Longfellow Deeds (Gary Cooper) inherits a fortune from a playboy uncle and then gives it all away to help the country's economy when he discovers that his so-called big-city business associates are swindlers and crooks. In a superb supporting cast George Bancroft's newspaper editor, Douglas Dumbrille's crooked attorney and Walter Catlett's alcoholic author stand out. Academy Award to Frank Capra (his second) for best direction.

COLUMBIA

Production & direction— Frank Capra
Screenplay (from story by Clarence Budington Kelland) —Robert Riskin

Photography—Joseph Walker
Art direction—Stephen Goosson
Music direction— Howard Jackson
Editing—Gene Havlick

PLAYERS: Gary Cooper, Jean Arthur, George Bancroft, Lionel Stander, Douglas Dumbrille, Raymond Walburn, H. B. Warner, Walter Catlett

MR. SMITH GOES TO WASHINGTON   U.S.A. (1939)

Frank Capra's last great social comedy of the 1930's deals with idealistic young Wisconsin Senator (James Stewart) who exposes and eventually defeats corrupt politician (Claude Rains) and his crooked business associates. Same message as before—Boy Scout idealism overcomes corruption in high places—but a popular film nonetheless and outstandingly well played, especially by such supporting players as Edward Arnold as crooked publisher, Guy Kibbee as state governor and Thomas Mitchell as newspaper correspondent.

COLUMBIA

Production & direction—
Frank Capra
Screenplay—Sidney Buchman
Story—Lewis R. Foster
Photography—Joseph Walker
Art direction—Lionel Banks
Music—Dimitri Tiomkin
Editing—Gene Havlick &
Al Clark

PLAYERS: Jean Arthur, James Stewart, Claude Rains, Edward Arnold, Guy Kibbee, Thomas Mitchell, Eugene Pallette, Beulah Bondi, H. B. Warner

MOANA   U.S.A. (1926)

Visually beautiful documentary about the everyday life of the people of Samoa, having as its centerpiece the painful tattooing ritual that every young Samoan youth must undergo in order to establish his manhood. Robert J. Flaherty was commissioned to make his second documentary by Paramount after the enormous success of *Nanook of the North*.

FAMOUS PLAYERS LASKY CORPORATION (PARAMOUNT)

Direction, screenplay & photography—Robert J. Flaherty & Frances Flaherty
Assistant—David Flaherty
Editing—Robert J. Flaherty
Subtitles—Julian Johnston & Robert J. Flaherty

PLAYERS: Reni, Matchi

MOBY DICK   Gt. Britain (1956)

Captain Ahab's epic search for the great white whale brilliantly translated into cinematic terms by John Huston. An ambitious, extraordinarily successful film that somehow manages to capture all the fatalism and superstition of Melville's great "destiny" novel and still remain a thrilling sea adventure. Only Gregory Peck, miscast and lacking tragic stature as Ahab, is wrong, otherwise the handpicked cast—Richard Basehart (Ishmael), Leo Genn (Starbuck), Frederick Ledebur (Queequeg) and Orson Welles (Father Maple)—is splendid. Brilliant whaling scenes and splendidly evoked period atmosphere; a unique success. New York Critics award to John Huston (best director, 1956).

MOULIN PICTURES/WARNER BROS.

Production & direction—
John Huston
Screenplay (from novel by Herman Melville)—Ray
Bradbury & John Huston
Photography (Technicolor)—
Oswald Morris
Art direction—Ralph Brinton
Music—Philip Stainton
Editing—Russell Lloyd

PLAYERS: Gregory Peck, Richard Basehart, Leo Genn, Orson Welles, Harry Andrews, Bernard Miles, Mervyn Johns, Noel Purcell, Frederick Ledebur

MODERN TIMES   U.S.A. (1936)
Chaplin's last silent film is a sociological satire on the perils of the machine age. Chaplin, a factory worker who tightens bolts on a moving belt, is hilariously involved with co-worker Chester Conklin and new girl friend Paulette Goddard. The slapstick, gags and stunts are ingeniously blended with moments of pathos. The film, although more uneven than either *City Lights* or *The Gold Rush*, remains one of Chaplin's most ambitious and meaningful works. The last scene in which Chaplin and Goddard walk hand in hand toward the horizon was the very last in which the little tramp—perhaps the most famous creation in any art medium of the 20th century—appeared on the screen.

UNITED ARTISTS

Production, direction & screenplay—Charles Chaplin
Assistant directors—Carter De Haven, Henry Bergman

Photography—R. H. Totheroh, Ira Morgan
Music—Charles Chaplin
Musical direction—Alfred Newman

PLAYERS: Charles Chaplin, Paulette Goddard, Henry Bergman, Chester Conklin, Stanley Sanford, Hank Mann, Louis Natheaux, Allan Garcia

MOMENT OF TRUTH, THE (Il Momento Della Verità)
                                                   Italy/Spain (1965)
Stylish movie tracing the career of a Spanish bullfighter from the time he arrives in a large Spanish city as an Andalusian peasant boy until his death as a famous matador in the bull ring. The conventional rags to riches story, although Rosi's emphasis on realism and honest observation of the bullfights (he films not only the skill and grace but also the blood and the death agonies of the bulls and horses) make it anything but conventional. It is perhaps the best picture about bullfighting ever made. Exquisite color work by Di Venanzo, who also worked with Fellini (8½, *Juliet of the Spirits*) and Antonioni (*La Notte*).

FEDERIZ (ROME)/A.S. FILM (MADRID)

Direction—Francesco Rosi
Screenplay—Francesco Rosi, Pedro Portabella, Ricardo Munoz Suay & Pedro Beltrantis

Photography (Technicolor)—Gianni Di Venanzo, Ajace Parolin, Pasquale de Santis
Music—Piero Piccioni
Editing—Mario Serandrei

PLAYERS: Miguel Mateo Miguelin, José Gomez Sevillano, Pedro Basauri Pedrucho, Linda Christian

MON ONCLE   France/Italy (1958)

Jacques Tati's amusing attempt to involve his pipe-smoking hero Monsieur Hulot in the perils of modern life by letting him loose in an ultra-modern Paris house and in an equally modern factory producing plastic hose. Slow-moving at times and not as funny as *Monsieur Hulot's Holiday* but far, far more amusing than the majority of film comedies. Tati's first in color.

SPECTA FILMS/GRAY FILM/ALTER FILM (PARIS) FILM DEL CENTAURO (ROME)

Direction, screenplay & dialogue *Photography (Eastmancolor)*—
 —Jacques Tati with the collab-   Jean Bourgoin
 oration of Jacques Lagrange, *Music*—Franck Barcellini,
 Jean L'Hôte   Alain Romans
Art direction—Henri Schmitt *Editing*—Suzanne Baron

PLAYERS: Jacques Tati, Jean-Pierre Zola, Alain Bécourt, Lucien Frégis, Dominique Marie, Betty Schneider, André Dino

MONKEY BUSINESS   U.S.A. (1931)

The Marx Brothers' third film but their first screen original and first made in Hollywood. An inventive, wisecracking movie concerned with the zany quartet's adventures as stowaways on board a trans-atlantic ocean liner and at a party in a New York country house. Brilliant set pieces include Harpo joining a Punch and Judy show, the quartet's attempted escape from the ship disguised as Maurice Chevalier, and an hilarious free-for-all with kidnappers in an old barn. Directed by Norman McLeod who also did *Horse Feathers*.

PARAMOUNT

Direction—Norman McLeod *Additional dialogue*—
Story—S. J. Perelman & Will B.   Arthur Sheekman
 Johnstone   *Photography*—Arthur L. Todd

PLAYERS: Groucho, Harpo, Chico & Zeppo Marx, Thelma Todd, Rockcliffe Fellowes, Tom Kennedy, Ruth Hall, Harry Woods, Ben Taggart

MONKEY BUSINESS   U.S.A. (1952)

Amusing screwball comedy about an absent-minded research chemist (Cary Grant) and his quest for the wonder drug that will restore people's youth. Some brilliantly funny scenes, particularly those in which Grant and wife Ginger Rogers revert to adolescence, and two delightful supporting performances from Charles Coburn as a drug manufacturer and Marilyn Monroe—in an early role before she reached stardom—as his secretary. The last comedy of any note that Hawks directed.

TWENTIETH CENTURY–FOX

Production—Sol C. Siegel
Direction—Howard Hawks
Screenplay (from story by Harry
  Segall)—Ben Hecht, I. A. L.
  Diamond, Charles Lederer

Photography—Milton Krasner
Art direction—Lyle Wheeler,
  George Patrick
Music—Leigh Harline
Editing—William B. Murphy

PLAYERS: Cary Grant, Ginger Rogers, Charles Coburn, Marilyn Monroe, Hugh Marlowe, Henri Letondal, Robert Cornthwaite

MONSIEUR HULOT'S HOLIDAY

(Les Vacances de Monsieur Hulot)   France (1953)
The first appearance of Jacques Tati's endearing pipe-smoking clown. Monsieur Hulot is observed as he takes an incident-packed and completely catastrophic holiday in a small seaside resort in Brittany. A lazy, charming little movie, full of impeccably timed slapstick and containing one of the funniest opening sequences in the history of the cinema: a crowd of confused holiday passengers rush idiotically from one wrong station platform to another as the loudspeaker blares out garbled instructions. Raymond Carl appears briefly but memorably as a bewildered hotel waiter.

CADY FILMS/DISCINA/ECLAIR JOURNAL

Direction—Jacques Tati
Screenplay & dialogue (with
  collaboration of P. Aubert &
  Jacques Lagrange)—Jacques
  Tati & Henri Marquet
Music—Alain Romans

Photography—Jacques
  Mercanton & Jean Mousselle
Art direction—Roger Briaucourt
  & Henri Schmitt
Editing—Suzanne Baron, Charles
  Bretoneiche & Grassi

PLAYERS: Jacques Tati, Nathalie Pascaud, Louis Perrault, Michèle Rolla, Suzy Willy, André Dubois, Valentine Camax, Lucien Frégis, Raymond Carl

MONSIEUR VERDOUX   U.S.A. (1947)

Chaplin's most unusual and complex film, a story of a modern Bluebeard who murders a number of rich women in order to provide a comfortable life for his invalid wife and children. A curious mixture of old-fashioned cinema and penetrating satire that is not so much a "comedy of murders" (the film's subtitle) as a scathing attack on a war-minded world and the ethics of modern business, Chaplin's point being that if war is perhaps the end result of diplomacy then murder is equally the logical extension of business. Underrated when it was first shown but now ranking as one of Chaplin's major works. Photographed by Rollie Totheroh (his last film for Chaplin) who had worked with him on no less than forty-two occasions between 1915 and 1947.

UNITED ARTISTS

*Production, direction &
  screenplay*—Charles Chaplin
Assistant directors—Robert Florey
  & Wheeler Dryden
Photography—R. H. Totheroh,
  Curt Courant & Wallace
  Chewing

Art direction—John Beckman
Music—Charles Chaplin
Musical direction & arrangement
  —Rudolph Schrager
Editing—Willard Nico

PLAYERS: Charles Chaplin, Mady Correll, Allison Roddan, Robert Lewis, Audrey Betz, Martha Raye, Isobel Elsom, Irving Bacon

MOON AND SIXPENCE, THE   U.S.A. (1942)
Based on the novel by Somerset Maugham which was inspired by the life of the artist Gauguin this Albert Lewin movie traces the later career of a 40-year-old Edwardian stockbroker (George Sanders) who suddenly deserts his wife and family in order to devote his life to painting. Much of the quality of Maugham's novel comes across in this faithful version. Herbert Marshall appears as the narrator author and there is a superb cameo from Florence Bates as the bighearted proprietress of a Tahitian hotel. Shot in monochrome except for one sequence in which the dead artist's work is revealed around the walls of his Tahitian home.

DAVID L. LOEW—ALBERT LEWIN INC./UNITED ARTISTS

Production—David L. Loew
Associate producer—
  Stanley Kramer
Direction—Albert Lewin
Screenplay—Albert Lewin

Photography—John Seitz
Art direction—F. Paul Sylos
Music—Dimitri Tiomkin
Editing—Richard L. Van Enger

PLAYERS: George Sanders, Herbert Marshall, Steve Geray, Doris Dudley, Eric Blore, Albert Basserman, Florence Bates

MOON IS BLUE, THE   U.S.A. (1953)
Comedy derived from the 1951 Broadway stage success reveals a young American girl (Maggie McNamara) and her experiences with

a couple of New York wolves (William Holden and David Niven). Strictly minor Preminger but Hugh Herbert's script is amusing and uses for the first time on the screen such previously forbidden words as "virgin," "seduction," and "mistress." The picture caused something of a censorship rumpus when first shown in 1953.

UNITED ARTISTS

Production & direction—
Otto Preminger
Screenplay (from his play)—
F. Hugh Herbert
*Photography—*Ernest Laszlo

Production design—
Nicolei Remisoff
*Music—*Herschel Burke Gilbert
Editorial supervision—
Otto Ludwig

PLAYERS: Maggie McNamara, William Holden, David Niven, Dawn Addams, Gregory Ratoff, Tom Tully

MORE THE MERRIER, THE U.S.A. (1943)
A beautifully made comedy set in Washington during the famous housing shortage and showing Government employee (Jean Arthur) who lets half her apartment to retired industrialist (Charles Coburn) who in turn sublets half of his half to young aircraft technician (Joel McCrea) with hilarious and romantic results. Smart, civilized, continuously funny and expertly directed by George Stevens (New York Critics Award for direction, 1943).

COLUMBIA

Production & direction—
George Stevens
*Screenplay—*Robert Russell,
Frank Ross, Richard Flounoy,
Lewis R. Foster
*Photography—*Ted Tetzlaff

*Story—*Robert Russell, Frank
Ross
*Art direction—*Lionel Banks
*Associate—*Rudolph Sternad
*Music—*Leigh Harline
*Editing—*Otto Meyer

PLAYERS: Jean Arthur, Joel McCrea, Charles Coburn, Richard Gaines, Bruce Bennett, Frank Sully, Clyde Fillmore, Stanley Clements, Don Douglas

MORGAN, A SUITABLE CASE FOR TREATMENT
Gt. Britain (1966)
Complex, highly original fantasy developed by David Mercer from his own play about a young working-class anarchist (David Warner) who spends most of his time living in a dream world inhabited by animals and whose ingenious efforts to win back his divorced wife (Vanessa

Redgrave)—they include trying to abduct her King Kong style from her wedding reception and trying to blow up her mother with a home-made bomb—cause him to drift from an amiable eccentricity into a maniacal and ultimately pitiful madness. For most of the time the film is hilariously funny, especially in the sequences involving the hero's Bolshevist mother (Irene Handl) and her wrestler boyfriend (Arthur Mullard), but beneath the humor the film is basically serious and comments frequently on the social stigma of mental illness and on society's rebuttal of the outsider.

A QUINTRA PRODUCTION

Production—Leon Clore   *Photography*—Larry Pizer &
Direction—Karel Reisz   Gerry Turpin
Screenplay—David Mercer   *Music*—John Dankworth
Art direction—Philip Harrison   *Editing*—Victor Proctor
PLAYERS: David Warner, Vanessa Redgrave, Robert Stephens, Irene Handl, Newton Blick, Nan Munroe, Bernard Bresslaw, Arthur Mullard

MOROCCO   U.S.A. (1931)
Marlene Dietrich's Hollywood debut as the sultry cabaret singer Amy Jolly who falls in love with Foreign Legionnaire Gary Cooper. Splendidly evoked desert atmosphere and a scintillating performance from Dietrich who won an Academy Award nomination as year's best actress. Josef von Sternberg had earlier guided Dietrich through *The Blue Angel* and, between 1931 and 1935, worked with her on no less than six occasions, making her one of the world's most popular stars.

PARAMOUNT

Direction—Josef von Sternberg   *Photography*—Lee Garmes
Screenplay (*based on novel* Amy   *Set designer*—Hans Dreier
  Jolly *by Benno Vigny*)—   *Editing*—Sam Winston
  Jules Furthman
PLAYERS: Gary Cooper, Marlene Dietrich, Adolphe Menjou, Ullrich Haupt, Juliette Compton, Francis MacDonald, Albert Conti, Eve Southern

MORTAL STORM, THE   U.S.A. (1940)
A prosperous middle-class German family, led by respected college professor (Frank Morgan), is torn apart and destroyed by Nazism. Despite a hackneyed script and artificial Cedric Gibbons sets, Borzage's handling is assured and the message comes across strongly. Seen in retrospect this is probably Hollywood's most impressive anti-Nazi movie.

Margaret Sullavan plays the professor's daughter and James Stewart (a pacifist) and Robert Young (a Nazi party member) are her lovers.

METRO–GOLDWYN–MAYER

Direction—Frank Borzage
Screenplay (from book by Phyllis Bottome—Claudine West, Andersen Ellis & George Froeschel

Photography—William Daniels
Art direction—Cedric Gibbons & Wade B. Rubottom
Music—Edward Kane
Editing—Elmo Veron

PLAYERS: Margaret Sullavan, James Stewart, Robert Young, Frank Morgan, Robert Stack, Bonita Granville, Irene Rich

MOST DANGEROUS GAME, THE (The Hounds of Zaroff)

U.S.A. (1932)

Superior horror film about the sadistic pleasures of a fanatical big-game hunter (Leslie Banks) who, bored with hunting animals, turns to human beings for his victims. Among the best films in the genre, expertly photographed and containing some genuinely frightening sequences, particularly those in which the victims of a shipwreck are hunted through jungle swamps by Zaroff's terrifying pack of hounds.

RKO RADIO

Production—Merian C. Cooper
Direction—Ernest B. Schoedsack, Irving Pichel
Screenplay (from novel by Richard Connell)— J. A. Creelman

Photography—Henry Gerrard
Art direction—Carroll Clark
Music—Max Steiner
Editing—Archie Marshek

PLAYERS: Leslie Banks, Fay Wray, Joel McCrea, Robert Armstrong, Hale Hamilton, Noble Johnson

MOTHER

U.S.S.R. (1926)

Pudovkin's film of Maxim Gorky's great novel about a heroic young revolutionary who, in the futile prewar revolution of 1906, gives his life fighting against the misery and poverty of Tsarist Russia and, in so doing, brings about his own mother's political awareness. Visually superb; Vera Baranovskaya's portrayal of the mother is one of the supreme acting performances of the silent cinema.

MEZHRABPOM–RUSS

Direction—Vsevolod Pudovkin
Assistants—Mikhail Doller, V. Strauss

Screenplay—Nathan Zarkhi
Photography—Anatoli Golovnya
Art direction—Sergei Kozlovsky

PLAYERS: Vera Baranovskaya, Nikolai Batalov, A. Chistyakov, Ivan Koval-Samborsky

MOULIN ROUGE   Gt. Britain (1952)
Beautifully colored but overlong film biography of the crippled French painter Toulouse Lautrec. Disappointingly routine for most of the time except for the opening 15 minutes when Huston and cameraman Oswald Morris brilliantly re-create all the noise, color and gaiety of the old Moulin Rouge. José Ferrer (Lautrec) played the role on his knees with his legs strapped behind his back.

ROMULUS/UNITED ARTISTS

Production—Jack Clayton   *Photography (Technicolor)*—
Direction—John Huston   Oswald Morris
Screenplay (from novel by   *Art direction*—Marcel Vertes
  Pierre LaMure)—John Huston,   *Music*—George Auric
  Anthony Veiller   *Editing*—Ralph Kemplen
PLAYERS: José Ferrer, Colette Marchand, Suzanne Flon, Zsa Zsa Gabor, Katherine Kath, Claude Nollier, Muriel Smith, Georges Lannes.

MUMMY, THE   U.S.A. (1932)
German cameraman Karl Freund's underrated horror classic gave Boris Karloff one of his more restrained horror roles as the 3,700-year-old mummified Egyptian priest Imhotep accidentally brought back to life by an English archeologist. The actual awakening of Karloff is a terrifying scene by any standards. Freund directed one more film, *Mad Love* (1935), a remake of *The Hands of Orlac*, before returning permanently to his more accustomed role behind the cameras.

UNIVERSAL

Direction—Karl Freund   Richard Schayer)—
Screenplay (from story by   John L. Balderston
  Nina Wilcox Putnam and   *Photography*—Charles Stumar
PLAYERS: Boris Karloff, Zita Johann, David Manners, Arthur Byron, Edward Van Sloan, Bramwell Fletcher, Noble Johnson, Leonard Mudie, Henry Victor

MURDERS IN THE RUE MORGUE   U.S.A. (1932)
Bizarre horror movie about a maniacal doctor (Bela Lugosi) who performs diabolical experiments with kidnapped women and a huge gorilla in order to prove his mad theories about evolution. Some moments of sadism but skillfully directed by Robert Florey who was

303

handed this assignment by Universal after *Frankenstein,* the plum directing job, had gone to James Whale. Photographed by Karl Freund who later that same year went on to direct his own horror movie, *The Mummy.*

Direction—Robert Florey   *Screenplay (from story by*
Dialogue—John Huston   *Edgar Allan Poe)*—
Photography—Karl Freund   Tom Reed, Dale van Avery

PLAYERS: Bela Lugosi, Sidney Fox, Leon Waycoff (later Ames), Bert Roach, Brandon Hurst, Noble Johnson, D'Arcy Corrigan, Betty Ross Clarke, Arlene Francis

MUSIC BOX, THE   U.S.A. (1932)

The plot of this celebrated Laurel and Hardy short consists of nothing more than Stan and Ollie unloading a piano from a horse and cart and then attempting to haul it up an enormously long flight of stone steps. James Parrott's handling of this basic gag was so ingenious, however, and the editing so brilliant that the film was named as best short subject of 1932, the only Laurel and Hardy film ever to win an Oscar. Parrott directed 20 of the Laurel and Hardy films, including *Two Tars, Night Owls* and *County Hospital.*

HAL ROACH/METRO—GOLDWYN—MAYER

Direction—James Parrott
PLAYERS: Stan Laurel and Oliver Hardy, Billy Gilbert, Charlie Hall

MUTINY ON THE BOUNTY   U.S.A. (1935)

Charles Laughton at his brilliant best as the tyrannical and sadistic Captain Bligh who puts the crew of HMS *Bounty* through every kind of misery before being deposed by first officer Fletcher Christian (Clark Gable) and set adrift, together with a group of non-mutineers, in an open boat. Efficiently directed by Frank Lloyd (this is perhaps his best film) and well played all around. This is Laughton's film from beginning to end despite the fact that the real-life Captain Bligh was nowhere near as brutal or perverted as the script and actor make him out to be. The film won the Academy Award as best production of the year and was remade, less effectively, in 1962 with Trevor Howard as Bligh and Marlon Brando as a foppish Fletcher Christian.

METRO—GOLDWYN—MAYER

Production—Irving G. Thalberg   *Direction*—Frank Lloyd
Associate producer—   *Photography*—Arthur Edeson
     Albert Lewin   *Art direction*—Cedric Gibbons

Music—Herbert Stothart Talbot Jennings,
Screenplay (from novel by Jules Furthman &
  Charles Nordhoff and Carey Wilson
  James Norman Hall)— *Editing*—Margaret Booth
PLAYERS: Clark Gable, Charles Laughton, Franchot Tone, Dudley
Digges, DeWitt Jennings, Movita, Mamo, Herbert Mundin, Donald
Crisp

MY CHILDHOOD (Among People) U.S.S.R. (1939)

The continuing story of Gorky's childhood traces his early working
life (he began earning his living at the age of nine) as a scullion in a
merchant's house, a dishwasher on a Volga river steamer, and as an
apprentice in a studio of aged icon painters. The film is basically
the second half of *The Childhood of Maxim Gorky*, again being set on
the Volga and including most of the characters who appeared in the
first film. The picture ends with Gorky taking leave of his grandparents
and setting off to find new work. Gorky is again played by Alexei
Lyarsky although in the last part of the trilogy (*My Universities*) he is
played by an older youth named Valbert. Both boys were killed during
fighting in the Second World War.

SOYUZDETFILM

Direction—Mark Donskoi *Photography*—Pyotr Yermolov
Screenplay (from Gorky's *Art direction*—I. Stepanov
  memoirs)—I. Gruzdev *Music*—Lev Schwartz
PLAYERS: Alexei Lyarsky, Varvara Massalitinova, Mikhail Troyanovsky

MY DARLING CLEMENTINE U.S.A. (1946)

A traditional, poetic Western set in Tombstone against a background
of the famous gunfight between Marshal Wyatt Earp and the Clanton
gang. One of John Ford's most imposing films, it was shot on the Utah-
Arizona border and has fine performances from Henry Fonda as Earp,
Walter Brennan as "Ole Man Clanton," and Victor Mature as the
drunken, consumptive "Doc" Holliday. Easily the best Western of
1946.

TWENTIETH CENTURY—FOX

Production—Samuel G. Engel *Screenplay (from story by*
Direction—John Ford   *Sam Hellman, based on book*
Photography—Joe MacDonald   Wyatt Earp, Frontier Marshal
Art direction—Lyle Wheeler,   *by Stuart N. Lake)*—Samuel G.
  James Basevi   Engel, Winston Miller
Music—Alfred Newman   *Editing*—Dorothy Spencer

PLAYERS: Henry Fonda, Linda Darnell, Victor Mature, Walter Brennan, Tim Holt, Cathy Downs, Ward Bond, Alan Mowbray, Jane Darwell, John Ireland, Grant Withers, Roy Roberts, Russell Simpson

MY FAIR LADY   U.S.A. (1964)

Professor Henry Higgins (Rex Harrison) transforms cockney flower girl Eliza Doolittle (Audrey Hepburn) into a well-spoken society lady to the accompaniment of one of the wittiest scores ever written for a musical comedy. George Cukor's film version of the 1956 Broadway hit is filmed more or less straight, but is none the worse for that. Harrison and Stanley Holloway (as Eliza's dustman father) repeat their original stage roles; newcomers include Hepburn herself and Wilfrid Hyde White as Colonel Pickering. Eight Oscars including best film, direction, actor (Harrison) and costumes.

WARNER BROS.

Production—Jack L. Warner
Direction—George Cukor
Screenplay (from play Pygmalion
    by George Bernard Shaw, &
    musical by Alan Jay Lerner
    and Frederick Loewe)—
    Alan Jay Lerner
Photography (Technicolor/
    Super Panavision 70)—
    Harry Stradling

Art direction—Gene Allen
Costumes, scenery &
    production design—
    Cecil Beaton
Music—Lerner (lyrics) &
    Loewe (music)
Music supervision—
    Andre Previn
Editing—William Ziegler

PLAYERS: Rex Harrison, Audrey Hepburn, Stanley Holloway, Wilfrid Hyde White, Gladys Cooper, Jeremy Brett, Theodore Bikel

MY LITTLE CHICKADEE   U.S.A. (1940)

W. C. Fields as card-playing rogue Cuthbert J. Twillie and Mae West as Flower Belle Lee team together in a burlesque of life in the Old West during the 1880's. This is the film in which Fields gets into bed with a goat thinking that it is Mae West and also in which he ruminates wistfully on how he struggled across Africa without a corkscrew "living for days on only food and water." Much hip swinging and wisecracking from Miss West, superb vaudeville comedy from Fields; a unique comedy that, like many of Fields' movies, improves with age.

UNIVERSAL

Production—Lester Cowan   Direction—Edward Cline

Original screenplay—Mae West 　*Art direction*—Jack Otterson
& W. C. Fields 　　　　　　　*Music*—Frank Skinner
Photography—Joseph Valentine *Editing*—Ed. Curtiss
PLAYERS: W. C. Fields, Mae West, Joseph Calleia, Dick Foran, Margaret Hamilton, George Moran, Si Jenks

MYSTERY OF THE WAX MUSEUM U.S.A. (1933)

Superior American horror movie of the early 1930's with Lionel Atwill in top form as a horribly disfigured sculptor who shapes wax models from corpses stolen from the morgue. The film, regarded as a minor classic by many critics, is remembered mainly because of one terrifying scene in which heroine Fay Wray dies a thousand deaths when she strikes at the masked face of the sculptor and watches it disintegrate to reveal the hideously charred features beneath. Remade some 20 years later, not ineffectively, as the 3-D *House of Wax* with Vincent Price in the Atwill role.

WARNER BROS.

Direction—Michael Curtiz 　*Screenplay (from play by*
Photography—Ray Rennahan 　*Charles S. Belden)*—
Editing—George Amy 　　　　Don Mullaly & Carl Erickson
PLAYERS: Lionel Atwill, Fay Wray, Glenda Farrell, Frank McHugh, Allen Vincent, Holmes Herbert, Monica Bannister

MY UNIVERSITIES U.S.S.R. (1940)

The last part of Donskoi's trilogy about the early life of Maxim Gorky is set this time in the slums of the Russian town of Kazan and concentrates for most of its length on Gorky's employment and rebellion against the sweated labor of a squalid bakery. The film jumps forward some nine or ten years in time from the earlier films and examines the early revolutionary stirrings within the great writer, played on this occasion by Y. Valbert. Donskoi directed all three films and his production team—cameraman Yermolov, designer Stepanov and composer Schwartz—also worked throughout the trilogy. Earlier films are *The Childhood of Maxim Gorky* and *My Childhood*.

SOYUZDETFILM

Direction—Mark Donskoi 　　*Photography*—Pyotr Yermolov
Screenplay—I. Gruzdev & 　　*Art direction*—I. Stepanov
Mark Donskoi 　　　　　　　*Music*—Lev Schwartz
PLAYERS: Y. Valbert, Stepan Kayukov, Nikolai Dorokhin, Lev Sverdlin

NAKED CITY, THE   U.S.A. (1948)

One of the best of Hollywood's semidocumentary thrillers of the late 1940's, this simple, straightforward story centers on two Homicide Bureau detectives (Barry Fitzgerald and Don Taylor) as they attempt to track down the killer of a New York model. Distinguished principally by Jules Dassin's taut direction and the camera work of William Daniels (Academy Award, 1948) who shot the greater part of the film on the streets of New York during a heat wave. Producer Mark Hellinger's last movie.

A UNIVERSAL–INTERNATIONAL PICTURE

Production—Mark Hellinger
Direction—Jules Dassin
Screenplay (from story by
  Malvin Ward)—Albert Maltz
  & Malvin Wald
Photography—William Daniels

Art direction—
  Bernard Herzbrun &
  John F. DeCuir
Music—Miklos Rozsa
Editing—Paul Weatherwax

PLAYERS: Barry Fitzgerald, Don Taylor, Howard Duff, Dorothy Hart, Ted De Corsia, House Jameson, Anne Sargent, Adelaide Klein

NAKED JUNGLE, THE   U.S.A. (1954)

Unusual science-fiction thriller set in the South American jungle at the turn of the century focuses on the relationship between a plantation owner (Charlton Heston) and the wife (Eleanor Parker) he has married by proxy and their combined efforts to defeat a massive army of advancing soldier ants. Producer George Pal and director Byron Haskin have been regularly associated with the science-fiction genre during the last 20 years, Pal producing such films as *Destination Moon, When Worlds Collide, War of the Worlds* and *The Time Machine,* and Haskin directing, among others, *War of the Worlds, Conquest of Space* and *Robinson Crusoe on Mars.*

PARAMOUNT

Production—George Pal
Direction—Byron Haskin
Screenplay (from story
  "Leiningen Versus the Ants"
  by Carl Stephenson)—
  Philip Yordan &
  Ranald MacDougall

Photography (Technicolor)—
  Ernest Laszlo
Art direction—Hal Pereira &
  Franz Bachelin
Music—Daniele Amfitheatrof
Editing—Everett Douglas

PLAYERS: Eleanor Parker, Charlton Heston, William Conrad, Abraham Sofaer, Norma Calderon, John Dierkes, Douglas Fowley

NANOOK OF THE NORTH   U.S.A. (1922)
The first feature-length documentary shows the daily life and struggle
for survival of an Eskimo hunter and his family. The 6-reel picture was
sponsored by the Revillion Fréres fur company and shot by explorer-
film-maker Robert Flaherty on location in Baffin Land between the
years 1920 and 1922. Flaherty tried five different distributors before
Pathé agreed to run the film at the Capitol Theater in New York,
where it became a commercial success and established his reputation
as a film-maker of the highest class.

REVILLON FRERES/PATHÉ

Direction, screenplay &   Subtitles—Carl Stearns Clancy
   photography—   & Robert J. Flaherty
   Robert J. Flaherty   Editing—Robert J. Flaherty
Assistant—Captain Thierry Mallet
PLAYERS: Nanook, his wife Nyla, and their children

NARROW MARGIN, THE   U.S.A. (1952)
Tough detective (Charles McGraw) escorts gangster's widow (Marie
Windsor) on a train journey from Chicago to Los Angeles in order to
protect her from the crime syndicate determined to kill her before she
can turn state's evidence. Way above the usual B thriller, neat and
well-constructed, among the best train films. Efficiently directed by
Richard Fleischer whose last B picture this was.

RKO RADIO

Production—Stanley Rubin   Photography—George E. Diskant
Direction—Richard Fleischer   Art direction—
Screenplay (from story by   Albert S. D'Agostino
   Martin Goldsmith & Jack   & Jack Okey
   Leonard)—Earl Felton   Editing—Robert Swink
PLAYERS: Charles McGraw, Marie Windsor, Jacqueline White, Gordon
Gebert, Queenie Leonard, David Clarke

NAVIGATOR, THE   U.S.A. (1924)
Classic Buster Keaton comedy about the efforts of a young millionaire
(Keaton) and his dumb girl friend (Kathryn McGuire) to survive when
they are stranded alone on a luxury ocean liner that caters to a
thousand passengers. Visually brilliant and financially (the film grossed
an estimated $2,000,000 on its first release) the most successful of all
Keaton's pictures.

BUSTER KEATON PRODUCTIONS INC./METRO—GOLDWYN

Nazarin

Production—Joseph M. Schenck
Direction—Buster Keaton,
   Donald Crisp
Screenplay—Clyde Bruckman,
   Jean Havez, Joseph Mitchell

Photography—Elgin Lessley,
   Byron Houck
Technical direction—
   Fred Gabourie
Electrical effects—
   Denver Harmon

PLAYERS: Buster Keaton, Kathryn McGuire, Frederick Vroom, Noble Johnson, Clarence Burton, H. M. Clugston

NAZARIN   Mexico (1958)
A saintly young parish priest in poverty-stricken Mexico at the turn of the century sets out to live the pure Christian life, but finds that his efforts only bring disaster to himself and to all the beggars, thieves and whores who come in contact with him. A stark, disturbing film in which Buñuel attacks bigotry, the hypocrisy of those who lead a spiritual life, and shows that both the Church and Christian values are hopelessly inept in a modern society.

MANUEL BARBACHANO PONCE
Direction—Luis Buñuel   *Photography*—
Screenplay (from novel by   Gabriel Figueroa
Benito Pérez Galdós)—   *Art direction*—
Luis Buñuel and   Edward Fitzgerald
Julio Alejandro   *Editing*—Carlos Savage
PLAYERS: Francisco Rabal, Marga Lopez, Rita Macedo, Ignacio Lopez
Tarso, Ofelia Guilmain, Luis Aceves Castañeda

NEVER GIVE A SUCKER AN EVEN BREAK   U.S.A. (1941)

W. C. Fields on the loose in Mexico selling wooden nutmegs to members of a Russian colony and becoming involved with wealthy man-eater Margaret Dumont who spends most of her time living on top of a mountain. Zany, confused and very, very funny; the last of Fields' quartet of Universal comedies and his last starring feature. The original story, if that is what it can be called, was credited to Otis Criblecoblis which was yet another of Fields' pseudonyms.

UNIVERSAL

Direction—Edward Cline   *Art direction*—Jack Otterson,
Screenplay—John T. Neville,   Richard H. Riedel
Prescott Chaplin   *Music*—Frank Skinner
Photography—Charles Van Enger   *Editing*—Arthur Hilton
PLAYERS: W. C. Fields, Gloria Jean, Billy Lenhart, Kenneth Brown,
Anne Nagel, Franklin Pangborn, Mona Barrie, Leon Errol, Margaret
Dumont

NEVER ON SUNDAY   Greece (1960)

Slight little comedy about an American tourist (Jules Dassin) who tries to reform, by education, the most popular prostitute (Melina Mercouri) on the waterfront of Piraeus in the port of Athens. Some amusing moments, but the film has enjoyed something of an inflated reputation over the years primarily because of Manus Hadjidakis' music score, the main theme of which became one of the most popular standards of the 1960's. Made on a shoestring in Greece by Dassin, several of whose later films also feature wife Melina Mercouri—i.e. *Phaedra, Topkapi, 10:30 p.m. Summer,* etc.

LOPERT PICTURES—MELINA FILM/UNITED ARTISTS

Production & direction—   *Photography*—Jacques Natteau
Jules Dassin   *Music*—Manos Hadjidakis
Original screenplay—Jules Dassin   *Editing*—Roger Dwyre

311

PLAYERS: Melina Mercouri, Jules Dassin, Georges Foundas, Tito Vandis, Mitsos Liguisos, Despo Diamantidou, Dimos Starrenios

NIGHT AT THE OPERA, A   U.S.A. (1935)

Groucho, Chico and Harpo involved (inevitably) with Margaret Dumont as a patron of opera and the superb Sig Rumann as the director of the New York opera company. Romantic and musical interludes sometimes get in the way of the gags, but there are some memorable moments: scores of people pouring into and then tumbling out of a tiny ship's cabin and a zany climax during a performance of grand opera. The first of the five Marx Bros. films at M-G-M and their first without Zeppo who had become their agent.

METRO–GOLDWYN–MAYER

Production—Irving G. Thalberg	Photography—Merritt B. Gerstad
Direction—Sam Wood	Art direction—Cedric Gibbons,
Screenplay—George S. Kaufman	Ben Carré & Edwin B. Willis
& Morrie Ryskind	Musical score—
Additional material—Al Boasberg	Herbert Stothart
Story—James Kevin McGuinness	Editing—William LeVanway

PLAYERS: Groucho, Harpo & Chico Marx, Margaret Dumont, Sig Rumann, Kitty Carlisle, Allan Jones, Walter King, Edward Keane

NIGHT OF THE DEMON   Gt. Britain (1957)

Jacques Tourneur's most distinguished venture into the horror genre since his Val Lewton films of the forties, a modernization of the M. R. James story "Casting the Runes" about the summoning up of demons and monsters from outside time and space. Understated and at its best when hinting at the presence of unknown terror, but marred ultimately by the appearance of an unconvincing monster (inserted at the studio's insistence, not Tourneur's) which seriously damages the carefully established mood.

SABRE FILMS

Production—Frank Bevis	Photography—Ted Scaife
Direction—Jacques Tourneur	Art direction—Ken Adam
Screenplay—Charles Bennett &	Music—Clifton Parker
Hal E. Chester	Editing—Michael Gordon

PLAYERS: Dana Andrews, Peggy Cummings, Niall MacGinnis, Athene Seyler, Maurice Denham, Liam Redmond, Reginald Beckwith, Rosamund Greenwood

NIGHT OF THE HUNTER   U.S.A. (1955)

A strange, often frightening little film, set in Missouri during the 1930's, about a psychopathic backwoods preacher's relentless pursuit of two children who alone can tell him the whereabouts of their dead father's money. One of the most poetic American films of the fifties, directed with great style by Charles Laughton (the only occasion he ever directed) and beautifully photographed by Stanley Cortez whose night scenes, particularly those depicting the children's nightmarish flight down the Ohio River, are comparable to his great work on Welles' *The Magnificent Ambersons.*

UNITED ARTISTS

Production—Paul Gregory   *Photography*—Stanley Cortez
Direction—Charles Laughton   *Art direction*—Hilyard Brown
Screenplay (*from novel by*   *Music*—Walter Schumann
   Davis Grubb)—James Agee   *Editing*—Robert Golden
PLAYERS: Robert Mitchum, Shelley Winters, Lillian Gish, Evelyn Varden, Peter Graves, Billy Chapin, Sally Jane Bruce, James Gleason

NIGHT OWLS   U.S.A. (1930)

Vintage Laurel and Hardy short is based, like so many of their early 2-reelers, almost entirely on a single joke: Stan and Ollie's hilarious attempts to break into and rob a locked house. Brilliantly inventive slapstick; Edgar Kennedy appears as a blackmailing cop and Anders Randolph as a police chief.

HAL ROACH/METRO–GOLDWYN–MAYER

Direction—James Parrott   *Story*—Leo McCarey
PLAYERS: Stan Laurel and Oliver Hardy, Edgar Kennedy, Anders Randolph

NIGHTMARE ALLEY   U.S.A. (1947)

Tyrone Power in the most satisfying role of his career as a ruthless young carnival barker who exploits a mind-reading and spiritualist act to the full before being cheated himself and sinking to the lowest depths of alcoholic degradation. This extraordinary movie perceptively examines the carnival and fake spiritualist rackets in America and looks considerably more impressive in retrospect than when first shown in 1947. The most accomplished film of director Edmund Goulding's later career.

TWENTIETH CENTURY–FOX

Production—George Jessel   *Direction*—Edmund Goulding

Screenplay (from novel by
William Lindsay Gresham)—
Jules Furthman
Photography—Lee Garmes

Art direction—Lyle Wheeler &
J. Russell Spencer
Music—Cyril J. Mockridge
Editing—Barbara McLean

PLAYERS: Tyrone Power, Joan Blondell, Coleen Gray, Helen Walker, Taylor Holmes, Mike Mazurki, Ian Keith

NIGHTS OF CABIRIA (Le Notti di Cabiria)   France/Italy (1957)
The hopes, fears and experiences of a happy-go-lucky and ever-optimistic Roman prostitute as she endeavours, with tragic results, to attain respectability. Brilliantly performed by Giulietta Masina (Fellini's wife) as the streetwalker who is never better than in the very last scene when, robbed of her life savings and deserted by the man she had hoped to marry, she smiles defiantly through her tears and begins the long trudge back to Rome and her old life. Sad, very moving, it is among Fellini's best.

DINO DE LAURENTIIS/FILMS MARCEAU

Production—Dino de Laurentiis
Direction—Federico Fellini
Photography—Aldo Tonti
Art direction—Piero Gherardi
Music—Nino Rota

Screenplay—Federico Fellini,
Ennio Flaiano, & Tullio Pinelli
Additional dialogue—
Pier Paolo Pasolini
Editing—Leo Cattozzo

PLAYERS: Giulietta Masina, Francois Perier, Amadeo Nazzari, Franca Marzi, Dorian Gray, Aldo Silvana, Mario Passante, Pina Gualandri

NINOTCHKA   U.S.A. (1939)
Cynical Lubitsch comedy featuring Greta Garbo in one of her most famous roles as the straight-laced Russian trade commissar who becomes romantically involved with a goodlooking capitalist (Melvyn Douglas) during her period of service in Paris. Overlong, but with a witty screenplay and delightful supporting performances from Sig Rumann, Felix Bressart and Alexander Granach as Russian emigrés.

METRO–GOLDWYN–MAYER

Production & direction—
Ernst Lubitsch
Screenplay (from original story
by Melchior Lengyel)—
Charles Brackett, Billy Wilder
& Walter Reisch

Photography—William Daniels
Art direction—Cedric Gibbons &
Randall Duell
Music—Werner Heymann
Editing—Gene Ruggiero

PLAYERS: Greta Garbo, Melvyn Douglas, Ina Claire, Bela Lugosi, Felix Bressart, Alexander Granach, Sig Rumann, Gregory Gaye

314

NO WAY OUT   U.S.A. (1950)

One of the last of Hollywood's postwar problem pictures; a well-written thriller on the conflict between a pathological Negro-hater (Richard Widmark) and a young colored intern (Sidney Poitier) who is accused of murder when Widmark's gangster brother dies on the operating table. Now all but forgotten, the film is blunter and more forthright than most of its kind. It comes from the same stable as *Pinky* (also produced by Zanuck) and made the previous year.

TWENTIETH CENTURY–FOX

Production—Darryl F. Zanuck
Direction—Joseph L. Mankiewicz
Screenplay—Joseph L.
    Mankiewicz & Lesser Samuels
Photography—Milton Krasner

Art direction—Lyle Wheeler &
    George W. Davis
Music—Alfred Newman
Editing—Barbara McLean

PLAYERS: Richard Widmark, Sidney Poitier, Linda Darnell, Stephen McNally, Mildred Joanne Smith, Harry Bellaver, Stanley Ridges, Dots Johnson

NO WAY TO TREAT A LADY   U.S.A. (1967)

Very black comedy with Rod Steiger as a psychopathic theater producer who roams New York in a variety of disguises strangling lonely women. George Segal is the detective investigating the case and Lee Remick is an intended victim, but this is Steiger's film without a doubt and his many-faced role allows him to display his considerable talent. Included in his range of impersonations: an Irish priest, a German plumber, a homosexual wig-seller, and a caricature of W. C. Fields.

SOL C. SIEGEL PRODUCTIONS/PARAMOUNT

Production—Sol C. Siegel
Direction—Jack Smight
*Screenplay (based on novel by
    William Goldman)*—John Gay
Music—Stanley Myers

Photography (Technicolor)—
    Jack Priestley
Art direction—Hal Pereira &
    George Jenkins
Editing—Archie Marshek

PLAYERS: Rod Steiger, George Segal, Lee Remick, Eileen Heckart, Murray Hamilton, Michael Dunn, Martine Bartlett, Barbara Baxley

NORA PRENTISS   U.S.A. (1947)

Ingenious though far-fetched Hollywood thriller about a respectable middle-class doctor (Kent Smith) who, hopelessly in love with a cabaret singer (Ann Sheridan), fakes his own death, suffers disfigurement in a car accident and is then accused and tried for his own murder. What makes these somewhat unlikely events so entertaining and believable are the superb performances, particularly Miss Sheridan, whose best film this was.

WARNER BROS.

Executive producer—
  Jack L. Warner
*Direction—*Vincent Sherman
Screenplay (from story by Paul
  Webster & Jack Sobell)—
  N. Richard Nash

Photography—
  James Wong Howe
*Art direction—*Anton Grot
*Music—*Franz Waxman
*Editing—*Owen Marks

PLAYERS: Ann Sheridan, Kent Smith, Bruce Bennett, Robert Alda, Rosemary DeCamp, John Ridgely, Robert Arthur, Wanda Hendrix

NORTH BY NORTHWEST   U.S.A. (1959)

Fast, immensely enjoyable Hitchcock tale about an innocent advertising executive (Cary Grant) who becomes involved in an international espionage plot. Witty script by Ernest Lehman and some of the most famous of all Hitchcock's set pieces—an assassination in the United Nations building, an attempted murder on a deserted prairie road, and an exciting chase over the Presidential stone faces of Mount Rushmore. Superbly done all around and in many ways the most entertaining of Hitchcock's movies.

METRO–GOLDWYN–MAYER

Production & direction—
  Alfred Hitchcock
*Screenplay—*Ernest Lehman
Photography (Technicolor)—
  Robert Burks

*Art direction—*William A.
  Horning, Robert Boyle, Merrill
  Pye
*Music—*Bernard Herrmann
*Editing—*George Tomasini

PLAYERS: Cary Grant, Eva Marie Saint, James Mason, Jessie Royce Landis, Leo G. Carroll, Philip Ober, Josephine Hutchinson, Martin Landau, Adam Williams, Carleton Young

NORTHWEST MOUNTED POLICE   U.S.A. (1940)

Cecil B. DeMille adventure set against the background of the Riel Rebellion in Canada in 1885 tells the pursuit of criminal (George Bancroft) by Texas Ranger (Gary Cooper). Less spectacular than the majority of DeMille's pictures, but with some notable Technicolor locations (this was the first time DeMille had used color throughout his film) and several enjoyable performances. Others in the cast: Madeleine Carroll as an Anglican nurse, Robert Preston and Preston Foster as Mounties, and Paulette Goddard as a half-breed girl.

316

Production & direction—
Cecil B. DeMille
Original screenplay—Alan Le
May, Jesse Lasky, Jr., &
C. Gardner Sullivan
Music—Victor Young

Photography (Technicolor)—
Victor Milner & W. Howard
Greene
Art direction—Hans Dreier &
Roland Anderson
Editing—Anne Bauchens

PLAYERS: Gary Cooper, Madeleine Carroll, Paulette Goddard, Preston Foster, Robert Preston, George Bancroft, Lynne Overman, Akim Tamiroff

NORTHWEST PASSAGE U.S.A. (1940)

Spencer Tracy as the legendary Major Rogers leading his rangers on an epic trek across the wild and uncharted Canadian woods in the eighteenth century. An exciting adventure story directed by King Vidor with heavy emphasis on realism and on the physical suffering endured by the pioneers. The film was originally intended as a two-part production, but the second part dealing with the mapping of a Northwest Passage was never put before the cameras.

Production—Hunt Stromberg
Direction—King Vidor
Screenplay (from novel by
Kenneth Roberts)—Laurence
Stallings, Talbot Jennings

Photography (Technicolor)—
Sidney Wagner, William V.
Skall
Art direction—Cedric Gibbons,
Malcolm Brown
Music—Herbert Stothart

PLAYERS: Spencer Tracy, Robert Young, Walter Brennan, Ruth Hussey, Nat Pendleton, Louis Hector, Robert Barrat, Lumsden Hare, Donald McBride, Isabel Jewell

NOTHING SACRED U.S.A. (1937)

Small-town girl (Carole Lombard), thought to be dying from radium poisoning but in reality as fit as a fiddle, is given the time of her life in New York by a large newspaper who hopes to gain publicity by following the "last weeks" of her life. A classic satire from a brilliant script; Ben Hecht's attacks on publicity methods and the gutter press are consistently on target. Others in the cast: Fredric March as the news reporter who accompanies Lombard on her fling, Walter Connolly as his editor, and Sig Rumann as a famous European specialist on radium poisoning.

Production–David Selznick
Direction–William A. Wellman
Screenplay (from story by James
   H. Street)–Ben Hecht

Photography (Technicolor)–
   W. Howard Greene
Art direction–Lyle Wheeler
Music–Raymond Scott Quintet
Editing–James E. Newcom

PLAYERS: Carole Lombard, Fredric March, Charles Winninger, Walter Connolly, Sig Rumann, Frank Fay, Maxie Rosenbloom

NOTORIOUS U.S.A. (1946)

South American espionage story about FBI agents Cary Grant and Ingrid Bergman who track down a group of Nazis operating in Rio de Janeiro. A tense, polished Hitchcock thriller, unfairly criticized when it was first shown but now ranked with his best work. An excellent portrait of a Fascist leader by Claude Rains and some outstandingly fine photography by cameraman Ted Tetzlaff who shortly afterward turned to directing with considerably less success.

RKO RADIO

Production & direction–
   Alfred Hitchcock
Screenplay (from theme by
   Hitchcock)–Ben Hecht
Photography–Ted Tetzlaff

Art direction–Albert S.
   D'Agostino, Carroll Clark
Music–Roy Webb
Editing–Theron Warth

PLAYERS: Ingrid Bergman, Cary Grant, Claude Rains, Louis Calhern, Leopoldine Konstantin, Reinhold Schunzel, Moroni Olsen, Ivan Triesault

NOUS SOMMES TOUS DES ASSASSINS France (1952)

Powerful anti-capital punishment film that examines the suffering and terror experienced by four men—a doctor, an ex-Resistance worker, a Corsican, and a child murderer—as they wait in the condemned cell during the long bleak weeks before their execution. Sordid and somewhat uneven but the playing is impressive and the message comes across strongly. Directed by former French barrister André Cayatte, it won the International Prize at the Cannes Film Festival in 1952.

U.G.C.

Direction–André Cayatte
Screenplay–André Cayatte &
   Charles Spaak
Photography–Jean Bourgoin

Art direction–
   Jacques Colombier
Editing–Paul Cayatte

PLAYERS: Marcel Mouloudji, Raymond Pellegrin, Antoine Balpêtre, Julien Verdier, Claude Laydu, Jacqueline Pierreux, Louis Seigner

NOW, VOYAGER U.S.A. (1942)

Neurotic young spinster (Bette Davis) whose tyrannical mother (Gladys Cooper) is driving her steadily toward a breakdown is cured of her emotional problems by psychiatrist (Claude Rains), but inherits a fresh set when she meets and falls in love with married Paul Henreid on a recuperatory South American cruise. A trite tale, skillfully rendered, and remembered not only as a Bette Davis vehicle but as the movie in which Paul Henreid performs his famous trick of lighting two cigarettes in his mouth at the same time. Max Steiner's romantic score was named best film music of 1942 by the Academy of Motion Picture Arts and Sciences.

WARNER BROS./FIRST NATIONAL

Production—Hal B. Wallis
Direction—Irving Rapper
Screenplay (based on novel by
  Olive Higgins Prouty)—
  Casey Robinson

Photography—Sol Polito
Music—Max Steiner
Art direction—Robert Haas
Editing—Warren Low

PLAYERS: Bette Davis, Paul Henreid, Claude Rains, Gladys Cooper, Bonita Granville, Ilka Chase, John Loder, Lee Patrick

NUN'S STORY, THE U.S.A. (1959)

Sensitive, extremely moving film about the spiritual struggles of a young Belgian nun whose desire to nurse the sick and learn more about medicine conflicts with the grim discipline of her religious order. The most impressive of all Hollywood-financed religious films, directed with taste and considerable skill by Fred Zinnemann, and notably well acted by Audrey Hepburn as the nun and Peter Finch in a brief role as an agnostic mission doctor working in the Congo. Exquisite color photography by Franz Planer.

WARNER BROS.

Production—Henry Blanke
Direction—Fred Zinnemann
Screenplay (based on book by
  Kathryn C. Hulme)—Robert
  Anderson

Photography (Technicolor)—
  Franz Planer
Art direction—Alexandre Trauner
Music—Franz Waxman
Editing—Walter Thompson

PLAYERS: Audrey Hepburn, Peter Finch, Edith Evans, Peggy Ashcroft,

Dean Jagger, Mildred Dunnock, Niall MacGinnis, Patricia Collinge, Eva Kotthaus

OCCUPE-TOI D'AMÉLIE   France (1949)
Consistently amusing French farce concerns the exploits of a young courtesan in the Paris of 1910. Full of the usual confusion—indiscreet bedroom scenes, hiding behind curtains, etc.—and filmed by Claude Autant-Lara as a stage play in three clearly defined acts with the camera occasionally going over the footlights to observe the audience and also into the dressing rooms to observe the players. Some dazzling costumes and sets, a stunning heroine (Danielle Darrieux), and a lascivious Balkan prince (Grégoire "Coco" Aslan).

LUX FILMS

Direction—Claude Autant-Lara   *Photography*—André Bac
Screenplay, adaptation &   *Art direction*—Max Douy
  dialogue (from play by   *Music*—René Cloërec
  Georges Feydeau)—Jean   *Editing*—Madeleine Gug
  Aurenche & Pierre Bost
PLAYERS: Danielle Darrieux, Jean Desailly, Louise Conte, Bervil, Armontel, Carette, Grégoire Aslan

OCTOBER   U.S.S.R. (1928)
Spectacular reconstruction of the events that took place in Russia between Lenin's secret return from exile and the Bolshevik seizure of power in 1917. Contains several of Eisenstein's most memorable scenes: the destruction of the Tsar's statue, the satirical observations of Kerensky during his first days of power in the Winter Palace, and the Raising of the Bridges during the St. Petersburg demonstrations. Superb lighting effects by Edouard Tisse; Eisenstein's third film and one of several made in Russia to commemorate the tenth anniversary of the Revolution.

SOVKINO (MOSCOW & LENINGRAD)

Screenplay & direction—Sergei   *Assistants*—Vladimir Nilsen,
  Eisenstein, Grigori Alexandrov   Vladimir Popov
Assistants—Maxim Strauch,   *Art direction*—Vasili Kovrigin
  Mikhail Gomarov, Ilya   *Music (for performance abroad)*
  Trauberg   —Edmund Meisel
Photography—Eduard Tissé
PLAYERS: Nikandrov, N. Popov

OH! MR. PORTER   Gt. Britain (1937)
Well-loved British comedy of the 1930's with stationmaster (Will Hay)
in charge of the derelict and supposedly haunted Bugleskelly railway
station and presumably being aided but mostly hindered by his two
assistants (Moore Marriott and Graham Moffatt). A vintage Hay comedy that is almost certainly his best; contains a hilarious climax on a
runaway railway engine named "Gladstone."

GAINSBOROUGH

Direction—Marcel Varnel   Art direction—Vetchinsky
Screenplay—J. O. C. Orton, Val   Music—Louis Levy
    Guest, Marriott Edgar   Editing—R. E. Dearing, Alfred
Photography—Arthur Crabtree   Roome
PLAYERS: Will Hay, Moore Marriott, Graham Moffatt, Sebastian Smith,
Agnes Lauchlan, Percy Walsh

OH! WHAT A LOVELY WAR   Gt. Britain (1969)
Joan Littlewood's 1963 musical about World War I adapted by Len
Deighton and Richard Attenborough (his first film as a director) into
screen terms, the Pierrot company of the stage show being ingeniously
replaced by Brighton pier on which the various scenes, except those
in the trenches, are played out. The tragedy of millions of wasted dead
is apparent in every frame of this deeply moving film, never more so
than in the final fadeout when, to the accompaniment of Jerome Kern's
"They Wouldn't Believe Me" the camera pulls back from a hillside and
reveals an infinity of white crosses. The huge cast includes almost every
major star of the British cinema; among them John Mills as Sir Douglas
Haig, Laurence Olivier as Sir John French, Michael Redgrave as Sir
Henry Wilson, and Maggie Smith, brilliant in a small scene.

ACCORD/PARAMOUNT

Production—Brian Duffy, Richard   Screenplay (based on Joan
    Attenborough   Littlewood/Theatre Workshop
Direction—Richard Attenborough   musical play, adapted from
Photography (Technicolor/   radio feature "The Long, Long
    Panavision)—Gerry Turpin   Trail" by Charles Chilton)—
Art direction—Harry White   Len Deighton
Music & musical direction—   Editing—Kevin Connor
    Alfred Ralston
PLAYERS: Ralph Richardson, John Gielgud, Kenneth More, John Mills,
Laurence Olivier, Michael Redgrave, Jack Hawkins, Maggie Smith,
Ian Holm, John Clements, Paul Daneman

OLD DARK HOUSE, THE   U.S.A. (1932)
Creaky horror vehicle adapted from J. B. Priestley's novel *Benighted*
and set in an old Welsh mansion where a group of travelers are forced
to seek shelter during a stormy night. Of interest primarily for the playing of an unbeatable cast. Among the hosts: Boris Karloff as a dumb,
murderous butler, Brember Wills as a pyromaniac dwarf, Ernest
Thesiger and Eva Moore as an insane brother and sister, and John
Dudgeon as a 100-year-old baronet locked in an upstairs room; among
the luckless visitors: Charles Laughton, Melvyn Douglas, Lilian Bond.
Directed by James Whale between his *Frankenstein* and *Invisible Man*
assignments.

UNIVERSAL

Direction—James Whale   *Dialogue*—R. C. Sherriff
Screenplay—Benn W. Levy   *Photography*—Arthur Edeson
PLAYERS: Boris Karloff, Melvyn Douglas, Charles Laughton, Gloria
Stuart, Lilian Bond, Ernest Thesiger, Eva Moore, Raymond Massey,
Brember Wills, John Dudgeon

OLIVER TWIST   Gt. Britain (1948)
David Lean's follow-up to his brilliant *Great Expectations* and only
marginally less effective. The characterizations—Alec Guinness's Fagin,
Francis L. Sullivan's Bumble, Robert Newton's Bill Sykes and Kay
Walsh's Nancy—are equal to any in the earlier picture and the opening
journey to the parish workhouse, the murder of Nancy and the long
sequence in "The Three Cripples" belong with the best scenes from all
his films. Many of the *Great Expectations* production team (cameraman Guy Green, art director John Bryan and editor Jack Harris) also
worked on this second movie. Others in the cast include John Howard
Davies as Oliver, Mary Clare as Mrs. Corney, Henry Stephenson as Mr.
Brownlow, and Anthony Newley as the Artful Dodger.

CINEGUILD

Production—Ronald Neame   *Sets*—John Bryan
Direction—David Lean   *Music*—Sir Arnold Bax
Screenplay—David Lean &   *Costumes*—Margaret Furse
  Stanley Haynes   *Editing*—Jack Harris
Photography—Guy Green
PLAYERS: Robert Newton, Alec Guinness, Kay Walsh, Francis L. Sulli-
van, Henry Stephenson, Mary Clare, John Howard Davies, Anthony
Newley, Peter Bull

322

Oliver Twist

OLYMPISCHE SPIELE 1936 (Olympia)   Germany (1936–38)
The 3-hour 40-minute record of the 1936 Berlin Olympic Games capturing not only the excitement and tension of the games themselves but
also the atmosphere of hysterical nationalism in which the games were
conducted. More poetic in vision than Ichikawa's technically accomplished *Tokyo Olympiad* (1965), although both films in their different
ways are great works of art. Leni Riefenstahl, who was commissioned
by Goebbels to make the film, used over 30 cameramen on the production and spent some two years in the cutting rooms.

LENI RIEFENSTAHL/TOBIS–FILMKUNST

Production, direction & editing—   *Photography—*Hans Ertl, Walter
  Leni Riefenstahl   Frentz, Guzzi Lantschner,
*Assistant—*Walter Ruttman   Kurt Neubert, Hans Scheib,
*Music—*Herbert Windt   Willy Zielke & others

ON THE BEACH   U.S.A. (1959)
American submarine commander (Gregory Peck) teamed with Aus-
tralian girl (Ava Gardner) and guilt-ridden scientist (Fred Astaire) in
Stanley Kramer's film version of Nevil Shute's novel about the last
months of civilization following the end of a nuclear Third World War.
The film is set in Australia, and in particular Melbourne where the inhabitants of the city wait quietly for the lethal radioactive fallout to
drift in from the Northern Hemisphere. The most effective scenes are
those depicting the long queues for suicide pills and those in which
Gregory Peck and his crew make an abortive journey to lifeless San
Francisco.

LOMITAS/UNITED ARTISTS

Production & direction—   *Art direction—*
  Stanley Kramer   Fernando Carrere
*Screenplay—*John Paxton &   *Production design—*
  James Lee Barrett   Rudolph Sternad
Photography—   *Music—*Ernest Gold
  Giuseppe Rotunno   *Editing—*Frederic Knudtson
PLAYERS: Gregory Peck, Ava Gardner, Fred Astaire, Anthony Perkins,
Donna Anderson, John Tate, Lola Brooks

ON THE BOWERY   U.S.A. (1956)
A powerful, often harrowing glimpse into the tragic lives of the alco-
holics and down-and-outers who inhabit the sidewalks and bars of New
York's Skid Row, a poverty-stricken district in the Lower East Side of

Manhattan. A major American documentary, made with great compassion by Lionel Rogosin who spent some eighteen months in the Bowery while making the film, shooting a great many of the scenes with concealed cameras.

A LIONEL ROGOSIN PRODUCTIONS, INC. RELEASE

Production & direction (in
  collaboration with Richard
  Bagley & Mark Sufrin)—
  Lionel Rogosin

Script—Mark Sufrin
Photography—Richard Bagley
Music—Charles Mills
Editing—Carl Lerner

ON THE TOWN   U.S.A. (1949)

Classic musical adapted from the Broadway show *Wonderful Town* about three American sailors (Gene Kelly, Frank Sinatra, Jules Munshin) on 24-hour shore leave in New York. The film ranges from the subways and museums to the top of the Empire State Building. Among its most exhilarating numbers are the opening "New York, New York, It's a Wonderful Town," Ann Miller's tap routine "Prehistoric Joe," and "We're Going on the Town," sung by the six leads as they swing out into a New York street to sample the city's night life. Mixed in with the realistic numbers is the "Miss Turnstiles" fantasy ballet danced by Kelly and Vera-Ellen when the latter comes to life from a subway advertisement. The first of three films co-directed by Kelly and Stanley Donen and along with the same team's *Singin' in the Rain*, the best musical ever made.

METRO–GOLDWYN–MAYER

Production—Arthur Freed
Direction—Stanley Donen,
  Gene Kelly
Screenplay (from their musical
  & Jerome Robbins' ballet
  Fancy Free)—Betty Comden
  & Adolph Green

Photography (Technicolor)—
  Harold Rosson
Art direction—Cedric Gibbons &
  Jack Martin Smith
Music—Leonard Bernstein
Lyrics—Betty Comden &
  Adolph Green
Editing—Ralph E. Winters

PLAYERS: Gene Kelly, Frank Sinatra, Betty Garrett, Ann Miller, Jules Munshin, Vera-Ellen, Florence Bates, Alice Pearce

ON THE WATERFRONT   U.S.A. (1954)

Elia Kazan's superb though slightly softened version of Budd Schulberg's novel about the corruption and brutal racketeering on New York's waterfront with Marlon Brando giving the finest performance of his career as the punch-drunk ex-boxer who takes up the cause of the longshoremen and eventually destroys the stranglehold of the "scab union" bosses. Good support from Rod Steiger as Brando's gangster brother, Karl Malden as a tough waterfront priest, and Lee J. Cobb as a racketeer and some bleak location photography by Boris Kaufman who, during the last fifteen years, has worked almost exclusively for Kazan and Sidney Lumet on New York-based productions. The music score is by Leonard Bernstein, making one of his rare contributions to original film music. The film was awarded eight Oscars, including best film, direction, actor (Brando), screenplay and photography.

HORIZON–AMERICAN PICTURE RELEASED BY COLUMBIA

Production–Sam Spiegel
Direction–Elia Kazan
Story & screenplay–
    Budd Schulberg
Photography–Boris Kaufman

Art direction–Richard Day
Musical score–
    Leonard Bernstein
Editing–Gene Milford

PLAYERS: Marlon Brando, Rod Steiger, Karl Malden, Lee J. Cobb, Eva Marie Saint, Leif Erickson, Pat Henning, James Westerfield

ONE HOUR WITH YOU   U.S.A. (1932)

Musical remake, co-directed by Ernst Lubitsch and George Cukor, of Lubitsch's own *The Marriage Circle,* updated to the 1930's and set in Paris instead of prewar Vienna. Maurice Chevalier and Jeanette Mac-Donald, along with Genevieve Tobin and Roland Young, replaced the original leads, and Victor Milner, who collaborated with Lubitsch on the majority of his Paramount films, was on camera. Other Lubitsch/ Milner collaborations: *The Love Parade, Monte Carlo, The Man I Killed, Trouble in Paradise, Design for Living, Desire.*

PARAMOUNT

Direction–Ernst Lubitsch &
    George Cukor
Screenplay (from play Only a
    Dream *by Lothar Schmidt*)–
    Samson Raphaelson

Photography–Victor Milner
Art direction–Hans Dreier
Music–Oscar Strauss &
    Richard A. Whiting
Lyrics–Leo Robin

PLAYERS: Jeanette MacDonald, Maurice Chevalier, Charles Ruggles, Genevieve Tobin, Roland Young, George Barbier

101 DALMATIANS   U.S.A. (1961)

Disney's most inventive cartoon feature of his later period relates how all the dogs in England, led by the Great Dane of Hampstead, rescue fifteen Dalmatian pups from the clutches of archvillainess Cruella de

Vil, a socialite who plans to turn them into a fur coat. Brisk, funny, often witty; based on the book by Dodie Smith and containing not only the usual exquisite animal characterizations but also some amusing human animation, notably Cruella herself and a couple of endearing robbers named Jasper and Horace.

WALT DISNEY PRODUCTIONS

Production—Walt Disney
Directors—Wolfgang Reitherman, Hamilton S. Luske, Clyde Geronimi
Story—Bill Peet

Art direction & production design—Ken Anderson
Music—George Bruns
Orchestration—Franklin Marks
Songs—Mel Leven

ONLY ANGELS HAVE WINGS U.S.A. (1939)

Characteristic Hawks adventure focuses on the relationship between expatriate fliers operating an airmail service in Central America. An uneven film, let down by a third-rate script, but redeemed by its stunningly photographed aerial scenes and by the enjoyable performances of Cary Grant and Richard Barthelmess as the fliers and Jean Arthur as the wisecracking female lead.

COLUMBIA

Production & direction—Howard Hawks
Screenplay (from story by Hawks)—Jules Furthman
Music—Dimitri Tiomkin

Photography—Elmer Dyer, Joseph Walker
Editing—Viola Lawrence
Special effects—Roy Davidson, Edwin C. Hahn

PLAYERS: Cary Grant, Jean Arthur, Richard Barthelmess, Rita Hayworth, Thomas Mitchell, Sig Rumann, Victor Kilian, John Carroll, Allyn Joslyn

OPEN CITY Italy (1945)

Brutally realistic account of the Italian resistance in Rome during the Nazi occupation. The first of Italy's neo-realistic masterpieces, scripted by Sergio Amidei and Federico Fellini (one of his earliest assignments) and shot for part of the time with concealed cameras while the German Army was still in Rome. A key film in the history of the cinema, superbly played by both professional and nonprofessional actors, particularly Aldo Fabrizi as a priest and Anna Magnani as a young widow.

EXCELSA FILM

Production & direction—Roberto Rossellini
Story—Sergio Amidei

Screenplay—Amidei, Fellini
Photography—Ubaldo Arata
Music—Renzo Rossellini

327

PLAYERS: Aldo Fabrizi, Anna Magnani, Marcello Pagliero, Maria Michi, Harry Feist, Giovanna Galletti, Vito Annicchiarico, Carla Rovere, Van Hulzen, C. Sindici

OSSESSIONE   Italy (1942)
Early Italian neo-realist movie, adapted from James M. Cain's *The Postman Always Rings Twice*, is about a wandering hobo who becomes infatuated with the proprietress of a wayside cafe and conspires with her to murder her husband. A bleak, powerful film, directed by Luchino Visconti (his first) and photographed entirely in the lowlands around Ferrara and in some of the shabbier streets of north Italian towns. An inferior American version of the novel was filmed by Tay Garnett in 1945.

ICI ROME

Direction—Luchino Visconti   *Photography*—Aldo Tonti
Screenplay—Mario Alicata,   Domenico Scala
   Antonio Pietrangeli, Gianni   *Art direction*—Gino Rosati
   Puccini, Giuseppe de Santis &   *Music*—Giuseppe Rosati
   Visconti   *Editing*—Mario Serandrei

PLAYERS: Clara Calamai, Massimo Girotti, Juan de Landa, Elia Marcuzzo, Dhia Cristani, Vittorio Duse

OTHELLO   Morocco (1952)
Visually among Orson Welles' most ornate and memorable films, this version of Shakespeare's tragedy contains a great performance from Welles himself as the jealous Moor and an equally fine one from Micheal MacLiammoir as Iago. The film was made over a period of three years (1949 to 1952), often under the most difficult conditions, one of its most imaginative sequences—the murder of Rodriguez—being staged in a Turkish bath because the men's costumes had been delayed in Rome. Filmed in Venice, Rome and among the old Arab citadels of Mogador in North Africa, it was joint winner of the Grand Prix at the 1952 Cannes Film Festival.

A MERCURY PRODUCTION

Production & direction—   *Art direction*—Alexandre Trauner
   Orson Welles   *Music*—Francesco Lavagnino,
Screenplay—Orson Welles   Alberto Barberis
Photography—Anchise Brizzi,   *Editing*—Jean Sacha, with Renzo
   G. R. Aldo, George Fanto, with   Lucidi, John Shepridge
   Obadan Troiani, Roberto Fusi

PLAYERS: Orson Welles, Micheal MacLiammoir, Suzanne Cloutier, Robert Coote, Hilton Edwards, Michael Lawrence, Fay Compton, Nicholas Bruce

OUR DAILY BREAD   U.S.A. (1934)
Depression movie about a jobless city couple (Tom Keene and Karen Morley) who, together with an out-of-work farmer (John Qualen), take over and make a success of a derelict farm, open up the land to the unemployed and establish a self-supporting rural community. A somewhat neglected picture, of interest primarily for its realism and honest approach to the problems of ordinary people during the bitter years of the 1930's. Marred ultimately by indifferent performances.
                              UNITED ARTISTS
Direction—King Vidor   Screenplay (from story by King
Photography—Robert Planck   Vidor, inspired by article in
Music—Alfred Newman   Reader's Digest)—Elizabeth
Editing—Lloyd Nossler   Hill
PLAYERS: Karen Morley, Tom Keene, John T. Qualen, Barbara Pepper, Addison Richards, Bill Engel

OUR HOSPITALITY   U.S.A. (1923)
Buster Keaton as a New York dandy caught up in a Southern family feud in 19th-century America. One of the best of his early features, enriched by superb period atmosphere and containing one of his most elaborate acrobatic gags in which he swings from a rope to rescue a girl from the top of a raging waterfall.
     BUSTER KEATON/JOSEPH M. SCHENCK PRODUCTIONS/METRO PICTURES
Production—Joseph M. Schenck   Photography—Elgin Lessley,
Direction—Buster Keaton, Jack   Gordon Jennings
  G. Blystone   Technical direction—
Screenplay—Clyde Bruckman,   Fred Gabourie
  Jean Havez, Joseph Mitchell
PLAYERS: Buster Keaton, Joe Roberts, Natalie Talmadge, Joe Keaton, Joseph Keaton Talmadge, Kitty Bradbury, Leonard Chapman, Craig Ward

OUT OF THE PAST   U.S.A. (1947)
Ex-crook turned private-eye (Robert Mitchum) and gangster boss (Kirk Douglas) become involved in murder and double-cross as they search in Mexico for femme fatale (Jane Greer) and $40,000. Tough,

very confusing Jacques Tourneur thriller, highly regarded in some quarters, not least for the quality of Nicholas Musuraca's outstanding photography.

RKO RADIO

Production—Warren Duff
Direction—Jacques Tourneur
Screenplay (from his novel)—
  Geoffrey Homes
Photography—Nicholas Musuraca

Art direction—Albert S.
  D'Agostino & Jack Okey
Music—Roy Webb
Editing—Samuel E. Beetley

PLAYERS: Robert Mitchum, Jane Greer, Kirk Douglas, Rhonda Fleming, Richard Webb, Steve Brodie

OUTCAST OF THE ISLANDS, AN — Gt. Britain (1952)

Stylish, underrated film version of Joseph Conrad's classic tale of the East Indies with Trevor Howard in brilliant form as the treacherous trader's agent Peter Willems who betrays without compunction all those around him and sinks finally to the lowest depths of degradation because of his infatuation with a native girl. Ralph Richardson featured as Captain Lingard and Robert Morley as Almayer, the pompous manager of a river trading post. The admirable location photography (the film was shot in Borneo and Ceylon) was by John Wilcox and the score by Brian Easdale.

LONDON FILMS

Production & direction—
  Carol Reed
Associate producer—
  Hugh Perceval
Screenplay—William Fairchild

Photography—John Wilcox
  in association with—
  Edward Scaife
Art direction—Vincent Korda
Music—Brian Easdale
Editing—Bert Bates

PLAYERS: Ralph Richardson, Trevor Howard, Robert Morley, Wendy Hiller, Kerima, George Coulouris, Wilfrid Hyde-White, Frederick Valk

OVERLANDERS, THE — Gt. Britain (1946)

Spectacular, semidocumentary movie set in World War II and about a small group of Australians (six men, two women and a child) who drive a thousand head of cattle across the deserts of Australia to Queensland when the northwest part of the continent is threatened with invasion by the Japanese. Tough, realistic, shot in its entirety in Australia.

EALING STUDIOS

Production—Michael Balcon
Direction & screenplay—
  Harry Watt

Photography—
  Osmond Borrodaile
Music—John Ireland
Editing—E. M. Inman Hunter

PLAYERS: Chips Rafferty, John Nugent Hayward, Daphne Campbell, Jean Blue, Helen Grieve, John Fernside, Peter Pagan, Frank Ransome

OX-BOW INCIDENT, THE   U.S.A. (1943)

Western drama of Nevada in the 1880's about three cowboys who are rounded up and savagely lynched for a murder they did not commit. Relentless, uncompromising film by erratic William Wellman is one of the most powerful indictments of prejudice and mob hysteria ever put on the screen. Fine performances from Dana Andrews, Anthony Quinn and Francis Ford as the three men, Henry Fonda as an unwilling lyncher, and Jane Darwell (particularly impressive) as the vicious old "Ma" Grier. Filmed in 1941 but not released by Fox until 1943.

TWENTIETH CENTURY–FOX

Production—Lamar Trotti
Direction—William A. Wellman
Screenplay (from novel by Walter
  Van Tilburg Clark)—Lamar
  Trotti

Photography—Arthur Miller
Art direction—Richard Day,
  James Basevi
Music—Cyril J. Mockridge
Editing—Allen McNeil

PLAYERS: Henry Fonda, Dana Andrews, Mary Beth Hughes, Anthony Quinn, William Eythe, Henry Morgan, Jane Darwell, Francis Ford, Victor Kilian

PALM BEACH STORY, THE   U.S.A. (1942)

Zany, tremendously fast comedy with Claudette Colbert as runaway wife who attempts to get $99,000 needed for husband Joel McCrea's engineering project. A brilliantly written, wildly funny film which pokes fun at the eccentric rich and which boasts a whole gallery of excellent performances from Rudy Vallee as a yacht-crazy millionaire and Mary Astor as his man-mad sister to William Demarest, Jack Norton and Roscoe Ates as members of the noisy Ale and Quail Club.

PARAMOUNT

Associate producer—Paul Jones
Direction & screenplay—
  Preston Sturges
Photography—Victor Milner

Art direction—Hans Dreier,
  Ernst Fegte
Music—Victor Young
Editing—Stuart Gilmore

PLAYERS: Claudette Colbert, Joel McCrea, Mary Astor, Rudy Vallee,

Sig Arno, Robert Warwick, Arthur Stuart Hull, Torben Meyer, Jimmy Conlin, Victor Potel, William Demarest, Jack Norton, Robert Greig, Roscoe Ates, Dewey Robinson, Chester Conklin, Sheldon Jeff, Franklin Pangborn

PANDORA AND THE FLYING DUTCHMAN   Gt. Britain (1951)
One of the great curiosities of the British cinema, based on the age-old legend of the Flying Dutchman and featuring James Mason as the doomed seaman and Ava Gardner as the young American girl who dies to save him. An unusual, pretentious, frequently dull film but one that lingers in the mind for its poetic qualities and exotic Technicolor photography. Shot on location in Spain by Albert Lewin who made some of the more unusual films to come out of Hollywood.

ROMULUS/BRITISH LION

Production & direction—
  Albert Lewin
Screenplay & story—
  Albert Lewin

Photography (Technicolor)—
  Jack Cardiff
*Production design—*John Bryan
*Music—*Alan Rawsthorne
*Editing—*Ralph Kemplen

PLAYERS: James Mason, Ava Gardner, Nigel Patrick, Sheila Sim, Harold Warrender, Mario Cabre, John Laurie, Pamela Kellino, Patricia Raine, Margarita D'Alvarez, Marius Goring, Abraham Sofaer

PANDORA'S BOX (Die Büchse der Pandora)   Germany (1928)
Pabst's intense and dispassionate study of the life of a doomed nymphomaniac chorus girl who destroys all those she comes into contact with before meeting her own death at the hands of Jack the Ripper in London's East End. Among the most erotic films ever made and containing the performance of a lifetime from the obscure American actress Louise Brooks. After *The Joyless Street*, Pabst's most accomplished silent film.

NERO FILM

*Direction—*G. W. Pabst
*Photography—*Günther Krampf
*Art direction—*Andrei Andreiev,
  Gottlieb Hesch

*Screenplay (from two plays by
  Frank Wedekind: Erdgeist
  and Büchse der Pandora)—*
  Ladislaus Vayda

PLAYERS: Louise Brooks, Fritz Kortner, Daisy D'Ora, Franz Lederer, Gustav Diessl, Siegfried Arno, Alice Roberts, Carl Groetz

PANIC IN THE STREETS   U.S.A. (1950)
Tense, exciting hunt for a plague carrier loose in the streets of New

Orleans. A fast-moving, semidocumentary film, among Kazan's best, which brilliantly captures the atmosphere of the New Orleans docks and underworld. Excellent performances from Richard Widmark as medical health officer and Paul Douglas as sceptical police captain, and two interesting minor ones from Jack Palance and Zero Mostel as the hunted criminals.

TWENTIETH CENTURY–FOX

Production–Sol C. Siegel
Direction–Elia Kazan
Screenplay–Richard Murphy
Story–Edna & Edward Anhalt
Adaptation–Daniel Fuchs

Photography–Joe MacDonald
Art direction–Lyle Wheeler,
    Maurice Ransford
Music–Alfred Newman
Editing–Harmon Jones

PLAYERS: Richard Widmark, Paul Douglas, Barbara Bel Geddes, Jack Palance, Zero Mostel, Dan Riss, Alexis Minotis, Guy Thomajan, Tommy Cook

PANIQUE   France (1946)

Brutal story of a vicious young crook who robs and murders an elderly woman in a fairground and then conspires with his girlfriend to put the blame for the crime on a bearded recluse who lives in the neighborhood. Some sharply observed backgrounds of the poorer quarters of a Paris suburb and a harrowing climax in which the recluse, brilliantly played by Michel Simon, is hounded to death by a bloodthirsty mob. Duvivier's first major postwar work.

RÉGINA

Direction–Julien Duvivier
Screenplay (from novel by
    Georges Simenon)–
    Charles Spaak &
    Julien Duvivier

Dialogue–Charles Spaak
Photography–Nicolas Hayer
Art direction–S. Pimenoff
Music–J. Ibert
Editing–Marthe Poncin

PLAYERS: Michel Simon, Viviane Romance, Paul Bernard, Charles Dorat, Max Dalban, Emile Drain, Marcel Pérès

PARTY GIRL   U.S.A. (1958)

Crime movie of Chicago in the early 1930's with Robert Taylor as crooked lawyer, Cyd Charisse as cabaret dancer, and Lee J. Cobb as bigtime racketeer. Directed by Nicholas Ray in garish Metrocolor and regarded very highly by many European critics. But, although competently done, it fails to measure up to the classic Raoul Walsh/ Michael Curtiz gangster movies of the thirties.

METRO–GOLDWYN–MAYER

Production—Joe Pasternak
Direction—Nicholas Ray
Screenplay (from story by
  Leo Katcher)—George Wells
Photography (Metrocolor/
  CinemaScope)—Robert Bronner
Art direction—
  William A. Horning &
  Randall Duell
Music—Jeff Alexander
Editing—John McSweeney Jr.

PLAYERS: Robert Taylor, Cyd Charisse, Lee J. Cobb, John Ireland, Kent Smith, Claire Kelly

PASSENGER, THE (Pasazerka)   Poland (1963)
Unfinished Polish film (director Andrzej Munk was killed in an automobile accident) about a German woman holidaying on an ocean liner who catches sight of a woman she thinks she once knew and remembers back 20 years to the war when she served as an overseer at Auschwitz concentration camp and the girl, a Polish Jewess, was an occupant. The film is told in two flashbacks, both covering the same events. The first, told by the German woman to her husband, is a romanticized version of the truth and describes how she tried to help the girl and care for her; the second, which is probably nearer the truth, reflects the woman's private thoughts and shows how her treatment of the girl was in fact brutal and sadistic. An extraordinary, frequently brilliant fragment of film (62 minutes) pieced together by some of Munk's colleagues who used still photographs to link the sequences that he had completed.

KAMERA UNIT (WILHELM HOLLENDER)/FILM POLSKI

Direction—Andrzej Munk
Screenplay—Andrzej Munk &
  Zofia Posmysz-Piasecka
Photography—
  Krzysztof Winiewicz
Art direction—Tadeusz Wybult
Music—Tadeusz Baird
Editing—Zofia Dwornik
Completed by—
  Witold Lesiewicz

PLAYERS: Aleksandra Slaska, Anna Ciepielewska, Jan Kreczmar, Marek Walczewski, Maria Koscialkowska

PASSPORT TO PIMLICO   Gt. Britain (1949)
An engaging little fantasy about a group of Pimlico residents who come across a fifteenth-century royal charter and discover that their street is really part of Burgundy instead of London. Some amusing moments especially when licensing hours and rationing are abolished and a beautiful little cameo from Margaret Rutherford as an eccentric professor of medieval history. One of Ealing's most famous films but one that has not lasted as well as some of their other comedies.

Production—Michael Balcon *Art direction*—Roy Oxley
Direction—Henry Cornelius *Music*—Georges Auric
Screenplay—T. E. B. Clarke *Editing*—Michael Truman
Photography—Lionel Banes
PLAYERS: Stanley Holloway, Barbara Murray, Raymond Huntley, Paul Dupuis, Basil Radford, Naunton Wayne, Margaret Rutherford, John Slater, Jane Hylton

PAT AND MIKE   U.S.A. (1952)

Hepburn and Tracy appearing for the third time under Cukor's direction as, respectively, a lady athlete who excels at golf and tennis and a pugnacious sports promoter who turns her into a champion. A good-humored little movie with a witty script that shows up some of the rackets of American professional sport. Excellent performances as always from the two leads and also from Aldo Ray (debut) as a dumb boxer.

METRO–GOLDWYN–MAYER

Production— *Photography*—William Daniels
  Lawrence Weingarten *Art direction*—Cedric Gibbons,
Direction—George Cukor Urie McCleary
Screenplay—Ruth Gordon, *Music*—David Raksin
  Garson Kanin *Editing*—George Boemler
PLAYERS: Spencer Tracy, Katharine Hepburn, Aldo Ray, William Ching, Sammy White, George Mathews, Loring Smith, Phyllis Povah

PATHER PANCHALI   India (1956)

Leisurely, carefully composed study of a poor Indian scholar and his family living the hardships of everyday existence in a small Bengali village. Nothing much happens and the camera does little more than record day-to-day village life, but the compassion and poetic feeling with which this life is observed, plus the beauty of the photography, raise the film to a remarkably high level of cinematic art. It proved to be one of the revelations of the 1950's and brought the Indian cinema, and particularly Satyajit Ray, into world prominence by winning a major prize at the 1956 Cannes Film Festival. Two additional films about the same family, *Aparajito* and *The World of Apu*, were made in 1957 and 1958 respectively.

GOVERNMENT OF WEST BENGAL

Production, direction & *Bidhutibhustan Bandapad-*
  screenplay (from novel by *haya)*—Satyajit Ray

Photography—Subrata Mitra   *Editing*—Dulal Dutta
Music—Ravi Shankar
PLAYERS: Kanu Banerjee, Karuna Banerjee, Subir Banerjee, Uma Das Gupta, Chunibala Devi

PATHS OF GLORY   U.S.A. (1957)

World War I movie by Stanley Kubrick tracing the court-martial and execution of three soldiers chosen as scapegoats for the failure of a suicidal French infantry attack. Like Milestone's *All Quiet on the Western Front,* the film condemns war, but differs from its predecessor in being more intellectual in its approach and concentrating equally on condemning the corruption of the French High Command. Derived from a novel by Humphrey Cobb which was supposedly based on a true incident in the French Army in 1916.

BRYNA/UNITED ARTISTS

Production—James B. Harris   *Screenplay*—Stanley Kubrick,
Direction—Stanley Kubrick   Calder Willingham &
Photography—George Krause   Jim Thompson
Music—Gerald Fried   *Editing*—Eva Kroll
PLAYERS: Kirk Douglas, Ralph Meeker, Adolphe Menjou, George Macready, Wayne Morris, Richard Anderson

PATTON   U.S.A. (1970)

Biographical war movie covering two years (1943–45) in the turbulent career of General George S. Patton, one of the most outspoken and controversial American commanders of World War II. An ambitious and perceptive American film (the most distinguished in the war genre since Kubrick's *Paths of Glory*) which at three hours is not a minute too long. George C. Scott (Academy Award-winning performance) plays Patton, Karl Malden is his colleague General Omar Bradley, and there is an amusing vignette portrayal by Michael Bates as Field Marshal Montgomery.

TWENTIETH CENTURY—FOX

Production—Frank McCarthy   *Screenplay (based on material*
Direction—Franklin J. Schaffner   *from the books* Patton:
Photography (DeLuxecolor/   Ordeal and Triumph *by*
  Dimension 150)—   *Ladislas Farago and* A
  Fred Koenekamp   Soldier's Story *by Omar N.*
Art direction—Urie McCleary,   *Bradley)*—Francis Ford
  Gil Parrondo   Coppola, Edmund H. North
Music—Jerry Goldsmith   *Editing*—Hugh S. Fowler

PLAYERS: George C. Scott, Karl Malden, Michael Bates, Stephen Young, Michael Strong, Cary Loftin, Albert Dumortier, Frank Latimore

PAWNBROKER, THE   U.S.A. (1964)

Rod Steiger gives one of the screen's great acting performances as pawnbroker Sol Nazerman, a man so embittered by his past experiences in a German concentration camp where his wife and children died that he has been left devoid of all human emotion. It takes yet another death—that of his young Puerto Rican assistant, shot while defending him during a robbery in his shop—to bring him face to face with reality and to make him care once more about the world around him. Punctuated by Resnais-styled flashbacks, the film is a powerful, frequently harrowing experience and among the major works of the contemporary American cinema. Few films have investigated the question of human responsibility so thoroughly or effectively as this one.

ELY LANDAU

Production—Philip Langner & Robert H. Lewis
Direction—Sidney Lumet
Photography—Boris Kaufman
Production design—
Richard Sylbert

Screenplay (based on novel by Edward Lewis Wallant)—
David Friedkin & Morton Fine
Music—Quincy Jones
Editing—Ralph Rosenblum

PLAYERS: Rod Steiger, Geraldine Fitzgerald, Jamie Sanchez, Brock Peters, Thelma Oliver, Marketa Kimbrell, Baruch Lumet, Juano Hernandez

PAWNSHOP, THE   U.S.A. (1916)

One of Chaplin's most brilliant two-reelers for Mutual with Charlie as a pawnshop assistant involved with a number of unusual customers, a rival assistant, and the pawnbroker's daughter Edna Purviance. Contains one of the most famous scenes in all Chaplin's films: that in which he appraises and dismantles an alarm clock, examining it first as a doctor, then, in succession, as a heart specialist, dentist, plumber, jeweler, etc. and finally handing the remaining parts back to the bewildered owner. Portly Henry Bergman made his first appearance in a Chaplin film as the owner of the pawnshop.

A MUTUAL COMEDY

Direction—Charles Chaplin
Screenplay—Charles Chaplin

Photography—R. H. Totheroh & W. C. Foster

PLAYERS: Charles Chaplin, Albert Austin, Henry Bergman, Eric Campbell, Frank J. Coleman, James T. Kelly, Edna Purviance, John Rand

PENNY SERENADE   U.S.A. (1941)

Little-known movie about the domestic problems of a small-town newspaper proprietor (Cary Grant) and his wife (Irene Dunne) when they lose their own child and later, at the age of six, their adopted daughter. Told in flashbacks as the wife remembers her married life the film is unashamedly sentimental, but the direction is so skillful (the film offers further evidence that Stevens was at his peak during this period) and the playing so assured that the whole thing works perfectly as superior cinematic entertainment. Edgar Buchanan, a favorite Stevens performer, appears in a sympathetic supporting role.

COLUMBIA

Production & direction—   *Art direction*—Lionel Banks
  George Stevens   *Music*—W. Franke Harling
Screenplay—Morris Ryskind   *Musical direction*—
Story—Martha Cheavens   M. W. Stoloff
Photography—Joseph Walker   *Editing*—Otto Meyer

PLAYERS: Cary Grant, Irene Dunne, Beulah Bondi, Edgar Buchanan, Ann Doran, Eva Lee Kuney, Leonard Willey, Wallis Clark, Walter Soderling

PEOPLE ON SUNDAY (Menschen am Sonntag)   Germany (1929)

Fresh, very simple little picture, shot on location and played by non-professional actors, tells of an ordinary day in the lives of four Berliners—a salesgirl, a commercial traveler, a driver, and a film extra—as they spend a day by the Wandsee. Put together independently the film is famous mainly because of the extraordinary talent working behind the cameras: Robert Siodmak, Billy Wilder, Fred Zinnemann and Edgar G. Ulmer.

FILM STUDIO (BERLIN)

Direction—Robert Siodmak   *Assistant directors*—Fred
Screenplay—Billy Wilder,   Zinnemann, Edgar G. Ulmer
  Robert Siodmak   *Photography*—Eugene Schufftan

PLAYERS: Brigitte Borchert, Christl Ehlers, Annie Schreyer, Wolfgang Von Waltersh Ausen, Erwin Splettstöber

PEOPLE WILL TALK   U.S.A. (1951)

Ambitious movie concerning a progressive doctor (Cary Grant) who uses humanity and psychiatry in addition to his medical skills to cure his patients and is consequently accused by his colleagues of using mystic powers in healing. Among the most unusual films to come out in the early 1950's, sophisticated, wittily scripted, and raising some important questions about psychosomatic medicine and the psychiatric treatment of the sick.

TWENTIETH CENTURY–FOX

Production–Darryl F. Zanuck
Direction–Joseph L. Mankiewicz
Screenplay (*from play and screenplay* Doctor Praetorius *by Curt Goetz*)–
    Joseph L. Mankiewicz
Photography–Milton Krasner

Art direction–Lyle Wheeler & George W. Davis
Music–Brahms's Academic Festival Overture & Wagner's Prize Song conducted by Alfred Newman
Editing–Barbara McLean

PLAYERS: Cary Grant, Jeanne Crain, Finlay Currie, Hume Cronyn, Walter Slezak, Sidney Blackmer, Basil Ruysdael, Katherine Locke

PEPE-LE-MOKO   France (1937)

Melodrama about a doomed thief (Jean Gabin) who finds temporary safety from the police in the Algerian Casbah. An over-romantic film that presents the criminal as a heroic outsider fighting against authority and which observes, perhaps better than any other prewar film, the background and environment in which he lives. The movie helped establish Jean Gabin as a world-famous actor and was remade, less effectively, in Hollywood as *Algiers* with Charles Boyer in the title role.

PARIS–FILM PRODUCTION

Direction–Julien Duvivier
Screenplay (*from detective novel by Roger Ashelbé*)–
    Julien Duvivier & Henri Jeanson
Dialogue–Henri Jeanson

Photography–J. Kruger, M. Fossard
Art direction–J. Krauss
Music–Vincent Scotto, Mohamed Yguerbuchen
Editing–Marguerite Beaugé

PLAYERS: Jean Gabin, Mireille Balin, Gabriel Gabrio, Lucas Gridoux, Marcel Dalio, Saturnin Fabre, Charpin

PERSONA   Sweden (1966)

An eminent actress in her early thirties suffers a nervous breakdown on stage and withdraws into a world of total silence. Sent by her psychiatrist to recuperate at his lonely seaside cottage she is attended by a young hospital nurse who, faced with a wall of silence, pours out her own frustrations and anxieties identifying herself so closely with her patient that the roles are gradually reversed and the women's personalities appear to merge. One of Ingmar Bergman's most difficult and complex works, brilliantly acted by Liv Ullmann (the patient) and Bibi Andersson (the nurse) who are on screen for almost the entire film. The title refers to the mask worn by actors in ancient times, especially in Greek drama.

SVENSK FILMINDUSTRI

Direction & screenplay—	*Art direction—*Bibi Lindström
Ingmar Bergman	*Music—*Lars Johan Werle
*Photography—*Sven Nykvist	*Editing—*Ulla Ryghe

PLAYERS: Bibi Andersson, Liv Ullmann, Gunnar Björnstrand, Margaretha Krook

PETRIFIED FOREST, THE U.S.A. (1936)

Thriller adapted from the stage play by Robert Sherwood about some gangsters who hold a group of people hostage in a desert gas-station cafe in Arizona. Melodramatic and disappointingly routine for the most part, but forever famous as the film which gave Humphrey Bogart his first big break as gangster Duke Mantee. Leslie Howard and Bette Davis (as a waitress) appear as two of the hostages and Joe Sawyer, in his familiar role, as one of the heavies.

WARNER BROS.

*Associate producer—*Henry Blanke	*Photography—*Sol Polito
*Direction—*Archie Mayo	*Art direction—*John Hughes
*Screenplay—*Charles Kenyon &	*Music—*Bernhard Kaun
Delmer Daves	*Editing—*Owen Marks

PLAYERS: Leslie Howard, Bette Davis, Genevieve Tobin, Dick Foran, Humphrey Bogart, Joseph Sawyer, Porter Hall, Charley Grapewin

PHANTOM OF THE OPERA, THE U.S.A. (1925)

Classic piece of hokum about a demented musician with a disfigured face who haunts the underground caves of the Paris Opera. One of the most famous American silent pictures, elegantly designed and partly photographed in the early Technicolor process. The highlight— Lon Chaney's horrific unmasking in the fifth reel—is one of the great moments in screen horror.

UNIVERSAL

*Production—*Carl Laemmle	*Art direction—*Dan Hall
*Direction—*Rupert Julian	*Screenplay (based on novel*
*Associate director—*Edward Sedgwick	*by Gaston Leroux)—*
Photography (Technicolor	Elliott J. Clawson
*sequences)—*Charles Van Enger	

340

The Phantom of the Opera

PLAYERS: Lon Chaney, Mary Philbin, Norman Kerry, Snitz Edwards, Gibson Gowland, John Sainpolis, Virginia Pearson, Arthur Edmund Carew

PHANTOM OF THE OPERA, THE   U.S.A. (1943)
Technicolor remake with Nelson Eddy and Susanna Foster leading the opera singers and Claude Rains, complete with sombrero, red-tipped cloak and blue mask, as the murdering Phantom. Not nearly as frightening as the silent version—due mainly to the opera overshadowing the horror—but once again exceptionally well-designed and photographed (Academy Awards for best color art direction and for best color photography). The film was remade for a third time in 1962 with Herbert Lom as the Phantom.

UNIVERSAL

Production—George Waggner   *Photography (Technicolor)*—
Direction—Arthur Lubin   Hal Mohr, W. Howard Green

Screenplay (from novel by
   Gaston Leroux)—Eric Taylor,
   Samuel Hoffenstein

Art direction—Alexander
   Golitzen, John B. Goodman
Music—Edmund Ward
Editing—Russell Schoengarth

PLAYERS: Nelson Eddy, Susanna Foster, Claude Rains, Edgar Barrier, Leo Carrillo, Jane Farrar, J. Edward Bromberg, Fritz Feld, Hume Cronyn

PHILADELPHIA STORY, THE   U.S.A. (1940)

Katharine Hepburn in superb form (her best prewar roles were invariably in Cukor or George Stevens films) as spoiled rich girl Tracy Lord whose impending second marriage is disrupted by first husband (Cary Grant) and by gossip columnist (James Stewart) who arrives with photographer (Ruth Hussey) to cover the marriage for his society sheet. Smart, sophisticated and beautifully played by all concerned, but Hepburn's film from first to last.

METRO–GOLDWYN–MAYER

Production—
   Joseph L. Mankiewicz
Direction—George Cukor
Screenplay (from play by
   Philip Barry)—
   Donald Ogden Stewart

Photography—
   Joseph Ruttenberg
Art direction—Cedric Gibbons
   & Wade B. Rubottom
Music—Franz Waxman
Editing—Frank Sullivan

PLAYERS: Katharine Hepburn, Cary Grant, James Stewart, Ruth Hussey, John Howard, Roland Young

PICNIC   U.S.A. (1955)

Movie version of William Inge's New York stage play about a wandering young hobo (William Holden) and his effect on some of the inhabitants of a small Kansas town during his brief stay there on Labor Day. The lazy summer holiday atmosphere is perfectly evoked and the picnic scenes wonderfully handled by director Joshua Logan who excelled himself with this film, removing all traces of its theatrical origins and making admirable use of his locations. Outstanding in a talented cast are Betty Field as an anxious mother of two daughters (Kim Novak, Susan Strasberg) and Rosalind Russell as a frustrated schoolmistress on the brink of spinsterhood. One of Columbia's most successful productions of the 1950's.

COLUMBIA

Production—Fred Kohlmar   Direction—Joshua Logan

Screenplay—Daniel Taradash   *Music*—George Duning
Photography (*Technicolor*)—   *Editing*—William A. Lyon &
   James Wong Howe   Charles Nelson
Art direction—William Flannery
PLAYERS: William Holden, Kim Novak, Betty Field, Susan Strasberg, Cliff Robertson, Rosalind Russell, Arthur O'Connell, Verna Felton, Reta Shaw

PICKPOCKET   France (1959)

Slow, somber study of a young thief who becomes a pickpocket not for gain but for the experience and excitement of the theft and to free himself from the society he despises. Director Robert Bresson concerns himself with the inner thoughts and motives of his leading character although his scenes showing the thief being trained by a master pickpocket are often more fascinating. A short (75-minute) rather gray film, played mostly by nonprofessionals.

AGNES DELAHAIE

Production—Agnès Delahaie   *Art direction*—
Direction, screenplay &   Pierre Charbonnier
   dialogue—Robert Bresson   *Music*—Lulli
Photography—   *Editing*—Raymond Lamy
   Léonce-Henry Burel
PLAYERS: Martin Lasalle, Pierre Leymarie, Jean Pelegri, Marika Green, Kassagi, Pierre Etaix, Dolly Seal

PICTURE OF DORIAN GRAY, THE   U.S.A. (1945)

Oscar Wilde's witty morality story about a man who sells his soul for eternal youth, remaining young while his portrait shows the stigma of age and corruption. A mannered, surprisingly sophisticated Hollywood adaptation, beautifully in period and superbly played by George Sanders as the cynical Lord Henry, Angela Lansbury as the dancehall entertainer Sybil Vane, and Hurd Hatfield as Dorian Gray. Shot in black-and-white (Academy Award, best photography, 1945) except for a few isolated scenes in Technicolor of the decaying portrait.

METRO—GOLDWYN—MAYER

Production—Pandro S. Berman   *Art direction*—Cedric Gibbons,
Direction—Albert Lewin   Hans Peters
Screenplay—Albert Lewin   *Music*—Herbert Stothart
Photography—Harry Stradling   *Editing*—Ferris Webster
PLAYERS: George Sanders, Hurd Hatfield, Donna Reed, Angela Lans-

bury, Peter Lawford, Lowell Gilmore, Richard Fraser, Douglas Walton, Morton Lowry, Miles Mander

PILGRIM, THE   U.S.A. (1923)
Short Chaplin feature (4 reels) with Charlie as an escaped convict masquerading as a minister in a small Western town. Not one of his best-known films but with several bright moments and some gentle satire of American rural types and small-town puritanism. The last Chaplin picture for First National and the last in which Edna Purviance appeared as his leading lady. Miss Purviance made her debut in the Chaplin film *A Night Out* in 1914 and played in no fewer than 34 Chaplin movies between 1915 and 1923.

FIRST NATIONAL

Direction—Charles Chaplin   *Screenplay*—Charles Chaplin
Associate director—Chuck Riesner   *Photography*—R. H. Totheroh
PLAYERS: Charles Chaplin, Edna Purviance, Mack Swain, Kitty Bradbury, Dinky Dean, Loyal Underwood, Mai Wells, Sydney Chaplin, Chuck Riesner

PINKY   U.S.A. (1949)
Quiet little movie concerning a fair-skinned colored girl (Jeanne Crain) living in the deep South who becomes a figure of hate and suspicion when she is left a large house by the old white woman (Ethel Barrymore) she has nursed in sickness. A serious, sometimes bitter, tale of racial intolerance, milder in tone than most of the films about this subject but equally as effective. Moving performances from Crain and Barrymore and a superb one from Ethel Waters as Pinky's Negro grandmother. The film was originally assigned to John Ford who worked on it for just one day before illness caused him to withdraw from the project.

TWENTIETH CENTURY–FOX

Production—Darryl F. Zanuck   *Photography*—Joe MacDonald
Direction—Elia Kazan   *Art direction*—Lyle Wheeler &
Screenplay (from novel by   J. Russell Spencer
  Cid Ricketts Sumner)—   *Music*—Alfred Newman
  Philip Dunne &   *Editing*—Harmon Jones
  Dudley Nichols
PLAYERS: Jeanne Crain, Ethel Barrymore, Ethel Waters, William Lundigan, Basil Ruysdael, Kenny Washington, Nina Mae McKinney, Griff Barnett, Evelyn Warden

344

PINOCCHIO   U.S.A. (1940)
Walt Disney's second full-length cartoon feature is about a wooden
puppet who is turned into a real boy. The film shows Disney at the
peak of his most creative period, although the most memorably drawn
sequences—Pinocchio's encounter with puppet-master Stromboli, his
journey with the dreaded coachman on Pleasure Island, and a storm
at sea—are invariably the ones that frighten children the most. Best
characters: Jiminy Cricket (Pinocchio's conscience), Figaro (the Cat),
Cleo (a glamorous goldfish), and J. Worthington Foulfellow (Honest
John), a roguish fox who is perhaps Disney's most crafty all-around
villain. This last character was made vocal by actor Walter Catlett.
Among the songs are "Give a Little Whistle," "Hi-diddle-dee-dee, An
Actor's Life for Me," and "When you Wish Upon a Star."

WALT DISNEY PRODUCTIONS/RKO RADIO

Production—Walt Disney
Supervising directors—Ben
  Sharpsteen, Hamilton Luske
Sequence directors—Bill Roberts,
  Norman Ferguson, Jack Kinney,
  Wilfred Jackson, T. Hee
Story adaptation (from folk
  tale by Carlo Coleddi)—
  Ted Sears, Webb Smith,

Joseph Sabo, Otto Englander,
  William Cottrell,
  Erdman Penner,
  Aurelios Battaglia
Music and lyrics—
  Leigh Harline,
  Ned Washington,
  Paul J. Smith

PIRATE, THE   U.S.A. (1948)
Sophisticated M-G-M period musical revolving around the Caribbean
romance between a young girl (Judy Garland) and the strolling player
(Gene Kelly) who impersonates the fabulous pirate she dreams of in
order to court her. Beautiful designs and a witty script; several of the
numbers show Kelly and director Vincent Minnelli at top form—
most notably the delightful "Be a Clown," a Kelly-Garland duo, and
Kelly's dazzling "Pirate Ballet." Other Cole Porter numbers include
"Nina" and "Mack the Black."

METRO—GOLDWYN—MAYER

Production—Arthur Freed
Direction—Vincente Minnelli
Screenplay (from play by
  S. N. Behrman)—
  Albert Hackett &
  Frances Goodrich

Photography (Technicolor)—
  Harry Stradling
Art direction—Cedric Gibbons &
  Jack Martin Smith
Music—Cole Porter
Editing—Blanche Sewell

PLAYERS: Judy Garland, Gene Kelly, Walter Slezak, Gladys Cooper, Reginald Owen, George Zucco, Nicholas Brothers, Lester Allen

PLACE IN THE SUN, A   U.S.A. (1951)

This George Stevens masterpiece (described by Chaplin as "one of the greatest films ever to come out of Hollywood") relates the story of a poor factory worker (Montgomery Clift) who becomes tragically involved with two women in different stratums of society—a plain working girl (Shelley Winters) who carries his illegitimate child and a spoilt society girl (Elizabeth Taylor) whose luxury world he craves for. The playing, especially of Clift, is very fine, but this is without doubt a director's film. The early sequences (shot in huge close-up) establishing the Clift-Taylor love affair and the later ones dealing with the murder on the lake are among the greatest moments of modern American cinema. Five Academy Awards including Oscars to Stevens and Franz Waxman for his music score.

PARAMOUNT

Production & direction—
  George Stevens
Screenplay (from novel An American Tragedy *by Theodore Dreiser)—*Michael Wilson & Harry Brown

*Photography—*William C. Mellor
*Art direction—*Hans Dreier & Walter Tyler
*Music—*Franz Waxman
*Editing—*William Hornbeck

PLAYERS: Montgomery Clift, Elizabeth Taylor, Shelley Winters, Anne Revere, Raymond Burr, Herbert Heyes, Keefe Brasselle, Shepperd Strudwick

PLAINSMAN, THE   U.S.A. (1937)

Gary Cooper (Wild Bill Hickok), Jean Arthur (Calamity Jane), and James Ellison (Buffalo Bill) are involved with a large-scale Indian uprising just after the Civil War. A traditional, romanticized Western very well handled by DeMille whose films about American history (*Union Pacific, Reap the Wild Wind, Unconquered,* etc.) are among the best and most underrated of his work. Excellent supporting performances from Charles Bickford as trader who smuggles guns to the Indians and Porter Hall as Jack McCall, the real-life killer who shot Hickok in the back during a saloon poker game.

PARAMOUNT

Production & direction—
  Cecil B. DeMille

*Photography—*Victor Milner, George Robinson

346

Planet of the Apes

Screenplay (based on unpublished original screen story by Courtney Riley Cooper, the book Wild Bill Hickok *by Frank J. Wilstach, and material compiled by Jeannie Macpherson)*—Waldemar Young, Harold Lamb, Lynn Riggs
Music—George Antheil
Editing—Anne Bauchens
PLAYERS: Gary Cooper, Jean Arthur, James Ellison, Charles Bickford, Helen Burgess, Porter Hall, Paul Harvey, Victor Varconi, John Miljan

PLANET OF THE APES   U.S.A. (1967)
Superior science-fiction movie about three American astronauts (led by Charlton Heston) who crash-land on a desolate planet ruled by intelligent apes (a planet that in reality is the earth some 2000 years hence when mankind has destroyed itself by atomic warfare and evolution has been reversed). Sometimes satirical, frequently exciting and, in its climactic scene, quite shattering. The anti-bomb message has rarely come across more strongly. Distinguished actors Maurice Evans, Kim Hunter and Roddy McDowall all appear in ape costume.

347

APJAC/TWENTIETH CENTURY–FOX

Production–Arthur P. Jacobs
Direction–Franklin J. Schaffner
Screenplay (*based on novel*
  Monkey Planet *by Pierre*
  Boulle)–Michael Wilson &
  Rod Serling

Photography (*Panavision/*
  DeLuxecolor)–Leon Shamroy
Art direction–Jack Martin Smith
  & William Creber
Music–Jerry Goldsmith
Editing–Hugh S. Fowler

PLAYERS: Charlton Heston, Roddy McDowall, Kim Hunter, Maurice
Evans, James Whitmore, James Daly, Linda Harrison, Robert Gunner

PLATINUM BLONDE   U.S.A. (1931)

Triangle comedy with Robert Williams as the bright young newspaperman sought after by New York society hostess (Jean Harlow) and
fellow reporter (Loretta Young). Includes some bright dialogue by
Robert Riskin whose first film for Capra this was and who worked with
Capra on some eleven occasions between 1931 and 1951. Other Capra/
Riskin collaborations: *American Madness, Lady for a Day, It Happened One Night, Broadway Bill, Mr. Deeds Goes to Town, Lost
Horizon, You Can't Take it With You, Meet John Doe, Riding High*
(a remake of *Broadway Bill*), and *Here Comes the Groom* (story only).

COLUMBIA

Direction–Frank Capra
Story–Harry E. Chandlee &
  Douglas W. Churchill
Adaptation–Jo Swerling

Dialogue–Robert Riskin
Photography–Joseph Walker
Editing–Gene Milford
Continuity–Dorothy Howell

PLAYERS: Loretta Young, Robert Williams, Jean Harlow, Reginald
Owen, Louise Closser Hale, Edmond Breese, Walter Catlett

PLAYTIME   France (1967)

Jacques Tati's third film about the awkward, well-meaning Parisian
Monsieur Hulot who, on this occasion, becomes catastrophically involved in such complexities of modern life as a glass-fronted airport, an
exhibition of modern equipment, a new restaurant, and a supermarket.
Three years in the making and costing $3,000,000 the film is overlong
and less immediately winning than *Monsieur Holot's Holiday* and *Jour
de Fête*. There is some very funny visual comedy, however, and, as
always in a Tati film, a charming music score.

SPECTA FILMS

Direction–Jacques Tati
Screenplay–Jacques Tati,
  Jacques Lagrange

Photography (*70 mm. Eastmancolor*)–Jean Badal, Andréas
  Winding

English dialogue—Art Buchwald   *Music*—Francis Lemarque
Production design—Eugène Roman   *Editing*—Gérard Pollicand
PLAYERS: Jacques Tati, Barbara Dennek, Jacqueline Lecomte, Valérie
Camille, France Rumilly, France Delahalle, Laure Paillette

POIL DE CAROTTE   France (1932)

Sensitive film shows the unhappy childhood of a small farm boy whose
loneliness and suffering at the hands of his parents drive him to the
verge of suicide. Some delightful backgrounds of pastoral France, two
fine performances from Catherine Fonteney and Harry Baur as the
parents and a brilliant one from Robert Lynen as the boy. Both Baur
and Lynen died tragically at the hands of the Nazis in World War II,
the former in a concentration camp and the latter in front of a firing
squad for his part in the Resistance.

FILM D'ART (VANDAL & DELAC)

Direction—Julien Duvivier   *Art direction*—Lucien Aguettand
Adaptation (from stories "Poil de   & Carré
  Carotte" & "La Bigote" by   *Photography*—Armand Thirard
  Jules Renard)—Julien Duvivier   & Monniot
Music—Alexandre Tansman   *Editing*—J.-P. le Chanois
PLAYERS: Robert Lynen, Harry Baur, Catherine Fonteney, Louis
Gauthier, Christiane Dor, Colette Segal, Simone Audry

POPPY   U.S.A. (1936)

W. C. Fields as Professor Eustace McGargle, a happy-go-lucky con-
fidence trickster/circus showman who tries to pass off his daughter
Poppy (Rochelle Hudson) as an heiress. After his Mr. Micawber this
is the most famous of all Fields' screen portrayals. This was the second
time that he played McGargle on the screen, the first being in 1925
when he appeared in *Sally of the Sawdust* (a retitled version of the
same story) for D. W. Griffith. *Poppy* was director Edward Sutherland's fifth film with Fields. Other Fields/Sutherland collaborations:
It's the Old Army Game, Tillie's Punctured Romance (1928), *International House, Mississippi, Follow the Boys.*

PARAMOUNT

Production—William LeBaron   *Art direction*—Hans Dreier &
Direction—A. Edward Sutherland   Bernard Herzbrun
Screenplay (from play by Dorothy   *Editing*—Stuart Heisler
  Donnelly)—Waldemar Young   *Music & lyrics*—Ralph Rainger &
  & Virginia Van Upp   Leo Robin, & Sam Coslow &
Photography—William Mellor   Frederick Hollander

PLAYERS: W. C. Fields, Rochelle Hudson, Richard Cromwell, Granville Bates, Catherine Doucet, Lynne Overman, Maude Eburne, Bill Wolfe

PORTRAIT OF JENNIE   U.S.A. (1949)

Struggling artist (Joseph Cotten) becomes infatuated with young girl (Jennifer Jones) he meets in Central Park only to find that she is a spirit, and that she died many years before. William Dieterle's later Hollywood films were largely undistinguished, but this curious little fantasy, although unashamed romantic hokum, has a haunting quality most skillfully put across. The photography, which makes imaginative use of color tints, was Joseph August's last assignment.

SELZNICK STUDIO

Production—David O. Selznick
Direction—William Dieterle
Screenplay (from novel by
   Robert Nathan)—Paul Osborn
   & Peter Bernies
Adaptation—Leonard Bercovici
Photography (color sequence
   Technicolor)—Joseph August

Art direction—J. McMillan
   Johnson, Joseph B. Platt
Music (based on themes by
   Claude Debussy)—
   Dimitri Tiomkin
Editing—Gerard Wilson

PLAYERS: Joseph Cotten, Jennifer Jones, Ethel Barrymore, Lillian Gish, Cecil Kellaway, David Wayne, Albert Sharpe, Henry Hull

POSSESSED   U.S.A. (1947)

Joan Crawford as a schizophrenic nurse, Van Heflin as her brutal lover, and Raymond Massey as the sympathetic husband of her loveless marriage. A glossy, superior psychological melodrama directed by the erratic Curtis Bernhardt and worthy of mention for the sheer professional skill with which it was put together. Art director Anton Grot, editor Rudi Fehr and composer Franz Waxman all worked regularly at the Warner studios during the 1940's.

WARNER BROS.

Production—Jerry Wald
Direction—Curtis Bernhardt
Screenplay (based on story by
   Rita Weiman)—Silvia Richards,
   Ranald MacDougall

Photography—Joseph Valentine
Art direction—Anton Grot
Music—Franz Waxman
Editing—Rudi Fehr

PLAYERS: Joan Crawford, Van Heflin, Raymond Massey, Geraldine Brooks, Stanley Ridges, John Ridgeley, Moroni Olsen, Erskine Sanford

PRISONER OF ZENDA, THE   U.S.A. (1937)

Ronald Colman, Douglas Fairbanks and Raymond Massey acting and fighting out Anthony Hope's famous Ruritanian romance under John Cromwell's vigorous direction. Some striking Lyle Wheeler sets and a rousing sword duel climax between hero Colman and villain Fairbanks. Remade with considerably less gusto by Richard Thorpe in 1952.

SELZNICK PRODUCTIONS/UNITED ARTISTS

Production—David Selznick
Direction—John Cromwell
Screenplay—John Balderston, Wells Root, Donald Ogden Stewart
Photography— James Wong Howe
Art direction—Lyle Wheeler
Music—Alfred Newman
Editing—Hal C. Kern

PLAYERS: Ronald Colman, Madeleine Carroll, Douglas Fairbanks, Jr., Mary Astor, C. Aubrey Smith, Raymond Massey, David Niven

PRIVATE LIFE OF HENRY VIII, THE   Gt. Britain (1933)

Alexander Korda's most famous British film of the 1930's traces, through a series of loosely connected episodes, the matrimonial misadventures of Henry VIII (Charles Laughton). Laughton's superb performance earned him an Oscar and helped the film become one of the biggest commercial successes of the period. The picture was shot in five weeks on a shoestring budget of £15,000, every member of the cast acting without salary and agreeing to share in the profit or loss.

LONDON FILM PRODUCTIONS

Direction—Alexander Korda
Screenplay—Lajos Biro & Arthur Wimperis
Photography—Georges Périnal
Art direction—Vincent Korda
Music—Kurt Schroeder
Editing—Stephen Harrison

PLAYERS: Charles Laughton, Robert Donat, Merle Oberon, Binnie Barnes, Lady Tree, Elsa Lanchester, Franklin Dyall, Miles Mander

PRIVATE LIVES OF ELIZABETH AND ESSEX   U.S.A. (1939)

Hollywood costume drama with Bette Davis as an infatuated middle-aged Queen Elizabeth and the handsome Errol Flynn as the ill-fated Earl of Essex, the object of her affection. Not the most successful of Warner's period adaptations (Michael Curtiz seemed particularly unhappy working from stage material), but interesting for the intelligent playing of Miss Davis and for the magnificent score. Korngold's other historical scores of this period include *The Adventures of Robin Hood* and *The Sea Hawk*.

351

WARNER BROS./FIRST NATIONAL

Production—Hal B. Wallis in association with Robert Lord
Direction—Michael Curtiz
Screenplay (based on play Elizabeth the Queen by Maxwell Anderson)—Norman Reilly Raine & Aeneas MacKenzie
Photography (Technicolor)—Sol Polito
Art direction—Anton Grot
Music—Erich Wolfgang Korngold
Musical direction—Leo F. Forbstein
Editing—Owen Marks

PLAYERS: Bette Davis, Errol Flynn, Olivia de Havilland, Donald Crisp, Vincent Price, Alan Hale, Henry Stephenson, Henry Daniell, Leo G. Carroll, Nanette Fabares (Fabray)

PROFESSIONALS, THE   U.S.A. (1966)

Robust Mexican Western set at the time of Pancho Villa and focusing on four adventurers who are hired by a millionaire to rescue his young wife from the clutches of Mexican guerrilla leader (Jack Palance). Somewhat similar to *The Magnificent Seven,* but more literate and generally more successful. Well played by everyone in the all-star cast although laconic Lee Marvin eventually dominates with his performance of a former Rough Rider. Stunning Mexican desert landscapes, a rousing Jarre score, and an amusingly witty last line.

PAX ENTERPRISES/COLUMBIA

Production & direction—Richard Brooks
Screenplay (based on novel A Mule for the Marquesa by Frank O'Rourke)—Richard Brooks
Photography (Technicolor/Panavision)—Conrad Hall
Art direction—Edward S. Haworth
Music—Maurice Jarre
Editing—Peter Zinner

PLAYERS: Lee Marvin, Burt Lancaster, Robert Ryan, Jack Palance, Claudia Cardinale, Ralph Bellamy, Woody Strode, Joe De Santis

PROWLER, THE   U.S.A. (1951)

Modest crime thriller about an unscrupulous cop (Van Heflin) who murders an elderly radio announcer so that he can marry the widow (Evelyn Keyes) and collect on the insurance. Very competent and built firmly in the *Double Indemnity* mold but never reaching that brilliant movie's high standard. Of interest primarily as one of the best of Joseph Losey's limited American output and as one of the last films to be photographed by ace cameraman Arthur Miller before retirement.

352

Production—S. P. Eagle
Direction—Joseph Losey
Assistant director—
Robert Aldrich
Photography—Arthur Miller
Art direction—Boris Leven

Screenplay (from original story
by Robert Thoeren & Hans
Wilhelm)—Dalton Trumbo,
Hugo Butler
Music—Lyn Murray
Editing—Paul Weatherwax

PLAYERS: Van Heflin, Evelyn Keyes, John Maxwell, Katherine Warren, Emerson Treacy, Madge Blake, Wheaton Chambers

PSYCHO   U.S.A. (1960)

Hitchcock's most famous postwar film and technically his most accomplished achievement, a gothic tongue-in-cheek thriller about the nightmarish activities of a homicidal psychopath who runs a lonely Arizona motel and lives with his unseen "mother" in an adjoining Victorian mansion. Contains two of Hitchcock's most grisly set pieces—the murder in the shower and the staircase killing of the private detective. It also has some of his most tantalizing red herrings, particularly in the early sequences when Janet Leigh is pursued by a suspicious traffic cop. Distinguished further by the sinister music score of Bernard Herrmann and by the playing of Anthony Perkins as the killer and Janet Leigh and Martin Balsam as his victims.

PARAMOUNT

Production & direction—
Alfred Hitchcock
Screenplay (from novel by
Robert Bloch)—Joseph Stefano
Photography—John L. Russell

Art direction—Joseph Hurley,
Robert Clatworthy &
George Milo
Music—Bernard Herrmann
Editing—George Tomasini

PLAYERS: Janet Leigh, Anthony Perkins, Vera Miles, John Gavin, Martin Balsam, John McIntire, Simon Oakland, Frank Albertson

PUBLIC ENEMY   U.S.A. (1931)

Key gangster movie of the early 1930's traces the rise, career and violent death of liquor racket gangster (James Cagney). Directed by William Wellman from a story by former Chicago news reporters John Bright and Kubec Glasmon and forever famous for the scene in which a disgruntled Cagney shoves a grapefruit into the face of startled floozie Mae Clark. Eddie Woods plays Cagney's buddy who "gets his" earlier in the film at the hands of rival gangsters.

WARNER BROS.

Direction—William A. Wellman   *Photography*—Dev Jennings
Screenplay & dialogue—   *Editing*—Edward McCormick
   Harvey Thew
PLAYERS: James Cagney, Eddie Woods, Jean Harlow, Beryl Mercer, Donald Cook, Joan Blondell, Leslie Fenton, Rita Flynn, Louise Brooks, Mae Clark

PUTTING PANTS ON PHILIP   U.S.A. (1927)
The first of Laurel and Hardy's short films, although not the first to be released. Ollie plays a small-town Southern gentleman named Piedmon Mumblethumber and Stan, complete with kilt, appears as his visiting nephew from Scotland. Director Clyde Bruckman did several other early Laurel and Hardy shorts, including *Call of the Cuckoo, The Battle of the Century* and *Leave 'Em Laughing.*

HAL ROACH

Direction—Clyde Bruckman
PLAYERS: Stan Laurel & Oliver Hardy

PYGMALION   Gt. Britain (1938)
Straight adaptation of Shaw's play about a cockney flower girl who is transformed by a professor of English into a lady of fashion. Not a particularly cinematic film, but marked by the wit and intelligence of its dialogue and the polished playing of Leslie Howard (Professor Higgins), Wendy Hiller (Eliza Doolittle), and Wilfrid Lawson as her outrageous dustman father. *My Fair Lady*, a musical version of the play, was staged in New York in 1956 and later filmed at Warners by George Cukor.

GABRIEL PASCAL PRODUCTIONS

Production—Gabriel Pascal   *Screenplay*—W. P. Lipscomb,
Direction—Anthony Asquith,   Cecil Lewis
   Leslie Howard   *Photography*—Harry Stradling
Original story & dialogue—   *Sets*—Laurence Irving
   George Bernard Shaw   *Music*—Arthur Honegger
                                     Editing—David Lean
PLAYERS: Leslie Howard, Wendy Hiller, Wilfrid Lawson, Marie Lohr, Scott Sunderland, Jean Cadell, David Tree, Esme Percy

QUAI DES BRUMES (Port of Shadows)   France (1938)
Disillusioned army deserter (Jean Gabin), searching the port of Le Havre for a ship that will take him to South America, becomes involved

in an impossible love affair with Michèle Morgan and with gangsters later responsible for his death. The pessimism of the French cinema of the 1930's has never been more accurately reflected than in this sordid tale with its drab and misty setting of factories, docks and working-class streets—all given a melancholy beauty by the camera of Eugene Schuftan. Hauntingly scored by Maurice Jaubert who also composed the music for Carné's *Drôle de Drame, Hôtel du Nord* and *Le Jour Se Lève.*

RABINOVICH

Direction—Marcel Carné
Screenplay, adaptation &
  dialogue (from novel by Pierre
  MacOrlan)—Jacques Prévert
Photography—Eugène Schuftan

Art direction—
  Alexandre Trauner
Music—Maurice Jaubert
Editing—René Le Hénaff

PLAYERS: Jean Gabin, Michel Simon, Michèle Morgan, Aimos, René Génin, Pierre Brasseur

QUAI DES ORFEVRES   France (1947)

Henri-Georges Clouzot's realistic little crime film revolves about police inspector (Louis Jouvet) and his investigation of the murder of an old movie producer. A well-written thriller raised to a higher plane by Clouzot's pessimistic observations of postwar Parisian life, particularly the sleazy music-hall world in which the story is set. Beautifully played by Jouvet, Bernard Blier as chief suspect, and Suzy Delair as his wife.

MAJESTIC FILMS

Direction—
  Henri-Georges Clouzot
Photography—Armand Thirard
Design—Max Douy
Music—Francis Lopez

Screenplay, adaptation &
  dialogue (from novel Legitime
  Defense *by S. A. Steeman)—*
  Clouzot, Jean Ferry
Editing—Charles Bretonneiche

PLAYERS: Louis Jouvet, Simone Renant, Bernard Blier, Suzy Delair, Charles Dullin

QUATORZE JUILLET   France (1932)

Little-known René Clair movie about a few hours in the life of a flower girl on the eve of France's annual holiday. Similar in mood and style to *Sous les Toits de Paris* and, though not as successful as that classic picture, contains much of its charm, capturing once again the feel of everyday life in the lower-class streets of Montmartre. Excellent performance by Paul Olivier as a drunken eccentric. Photographed by

Georges Périnal (his last film for Clair) who had earlier worked on *Sous les Toits de Paris, A Nous la Liberté* and *Le Million.*

FILMS SONORES TOBIS

Direction, screenplay & dialogue
—René Clair
Photography—Georges Périnal

Art direction—Lazare Meerson
Music—Maurice Jaubert
Sound editing—René Le Hénaff

PLAYERS: Annabella, Georges Rigaud, Pola Illery, Raymond Cordy, Paul Olivier, Raymond Aimos, Thomy Bourdelle

QUEEN CHRISTINA   U.S.A. (1933)

Costume romance about the tragic love of 17th-century Swedish Queen (Greta Garbo) for Spanish envoy (John Gilbert). Routine and uninspired for the most part although the set designs are impressive and Garbo's performance unforgettable. The final scene on the prow of the ship taking Christina into exile, in which the camera dollies into a huge close-up of Garbo's face, is among the most famous last shots in movie history.

METRO—GOLDWYN—MAYER

Direction—Rouben Mamoulian
Screenplay—H. M. Harwood &
   Salka Viertel
Dialogue—S. N. Behrman
Story—Salka Viertel &
   Margaret R. Levino

Photography—William Daniels
Art direction—Alexander
   Toluboff & Edwin B. Willis
Music—Herbert Stothart
Editing—Blanche Sewell

PLAYERS: Greta Garbo, John Gilbert, Ian Keith, Lewis Stone, Elizabeth Young, C. Aubrey Smith, Reginald Owen

QUEEN KELLY   U.S.A. (1928)

Gloria Swanson as an innocent young convent girl, Walter Byron as the Ruritanian prince who seduces her, and Seena Owen as a mad queen who slinks naked around a vast, extravagantly decorated palace. One of the most erotic and bizarre of all American silent films, often vulgar but frequently displaying the full range of von Stroheim's remarkable talent. The film was unfinished (production halted when sound arrived) and released in a shortened version in which the convent girl meets her death in the palace moat. During the 1960's, however, a further 20 minutes of film were uncovered in which Miss Swanson is found not to be dead after all, but continuing her strange adventures in an African brothel.

GLORIA SWANSON/JOSEPH KENNEDY PRODUCTION FOR UNITED ARTISTS

Queen Christina

Direction & screenplay—
Erich von Stroheim
*Photography—*Ben Reynolds &
Hal Mohr

*Art direction—*Richard Day &
Erich von Stroheim
*Editing—*Viola Lawrence

PLAYERS: Gloria Swanson, Walter Byron, Seena Owen, Sidney Bracey, William von Brincken

QUEEN OF SPADES, THE   Gt. Britain (1948)

Penniless young Russian officer (Anton Walbrook), obsessed with the idea of making his fortune at the game of faro, attempts to wrest the secret of winning cards from aged countess (Edith Evans) who, years before, had sold her soul for the same reason. Britain's most stylish and successful costume film of the 1940's. Best sequence: the final card game when Walbrook, on the verge of winning a fortune, turns up not the winning card but the Queen of Spades, transformed in one classic moment of horror into the face of the dead countess.

WORLD SCREENPLAYS

Production—
Anatole de Grunwald
*Direction—*Thorold Dickinson
Screenplay (based on story by
*Alexander Pushkin)—*Rodney
Ackland & Arthur Boys

*Photography—*Otto Heller
*Art direction—*William Kellner
*Design—*Oliver Messel
*Music—*Georges Auric
*Editing—*Hazel Wilkinson

PLAYERS: Edith Evans, Anton Walbrook, Yvonne Mitchell, Ronald Howard, Mary Jerrold, Anthony Dawson, Miles Malleson, Michael Medwin

QUIET MAN, THE   U.S.A. (1952)

Cheerful love story set in a never-never Ireland with ex-boxer (John Wayne) returning to his native Galway to court fiery, red-haired Maureen O'Hara and fight bullying squire (Victor McLaglen). Some delightful scenes: the village steeplechase for the prize of a lady's bonnet, Wayne's humorous courtship of his colleen, and the final all-out fistfight around the village. There are a number of mischievous supporting performances—Ward Bond as the local priest, Mildred Natwick as a merry widow, and Barry Fitzgerald as a marriage broker who is also a bookie. Winton Hoch's lovely location photography won him his third Academy Award in six years and Ford also received an Oscar (his fourth) for his direction.

Production–John Ford, Merian C. Cooper

Direction–John Ford

Screenplay (*from story by Maurice Walsh*)–Frank S. Nugent

Photography (*Technicolor*)–Winton C. Hoch

Photography (*Second unit*)–Archie Stout

Art direction–Frank Hotaling

Music–Victor Young

Editing–Jack Murray

PLAYERS: John Wayne, Maureen O'Hara, Barry Fitzgerald, Ward Bond, Victor McLaglen, Mildred Natwick, Francis Ford, Eileen Crowe, May Craig, Arthur Shields

RANCHO NOTORIOUS U.S.A. (1952)

A bizarre little Western by director Fritz Lang—his third and last—focusing on Arthur Kennedy and his hunt for the outlaws who killed his sweetheart. Notable mainly for Lang's stylized direction and for Marlene Dietrich's splendid portrait of an ex-saloon hostess who runs a hideaway ranch for outlaws on the Mexican border. One of the first films to use a ballad song (The ballad of Chuck-a-Luck) as a music score.

RKO RADIO

Production–Howard Welsch

Direction–Fritz Lang

Screenplay (*from story "Gunsight Whitman" by Silvia Richards*)–Daniel Taradash

Photography (*Technicolor*)–Hal Mohr

Art direction–Robert Priestley

Music–Emil Newman

Editing–Otto Ludwig

PLAYERS: Marlene Dietrich, Arthur Kennedy, Mel Ferrer, Gloria Henry, William Frawley, Lisa Ferraday, John Raven, Jack Elam

RASHOMON Japan (1950)

Japanese masterpiece reconstructing, from four different points of view, the murder of a nobleman and the rape of his wife in 8th-century Japan. The incident is recalled by the bandit who supposedly committed the crime, a woodcutter, the dead nobleman (whose thoughts are reflected through a medium representing the dead man's spirit), and his wife. Each version of the story is distorted, and the complete truth, which lies somewhere in between all four stories, is never uncovered. The film introduced the Japanese cinema to western audiences and won the Grand Prize at the 1951 Venice Film Festival. It is taken from episodes in two stories by Ryunosuke Akutagawa, one of the foremost names in modern Japanese literature.

DAIEI (JINGO MINORU/MASAICHI NAGATA)

Direction—Akira Kurosawa   *Photography*—Kazuo Miyagawa
Screenplay—Shinobu Hashimoto   *Music*—Fumio Hayasaka
  & Akira Kurosawa   *Art direction*—So Matsuyama
PLAYERS: Toshiro Mifune, Masayuki Mori, Takashi Shimura, Machiko Kyo, Minoru Chiaki

REAP THE WILD WIND   U.S.A. (1942)
One of DeMille's best films, set in Key West, Florida, in the 1840's, and dealing with the pirate wreckers who plunder the cargoes of the majestic ships wrecked on the Florida reefs. A romantic, sometimes surprisingly refined swashbuckler, beautifully in period (art directors Hans Dreier and Roland Anderson and costume designer Natalie Visart again serve DeMille well) and handsomely photographed in Technicolor. The highlight is a magnificent undersea battle with a giant squid, one of the most effective studio monsters since King Kong. Raymond Massey, splendid as the heavy, dominates a cast headed by Ray Milland and John Wayne and such DeMille regulars as Paulette Goddard, Robert Preston and Lynne Overman.

PARAMOUNT

Production & direction—   *Photography (Technicolor)*—
  Cecil B. DeMille   Victor Milner, William V.
Screenplay (from Saturday   Skall
  Evening Post story by Thelma   *Art direction*—Hans Dreier,
  Strabel)—Alan LeMay, Charles   Roland Anderson
  Bennett, Jesse Lasky, Jr.   *Music*—Victor Young
         Editing—Anne Bauchens
PLAYERS: Ray Milland, Paulette Goddard, John Wayne, Raymond Massey, Robert Preston, Susan Hayward, Lynne Overman, Charles Bickford

REAR WINDOW   U.S.A. (1954)
Superior Hitchcock movie about an injured magazine photographer, restricted to his Manhattan apartment because of a broken leg, who suspects that a murder has been committed in a neighboring flat. An original picture, confined throughout to one set—the photographer's apartment and the courtyard and windows of the opposite block. It is directed and written with considerable distinction. James Stewart plays

the photographer, Grace Kelly his smart New York girlfriend, and Raymond Burr, complete with white hair and spectacles, the killer.

Production & direction—
Alfred Hitchcock
*Screenplay (from short story by Cornell Woolrich)—*John Michael Hayes

Photography (Technicolor)—
Robert Burks
*Music—*Franz Waxman
*Editing—*George Tomasini

PLAYERS: James Stewart, Grace Kelly, Wendell Corey, Thelma Ritter, Raymond Burr, Judith Evelyn, Ross Bagdasarian, Georgine Darcy

REBECCA   U.S.A. (1940)

Hitchcock's celebrated film version of Daphne du Maurier's romantic novel about a newlywed young girl (Joan Fontaine) who finds that her husband (Laurence Olivier) is still dominated by the spirit of his dead first wife. Melodramatic, glossy and not really Hitchcock material, but very well made and acted (particularly by Judith Anderson as the sinister housekeeper). Impeccably designed by Lyle Wheeler whose huge Cornish mansion, Mandalay, remains one of his finest creations. George Barnes, a leading Hollywood cameraman of the thirties and forties, won his sole Academy Award for his work on this film.

DAVID O. SELZNICK/UNITED ARTISTS

*Production—*David O. Selznick
*Direction—*Alfred Hitchcock
*Screenplay—*Robert E. Sherwood, Joan Harrison

*Photography—*George Barnes
*Art direction—*Lyle Wheeler
*Music—*Franz Waxman
*Editing—*Hal C. Kern

PLAYERS: Laurence Olivier, Joan Fontaine, George Sanders, Judith Anderson, Nigel Bruce, C. Aubrey Smith, Reginald Denny, Gladys Cooper, Leo G. Carroll

REBEL WITHOUT A CAUSE   U.S.A. (1955)

The problems and frustrations of three American juvenile delinquents (James Dean, Natalie Wood, Sal Mineo) examined in a perceptive movie that breaks away from the conventional mold by showing that delinquency exists not only in slum areas but also in the middle-class, more affluent sections of society. Based on eight months' exhaustive research among policemen, judges, youth leaders and juvenile welfare officers. The second of Dean's three films and his best screen performance.

Production—David Weisbart
Direction—Nicholas Ray
Screenplay (*from adaptation by*
  Irving Shulman of story by
  Nicholas Ray)—Stewart Stern

Photography (*Warnercolor/*
  CinemaScope)—Ernest Haller
Art direction—Malcolm Bert
Music—Leonard Rosenman
Editing—William Ziegler

PLAYERS: James Dean, Natalie Wood, Jim Backus, Ann Doran, Rochelle Hudson, William Hopper, Sal Mineo

RED BADGE OF COURAGE, THE   U.S.A. (1951)
An affectionate version of Stephen Crane's Civil War novel about a young farm boy who struggles against doubts and fears before fighting in his first battle. Uneven, ragged (the film was cut by the studio from 80 minutes to 69), occasionally brilliant and with some effectively staged battle scenes. One of the more interesting war pictures, but unfortunately not the masterpiece that Dore Schary and director John Huston intended.

METRO–GOLDWYN–MAYER

Production—Dore Schary
Direction—John Huston
Screenplay—John Huston
Photography—Harold Rosson

Art direction—Cedric Gibbons,
  Hans Peters
Music—Bronislau Kaper
Editing (*supervised by Margaret
  Booth*)—Ben Lewis

PLAYERS: Audie Murphy, Bill Mauldin, John Dierkes, Royal Dano, Arthur Hunnicutt, Tim Durant, Douglas Dick, Andy Devine

RED BALLOON, THE   France (1956)
Delightful 35-minute fantasy about the adventures of a little boy (Lamorisse's own six-year-old son) and a big red balloon he rescues from a lamppost. The most refreshing film of 1956 is photographed entirely in the picturesque back streets and narrow alleys of Old Montmartre.

FILMS MONTSOURIS

Production, direction &
  screenplay—Albert Lamorisse

Photography (*Technicolor*)—
  Edmond Sechan
Music—Maurice Le Roux

PLAYERS: Pascal Lamorisse, the children of Menilmontant, and all the balloons of Paris.

RED DESERT, THE (Deserto Rosso)   Italy/France (1964)
Penetrating and detailed study of acutely depressed married woman

(Monica Vitti) living in the industrialized north of Italy whose neurosis stems not only from the mental effects of a car accident but also from her inability to live in and resist the overpowering pressures of modern industrial society. A pessimistic, slow but nonetheless remarkable film enhanced by the extraordinary color photography of Carlo Di Palma (it was Antonioni's first film in color) and by the intensity of Monica Vitti's performance. Also in the cast: Carlo Chionetti as the woman's dispassionate engineer husband and Richard Harris as her lover.

FILM DUEMILA/CINEMATOGRAFICA FEDERIZ (ROME)/FRANCORIZ (PARIS)

Direction—
  Michelangelo Antonioni
*Screenplay—*Antonioni &
  Tonino Guerra

Photography (Eastmancolor)—
  Carlo Di Palma
*Art direction—*Piero Poletto
*Music—*Giovanni Fusco
*Editing—*Eraldo Da Roma

PLAYERS: Monica Vitti, Richard Harris, Carlo Chionetti, Xenia Valderi, Rita Renoir, Aldo Grotti, Valerio Bartoleschi

RED DUST   U.S.A. (1932)
Lively M-G-M comedy drama with smart-talking prostitute (Jean Harlow) involved with rubber planter (Clark Gable) in prewar Saigon. The film is best remembered for Harlow's shrewd and engaging performance (it was in this picture that she proved herself to be a superb comedienne). This was the second of her six films with Gable. Others: *The Secret Six* (1931), *Hold Your Man* (1933), *China Seas* (1935), *Wife vs Secretary* (1936), *Saratoga* (1937).

METRO–GOLDWYN–MAYER

Production & direction—
  Victor Fleming
*Photography—*Harold Rosson

*Screenplay (from play by Wilson Collison)—*John Lee Mahin
*Editing—*Blanche Sewell

PLAYERS: Clark Gable, Jean Harlow, Gene Raymond, Mary Astor, Donald Crisp, Tully Marshall, Forrester Harvey

RED RIVER   U.S.A. (1948)
The epic story of a cattle trek over the Chisholm Trail from Texas to Kansas. Beautifully photographed scenes of cattle crossing prairies and rivers, a thrilling cattle stampede, and a fine performance from John Wayne (his best away from John Ford) as a ruthless cattle king. Howard Hawks' first Western and along with *My Darling Clementine* and *She Wore a Yellow Ribbon* the best of the whole decade.

MONTEREY PRODUCTIONS/UNITED ARTISTS

The Red Shoes

Production & direction—
  Howard Hawks
Screenplay (from novel The
  Chisholm Trail *by Borden
  Chase)—*Borden Chase,
  Charles Schnee

*Photography—*Russell Harlan
Art direction—
  John Datu Arensma
*Music—*Dimitri Tiomkin
*Editing—*Christian Nyby

PLAYERS: John Wayne, Montgomery Clift, Joanne Dru, Walter Brennan, Coleen Gray, John Ireland, Noah Berry, Jr., Harry Carey, Sr., Chief Yowlachie, Harry Carey, Jr., Mickey Kuhn, Paul Fix, Hank Warden

RED SHOES, THE   Gt. Britain (1948)
Beautifully photographed ballet story about a young ballerina who finds herself torn between her passion for dancing and her love for her composer-husband. An ambitious, sometimes self-conscious picture, hampered by its trite story, but redeemed by the sharp, exciting music of Brian Easdale, the superb dancing of Moira Shearer, Leonide Massine and Robert Helpmann, and a fine performance by Anton Walbrook

as an impresario. The final 20-minute ballet was composed specially for the film and is based on the Hans Christian Andersen story about the magic red shoes that danced a little girl to death.

ARCHERS

Production, direction &
screenplay—Michael Powell,
Emeric Pressburger
Original screenplay—
Emeric Pressburger
Additional dialogue—
Keith Winter

Photography (Technicolor)—
Jack Cardiff
Production design—
Hein Heckroth
Art direction—Arthur Lawson
Music—Brian Easdale
Editing—Reginald Mills

PLAYERS: Moira Shearer, Leonide Massine, Robert Helpmann, Anton Walbrook, Marius Goring, Jean Short, Gordin Littman, Julia Lang, Bill Shine, Austin Trevor, Esmond Knight

REMBRANDT   Gt. Britain (1936)
Slow, carefully scripted account of the last years of Rembrandt's life from the death of his wife to his own death in 1669. An ambitious, rather austere film (it was one of Korda's commercial failures) made notable by Charles Laughton's virtuoso performance and by Vincent Korda's magnificent Dutch interiors. Gertrude Lawrence made one of her rare screen appearances as Rembrandt's housekeeper.

LONDON FILMS

Production & direction—
Alexander Korda
Screenplay—Carl Zuckmayer,
Arthur Wimperis, June Head
Photography—Georges Périnal

Settings—Vincent Korda
Music—Geoffrey Toye
Editing—Francis Lyon
Supervising editor—
William Hornbeck

PLAYERS: Charles Laughton, Gertrude Lawrence, Elsa Lanchester, John Bryning, Richard Gofe, Meinhart Maur, Walter Hudd, John Clements

RENDEZ-VOUS DE JUILLET   France (1949)
Jacques Becker looks at the wild and disordered lives of a group of jazz-loving Left Bank adolescents growing up in postwar Paris. Basically nothing more than a series of sketches, the film does not rank with Becker's best work, but is nonetheless admirable for the way in which it captures the hopes, obsessions and emotional frustrations of its characters and for its often sympathetic feeling toward the young in their revolt against orthodoxy. Daniel Gélin as a sober young would-be explorer, and Brigitte Auber and Nicole Courcel as aspiring actresses, head the cast.

365

Direction—Jacques Becker
Screenplay—Becker & Maurice
Griffe
Adaptation & dialogue—
Jacques Becker

Photography—Claude Renoir
Art direction—
Robert Jules Garnier
Music—Jean Wiener & Mezz
Mezzrow
Editing—Marguerite Renoir

PLAYERS: Daniel Gélin, Bernard Lajarrige, Maurice Ronet, Pierre Trabaud, Nicole Courcel, Brigitte Auber, Louis Seigner

RICHARD III   Gt. Britain (1955)

The third and best of Laurence Olivier's filmed Shakespearean plays with Olivier himself outstanding as the treacherous hunchback Duke of Gloucester who woos, schemes and murders his way to the throne of England. Impeccably in period and distinguished both by its playing—Ralph Richardson (Buckingham), John Gielgud (Clarence), Cedric Hardwicke (Edward IV)—and by Olivier's bold direction technique; i.e., Richard talking straight at the camera and confiding his evil machinations to the audience. Several of Olivier's collaborators on his two earlier Shakespeare films also worked on this production.

LONDON FILMS

Production & direction (adapted
from Shakespeare)—Laurence
Olivier
Text advisor—Alan Dent
Production design—Roger Furse

Photography (VistaVision/
Technicolor)—Otto Heller
Art direction—Carmen Dillon
Music—William Walton
Editing—Helga Cranston

PLAYERS: Laurence Olivier, John Gielgud, Ralph Richardson, Cedric Hardwicke, Claire Bloom, Mary Kerridge, Pamela Brown, Alec Clunes, Michael Gough, Stanley Baker, Norman Wooland, Helen Hayes

RIDE THE HIGH COUNTRY   U.S.A. (1961)

Downbeat Western about a pair of middle-aged gunmen who regain their self-respect by riding the trail once more as escorts to a gold shipment. The film brought critical acclaim to Peckinpah and also to its two stars, Joel McCrea and Randolph Scott, who were 57 and 59 respectively at the time of shooting and who came out of semiretirement especially to play in the picture. *The* "sleeper" and arguably the best Western of the 1960's.

METRO—GOLDWYN—MAYER

Production—Richard E. Lyons
Direction—Sam Peckinpah

Screenplay—N. B. Stone, Jnr.
Music—George Bassman

Photography (CinemaScope/   *Art direction*—George W. Davis,
Metrocolor)—Lucien Ballard   Leroy Coleman
PLAYERS: Randolph Scott, Joel McCrea, Ronald Starr, Mariette Hart-
ley, James Drury, R. G. Armstrong, Edgar Buchanan, Jenie Jackson

RIFIFI   France (1955)
Crime thriller about a major jewel robbery in a famous Paris store and
the bloody gang war that follows when two rival gangs fight it out
with guns and razors. The actual robbery—an enthralling 20-minute
sequence played in silence—is brilliantly done, but the rest of the film
is no better than any one of a dozen routine American thrillers and
bears little comparison to Huston's classic robbery movie *The Asphalt
Jungle*. Dassin, who won the 1955 Cannes Award for best direction,
appears in the film as one of the thieves.

INDUS FILMS–S. N. PATHÉ CINEMA–PRIMA FILM

Direction—Jules Dassin   *Photography*—Philippe Agostini
Screenplay—Rene Wheeler,   *Art direction*—Auguste Capelier
    Jules Dassin,   *Music*—Georges Auric
    Auguste le Breton   *Editing*—Roger Dwyre
PLAYERS: Jean Servais, Carl Mohner, Robert Manuel, Perlo Vita, Magali
Noel, Marie Sabouret, Robert Hossein

RINK, THE   U.S.A. (1916)
Classic Mutual two-reeler with humble waiter (Charlie Chaplin) saving Edna Purviance from the unwelcome attentions of flirtatious Mr.
Stout (Eric Campbell) at a skating party. Full of the usual impeccably
timed Chaplin slapstick and climaxed by a free-for-all with everyone
on roller skates and crashing into each other. Henry Bergman in his
third Chaplin film appeared as Mrs. Stout.

A MUTUAL COMEDY

Direction—Charles Chaplin   *Photography*—R. H. Totheroh
Screenplay—Charles Chaplin   and W. C. Foster
PLAYERS: Charles Chaplin, Albert Austin, Lloyd Bacon, Henry Berg-
man, Eric Campbell, Frank J. Coleman, James T. Kelly, Charlotte
Mineau

RIO BRAVO   U.S.A. (1959)
Sheriff (John Wayne) enlists alcoholic deputy (Dean Martin), crippled
old-timer (Walter Brennan), and gunslinger (Ricky Nelson) to help
him prevent a rancher and his gang from rescuing one of their number
being held in the jail of a small Texas border town. An immensely

engaging Hawks Western with some crisply edited bursts of action and one of Tiomkin's most melodic Western scores. Despite its un-doubted entertainment value it is not the classic it is often made out to be and is far below the standard of George Stevens' *Shane* and Sam Peckinpah's *Guns in the Afternoon*.

ARMADA PRODUCTIONS/WARNER BROS.

Production & direction—
Howard Hawks
Screenplay (from story by B. H.
Campbell)—Jules Furthman,
Leigh Brackett

Photography (Technicolor)—
Russell Harlan
Music—Dimitri Tiomkin
Art direction—Leo K. Kuter
Editing—Folmar Blangsted

PLAYERS: John Wayne, Dean Martin, Ricky Nelson, Angie Dickinson, Walter Brennan, Ward Bond, John Russell, Pedro Gonzalez-Gonzalez

RIO GRANDE   U.S.A. (1950)

The last in John Ford's trilogy of cavalry films, set in the post-Civil War period and featuring John Wayne as a U.S. Cavalry colonel who leads the fight against the Apaches along the Mexican border. A sprawl-ing, oversentimental film, inferior to both *Fort Apache* and *She Wore a Yellow Ribbon*, but sporadically interesting for its well-staged action sequences. Maureen O'Hara is Wayne's wife, Claude Jarman his en-listed son, and an assortment of Ford regulars (Victor McLaglen, Harry Carey Jr., Ben Johnson) are cavalry personnel.

ARGOSY PICTURES—REPUBLIC

Production—John Ford,
Merian C. Cooper
Direction—John Ford
Photography—Bert Glennon
Second-Unit—Archie Stout
Art direction—Frank Hotaling

Screenplay (from story
Mission With No Record *by*
James Warner Bellah)—
James Kevin McGuinness
Music—Victor Young
Editing—Jack Murray

PLAYERS: John Wayne, Maureen O'Hara, Ben Johnson, Claude Jarman, Jr., Harry Carey Jr., Chill Wills, J. Carroll Naish, Victor McLaglen, Grant Withers, Peter Ortiz

RIOT IN CELL BLOCK 11   U.S.A. (1954)

Powerful documentary-style indictment of the conditions and need for reform in America's penal institutions. Neville Brand gives a ferocious performance as the long-term prisoner who sets off a riot and Emile Meyer gives a quieter but equally assured portrayal of a sympathetic warder. Actually shot inside the walls of Folsom State Prison in California.

Production—Walter Wanger   *Art direction*—David Milton
Direction—Don Siegel   *Music*—Herschel Burke Gilbert
Screenplay—Richard Collins   *Editing*—Bruce P. Pierce
Photography—Russell Harlan
PLAYERS: Neville Brand, Emile Meyer, Frank Faylen, Leo Gordon, Robert Osterloh, Paul Frees, Don Keefer

RISE AND FALL OF LEGS DIAMOND, THE   U.S.A. (1960)
The career of Jack "Legs" Diamond, a lesser-known "protection" racketeer who prospered in New York during prohibition days. Fast-paced but (although highly regarded by many critics) very much a minor work when compared with the Raoul Walsh and Michael Curtiz classics of the 1930's. Ray Danton plays Diamond, Karen Steele is his moll, and the camera work is by Lucien Ballard who earlier worked with Boetticher on *The Magnificent Matador, Arruza* and *Buchanan Rides Alone.*

A UNITED STATES PRODUCTIONS PICTURE/WARNER BROS.
Production—Milton Sperling   *Art direction*—Jack Poplin
Direction—Budd Boetticher   *Music*—Leonard Rosenman
Screenplay—Joseph Landon   *Editing*—Folmar Blangsted
Photography—Lucien Ballard
PLAYERS: Ray Danton, Karen Steele, Elaine Stewart, Jesse White, Simon Oakland, Robert Lowrey, Judson Pratt

RIVER, THE   India (1950)
Enchanting version of Rumer Godden's novel about three teen-age girls and their first uncertain experience of love as they grow up beside the River Ganges in India. One of Renoir's most beautiful pictures (his first in color), leisurely, poetic, full of atmosphere and handsomely photographed by his nephew Claude, this being the fourth time they had worked together since their initial collaboration on *Toni* in 1935.

THEATER GUILD
Direction—Jean Renoir   *Art direction*—Eugène Lourié,
Screenplay, adaptation &   Basi Chandra Gupta
   dialogue—Jean Renoir,   *Music arranged by*
   Rumer Godden   M.-A Parata Sarati
Photography (Technicolor)—   *Editing*—Georges Gale
   Claude Renoir
PLAYERS: Nora Swinbourne, Esmond Knight, Arthur Shields, Thomas E. Breen, Patricia Walters, Radha, Adrienne Corri

ROARING TWENTIES, THE U.S.A. (1939)

High-grade, very tough Warner crime melodrama with James Cagney and Humphrey Bogart as a couple of ruthless prohibition bootleggers and Jeffrey Lynn as their ex-Army buddy-turned-lawyer who is eventually responsible for their destruction. Among the best and most exciting in the genre, directed with great efficiency by Raoul Walsh who was as skillful at directing Warner gangster movies (*High Sierra, White Heat*) as Michael Curtiz was at directing Warner swashbucklers. Jerry Wald (later producer) and Robert Rossen (later director) both contributed to the smartly tailored script which was based on an original story by Mark Hellinger.

WARNER BROS./FIRST NATIONAL

Executive producer—
  Hal B. Wallis
Associate producer—
  Samuel Bischoff
Direction—Raoul Walsh
Photography—Ernest Haller

Screenplay—Jerry Wald, Richard
  Macaulay & Robert Rossen
Art direction—Max Parker
Music—Heinz Roemheld &
  Ray Heindorf
Editing—Jack Killifer

PLAYERS: James Cagney, Priscilla Lane, Humphery Bogart, Gladys George, Jeffrey Lynn, Frank McHugh, Paul Kelly, Elisabeth Risdon

ROBERTA U.S.A. (1935)

Astaire and Rogers with a new director and combining with Irene Dunne in the third of their successful romantic musicals of the thirties. Not the best in the series but some fine Jerome Kern music ("Smoke Gets in Your Eyes," "Lovely to Look At") and a scintillating Astaire-Rogers tap routine to "I'll Be Hard to Handle."

RKO RADIO

Production—Pandro S. Berman
Direction—William Seiter
*Screenplay (from play, book
  and lyrics by Otto Harbach
  and music by Jerome Kern)*—
  Jane Murfin, Sam Mintz &
  Allan Scott

Additional dialogue—
  Glenn Tryon
Photography—
  Edward Cronjager
Art direction—Van Nest Polglase
  & Carroll Clark
Editing—William Hamilton

PLAYERS: Irene Dunne, Fred Astaire, Ginger Rogers, Randolph Scott, Helen Westley, Claire Dodd, Victor Varconi

ROBINSON CRUSOE ON MARS U.S.A. (1964)

Superior science-fiction vehicle cleverly and faithfully adapted from

Defoe's tale of Robinson Crusoe, and featuring Paul Mantee as an American astronaut who is marooned on Mars with a pet monkey and a stranger from another planet. The magnificent landscapes of Death Valley served for the Martian terrain and offered ace color cameraman Winton C. Hoch his best opportunity since working with John Ford on *She Wore a Yellow Ribbon*, *The Quiet Man* and *The Searchers*. Directed by science-fiction expert Byron Haskin.

PARAMOUNT

Production—Aubrey Schenck
Direction—Byron Haskin
Screenplay (*based on novel*
   Robinson Crusoe *by Daniel*
   Defoe)—Ib Melchior &
   John C. Higgins

Photography (*Technicolor/*
   Techniscope)—
   Winton C. Hoch
Art direction—Hal Pereira &
   Arthur Lonergan
Music—Van Cleave
Editing—Terry Morse

PLAYERS: Paul Mantee, Vic Lundin, Adam West

ROCCO AND HIS BROTHERS   Italy/France (1960)

Ambitious 3-hour Italian picture about a large peasant family from the impoverished South and their bitter, often humiliating, experiences as they try to make a new life in the industrialized northern city of Milan. An episodic, violent, frequently brilliant film, notable mainly for the playing of its international cast, particularly Katina Paxinou as the ambitious mother and for its realistic evocation of life in the slums of a big city. Directed by Luchino Visconti who himself was born and raised in Milan.

TITANUS (ROME)/LES FILMS MARCEAU (PARIS)

Direction—Luchino Visconti
Photography—Giuseppe Rotunno
Art direction—Mario Garbuglia
Music—Nino Rota
Editing—Mario Serandrei

Screenplay (*inspired by*
   Giovanni Testori's "Il
   Ponte della Ghisolfa")—
   Luchino Visconti,
   Vasco Pratolini &
   Suso Cecchi D'Amico

PLAYERS: Alain Delon, Renato Salvatori, Annie Girardot, Katina Paxinou, Roger Hanin, Paolo Stoppa, Suzy Delai, Claudia Cardinale, Max Cartier

ROMAN HOLIDAY   U.S.A. (1953)

Stylish, romantic little fairy tale about a young princess who escapes for 24 hours from the duties of an Italian state visit to enjoy herself

371

Rocco and His Brothers

more informally in the company of an American newspaperman. A well-written, but sometimes slow film, reminiscent in many ways of Capra's *It Happened One Night*. Very well played by Audrey Hepburn as the princess (an enchanting performance for which she won an Oscar), Gregory Peck as the journalist, and Eddie Albert as his bewildered photographer.

PARAMOUNT

Production & direction—
 William Wyler
Screenplay (from story by
 Ian McLellan Hunter)—
 Ian McLellan Hunter,
 John Dighton

*Photography—*Franz Planer,
 Henri Alekan
*Art direction—*Hal Pereira,
 Walter Tyler
*Music—*Georges Auric
*Editing—*Robert Swink

PLAYERS: Gregory Peck, Audrey Hepburn, Eddie Albert, Hartley Power, Harcourt Williams, Margaret Rawlings, Tullio Carminati

ROMMEL–DESERT FOX   U.S.A. (1951)

Above average war movie about the last years in the life of Field Marshal Erwin Rommel. Somewhat oversimplified but effectively played by James Mason and directed with great authority by Henry Hathaway whose handling of the pre-credit commando raid sequence is especially notable.

TWENTIETH CENTURY–FOX

Production—Nunnally Johnson
Direction—Henry Hathaway
Screenplay (from the book
  Rommel by Desmond Young)—
  Nunnally Johnson

Photography—Norbert Brodine
Art direction—Lyle Wheeler,
  Maurice Ransford
Editing—James B. Clark

PLAYERS: James Mason, Cedric Hardwicke, Jessica Tandy, Luther Adler, Everett Sloane, Leo G. Carroll, George Macready, Richard Boone

ROOM AT THE TOP   Gt. Britain (1959)

The meteoric rise of working-class accountant Joe Lampton (Laurence Harvey) who makes it to the top in one bounce by marrying rich industrialist's daughter (Heather Sears). The film's great performance comes from Simone Signoret (Academy Award, best actress, 1959) as the tragic middle-aged mistress he discards on the way. A now dated picture, but still a significant one in that it pioneered the new British realism and also established a much franker attitude toward sex. Shot in and around the Yorkshire city of Bradford and directed by Jack Clayton whose only previous directorial assignment had been the short *The Bespoke Overcoat.*

A REMUS FILM

Production—John & James Woolf
Direction—Jack Clayton
Screenplay (from novel by
  John Braine)—Neil Paterson

Photography—Freddie Francis
Art direction—Ralph Brinton
Music—Mario Nascimbene
Editing—Ralph Kemplen

PLAYERS: Simone Signoret, Laurence Harvey, Heather Sears, Donald Wolfit, Donald Houston, Hermione Baddeley, Ambrosine Phillpotts, Raymond Huntley

ROPE   U.S.A. (1948)

Alfred Hitchcock's famous "10-minute take" adaptation of Patrick Hamilton's play about two young homosexuals (Farley Granger and John Dall) who murder a college friend in order to prove themselves superior to conventional morality and then entertain the dead boy's parents, his fiancée and also their former college professor (James Stewart) to cocktails in the very room in which they have hidden the body. The film is set entirely in a New York apartment between the hours of 7:30 and 9:15 P.M. The "10-minute take" refers to scenes shot with the entire role of film in the camera magazine—some ten minutes of screen time. Hitchcock used a consistently mobile camera and excluded all the usual cuts and dissolves, but this tended to make the film slow-moving and even tedious and the technique was never used again after this occasion. The screenplay is based on the Leopold and Loeb murder case of the 1920's (see also *Compulsion*) and the film is of additional interest for being Hitchcock's first in color.

TRANSATLANTIC PICTURES/WARNER BROS.

Production—Sidney Bernstein, Alfred Hitchcock
Direction—Alfred Hitchcock
Screenplay—Arthur Laurents
Adaptation—Hume Cronyn
Art direction—Perry Ferguson
Photography (Technicolor)—Joseph Valentine, William V. Skall
Music (based on theme by Poulenc)—Leo F. Forbstein
Editing—William H. Ziegler

PLAYERS: James Stewart, Farley Granger, John Dall, Joan Chandler, Sir Cedric Hardwicke, Constance Collier, Edith Evanson, Douglas Dick

ROSE TATTOO, THE   U.S.A. (1955)
Lonely, middle-aged Italian widow (Anna Magnani) finds in oafish truck driver (Burt Lancaster) a physical substitute for the dead husband she mourns so deeply. Set in the Italian quarter of a small town in the Gulf of Mexico this film is strictly canned theater, but Magnani's performance and James Wong Howe's glittering black-and-white photography make for an interesting work. Directed by Daniel Mann who, during the 1950's, adapted several Broadway plays into screen terms, among them *Come Back, Little Sheba, Teahouse of the August Moon* and *Hot Spell*.

PARAMOUNT

Production—Hal B. Wallis
Direction—Daniel Mann
Screenplay (from his own play)—Tennessee Williams
Photography—James Wong Howe
Art direction—Hal Pereira & Tambi Larsen
Music—Alex North
Editing—Warren Low

PLAYERS: Anna Magnani, Burt Lancaster, Marisa Pavan, Ben Cooper, Virginia Grey, Jo Van Fleet, Sandro Giglio, Mimi Aguglia

ROSEMARY'S BABY   U.S.A. (1968)
Chillingly effective version of Ira Levin's best-selling novel in which
a happily married young couple (Mia Farrow and John Cassavetes)
become inextricably involved in witchcraft and Satanism when they
move into an old New York apartment building. A psychological horror
thriller of the highest class, reminiscent in many ways of Hitchcock,
depending for much of its success on Levin's original novel and on the
talented technicians and players who transferred it to the screen.
Impressive performances from the two principals and suitably creepy
ones from Sidney Blackmer as the leader of the coven and Ruth Gordon
(Academy Award, best supporting actress, 1968) as his flamboyant
wife.

PARAMOUNT/WILLIAM CASTLE ENTERPRISES

Production—William Castle   Art direction—Joel Schiller
Direction—Roman Polanski   Music—Krzysztof Komeda
Screenplay—Roman Polanski   Editing—Sam O'Steen &
Photography (Technicolor)—   Bob Wyman
   William Fraker
PLAYERS: Mia Farrow, John Cassavetes, Ruth Gordon, Sidney Blackmer,
Maurice Evans, Ralph Bellamy, Angela Dorian, Patsy Kelly, Elisha
Cook

ROUND UP, THE (Szegénylegények)   Hungary (1965)
Stark Hungarian film set during the aftermath of the ill-fated Kossuth-
led revolution of March, 1848 and dealing with a group of revolutionary
guerrillas who are rounded up and imprisoned in a large camp on the
Hungarian plains. Here they are interrogated, psychologically tortured
and tricked into informing on each other in the hope that one of them
will eventually betray their leader who is still at large. A slow, oppressive, terrifyingly cruel film, among the major works to emerge
from the contemporary Hungarian cinema.

STUDIO IV, MAFILM

Direction—Miklós Jancsó   Photography (AgfaScope)—
Screenplay—Gyula Hernádi   Tamás Somló
Art direction—Tamás Banovich   Editing—Zoltan Farkas
PLAYERS: János Görbe, Tibor Molnár, András Kozák, Gábor Agárdy,
Zoltán Latinovits, István Avar, Lajos Oze

RUGGLES OF RED GAP   U.S.A. (1935)
Charles Laughton in the best of his early American roles as an English

valet who is lost by his master to an American family in a poker game and thus thrown into a one-horse town in the West where he eventually achieves his independence. An amusing, high-spirited comedy that satirizes both American snobbery and English aristocracy. Excellent supporting cameos from check-suited Charlie Ruggles and Mary Boland as the valet's American owners and Roland Young as a somewhat decadent English earl. First filmed in 1923 with Edward Everett Horton as Ruggles and later remade as *Fancy Pants* (1950) with Bob Hope.

PARAMOUNT

Production—	*Adaptation (from novel by*
Arthur Hornblow, Jr.	*Harry Leon Wilson)—*
*Direction—*Leo McCarey	Humphrey Pearson
*Screenplay—*Walter DeLeon &	*Art direction—*Hans Dreier &
Harlan Thompson	Robert Odell
*Photography—*Alfred Gilks	*Editing—*Edward Dmytryk

PLAYERS: Charles Laughton, Mary Boland, Charlie Ruggles, Zasu Pitts, Roland Young, Leila Hyams, Maude Eburne

RUN OF THE ARROW   U.S.A. (1957)

Brutal Western about a Southern soldier who, after firing the last shot of the American Civil War, rejects the white man's civilization which has caused him so much bitterness and starts a new life among the Sioux Indians. Underrated when it first appeared, but now regarded by many critics as one of the most important Westerns of the 1950's. Rod Steiger plays the leading role and Jay C. Flippen appears in a supporting part as an old Indian scout.

RKO RADIO

Production & direction—	*Art direction—*
Samuel Fuller	Albert S. D'Agostino
*Screenplay—*Samuel Fuller	& Jack Okey
Photography (Technicolor/	*Music—*Victor Young
*RKO Scope)—*Joseph Biroc	*Editing—*Gene Fowler, Jr.

PLAYERS: Rod Steiger, Sarira Montiel, Brian Keith, Ralph Meeker, Jay C. Flippen, Charles Bronson, Olive Carey

SABOTAGE   Gt. Britain (1936)

Uneven Hitchcock thriller tracing the attempts of master saboteur (Oscar Homolka) and his gang of anarchistic agitators to destroy London. Some famous moments—a murder scene played in silence in which Sylvia Sidney kills her husband with a knife and the one in which a young boy unknowingly carries a time bomb across London—but over all a disappointing work. The film was adapted from Joseph Conrad's *The Secret Agent* and is not to be confused with Hitchcock's own film of that title made the same year but with a different story. Hitchcock's *Saboteur*, shot during the early Hollywood period, further adds to the confusion of titles.

SHEPHERD, GAUMONT–BRITISH PICTURES

Production–Michael Balcon
Direction–Alfred Hitchcock
Screenplay–Charles Bennett
Dialogue–Ian Hay, Helen
  Simpson, E. V. H. Emmett

Photography–Bernard Knowles
Art direction–Otto Werndorff
  & Albert Jullion
Music–Louis Levy
Editing–Charles Frend

PLAYERS: Sylvia Sidney, Oscar Homolka, Desmond Tester, John Loder, Joyce Barbour, Matthew Boulton, S. J. Warmington, William Dewhurst

SABOTEUR   U.S.A. (1942)
The least effective of Hitchcock's early American films is about a factory worker (Robert Cummings) suspected of sabotage who is hunted across America before he can establish his innocence. Routine, uneven, poorly acted, but worthy of mention for its memorably filmed climactic fight in the torch of the Statue of Liberty.

UNIVERSAL

Production–Frank Lloyd,
  Jack H. Skirball
Direction–Alfred Hitchcock
Art direction–Jack Otterson
Music–Charles Previn,
  Frank Skinner

Photography–Joseph Valentine
*Screenplay (from an original
  subject by Hitchcock)*–
  Peter Viertel, Joan Harrison,
  Dorothy Parker
Editing–Otto Ludwig

PLAYERS: Robert Cummings, Priscilla Lane, Otto Kruger, Alan Baxter, Alma Kruger, Vaughan Glazer, Dorothy Peterson

SAFETY LAST,   U.S.A. (1923)
Hard-up city clerk (Harold Lloyd), anxious to impress his small-town girlfriend, offers to climb a skyscraper for $1,000 in order to attract publicity for his store. The film's climax when Lloyd becomes entangled with a gigantic clock, a painter's lift, some windows and a mouse while dangling precariously some twenty stories above the ground is one of the silent cinema's most cleverly sustained comedy sequences. Mildred Davies, Lloyd's real-life wife, appeared in the film as the girlfriend.

HAL ROACH, ASSOCIATES
Direction—Fred Newmayer &   *Screenplay*—Harold Lloyd &
  Sam Taylor   Hal Roach
Photography—Walter Lundon   *Editing*—Fred L. Guiol
PLAYERS: Harold Lloyd, Mildred Davies, Bill Strothers, Noah Young,
W. B. Clarke

ST. VALENTINE'S DAY MASSACRE, THE   U.S.A. (1967)
Director Roger Corman's first big-budget film, a semidocumentary
reconstruction of the rivalry between Al Capone's South Side gang
and Bugs Moran's North Side outfit in 1928 Chicago, a rivalry that
culminated on St. Valentine's Day, 1929 when seven of Moran's gang
were trapped in a garage and wiped out by Capone's men disguised
as policemen. The performances are only average, but the Chicago of
the late twenties is lovingly re-created and the action sequences, of
which there are many, are as efficiently handled as any in the Curtiz-
Walsh movies of the 1930's. Jason Robards appeared as Capone and
Ralph Meeker as Moran.
                LOS ALTOS/TWENTIETH CENTURY–FOX
Production & direction—   *Art direction*—Jack Martin Smith
  Roger Corman   & Philip Jefferies
Screenplay—Howard Browne   *Music*—Fred Steiner
Photography (*DeLuxecolor*/   *Musical direction*—
  Panavision)—   Lionel Newman
  Milton Krasner   *Editing*—William B. Murphy
PLAYERS: Jason Robards, George Segal, Ralph Meeker, Jean Hale,
Clint Ritchie, Frank Silvera, Michele Guayini, Joseph Campanella

SAMSON & DELILAH   U.S.A. (1950)
DeMille biblical spectacular about the love of Danite strong man
(Victor Mature) for Philistine temptress (Hedy Lamarr). The hackneyed screenplay and crude playing are totally redeemed by DeMille's
robust handling of the spectacle—a fight with a lion, the wrecking of
an army with a jawbone of an ass, and the destruction of a Philistine
temple—and also by George Barnes' Technicolor camera work and
Victor Young's romantic music score. Young, who was Paramount's
leading composer/arranger in the 1940's, scored all six DeMille films
made between 1940 and 1952; namely, *Northwest Mounted Police*
(1940), *Reap the Wild Wind* (1942), *The Story of Dr. Wassell* (1944)
Unconquered (1947), *Samson and Delilah* (1950) and *The Greatest
Show on Earth* (1952).

Production & direction—
Cecil B. DeMille
*Screenplay (based on treatment
by Harold Lamb of Bible
story & Vladimir Jabotinsky's
novel* Judge and Fool)—Jesse L.
Lasky, Jr., Fredric M. Frank

Photography (Technicolor)—
George Barnes
*Music—*Victor Young
*Editing—*Anne Bauchens
*Art direction—*Hans Dreier &
Walter Tyler

PLAYERS: Victor Mature, Hedy Lamarr, George Sanders, Angela Lansbury, Henry Wilcoxon, Olive Deering, Fay Holden, Julia Faye, Russell Tamblyn

SAN FRANCISCO   U.S.A. (1936)
One of the most popular films to come from Metro during the 1930's, this robust piece of hokum is set on the Barbary Coast and traces the intertwined lives of saloon owner (Clark Gable), opera singer (Jeanette MacDonald), and two-fisted priest (Spencer Tracy) during the months preceding the earthquake of 1906. The earthquake itself, which comes at the end of the film, is magnificently staged and edited, demonstrating director Van Dyke's considerable skill as a film technician.

METRO–GOLDWYN–MAYER (A W. S. VAN DYKE PRODUCTION)

*Production—*John Emerson &
Bernard H. Hyman
*Direction—*W. S. Van Dyke
*Screenplay (based on story by
Robert Hopkins)—*Anita Loos

*Photography—*Oliver T. Marsh
*Art direction—*Cedric Gibbons
Musical direction—
Herbert Stothart
*Musical Score—*Edward Ward
*Editing—*Tom Held

PLAYERS: Clark Gable, Jeanette MacDonald, Spencer Tracy, Jack Holt, Jessie Ralph, Ted Healy, Shirley Ross, Margaret Irving, Harold Huber

SANDS OF IWO JIMA   U.S.A. (1949)
Realistic account of how the U.S. Marines took the Japanese-held islands of Tarawa and Iwo Jima during World War Two. Full of the usual hackneyed stock characters, including the tough sergeant with the heart of gold (well played by John Wayne), but historically important for its extensive use of authentic combat material.

REPUBLIC/A HERBERT J. YATES PRODUCTION

Associate producer—
Edmund Grainger
*Direction—*Allan Dwan

*Screenplay—*Harry Brown,
James Edward Grant
*Photography—*Reggie Lanning

379

Art direction—James Sullivan   *Editing*—Richard L. Van Enger
Music—Victor Young
PLAYERS: John Wayne, John Agar, Adele Mara, Forrest Tucker, Wally Cassell, James Brown, Richard Webb, Arthur Franz, Julie Bishop, James Holden, Peter Coe

SATURDAY NIGHT & SUNDAY MORNING   Gt. Britain (1960)
A few months in the life of rebellious, hard-drinking factory worker Arthur Seaton (superbly played by Albert Finney) as he drinks and sleeps his way through the pubs and married beds of working-class Nottingham before being tamed by a simple suburban girl (Shirley Ann Field). The working-class atmosphere and backgrounds of industrial Britain have rarely been more accurately observed than in this film and although the majority of Britain's realistic pictures of the early 1960's now appear dated, this one stands up better than most. The film marked Karel Reisz's debut as a feature director and was photographed by Freddie Francis who, the same year, won an Academy Award for his work on Jack Cardiff's *Sons and Lovers*.

A WOODFALL PRODUCTION

Executive producer—
  Harry Saltzman
Production—Tony Richardson
Direction—Karel Reisz
Photography—Freddie Francis

Screenplay (adapted from his novel)—Alan Sillitoe
Music—Johnny Dankworth
Art direction—Ted Marshall
Editing—Seth Holt

PLAYERS: Albert Finney, Shirley Ann Field, Rachel Roberts, Hylda Baker, Norman Rossington, Bryan Pringle, Robert Cawdron, Edna Morris

SAVAGE EYE, THE   U.S.A. (1959)
Documentary look at the more degrading aspects of the American urban scene traces the experiences of a recently divorced woman as she wanders through the bars and streets of Los Angeles observing, in her pessimistic mood, only the seedy and more unpleasant side of city life—the cheap rooming houses, striptease shows, wrestling matches, poker halls, beauty parlors, etc. Made over a period of four years by a large team of technicians headed by Ben Maddow, Sidney Meyers and Joseph Strick.

CITY FILMS CORPORATION

Direction—Joseph Strick,
  Ben Maddow & Sidney Meyers
Screenplay—Ben Maddow

Photography—Jack Couffer,
  Helen Levitt &
  Haskell Wexler

Music—Leonard Rosenman   *Editing*—Sidney Meyers
PLAYERS: Barbara Baxley, Gary Merrill, Herschel Bernardi, Jean
Hidey, Elizabeth Zemach

SAWDUST AND TINSEL (Gycklarnas Afton)   Sweden (1953)
Powerful Bergman exercise in physical and spiritual degradation is
built around an unsuccessful traveling circus in turn-of-the-century
Sweden and tells of the humiliation suffered by the aging proprietor
at the hands of his young mistress and her actor lover. The most
brutal and depressing of Bergman's early films recalls in its fatalism
the great German silent films of the 1920's. Harriet Andersson con-
tributes an outstanding performance as the callous mistress.
                    SANDREWS (RUNE WALDEKRANZ)
Direction & screenplay—   *Art direction*—Bibi Lindström
   Ingmar Bergman   *Music*—Karl-Birger Blomdahl
Photography—Sven Nykvist &   *Editing*—Carl-Olov Skeppstedt
   Hilding Bladh
PLAYERS: Harriet Andersson, Ake Grönberg, Hasse Ekman, Anders Ek,
Gudrun Brost, Annika Tretow, Gunnar Björnstrand, Erik Strandmark

SCARFACE   U.S.A. (1932)
Violent account of the criminal career of gangster Al Capone. One of
the best of America's crime thrillers of the thirties, brilliantly directed
and expertly performed by Paul Muni as Capone, Ann Dvorak as his
sluttish sister, and Karen Morley as his mistress. The movie is also
historically interesting for the early appearance of Boris Karloff as a
hoodlum and George Raft as Capone's coin-flipping bodyguard.
                    HUGHES PRODUCTION/UNITED ARTISTS
Production—Howard Hughes,   *Adaptation & dialogue*—
   Howard Hawks   Seton I. Miller,
Direction—Howard Hawks   John Lee Mahin,
Screenplay (*from novel by*   W. R. Burnett
   Armitage Trail*)*—Ben Hecht   *Music*—Adolph Tandler,
Photography—Lee Garmes,   Gus Arnheim
   L. William O'Connell   *Editing*—Edward Curtiss
PLAYERS: Paul Muni, Ann Dvorak, Karen Morley, Osgood Perkins,
Boris Karloff, C. Henry Gordon, George Raft, Purnell Pratt, Vince
Barnett, Ines Palange

SCARLET EMPRESS, THE   U.S.A. (1934)
Director Josef von Sternberg's version of the rise of Catherine the

381

Great (Marlene Dietrich) to the throne of Russia. Some inferior dialogue, but in every other way—direction, sets, costumes, editing, etc.—one of the finest and most convincing costume pictures ever made in Hollywood. Bert Glennon, in the last of his four pictures with Sternberg, contributed some of the most stunning photography of his career—not least in the bravura climax when Dietrich leads her army on horseback up the palace stairway to the throne room. Sam Jaffe played the mad Grand Duke Peter and the film was the last but one of the six Paramount films made by Sternberg and Dietrich during the thirties.

PARAMOUNT

Direction—Josef von Sternberg
Screenplay (based on diary of
  Catherine the Great)—
  Manuel Komroff
Photography—Bert Glennon
Set design and décor—
  Hans Dreier, Peter Ballbusch,
  Richard Kollorsz

Music (based on themes by
  Tschaikowsky and
  Mendelssohn) arranged by—
  John M. Leipold &
  W. Frank Harling
Titles and effects—
  Gordon Jennings
Costumes—Travis Banton

PLAYERS: Marlene Dietrich, John Lodge, Sam Jaffe, Louise Dresser, Maria Sieber, C. Aubrey Smith, Ruthelma Stevens, Olive Tell

SCARLET STREET   U.S.A. (1945)
Fatalistic thriller about a respectable little store cashier (Edward G. Robinson) who becomes infatuated with and eventually murders a whore (Joan Bennett) and then allows her pimp boyfriend (Dan Duryea) to be executed for the crime. One of Lang's bleakest works, impressively played and enhanced considerably by Milton Krasner's superior lensing of rain-filled Manhattan streets at night. Based on the play *La Chienne*, filmed in 1931 in France by Jean Renoir.

DIANA PRODUCTIONS–UNIVERSAL

Production & direction—
  Fritz Lang
Screenplay (from novel and play
  La Chienne *by Georges de la*
  Fouchardiere, with Mouezy-
  Eon)—Dudley Nichols

Photography—Milton Krasner
Special photographic effects—
  John P. Fulton
Art direction—Alexander Golitzen
Music—Hans J. Salter
Editing—Arthur Hilton

PLAYERS: Edward G. Robinson, Joan Bennett, Dan Duryea, Margaret Lindsay, Rosalind Ivan, Samuel S. Hinds, Jess Barker, Arthur Loft

SCOTT OF THE ANTARCTIC   Gt. Britain (1948)
The tragic story of Captain Scott's heroic but ill-fated 1909 expedition

to the South Pole. A long, ambitious and ultimately rather tedious film redeemed by some fine Technicolor Antarctic landscapes and a majestic music score by Vaughan Williams. John Mills in the title role is supported by Harold Warrender (Dr. Wilson), Reginald Beckwith (Bowers), James Robertson Justice ('Taff' Evans) and Derek Bond as the gallant Oates who commits suicide by walking out into a blizzard. Kenneth More and John Gregson, two of Britain's top box-office stars of the 1950's, appear in minor roles.

EALING STUDIOS

Production—Michael Balcon
Direction—Charles Frend
Screenplay—Walter Meade & Ivor Montagu
Photography (Technicolor)— Jack Cardiff, Osmond Borrodaile & Geoffrey Unsworth

Additional dialogue— Mary Hayley Bell
Art direction—Arne Akermark
Special effects art direction— Jim Morahan
Music—Vaughan Williams
Editing—Peter Tanner

PLAYERS: John Mills, Derek Bond, Harold Warrender, James Robertson Justice, Reginald Beckwith, Diana Churchill, Anne Firth, Kenneth More, Norman Williams, John Gregson

SEA HAWK, THE   U.S.A. (1940)
Exhilarating period adventure with Errol Flynn as romantic English sea captain fighting for Elizabeth against the crafty Spaniards and winning not the hand of Olivia de Havilland as was usual in Warner films of this time but of lesser-known Brenda Marshall. Climaxed by a furious duel between Flynn and spy-villain Henry Daniell and directed with great style by Michael Curtiz who between 1935 and 1940 was responsible for some half dozen Flynn period adventures—*Captain Blood, The Charge of the Light Brigade, The Prince and the Pauper, The Adventures of Robin Hood, The Private Lives of Elizabeth and Essex,* and *The Sea Hawk.* Erich Wolfgang Korngold wrote the music for all but one of these films (*The Charge of the Light Brigade,* scored by Max Steiner, being the exception) and ace cameraman Sol Polito photographed all but *Captain Blood.*

WARNER BROS./FIRST NATIONAL

Executive producer— Hal B. Wallis
Associate producer— Henry Blanke
Direction—Michael Curtiz
Photography—Sol Polito

Original screenplay—Howard Koch & Seton I. Miller
Art direction—Anton Grot
Music— Erich Wolfgang Korngold
Editing—George Amy

PLAYERS: Errol Flynn, Brenda Marshall, Claude Rains, Donald Crisp, Flora Robson, Alan Hale, Henry Daniell, Una O'Connor

SEA WOLF, THE   U.S.A. (1941)
The fine performance of Edward G. Robinson as the sadistic sea captain threatened with approaching blindness stands out in this technically expert, finely written version of Jack London's turn-of-the-century sea drama. Barry Fitzgerald as a cockney cook with one leg and John Garfield as an ex-convict are others on board the scavenger ship *Ghost* and Gene Lockhart is a splendid drunken ship's doctor. Among Michael Curtiz's most underrated films.

WARNER BROS.

Executive producer—Hal B. Wallis   *Photography*—Sol Polito
Associate producer—   *Art direction*—Anton Grot
  Henry Blanke   *Music*—
Direction—Michael Curtiz   Erich Wolfgang Korngold
Screenplay—Robert Rossen   *Editing*—George Amy
PLAYERS: Edward G. Robinson, Ida Lupino, John Garfield, Alexander Knox, Gene Lockhart, Barry Fitzgerald, Stanley Ridges, Howard Da Silva

SEARCH, THE   U.S.A. (1948)
Part-documentary film concerns itself with the plight of thousands of refugee children in postwar Europe, and in particular with one 9-year-old Czech boy and his mother's desperate search for him among the scattered ruins of Germany. Not up to the standard of De Sica's wholly realistic films of the period but compassionate in its observation of the problem. Well played by Ivan Jandl as the boy, Montgomery Clift (debut) as the American soldier who befriends him, and Aline Mac-Mahon (superb) as the tireless officer of UNRRA, the organization formed to rehabilitate the displaced children of Europe. The film was shot in Switzerland and the American Zone of Germany and established Fred Zinnemann as a director of the front rank.

PRAESENS FILM/METRO–GOLDWYN–MAYER

Production—Lazar Wechsler   *Photography*—Emil Berna
Direction—Fred Zinnemann   *Music*—Robert Blum
Screenplay—Richard Schweizer   *Editing*—Herman Haller
  & David Wechsler
PLAYERS: Montgomery Clift, Aline MacMahon, Ivan Jandl, Jarmila Novotna, Wendell Corey, Mary Patton

SEARCHERS, THE   U.S.A. (1956)
Superbly photographed Western about the five-year search by an em-
bittered ex-Confederate soldier (John Wayne) and a half-breed Indian
boy (Jeffrey Hunter) for a young white girl kidnapped by a Comanche
war party. Photographed in Monument Valley by Winton Hoch (a
Ford cameraman between 1948 and 1956) and vigorously performed
by the Ford regulars, particularly supporting players Olive Carey and
John Qualen as a pair of veteran Swedish settlers and Ward Bond as a
Texas Ranger who is also a preacher. A rambling but characteristic
Ford work that, after *Wagonmaster,* stands as his best Western of the
1950's.

C. V. WHITNEY/WARNER BROS.

Production—Merian C. Cooper   *Photography (Technicolor/*
  & C. V. Whitney   *VistaVision)*—Winton C. Hoch
Direction—John Ford   *Art direction*—Frank Hotaling &
Screenplay (from novel by Alan   James Basevi
  Le May)—Frank S. Nugent   *Music*—Max Steiner
                                       Editing—Jack Murray

PLAYERS: John Wayne, Jeffrey Hunter, Vera Miles, Ward Bond, Natalie
Wood, John Qualen, Olive Carey, Henry Brandon

SECONDS   U.S.A. (1966)
Middle-aged banker (played first by John Randolph and later by Rock
Hudson) becomes tragically involved with a secret organization in
New York which offers him a chance of rejuvenation by arranging for
his "death" and transforming him by plastic surgery and physical and
mental conditioning into a younger man. Nightmarish Frankenheimer
thriller, uneven, slow at times, but the opening in a New York subway
and the final horrors on the operating table are beautifully handled.
There are two admirable character cameos from Will Geer and Jeff
Corey as the sinister brains behind the organization.

PARAMOUNT—JOEL—GIBRALTAR

Production—Edward Lewis   *Photography*—
Direction—John Frankenheimer   James Wong Howe
Screenplay (based on novel by   *Art direction*—Ted Haworth
  David Ely)—   *Music*—Jerry Goldsmith
  Lewis John Carlino   *Editing*—Ferris Webster &
                                          David Webster

PLAYERS: Rock Hudson, John Randolph, Salome Jens, Will Geer, Jeff
Corey, Richard Anderson, Murray Hamilton, Karl Swenson

SECRET AGENT, THE   Gt. Britain (1936)

Ironic little Hitchcock thriller, adapted from two of Somerset Maugham's Ashenden stories ("The Traitor" and "The Hairless Mexican"), tells about a secret agent (John Gielgud) who, during the First World War, reluctantly agrees to dispose of a spy operating in Switzerland but succeeds only in killing an innocent tourist. Minor league Hitchcock, although there are sequences of considerable tension, i.e. the opening scene in London during a bomb raid, and the buildup to the murder itself, plus a rewarding performance from Peter Lorre as a bizarre Mexican assassin.

GAUMONT BRITISH

Production—Michael Balcon
Direction—Alfred Hitchcock
Screenplay (from play by Campbell Dixon adapted from Somerset Maugham's Ashenden)—Charles Bennett

Dialogue—Ian Hay, Jesse Lasky Jr.
Photography—Bernard Knowles
Art direction—Otto Werndorff & Albert Jullion
Music—Louis Levy
Editing—Charles Frend

PLAYERS: Madeleine Carroll, John Gielgud, Peter Lorre, Robert Young, Percy Marmont, Florence Kahn, Lilli Palmer, Charles Carson, Michael Redgrave

SECRET PEOPLE   Gt. Britain (1952)

Intelligent attempt by Thorold Dickinson to investigate the moral right to use violence to further the cause of freedom and justice. The confused story revolves around a naturalized young Englishwoman (Valentina Cortesa) who is persuaded by her former lover (Serge Reggiani) to join in an assassination attempt against the dictator of their old country when he visits London. Although not wholly successful the film stands out from most British movies of this period which were invariably war dramas glorifying the exploits of naval commanders and R.A.F. pilots during World War II. Well played by Cortesa and Reggiani; Audrey Hepburn appeared in a supporting role as Cortesa's younger sister.

EALING STUDIOS

Production—Sidney Cole
Direction—Thorold Dickinson
Screenplay—Thorold Dickinson, Wolfgang Wilhelm

Photography—Gordon Dines
Art direction—William Kellner
Music—Roberto Gerhard
Editing—Peter Tanner

PLAYERS: Valentina Cortesa, Serge Reggiani, Charles Goldner, Audrey Hepburn, Angela Fouldes, Megs Jenkins, Irene Worth, Reginald Tate

SECRETS OF A SOUL (Geheimnisse einer Seele) Germany (1926) Ambitious attempt by G. W. Pabst to film a Freudian case history includes a remarkably photographed dream sequence and a good performance from Werner Krauss as the elderly doctor who is cured of his nightmares and fears of impotency by psychoanalysis. Dr. Hanns Sachs and Dr. Karl Abraham, two of Freud's collaborators, worked as Pabst's assistants on the film.

NEUMANN–FILM PRODUKTION

Direction–G. W. Pabst
Screenplay–Colin Ross &
  Hans Neumann

Photography–Guido Seeber,
  Curt Oertel, Robert Lach
Art direction–Erno Metzner

PLAYERS: Werner Krauss, Ruth Weyher, Ilka Grüning, Hertha von Walther, Pawel Pawlow, Jack Trevor

SENSO   Italy (1954)
Set during the war between Italy and Austria in the 1860's and centering on the doomed love affair between a dissolute young Austrian officer (Farley Granger) and a Venetian countess (Alida Valli) whose desperate infatuation for the younger man leads her to betray her fellow Italian patriots. Memorable primarily for the exquisite color photography of G. R. Aldo (one of Italy's greatest cameramen) who died during the shooting, with Robert Krasker taking over. The outdoor scenes of Venice and the delicate interiors rank with the finest color scenes ever filmed.

LUX FILMS

Direction–Luchino Visconti
Screenplay (from short story by
  Camille Boito)–Luchino
  Visconti, Suso Cecchi d'Amico
Art direction–Ottavio Scotti

Photography (Technicolor)–
  G. R. Aldo, Robert Krasker
Music–from Anton Bruckner's
  Seventh Symphony
Editing–Mario Serandrei

PLAYERS: Alida Valli, Farley Granger, Massimo Girotti, Heinz Moog, Rina Morelli, Sergio Fantoni

SERVANT, THE   Gt. Britain (1963)
Brilliantly written (Pinter) and directed (Losey) film about a rich, pleasure-loving young London bachelor (James Fox) who is corrupted and morally destroyed by the vicious lower-class underling (astonishingly well-played by Dirk Bogarde) he employs as his manservant. A disturbing and most remarkable film of considerable depth and insight, and ranking second only to Accident as Losey's most impressive work. Wendy Craig is the young man's fiancée and Sarah Miles is the

The Servant

servant's mistress. Designed by Richard MacDonald, who worked on the majority of Losey's films including *The Criminal, Eve* and *Modesty Blaise*.

SPRINGBOK/ELSTREE

Production—Josephy Losey & Norman Priggen
Direction—Joseph Losey
Photography—Douglas Slocombe
Art direction—Ted Clements

Screenplay (based on novel by Robin Maugham)— Harold Pinter
Music—John Dankworth
Editing—Reginald Mills

PLAYERS: Dirk Bogarde, James Fox, Wendy Craig, Sarah Miles, Catherine Lacey, Richard Vernon, Ann Firbank, Doris Knox, Patrick Magee

SET-UP, THE U.S.A. (1949)

The best of all pictures about the boxing racket follows 80 minutes (the film's exact running time) in the life of an aging middleweight (Robert Ryan) before, during and after his last fight. No other film has managed to portray the shabbiness and degrading aspects of professional boxing, nor observed so accurately the sadism and blood lust of the spectators.

RKO RADIO

Production—Richard Goldstone
Direction—Robert Wise
Screenplay (from poem by Joseph Moncure March)— Art Cohn

Photography—Milton Krasner
Art direction—Albert S. D'Agostino & Jack Okey
Music direction— C. Bakaleinikoff
Editing—Roland Cross

PLAYERS: Robert Ryan, Audrey Totter, George Tobias, Alan Baxter, Wallace Ford, Percy Helton, Hal Bieberling, Darryl Hickman

SEVEN BRIDES FOR SEVEN BROTHERS U.S.A. (1954)

Robust Hollywood musical (the last great original of the 1950's) about seven Oregon backwoods boys who, influenced by the story of the rape of the Sabine women, kidnap seven girls from the local township and make them their brides. A vigorous, lively film carried along by its memorable music score and the sheer exuberance of its dancing. Among the best numbers are a brilliantly acrobatic square dance, the slow "Lonesome Polecat" lament, and "Sobbin' Women."

METRO–GOLDWYN–MAYER

389

Production–Jack Cummings	*Photography* (*Anscocolor/*
Direction–Stanley Donen	*CinemaScope*)–
Screenplay (*based on story*	George J. Folsey
"Sobbin' Women" by Stephen	*Music*–Gene de Paul
Vincent Benét)–Albert Hackett,	*Lyrics*–Johnny Mercer
Frances Goodrich & Dorothy	*Musical direction*–
Kingsley	Adolph Deutsch
Art direction–Cedric Gibbons &	*Choreography*–Michael Kidd
Urie McCleary	*Editing*–Ralph E. Winters

PLAYERS: Howard Keel, Jane Powell, Jeff Richards, Russ Tamblyn, Tommy Rall, Marc Platt, Matt Mattcox

SEVEN CHANCES U.S.A. (1925)

Buster Keaton, heir to a fortune, finds that he has to find a bride within 24 hours in order to claim his inheritance. A fast-moving six-reel comedy, containing some of Keaton's funniest gags and culminating in a hilarious chase in which Buster is pursued through town and country by hordes of would-be brides, and a wonderfully staged landslide.

BUSTER KEATON PRODUCTIONS INC./METRO–GOLDWYN PICTURES

Production–Joseph M. Schenck	*Screenplay* (*based on comedy by*
Direction–Buster Keaton	*Roi Cooper Megrue, produced*
Photography–Elgin Lessley,	*by David Belasco*)–
Byron Houck	Clyde Bruckman, Jean Havez,
Technical direction–	Joseph Mitchell
Fred Gabourie	

PLAYERS: Buster Keaton, Ray Barnes, Snitz Edwards, Ruth Dwyer, Frankie Raymond, Jules Cowles, Erwin Connelly, Jean Havez

SEVEN DAYS IN MAY U.S.A. (1964)

Political thriller about a demagogic four-star general (Burt Lancaster) who, together with other military leaders, attempts to overthrow the liberal President of the United States (Fredric March) who is about to sign a Russian-American disarmament pact. Not as exciting or imaginative as Frankenheimer's earlier *The Manchurian Candidate* but compelling nonetheless and way ahead of the usual thriller. Others in a high-grade cast include Kirk Douglas as the colonel who uncovers the coup, Ava Gardner as a Washington socialite, and Edmond O'Brien (superb) as a boozy old Southern senator. Distinguished Hollywood producer John Houseman (*They Live by Night, Julius Caesar, The Bad and the Beautiful*) appears in one scene as a disloyal admiral.

SEVEN ARTS–JOEL–JOHN FRANKENHEIMER PRODUCTIONS/PARAMOUNT

Production–Edward Lewis
Direction–John Frankenheimer
Screenplay (from novel by
Fletcher Knebel & Charles
W. Bailey II)–Rod Serling

Photography–
Ellsworth Fredericks
Art direction–Cary Odell
Editing–Ferris Webster

PLAYERS: Burt Lancaster, Kirk Douglas, Fredric March, Ava Gardner, Edmond O'Brien, Martin Balsam, George Macready, Whit Bissell, Hugh Marlowe

SEVEN DAYS TO NOON   Gt. Britain (1950)

Thriller about a top British scientist who steals an atom bomb and threatens to destroy London in seven days (at noon on Sunday) unless the Prime Minister agrees to stop making atomic weapons. Some impressive scenes of a deserted, evacuated London and a number of excellent performances from a largely unknown cast: Barry Jones as the scientist, Olive Sloane as the boozy old show girl he forces to help him, and André Morrell as a Scotland Yard man. Tense, slick, made with some style by John Boulting.

LONDON FILMS/BRITISH LION

Production & editing–
Roy Boulting
Direction–John Boulting
Photography–Gilbert Taylor

Screenplay (from original story
by Paul Dehn & James
Bernard)–Roy Boulting
Art direction–John Elphick
Music–John Addison

PLAYERS: Barry Jones, Olive Sloane, André Morrell, Sheila Manahan, Hugh Cross, Joan Hickson, Ronald Adam, Marie Ney, Russell Waters, Frederick Allen, Geoffrey Keen

SEVEN SAMURAI   Japan (1954)

Three-hour Kurosawa epic, set in medieval Japan, revolving around seven samurai warriors who are employed by the inhabitants of a small village to protect them from a band of plundering brigands. An expensive (in 1954 it was the costliest picture ever made in Japan), painstaking (over a year in production), altogether extraordinary film which, in its ferocious climactic battle sequences in a muddy compound in pouring rain, reaches great heights of cinematic achievement. Remade by John Sturges as the Western *The Magnificent Seven* (1960).

TOHO (SHOJIRO MOTOKI)

Direction–Akira Kurosawa   *Photography*–Asakazu Nakai

Screenplay—Shinobu Hashimoto,   *Art direction*—So Matsuyama
   Hideo Oguni, Akira Kurosawa   *Music*—Fumio Hayasaka
PLAYERS: Takashi Shimura, Toshiro Mifune, Yoshio Inaba, Seiji Miya-
guchi, Minoru Chiaki, Daisuke Kato, Ko Kimura

SEVEN YEAR ITCH, THE   U.S.A. (1955)
Shy, middle-aged New York husband (Tom Ewell), a summer bachelor
during his wife's vacation, becomes romantically involved with the sexy
model (Marilyn Monroe) living in the upstairs apartment. An uneven
Billy Wilder film spoiled and slowed up by being shot in the Cinema-
Scope process, but with quite a few bright moments and a delicious
performance from Monroe. Directed and co-scripted (with George
Axelrod) by Wilder from Axelrod's own Broadway stage hit.

TWENTIETH CENTURY–FOX

Production—Charles K. Feldman,   *Photography* (*DeLuxecolor/*
   Billy Wilder   *CinemaScope*)—
Direction—Billy Wilder   Milton Krasner
Screenplay—Billy Wilder,   *Art direction*—Lyle Wheeler,
   George Axelrod   George W. Davis
Music—Alfred Newman   *Editing*—Hugh S. Fowler
PLAYERS: Marilyn Monroe, Tom Ewell, Evelyn Keyes, Sonny Tufts,
Robert Strauss, Oscar Homolka, Marguerite Chapman, Victor Moore

SEVENTH SEAL, THE   Sweden (1957)
Disillusioned knight (Max von Sydow) is claimed by Death as he returns from the Crusades to his plague-stricken homeland but pleads for
more time to solve the mysteries of suffering and mortality. Death
agrees to play a game of chess, allowing the knight extra life only as
long as the game is in progress. By the end of the film the knight has
encountered superstition, fear and cruelty and is no nearer the truth
than he was at the beginning of his quest. Bergman himself offers no
answers, but the final dance of death and the mood of the film as a
whole is one of pessimism and despair. A stark, enormously powerful
film—a masterpiece.

SVENSK FILMINDUSTRI

Direction & screenplay—   *Art direction*—P. A. Lundgren
   Ingmar Bergman   *Music*—Erik Nordgren
Photography—Gunnar Fischer   *Editing*—Lennart Wallén
PLAYERS: Max von Sydow, Gunnar Björnstrand, Nils Poppe, Bibi
Andersson, Bengt Ekerot, Ake Fridell, Inga Gill, Erik Strandmark,
Gunnel Lindblom, Inga Landgré

SEVENTH VICTIM, THE   U.S.A. (1943)
Oppressive little horror movie in which Kim Hunter becomes involved
with a cult of devil worshippers as she searches for her missing sister
in New York City. Short on physical horror but impressive in the way it
subtly suggests the presence of hidden evil. Former editor Mark Robson's first directorial assignment and Val Lewton's most underrated
movie.

RKO RADIO

Production—Val Lewton
Direction—Mark Robson
Screenplay—Charles O'Neal &
    DeWitt Bodeen
Music—Roy Webb

Photography—
    Nicholas Musuraca
Art direction—Albert S.
    D'Agostino & Walter E. Keller
Editing—John Lockert

PLAYERS: Tom Conway, Jean Brooks, Isobel Jewell, Kim Hunter,
Evelyn Brent, Erford Gage

SHADOW OF A DOUBT   U.S.A. (1943)
Understated thriller about a psychotic widow murderer loose in a quiet
American town. Rich in small-town detail (the picture was shot mainly
on location in Santa Rosa, California) and beautifully written by
Thornton Wilder whose natural, overlapping dialogue helped to give
the film its realistic atmosphere. MacDonald Carey plays the detective,
Joseph Cotten the killer, and Teresa Wright his terrified niece. One of
Hitchcock's best pictures of his early American period.

UNIVERSAL

Production—Jack H. Skirball
Direction—Alfred Hitchcock
Screenplay (from story by
    Gordon McDonnell)—
    Thornton Wilder, Alma
    Reville, Sally Benson

Photography—Joseph Valentine
Art direction—John B. Goodman,
    Robert Boyle
Music—Dimitri Tiomkin
Editing—Milton Carruth

PLAYERS: Joseph Cotten, Teresa Wright, MacDonald Carey, Patricia
Collinge, Henry Travers, Hume Cronyn, Wallace Ford, Janet Shaw

SHAKESPEARE WALLAH   India (1965)
Indian film, spoken in English, about the experiences of a group of
actors as they travel across India scratching a living by bringing Shakespeare to the unenthusiastic provinces. Too slow-paced but the mood
and atmosphere of life in India today is beautifully caught and there
is an occasional fascinating glimpse of life as it used to be under British
rule. The three principal actors—Geoffrey Kendal, Laura Liddell and

Felicity Kendal—who play the father, mother and daughter actually run a theatrical touring company in India. Directed by American James Ivory.

MERCHANT/IVORY

Production—Ismail Merchant   *Photography*—Subrata Mitra
Direction—James Ivory   *Music*—Satyajit Ray
Screenplay—R. Prawer Jhabvala   *Editing*—Amit Bose
  & James Ivory
PLAYERS: Felicity Kendal, Shashi Kapoor, Geoffrey Kendal, Laura Liddell, Madhur Jaffrey, Utpal Dutt, Jim Tytler

SHALL WE DANCE?   U.S.A. (1937)
The seventh Astaire and Rogers film is directed once more by Mark (*Gay Divorcee, Top Hat*) Sandrich, but scored this time by George and Ira Gershwin. More uneven and less assured than the earlier films, but the staging of the musical numbers, among them "They Can't Take That Away From Me," "Let's Call the Whole Thing Off" and "They All Laughed," is as delightful as ever.

RKO RADIO

Production—Pandro S. Berman   *Photography*—David Abel
Direction—Mark Sandrich   *Art direction*—Van Nest Polglase
Screenplay (*from story by Lee*   *Music*—George Gershwin
  Loeb & Harold Buchman)—   *Lyrics*—Ira Gershwin
  Allan Scott, Ernest Pagano,   *Dance direction*—Hermes Pan
  P. J. Wolfson   *Editing*—William Hamilton
PLAYERS: Fred Astaire, Ginger Rogers, Edward Everett Horton, Eric Blore, Jerome Cowan, Ketti Gallian, William Brisbane

SHAME, THE (Skammen)   Sweden (1968)
Degradation, persecution and despair figure prominently in this study of a middle-aged married couple (a pair of retired musicians) whose lives are shattered when the remote island on which they live is engulfed by the civil war that is ravaging the mainland. The film's theme is the effect of war on human beings; its starkness, power, and above all its profound pessimism make it one of Ingmar Bergman's most uncomfortable works. Max von Sydow plays the husband and Liv Ullman his wife.

SVENSK FILMINDUSTRI

Production—Lars-Owe Carlberg   *Screenplay*—Ingmar Bergman
Direction—Ingmar Bergman   *Photography*—Sven Nykvist

394

Art direction—P. A. Lundgren   *Editing*—Ulla Ryghe
PLAYERS: Liv Ullmann, Max von Sydow, Gunnar Björnstrand, Sigge
Fürst, Birgitta Valberg, Hans Alfredson, Ingvar Kjellson, Raymond
Lundberg

SHANE   U.S.A. (1953)
Classic Western about a mysterious gunman (Alan Ladd) who rides
into a Wyoming valley, helps the homesteaders in their fight against the
cattlemen, then rides out again as mysteriously as he came. A slow-
moving, near perfect film built firmly in the romantic tradition, but
brilliantly evoking the feeling of frontier life in the American West
during the 1880's. Contains many of George Stevens' most brilliant set
pieces such as the murder of homesteader Elisha Cook in the muddy
street outside the saloon, the fistfight in the barroom, the funeral on the
hill, and the climactic gun battle. Van Heflin, Jean Arthur and Edgar
Buchanan appear as settlers, Emile Meyer and John Dierkes as cattlemen, and Jack Palance as a professional gunfighter. The considerable
beauty of the settings is admirably captured in Loyal Griggs' Academy
Award-winning photography.
                              PARAMOUNT
Production & direction—   *Photography (Technicolor)*—
  George Stevens   Loyal Griggs
Screenplay (from novel by Jack   *Art direction*—Hal Pereira,
  Schaefer)—A. B. Guthrie, Jr.   Walter Tyler
Additional dialogue—Jack Sher   *Editing*—William Hornbeck,
Music—Victor Young   Tom McAdoo
PLAYERS: Alan Ladd, Jean Arthur, Van Heflin, Jack Palance, Brandon
De Wilde, Ben Johnson, Emile Meyer, Elisha Cook, Jr.

SHANGHAI EXPRESS   U.S.A. (1932)
Notorious prostitute Shanghai Lily (Marlene Dietrich) saves a former
lover from revolutionaries in exotic China. A colorful, brilliantly directed
Oriental extravaganza set mainly aboard a train traveling from Peking
to Shanghai and containing one of Dietrich's richest performances.
Sternberg's third American film with his star and their greatest com-
mercial success.
                              PARAMOUNT
Direction—Josef von Sternberg   *Photography*—Lee Garmes
Screenplay (based on story by   *Set designer*—Hans Dreier
  Harry Hervey)—Jules Furthman   *Gowns*—Travis Banton

SHCHORS U.S.S.R. (1939)

Heroic account of the civil war activities of Nikolai Shchors, the young Ukrainian partisan leader who, in 1919, fought the Germans, Poles and antirevolutionaries in the Ukraine and became a hero of his country. A long, shapeless epic given stature by its impressive battle scenes, particularly the wonderfully staged crossing of the frozen river Desna and by Dovzhenko's portrayal of the natural beauty of the Ukrainian countryside. Made on the advice of Stalin who asked for a "Ukrainian *Chapayev*" and highly regarded in Russia where it is often discussed in the same terms as Dovzhenko's silent masterpiece *Earth*.

KIEV STUDIO

Direction & screenplay—
  Alexander Dovzhenko
Co-director—Yulia Solntseva
Assistant—Lazar Bodik

Photography—Yuri Yekelchik
Art direction—Mauritz Umansky
Music—Dmitri Kabalevsky

PLAYERS: Yevgeni Samoilov, Ivan Skuratov, Hans Klering

SHE DONE HIM WRONG U.S.A. (1933)

Rich comedy, set on the Bowery during the 1890's, with Mae West in perhaps her most famous screen role as blond, diamond-loving Lady Lou and Cary Grant as a detective disguised as a member of the Salvation Army. This is the film containing Miss West's famous invitation "Come up 'n' see me sometime" and in which she sings "Easy Rider," "A Guy What Takes His Time" and "Frankie and Johnny." Based on her own play *Diamond Lil.*

PARAMOUNT

Direction—Lowell Sherman
Screenplay—Harvey Thew &
  John Bright

Photography—Charles Lang
Art direction—Robert Usher
Editing—Alexander Hall

PLAYERS: Mae West, Cary Grant, Gilbert Roland, Noah Beery, Rafaela Ottiano, Owen Moore

SHE WORE A YELLOW RIBBON U.S.A. (1949)

Retiring captain Nathan Brittles and the U.S. Cavalry put down a large-scale Indian uprising just after the Civil War. A romantic, richly photographed piece with scenes of great beauty—towering red mountains, glowing sunsets, and long columns of men riding across prairies—marred occasionally by the director's excess of sentiment. One of Ford's major works, lovingly made and with an array of good performances from his regulars: John Wayne (Brittles), Harry Carey, Jr., George O'Brien, Arthur Shields, etc.

ARGOSY PICTURES/RKO

Production—John Ford, Merian C. Cooper
Direction—John Ford
Screenplay (from story "War Party" by James Warner Bellah)—Frank S. Nugent, Laurence Stallings

Photography (Technicolor)—Winton C. Hoch
Second unit—Charles P. Boyle
Art direction—James Basevi
Music—Richard Hageman
Editing—Jack Murray

PLAYERS: John Wayne, Joanne Dru, John Agar, Ben Johnson, Harry Cary Jr., Victor McLaglen, Mildred Natwick, George O'Brien, Arthur Shields, Francis Ford, Harry Woods

SHERLOCK JUNIOR   U.S.A. (1924)

Buster Keaton as timid little film projectionist who imagines himself taking part in the detective picture he is showing at the local movie house. An outstanding silent comedy, fast, brilliantly timed, with almost a gag a minute. Highlights: Keaton walking down the theater aisle and into the picture on the screen, and then becoming involved in a wild chase, firstly on a motorcycle without a driver and secondly in a car which finishes in a river.

BUSTER KEATON/JOSEPH M. SCHENCK PRODUCTIONS/
METRO PICTURES

Production—Joseph M. Schenck
Direction—Buster Keaton
Screenplay—Clyde Bruckman, Jean Havez, Joseph Mitchell

Photography—Elgin Lessley, Byron Houck
Technical direction—Fred Gabourie
Costumes—Clare West

PLAYERS: Buster Keaton, Kathryn McGuire, Joe Keaton, Ward Crane, Jane Connelly, Erwin Connelly, Ford West, George Davis

SHOESHINE   Italy (1948)

This pessimistic Italian neo-realist film tells of two young Roman street urchins, working as shoeshine boys to ward off starvation, who become involved in a black-market racket and finish up in the grim Regina Coeli prison. A shattering film which spotlighted the plight of hundreds of boys in war-shattered Europe and which bitterly attacked the inadequacies of city authorities hampered by a shortage of food, schools and hospitals. Made with deep compassion by Vittorio de Sica and shot in the streets of Rome with nonprofessional actors. A landmark of the Italian cinema.

ALFA CINEMATOGRAFICA (W. TAMBURELLA)

Production—
Paolo W. Tamburella
Direction—Vittorio de Sica
Photography—Anchise Brizzi
Music—Alessandro Cicognini

Original screenplay—
Sergio Amidei, Adolfe Franci,
C. G. Viola, Cesare Zavattini
Sets—Ivo Battelli

PLAYERS: Rinaldo Smordoni, Franco Interlenghi, Aniello Mele, Bruno Ortensi, Pacifico Astrologo, Francesco de Nicola, Antonio Carlino, Enrico de Silva

SHOULDER ARMS   U.S.A. (1918)

Brilliant satire on army life with Chaplin as an incompetent private in the trenches during World War I. A characteristic combination of slap-stick, pathos and irony, filmed in 1918 when the war was still in progress and, until *The Gold Rush* (1925), the movie considered by most critics to be Chaplin's masterwork. Highlight: Charlie disguised as a tree trying to delude the enemy.

FIRST NATIONAL

Direction—Charles Chaplin
Screenplay—Charles Chaplin

Photography—R. H. Totheroh

PLAYERS: Charles Chaplin, Albert Austin, Henry Bergman, Sydney Chaplin, Park Jones, Edna Purviance, Loyal Underwood, Jack Wilson, Tom Wilson

SIGN OF THE CROSS, THE   U.S.A. (1932)

Cecil B. DeMille mixes sex, sadism and religion in a story about the coming of Christianity to ancient Rome. Charles Laughton, magnifi-cently decadent as an effeminate Nero and Claudette Colbert as his empress Poppaea appear for the pagans, and Elissa Landi as a Christian girl and Fredric March as a converted Roman commander for the Christians. Spectacular (the burning of Rome, the climactic feeding of the Christians to the lions) and very similar in theme to Henryk Sien-kiewicz's *Quo Vadis,* but far more erotic, especially in the sequence when Miss Colbert bathes in a pool filled with asses' milk.

Production & direction—   *Photography*—Karl Struss
   Cecil B. DeMille   *Art direction*—Mitchell Leisen
Screenplay (adapted from play   *Music*—Rudolph Kopp
   by Wilson Barrett)—Waldemar   *Editing*—Anne Bauchens
   Young & Sidney Buchman
PLAYERS: Charles Laughton, Claudette Colbert, Fredric March, Elissa Landi, Ian Keith, Vivian Tobin, Harry Beresford, Ferdinand Gottschalk

SILENCE, THE (Tystnaden)   Sweden (1963)
Loneliness, love and sexual obsession studied in depth by Ingmar Bergman as he looks at the incestuous love-hate relationship of two sisters stranded for a night in a deserted foreign hotel. Ingrid Thulin plays the older, consumptive sister and Gunnel Lindblom the younger woman trying desperately to free herself from the lesbian relationship. Impeccable photography by Sven Nykvist who worked on Bergman's previous films in his "chamber" trilogy (*Winter Light* and *Through a Glass Darkly*) as well as on the majority of his other films of the 1960's, e.g. *Now About These Women, Persona, Hour of the Wolf.*

SVENSK FILMINDUSTRI

Direction & screenplay—   *Music*—Johann Sebastian Bach's
   Ingmar Bergman   "The Goldberg Variations"
Photography—Sven Nykvist   *Editing*—Ulla Ryghe
Art direction—P. A. Lundgren
PLAYERS: Ingrid Thulin, Gunnel Lindblom, Birger Malmsten, Jörgen Lindström, Håkan Jahnberg

SILK STOCKINGS   U.S.A. (1957)
The old *Ninotchka* story about the female Russian commissar who falls under the spell of gay capitalistic Paris is updated and adapted into a Cole Porter musical with elegant dancer Cyd Charisse in the original Garbo role and Fred Astaire as an American film producer in the Melvyn Douglas part. Some amusing wisecracks about the American and Russian ways of life, a sparkling little cameo from Janis Paige as an ex-swimming star, and a witty skit on big screen techniques entitled "Stereophonic Sound." Very much underrated; Mamoulian's last film.

METRO–GOLDWYN–MAYER

Production—Arthur Freed   *Photography (Metrocolor)*—
Direction—Rouben Mamoulian   Robert Bronner

Screenplay (*suggested by*
Ninotchka *by Melchoir*
Lengyel)—Leonard Gershe,
Leonard Spigelgass
Book of original musical play—
George S. Kaufman, Leveen
McGrath, Abe Burrows

Art direction—William A.
Horning, Randall Duell
Music & lyrics—Cole Porter
Musicial supervision—
Andre Previn
Editing—Harold F. Kress

PLAYERS: Fred Astaire, Cyd Charisse, Janis Paige, Peter Lorre, George
Tobias, Jules Munshin, Joseph Buloff

SINGIN' IN THE RAIN   U.S.A. (1952)

A witty, boisterous musical satire on Hollywood in the twenties. One
of the best screen musicals ever made, noisy, tuneful, directed in great
style by Kelly and Donen from a sparkling script by Betty Comden and
Adolph Green. Among the musical highlights are Gene Kelly's famous
dance sequence in the pouring rain and Donald O'Connor's equally inventive knockabout solo "Make Em Laugh." Jean Hagen's delicious
squeaky-voiced silent movie queen was an unexpected additional gem.

METRO–GOLDWYN–MAYER

Production—Arthur Freed
Direction—Gene Kelly,
Stanley Donen
Original screenplay—
Betty Comden, Adolph Green
Photography (*Technicolor*)—
Harold Rosson

Art direction—Cedric Gibbons,
Randall Duell
Music—Nacio Herb Brown,
Roger Edens
Lyrics—Arthur Freed,
Al Hoffman, Al Goodhart,
Betty Comden, Adolph Green
Editing—Adrienne Fazan

PLAYERS: Gene Kelly, Debbie Reynolds, Jean Hagen, Donald O'Connor,
Millard Mitchell, Cyd Charisse, Rita Moreno, Douglas Fowley, Madge
Blake, Kathleen Freeman, Dawn Adams

SINGING FOOL, THE   U.S.A. (1928)

Warner's musical follow-up to *The Jazz Singer* concerns a singing
waiter (Al Jolson) being two-timed by worthless Josephine Dunn but
saved eventually by kindhearted cigarette girl (Betty Bronson). Conventional, cloyingly sentimental and generally undistinguished, but this
is the one in which black-faced Al Jolson sings "Sonny Boy" and for this
scene alone it will always be of historic importance. Other songs in the
picture include "It All Depends on You," "I'm Sittin' on Top of the
World" and "There's a Rainbow Round my Shoulder."

WARNER BROS.

Direction—Lloyd Bacon
Screenplay—G. Graham Baker
Story—Leslie S. Barrow
Photography—Byron Haskin
Musical score by Vitaphone Symphony Orchestra, conducted by Louis Silvers
PLAYERS: Al Jolson, Betty Bronson, Josephine Dunn, Davey Lee, Reed Holmes, Edward Martindel, Arthur Houseman

SITTING PRETTY   U.S.A. (1948)

Diverting American domestic comedy with Robert Young and Maureen O'Hara as young suburban couple and Clifton Webb as unconventional self-acknowledged "genius" hired as baby-sitter for their three children. Some well-drawn small-town detail and a brilliantly funny performance from Webb who, by his expert timing, often makes a good script sound inspired. The film seems funnier now than it did when it was first shown, probably because domestic comedies are rare in Hollywood these days. Richard Haydn adds an excellent cameo as the town busybody. Webb later repeated his Belvedere characterization in a couple of sequels—*Mr. Belvedere Goes to College* and *Mr. Belvedere Rings the Bell*.

TWENTIETH CENTURY–FOX

Production—Samuel G. Engel
Direction—Walter Lang
Screenplay (based on novel by Gwen Davenport)— F. Hugh Herbert
Photography—Norbert Brodine
Art direction—Lyle Wheeler & Leland Fuller
Music—Alfred Newman
Editorial supervision— Harmon Jones
PLAYERS: Robert Young, Maureen O'Hara, Clifton Webb, Richard Haydn, Louise Allbritton, Randy Stuart, Ed Begley, Larry Olsen

SIX OF A KIND   U.S.A. (1934)

Two couples (Charlie Ruggles and Mary Boland with George Burns and Gracie Allen) plus a Great Dane and a suitcase containing $50,000 go on an incident-packed motor trip across the United States. Despite the excellence of the four stars, the picture belongs entirely to W. C. Fields whose Nevada sheriff John Hoxley is among his most amusing screen characterizations. During the picture Fields plays his famous game of billiards and ruminates on the fact that everything really pleasant in life is "either illegal, immoral or fattening." Directed by Leo McCarey who, a year earlier, had guided the Marx Brothers through *Duck Soup*.

PARAMOUNT

401

Direction—Leo McCarey
Screenplay (*from original story*
by Keene Thompson &
Douglas MacLean)—Walter
DeLeon & Harry Ruskin

Photography—Henry Sharp
Art direction—Hans Dreier &
Robert Odell
Editing—LeRoy Stone

PLAYERS: Charlie Ruggles, Mary Boland, W. C. Fields, George Burns, Gracie Allen, Alison Skipworth, Bradley Page, Grace Bradley

SMILES OF A SUMMER NIGHT (Sommarnattens Leende)
Sweden (1955)
Turn-of-the-century comedy of manners about a collection of wives, husbands, mistresses and lovers who work out their destinies during a summer night party at a country mansion. A witty, sophisticated entertainment, not among Bergman's major works but visually (Fischer's glittering camera work and Lundgren's stylish décor) as good as anything he has ever done. Delightful performances from some of Sweden's loveliest actresses: Ulla Jacobsson, Eva Dahlbeck, Harriet Andersson.

SVENSK FILMINDUSTRI

Direction & screenplay—
Ingmar Bergman
Photography—Gunnar Fischer

Art direction—P. A. Lundgren
Music—Erik Nordgren
Editing—Oscar Rosander

PLAYERS: Ulla Jacobsson, Gunnar Björnstrand, Eva Dahlbeck, Jarl Kulle, Margit Carlqvist, Harriet Andersson, Ake Fridell, Björn Bjelvenstam

SNAKE PIT, THE   U.S.A. (1948)
Anatole Litvak's disturbing film about a young woman writer who has a mental breakdown and becomes a patient in a mental home. A stark, depressing social document which contains some harrowing scenes and shows the appalling overcrowding and squalor in some American mental institutions. An important film, intelligently written and with an unforgettable performance by Olivia de Havilland as the young girl.

TWENTIETH CENTURY–FOX

Production—Robert Bassler,
Anatole Litvak
Direction—Anatole Litvak
Screenplay (*from novel by Mary
Ward*)—F. Partos, Millen Brand

Photography—Leo Tover
Art direction—Lyle Wheeler,
Joseph C. Wright
Music—Alfred Newman
Editing—Dorothy Spencer

PLAYERS: Olivia de Havilland, Mark Stevens, Leo Genn, Celeste Holm, Glenn Langan, Helen Craig, Leif Erickson, Beulah Bondi, Lee Patrick, Howard Freeman, Natalie Schafer, Ruth Donnelly

Snow White and the Seven Dwarfs

SNOW WHITE AND THE SEVEN DWARFS   U.S.A. (1938)
First full-length cartoon by Walt Disney is adapted from fairy story
by the Brothers Grimm and features some of Disney's most inventive
(the animals of the forest, the wicked queen and the dwarfs themselves) and banal (Snow White and her cardboard prince) animation.
A unique entertainment helped commercially by such hit songs as "Hi-
Ho," "Whistle While You Work" and "Someday My Prince Will Come."
The seven dwarfs are Doc, Happy, Sleepy, Grumpy, Dopey, Sneezy
and Bashful.

WALT DISNEY PRODUCTIONS/RKO RADIO

Production (Technicolor)—
  Walt Disney
*Supervising director—*Dave Hand
*Sequence directors—*Perce
  Pearce, William Cottrell, Larry
  Morey, Wilfred Jackson,
  Ben Sharpsteen

Supervising animators—
  Hamilton Luske, Fred Moore,
  Vladimir Tytla,
  Herman Ferguson
*Music—*Frank Churchill,
  Leigh Harline, Paul Smith

SO CLOSE TO LIFE (Nära Livet)   Sweden (1957)
Three women in a maternity ward in a Swedish hospital are studied

403

under the Ingmar Bergman microscope before, during, and after the birth of their babies. An intense and, in one sequence, quite harrowing film, isolated because of its documentary style from Bergman's other works. Strikingly well played by Ingrid Thulin as the woman whose marriage is failing and who loses her baby through miscarriage, Eva Dahlbeck, whose eagerly awaited child dies at birth, and Bibi Andersson as the apprehensive unmarried girl who, alone of the three, leaves the hospital a happier and more mature person. Rarely has a director been so well served by his actresses as in this film.

NORDISK TONEFILM

Direction—Ingmar Bergman	*Photography*—Max Wilén
Screenplay (*from her short story*	*Art direction*—Bibi Lindström
"*Det vänliga, värdiga*") —	*Editing*—Carl-Olov Skeppstedt
Ulla Isaksson	

PLAYERS: Ingrid Thulin, Eva Dahlbeck, Bibi Andersson, Barbro Hiort af Ornäs, Max von Sydow, Erland Josephson, Inga Landgré, Ann-Mari Gyllenspetz

SOLID GOLD CADILLAC, THE U.S.A. (1956)

Judy Holliday at the top of her dumb-blonde form as a naive unemployed actress who creates chaos in a large business organization (in which she owns ten shares) when she attends a stockholders' meeting and suggests that the directors are corrupt and overpaid. The film is built firmly in the prewar Capra mold (simple idealism triumphs over corruption) and is further distinguished by the comedy playing of the male members of the cast—Paul Douglas as the bluff, amiable ex-president of the company and Fred Clark and John Williams as a couple of crooked directors. Based on a Broadway play in which Josephine Hull played the leading role.

COLUMBIA

Production—Fred Kohlmar	*Photography*—Charles Lang
Direction—Richard Quine	*Art direction*—Ross Bellah
Screenplay (*from play by George*	*Music*—Cyril Mockridge
S. *Kaufman & Howard*	*Editing*—Charles Nelson
Teichmann)—Abe Burrows	

PLAYERS: Judy Holliday, Paul Douglas, Fred Clark, John Williams, Hirman Sherman, Neva Patterson

SOME LIKE IT HOT U.S.A. (1959)

Saxophonist (Tony Curtis) and bass player (Jack Lemmon) witness the St. Valentine's Day Massacre and are forced to masquerade as an all-girl dance band in order to escape the evil attentions of a mobster (George Raft) and his cronies. Billy Wilder's funniest and fastest comedy, deliciously performed not only by Curtis and Lemmon but also by Marilyn Monroe as the dance band's lead singer and Joe E. Brown as a lascivious old millionaire. Arguably the wittiest and most amusing American film of the 1950's.

A MIRISCH CO. PRESENTATION/UNITED ARTISTS

Production & direction
   Billy Wilder
*Screenplay (suggested from
   story by R. Thoeren &
   M. Logan)*—Billy Wilder &
I. A. L. Diamond

Photography—Charles B. Lang
Art direction—Ted Haworth
Music—Adolph Deutsch
Editing—Arthur Schmidt

PLAYERS: Marilyn Monroe, Tony Curtis, Jack Lemmon, George Raft, Pat O'Brien, Joe E. Brown, Nehemiah Persoff, Joan Shawlee

SOMEBODY UP THERE LIKES ME   U.S.A. (1956)
Boxing movie traces the turbulent career of Rocky Graziano, a rebellious New York delinquent who overcame the disadvantages of his early life by entering the fight game and boxing his way to the middleweight championship of the world. Not in any way another *Set-Up*, but the slum backgrounds are well observed (the film was shot in New York's Lower East Side and Brooklyn), Ernest Lehman's script intelligent, and the performance of Paul Newman in his first serious role is outstanding. Produced by Charles Schnee whose most interesting contributions to the American cinema were as a scriptwriter, e.g. *Red River* (Hawks), *The Next Voice You Hear* (Wellman), and *The Bad and the Beautiful* (Minnelli).

METRO—GOLDWYN—MAYER

Production—Charles Schnee
Direction—Robert Wise
*Screenplay (based on auto-
   biography of Rocky Graziano
   written with Rowland
   Barber)*—Ernest Lehman

Photography—
   Joseph Ruttenberg
Art direction—Cedric Gibbons
   & Malcolm Brown
Music—Bronislau Kaper
Editing—Albert Akst

PLAYERS: Paul Newman, Pier Angeli, Everett Sloane, Eileen Heckart, Sal Mineo, Harold J. Stone, Joseph Buloff

SONG OF THE SOUTH   U.S.A. (1946)
Walt Disney adaptation of the *Tales of Uncle Remus* is much too whimsical and soft centered, but with some genuine moments of charm.

Interesting, also, for being one of the first movies to combine live action with animation, this technique being especially effective in the sequence built around the song "Zip-a-Dee-Doo-Dah," sung by Uncle Remus (James Baskett) against a cartoon background and with animated birds perching on his shoulder. The three Brer Rabbit stories in the film include "The Tar Baby" and feature the characters Brer Rabbit, Brer Fox and Brer Bear.

WALT DISNEY PRODUCTIONS/RKO RADIO

Production—Walt Disney
Associate producer—Perce Pearce
Direction (live action)—
  Harve Foster
Direction (animation)—
  Wilfred Jackson
Screenplay—Dalton Reymond,
  Morton Grant, Maurice Rapf
*Original story (based on
  Tales of Uncle Remus by
  Joel Chandler Harris)*—
  Dalton Reymond

Photography (Technicolor)—
  Gregg Toland
Art direction—Perry Ferguson
Editing—William M. Morgan
Photoplay score—
  Daniel Amfitheatrof
Music direction—
  Charles Wolcott
Cartoon score—Paul J. Smith
Vocal arrangements—Ken Darby
Orchestrations—Edward Plumb

PLAYERS: Ruth Warrick, Bobby Driscoll, James Baskett, Luana Patten, Lucile Watson, Hattie McDaniel, Eric Rolf.

SORRY, WRONG NUMBER   U.S.A. (1948)
Barbara Stanwyck suffering magnificently as a bedridden hypochondriac heiress accidentally overhears a crossed-line telephone conversation planning her murder. Contrived and with some loopholes in the basic plot, but Anatole Litvak's flashback technique in which he expands the characters of the heiress and her murderous husband (Burt Lancaster) is extremely effective. The whole film is a superior example of the well-made suspense thriller turned out by Hollywood during the 1940's. Remarkable also for a downbeat ending in which the heroine, after living in a state of terror for some two hours, *is* finally murdered.

PARAMOUNT

Production—Hal Wallis &
  Anatole Litvak
Direction—Anatole Litvak
*Screenplay (based on her
  radio play)*—Lucille Fletcher
Photography—Sol Polito

Art direction—Hans Dreier &
  Earl Hedrick
Special photographic effects—
  Gordon Jennings
Music—Franz Waxman
Editing—Warren Low

SOUND BARRIER, THE   Gt. Britain (1952)
David Lean looks at the lives of a wealthy manufacturer (Ralph Richardson), his designer (Joseph Tomelty), and two pilots (Nigel Patrick and John Justin) as they risk their lives and reputations in trying to produce a plane that will fly faster than sound. Mankind's incredible technical advances of the last 20 years (space travel, moon landings, etc.) have made this film a period piece although the basic premise—man's continuing willingness to risk his life in conquering the unknown—remains the same. The film's main virtues are its brilliantly photographed flying scenes and an excitingly edited pre-credit sequence in which an out-of-control Spitfire swoops low over the cliffs.

LONDON FILMS/BRITISH LION

Production & direction—
    David Lean
Story & screenplay—
    Terence Rattigan
*Photography—*Jack Hildyard
*Art direction—*Joseph Bato

*Sets designed by—*Vincent Korda
*Music—*Malcolm Arnold
Associate producer—
    Norman Spencer
*Editing—*Geoffrey Foot

PLAYERS: Ralph Richardson, Ann Todd, Nigel Patrick, John Justin, Dinah Sheridan, Joseph Tomelty, Denholm Elliott, Jack Allen

SOUS LES TOITS DE PARIS   France (1930)
Slender, charming René Clair movie (his first talkie) concerning the loves and rivalries of a small group of Parisians living in the poorer quarters of the city. The story matters little; what counts is Clair's romantic impression of the people who live in his beloved Paris and, on a more technical level, his ingenious use of natural sound to give added dimension to his scenes. Like Rouben Mamoulian in the United States, Clair was one of the first directors to appreciate and experiment with sound and image.

FILMS SONORES TOBIS

Direction, screenplay &
    *dialogue—*René Clair
*Assistant directors—*Georges
    Lacombe, Marcel Carné,
    Houssin, de Schaak
*Photography—*Georges Périnal
    & Georges Raulet

*Art direction—*Lazare Meerson
*Costumes—*René Hubert
Musical direction—
    Armand Bernard
*Original songs—*Raoul Moretti,
    R. Nazelles
*Sound editing—*René Le Hénaff

Albert Préjean, Pola Illery, Gaston Modot, Edmond Gréville, Bill Bocket, Paul Olivier, Jane Pierson, Aimos

SOUTHERNER, THE   U.S.A. (1945)

Considered by many critics to be the best of Renoir's American films, this picture revolves around a young farmer and his family and their struggle to earn a modest living from growing cotton on a derelict Texas farm. The film has a certain affinity with *The Grapes of Wrath* in its feeling for the men who work the soil. It is sympathetically played by Zachary Scott and Betty Fields as the young couple and Beulah Bondi as the quarrelsome old grandmother who lives with them and their children.

UNITED ARTISTS

Production—David J. Lowe & Robert Hakim
Direction, screenplay & dialogue (from novel Hold Autumn in Your Hand *by George Perry)*—Jean Renoir

Photography—Lucien Andriot
Art direction—Eugène Lourie
Music—Werner Janssen
Editing—Gregg Tallas

PLAYERS: Zachary Scott, Betty Field, J. Carrol Naish, Beulah Bondi, Percy Kilbride, Blanche Yurka

SPANISH MAIN, THE   U.S.A. (1945)

A witty spoof of the Hollywood swashbuckler, directed with great relish by Frank Borzage, containing a gem of a performance from Walter Slezak as a richly comic villain. Paul Henreid and Maureen O'Hara play hero and heroine respectively and Binnie Barnes is featured as the pirate Anne Bonney.

RKO RADIO

Production—Edmund Grainger
Direction—Frank Borzage
Screenplay—
   George Worthington Yates
   & Herman J. Mankiewicz
Story—Aeneas Mackenzie

Photography (Technicolor)—
   George Barnes
Art direction—Albert S.
   D'Agostino & Carroll Clark
Music—Hans Eisler
Editing—Ralph Dawson

PLAYERS: Paul Henreid, Maureen O'Hara, Walter Slezak, Binnie Barnes, John Emery, Barton MacLane, J. M. Kerrigan

SPARTACUS   U.S.A. (1960)

Realistic 198-minute epic about the rebellion of the slaves under Spar-

408

tacus during the last decades of the tyrannical Roman republic. Slackens off a bit after a promising start, but still impressive when compared with other films in this hackneyed genre. Alternately intelligent and banal but never boring, thanks to Kubrick's handling and the stunning performances of the British male contingent in the cast. Laurence Olivier is the political militarist Crassus, Charles Laughton a liberal senator, and Peter Ustinov (Academy Award, best supporting actor, 1960) the nervous owner of a school for gladiators. Cameraman Russell Metty received an Oscar for his color photography.

BRYNA/UNIVERSAL

Production—Edward Lewis
Direction—Stanley Kubrick
Screenplay (based on novel
 by Howard Fast)—
 Dalton Trumbo
Music—Alex North

Photography (Technicolor/
 Super Technirama 70)—
 Russell Metty
Art direction—Alexander
 Golitzen & Eric Orbom
Editing—Robert Lawrence

PLAYERS: Kirk Douglas, Laurence Olivier, Jean Simmons, Charles Laughton, Peter Ustinov, John Gavin, Nina Foch, Herbert Lom, John Ireland, John Dall

SPELLBOUND   U.S.A. (1945)

One of the first pictures about psychoanalysis; a glossy, pretentious melodrama with Gregory Peck as an amnesiac who subconsciously believes himself to be a murderer and Ingrid Bergman as the beautiful, somewhat improbable psychiatrist who cures him. Directed with some style by Hitchcock but not one of his best films. Remembered mainly for its famous trick effects—the revolver exploding straight at the audience and Salvador Dali's dream sequence—and for Miklos Rozsa's lush music score.

SELZNICK INTERNATIONAL

Production—David O. Selznick
Direction—Alfred Hitchcock
Screenplay (based on The
 House of Dr. Edwardes by
 Francis Beeding)—
 Ben Hecht
Adaptation—Angus McPhail

Photography—Georges Barnes
Special effects—Jack Cosgrove
Art direction—James Basevi,
 John Ewing
Music—Miklos Rozsa
Editing—William Ziegler,
 Hal C. Kern

PLAYERS: Ingrid Bergman, Gregory Peck, Jean Acker, Rhonda Fleming, Donald Curtis, John Emery, Leo G. Carroll, Norman Lloyd, Michael Chekov

SPIDERS, THE (Die Spinnen)   Germany (1919)
Released in two parts: *Der Goldene See* and *Das Brillanten Schiff*
Early Fritz Lang film about an organized gang of supercriminals seeking world domination. The picture, which helped the Decla studio
become one of the leading production companies in Germany, was
released in two parts, the first dealing with the Spiders' search for the
fabulous treasure of the Incas buried at the "Golden Sea," and the
second with the quest for a precious diamond which, according to
legend, makes its owner the Emperor of Asia. Lang wrote scripts for
two further episodes—*The Secret of the Sphinx* and *For the Sake of
Asia's Imperial Crown*—but these were never put into production.
Ressel Orla played Lio Sha, the anarchistic millionairess who directs
the Spider organization.

DECLA

Direction & screenplay—   *Photography (Das Brillanten*
  Fritz Lang   *Schiff)*—Emil Schünemann
Photography (Der Goldene   *Art direction*—Otto Hunte,
  See)—Karl Freund   Carl Ludwig Kirmse
PLAYERS: Carl de Vogt, Ressel Orla, Lil Dagover, Paul Morgan, Georg
John, Friedrich Kuehne, Bruno Lettinger, Paul Biensfeldt

SPIONE   Germany (1928)
Silent movie centering on the activities of a respectable German bank
director who is secretly the crippled, all-powerful head of a vast gang
of international spies. Fritz Lang returned here to the world of *The
Spiders* and *Dr. Mabuse* and once again cast Rudolph Klein-Rogge
(Mabuse in the 1922 film) as his supercriminal. The film is technically
superior to its predecessors, but remains one of the least-known of
Lang's silent works. Shot in 100 days in Berlin and later novelized by
Thea von Harbou, Lang's wife and co-scriptwriter.

FRITZ LANG FILM G.M.B.H.–UFA

Production & direction—   *Photography—*
  Fritz Lang   Fritz Arno Wagner
Screenplay—Fritz Lang &   *Art direction*—Otto Hunte,
  Thea von Harbou   Karl Vollbrecht
                                         Music—Werner R. Heymann
PLAYERS: Rudolph Klein-Rogge, Gerda Maurus, Willy Fritsch, Lupu
Pick, Fritz Rasp, Lien Deyers, Craighall Sherry, Julius Falkenstein

SPIRAL STAIRCASE, THE   U.S.A. (1946)
High-grade gothic thriller focuses on the activities of a homicidal

maniac in turn-of-the-century New England. German director Robert Siodmak and his talented cameraman Nicholas Musuraca enjoy themselves immensely during the more eerie passages using shadowy interiors, stormy rain-swept streets, and close-ups of human eyes with great effect. Excellent performance from Dorothy McGuire as the dumb girl next on the killer's list. High spot: a murder sequence in a room above a nickelodeon.

RKO RADIO

Production—Dore Schary
Direction—Robert Siodmak
Screenplay (*based on novel*
  Some Must Watch *by Ethel*
  Lina White)—Mel Dinelli
Photography—Nicholas Musuraca

Art direction—
  Albert S. D'Agostino
Music—Roy Webb
Editing—Harry Marker,
  Harry Gerstad

PLAYERS: Dorothy McGuire, George Brent, Ethel Barrymore, Kent Smith, Rhonda Fleming, Gordon Oliver, Elsa Lanchester, Sara Allgood, Rhys Williams

SPLENDOR IN THE GRASS   U.S.A. (1961)

Elia Kazan looks at the anguished, ultimately bitter love affair of two young people living in a small Kansas town in the 1920's and at the same time examines the puritanism and inhibitions of the Midwestern community that surrounds them. Ambitious in concept and one of the few intelligent screen originals to come out of Hollywood in the sixties. Warren Beatty and Natalie Wood play the lovers and Pat Hingle adds a stunning cameo as Beatty's neurotic, selfmade tycoon father.

WARNER BROS./N.B.I. PICTURES

Production & direction—
  Elia Kazan
Screenplay—William Inge
Art direction—Richard Sylbert

Photography (*Technicolor*)—
  Boris Kaufman
Music—David Amram
Editing—Gene Milford

PLAYERS: Natalie Wood, Warren Beatty, Pat Hingle, Audrey Christie, Barbara Loden

SQUAW MAN, THE   U.S.A. (1914)

Early DeMille Western about an Englishman (Dustin Farnum) who becomes involved with cattle rustlers and an Indian girl in Wyoming during the lawless days of the early West. Billy Elmer plays the heavy, and Red Wing the young Indian girl whom Farnum marries. The film was adapted from a stage play by Edwin Milton Royle and remade twice by DeMille, first in 1918 with Elliott Dexter in the Farnum

411

role and then as a talkie in 1931 with Warner Baxter. Together with *The Spoilers,* released the same year, it ranks as one of the earliest of the ambitious Westerns and among the very first films to be made in Hollywood—DeMille's studio then being nothing more than a rented barn at 6284 Selina Avenue.

JESSE L. LASKY FEATURE PLAY CO.

Production & direction—
Cecil B. DeMille &
Oscar C. Apfel

Screenplay—DeMille & Apfel
Photography—Alfred Gandolfi
Editing—Mamie Wagner

PLAYERS: Dustin Farnum, Monroe Salisbury, Winifred Kingston, Red Wing, Billy Elmer, Dick La Strange, Foster Knox, Joe E. Singleton

STAGECOACH   U.S.A. (1939)

John Ford's exciting account of a stagecoach journey across the plains of Arizona in the 1870's, shot in Monument Valley (a favorite location to which Ford returned in the 1950's), and climaxed by a brilliantly edited Apache chase across a stretch of salt flats. Among the passengers: Thomas Mitchell (Academy Award, best supporting actor 1939) as a drunken doctor; John Carradine as a professional gambler; Claire Trevor as a whore, and John Wayne as the outlaw Ringo Kid— the first major role of his career and also the first of his 14 films with Ford. The only classic Western of the 1930's.

WANGER—UNITED ARTISTS

Production & direction—
John Ford
Screenplay (from story "Stage to Lordsburg" by Ernest Haycox)—Dudley Nichols
Photography—Bert Glennon
Art direction—Alexander Toluboff

Music (adapted from American folk tunes of early 1880's)—
Richard Hageman, W. Franke Harling, John Leipold; Leo Shuken, Louis Gruenberg
Editing—Dorothy Spencer, Walter Reynolds

PLAYERS: John Wayne, Claire Trevor, John Carradine, Thomas Mitchell, Andy Devine, Donald Meek, Louise Platt, Tim Holt

STAND-IN   U.S.A. (1937)

One of the wittiest of the early spoofs of Hollywood. Leslie Howard plays an efficiency expert sent from New York to investigate the financial position of Colossal Pictures. Humphrey Bogart appears as a drunken producer and Joan Blondell is featured as a wisecracking stand-in for the company's leading star. There is also an amusing cameo from Alan Mowbray as a temperamental movie director named Koslofski.

A WALTER WANGER PRODUCTION/UNITED ARTISTS

Production—Walter Wanger   *Photography*—Charles Clarke
Direction—Tay Garnett   *Art direction*—
Screenplay (*based on* Saturday   Alexander Toluboff
  Evening Post *serial by Clarence*   *Music*—Heinz Roemheld
  Budington Kelland)—   *Editing*—Otho Lovering &
  Gene Towne & Graham Baker   Dorothy Spencer
PLAYERS: Leslie Howard, Joan Blondell, Humphrey Bogart, Alan Mowbray, Marla Shelton, C. Henry Gordon, Jack Carson, Tully Marshall

STAR IS BORN, A   U.S.A. (1937)
Satire on Hollywood directed with skill and insight by William Wellman and beautifully acted by Fredric March as the Hollywood actor on the way down because of drink and Janet Gaynor as the young girl he discovers and turns into a star. A wittily scripted film with an Oscar-winning original story by Wellman and Robert Carson and some early Technicolor photography by W. Howard Greene.

SELZNICK/UNITED ARTISTS

Production—David O. Selznick   *Photography* (*Technicolor*)—
Direction—William Wellman   W. Howard Greene
Screenplay (*from original story*   *Art direction*—Lyle Wheeler,
  by Wellman & Carson)—   Edward Boyle
  Dorothy Parker,   *Music*—Max Steiner
  Alan Campbell, Robert Carson   *Editing*—Hal C. Kern,
                                     Anson Stevenson
PLAYERS: Janet Gaynor, Fredric March, Adolphe Menjou, May Robson, Andy Devine, Lionel Stander, Elizabeth Jenns, Edgar Kennedy, Owen Moore

STAR IS BORN, A   U.S.A. (1954)
Same story, but remade as a musical drama with Judy Garland as a blues singer replacing Janet Gaynor and James Mason in the drunken actor role. Smart, ironic, technically expert (the film was one of the first to demonstrate the possibilities of CinemaScope) and packed with superb music, including the song "The Man That Got Away" and the exciting 20-minute production number "Born in a Trunk." A performance of great pathos from Garland, a brilliantly underplayed one from Mason, and two expert supporting portrayals from Jack Carson as the Hollywood publicity man (played by Lionel Stander in the first version) and Charles Bickford as the sympathetic studio head (Adolphe

413

Menjou's original role). One of Cukor's best films and one of the few occasions when a remake has proved better than the original.

WARNER BROS.

Production—Sidney Luft
Direction—George Cukor
Screenplay (from screenplay of
   the 1937 film)—Moss Hart
Photography (Technicolor/
   CinemaScope)—Sam Leavitt

Art direction & costumes—
   Gene Allen, Irene Sharaff
Music & lyrics—Harold Arlen,
   Ira Gershwin
Editing—Folmar Blangsted

PLAYERS: Judy Garland, James Mason, Jack Carson, Charles Bickford, Tommy Noonan, Lucy Marlow, Amanda Blake, Irving Bacon

STARS IN MY CROWN   U.S.A. (1950)

A nostalgic little picture, directed with great affection by Jacques Tourneur, about life in a small Tennessee town at the turn of the century. Basically nothing more than a series of remembered incidents from a man's childhood, the film is an excellent example of the small budget picture made by M-G-M and RKO in the late forties and early fifties, a type of film long since abandoned by the major studios.

METRO–GOLDWYN–MAYER

Production—William H. Wright
Direction—Jacques Tourneur
Screenplay (from novel &
   adaptation by Joe David
   Brown)—Margaret Fitts

Photography—
   Charles Schoenbaum
Art direction—Cedric Gibbons,
   Eddie Imazu
Music—Adolph Deutsch
Editing—Gene Ruggiero

PLAYERS: Joel McCrea, Ellen Drew, Dean Stockwell, Alan Hale, Lewis Stone, James Mitchell, Amanda Blake, Juano Hernandez, Charles Kemper, Connie Gilchrist, Ed Begley, Jack Lambert, Arthur Hunnicutt

STATE OF THE UNION   U.S.A. (1948)

A somewhat neglected Capra movie; Spencer Tracy plays an American businessman who becomes the Republican party's Presidential candidate, and then revolts against the corrupt political backers, led by Adolphe Menjou and bitchy newspaper owner Angela Lansbury, who helped him gain the nomination. Tracy's final TV speech in which he attacks political dishonesty echoes once again the famous "idealism versus corruption" theme of the Capra films of the 1930's.

METRO–GOLDWYN–MAYER/A LIBERTY PRODUCTION

Production & direction—
Frank Capra
Screenplay (based on play by
Howard Lindsay & Russell
Crouse)—Anthony Veiller &
Myles Connolly
Photography—George J. Folsey
Art direction—Cedric Gibbons &
Urie McCleary
Music—Victor Young
Editing—William Hornbeck

PLAYERS: Spencer Tracy, Katharine Hepburn, Angela Lansbury, Van Johnson, Adolphe Menjou, Lewis Stone, Howard Smith, Charles Dingle

STEAMBOAT BILL JR.   U.S.A. (1928)

Keaton's last independently produced film. He appears as a delicate college boy who becomes involved in the feud between his father, a rugged steamboat captain (Ernest Torrence), and his father's rival, a riverboat owner (Tom McGuire). Marvelous location photography (the film was set in an old river town in the South) and a virtuoso, splendidly staged climax during a Mississippi cyclone.

BUSTER KEATON PRODUCTIONS INC./UNITED ARTISTS

Production—Joseph M. Schenck
Direction—Charles F. Reisner
Screenplay—Carl Harbaugh
Photography—J. Devereux
Jennings, Bert Haines
Editing—J. Sherman Kell

PLAYERS: Buster Keaton, Ernest Torrence, Tom Lewis, Tom McGuire, Marion Byron, Joe Keaton

STELLA   Greece (1955)

Greek melodrama about the loves of a sensuous cabaret singer (played by Melina Mercouri) whose insatiable sexual appetite and passionate affair with a football player lead eventually to her own destruction. Set almost entirely in the streets, cafes and tenements of working-class Athens and scored with *bouzouki* music by the then unknown Manos Hadjidakis. Michael Cacoyannis' second movie.

MILLAS PRODUCTIONS

Direction & screenplay—
Michael Cacoyannis
Photography—Costa Theodorides
Art direction—Yanni Tsarouchi
Music—Manos Hadjidakis

PLAYERS: Melina Mercouri, Georges Foundas, Aleko Alexandrakis, Sofia Vembo

STORM OVER ASIA   U.S.S.R. (1928)

Set in the steppes of Central Asia at the time of the Mongols' fight against the English army of occupation this Pudovkin film centers on the exploits of a young Mongol trapper who is thought to be the direct descendant of Genghis Khan. The climactic charge of the Mongol cavalry and the factual sequences dealing with an Asian fur market and the Festival of the Lamas are especially notable and the photography by Golovnya (Pudovkin's regular cameraman) often inspired. Originally called *The Heir to Genghis Khan*.

MEZHRABPOMFILM

Direction—Vsevolod Pudovkin

Assistants—A. Ledashev & L. Bronstein

Photography—Anatoli Golovnya

Screenplay (from story by I. Novokshonov)—Osip Brik

Art direction—Sergei Kozlovsky & M. Aaronson

PLAYERS: Valeri Inkizhinov, A. Dedintsev, Anna Studakevich, V. Tsoppi, Boris Barnet

STORM WARNING U.S.A. (1950)

An isolated attempt by Warner Bros. to return to the social thriller of the thirties. Intelligently scripted and rather surprisingly cast with Ginger Rogers as a girl who witnesses a Ku Klux Klan murder in a small Southern town and Doris Day as her sister who is married to one of the killers. Vigorous, tense, realistic, one of the few quality movies that Stuart Heisler directed.

WARNER BROS.

Production—Jerry Wald

Direction—Stuart Heisler

Screenplay—Richard Brooks, Daniel Fuchs

Photography—Carl Guthrie

Art direction—Leo K. Kuter

Music—Daniele Amphitheatrof

Editing—Clarence Kolster

PLAYERS: Ginger Rogers, Ronald Reagan, Doris Day, Steve Cochran, Hugh Sanders, Lloyd Gough, Raymond Greenleaf, Ned Glass, Walter Baldwin, Paul F. Burns

STORY OF G.I. JOE, THE U.S.A. (1945)

The experiences of a small group of World War II infantrymen from the days of their first action in Tunisia to the fall of Cassino and the march on Rome. Based on the writings of Pulitzer Prize-winning correspondent Ernie Pyle (later killed in the fighting at Iwo Jima) and admirably directed by William Wellman whose directorial skill has never been more evident than in the sequence showing some Nazi snipers being ferreted out of a ruined Italian church. Burgess Meredith plays Pyle and Robert Mitchum, in an early role, appears as a war-weary sergeant.

416

Production—Lester Cowan *Art direction*—James Sullivan
Direction—William Wellman *Music*—Ann Ronell &
Screenplay—Leopold Atlas, Guy Louis Applebaum
  Endore & Philip Stevenson *Editing*—Otho Lovering
Photography—Russell Metty
PLAYERS: Burgess Meredith, Robert Mitchum, Freddie Steele, Wally Cassell, Jimmy Lloyd, Jack Reilly, Bill Murphy

STORY OF LOUIS PASTEUR, THE   U.S.A. (1936)

The first, and in many ways the most impressive, of the Dieterle-directed Warner biographies of the thirties—a slow, thoughtful, carefully staged account of the later years in the life of the great French chemist concentrating not only on his battle with anthrax and hydrophobia but also on his fight against the bigotry of his own profession. Paul Muni won an Academy Award for his performance as Pasteur and later appeared again for Dieterle in *The Life of Emile Zola* and *Juarez*.

FIRST NATIONAL–COSMOPOLITAN/WARNER BROS.
Direction—William Dieterle *Art direction*—Robert Haas
Original screenplay—Sheridan *Music direction*—
  Gibney & Pierre Collings Leo F. Forbstein
Photography—Tony Gaudio *Editing*—Ralph Dawson
PLAYERS: Paul Muni, Josephine Hutchinson, Anita Louise, Donald Woods, Fritz Leiber, Henry O'Neill, Porter Hall, Raymond Brown, Akim Tamiroff

STORY OF VERNON AND IRENE CASTLE   U.S.A. (1939)

Ninth, and last, of the prewar Astaire-Rogers vehicles traces the show-biz career of a famous American dance team of the early 1900's. A pleasant score, but the formula was wearing a little thin and the Busby Berkeley/Judy Garland musicals at Metro were beginning to be more popular with movie audiences.

RKO RADIO
Production—George Haight *Adaptation*—Oscar Hammerstein,
Direction—H. C. Potter Dorothy Yost
Screenplay (*based on the stories* *Photography*—Robert deGrasse
  "My Husband" & *"My Memo-* *Musical direction*—
  ries of Vernon Castle" by Irene Victor Baravalle
  Castle)—Richard Sherman *Editing*—William Hamilton
PLAYERS: Fred Astaire, Ginger Rogers, Edna May Oliver, Walter Brennan, Lew Fields, Etienne Girardot, Janet Beecher

STRANGE LOVE OF MARTHA IVERS, THE   U.S.A. (1946)
Barbara Stanwyck as a murderess, Judith Anderson as her victim, Kirk
Douglas as her attorney husband, and Van Heflin as her gambler lover.
A polished psychological thriller, well acted and efficiently directed,
but given extra quality by Robert Rossen's cynical, smartly tailored
screenplay. This was Rossen's penultimate writing assignment (his last
was *Desert Fury*) before turning to directing his own scripts with
Johnny O'Clock in 1947.

PARAMOUNT

Production—Hal Wallis

Direction—Lewis Milestone

Screenplay (from original story
  by Jack Patrick)—
  Robert Rossen

Photography—Victor Milner

Art direction—Hans Dreier &
  John Meehan

Music—Miklos Rozsa

Editing—Archie Marshek

PLAYERS: Barbara Stanwyck, Van Heflin, Kirk Douglas, Lizabeth Scott,
Judith Anderson, Roman Bohnen, Darryl Hickman, Janis Wilson

STRANGER, THE   U.S.A. (1946)
Exciting though not altogether successful thriller follows the attempts
of War Crimes commissioner (Edward G. Robinson) to track down a
fugitive Nazi (Welles) posing as a schoolteacher in a small town in
Connecticut. Not in any way a major Welles work although, as in all
his films, there are some splendid moments, e.g. the tracking of a fugitive in the opening reel and the climax in which the teacher is speared
to death by one of the revolving sword-bearing effigies on the town
clock tower. Coscripted by John Huston and produced by S. P. Eagle
who, under his real name of Sam Spiegel, later produced such pictures
as *On the Waterfront, The Bridge on the River Kwai* and *Lawrence of
Arabia*.

INTERNATIONAL PICTURES/UNITED ARTISTS

Production—S. P. Eagle

Direction—Orson Welles

Original screenplay—
  Victor Trivas

Photography—Russell Metty

Art direction—Perry Ferguson

Adaptation & dialogue—
  Anthony Veiller, John Huston
  & Orson Welles

Music—Bronislaw Kaper

Editing—Ernst Nims

PLAYERS: Orson Wells, Loretta Young, Edward G. Robinson, Philip
Merivale, Richard Long, Byron Keith, Billy House

STRANGERS ON A TRAIN   U.S.A. (1951)
Striking Hitchcock thriller with Robert Walker in one of his finest roles

as a wealthy psychopath who tries to "swap" murders with a famous tennis player he meets on a train. Very well written—the script was partly by Raymond Chandler—and containing some of Hitchcock's most imaginative sequences, notably a murder in an amusement park photographed through a pair of fallen spectacles, and the thrilling climax on an out-of-control carousel. The picture was the first of Hitchcock's 12 films with cameraman Robert Burks.

WARNER BROS.

Production & direction—
  Alfred Hitchcock
Screenplay (based on novel by
  Patricia Highsmith)—Raymond
  Chandler, Czenzi Ormonde

Adaptation—Whitfield Cook
Photography—Robert Burks
Art direction—Ted Haworth
Music—Dimitri Tiomkin
Editing—William H. Ziegler

PLAYERS: Robert Walker, Farley Granger, Ruth Roman, Leo G. Carroll, Patricia Hitchcock, Laura Elliott, Marion Lorne, Jonathan Hale

STREET WITH NO NAME, THE   U.S.A. (1948)

Another in Fox's long line of semidocumentary thrillers with William Keighley trying to repeat the success of Henry Hathaway before him with a story about an FBI agent (Mark Stevens) who infiltrates and then smashes a gang of criminals. Not quite up to the standard of *The House on 92nd Street* or *Kiss of Death,* but the battle of wills between Stevens and the gang leader (Richard Widmark) is well observed. Joe MacDonald's photography is thoroughly realistic.

TWENTIETH CENTURY–FOX

Production—Samuel G. Engel
Direction—William Keighley
Screenplay & story—
  Harry Kleiner
Photography—Joe MacDonald

Art direction—Lyle Wheeler &
  Chester Gore
Music direction—
  Lionel Newman
Editing—William Reynolds

PLAYERS: Mark Stevens, Richard Widmark, Lloyd Nolan, Barbara Lawrence, Ed Begley, Donald Buka, Joseph Pevney, John McIntire

STREETCAR NAMED DESIRE, A   U.S.A. (1951)

Impressive film about the final degradation of Tennessee Williams' faded Southern belle Blanche du Bois (Vivien Leigh) who finishes her days an alcoholic slut in her sister's sleazy apartment in the slum district of New Orleans. Directed with great authority by Elia Kazan who also directed the 1947 New York stage version, but notable primarily for the remarkable quality of the acting which in 1951 was the most powerful ever seen on American screens. Others in the cast: Kim

Hunter as the doomed heroine's sister, Marlon Brando as her brutal Polack brother-in-law, and Karl Malden as the aging lover who gives her a last brief chance of happiness. The film won five Oscars, including awards to Leigh, Hunter and Malden, and was named best of the year by the New York Film Critics.

WARNER BROS.

Production—Charles K. Feldman

Direction—Elia Kazan

Screenplay (from his play)—
 Tennessee Williams

Adaptation—Oscar Saul

Photography—Harry Stradling

Art direction—Richard Day &
 George James Hopkins

Music—Alex North

Editing—David Weisbart

PLAYERS: Vivien Leigh, Marlon Brando, Kim Hunter, Karl Malden, Rudy Bond, Nick Dennis

STRIKE (Stachka)   U.S.S.R. (1924)

The evolution of an industrial strike in pre-1917 Russia and the tragic aftermath when the strikers are murdered in the streets by mounted police. Eisenstein's first full-length film, brilliantly organized and notable for its dynamic experiments in film editing techniques that were later developed even more excitingly in *Battleship Potemkin* and *October*. Photographed by Eduard Tissé, the cameraman on all of Eisenstein's subsequent works.

1ST GOSKINO

Direction—Sergei M. Eisenstein

Screenplay—The Proletkult
 Collective (Valeri F. Pletniov,
 S. M. Eisenstein,
 I. Kravchinovski, etc.)

Photography—Eduard Tissé

Art direction—Vasili Rakhals

Assistant direction—
 G. Alexandrov,
 I. Kravchinovski, A. Levshin

Assistant cameramen—V. Popov,
 V. Khvatov

PLAYERS: Maxim Shtraukh, Grigori Alexandrov, Mikhail Gomorov, I. Ivanov, I. Klukvin, A. Antonov

STRIKE UP THE BAND   U.S.A. (1940)

Second of the four Judy Garland musicals directed by Busby Berkeley between 1939 and 1942—a strictly formularized success story about a group of high-school youngsters who, led by drumming wizard Mickey Rooney and singer Judy Garland, form their own juvenile band and rise to national fame. Schmaltzy, brash and consistently overloud, but Garland's rendering of the charming "Our Love Affair" and Berkeley's brilliant staging of the 5-minute "La Conga" are compensations.

METRO–GOLDWYN–MAYER

Production—Arthur Freed
Direction—Busby Berkeley
Screenplay—John Monks, Jr.,
Fred Finklehoffe
Photography—Ray June

Lyrics & music—Roger Edens,
George & Ira Gershwin,
Arthur Freed
Editing—Ben Lewis

PLAYERS: Mickey Rooney, Judy Garland, Paul Whiteman, June Preisser, William Tracy, Larry Nunn, Margaret Early, Ann Shoemaker

STRONG MAN, THE   U.S.A. (1926)

Strong man's assistant Harry Langdon becomes involved in all kinds of ridiculous adventures during his search for the girl who wrote him love letters during his army service in Belgium. A wealth of slapstick, also pathos, and with a memorable climax in a lawless mining town when Langdon stands in for his boss and literally brings a saloon down about his ears. Directed by Frank Capra whose first feature this was.

HARRY LANGDON CORPORATION/FIRST NATIONAL

Direction—Frank Capra
Screenplay—Hal Conklin &
Robert Eddy

Story—Arthur Ripley
Photography—Elgin Lessley &
Glenn Kershner

PLAYERS: Harry Langdon, Gertrude Astor, William V. Mong, Robert McKim, Priscilla Bonner, Arthur Thalasso

SULLIVAN'S TRAVELS   U.S.A. (1942)

Third and best of the brilliant comedies made by Preston Sturges at Paramount during his remarkably creative five-year period between 1940 and 1944. Joel McCrea (a favorite Sturges performer) appears as a top comedy-film director who yearns to make a realistic masterpiece called *Brother Where Art Thou* and goes out on the road dressed as a tramp in order to find real-life material. A witty, original entertainment containing some sharp satire on the morals of Hollywood and on American society as a whole. Blonde Veronica Lake featured as McCrea's wisecracking traveling companion.

PARAMOUNT

Production—Paul Jones
Direction—Preston Sturges
Photography—John Seitz

Original screenplay—
Preston Sturges
Editing—Stuart Gilmore

PLAYERS: Joel McCrea, Veronica Lake, Robert Warwick, William Demarest, Margaret Hayes, Porter Hall, Franklin Pangborn, Eric Blore

SUMMER HOLIDAY   U.S.A. (1948)
Stylish, richly colored Mamoulian musical, much underrated when it
first appeared, about the ecstasies and heartaches of an adolescent
(Mickey Rooney) growing up in small-town America at the turn of the
century. Some delightful performances, especially from Agnes Moorehead as a spinster aunt and Frank Morgan as a drunken uncle, and
some of Mamoulian's most inventive musical numbers, e.g., "The
Stanley Steamer Song" built around a family outing in a new motorcar
and "You Mustn't Be Afraid to Fall in Love," a Mickey Rooney/Gloria
DeHaven duet culminating in a lyrical polka danced across a bright
green lawn.

                         METRO–GOLDWYN–MAYER
Production–Arthur Freed   *Photography (Technicolor)*–
Direction–Rouben Mamoulian   Charles Schoenbaum
Screenplay (adapted by Irving   *Art direction*–Cedric Gibbons &
  Brecher & Jean Holloway from   Jack Martin Smith
  Eugene O'Neill's play Ah   *Music direction*–Lennie Hayton
  Wilderness)–Frances   *Editing*–Albert Akst
  Goodrich & Albert Hackett
PLAYERS: Mickey Rooney, Gloria DeHaven, Walter Huston, Frank
Morgan, Butch Jenkins, Marilyn Maxwell, Agnes Moorehead, Selena
Royle

SUMMER INTERLUDE (Sommarlek)   Sweden (1950)
A tragic summer love affair of long ago remembered with nostalgia by
a 30-year-old ballerina and contrasted, through a series of flashbacks,
with her current, less idyllic relationship with a Stockholm journalist.
A minor Bergman opus made at a time when he was concerning himself
with the problems and anguish of young love. Lovely performance
from Maj-Britt Nilsson as the ballerina and some exquisite location
photography of the skerries around Stockholm.

                          SVENSK FILMINDUSTRI
Direction–Ingmar Bergman   *Art direction*–Nils Svenwall
Screenplay–Ingmar Bergman &   *Music*–Erik Nordgren
  Herbert Grevenius   *Editing*–Oscar Rosander
Photography–Gunnar Fischer
PLAYERS: Maj-Britt Nilsson, Birger Malmsten, Alf Kjellin, Annalisa
Ericson, Georg Funkquist, Stig Olin, Renée Björling, Mimi Pollak

SUMMER STOCK   U.S.A. (1950)
Lively M-G-M musical has New England farm owner (Judy Garland)

                                422

involved with Gene Kelly and his troupe of road-show players when they take over her barn as a summer theater. The songs are not as familiar as those in Metro's more ambitious musicals of the period but there are still some charming Garland solos ("If You Feel Like Singing" and "Happy Harvest") and vigorous Kelly routines ("You Wonderful You," a duo with Garland, "Portland Fancy" and "Dig for Your Dinner"). After *Good News* Charles Walters' best early musical.

METRO–GOLDWYN–MAYER

Production–Joe Pasternak
Direction–Charles Walters
Screenplay–George Wells &
   Sy Gomberg
Story–Sy Gomberg

Photography (Technicolor)–
   Robert Planck
Art direction–Cedric Gibbons &
   Jack Martin Smith
Music direction–Johnny Green
Editing–Albert Akst

PLAYERS: Judy Garland, Gene Kelly, Eddie Bracken, Gloria de Haven, Marjorie Main, Phil Silvers, Ray Collins, Nita Bieber

SUMMER WITH MONIKA (Sommaren med Monika)
Sweden (1952)

Relatively simple Bergman work about the brief, ultimately bitter romance of a 19-year-old boy from a respectable home and a trollop from the poorer quarter of Stockholm, who enjoy one enchanted summer together before an unwanted baby and the restrictions of their shabby flat cause the girl to revert to her sluttish ways. Bleak and despairing, but commendably honest in its observation of the ecstasies and agonies of a first sexual experience. Superb performance by Harriet Andersson as the sensual Monika.

SVENSK FILMINDUSTRI

Direction–Ingmar Bergman
*Screenplay (from novel by
   Fogelström)*–Ingmar Bergman,
   P. A. Fogelström

Photography–Gunnar Fischer
Art direction–Nils Svenwall,
   P. A. Lundgren
Music–Erik Nordgren
Editing–Tage Holmberg

PLAYERS: Harriet Andersson, Lars Ekborg, John Harryson, Georg Skarstedt, Dagmar Ebbeson, Ake Fridell, Naemi Briese

SUMMERTIME
Gt. Britain (1955)

Outstanding adaptation of Arthur Laurents' celebrated play *The Time of the Cuckoo* about the sad little love affair between an aging American spinster (Katharine Hepburn) and a married Italian (Rossano Brazzi) during her vacation in Venice. While made with impeccable

423

Summer With Monika

craftsmanship by Lean, the film is most distinguished by the performance of Miss Hepburn whose playing brilliantly suggests all the frustrations and loneliness of a single woman nearing middle age, and by
Jack Hildyard's beautiful Eastmancolor panoramas of Venice.

LONDON FILMS/LOPORT FILM PRODUCTIONS

Production—Ilya Loport
Direction—David Lean
Screenplay—David Lean,
   H. E. Bates

Photography (*Eastmancolor*)—
   Jack Hildyard
Art direction—Vincent Korda
Music—Alessandro Cicognini
Editing—Peter Taylor

PLAYERS: Katharine Hepburn, Rossano Brazzi, Isa Miranda, Darren
McGavin, Mari Aldon, Jack Rose, Macdonald Parke, Jeremy Spenser

SUN SHINES BRIGHT, THE   U.S.A. (1953)
Slight, folksy little picture derived from three of Irvin S. Cobb's "Judge
Priest" stories about life in a small Kentucky town in the 1890's. A
neglected minor masterpiece directed by John Ford who, twenty years
earlier, had filmed some of Cobb's other stories under the title *Judge
Priest* with Will Rogers in the starring role. In this film Charles Win-

ninger plays Judge Priest, Stepin Fetchit his Negro servant, and Milburn Stone his political rival. Said to be Ford's personal favorite of all his own films.

REPUBLIC

Production—John Ford, Merian C. Cooper
Direction—John Ford
Screenplay (from stories "The Sun Shines Bright," "The Mob from Massac" and "The Lord Provides" by Irvin S. Cobb)— Laurence Stallings
Photography—Archie Stout
Art direction—Frank Hotaling
Music—Victor Young
Editing—Jack Murray

PLAYERS: Charles Winninger, Arleen Whelan, John Russell, Stepin Fetchit, Russell Simpson, Ludwig Stossel, Francis Ford, Paul Hurst, Milburn Stone

SUNDAY DINNER FOR A SOLDIER   U.S.A. (1944)
Endearing little Hollywood wartime movie about an impoverished, parentless Florida family living on a ramshackle houseboat and the struggles and financial sacrifices they have to make in order to entertain an unknown American soldier at Sunday dinner. A tearful tale but rescued from excessive sentimentality by an honest script and by Lloyd Bacon's firm control of his material. Despite the restrictions and obvious pitfalls of the Hollywood studio system, films such as this one sometimes made the system worth while. Anne Baxter plays the eldest daughter who struggles to keep the family together, Charles Winninger her irresponsible old grandfather, and John Hodiak the soldier.

TWENTIETH CENTURY–FOX

Production—Walter Morosco
Direction—Lloyd Bacon
Screenplay (based on story by Martha Cheavens)—Wanda Tuchock & Melvin Levy
Photography— Joseph MacDonald
Art direction—Lyle Wheeler & Russell Spencer
Editing—J. Watson Webb

PLAYERS: Anne Baxter, John Hodiak, Charles Winninger, Anne Revere, Connie Marshall, Chill Wills, Robert Bailey, Bobby Driscoll, Jane Darwell

SUNDAY IN AUGUST   Italy (1950)
Neo-realist comedy made up of a half dozen sketches about the people who leave Rome for the nearby seaside resort at Ostia on a hot Sunday afternoon in August. Modest, frequently amusing, and with some honest observations of everyday life; performed by a cast made up

almost entirely of nonprofessional actors. The first feature of former documentary-maker Luciano Emmer.

Production—Sergio Amidei
Direction—Luciano Emmer
Screenplay—Franco Brusati,
   Luciano Emmer, Giulio
   Macchi, Cesare Zavattini

Photography—Domenico Scala,
   Leonida Barboni
Music—Roman Vlad
Editing—Jolanda Benvenuti

PLAYERS: Anna Baldini, Franco Interlenghi, Elvy Lissiak, Massimo Serato, Corrado Verga, Ave Ninchi, Marcello Mastroianni

SUNRISE   U.S.A. (1927)

Silent movie concerning the tragic experiences of a happily married young farmer (George O'Brien) who is enticed away from his pretty young wife (Janet Gaynor) and almost driven to murder by a city girl (Margaret Livingstone). Murnau's most famous American film is distinguished mainly by its visual qualities, i.e. the lyrical monochrome photography of Charles Rosher and Karl Struss (Academy Award, best photography, 1927) and the stylized designs of Rochus Gliese whose single set of the town center was over a mile long.

Direction—F. W. Murnau
Screenplay (based on short story
   "A Trip to Tilsit" by Hermann
   Sudermann)—Carl Mayer
Designer—Rochus Gliese

Photography—Charles Rosher,
   Karl Struss
Musical score—Hugo Riesenfeld
Editing & titles—Katherine
   Hilliker, H. H. Caldwell

PLAYERS: George O'Brien, Janet Gaynor, Margaret Livingstone, Bodil Rosing, J. Farrell MacDonald, Ralph Sipperly, Jane Winton

SUNSET BOULEVARD   U.S.A. (1950)

One of the most famous of Billy Wilder's early movies and still the wittiest film about Hollywood ever made; an ironic, acidly scripted tale of a faded silent-movie queen (Gloria Swanson) who hires a struggling writer (William Holden) to be her gigolo and to write the screenplay for her comeback picture. Miss Swanson (superb throughout) is supported by Erich von Stroheim as her butler-chauffeur (formerly her director-husband), Fred Clark as an ulcerated producer and, in a brief role, Cecil B. DeMille as himself. The film's greatest asset is its screenplay which deservedly won Wilder and Charles Brackett an Oscar and which was the last script on which these two talented writers collaborated. Other Brackett/Wilder collaborations: *Bluebeard's Eighth Wife, What a Life, Midnight, Ninotchka, Arise My Love, Hold Back the Dawn, Ball of Fire, The Major and the Minor, Five Graves to Cairo, The Lost Weekend, The Emperor Waltz, A Foreign Affair.*

PARAMOUNT

Direction—Billy Wilder
Screenplay—Charles Brackett, Billy Wilder & D. M. Marshman, Jr.
Photography—John F. Seitz

Art direction—Hans Dreier & John Meehan
Music—Franz Waxman
Editing—Doane Harrison & Arthur Schmidt

PLAYERS: Gloria Swanson, William Holden, Erich von Stroheim, Nancy Olson, Fred Clark, Lloyd Gough, Jack Webb

SUSPICION   U.S.A. (1941)

The first of Hitchcock's four films with Cary Grant focuses on a wealthy young wife (Joan Fontaine) who believes that her irresponsible playboy husband is slowly trying to murder her. Slickly done and with some effective moments of tension but generally substandard Hitchcock. Particularly unsatisfactory is the forced happy ending when would-be killer Grant (thought by the studio to be too popular an actor to be cast as a murderer) is shown to be completely innocent.

RKO RADIO

Direction—Alfred Hitchcock
Screenplay (from Francis Iles's Before the Fact)— Samson Raphaelson, Joan Harrison, Alma Reville

Photography—Harry Stradling
Art direction—Van Nest Polglase
Music—Franz Waxman
Editing—William Hamilton

PLAYERS: Cary Grant, Joan Fontaine, Nigel Bruce, Cedric Hardwicke, Dame May Whitty, Isabel Jeans, Heather Angel, Auriol Lee, Reginald Sheffield, Leo G. Carroll

SWAMP WATER   U.S.A. (1941)

Set in Georgia's desolate Okefenokee swamp, this atmospheric little melodrama is of historic interest as being the first of Jean Renoir's five American movies. The story concerns a suspected murderer (Walter Brennan) hiding out in the swamplands and the efforts of a young local boy (Dana Andrews) to prove his innocence. Remade in 1952 as *Lure of the Wilderness* with Walter Brennan repeating his role of the fugitive.

TWENTIETH CENTURY–FOX (IRVING PICHEL)

427

Direction—Jean Renoir
Screenplay, adaptation &
   dialogue (from story by
   Vereen Bell)—Dudley Nichols
Photography—J. Peverell Marley
Art direction—Thomas Little
Music—David Buttolph
Editing—Walter Thompson

PLAYERS: Walter Brennan, Walter Huston, Dana Andrews, John Carradine, Anne Baxter, Virginia Gilmore

SWEET SMELL OF SUCCESS, THE   U.S.A. (1957)

Acidly scripted study of the power of the press and the way it is corrupted when a sadistic, all-powerful New York columnist (Burt Lancaster) and his Broadway press agent (Tony Curtis) dig among the gossip empires of Broadway in order to smear and even ruin the reputation of anyone who gets in their way. The story itself (Lancaster's preoccupation with keeping his kid sister from marrying a young jazz musician) is unremarkable, but the atmosphere of the chic bistros and glittering streets of Time Square and Broadway is beautifully caught by British director Alexander Mackendrick whose only American film this is and who, like Peter Yates and John Schlesinger after him, settled down immediately to the American scene. Crisp monochrome camera work and an excellent jazz score.

A NORMA–CURTLEIGH PRODUCTIONS PICTURE/UNITED ARTISTS

Production—James Hill
Executive producer—
   Harold Hecht
Direction—
   Alexander Mackendrick
Photography—
   James Wong Howe
Screenplay (from novelette by
   Ernest Lehman)—Clifford
   Odets & Ernest Lehman
Art direction—Edward Carrere
Music—Elmer Bernstein
Editing—Alan Crosland, Jr.

PLAYERS: Burt Lancaster, Tony Curtis, Susan Harrison, Marty Milner, Sam Levene, Barbara Nichols, Jeff Donnell, Joseph Leon

SWING TIME   U.S.A. (1936)

Musical directed by George Stevens has gambler Fred Astaire wooing and winning Ginger Rogers after singing and dancing his way through several notable Jerome Kern songs including "Pick Yourself Up" and the Academy Award-winning "The Way You Look Tonight" (best song, 1936). Other top musical numbers: "A Fine Romance," "Waltz in Swing Time," a Rogers-Astaire dance duet, and the magnificent "Bojangles of Harlem," one of the most accomplished of all Astaire's dance routines.

RKO RADIO

Production—Pandro S. Berman	*Story*—Erwin Gelsey
Direction—George Stevens	*Photography*—David Abel
Screenplay—Howard Lindsay,	*Music*—Jerome Kern
Allan Scott	*Editing*—Henry Berman

PLAYERS: Fred Astaire, Ginger Rogers, Victor Moore, Helen Broderick, Eric Blore, Betty Furness

TABU   U.S.A. (1931)

Visually beautiful movie made by two most individual talents—German director F. W. Murnau who financed and directed the major part of the picture and Robert J. Flaherty the documentary film-maker responsible for *Nanook of the North* and *Moana*. The story, a simple one of two young Polynesian lovers who defy the tabu of their tribe, was filmed entirely in the South Seas and acted by a native cast. There was some dissent between the two directors during the making of the film and Flaherty left before filming was completed. Murnau was later killed in an automobile accident just prior to the film's premiere.

PARAMOUNT

Production—F. W. Murnau	*Assistant*—David Flaherty
Direction & screenplay—F. W.	*Photography*—Floyd Crosby
Murnau & Robert J. Flaherty	*Music*—Hugo Riesenfeld
Story—Robert J. Flaherty	

PLAYERS: Reri (Anna Chevalier), Matahi & Bill Bambridge

TAKE ME OUT TO THE BALL GAME   U.S.A. (1949)

Sparkling Metro musical of the late forties revolving around the activities of a turn-of-the-century baseball team led by Gene Kelly, Frank Sinatra and Jules Munshin. Somewhat overshadowed by the more ambitious musicals of the period—Minnelli's *The Pirate* and Kelly and Donen's *On the Town*, for instance—but lively enough, and with several splendidly staged numbers, including two exuberant Kelly/Sinatra duos—"Yes Indeedy" and "Take Me Out to the Ball Game" and the humorous "O'Brien to Ryan to Goldberg." Story by Kelly and Donen who also staged the numbers; direction by Busby Berkeley, whose last film as a director this was although he later worked as choreographer on such films as *Call Me Mister* at Fox, *Two Tickets to Broadway* at RKO and *Easy to Love* at M-GM.

METRO—GOLDWYN—MAYER

Production—Arthur Freed	*Screenplay (from story by Gene*
Direction—Busby Berkeley	*Kelly & Stanley Donen*)—
	Harry Tugend & George Wells

Photography (Technicolor)—
George Folsey
*Art direction—*Cedric Gibbons &
Daniel B. Cathcart
*Music—*Adolph Deutsch

*Lyrics—*Betty Comden,
Adolph Green, & Roger Edens
*Choreography—*Gene Kelly &
Stanley Donen
*Editing—*Blanche Sewell

PLAYERS: Frank Sinatra, Gene Kelly, Esther Williams, Betty Garrett, Edward Arnold, Jules Munshin, Richard Lane, Tom Dugan

TALES OF MANHATTAN   U.S.A. (1942)
Episodic film tracing the history of an evening tailcoat from the time it is first worn by a rich matinee idol (Charles Boyer) till it is finally owned by a group of poor American Negroes. Among the others who own the coat are Edward G. Robinson as a Bowery down-and-outer and Charles Laughton as a poor composer who needs it to conduct a symphony orchestra in front of a socialite audience. The film boasted 9 top-line stars, 44 leading character players, and 10 scriptwriters.

TWENTIETH CENTURY—FOX

*Production—*Boris Morros,
S. P. Eagle
*Direction—*Julien Duvivier
Original stories & screenplay—
Ben Hecht, Ferenc Molnar,
Donald Ogden Stewart,

Samuel Hoffenstein, Alan
Campbell, Ladislas Fodor,
L. Vadnai, L. Gorog, Lamar
Trotti, Henry Blankfort
*Photography—*Joseph Walker
*Music—*Sol Kaplan

PLAYERS: Charles Boyer, Rita Hayworth, Ginger Rogers, Henry Fonda, Charles Laughton, Edward G. Robinson, Paul Robeson, Thomas Mitchell, Eugene Pallette, Cesar Romero, Roland Young, Elsa Lanchester, George Sanders, James Gleason

TALK OF THE TOWN, THE   U.S.A. (1942)
Cary Grant amiably teamed with Jean Arthur and Ronald Colman in an engaging comedy of the early forties. Grant plays a jailbreaker unjustly accused of murder and arson who finds temporary safety in the home of law-school dean (Colman) and his scatterbrained landlady (Arthur). A witty, sophisticated movie, deliciously played; the second in a delightful trio of comedies made by Stevens during the early war period. Others: *Woman of the Year* and *The More the Merrier*.

COLUMBIA

Production & direction—
George Stevens
*Photography—*Ted Tetzlaff

Screenplay (based on story by
*Sidney Harmon)—*Irwin Shaw
& Sidney Buchman

Adaptation by—Dale Van Every   *Musical direction*—M. W. Stoloff
Art direction—Lionel Banks   *Editing*—Otto Meyer
Music—Fredrick Hollander
PLAYERS: Cary Grant, Jean Arthur, Ronald Colman, Edgar Buchanan,
Glenda Farrell, Charles Dingle, Emma Dunn, Rex Ingram

TASTE OF HONEY, A   Gt. Britain (1961)
Shapeless but sympathetic Richardson movie about the experiences of
a young girl (Rita Tushingham) and her sluttish mother (Dora Bryan)
in a drab canal town in the industrial North of England. Sometimes
brilliant, often amateurish, but always stunning to look at (cameraman
Walter Lassally is equally at home among the shabby streets and wet
pavements of Salford as in the sun-soaked islands of Greece). Strikingly well played not only by the two leads but also by Robert Stephens
and Murray Melvin in supporting roles. The film is scored by John
Addison who wrote the music for several other Richardson pictures,
including *The Entertainer, The Loneliness of the Long Distance Run-
ner* and *Tom Jones.*

A WOODFALL FILM

Production & direction—   *Photography*—Walter Lassally
   Tony Richardson   *Art direction*—Ralph Brinton
Screenplay (adapted from play   *Music*—John Addison
   by Shelagh Delaney)—Shelagh   *Editing*—Antony Gibbs
   Delaney & Tony Richardson
PLAYERS: Dora Bryan, Rita Tushingham, Robert Stephens, Murray
Melvin, Paul Danquah, David Boliver, Moira Kaye, Herbert Smith

TEN COMMANDMENTS, THE   U.S.A. (1923)
Double-story DeMille opus telling first, in early two-color Technicolor,
of the events that led to Moses' receiving the Ten Commandments on
Mount Sinai and then a triangular story showing the importance of the
Commandments in modern life. The film was the first of DeMille's
religious blockbusters and cost Paramount some 1½ million dollars to
produce. Its highlights—the Exodus and the crossing of the Red Sea—
were superbly photographed by a large team of distinguished cameramen led by color specialist Ray Rennahan, Bert Glennon (later a regular with both von Sternberg and Ford), and J. Peverell Marley who
also worked with DeMille on his 1956 remake. Theodore Roberts
played Moses, Charles de Roche appeared as Rameses, and Estelle

431

Taylor as Miriam. The cast of the modern story was headed by Richard Dix, Rod La Rocque and Leatrice Joy.

FAMOUS PLAYERS–LASKY CORP./PARAMOUNT

Production & direction—
  Cecil B. DeMille
*Screenplay (adapted from Book
  of Exodus & a modern story
  by Miss Macpherson)—*
  Jeanie Macpherson
*Photography—*Bert Glennon

*Assistants—*Edward S. Curtis,
  J. Peverell Marley, Fred
  Westerberg, Archibald J.
  Stout & Donald Biddle
  Keyes
Color photography—
  Ray Rennahan
*Editing—*Anne Bauchens

PLAYERS: Theodore Roberts, Charles de Roche, Estelle Taylor, Julia Faye, Terrence Moore, James Neill, Lawson Butt, Richard Dix, Rod La Rocque, Leatrice Joy, Edythe Chapman

TEN COMMANDMENTS, THE   U.S.A. (1956)
DeMille's remake (at 3 hours 41 minutes his longest film) concentrates this time entirely on the life of Moses. The spectacular highlights once again include the Exodus from Egypt and the crossing of the Red Sea. The early sequences dealing with the building of the Pyramids also are well handled. A sprawling giant of a movie, let down by a banal script and some appalling casting—Anne Baxter (Nefretiri), John Derek (Joshua), Edward G. Robinson (Dathan) and Yvonne De Carlo (Sephora). Only Charlton Heston as Moses and Yul Brynner as Rameses give their parts stature.

PARAMOUNT PICTURES INC.

Production & direction—
  Cecil B. DeMille
*Photography—(Technicolor/
  VistaVision)—*Loyal Griggs
Additional photography—
  J. Peverell Marley,
  John Warren, Wallace Kelley
*Art direction—*Hal Pereira,
  Walter Tyler & Albert Nozaki
*Music—*Elmer Bernstein
*Editing—*Anne Bauchens

*Screenplay (from Dorothy Clarke
  Wilson's novel* Prince of Egypt,
  Rev. J. H. Ingraham's novel
  Pillar of Fire *and Rev. G. E.
  Southon's* On Eagle's Wings,
  *in accordance with the ancient
  texts of Josephus, Eusebius,
  Philo,* The Midrash, *& The
  Holy Scriptures)—*Aeneas
  MacKenzie, Jesse L. Lasky, Jr.,
  Jack Gariss & Fredric M. Frank

PLAYERS: Charlton Heston, Yul Brynner, Anne Baxter, Edward G. Robinson, Yvonne De Carlo, Debra Paget, John Derek, Sir Cedric Hardwicke, Nina Foch, Vincent Price, John Carradine

TERESA   U.S.A. (1951)
Little-known film about the problems facing a young GI when he
brings home to his New York family and his overly possessive mother
the Italian peasant girl he has married during his war service in
Europe. Not one of Zinnemann's major works but with some impressive
scenes, particularly those showing American troops in combat in Italy
and those depicting the misery and poverty of life in an overcrowded
New York tenement building. John Ericson plays the GI, Pier Angeli is
his bride, and Patricia Collinge his mother.

METRO–GOLDWYN–MAYER

Production–Arthur M. Loew   Photography–William J. Miller
Direction–Fred Zinnemann   Art direction–Leo Kerz
Screenplay (from story by Alfred Music–Louis Applebaum
  Hayes & Stewart Stern)–   Editing–Frank Sullivan
  Stewart Stern

PLAYERS: Pier Angeli, John Ericson, Patricia Collinge, Richard Bishop,
Peggy Ann Garner, Ralph Meeker, Bill Mauldin, Rod Steiger

TERMINUS   Gt. Britain (1961)
A 35-minute documentary about a day in the life of London's Waterloo
Station. Excellently done and containing some amusing concealed-
camera observations of people in the rush hour, studying timetables,
searching for lost property, etc., although the scene that remains longest in the memory—a little boy alone in the station crying desperately
for his parents—is obviously stage managed. Directed by John Schlesinger later of Darling and Midnight Cowboy fame.

A BRITISH TRANSPORT COMMISSION FILM

Production–Edgar Anstey   Photography–Ken Phipps
Script & direction–   Music–Ron Grainer
  John Schlesinger   Editing–Hugh Raggett

THEM!   U.S.A. (1954)
Superior science-fiction thriller about giant 15-ft. ants which come out
of the New Mexico desert (where atomic tests have been taking place)
and create havoc before meeting their doom in the sewers of Los
Angeles. Efficiently directed and notable both for its opening 30 minutes which contain considerable tension, and also, more surprisingly,
for the appearance of the ants themselves which belong with the most
effective monsters ever created in a Hollywood studio. Ranks with

Invasion of the Body Snatchers and *War of the Worlds* as one of the best science-fiction movies of the 1950's.

WARNER BROS.

Direction—Gordon Douglas
Screenplay (*from story by*
  George Worthing Yates)—
  Ted Sherdeman

Photography—Sid Hickox
Music—Bronislau Kaper
Art direction—Stanley Fleischer
Editing—Thomas Reilly

PLAYERS: James Whitmore, Edmund Gwenn, Joan Weldon, James Arness, Onslow Stevens, Sandy Descher, Mary Ann Hokanson, Chris Drake

THÉRÈSE DESQUEYROUX   France (1962)

Flashback examination by Georges Franju of the spiritual dilemma of a young French wife who finds herself suffocating from boredom and unable to realize her submerged personality in her bourgeois husband's provincial society. A melancholy, deeply depressing film shot against the pine trees and marshes of the desolate Landes district in south-western France. Adapted by François Mauriac, his son Claude, and Franju from the former's celebrated novel and beautifully played by Emmanuèle Riva (best actress, Venice, 1962) as the wife and Philippe Noiret as her husband.

FILMEL

Direction—Georges Franju
Screenplay—François Mauriac,
  Claude Mauriac & Franju
Photography—Christian Matras

Art direction—Jacques Chalvet
Music—Maurice Jarre
Editing—Gilbert Natot

PLAYERS: Emmanuèle Riva, Philippe Noiret, Edith Scob, Sami Frey, Jeanne Perez, Lucien Nat

THEY LIVE BY NIGHT   U.S.A. (1947)

A boy criminal (Farley Granger), on the run with a couple of hardened convicts, makes a futile attempt to live down his past and start a new life with the young girl (Cathy O'Donnell) who shelters him from the police. A small-scale, deeply felt movie that captures with infinite skill all the tragedy and hopelessness of a doomed love affair in a hostile society. Nicholas Ray's first movie, expertly played by the then unknown principals and by Howard da Silva (a fine cameo of a one-eyed killer) and Jay C. Flippen as a pair of jailbreakers.

RKO RADIO (A DORE SCHARY PRESENTATION)

Production—John Houseman   *Direction*—Nicholas Ray

Screenplay *(from adaptation by Nicholas Ray of novel* Thieves Like Us *by Edward Anderson)* Charles Schnee
Photography—George E. Diskant

Art direction—Albert S. D'Agostino & Al Herman
Music—Leigh Harline
Editing—Sherman Todd

PLAYERS: Cathy O'Donnell, Farley Granger, Howard Da Silva, Jay C. Flippen, Helen Craig, Will Wright

THEY SHOOT HORSES, DON'T THEY?   U.S.A. (1969)

A disturbing look at the hopes, fears and disillusionments of some of the participants in one of the famous dance marathons of the depression years. Not of the stature of Ford's classic *The Grapes of Wrath,* the most heartrending film ever made about the misery of the thirties, but still one of the more interesting American movies of recent years and the most ambitious work to date of Sydney Pollack, a director whose previous films include *This Property Is Condemned, The Scalphunters* and *Castle Keep.* Jane Fonda as a Hollywood hopeful and Red Buttons as an aging sailor lead those contesting for the $1,500 prize and there is an Oscar-winning performance from Gig Young (best supporting actor, 1969) as the master of ceremonies.

PALOMAR PICTURES

Production—Irwin Winkler, Robert Chartoff
Direction—Sydney Pollack
Screenplay (based on novel by Horace McCoy)—James Poe, Robert E. Thompson

Photography (DeLuxecolor/ Panavision)—Philip H. Lathrop
Production design— Harry Horner
Music—John Green
Editing—Fredric Steinkamp

PLAYERS: Jane Fonda, Michael Sarrazin, Susannah York, Gig Young, Red Buttons, Bonnie Bedelia, Michael Conrad, Bruce Dern, Al Lewis

THEY WERE EXPENDABLE   U.S.A. (1945)

Considered one of the best American films to come out of World War II, this restrained, documentary-style John Ford picture follows the gallant fight of a squadron of motor torpedo boats in the Philippines during the early days of the war. Robert Montgomery gives one of the best performances of his career as the squadron commander and Joseph August, whose last film for Ford this was, contributed some beautiful camera work. August worked on some 14 films during his 20-year association with Ford, the most memorable being *The Informer* and *Mary*

435

of Scotland. He died in 1947, aged 57, after working on *Portrait of Jennie* for Selznick.

METRO–GOLDWYN–MAYER

Production & direction— John Ford
Associate producer—Cliff Reid
Screenplay (*from book by William L. White*)— Frank W. Wead
Photography—Joseph H. August
Art direction—Cedric Gibbons & Malcolm F. Brown
Music—Herbert Stothart
Editing—Douglas Biggs

PLAYERS: Robert Montgomery, John Wayne, Donna Reed, Jack Holt, Ward Bond, Louis Jean Heydt, Marshall Thompson, Russell Simpson

THEY WON'T FORGET   U.S.A. (1937)

Disturbing melodrama of the deep South with Edward Norris as a Yankee schoolteacher who is convicted and eventually lynched for a murder he did not commit and Claude Rains (his best-ever performance) as an unscrupulous district attorney who sees a chance of gaining political prestige if he secures a conviction. Among the most powerful and uncompromising films about prejudice ever made and easily LeRoy's best film of the thirties. Lana Turner made her debut in the picture as a murdered schoolgirl.

WARNER BROS.

Production & direction— Mervyn LeRoy
Photography—Arthur Edeson
Art direction—Robert Haas
Music—Adolph Deutsch
Screenplay (*from novel* Death in the Deep South *by Ward Greene*)—Robert Rossen & Aben Kandel
Editing—Thomas Richards

PLAYERS: Claude Rains, Gloria Dickson, Edward Norris, Otto Kruger, Lana Turner, Elisha Cook, Jr., Cy Kendall, Allyn Joslyn

THIEF, THE   U.S.A. (1952)

A suspenseful, uncomplicated spy thriller told completely without dialogue about a nuclear physicist (Ray Milland) who microfilms top-secret documents for a foreign spy ring. The year's most unusual movie, dominated inevitably by its camera work and sound effects, with a thrilling police chase on the roof of the Empire State Building for a climax.

UNITED ARTISTS

Production—Clarence Greene
Direction—Russell Rouse
Screenplay—Clarence Greene, Russell Rouse

Photography—Sam Leavitt   *Music*—Herschel Burke Gilbert
Production design—   *Editing*—Chester Shaeffer
  Joseph St. Amand
PLAYERS: Ray Milland, Martin Gabel, Rita Gam, Harry Bronson, John
McKutcheon, Rita Vale, Rex O'Malley, Joe Conlin

THING FROM ANOTHER WORLD, THE   U.S.A. (1951)
A group of American airmen and scientists versus an 8-ft. "intellectual
carrot" which has arrived from outer space, complete with flying
saucer, in the frozen wastes of the North Pole. One of the earliest in
the postwar science-fiction cycle and, like most films in this genre, at
its best in the early tension-building sequences before the monster is
seen. An eerie Tiomkin score, excellent Harlan snowscapes, and crisp
direction from Christian Nyby, Hawks' editor on *To Have and Have
Not, The Big Sleep, Red River* and *The Big Sky*.
                WINCHESTER PRODUCTIONS/RKO RADIO
Production—Howard Hawks   *Photography*—Russell Harlan
Direction—Christian Nyby   *Art direction*—
*Screenplay (from story "Who   Albert S. D'Agostino
  Goes There" by John W.*   *Music*—Dimitri Tiomkin
  Campbell, Jr.)—   *Editing*—Roland Cross
  Charles Lederer
PLAYERS: Margaret Sheridan, Kenneth Tobey, Robert Cornthwaite,
Douglas Spencer, James Young, Dewey Martin, Robert Nichols, Wil-
liam Self, Eduard Franz, Sally Creighton, James Arness (The Thing)

THINGS TO COME   Gt. Britain (1936)
H. G. Wells' story of the world from the devastating World War of
1940 to the mechanized Utopia of 2035. Ambitiously produced, with
some magnificent Vincent Korda sets, but let down badly by Wells'
own labored script and some atrocious acting. Like most of Korda's
productions of the thirties the film has worn badly, although some of
the spectacle still works. Sir Arthur Bliss' memorable score remains as
fresh as ever.
                        LONDON FILMS
Production—Alexander Korda   *Photography*—Georges Périnal
Direction—   *Art direction*—Vincent Korda
  William Cameron Menzies   *Music*—Sir Arthur Bliss
Screenplay (from his novel)—   *Editing*—Charles Crichton,
  H. G. Wells   Francis Lyon

437

PLAYERS: Raymond Massey, Edward Chapman, Ralph Richardson, Margaretta Scott, Cedric Hardwicke, Maurice Braddell, Sophie Stewart, Derrick de Marney, Ann Todd

THIRD MAN, THE   Gt. Britain (1949)
Based on a Graham Greene original this classic thriller centers on the tracking down of a penicillin racketeer in the ruins of postwar Vienna. Its basic story line is simple, but the buildup is fascinatingly complex. Director Carol Reed (for his evocation of the mood of a shattered, once-proud city) and Robert Krasker (for his location photography) helped make it one of the most stylish and satisfying of all British postwar films. Orson Welles appears as the racketeer Harry Lime, Valli as his Czech mistress, and Joseph Cotten as the American writer who assists military police officer Trevor Howard in tracking him down. The most celebrated sequences are the meeting between Welles and Cotten on the big wheel in a deserted fairground and the climactic chase through the sewers. The haunting zither music by Anton Karas became famous the world over.

CAROL REED/LONDON FILMS (ALEXANDER KORDA)

Direction—Carol Reed   *Art direction*—Vincent Korda
Screenplay—Graham Greene   *Music*—Anton Karas
Photography—Robert Krasker   *Editing*—Oswald Hafenrichter
PLAYERS: Orson Welles, Joseph Cotten, Valli, Trevor Howard, Bernard Lee, Wilfrid Hyde White

THIRTY-NINE STEPS, THE   Gt. Britain (1935)
One of Hitchcock's earliest chase films based loosely on John Buchan's novel and featuring Robert Donat as Richard Hannay who becomes involved in a murder and is pursued across Scotland by both the police and a dangerous spy ring. Full of last-minute escapes (the flight from a train on the Forth Bridge is especially exciting) and played in exactly the right key by Robert Donat and Madeleine Carroll who share an amusing scene when they are forced to spend the night together handcuffed by the wrist.

GAUMONT BRITISH

Production—Michael Balcon   *Photography*—Bernard Knowles
Direction—Alfred Hitchcock   *Art direction*—Otto Werndorff,
Screenplay & adaptation—   Albert Jullion
   Charles Bennett, Alma Reville   *Music*—Louis Levy
Additional dialogue—Ian Hay   *Editing*—Derek N. Twist

438

PLAYERS: Robert Donat, Madeleine Carroll, Lucie Mannheim, Godfrey Tearle, Peggy Ashcroft, John Laurie, Helen Haye, Frank Cellier, Wylie Watson

THIS GUN FOR HIRE U.S.A. (1942)

Alan Ladd in his first major role as an unsmiling professional killer who becomes involved with a blond cabaret girl (Veronica Lake) and also with a pair of fifth columnists (Laird Cregar and Tully Marshall) selling poison gas formulas to the Japanese. A short, unpretentious little thriller scripted by two of Hollywood's most accomplished scriptwriters from the novel by Graham Greene. Excellent black-and-white camera work by John Seitz, especially in the railway yard sequences.

PARAMOUNT

Production—Richard Blumenthal   Screenplay—Albert Maltz &
Direction—Frank Tuttle   W. R. Burnett
Photography—John Seitz   Editing—Archie Marshek
PLAYERS: Veronica Lake, Alan Ladd, Robert Preston, Laird Cregar, Tully Marshall, Marc Lawrence, Olin Howlin, Roger Imhof, Pamela Blake, Frank Ferguson, Victor Kilian

THIS HAPPY BREED Gt. Britain (1944)

David Lean's version of Noel Coward's play about an ordinary suburban family living in a house in Clapham between the wars. A nostalgic, well-written saga of family life which overcomes the limitations of its setting (the action takes place most entirely within the house) by some imaginative and mobile camera work. By far the best British film of 1944, photographed in subdued Technicolor and beautifully played by the entire cast, particularly Celia Johnson and Robert Newton as the parents.

TWO CITIES—CINEGUILD

Production—Noel Coward   Photography (Technicolor)—
Direction—David Lean   Ronald Neame
Associate producer—   Art direction—C. P. Norman
   Anthony Havelock-Allan   Music direction—
Screenplay (based on his stage   Muir Mathieson
   play)—Noel Coward   Editing—Jack Harris
PLAYERS: Robert Newton, Celia Johnson, John Mills, Kay Walsh, Stanley Holloway, Amy Veness, Alison Leggatt, Eileen Erskine, John Blythe, Guy Veryney

THIS SPORTING LIFE   Gt. Britain (1963)

This impressive addition to Britain's "new realism" movies of the
1960's hinges on a rebellious ex-miner turned rugby footballer (Richard
Harris) and his tortured relations with the widow (Rachel Roberts)
in whose house he lodges. A perceptive, often complex study of the
contemporary anti-hero, more ambitious than most films of its kind
and observing the Rugby League scene and the game itself with a
shrewd eye. Excellent supporting cameos from Alan Badel as a small-
town tycoon and William Hartnell as an old talent scout. The first
feature of Lindsay Anderson.

    INDEPENDENT ARTISTS/A JULIAN WINTLE–LESLIE PARKYN PRODUCTION

Production–Karel Reisz   *Photography*–Denys Coop
Direction–Lindsay Anderson   *Art direction*–Alan Withy
Screenplay (from his own   *Music*–Roberto Gerhard
    novel)–David Storey   *Editing*–Peter Taylor

PLAYERS: Richard Harris, Rachel Roberts, Alan Badel, William Hartnell, Colin Blakely, Vanda Godsell, Anne Cunningham, Jack Watson,
Arthur Lowe

THREE AGES, THE   U.S.A. (1923)

An uneven but witty parody of *Intolerance* in which Buster Keaton
relates, in parallel action, the triumphs and tragedies of love in the
Stone Age, Imperial Rome, and the 1920's. Despite its unevenness the
film contains some highly inventive slapstick moments—Keaton encountering a troglodyte (Wallace Beery), a giant cavewoman (Blanche
Payson) and, in the Rome sequence, winning a chariot race with the
aid of sleigh runners. Historically important as the first feature that
Keaton had a hand in directing.

    BUSTER KEATON/JOSEPH M. SCHENCK PRODUCTIONS/METRO PICTURES

Production–Joseph M. Schenck   *Photography*–William McGann,
Direction–Buster Keaton,   Elgin Lessley
    Eddie Cline   *Technical direction*–
Screenplay–Clyde Bruckman,   Fred Gabourie
    Jean Havez, Joseph Mitchell

PLAYERS: Buster Keaton, Wallace Beery, Margaret Leahy, Joe Roberts,
Lilian Lawrence, Horace Morgan, Oliver Hardy

THREEPENNY OPERA, THE (Die Dreigroschenoper)
                                                      Germany (1931)

Pabst's second sound film: a curious musical fantasy of crime and sex in the Soho underworld of the 1890's. Notable Andreiev sets of the Thames-side docks and Soho slums and stunning low-key photography by Fritz Arno Wagner who with this film demonstrated once again that he was one of the most talented cameramen in world cinema.

DEUTSCH–FIRST NATIONAL

Direction–G. W. Pabst
Screenplay (*from the play*
  by Bertolt Brecht and Kurt
  Weill (*music*), *derived from*
  The Beggar's Opera *by*

John Gay)–Leo Lania,
  Ladislaus Vajda, Béla Balázs
Photography–Fritz Arno Wagner
Art direction–André Andreiev
Music–Kurt Weill

PLAYERS: Rudolph Forster, Carola Neher, Reinhold Schünzel, Fritz Rasp, Valeska Gert, Lotte Lenya, Hermann Thimig, Ernst Busch

3:10 TO YUMA   U.S.A. (1957)

Delmer Daves' answer to *High Noon:* a tense, "chamber" Western centering on the psychological conflict between two men, one a renegade outlaw (Glenn Ford) who has been captured by the law, the other an honest but poor rancher (Van Heflin) who, because he needs the reward money, agrees to escort the outlaw to Contention City and put him on the train that will take him to the jail in Yuma. Taut, economical, it is among the best examples of the small-scale Western.

COLUMBIA

Production–David Heilweil
Direction–Delmer Daves
Screenplay (*based on story*
  by Elmore Leonard)–
  Halsted Welles

Photography–
  Charles Lawton, Jr.
Art direction–Frank Hotaling
Music–George Duning
Editing–Al Clark

PLAYERS: Glenn Ford, Van Heflin, Felicia Farr, Leora Dana, Henry Jones, Richard Jaeckel, Robert Emhardt, Sheridan Comerate

THRONE OF BLOOD   Japan (1957)

Japanese version of *Macbeth* transferred by Akira Kurosawa from Scotland to 16th-century Japan and featuring Toshiro Mifune (Kurosawa's star of *Rashomon* and *Seven Samurai*) as warlord Macbeth and Isuzo Yamada as his ambitious wife. A moody, bleak, brilliantly staged film with an extraordinary climax when Mifune is pinned to the wall by arrows and shot to death by his own archers. The picture was an expensive production—not the least contributory factor to its overall cost being the full-scale replica of a Japanese castle built by Kurosawa on the slopes of Mount Fuji.

441

Through a Glass Darkly

TOHO

Direction—Akira Kurosawa   Shinobu Hashimoto &
Screenplay (from play Macbeth   Akira Kurosawa
  by William Shakespeare)—   *Photography*—Asaichi Nakai
  Hideo Oguni, Ryuzo Kikushima,   *Music*—Masaru Sato
PLAYERS: Toshiro Mifune, Isuzu Yamada, Takashi Shimura, Minoru
Chiaki

THROUGH A GLASS DARKLY (Såsom i en Spegel)

Sweden (1961)

Ingmar Bergman raises once again his questions about the significance
of God and the meaning of life as he studies a family of four—a dissatisfied novelist, his adolescent son, his daughter recently released
from hospital, and her young doctor husband—holidaying in a family
house on a desolate island in the Baltic. Intense, complex, deeply
depressing but without question one of Bergman's most important
works. Some chillingly bleak landscapes by Sven Nykvist and brilliant

442

performances as always from the Bergman repertory company, particularly Gunnar Björnstrand as the novelist father and Harriet Andersson as his schizophrenic daughter who declines into madness after believing that God has revealed himself to her.

SVENSK FILMINDUSTRI

Direction & screenplay—	*Music—*Bach (Suite No. 2 in
Ingmar Bergman	D Major for violoncello)
*Photography—*Sven Nykvist	*Editing—*Ulla Ryghe
*Art direction—*P. A. Lundgren	

PLAYERS: Harriet Andersson, Max von Sydow, Gunnar Björnstrand, Lars Passgård

TILLIE'S PUNCTURED ROMANCE   U.S.A. (1914)

The longest (6-reels) and best-known of Chaplin's 35 comedies for Keystone. Marie Dressler repeats her stage performance as the innocent country girl who is swindled out of her money by city slicker Charlie Chaplin complete with genuine villainous mustache. The film took 14 weeks to shoot and was the first successful feature comedy. It made Chaplin a star even though he actually supported Miss Dressler in the picture.

A KEYSTONE FEATURE

*Direction—*Mack Sennett	*Edgar Smith, music by*
Adaptation (from Tillie's	*A. Baldwin Sloane)—*
Nightmare, *a musical comedy*	Hampton Del Ruth
with book and lyrics by	

PLAYERS: Charles Chaplin, Marie Dressler, Mabel Normand, Phyllis Allen, Billie Bennett, Charles Bennett, Joe Bordeaux, Charles Chase

TIME OUT OF WAR   U.S.A. (1954)

Poetic, 20-minute film about three tired Civil War soldiers (two Yankees and one Southerner) who, one hot afternoon, call a truce for an hour and smoke, fish and drink together. One of the cinema's strongest pleas against the horror and brutality of war and one of the few really successful short films of the fifties.

SANDERS BROS. PRODS.

*Direction—*Denis Sanders	*Photography—*Terry Sanders
Script (adapted from story	*Assistant director—*
"Pickets" by Robert W.	Rita Montgomery
*Chambers)—*Denis Sanders	*Music—*Frank Hamilton

PLAYERS: Barry Atwater, Robert Sherry, Alan Cohen

TIME WITHOUT PITY
Gt. Britain (1957)

Hysterical race-against-time thriller with alcoholic (Michael Redgrave) trying desperately to save his son from the condemned cell by attempting to prove that megalomaniac car tycoon (Leo McKern) is the real killer. Extravagant and overacted, but Losey began to get into stride with this one. The script's frequent attacks on the squalid ritual of capital punishment make it an interesting little work.

HARLEQUIN

Executive producer—Leon Clore
Producers—John Arnold &
  Anthony Simmons
Direction—Joseph Losey
Photography—Freddie Francis
Art direction—Bernard Sarron
Screenplay (based on play
  Someone Waiting by Emlyn
  Williams)—Ben Barzman
Music—Tristram Cary
Editing—Alan Osbiston

PLAYERS: Michael Redgrave, Ann Todd, Leo McKern, Peter Cushing, Alec McCowen, Renee Houston, Paul Daneman, Lois Maxwell

TIREZ SUR LE PIANISTE
France (1960)

Engaging spoof of the run-of-the-mill Hollywood crime movie, a tragicomedy about a once-famous concert pianist (Charles Aznavour) who takes refuge from his past by playing in a Paris bistro where he becomes enmeshed in the personal lives of his brothers and the gangster world that surrounds them. Truffaut's inventive use of the mobile camera, his employment of cinematic tricks, and his bold and abrupt changes of mood (farce one minute, tragedy the next) make the film one of the most enjoyable of the New Wave productions even though it is somewhat overshadowed by the more famous films (Les Quatre Cents Coups, Jules et Jim) of his early career.

FILMS DE LA PLEIADE

Direction—François Truffaut
Screenplay (from novel
  Down There by David
  Goodis)—François Truffaut
  & Marcel Moussy
Photography—Raoul Coutard
Music—Georges Delerue
Editing—Claudine Bouche &
  Cecile Decugis

PLAYERS: Charles Aznavour, Marie Dubois, Nicole Berger, Michèle Mercier, Alex Joffé, Albert Rémy

TO BE OR NOT TO BE
U.S.A. (1942)

Uneven but often brilliant wartime comedy about a group of touring actors mixed up in espionage in Occupied Warsaw. It created something of a sensation because it dared to poke fun at the Nazi regime. Unfairly criticized at the time, it now appears as one of the brightest of all Lubitsch's later works. Jack Benny and Carole Lombard (her last film before she was killed in a plane crash) head the cast and there is admirable support from Sig Rumann as a Gestapo chief.

UNITED ARTISTS

Production & direction—
Ernst Lubitsch
Screenplay (from story by
Ernst Lubitsch & Melchior
*Lengyel)—*Edwin Justus Mayer

*Photography—*Rudolph Mate
*Music—*Werner Heymann
Production design—
Vincent Korda
*Editing—*Dorothy Spencer

PLAYERS: Carole Lombard, Jack Benny, Robert Stack, Sig Rumann, Felix Bressart, Stanley Ridges

TO CATCH A THIEF   U.S.A. (1955)
Ex-jewel thief Cary Grant, suspected by the police of committing a series of new robberies, comes out of retirement in order to catch the impostor who is copying his methods. A lightweight Hitchcock vehicle set against lush Riviera backgrounds and photographed in Academy Award-winning style by Robert Burks (best color photography, 1955). Some typically debonair playing by Grant and a very sexy performance by Grace Kelly (her last film for Hitchcock) as his ice-cool British girlfriend.

PARAMOUNT

Production & direction—
Alfred Hitchcock
Screenplay (from novel by
David Dodge)—
John Michael Hayes

Photography (Technicolor)—
Robert Burks
*Art direction—*Hal Pereira,
J. McMillan Johnson
*Music—*Lyn Murray
*Editing—*George Tomasini

PLAYERS: Cary Grant, Grace Kelly, Charles Vanel, Jessie Royce Landis, Brigitte Auber, Rene Blancard, John Williams, Georgette Anys, Roland Lesaffre, Jean Hebey

TO HAVE AND HAVE NOT   U.S.A. (1945)
Tough, cynical expatriate Harry Morgan (Humphrey Bogart), based in Martinique where he hires out his cabin cruiser for fishing trips, becomes committed once more when he joins forces with the underground in the fight against Vichy. A very loose and, for a Hawks film, surprisingly unsatisfactory version of Hemingway's novel which was

subsequently more efficiently filmed by Michael Curtiz as *The Breaking Point* (1950). The compensations, however, are in the playing, particularly of Bogart and his slinky girlfriend Lauren Bacall, this being the first time they had played together.

WARNER BROS.–FIRST NATIONAL

Production & direction–
  Howard Hawks
Screenplay–Jules Furtherman &
  William Faulkner

Photography–Sid Hickox
Art direction–Charles Novi
Music–Franz Waxman
Editing–Christian Nyby

PLAYERS: Humphrey Bogart, Walter Brennan, Lauren Bacall, Dolores Moran, Hoagy Carmichael, Walter Molnar, Sheldon Leonard, Marcel Dalio

TOKYO OLYMPIAD   Japan (1965)

Japanese documentary of the 1964 Olympic Games shot by 164 cameramen and edited down eventually from 70 hours of film to 130 minutes' running time. Ichikawa contrasts sound with silence to great effect and frequently uses close-ups, camera freezes and slow motion to emphasize the strain that goes into an event not only during the event itself but also in the agonizing minutes that precede it. The 100 meters in slow motion, the restlessness of a Soviet shot putter, and the last miles of the marathon stand out as great moments from a great film.

ORGANIZING COMMITTEE OF THE GAMES OF THE 18TH OLYMPIAD/TOHO
(SUKETARU TAGUCHI)

Direction–Kon Ichikawa
Script–Natto Wada,
  Yoshio Shirasaka,
  Shuntaro Tanikawa,
  Kon Ichikawa
Art direction–Yusaka Kamekura

Photography (Eastmancolor)–
  Shigeo Hayashida,
  Kazuo Miyagawa,
  Juichi Nagano,
  Kinji Nakamura,
  Tadashi Tanaka
Music–Toshiro Mayuzumi

TOL'ABLE DAVID   U.S.A. (1921)

Early silent classic of American rural life with Richard Barthelmess in perhaps the best role of his distinguished career as the youngest son of a mountain family who takes over the responsibilities of the household when his elder brother is crippled and his father murdered by a gang of outlaws. A leisurely tale simply and poetically told by Henry King with an emphasis on the beauty of the surrounding countryside (the exteriors were shot on locations near his own home) and on the way of life of the community. The film established King as a director of the front rank and proved to be one of the biggest box-office successes of the early 1920's. Joseph Hergesheimer's story had been originally owned by D. W. Griffith, but Barthelmess purchased the property and together with director King formed Inspiration Pictures.

FIRST NATIONAL/INSPIRATION PICTURES
Direction—Henry King   *Screenplay (from novel by*
Photography—Henry Cronjager   *Joseph Hergesheimer)*—
                                       Edmund Goulding
PLAYERS: Richard Barthelmess, Ernest Torrence, Gladys Hulette, Warner Richmond, Edmund Gurney, Lawrence Eddinger, Forrest Robinson, Walter P. Lewis

TOM JONES   Gt. Britain (1963)
Boisterous adaptation of Henry Fielding's 18th-century classic with Albert Finney as the philandering illegitimate hero of the title and Diane Cilento, Susannah York and Joan Greenwood as some of the women he loves and leaves during his amorous escapades in the West Country and London. For most of the time the film concentrates on the bawdier aspects of the period, amusingly epitomized by the bottom-pinching squire (Hugh Griffith), although occasionally the cruelty is also stressed as in the horrifyingly realistic stag-hunt sequence. Most memorable scene: the over-dinner seduction of Tom by Joyce Redmond as a lady of easy virtue at a wayside inn.

WOODFALL PRODUCTION/UNITED ARTISTS
Production & direction—   *Photography (Eastmancolor)*—
  Tony Richardson   Walter Lassally
Screenplay—John Osborne   *Music*—John Addison
Art direction—Ted Marshall   *Editing*—Antony Gibbs
PLAYERS: Albert Finney, Hugh Griffith, Susannah York, Diane Cilento, Dame Edith Evans, Joan Greenwood, Joyce Redmond, George Devine

TONI   France (1934)
Realistic picture about tragic love of an Italian immigrant for French village girl. One of Renoir's most impressive early works, shot without sets or professional actors in a small community near Marseilles, and now historically important as one of the first influences on the Italian neo-realism movement of the forties.

FILMS D'AUJOURD'HUI (MARCEL PAGNOL)
Direction—Jean Renoir   *Photography*—Claude Renoir

447

Screenplay (from an idea by
  J. Levert)—Jean Renoir,
  Carl Einstein
Art direction—Bourelly
PLAYERS: Charles Blavette, Célia Montalvan, Jenny Hélia, Edouard Delmont, Andrex, Max Dalban

Music—Eugène Bozza
Editing—Marguerite Renoir,
  Suzanne de Troeye

TOP HAT   U.S.A. (1935)

Fred Astaire falling in love once more with redheaded Ginger Rogers in the most famous and tuneful of all their prewar musicals. Familiar story, magnificent Berlin score and superb choreography by Hermes Pan. Top numbers: "Cheek to Cheek," "Top Hat, White Tie and Tails," "Isn't This a Lovely Day" (danced by Astaire and Rogers in a deserted bandstand) and the climactic "Piccolino" production number.

RKO RADIO

Production—Pandro S. Berman
Direction—Mark Sandrich
Screenplay (from story by
  Dwight Taylor)—Dwight
  Taylor & Allan Scott

Photography—David Abel
Music & lyrics—Irving Berlin
Dance direction—Hermes Pan
Editing—William Hamilton

PLAYERS: Fred Astaire, Ginger Rogers, Edward Everett Horton, Helen Broderick, Erik Rhodes, Eric Blore

TOUCH OF EVIL   U.S.A. (1958)

Baroque thriller in which a corrupt police chief (Welles), a narcotics investigator (Charlton Heston), and an underworld boss (Akim Tamiroff) become caught up in murder in a small town on the Mexican border. Despite a highly complex and almost unfathomable plot, this is a visually brilliant film, with Welles in exceptional form as the crooked Hank Quinlan and Marlene Dietrich contributing a nostalgic few moments as a cigar-smoking proprietress of a broken-down Mexican brothel. The movie reunited Welles with cameraman Russell Metty who had previously worked on *The Stranger* some twelve years earlier.

UNIVERSAL

Production—Albert Zugsmith
Direction—Orson Welles
Screenplay (from novel Badge
  of Evil *by Walt Masterson)*—
  Orson Welles
Photography—Russell Metty

Art direction—
  Alexander Golitzen &
  Robert Clatworthy
Music—Henry Mancini
Editing—Virgil Vogel &
  Aaron Stell

PLAYERS: Orson Welles, Charlton Heston, Janet Leigh, Joseph Calleia, Akim Tamiroff, Joanna Moore, Ray Collins, Marlene Dietrich

TOWED IN A HOLE U.S.A. (1933)
Laurel and Hardy two-reeler in which the ever-optimistic pair appear as a couple of hard-up fishmongers who decide to go into the boating business. The entire film revolves around the efforts of Stan and Ollie to fix up and paint an old boat. Little dialogue is used and most of the humor springs from such slapstick situations as the one in which Stan saws methodically away at the boat's mast while Ollie, perched somewhat perilously, paints the top. Despite its predictability the film is one of the funniest of the pair's later shorts and is not dissimilar to *Busy Bodies* released later the same year.
HAL ROACH/METRO–GOLDWYN–MAYER

Direction—George Marshall
PLAYERS: Stan Laurel and Oliver Hardy, Billy Gilbert

TRAIL OF THE LONESOME PINE U.S.A. (1936)
Well-made Western-style drama about a feud between two Kentucky mountain families. Not Henry Hathaway's best film by any means, but historically significant as the first full-length outdoor picture to be photographed in Technicolor. Released by Paramount a year after the first all-Technicolor feature *Becky Sharp*.
PARAMOUNT

Production—Walter Wanger
Direction—Henry Hathaway
Screenplay (from novel by John Fox, Jr.)—
Grover Jones
Adaptation—Harvey Thew &
Horace McCoy

Photography (Technicolor)—
Robert C. Bruce,
W. Howard Greene
Art direction—
Alexander Toluboff
Music direction—Boris Morros
Editing—Robert Bischoff

PLAYERS: Sylvia Sidney, Henry Fonda, Fred MacMurray, Fred Stone, Nigel Bruce, Beulah Bondi

TRAIN, THE U.S.A. (1964)
The conflict between a German colonel (Paul Scofield) who, during the last days of the Nazi occupation of France, attempts to smuggle a train-load of priceless paintings into Germany and Resistance leader (Burt Lancaster) who is instructed to use all means at his disposal to stop him. The value placed upon art as against that on human life is thoroughly explored by John Frankenheimer and his scriptwriters in a

movie that is perhaps the best of all contemporary train films and which is climaxed by a spectacular three-train smashup. Veteran actor Michel Simon appears briefly as an aged French locomotive engineer.

UNITED ARTISTS–ARIANE–DEAR FILMS

Production–Jules Bricken
Direction–John Frankenheimer
Photography–Jean Tournier,
  Walter Wottitz
Production design–Willy Holt
Music–Maurice Jarre

Screenplay (*based on novel*
  Le Front de l'Art *by Rose*
  Valland)–Franklin Coen,
  Frank Davis, Walter Bernstein
Editing–David Bretherton,
  Gabriel Rongier

PLAYERS: Burt Lancaster, Paul Scofield, Jeanne Moreau, Michel Simon, Suzanne Flon, Charles Millot, Albert Rémy, Jacques Marin

TRAMP, TRAMP, TRAMP   U.S.A. (1926)

Harry Langdon's first feature-length (62 minutes) comedy, part scripted though not (as is sometimes thought) directed by Frank Capra, about the adventures of a young man (Langdon) when he attempts to win a transcontinental walking race organized by a wealthy shoe manufacturer known as "the sole of the nation." Joan Crawford, in an early role, appears as Langdon's leading lady and Tom Murray is featured as a tough walking champion.

HARRY LANGDON CORPORATION/FIRST NATIONAL

Direction–Harry Edwards
Screenplay–Frank Capra,
  Tim Whelan, Hal Conklin,

  J. Frank Holliday,
  Gerald Duffy & Murry Roth
Photography–Elgin Lessley

PLAYERS: Harry Langdon, Joan Crawford, Tom Murray, Edward Davis, Alec B. Francis, Carlton Griffith

TREASURE ISLAND   U.S.A. (1934)

Sprightly Hollywood version of Robert Louis Stevenson's classic about pirates and buried treasure. Jackie Cooper's too Americanized Jim Hawkins is compensated for by Lionel Barrymore's vastly enjoyable Billy Bones and Wallace Beery's full-blooded, slightly sentimental Long John Silver. A well-mounted film, remarkably faithful to the original novel, ably directed by Victor Fleming.

METRO-GOLDWYN–MAYER

Direction–Victor Fleming
Screenplay–John Lee Mahin
Photography–Ray June, Clyde
  DeVinna, Harold Rosson

Art direction–Cedric Gibbons,
  Merrill Pye, Edwin B. Willis
Music–Herbert Stothart
Editing–Blanche Sewell

PLAYERS: Wallace Beery, Jackie Cooper, Lionel Barrymore, Otto Kruger, Lewis Stone, Nigel Bruce, Charles "Chic" Sale

TREASURE ISLAND   Gt. Britain (1950)
Disney's more enjoyable remake dominated by Robert Newton's out-rageous eye-rolling portrait of Silver, one of the most entertaining ham performances in screen history. Some nicely observed period detail, good Technicolor photography, and several tongue-in-cheek perform-ances from a talented British supporting cast: Finlay Currie (Billy Bones), John Laurie (Blind Pew), Francis de Wolffe (Black Dog), Geoffrey Keen (Israel Hands). The first of Disney's so-called "live-action" films.

WALT DISNEY

Production—Perce Pearce
Direction—Byron Haskin
Screenplay (from novel by
   Robert Louis Stevenson)—
   Lawrence E. Watkins

Photography (Technicolor)—
   F. A. Young
Production design—
   Thomas Morahan
Music—Clifton Parker
Editing—Alan L. Jaggs

PLAYERS: Robert Newton, Bobby Driscoll, Basil Sydney, Walter Fitz-gerald, Denis O'Dea, Finlay Currie, Ralph Truman, Geoffrey Keen, Geoffrey Wilkinson, John Laurie, Francis de Wolffe

TREASURE OF THE SIERRA MADRE, THE   U.S.A. (1948)
John Huston's first postwar film, a penetrating look at the effects of greed on the characters of three men (Walter Huston, Humphrey Bogart and Tim Holt) as they risk danger both from bandits and from each other while prospecting for gold in the Mexican hills of the Sierra Madre. The film belongs with Huston's most ambitious works and although not so completely successful as either *The Maltese Falcon* or *The Asphalt Jungle* contains several of his finest sequences, e.g. the early scene-setting in 1920 Tampico, the murder of Bogart by bandits and the ironic ending when the gold is scattered unknowingly into the desert. Walter Huston contributes a fine performance as the oldest of the prospectors and Alfonso Bedoya is the very personifica-tion of evil as a Mexican bandit chief named "Gold Hat." Academy Awards went to John Huston for both writing and direction and to Walter Huston as best supporting actor, 1948.

WARNER BROS.—FIRST NATIONAL

A *Trip to the Moon*

Production—Henry Blanke
Direction—John Huston
Screenplay (based on novel by
 B. Traven)—John Huston

Photography—Ted McCord
Art direction—John Hughes
Music—Max Steiner
Editing—Owen Marks

PLAYERS: Humphrey Bogart, Walter Huston, Tim Holt, Bruce Bennett, Barton MacLane, Alfonso Bedoya, A. Soto Rangel, Manuel Donde

TREE GROWS IN BROOKLYN, A   U.S.A. (1945)
Elia Kazan's first film as a director: a slow, sober but beautifully realized account of a young girl growing up with her family in a Brooklyn tenement in the early 1900's. Not in any way indicative of Kazan's later, more ambitious work, but the scenes of family life are tenderly observed and the acting, especially of Dorothy McGuire as the hard-working mother and James Dunn as the drunken irresponsible father, is highly impressive.

TWENTIETH CENTURY–FOX

Production–Louis D. Lighton   Photography–Leon Shamroy
Direction–Elia Kazan   Art direction–Lyle Wheeler
Screenplay (from novel by   Music–Alfred Newman
  Betty Smith)–Tess Slesinger   Editing–Dorothy Spencer
  & Frank Davis
PLAYERS: Dorothy McGuire, Joan Blondell, James Dunn, Lloyd Nolan,
Peggy Ann Garner, Ted Donaldson, James Gleason

TRIP TO THE MOON, A (Le Voyage dans la Lune) France (1902)
Almost certainly the first screen fantasy, this 16-minute French film
is a combination of Jules Verne's *From the Earth to Moon* and H.
G. Wells' *First Man on the Moon*. It consists of 30 scenes showing
the journey of some earthmen (shot by space gun) to the moon, their
landing, encounter with a race of "Selenites" and eventual return to
earth. Considerably longer than most films of its day and costing some
10,000 francs, the picture is perhaps the most imaginative of all the
450 films (approximate) made by Georges Méliès between 1896 and
1908.

Production & direction–   Photography–Lucien Tainguy
  Georges Méliès
PLAYERS: Georges Méliès, dancers from the Theatre du Chetelet, acro-
bats from the Folies Bergeres

TRIUMPH OF THE WILL (Triumph des Willens) Germany (1934)
Leni Riefenstahl's shattering documentary of the 1934 Nuremberg
rallies, commissioned by Hitler and shot with 30 cameras by a crew of
over 100. One of the most impressive propaganda films ever made and
a permanent historical record of the mass hysteria created by the Nazi
machine in Germany during the 1930's. An overwhelming and frightening experience.

WALTER TRAUT, WALTER GROSKOPF
Direction & editing–   Photography–Sepp Allgeier
  Leni Riefenstahl   Assistants–Erna Peters,
In charge of production–   Guzzi & Otto Lantschner,
  Walter Traut, Walter Groskopf   Walter Prager
                                 Music–Herbert Windt

TROUBLE IN PARADISE   U.S.A. (1932)
Herbert Marshall and Miriam Hopkins serving Ernst Lubitsch well as
a couple of charming society crooks who meet up in Venice where they
plan to rob a rich widow (Kay Francis) of her jewelry. Scripted by

Samson Raphaelson who worked regularly with Lubitsch during the thirties and forties, this is considered by many critics to be the most sophisticated and successful of the director's comedies. Said to be Lubitsch's favorite of all his films.

PARAMOUNT

Direction—Ernst Lubitsch
Photography—Victor Milner
Art direction—Hans Dreier
Music—W. Franke Harling

Screenplay (from play The Honest Finder *by Laszlo Aladar, adapted by Grover Jones)*—Samson Raphaelson

PLAYERS: Kay Francis, Herbert Marshall, Miriam Hopkins, Charlie Ruggles, Edward Everett Horton, Robert Greig

TROUBLE WITH HARRY, THE   U.S.A. (1956)

A macabre little Hitchcock comedy about the efforts of a small New England community to dispose of an unwanted corpse. Dry, witty, and leisurely played by a little known cast (one of the major roles was played by the then unknown Shirley MacLaine) and stunningly photographed by Robert Burks whose Technicolor exteriors of Vermont in the fall rank with his best work. One of Hitchcock's most personal films and also one of his rare commercial failures.

PARAMOUNT

Production & direction—
Alfred Hitchcock
Screenplay (from novel by Jack Trevor Story)—
John Michael Hayes

Photography (Technicolor)—
Robert Burks
Art direction—Hal Pereira, John Goodman
Music—Bernard Herrmann
Editing—Alma Macrorie

PLAYERS: Edmund Gwenn, John Forsythe, Shirley MacLaine, Mildred Natwick, Jerry Mathers, Mildred Dunnock, Royal Dano, Parker Fennelly, Barry Macollum

TRUE GRIT   U.S.A. (1969)

An Oscar-winning performance by John Wayne as the one-eyed drunken marshal Rooster Cogburn who is hired by a young teenage girl (Kim Darby) to track down the killer of her father. The film, photographed on location near Montrose, Colorado, the Dallas Divide and Blue Mesa Reservoir, helped re-establish veteran Henry Hathaway as a major Western director. Most celebrated sequence: Wayne, reins clenched between his teeth and a gun whirling in each hand, charging and disposing of four outlaws.

Production—Hal B. Wallis   *Photography* (*Technicolor*)—
Direction—Henry Hathaway   Lucien Ballard
Screenplay (*based on novel by*   *Art direction*—Walter Tyler
  Charles Portis)—   *Music*—Elmer Bernstein
  Marguerite Roberts   *Editing*—Warren Low
PLAYERS: John Wayne, Glen Campbell, Kim Darby, Jeremy Slate, Robert Duvall, Dennis Hopper, Alfred Ryder, Strother Martin

TWELVE ANGRY MEN   U.S.A. (1957)

Filmed TV play with honest juror Henry Fonda pleading, arguing and eventually convincing the other eleven members of the jury that the 18-year-old Negro youth whose trial they have just presided over may, after all, just possibly be innocent of murder. A claustrophobic film set almost entirely in a sweltering New York jury room where the hatreds and prejudices of the twelve men rise dramatically to the surface as they are forced to discuss what they had thought to be an open-and-shut case. Directed by Sidney Lumet (his first film) from a screenplay by Reginald Rose who was later responsible for the excellent TV series *The Defenders*. Of the talented but then little-known cast E. G. Marshall, Lee J. Cobb, Ed Begley, Jack Warden and Martin Balsam (brilliant as the flustered jury foreman) emerge with the most distinction.

ORION—NOVA/UNITED ARTISTS

Production—Henry Fonda &   *Photography*—Boris Kaufman
  Reginald Rose   *Art direction*—Robert Markell
Direction—Sidney Lumet   *Music*—Kenyon Hopkins
Screenplay—Reginald Rose   *Editing*—Carl Lerner
PLAYERS: Henry Fonda, Lee J. Cobb, Ed Begley, E. G. Marshall, Jack Warden, Martin Balsam, John Fielder, Jack Klugman

TWELVE O'CLOCK HIGH   U.S.A. (1949)

Henry King's quiet, thoughtful war film about a badly battered American bomber group stationed in England during World War II. An honest, perceptive picture of men under stress with an ambitious script and an outstanding performance by Gregory Peck as the ruthless general who restores morale. Gary Merrill, Millard Mitchell and Hugh Marlowe head the rest of the notable all-male cast. Dean Jagger won an Academy Award for his supporting performance as a sympathetic adjutant.

Twelve O'Clock High

TWENTIETH CENTURY–FOX

Production—Darryl F. Zanuck
Direction—Henry King
Screenplay (from their novel)—
  Sy Bartlett & Beirne Lay, Jr.
Photography—Leon Shamroy

Art direction—Lyle Wheeler &
  Maurice Ransford
Music—Alfred Newman
Editing—Barbara McLean

PLAYERS: Gregory Peck, Hugh Marlowe, Gary Merrill, Millard Mitchell, Dean Jagger, Robert Arthur, Paul Stewart, John Kellogg, Bob Patten

TWO FLAGS WEST U.S.A. (1950)

An unusual, almost forgotten Western set on an isolated frontier post in the closing stages of the Civil War and centering on a group of Confederate prisoners who buy their liberty by agreeing to fight with Northern troops against the Indians. A minor, sometimes exciting Robert Wise film with an interesting script that intelligently mirrors all the bitterness and frustration of the Civil War. Finely played by Joseph Cotten as a Confederate colonel and Jeff Chandler as a bitter Northern officer.

*Production—*Casey Robinson   *Photography—*Leon Shamroy
*Direction—*Robert Wise   *Art direction—*Lyle Wheeler,
Screenplay (from story by   Chester Gore
   Frank S. Nugent & Curtis   *Music—*Hugo Friedhofer
   *Kenyon)—*Casey Robinson   *Editing—*Louis Loeffler

PLAYERS: Joseph Cotten, Linda Darnell, Jeff Chandler, Cornel Wilde, Dale Robertson, Jay C. Flippen, Noah Beery, Harry Von Zell, John Sands, Arthur Hunnicutt

TWO TARS   U.S.A. (1928)

A two-reeler with Laurel and Hardy as a pair of well-intentioned sailors who take a couple of girls out for a peaceful Sunday drive and become involved in a massive and terrifyingly destructive traffic jam. This last chaotic sequence, in which something like 100 cars are destroyed, belongs with the funniest of their destructive scenes and the film itself with the best of all their two-reelers. George Stevens, who later became one of America's greatest directors with such films as *A Place in the Sun, Giant* and *Shane,* is the cameraman.

*Direction—*James Parrott   *Photography—*George Stevens
PLAYERS: Stan Laurel and Oliver Hardy, Edgar Kennedy, Charles Hall

2001: A SPACE ODYSSEY   Gt. Britain (1968)

This most intelligent science-fiction film of all time is a strikingly beautiful picture that works equally well on two levels: first, as a serious and authentic prediction of the future of space travel and, second and more disturbingly, as an intellectual speculation on the possibility of extraterrestrial life. The story—the discovery on the moon of a centuries-old black monolith and of the subsequent fact-finding journey to Jupiter from which the monolith originated—ends enigmatically when the only surviving astronaut to reach the planet finds himself hopelessly lost in another dimension. The score is made up entirely of classical music and includes "The Blue Danube" waltz which is used to accompany the journeys by the spacecraft between earth and moon, and the now famous opening and closing bars of "Also Sprach Zarathustra." A unique success and one of the great technical achievements of recent years.

Production & direction—   *Special photographic effects—*
  Stanley Kubrick   Stanley Kubrick

Screenplay (based on short story "The Sentinel" by Arthur C. Clarke)—Stanley Kubrick & Arthur C. Clarke
Photography (Super Panavision/ Cinerama/Metrocolor)— Geoffrey Unsworth
Additional photography— John Alcott
Art direction—John Hoesli

Production design— Tony Masters, Harry Lange & Ernie Archer
Special effects—Wally Veevers, Douglas Trumbull, Con Pederson & Tom Howard
Music—Richard Strauss, Johann Strauss, Aram Khachaturian, Gyorgy Ligeti
Editing—Ray Lovejoy

PLAYERS: Keir Dullea, Gary Lockwood, William Sylvester, Daniel Richter, Douglas Rain, Leonard Rossiter, Margaret Tyzack, Robert Beatty, Sean Sullivan, Frank Miller, Penny Brahms

UGETSU MONOGATARI
Japan (1953)

Two Japanese peasants—one a potter, the other a farmer—decide to leave their homes and wives in order to profit by the civil war raging in Japan during the closing years of the 16th century. Eventually, after adventure and misadventure, both return home chastened by their experiences. A simple, poetically told morality tale, colorfully subtitled "Tales of the Pale Moon after the Rain" and directed by Kenji Mizoguchi (his last film) from an 18th-century novel.

DAIEI

Production—Masaich Nagata
Direction—Kenji Mizoguchi
Photography—Kazuo Miyagawa
Art direction—Kisaku Ito

Screenplay (from novel by Akinari Veda)—Matsutaro Kawaguchi & Giken Yoda
Music—Fumio Hayasaka

PLAYERS: Machikokyo, Mitsuko Mito, Kinuyo Tanaka, Masayuki Mori, Sakae Ozawa

UMBERTO D
Italy (1952)

A simple and very somber film about the tragedies and loneliness of old age played, like all of De Sica's realistic films, by nonprofessional actors. A retired government official (Carlo Battisti) finds it impossible to exist on his meager pension and is driven to the verge of suicide. All the mental and physical despair of old age is in this film and there is not a single concession to commercialism. A major work that completes a trio of masterpieces begun by De Sica with *Shoeshine* and *The Bicycle Thief*.

RIZZOLI—DE SICA—AMATO

Direction—Vittorio De Sica

Screenplay—Cesare Zavattini

Photography—G. R. Aldo   Music—Alessandro Cicognini
Art direction—Virgilio Marchi   Editing—Eraldo Da Roma
PLAYERS: Carlo Battisti, Maria Pia Casilio, Ileana Simova, Lina Gennari,
Elena Rea, Memmo Cartenuto

UMBRELLAS OF CHERBOURG, THE

(Les Parapluies de Cherbourg)   France/W. Germany (1964)
Charming, all-singing fairy tale by Jacques Demy about the young girl
from the umbrella shop in Cherbourg who marries another man while
her lover (the father of her unborn child) is serving in the army in
Algeria. A slender tale, but Rabier's color compositions and Evein's
designs are stunningly beautiful and Legrand's score wide-ranging in
its themes. Catherine Deneuve plays the girl, Nino Castelnuovo her
lover, and Marc Michel the man she eventually marries.

PARC FILM/MADELEINE FILM (PARIS)/BETA FILMS (MUNICH)
(MAG BODARD)

Direction, screenplay &   Art direction—Bernard Evein
  dialogue—Jacques Demy   Music—Michel Legrand
Photography (Eastmancolor)—   Editing—Anne-Marie Cotret
  Jean Rabier
PLAYERS: Anne Vernon, Catherine Deneuve, Marc Michel, Nino Castel-
novo, Mireille Perry, Ellen Farner, Dorothée Blank

UN CARNET DE BAL   France (1937)

Bittersweet French movie about a lonely young widow (Marie Bell)
who decides to trace her former suitors when she comes across their
names on an old dance program. Some moments of exquisite beauty
and superb performances from an all-star, and sadly unrepeatable, cast:
Raimu as a small-town mayor, Louis Jouvet as a night-club owner, and
Harry Baur as a monk. Duvivier's most romantic prewar movie is
charmingly scored by Maurice Jaubert whose waltz theme was one of
the most famous film compositions of the thirties. Other major Jaubert
scores: L'Atalante (Vigo), Drôle de Drame, Quai des Brumes, Le Jour
Se Lève (Carné) and La Fin du Jour (Duvivier).

SIGMA (P. FROGERAIS)

Direction—Julien Duvivier   Dialogue—Bernard Zimmer,
Screenplay—Julien Duvivier   H. Jeanson, Jean Sarment
Adaptation—Julien Duvivier,   Art direction—S. Piménoff,
  Jean Sarment, Pierre Wolff,   J. Douarinou
  Yves Mirande, Bernard Zimmer   Music—Maurice Jaubert
Photography—Michel Kelber   Editing—A. Versein

PLAYERS: Marie Bell, Françoise Rosay, Harry Baur, Pierre Blanchar, Raimu, Louis Jouvet, Fernandel, Pierre Richard-Willm, Milly Mathis, Robert Lynen

UN CONDAMNE À MORT S'EST ECHAPPE
(A Man Escaped)   France (1956)
Set in Lyons in 1943, this quiet, unemotional film recounts the pains-taking efforts of a French secret service agent to escape from the Nazi prison of Fort Montluc. On one level it is a gripping escape adventure, on another it is an austere study of a man's spiritual reaction to his captivity and isolation. Based on a true story and played by non-professionals.

S.N.E. GAUMONT/N.E.F.

Direction, screenplay & dialogue   *Art direction—*
  (from André Devigny's   Pierre Charbonnier
  account of his escape)—   *Music—*Mozart (C Minor Mass)
  Robert Bresson   *Editing—*Raymond Lamy
*Photography—*Léonce-Henry Burel

PLAYERS: François Leterrier, Charles le Clainche, Maurice Beerblock, Roland Monod, Jacques Ertaud, Roger Tréherne

UNCONQUERED   U.S.A. (1947)
A large-scale pioneering adventure set in 1763 when Pittsburgh was still a fort on the Ohio River. A somewhat incredible story with much banal dialogue but with superb sets and period detail, and a brilliantly filmed climactic siege of Fort Pitt by the Seneca Indians. Gary Cooper is a Virginia militiaman, Paulette Goddard a bond slave, and Howard da Silva the trader who sells tomahawks to the Indians. Magnificent Tech-nicolor photography of Pittsburgh's forest areas and Idaho's Snake River. DeMille's last venture west.

PARAMOUNT

Production & direction—   *Photography (Technicolor)—*
  Cecil B. DeMille   Ray Rennahan
Screenplay (from novel by Neil   *Art direction—*Hans Dreier,
  *H. Swanson)—*Charles Bennett,   Walter Tyler
  Frederic M. Frank,   *Music—*Victor Young
  Jesse Lasky, Jr.   *Editing—*Anne Bauchens

PLAYERS: Gary Cooper, Paulette Goddard, Howard da Silva, Boris Karloff, Cecil Kellaway, Ward Bond, Henry Wilcoxon, C. Aubrey Smith

UNDERWORLD
U.S.A. (1927)

Gangster film—one of the first and best of its kind—by Josef von Sternberg featuring George Bancroft as a big-time hoodlum, Evelyn Brent as his girlfriend "Feathers," and Clive Brook as an alcoholic lawyer. Distinguished mainly by its economical direction and the imaginative lighting of Bert Glennon, a cameraman who later worked with von Sternberg on *The Last Command, Blonde Venus* and, most notably, *The Scarlet Empress.*

FAMOUS PLAYERS—LASKY—PARAMOUNT

Production—Hector Turnbull   *Adaptation*—Charles Furthman
Direction—Josef von Sternberg   *Photography*—Bert Glennon
Screenplay (*based on story by*   *Set designer*—Hans Dreier
   Ben Hecht)—Robert N. Lee   *Titles*—George Marion, Jr.
PLAYERS: Clive Brook, Evelyn Brent, George Bancroft, Larry Semon, Fred Kohler, Helen Lynch, Jerry Mandy

UNE PARTIE DE CAMPAGNE
   (A Day in the Country)   France (1936 but released 1946)

Poetic 40-minute Renoir film based on two short stories by Guy de Maupassant tells of a boy and girl who have a brief love affair during one summer Sunday afternoon in the country and who return to the scene some 14 years later only to find that the magic of the afternoon has been lost forever. The picture was originally intended to be of feature length, but circumstances permitted Renoir to shoot only the first and last sequences and these were put together and released as one film in 1946.

PIERRE BRAUNBERGER PRODS.

Direction—Jean Renoir   *Music*—Joseph Kosma
Screenplay—Jean Renoir   *Editing*—Marguerite Renoir
Photography—Claude Renoir
PLAYERS: Sylvia Bataille, Georges Darnoux, Gabriello, Jeanne Marken, Paul Temps, Jacques Brunius, Jean Renoir

UNFAITHFUL, THE
U.S.A. (1947)

Ann Sheridan in superb form as a lonely wartime wife who is unfaithful to her soldier husband (Zachary Scott) just once and then pays for it in full when she becomes involved in murder and blackmail. A superior glossy melodrama with excellent San Francisco locations. Lew Ayres plays the defense counselor, Jerome Cowan a prosecuting attorney, and Eve Arden an acid-tongued relative.

Production—Jerry Wald
Direction—Vincent Sherman
Screenplay—David Goodis,
   James Gunn

Photography—Ernest Haller
Art direction—Leo K. Kuter
Music—Max Steiner
Editing—Alan Crosland, Jr.

PLAYERS: Ann Sheridan, Lew Ayres, Zachary Scott, Eve Arden, Jerome Cowan, Steven Geray, John Hoyt

UNFAITHFULLY YOURS   U.S.A. (1948)

Polished Sturges comedy about a celebrated orchestra conductor (Rex Harrison) who believes that his beautiful wife (Linda Darnell) has been unfaithful to him and who imagines, while conducting music by Wagner, Rossini and Tchaikovsky, the different ways that he can gain his revenge. An often amusing film, but the superb talent that had made six comic masterpieces in the astonishingly short period between 1940 and 1944 had by now burnt itself out and Sturges made only two more films—*The Beautiful Blonde from Bashful Bend* and *The Diary of Major Thompson,* both of which were dismal flops—before his death in 1959 at the age of 61.

Production, direction &
   screenplay—Preston Sturges
Art direction—Lyle Wheeler &
   Joseph C. Wright

Photography—Victor Milner
Music direction—
   Alfred Newman
Editing—Robert Fritch

PLAYERS: Rex Harrison, Linda Darnell, Rudy Vallee, Barbara Lawrence, Kurt Kreuger, Lionel Stander, Edgar Kennedy

UNINVITED, THE   U.S.A. (1944)

Adult, occasionally frightening but also rather quaint, little thriller about the exorcising of an evil spirit from an eerie house on the Cornish coast. Marred by a typically phony and over-cute Hollywood-styled Cornish village, but directed with restraint by Lewis Allen (debut) who refrained from showing the ghost until the very end. Photographed with considerable subtlety by Charles Lang whose high-key camera work won a 1944 Academy Award nomination. Heralded at the time as "Hollywood's first attempt at a serious ghost story."

Associate producer—
   Charles Brackett
Direction—Lewis Allen

Screenplay (from novel by
   Dorothy Macardle)—
   Dodie Smith & Frank Partos

Photography—Charles Lang *Music*—Victor Young
Art direction—Hans Dreier & *Editing*—Doane Harrison
  Ernst Fegte
PLAYERS: Ray Milland, Ruth Hussey, Gail Russell, Cornelia Otis Skinner,
Donald Crisp, Dorothy Stickney, Barbara Everest, Alan Napier

UNION PACIFIC   U.S.A. (1939)

DeMille's boisterous, fast-moving Western epic about the building of
the Union Pacific railway. Some well-staged spectacular sequences, including a train wreck and an exciting Indian attack, and some enjoyable performances from a talented cast letting their hair down: Joel
McCrea as a troubleshooter, Barbara Stanwyck as an Irish postmistress,
and Lynne Overman and Akim Tamiroff as a pair of grizzled old body-
guards. DeMille's last film in monochrome.

PARAMOUNT

Production & direction— *Photography*—Victor Milner,
  Cecil B. DeMille Dewey Wrigley
Screenplay (from story by Ernest *Art direction*—Hans Dreier,
  Haycox)—Jack Cunningham, Roland Anderson
  Walter DeLeon, C. Gardner *Music*—George Antheil
  Sullivan, Jesse Lasky, Jr. *Editing*—Anne Bauchens
PLAYERS: Barbara Stanwyck, Joel McCrea, Robert Preston, Lynne Over-
man, Akim Tamiroff, Brian Donlevy, Anthony Quinn, Evelyn Keyes

UNION STATION   U.S.A. (1950)

Efficient, tightly edited Paramount thriller played against the background of crowded Union Station tells of the efforts of railway cop
(William Holden) and Irish police inspector (Barry Fitzgerald) to
track down a kidnapper. Of interest primarily as being the only film
of any quality that the late and great cameraman Rudolph Mate made
during his less than distinguished 16-year period (1948–1964) as a
director.

PARAMOUNT

Production—Jules Schermer *Photography*—Daniel L. Fapp
Direction—Rudolph Mate *Art direction*—Hans Dreier &
Screenplay (from novel by Earl Hedrick
  Thomas Walsh)— *Music*—Irvin Talbot
  Sidney Boehm *Editing*—Ellsworth Hoaglund
PLAYERS: William Holden, Nancy Olson, Barry Fitzgerald, Lyle
Bettger, Jan Sterling, Ailene Roberts, Herbert Heyes

463

UNKNOWN SOLDIER, THE
Finland (1955)

The experiences of a machine-gun detachment of Finnish conscripts during the Russo-Finnish war of 1941–44. Long, episodic and depressing in its realistic emphasis on death and destruction, the film nevertheless triumphantly achieves what it sets out to do; namely, to show the full horror of war and its effects on the men concerned in the fighting. Ranks with *All Quiet on the Western Front, Westfront 1918* and *Paths of Glory* as one of the great antiwar films. Played by nonprofessionals.

SVOMEN FILM ITEOLLISUUS

Production—Toivo Särkkä
Direction (*adapted from novel by Väinö Linna*)—Edvin Laine
Photography—Pentti Unho, Osmo Harkimo, Olavi Tuomi, Antero Ruuhonen

Art direction—Aarre Koivisto
Music—Jean Sibelius, Anti Sonninen
Editing—Armas Vallasvuo, Osmo Harkimo, Aarre Koivisto

PLAYERS: Kosti Klemelä, Jussi Jurkka, Matti Ranin, Heikki Savolainen, Veikko Sinisalo

UNSUSPECTED, THE
U.S.A. (1947)

One of the least known of Michael Curtiz's late Warner films, this expert little murder mystery centers on a radio storyteller (Claude Rains) who plans and commits murder in order to get his hands on his ward's millions. A superior example of its kind, marked especially by Anton Grot's rich interiors. Rains (in his element) is well supported by Joan Caulfield as his ward, Audrey Totter as his designing niece, Fred Clark as a detective, and Jack Lambert as a hired killer.

WARNER BROS.

Production—Charles Hoffman
Direction—Michael Curtiz
Screenplay—Ranald MacDougall
Photography—Woody Bredell
Art direction—Anton Grot

Adaptation (*from story by Charlotte Armstrong*)—
Bess Meredyth
Music—Franz Waxman
Editing—Frederick Richards

PLAYERS: Claude Rains, Joan Caulfield, Audrey Totter, Constance Bennett, Hurd Hatfield, Michael North

VAGABOND, THE
U.S.A. (1916)

Chaplin as an impoverished violinist, Edna Purviance as the gypsy girl he loves, and artist Lloyd Bacon as the rival for her affections. The third of the Mutual two-reelers, still amusing but more ambitious and dramatic than usual, is a forerunner of such later works as *A Dog's Life* and *The Kid.* Lloyd Bacon appeared in several of Chaplin's comedies for Mutual and later became a director himself, making such distinguished musicals as *The Singing Fool* and *42nd Street.* His last appearance for Chaplin was in *The Rink* (1916).

A MUTUAL COMEDY

Direction—Charles Chaplin   *Photography*—R. H. Totheroh &
Screenplay—Charles Chaplin   W. C. Foster
PLAYERS: Charles Chaplin, Albert Austin, Lloyd Bacon, Eric Campbell, Frank J. Coleman, James T. Kelly, Charlotte Mineau, Edna Purviance, John Rand, Leo White (in two roles)

VANISHING PRAIRIE, THE   U.S.A. (1954)
The second of Walt Disney's feature-length "True Life Adventures" is a look at wildlife still surviving on the great American prairies bounded by the Mississippi, the Gulf of Mexico, the Rocky Mountains, and the Canadian Plains. Mountain lions, coyotes, bison, cougars, prairie dogs, and many others are observed in superb Technicolor by eleven of Disney's skilled photographers. What spoils an otherwise rewarding documentary is the vulgar commentary and the over-smart matching of music to the animals' movements. Some highlights: a herd of bison stampeding before a prairie fire, a coyote killing a rattlesnake, and birds performing a ritual dance at mating time.

WALT DISNEY PRODUCTIONS

Director—James Algar   Simon, N. Paul Kenworthy, Jr.,
Script—James Algar,   Cleveland P. Grant, Lloyd
  Winston Hibler, Ted Sears   Beebe, Herb Crisler, Dick
Associate producer—   Borden, Warren Garst, Murl
  Ben Sharpsteen   Deusing, Olin Sewall
Narration—Winston Hibler   Pettingill, Jr., Stuart V. Jewell
Photography (Technicolor)—   *Musical director*—Paul Smith
  Tom McHugh, James R.   *Editing*—Lloyd Richardson

VARIETY (Variete)   Germany (1925)
Sordid story of love, jealousy and murder among a group of second-rate variety performers. Some fine acting, especially from Emil Jannings as a trapeze artist, and some skillfully evoked side-show atmosphere, but of interest primarily for the mobile camera work of Karl Freund whose virtuoso photography of the trapeze acts—the camera flies through the air with the performers—is nearly as impressive as his photography of Murnau's *The Last Laugh* a year earlier.

Direction—E. A. Dupont   *Photography*—Karl Freund
Screenplay (from novel by Felix   *Art direction*—Oscar Werndorff
  Hollander)—Leo Birinski
PLAYERS: Emil Jannings, Lya de Putti, Warwick Ward, Mady Delschaft, Georg John, Kurt Gerron

VERA CRUZ   U.S.A. (1954)
Large-scale rollicking swashbuckler about two American adventurers—a Southern colonel (Gary Cooper) and a renegade outlaw (Burt Lancaster)—who, after the Civil War, sell their services to Mexico during the Juarez revolution. Robert Aldrich's second Western of 1954, marked by an excellent Friedhofer score and the presence of George Macready (Maximilian), Ernest Borgnine, Jack Elam and Charles Bronson (Lancaster's assorted villains) in the supporting cast.

Production—James Hill   *Photography (Technicolor/*
Direction—Robert Aldrich   *Superscope)*—Ernest Laszlo
Screenplay—Roland Kibbee &   *Art direction*—Al Ybarra
  James R. Webb   *Music*—Hugo Friedhofer
Story—Borden Chase   *Editing*—Alan Crosland
PLAYERS: Gary Cooper, Burt Lancaster, Denise Darcel, Cesar Romero, Sarita Montiel, George Macready, Ernest Borgnine, Morris Ankrum, Jack Elam, Charles Bronson

VERTIGO   U.S.A. (1958)
Considered by some critics to be Hitchcock's masterpiece. This intriguing film is both an elaborately constructed murder story (dealing with a carefully planned wife murder in which an ex-cop who has retired from the force because he suffers from vertigo is the innocent pawn) and also a fascinating study in sexual obsession. This secondary theme seems to have interested Hitchcock more than the main story line and the scenes in which James Stewart (the cop) tries to re-create the image of a woman he has loved but lost in death by reclothing and restyling the hair, etc. of a live woman who closely resembles her are the most fascinating part of an extremely complex and brilliantly directed film.

Production & direction—   *Photography (Technicolor)*—
  Alfred Hitchcock   Robert Burks

Screenplay (*from novel by Boileau & Narcejac* D'Entre les Morts)—Alec Coppel & Samuel Taylor

Art direction—Hal Pereira & Henry Bumstead
Music—Bernard Herrmann
Editing—George Tomasini

PLAYERS: James Stewart, Kim Novak, Barbara Bel Geddes, Henry Jones, Tom Helmore, Raymond Bailey, Ellen Corby, Konstantin Shayne, Lee Patrick

VIRGIN SPRING, THE   Sweden (1959)
Ingmar Bergman's version of a 14th-century folktale about a young virgin (Birgitta Pettersson) who, while on a holy errand to her local church, is raped and murdered by three herdsmen and then avenged by her grief-stricken father (Max von Sydow). After *The Seventh Seal*, the darkest and most horrifying of Bergman's medieval films, the brutal realism of the rape and murder sequences causing considerable censorship controversy when the picture was first shown in 1959. Photographed by Sven Nykvist, cameraman on the majority of Bergman's later works.

SVENSK FILMINDUSTRI

Direction—Ingmar Bergman
Screenplay (*from 14th-century ballad "Töres Dotter I Vänge"*)
—Ulla Isaksson

Photography—Sven Nykvist
Art direction—P. A. Lundgren
Music—Erik Nordgren
Editing—Oscar Rosander

PLAYERS: Max von Sydow, Birgitta Valberg, Gunnel Lindblom, Birgitta Pettersson, Axel Düberg, Tor Isedal, Allan Edwall, Ove Porath

VIRIDIANA   Spain/Mexico (1961)
Religious bigotry and Christian myths are attacked by Luis Buñuel as he follows the experiences of a young novice who, before taking her final vows, makes a last excursion into the outside world. Like the priest's charity in *Nazarin* her saintliness and eagerness to do good result in violence and unhappiness. By the end of a powerful film, her elderly uncle has died because of his love for her, his already neglected estate has been ruined by her attempts to convert it into a rest home for beggars, and she herself has been raped and degraded. Of all Buñuel's masterpieces this is the one that disturbs most.

UNINCI S.A./FILMS 59 (MADRID)/GUSTAVO ALATRISTE (MEXICO)

Direction—Luis Buñuel
Screenplay—Luis Buñuel & Julio Alejandro
Photography—José F. Agayo

Art direction—Francisco Canet
Music—from Handel's *Messiah*
Editing—Pedro del Rey

PLAYERS: Silvia Pinal, Francisco Rabal, Fernando Rey, Margarita Lozano, Victoria Zinny, Teresa Rabal, José Calvo, Joaquín Roa

VIVA MARIA   France/Italy (1965)
Lighthearted, refreshing piece of nonsense built around the amours and revolutionary activities of a pair of music-hall artistes (Brigitte Bardot and Jeanne Moreau) touring South America with a circus company at the turn of the century. Stylishly done and thoroughly enjoyable from beginning to end, although nothing quite matches up to the early sequence in which Bardot and Moreau accidentally discover the art of striptease when the former's costume splits apart on stage. Excellent photography and a melodic, often witty, music score.

NOUVELLES EDITIONS DE FILMS/O. DANCIGERS/PROD. ARTISTES
ASSOCIÉS (PARIS)/VIDES FILMS (ROME)

Direction—Louis Malle
Screenplay & dialogue—Louis Malle & Jean-Claude Carrière
Photography (Eastmancolor/ Panavision)—Henri Decaë

Art direction—Bernard Evein
Music—Georges Delerue
Editing—Kenout Peltier & Suzanne Baron

PLAYERS: Brigitte Bardot, Jeanne Moreau, George Hamilton, Gregor von Rezzori, Paulette Dubois, Claudio Brook

VIVA ZAPATA   U.S.A. (1952)
The story of the rise to power, exploits and final assassination of Emiliano Zapata (Marlon Brando), the Mexican peasant leader who, with Pancho Villa, helped overthrow the Diaz regime in 1911. The most exciting of all Kazan's films; the two assassination scenes—first President Madero, then Zapata himself—are beautifully handled and the long, build-up sequence in which hundreds of peasants appear silently from the hills to rescue their leader is a tour de force. The supporting cast includes Anthony Quinn as Zapata's brother, Joseph Wiseman as a treacherous revolutionary, and Frank Silvera as General Huerta.

TWENTIETH CENTURY—FOX

Production—Darryl F. Zanuck
Direction—Elia Kazan
Screenplay (from story by Edgcumb Pichon—Zapata the Unconquered)—John Steinbeck

Photography—Joe MacDonald
Art direction—Lyle R. Wheeler & Leland Fuller
Music—Alex North
Editing—Barbara McLean

PLAYERS: Marlon Brando, Jean Peters, Anthony Quinn, Joseph Wiseman, Arnold Moss, Frank Silvera, Mildred Dunnock, Alan Reed

WAGES OF FEAR, THE
(Le Salaire de la Peur)   France/Italy (1953)
Tension movie of the highest class centering on four Europeans who, in order to escape from the squalid little South American oil town in which they are stranded, agree to drive two trucks loaded with nitroglycerine over 300 miles of treacherous roads to a burning oil well. The scenes of the nightmare ride (about two thirds of the film) are justifiably famous and directed with considerable skill. Clouzot's early scene-setting and his examination of the men's characters as they while away their time listlessly in the oppressive heat and in the only bar in town is very effectively done. The bitterly ironic ending is exactly right and perfectly complements all that has gone before. Excellent portrayals from Yves Montand, Folco Lulli and Peter van Eyck as three of the truck drivers and a great one from Charles Vanel as an aging gangster who eventually cracks under the strain of the drive. Vanel was named best actor of the year at the 1953 Cannes Film Festival and the film itself deservedly received the Grand Prix.

C.I.C.C./FILMSONOR/VERA FILM/FONO ROMA

Direction—Henri-Georges Clouzot *Photography*—Armand Thirard
Screenplay, adaptation &   *Art direction*—René Renoux
 dialogue (from novel by   *Music*—Georges Auric
 Georges Arnaud)—Clouzot & *Editing*—Henri Rust,
 Jérôme Géronimi   Madeleine Gug, E. Muse
PLAYERS: Yves Montand, Charles Vanel, Véra Clouzot, Folco Lulli, Peter Van Eyck, William Tubbs

WAGONMASTER
               U.S.A. (1950)
Leisurely, poetic film about a small wagon train of Mormons who, during the 1870's, cross the deserts and mountains of the Southwest United States to establish new homes in Utah. Beautifully played by the Ford stock company, particularly Ward Bond and Jane Darwell as Mormon elders, and outstandingly well photographed. The best of all Ford's Westerns and together with *The Sun Shines Bright* and *The Quiet Man* the most personal of all his films.

ARGOSY PICTURES—RKO RADIO

Production—John Ford,   *Photography*—Bert Glennon
 Merian C. Cooper   *Second unit*—Archie Stout
Direction—John Ford   *Art direction*—James Basevi
Screenplay (from story by John *Music*—Richard Hageman
 Ford)—Frank S. Nugent,   *Editing*—Jack Murray
 Patrick Ford

469

PLAYERS: Ben Johnson, Harry Carey Jr., Joanne Dru, Ward Bond, Charles Kemper, Alan Mowbray, Jane Darwell, Ruth Clifford, Russell Simpson, Kathleen O'Malley, James Arness

WAITING WOMEN (Kvinnors Väntan)   Sweden (1952)
Ingmar Bergman explores in flashback the marital experiences of three women who, as they wait for their husbands to return on the evening train from Stockholm, discuss some of the emotional climaxes in their married lives. Less ambitious than Bergman's later films, but with some penetrating comments on the relationships between the sexes and a brilliant scene of high comedy when Eva Dahlbeck and her middle-aged husband (Gunnar Björnstrand) are forced to spend the night together in a broken-down elevator. Strikingly well played by the three women involved—Eva Dahlbeck, Anita Björk and Maj-Britt Nilsson.
                           SVENSK FILMINDUSTRI
Screenplay & direction—   *Art direction—*Nils Svenwall
  Ingmar Bergman   *Music—*Erik Nordgren
*Photography—*Gunnar Fischer   *Editing—*Oscar Rosander
PLAYERS: Anita Björk, Maj-Britt Nilsson, Eva Dahlbeck, Gunnar Björnstrand, Birger Malmsten, Jarl Kulle, Karl-Arne Holmsten

WALK IN THE SUN, A   U.S.A. (1945)
The story of a platoon of U.S. infantrymen who march six miles from an Italian beachhead to capture a Nazi-held farmhouse. A poetic, perceptive and very moving film primarily concerned with the effects of war on ordinary men. Notable direction from Lewis Milestone and a beautifully constructed script by Robert Rossen. One of the most distinguished American war films ever made.
                         TWENTIETH CENTURY—FOX
Production & direction—   *Photography—*Russell Harlan
  Lewis Milestone   *Art direction—*Max Bertisch
Screenplay (from novel by Harry *Music—*Fredric Efrem
  *Brown)—*Robert Rossen   *Editing—*W. Duncan Mansfield
PLAYERS: Dana Andrews, Richard Conte, Sterling Holloway, George Tyne, John Ireland, Herbert Rudley, Richard Benedict, Lloyd Bridges

WAR AND PEACE   U.S.A./Italy (1956)
A 3½-hour version of Tolstoy's majestic classic tracing the fortunes of a group of Russian aristocrats during the period of Napoleon's invasion and subsequent retreat from Moscow. An impossible novel to condense, but the film has its impressive moments, e.g. the beautifully designed

470

ballroom scene in Moscow, the more spectacular later sequences depicting the battles of Austerlitz and Borodino, and the grim winter retreat of the French Army across Russia. The performances are uneven, but Herbert Lom's Napoleon and Oscar Homolka's blustering peasant general Kutuzov are more than satisfactory. Audrey Hepburn (Natasha), Mel Ferrer (Prince Andrei) and Henry Fonda (Pierre) play the three leading characters around whom the massive story revolves.

PONTI DE LAURENTIIS/PARAMOUNT

Production—Dino de Laurentiis
Direction—King Vidor
Screenplay—Bridget Boland,
  Robert Westerby, King Vidor,
  Ivo Perilli, Mario Camerini &
  Ennio De Concini

Photography (Technicolor/
  VistaVision)—Jack Cardiff &
  Aldo Tonti
Art direction—Piero Gherardi
Music—Nino Rota
Editing—Leo Catozzo &
  Stuart Gilmore

PLAYERS: Audrey Hepburn, Henry Fonda, Mel Ferrer, Vittorio Gassman, Herbert Lom, Oscar Homolka, Anita Ekberg, John Mills, Helmut Dantine, Barry Jones, Jeremy Brett, Wilfrid Lawson

WAR AND PEACE   U.S.S.R. (1968)

Sergei Bondarchuk's colossal Russian remake, 6 hours 11 minutes long, is, like Vidor's version, memorable mainly for its spectacular scenes which fully deserve the accolade of being among the most stunning ever filmed. The picture took five years to make and was released in the Soviet Union in four separate segments—"Natasha," "Austerlitz," "Borodino" and "The Burning of Moscow," each episode running for approximately two hours. The American and European version was edited down from 8½ hours and released in two parts: the first combining episodes 1 and 2, the second episodes 3 and 4. Ludmila Savelyeva played Natasha, Vyacheslav Tikhonov was featured as Andrei, and Bondarchuk himself appeared as the idealistic Pierre.

MOSFILM

Direction—Sergei Bondarchuk
Screenplay (based on novel by
  Leo Tolstoy)—Sergei
  Bondarchuk, Vasily Solovyov
Photography (Sovcolor) 70 mm.
  —Anatoly Petritsky with
  Dmitri Korzhikin, A. Zenyan
Music—Vyacheslav Ovchinnikov

Art direction—Mikhail Bogdanov,
  Gennady Myasnikov
Special effects photography—
  G. Aizenberg
Special effects at Schöngraben &
  Austerlitz—Alexander
  Shelenkov, Chen-Yu-Lan
Editing—Tatiana Likhacheva

471

PLAYERS: Ludmila Savelyeva, Sergei Bondarchuk, Vyacheslav Tikhonov, Anastasia Vertinskaya, Vasily Lanovoi, Viktor Stanitsin, Oleg Tabakov, Anatoly Ktorov

WAR IS OVER, THE (La Guerre Est Finie) France/Sweden (1966)

The fears, anxieties and memories of an aging professional revolutionary (Yves Montand) who, after resisting the Franco regime for some 25 years during his exile in Paris, is at last becoming disillusioned with the cause. Basically a political melodrama, the film is the least complex and easiest to follow of Alain Resnais' work although, as in his earlier films, the complexities of time and memory are fully explored. Beautiful performances from Montand and from Ingrid Thulin as his mistress.

SOFRACIMA (PARIS)/EUROPA FILM (STOCKHOLM)

Direction—Alain Resnais	Art direction—Jacques Saulnier
Screenplay—Jorge Semprun	Music—Giovanni Fusco
Photography—Sacha Vierny	Editing—Eric Pluet

PLAYERS: Yves Montand, Ingrid Thulin, Michel Piccoli, Geneviève Bujold, Dominique Rozan, Francoise Bertin

WAR LORD, THE U.S.A. (1966)

Charlton Heston stars as a Norman war lord who claims his primitive right to share a peasant girl (Rosemary Forsyth) on her wedding night and then incurs the hatred of the Druid villagers by refusing to give her back to her husband. There are some well-handled siege and battle scenes, but this is not an epic in the true sense of the word; it is more a small personal story within an epic framework, deriving as it does from Leslie Stevens' stage play *The Lovers*. The mood and atmosphere of a brutal period are realistically evoked and the color photography by Russell Metty is outstanding.

COURT/UNIVERSAL–INTERNATIONAL

Production—Walter Seltzer	Photography (Technicolor/
Direction—Franklin Schaffner	Panavision)—Russell Metty
Screenplay—John Collier &	Art direction—Alexander
Millard Kaufman	Golitzen & Henry Bumstead
Music—Jerome Moross	Editing—Folmar Blangsted

PLAYERS: Charlton Heston, Richard Boone, Rosemary Forsyth, Maurice Evans, Guy Stockwell, Nial MacGinnis, Henry Wilcoxon

WAR OF THE WORLDS, THE U.S.A. (1953)

The most ambitious, technically at least, of all Hollywood's science-fiction movies of the fifties with the invasion of H. G. Wells' Martians transferred from peaceful, early-20th-century Surrey to postwar nuclear America. Some well-staged scenes of mass destruction although the Martians themselves, revealed only in one eerie scene as they grope their way around an abandoned house, are something of a disappointment. Directed by Byron Haskin, the man responsible for several other not-to-be despised films in the fantasy genre, including *The Naked Jungle* and *Robinson Crusoe on Mars*.

PARAMOUNT

Production—George Pal
Direction—Byron Haskin
Screenplay (from novel by H. G. Wells)—Barre Lyndon
Music—Leith Stevens

Photography (Technicolor)—George Barnes
Art direction—Hal Pereira, Albert Nozaki
Editing—Everett Douglas

PLAYERS: Gene Barry, Ann Robinson, Henry Brandon, Les Tremayne, Bob Cornthwaite, Sandro Giglio, Lewis Martin, Jack Kruschen, Bill Phipps

WAXWORKS (Das Wachsfigurenkabinett)   Germany (1924)
Macabre three-episode German thriller, directed by former set designer Paul Leni, about a young poet who is employed by the proprietor of a fairground wax museum to write stories about his three principal wax figures—Haroun-al-Raschid (Emil Jannings), Ivan the Terrible (Conrad Veidt), and Springheel Jack, alias Jack the Ripper (Werner Krauss). Splendidly played by the three principals, although the film is most distinguished by its frequently distorted sets and by the stylized camera work of Helmar Lerski. The picture was originally planned as a four-episode film, but the last segment about Rinaldo Rinaldini, whose wax figure can be seen in the film, was abandoned. Wilhelm Dieterle (later to be known as director William Dieterle) appeared as the poet.

NEPTUN—FILM

Direction—Paul Leni
Screenplay—Henrik Galeen
Photography—Helmar Lerski

Art direction—Paul Leni & Ernst Stern

PLAYERS: Emil Jannings, Conrad Veidt, Werner Krauss, Wilhelm Dieterle, Olga Belajeff, John Gottowt, Ernst Legal, Georg John

WAY DOWN EAST   U.S.A. (1920)
Creaky Victorian melodrama about the unhappy experiences of a country girl (Lillian Gish) who suffers terribly at the hands of both

her city playboy husband and a puritanical New England farming family. Richard Barthelmess (the Chinaman in *Broken Blossoms*) again plays the girl's lover and, in a brilliantly filmed climax, saves her from certain death when she is trapped on a fast-flowing river of breaking ice. Photographed by G. W. Bitzer and Hendrick Sartov who also worked together on Griffith's *Broken Blossoms, The White Rose* and *America.* The film was made at Griffith's Mamaroneck studios in New York, the ice-flow climax being shot on the Connecticut River.

UNITED ARTISTS

Direction—D. W. Griffith
Screenplay (*from stage play by Lottie Blair Parker*)—
Anthony Paul Kelly
Photography—G. W. Bitzer & Hendrick Sartov

Technical direction—
Frank Wortman
Art direction—Charles O. Seessel & Clifford Pember
Music arranged by—Louis Silvers & William F. Peters

PLAYERS: Lillian Gish, Mrs. David Landau, Josephine Bernard, Mrs. Morgan Belmont, Patricia Fruen, Florence Short, Richard Barthelmess, Lowell Sherman

WAY OUT WEST   U.S.A. (1937)

The majority of the Laurel and Hardy features were mediocre compared with their two-reelers, but this one is a gem and far and away their best. Directed by James Horne the film deals with the attempts of Ollie and Stan to deliver the deed to a gold mine to the daughter of their ex-partner and of the efforts of villainous saloon owner (James Finlayson) to swindle them by passing off his girlfriend (Sharon Lynne) as the rightful heiress. It was in this film that Laurel and Hardy sang the comic song "In the Blue Ridge Mountains of Virginia."

STAN LAUREL PRODUCTIONS FOR HAL ROACH/METRO–GOLDWYN–MAYER

Direction—James Horne
Photography—Art Lloyd & Walter Lundin

Screenplay—Jack Jevne, Charles Rogers, James Parrott & Felix Adler

PLAYERS: Laurel and Hardy, Sharon Lynne, James Finlayson, Rosina Lawrence, Stanley Fields, Vivien Oakland, Chill Wills, The Avalon Boys, Mary Gordon

WAY TO THE STARS, THE   Gt. Britain (1945)

Honest, rather stiff film about day-to-day life on a British airfield during World War II. Now very much a period piece, although the observations of wartime relationships between British and Americans fliers remain interesting and Nicholas Brodzsky's romantic score still evokes nostalgic memories. Among the cast are Michael Redgrave and John Mills as RAF pilots, Douglass Montgomery and Bonar Colleano as American fliers, and 16-year-old Jean Simmons making her film debut in a brief scene singing "Let Him Go, Let Him Tarry."

TWO CITIES

Production—Anatole de Grunwald   Photography—Derek Williams
Direction—Anthony Asquith   Art direction—Paul Sheriff
Screenplay—Terence Rattigan   Music—Nicholas Brodzsky
Poems—John Pudney   Editing—Fergus McDonell
PLAYERS: Michael Redgrave, Rosamund John, Douglass Montgomery, Renee Asherson, Stanley Holloway, Basil Radford, Felix Aylmer, Bonar Colleano, Joyce Carey, Trevor Howard

WEEK-END   France/Italy (1967)
The violence and materialistic values of modern capitalistic society attacked by Jean-Luc Godard as he follows a young French bourgeois couple on a nightmarish motoring week-end across the French countryside which is seen symbolically as a holocaust of corpses and burning cars. Perhaps no other contemporary movie has attacked the sickness of our age so wittily and perceptively as this one. Photographed in color by Raoul Coutard, Godard's cameraman on, among others, *A Bout de Souffle, Une Femme est une Femme, Vivre Sa Vie, Les Carabiniers, Alphaville.*

COMACICO/COPERNIC/LIRA FILMS (PARIS)/ASCOT CINERAID (ROME)
MIRISCH—SEVEN ARTS/UNITED ARTISTS

Direction—Jean-Luc Godard   Music—Antoine Duhamel;
Screenplay—Jean-Luc Godard   Mozart's Piano Sonata K. 576
Photography (Eastmancolor)—   Editing—Agnès Guillemot
   Raoul Coutard
PLAYERS: Mireille Darc, Jean Yanne, Jean-Pierre Kalfon, Valérie Lagrange, Jean-Pierre Léaud, Yves Beneyton, Paul Gégauff, Daniel Pommereulle

WEST SIDE STORY   U.S.A. (1961)
A modern and musical Romeo and Juliet story choreographed by Jerome Robbins and set in the slums of Manhattan's Upper West Side where the rival street gangs of the native New Yorkers (the Jets) and the immigrant Puerto Ricans (the Sharks) battle continually for supremacy. Falls away somewhat after a brilliant opening ten minutes,

475

West Side Story

but still far ahead of other stage-adapted musicals. The best *film* musical since Kelly and Donen's *On the Town* (1949) and *Singin' in the Rain* (1952). Most notable numbers are "Tonight," "Maria," "Somewhere," the satirical "Gee, Officer Krupke!" and the exhilarating rooftop dance "America." Based on Leonard Bernstein's 1957 Broadway hit and shot mostly on location in New York. Ten, and for once deserved, Academy Awards, including best film, best direction (Wise & Robbins), and best color photography.

MIRISCH–SEVEN ARTS/UNITED ARTISTS

Production–Robert Wise
Direction–Robert Wise &
    Jerome Robbins
Screenplay–Ernest Lehman
Book–Arthur Laurents

Photography (*Technicolor/*
    Panavision 70)–
    Daniel L. Fapp
Production design–Boris Leven
Choreography–Jerome Robbins

Music—Leonard Bernstein   *Music conductor*—Johnny Green
Lyrics—Stephen Sondheim   *Editing*—Thomas Stanford
PLAYERS: Natalie Wood, Richard Beymer, Russ Tamblyn, Rita Moreno, George Chakiris, Simon Oakland

WESTERNER, THE   U.S.A. (1940)
Stolid, underrated, unusually realistic Western about a dispute between farmers and cattlemen over land rights in frontier Texas. Magnificently photographed by the great Gregg Toland (the fifth of his seven films for Wyler) and excellently played by Walter Brennan as the crooked Judge Roy Bean (Academy Award, best supporting actor, 1940).

GOLDWYN/UNITED ARTISTS

Production—Samuel Goldwyn   *Photography*—Gregg Toland
Direction—William Wyler   *Additional exteriors*—
Screenplay (from story by Stuart   Archie Stout
   N. Lake)—Jo Swerling,   *Music*—Dimitri Tiomkin
   Niven Busch   *Editing*—Daniel Mandell
PLAYERS: Gary Cooper, Walter Brennan, Fred Stone, Doris Davenport, Forrest Tucker, Lillian Bond, Paul Hurst, Chill Wills

WESTFRONT 1918   Germany (1930)
Famous German film about the agonies suffered by young soldiers in trench warfare during World War I was made and released the same year as Milestone's classic *All Quiet on the Western Front* and suffering inevitably in comparison. It is memorable nonetheless and belongs with the great antiwar films of all time. Directed by G. W. Pabst whose use of a mobile camera added considerably to the realism of the battle scenes.

NEROFILM

Direction—G. W. Pabst   *Photography*—
Screenplay (from the novel Vier   Fritz Arno Wagner,
   von der Infanterie *by Ernst*   Charles Métain
   Johannsen)—Ladislaus Vajda,   *Art direction*—Ernö Metzner
   Peter Martin
PLAYERS: Fritz Kampers, Gustav Diessl, Hans Joachim Moebis, Claus Clausen, Gustav Püttjer, Jackie Monnier

WHAT EVER HAPPENED TO BABY JANE?   U.S.A. (1961)
Bette Davis as drunken half-mad ex-child star, Joan Crawford as crippled

477

sister she sadistically tortures, and Victor Buono as the gross pianist she hires to accompany her on her comeback. Grand Guignol at its most effective, set for most of the time in a decaying Hollywood mansion and handled with considerable style by Robert Aldrich who attempted to repeat the formula three years later with *Hush . . . Hush, Sweet Charlotte.* This was Ernest Haller's next to last picture with Bette Davis, an association which began in 1932 and lasted 32 years.

Davis/Haller pictures: *The Rich Are Always With Us, Dangerous, That Certain Woman, Jezebel, Dark Victory, All This and Heaven Too, The Bride Came C.O.D., In This Our Life, Mr. Skeffington, A Stolen Life* (also photographed by Sol Polito), *Deception, Winter Meeting, What Ever Happened to Baby Jane?, Dead Ringer.*

A SEVEN ARTS ASSOCIATES & ALDRICH PRODUCTION/WARNER BROS.

Executive producer—
  Kenneth Hyman
Associate producer & director—
  Robert Aldrich
*Photography—*Ernest Haller

Screenplay (based on novel by
  *Henry Farrell)—*Lukas Heller
*Art direction—*William Glasgow
*Musical score—*Frank DeVol
*Editing—*Michael Luciano

PLAYERS: Bette Davis, Joan Crawford, Victor Buono, Marjorie Bennett, Maidie Norman, Anna Lee, Barbara Merrill, Julie Allred

WHAT PRICE GLORY   U.S.A. (1926)

Partly dramatic, frequently humorous war movie detailing the amorous exploits of two American marines during their service in World War I. Mixed in with the boisterous comedy are some realistic battle sequences, moments of pathos and strong antiwar attitudes. Based on the stage play and directed by former actor Raoul Walsh, whose early screen roles included playing Lincoln's assassin John Wilkes Booth in *The Birth of a Nation.* Edmund Lowe and Victor McLaglen play the parts of Captain Flagg and Sergeant Quirt of the U.S. Marines and Dolores Del Rio is their French sweetheart.

FOX FILM CORP.

*Direction—*Raoul Walsh
Screenplay (based on play by
  Laurence Stallings & Maxwell
  Anderson)—
  James T. O'Donohoe

*Photography—*John Marta,
  Barney McGill & John Smith
Art direction—
  William S. Darling
*Editing—*Rose Smith

PLAYERS: Victor McLaglen, Dolores Del Rio, Edmund Lowe, William V. Mong, Phyllis Haver, Elena Jurado

478

WHISKY GALORE   Gt. Britain (1948)

The whisky-starved inhabitants of the island of Todday in the Outer Hebrides, deprived of their national beverage because of war rationing, make a daring moonlight raid on a wrecked cargo ship and smuggle some 50,000 cases of whisky past the local home guard. An early Ealing comedy, full of simple, childlike humor and packed with amusing little cameos, the most notable being Basil Radford's portrait of a teetotal and highly conscientious home-guard officer. Alexander Mackendrick's directorial debut.

EALING STUDIOS

Production—Michael Balcon
Direction—
  Alexander Mackendrick
Photography—Gerald Gibbs
Art direction—Jim Morahan

Screenplay (from novel by
  Mackenzie)—Compton
  Mackenzie & Angus Macphail
Music—Ernest Irving
Editing—Joseph Sterling

PLAYERS: Basil Radford, Catherine Lacey, Bruce Seton, Joan Greenwood, Wylie Watson, Gabriella Blunt, Gordon Jackson, Jean Cadell, James Robertson Justice

WHITE HEAT   U.S.A. (1949)

James Cagney as an unbalanced killer (his first gangster role since his Eddie Bartlett in *The Roaring Twenties* ten years earlier) causes havoc with his gang of hoodlums as they commit a series of holdups across the United States. Veteran Raoul Walsh proved that his flair for this kind of movie hadn't deserted him even though this was in fact his last major film in the genre. Margaret Wycherley plays Cagney's tough old ma, Virginia Mayo the moll he slaps around, and Edmond O'Brien is an undercover police officer.

WARNER BROS.

Production—Louis F. Edelman
Direction—Raoul Walsh
Screenplay (suggested by
  story by Virginia Kellogg)—
  Ivan Goff & Ben Roberts

Photography—Sid Hickox
Art direction—Edward Carrere
Music—Max Steiner
Editing—Owen Marks

PLAYERS: James Cagney, Virginia Mayo, Edmond O'Brien, Margaret Wycherly, Steve Cochran, John Archer, Wally Cassell

WHO'S AFRAID OF VIRGINIA WOOLF   U.S.A. (1966)

Film version of Edward Albee's ferocious play about marital relationships; a study of the ceaseless conflict between a middle-aged college professor (Richard Burton) and his blowsy, shrewish wife (Elizabeth Taylor) who between them trap and almost destroy two young campus innocents (George Segal and Sandy Dennis) during one of their vicious no-holds-barred evenings of drunken "fun and games." Brilliantly played, Elizabeth Taylor winning her second Academy Award for her portrayal of the dominating wife.

WARNER BROS.

Production—Ernest Lehman
Direction—Mike Nichols
Screenplay—Ernest Lehman
Photography—Haskell Wexler

Production design—
Richard Sylbert
Music—Alex North
Editing—Sam O'Steen

PLAYERS: Elizabeth Taylor, Richard Burton, George Segal, Sandy Dennis

WILD BUNCH, THE   U.S.A. (1969)

Sam Peckinpah is at his brilliant best in this violent Western about the last days of an outlaw gang in Texas and Mexico during the early years of this century. The opening and closing massacres, parts of which are filmed in slow motion, have earned the film a reputation for excessive violence, but it is perhaps more effective in its quieter passages reflecting on the predicament of a group of men whose time has long since passed and who can now prepare themselves only for death. The performances are fine (particularly William Holden's jaded gang-leader Pike and Emilio Fernandez's smiling Mexican bandit Mapache) and Lucien Ballard's landscapes magnificent.

WARNER-BROS.–SEVEN ARTS

Production—Phil Feldman
Direction—Sam Peckinpah
*Screenplay (from story by
    Walon Green & Roy N.
    Sickner)*—Walon Green &
    Sam Peckinpah

Photography (Technicolor)—
    Lucien Ballard
Art direction—Edward Carrere
Music—Jerry Fielding
Editing—Louis Lombardo

PLAYERS: William Holden, Ernest Borgnine, Robert Ryan, Edmond O'Brien, Warren Oates, Jaime Sanchez, Emilio Fernandez, Ben Johnson, Strother Martin, Albert Dekker, L. Q. Jones

WILD ONE, THE   U.S.A. (1953)

The hostilities and prejudices aroused in the inhabitants of a small Southern town invaded suddenly by a gang of motorcycle hoodlums led by black-leathered Marlon Brando. Something of a period piece now, it is still interesting for Brando's performance and for Lee Marvin's minor portrait of a rival gang leader. Directed by German-born Laslo Benedek who, a year earlier, had directed *Death of a Salesman* for Kramer.

COLUMBIA

Production—Stanley Kramer
Direction—Laslo Benedek
Screenplay (*based on story by Frank Rooney*)—
John Paxton

Photography—Hal Mohr
Art direction—Walter Holscher
Music—Leith Stevens
Editing—Al Clark

PLAYERS: Marlon Brando, Mary Murphy, Robert Keith, Lee Marvin, Jay C. Flippen, Hugh Sanders

WILD RIVER   U.S.A. (1960)

Minor Elia Kazan movie portraying the conflict between the Tennessee Valley Authority and an 80-year-old woman who refuses to give up her island home to make way for the Tennessee River flood-prevention dam. Set in the 1930's and based on characters and incidents in two separate novels. Jo Van Fleet, whom Kazan earlier directed to an Academy Award in *East of Eden*, plays the old woman and Montgomery Clift a TVA agent. Distinguished color location work by underrated cameraman Ellsworth Fredericks.

TWENTIETH CENTURY—FOX

Production & direction—
Elia Kazan
Screenplay (*from* Mud on the Stars *by William Bradford Huie and* Dunbar's Cove *by Borden Deal*)—Paul Osborn

Photography (*DeLuxecolor/CinemaScope*—
Ellsworth Fredericks
Art direction—Lyle R. Wheeler & Herman Blumenthal
Music—Kenyon Hopkins
Editing—William Reynolds

PLAYERS: Montgomery Clift, Lee Remick, Jo Van Fleet, Albert Salmi, Jay C. Flippen

WILD STRAWBERRIES (Smultronstället)   Sweden (1957)

The story of 24 hours in the life of an aged Stockholm professor who, as he travels by car to receive an honorary doctorate at a university, recollects his past experiences and becomes aware, for the first time, of his failings and shortcomings and the reasons for his wretched loneliness. A profound, cleverly constructed film that mixes flashbacks and dream sequences with reality and that reveals, with each new character it introduces—the professor's son, his daughter-in-law, a young girl hitchhiker, etc.—a new side to the old man's personality. Still the best of Bergman's "modern" films and wonderfully performed by veteran actor/director Victor Sjöström as the professor.

SVENSK FILMINDUSTRI

Screenplay & direction—
  Ingmar Bergman
*Photography—*Gunnar Fischer

*Art direction—*Gittan Gustafsson
*Music—*Erik Nordgren
*Editing—*Oscar Rosander

PLAYERS: Victor Sjöström, Ingrid Thulin, Bibi Andersson, Gunnar Björnstrand, Folke Sundquist, Björn Bjelvenstam, Naima Wifstrand, Jullan Kindahl

WILL PENNY   U.S.A. (1967)

Downbeat Western with Charlton Heston in one of his most accomplished roles as an illiterate, middle-aged cowboy roaming across the Old West from one cattle drive to the next, trying desperately to come to terms with his ever-increasing loneliness. The plot of the film—Heston's involvement with a pioneer woman and with a fanatical preacher whose son he has killed in self-defense—is of secondary importance. What gives the film its stature is its portrait of the West as it really was, a dirty, lonely, unromantic place made up of small bleak townships. This authentic view of the West puts the movie on a par with some of the early Hart Westerns and also with such later classics as *The Gunfighter* and *Shane*. The photography is by Lucien Ballard whose most distinguished work of the last ten years has usually been in the Western genre, i.e. *Guns in the Afternoon, The Wild Bunch, True Grit,* etc.

PARAMOUNT/AN ENGEL/GRIES/SELTZER PRODUCTION

*Production—*Fred Engel &
  Walter Seltzer
*Direction—*Tom Gries
Photography (Technicolor)—
  Lucien Ballard

*Screenplay—*Tom Gries
*Art direction—*Hal Pereira &
  Roland Anderson
*Music—*David Raksin
*Editing—*Warren Low

PLAYERS: Charlton Heston, Joan Hackett, Donald Pleasance, Lee Majors, Anthony Zerbe, Jon Francis, Bruce Dern, Gene Rutherford

WINCHESTER 73   U.S.A. (1950)

A well-constructed Western about an 1873 Winchester rifle—"The Gun That Won the West"—which is won and lost by James Stewart in a shooting competition and which passes through many hands before returning to its rightful owner. Some excitingly staged action scenes include a cliff-top rifle duel and two impressive performances from John McIntire as an Indian trader and Dan Duryea as a half-crazy outlaw killer. The first of Anthony Mann's eight pictures (most of them Westerns) with James Stewart and along with *The Gunfighter* and *Broken Arrow* one of the most important Westerns of the early fifties.

UNIVERSAL–INTERNATIONAL

Production—Aaron Rosenberg
Direction—Anthony Mann
Screenplay (*from story by Stuart N. Lake*)—
  Robert L. Richards,
  Borden Chase

Photography—William Daniels
Art direction—Bernard
  Herzbrun, Nathan Juran
Musical direction—
  Joseph Gershenson
Editing—Edward Curtiss

PLAYERS: James Stewart, Shelley Winters, Dan Duryea, Stephen McNally, Millard Mitchell, Charles Drake, John McIntire, Will Geer, Jay C. Flippen

WIND ACROSS THE EVERGLADES   U.S.A. (1958)

One of the best but least known of Nicholas Ray's films, this intelligent picture centers on the attempts of a young Bostonian schoolteacher (Christopher Plummer) to preserve wild bird life in turn-of-the century Florida and on his clash with a red-bearded snake charmer called Cottonmouth (Burl Ives) who lives in the Everglades with his piratical crew of poachers. An unusual, beautifully photographed little work; Gypsy Rose Lee appears in a minor role as the owner of a sordid Miami saloon.

WARNER BROS. (SCHULBERG PRODUCTIONS)

Production—Stuart Schulberg
Direction—Nicholas Ray
Photography (*Technicolor*)—
  Joseph Brun

Screenplay—Budd Schulberg
Art direction—Richard Sylbert
Editing—George Klotz &
  Joseph Zigman

PLAYERS: Burl Ives, Christopher Plummer, Gypsy Rose Lee, Tony Galento, Emmett Kelly, Sammy Renick

WINDFALL IN ATHENS   Greece (1954)

A winning lottery ticket, lost by a Greek girl while bathing in a swimming pool, involves her in a romance with the young cabaret singer who claims the prize. A lighthearted little fairy tale important because it put Greek films on the international map. Shot in only five weeks by Michael Cacoyannis (his first film) on location in Athens.

483

Direction—Michael Cacoyannis   *Photography*—Alvize Orfanelli
Original story & screenplay—   *Art direction*—Yanni Tsarouchi
  Michael Cacoyannis   *Music*—Andrea Anagnosti
PLAYERS: Ellie Lambetti, George Pappas, Dimitri Horn, Tasso Cavvadia, Sappho Notara, Margarita Papageorgiou

WINDOW, THE   U.S.A. (1948)

Imaginative 10-year-old Bobby Driscoll, well known in his district as a teller of tall stories, witnesses a murder and is nearly killed because neither the police nor his parents will believe him. A modest, taut thriller from RKO, among the most impressive sleepers of the late 1940's. Arthur Kennedy and Barbara Hale are the boy's parents, and Paul Stewart and Ruth Roman the killers. Directed by former cameraman Ted Tetzlaff.

RKO RADIO

Production—Frederic Ullman, Jr.   *Art direction*—Walter E. Keller &
Direction—Ted Tetzlaff   Sam Corso
Screenplay—Mel Dinelli   *Music*—Roy Webb
Photography—William Steiner   *Editing*—Frederic Knudtson
PLAYERS: Barbara Hale, Arthur Kennedy, Bobby Driscoll, Paul Stewart, Ruth Roman

WINGS   U.S.A. (1927)

Ambitious aviation movie with a hackneyed plot about two American pilots (Charles "Buddy" Rogers and Richard Arlen) who find themselves rivals for the affections of small-town girl Clara Bow. The story line matters little, however. More important are the expertly staged action sequences which incorporate some of the most spectacular stunt flying then seen on the screen. The film, first to win a Hollywood Oscar, was directed by William A. Wellman who served with the Lafayette Escadrille during the First World War. Wellman also directed numerous other air movies (*Man with Wings, The High and the Mighty* and *Lafayette Escadrille* among them) during his career.

PARAMOUNT

Production—Lucien Hubbard   *Screenplay*—Hope Loring &
Direction—William A. Wellman   Louis D. Lighton
Story—John Monk Saunders   *Photography*—Harry Perry
                             Editing—Lucien Hubbard
PLAYERS: Charles "Buddy" Rogers, Clara Bow, Richard Arlen, Gary Cooper, Jobyna Ralston, El Brendel, Richard Tucker

Winter Light

WINTER LIGHT (Nattvardsgästerna)   Sweden (1962)
Somber Bergman "chamber" film tracing a single day in the life of a
tormented Swedish pastor who has lost his faith in God through the
death of his wife and who is himself searching desperately for the
spiritual guidance he is unable to give to his parishioners. Bergman
at his most economical and severe; bleak North Sweden settings, impeccable Nykvist photography, fine performances. The second in
Bergman's trio of films explaining his views on man's relationship with
God. Others in the trilogy: *Through a Glass Darkly* and *The Silence*.

SVENSK FILMINDUSTRI

Direction & screenplay—   *Art direction*—P. A. Lundgren
   Ingmar Bergman   *Editing*—Ulla Ryghe
Photography—Sven Nykvist

PLAYERS: Gunnar Björnstrand, Ingrid Thulin, Max von Sydow, Gunnel
Lindblom, Allan Edwall, Olof Thunberg, Elsa Ebbesen, Kolbjörn
Knudsen

WIZARD OF OZ, THE   U.S.A. (1939)
Handsomely mounted film with Judy Garland as the girl who finds
herself in the never-never land of Oz and Ray Bolger (the Straw
Man), Bert Lahr (the Cowardly Lion), and Jack Haley (the Tin

485

Woodman) traveling with her to the Emerald City. Some fine Ham-burg/Arlen songs—"Ding Dong the Witch Is Dead," "We're Off to See the Wizard," and especially "Over the Rainbow"—and delightful performances not only from the principals but also from Margaret Hamilton as the razor-faced wicked Witch of the West and Frank Morgan as the Wizard. The film was photographed in both mono-chrome and Technicolor—the opening scenes, which include a superbly photographed tornado, and closing moments being in black-and-white, and the fantasy sequences (the greater part of the film) in color.

METRO—GOLDWYN—MAYER

Production—Mervyn LeRoy
Direction—Victor Fleming
Screenplay—Noel Langley,
  Florence Ryerson,
  Edgar Allan Woolf
Adaptation (*from* The
  Wonderful Wizard of Oz *by*
  L. *Frank Baum*)—Noel Langley

Photography (*Technicolor*)—
  Harold Rosson
Art direction—Cedric Gibbons
Musical Adaptation—
  Herbert Stothart
Editing—Blanche Sewell
Lyrics (*songs*)—E. Y. Harburg
Music (*songs*)—Harold Arlen

PLAYERS: Judy Garland, Frank Morgan, Ray Bolger, Bert Lahr, Jack Haley, Billie Burke, Margaret Hamilton, Charles Grapewin, Clara Bondick, The Singer Midgets as the Munchkins

WOMAN IN A DRESSING GOWN   Gt. Britain (1957)
Modest, well-observed triangular drama featuring Anthony Quayle as a middle-aged suburban husband torn between his office secretary (Sylvia Sims) and his sluttish but well-meaning wife (Yvonne Mitchell). A familiar story raised well out of the normal rut by the honesty of Ted Willis's screenplay and the performance of Miss Mitchell who deservedly won the best actress award at the 1957 Berlin Film Festival.

ASSOCIATED BRITISH

Production—Frank Godwin &
  J. Lee Thompson
Direction—J. Lee Thompson
Original story & screenplay—
  Ted Willis

Photography—Gilbert Taylor
Art direction—Robert Jones
Music arranged & conducted
  by—Louis Levy
Editing—Richard Best

PLAYERS: Yvonne Mitchell, Anthony Quale, Sylvia Sims, Andrew Ray, Carole Lesley, Michael Ripper, Nora Gordon, Marianne Stone

WOMAN IN THE MOON, THE (Frau im Mond) Germany (1929)
Fritz Lang's last silent film, a 2½-hour science-fiction melodrama

about a manned rocket flight to the moon, is marred somewhat by a weak story line and poor characterization, but redeemed by the realism of its rocket interiors and exciting photography of the lunar landscapes. Professor Oberth and Professor Ley acted as Lang's technical advisers on the film. Oberth remained in Germany and became a Nazi, but Ley fled the country to work as a rocket expert in the United States.

FRITZ-LANG–FILM G.M.B.H.–UFA

Production & direction—
Fritz Lang
*Screenplay—*Fritz Lang,
Thea von Harbou
*Photography—*Curt Courant,
Oskar Fischinger,
Otto Kanturek

Special effects—
Konstantin Tschetwerikoff
Technical advisors—
Hermann Oberth, Willy Ley
*Art direction—*Otto Hunte,
Emil Hasler, Karl Vollbrecht
*Music—*Willy Schmidt-Gentner

PLAYERS: Gerda Maurus, Willy Fritsch, Fritz Rasp, Gustav von Wangenheim, Klaus Pohl, Gustl Stark-Gstettenbaur, Margarete Kupfer, Tilla Durieux

WOMAN IN THE WINDOW, THE   U.S.A. (1944)
Neatly made thriller with meek New York psychology professor (Edward G. Robinson) becoming involved in murder and blackmail during his family's summer vacation in the country. Crisp direction by Fritz Lang and some impressive Milton Krasner camera work but suffers eventually from a too cute final scene in which the whole story is revealed to have been nothing but a dream. Dan Duryea (superb) plays a blackmailer and Joan Bennett the girl whose portrait starts the chain of events in motion.

CHRISTIE CORP.–INTERNATIONAL PICTURES–RKO RADIO

*Production—*Nunnally Johnson
*Direction—*Fritz Lang
Screenplay (from novel Once
Off Guard *by J. H. Wallis)—*
Nunnally Johnson

*Photography—*Milton Krasner
*Art direction—*Duncan Cramer
*Music—*Arthur Lang
*Editing—*Marjorie Johnson

PLAYERS: Edward G. Robinson, Joan Bennett, Raymond Massey, Dan Duryea, Edmond Breon, Thomas E. Jackson, Arthur Loft, Dorothy Peterson

WOMAN OF THE YEAR   U.S.A. (1942)
Spencer Tracy as baseball correspondent marrying and constantly bickering with "Woman of the Year" Katharine Hepburn, an international affairs correspondent on the same newspaper. The old theme

of husband versus career wife is made brilliantly funny by the delicious Lardner/Kanin screenplay, George Stevens' expert comedy direction, and the faultlessly timed performances of the two principals.

METRO–GOLDWYN–MAYER

Production–
  Joseph L. Mankiewicz
*Direction–*George Stevens
*Original screenplay–*Ring
  Lardner, Jr., Michael Kanin

*Photography–*Joseph Ruttenberg
*Art direction–*Cedric Gibbons,
  Randall Duell
*Music–*Franz Waxman
*Editing–*Frank Sullivan

PLAYERS: Spencer Tracy, Katharine Hepburn, Fay Bainter, Reginald Owen, Minor Watson, William Bendix, Ludwig Stoessel, Gladys Blake

WORDS AND MUSIC   U.S.A. (1948)

Musical biography of songwriters Richard Rodgers (played by Tom Drake) and Lorenz Hart (Mickey Rooney) is completely uninspired during its straight passages but always entertaining when the music takes over. Guest stars include Gene Kelly and Vera-Ellen (who dance the climactic "Slaughter on Tenth Avenue"), June Allyson ("Thou Swell"), Lena Horne ("Where or When," "The Lady Is a Tramp") and Judy Garland ("I Wish I Were in Love Again" with Rooney and "Johnny One-Note"). The film was lensed by Charles Rosher and Harry Stradling, two of Metro's leading cameramen. Stradling particularly was associated with musicals during the peak period of the late 1940's, i.e. *Till the Clouds Roll By* (with George Folsey), *The Pirate* and *Easter Parade.*

METRO–GOLDWYN–MAYER

*Production–*Arthur Freed
*Direction–*Norman Taurog
*Screenplay–*Fred Finklehoffe
*Story–*Guy Bolton &
  Jean Halloway
Photography (Technicolor)–
  Charles Rosher &
  Harry Stradling

*Art direction–*Cedric Gibbons &
  Jack Martin Smith
Musical direction–
  Lennie Hayton
*Music–*Richard Rodgers &
  Lorenz Hart
*Editing–*A. Akst &
  Ferris Webster

PLAYERS: June Allyson, Perry Como, Judy Garland, Lena Horne, Gene Kelly, Mickey Rooney, Tom Drake, Ann Sothern, Cyd Charisse, Betty Garrett, Janet Leigh, Marshall Thompson, Mel Torme, Vera-Ellen, Jeanette Nolan, Richard Quine, Clinton Sundberg

WORLD OF APU, THE   India (1958)

The third part of Satyajit Ray's trilogy centers on the now grown-up son of the original peasant family, tracing his attempt to earn a living as a writer, his idyllic marriage which ends tragically with his wife's death in childbirth, and his eventual reconciliation with the son he had refused to love. A slow, spiritual, beautiful acted Indian film that brings to a triumphant close one of the most impressive trilogies in the history of the cinema.

SATYAJIT RAY PRODUCTIONS, CALCUTTA

Production, direction &
screenplay (from novel by
Bidhutibhustan Bandapad-
haya)—Satyajit Ray

Photography—Subrata Mitra
Music—Ravi Shankar
Editing—Dulal Dutta

PLAYERS: Soumitra Chatterjee, Sharmila Tagore, Shapan Mukherjee, S. Aloke Chakraverty

WRONG MAN, THE   U.S.A. (1957)

Hitchcock's most underrated film, based on a true police case, is about a jazz musician who is arrested and jailed for a robbery he did not commit. A depressing but most accomplished picture, shot in and around New York City and almost documentary in its presentation of police procedure. Excellently played by Henry Fonda as the wrongly accused man and Vera Miles as his wife.

WARNER BROS.

Production & direction—
   Alfred Hitchcock
Photography—Robert Burks
Art direction—Paul Sylbert,
   William L. Kuehl
Music—Bernard Herrmann

Screenplay (from "The True
   Story of Christopher Emmanuel
   Balestrero" by Anderson)—
   Maxwell Anderson,
   Angus McPhail
Editing—George Tomasini

PLAYERS: Henry Fonda, Vera Miles, Anthony Quayle, Harold J. Stone, Charles Cooper, John Heldabrand, Richard Robbins, Esther Minciotti

WUTHERING HEIGHTS   U.S.A. (1939)

Romantic version of Emily Brontë's tragic love story of the Yorkshire moors is dominated by Laurence Olivier's Heathcliff and by the inspired monochrome camera work of Gregg Toland. Full of suitably gloomy James Basevi interiors and well adapted by Ben Hecht and Charles MacArthur who retained much of the original dialogue in their screenplay. Voted best film of the year by the New York Film Critics (in preference to *Gone With the Wind*) and said to be Goldwyn's favorite of all his productions.

GOLDWYN/UNITED ARTISTS

Production—Samuel Goldwyn
Direction—William Wyler
Screenplay—Ben Hecht &
  Charles MacArthur
Photography—Gregg Toland
Art direction—James Basevi
Music—Alfred Newman
Editing—Daniel Mandell

PLAYERS: Laurence Olivier, Merle Oberon, David Niven, Flora Robson, Donald Crisp, Hugh Williams, Geraldine Fitzgerald, Leo G. Carroll, Cecil Humphreys, Miles Mander

YANKEE DOODLE DANDY   U.S.A. (1942)

James Cagney struts, dances and sings his way to the 1942 Academy Award as George M. Cohan, one of America's most popular composer/entertainers of the early 1900's. A schmaltzy but above average musical biography distinguished not only by Cagney's bouncing performance and Curtiz's direction but by several evergreen numbers—most notably the title song and the patriotic "Over There." Joan Leslie plays Cohan's wife and Walter Huston appears as George M. Cohan, Sr.

WARNER BROS.

Executive producer—
  Hal B. Wallis
Direction—Michael Curtiz
Screenplay (from original story
  by Robert Buckner)—Robert
  Buckner & Edmund Joseph
Photography—
  James Wong Howe
Art direction—Carl Jules Weyl
Music & lyrics—
  George M. Cohan
Music direction—
  Leo F. Forbstein
Dance numbers staged by—
  LeRoy Prinz & Seymour Felix
Editing—George Amy

PLAYERS: James Cagney, Joan Leslie, Walter Huston, Richard Whorf, Irene Manning, George Tobias, Rosemary De Camp

YEARLING, THE   U.S.A. (1946)

Lush Technicolor version of Marjorie Kinnan Rawlings' prizewinning novel about a farmer's son growing into manhood on a small farm in the wild Florida backwoods. Gregory Peck and Jane Wyman as the boy's parents are supported by animals of every description, including dogs, bears, snakes, birds and the pet fawn of the title. Overlong and oversentimental (with sunsets and heavenly choirs) the film is still not without moments of freshness. The chase of an old bear by man and dogs is particularly skilfully handled.

METRO—GOLDWYN—MAYER

Production—Sidney Franklin
Direction—Clarence Brown
Screenplay—Paul Osborn
Photography (Technicolor)—
  Charles Rosher, Leonard Smith
  & Arthur Arling

Art direction—Cedric Gibbons   *Music*—Herbert Stothart
   & Paul Groesse   *Editing*—Harold Kress
PLAYERS: Gregory Peck, Jane Wyman, Claude Jarman Jr., Chill Wills, Clem Bevans, Margaret Wycherly, Henry Travers, Forrest Tucker

YOU CAN'T CHEAT AN HONEST MAN   U.S.A. (1939)
Another of W. C. Fields' original screen "stories," this time about a circus proprietor who is just one step ahead of the local sheriff and whose show is permanently in financial difficulties. Adding to the complications are Edgar Bergen and his ventriloquist dummies Charlie McCarthy and Mortimer Snerd. Slapstick nonsense, funny and expertly rendered; the first of four films made by Fields for Universal.

UNIVERSAL

Production—Lester Cowan   *Photography*—Milton Krasner
Direction—George Marshall   *Art direction*—Jack Otterson
Screenplay (from original story   *Musical direction*—
   by Charles Bogle (W. C.   Charles Previn
   Fields)—George Marion, Jr.,   *Editing*—Otto Ludwig
   Richard Mack & Everett Freeman
PLAYERS: W. C. Fields, Edgar Bergen, Charlie McCarthy, Mortimer Snerd, Constance Moore, Mary Forbes, Thurston Hall, Princess Baba

YOU CAN'T TAKE IT WITH YOU   U.S.A. (1938)
Oscar-winning version of the Moss Hart/George S. Kaufman stage hit; an amusing tale about the escapades of an eccentric family (led by retired businessman Lionel Barrymore) and hitting out, like Capra's earlier social comedies, at wealth and American tycoons and coming down firmly on the side of the little man in his fight against big business. Jean Arthur and James Stewart play the romantic leads and Capra's direction earned him his third Academy Award in five years.

COLUMBIA

Production & direction—   *Art direction*—Stephen Goosson
   Frank Capra   & Lionel Banks
Screenplay—Robert Riskin   *Music*—Dimitri Tiomkin
Photography—Joseph Walker   *Editing*—Gene Havlick
PLAYERS: Lionel Barrymore, Jean Arthur, James Stewart, Spring Byington, Ann Miller, Mischa Auer, Edward Arnold, Halliwell Hobbes, Samuel S. Hinds

YOUNG AND INNOCENT   Gt. Britain (1937)
Another of Hitchcock's double-chase films with hero Derrick de

Marney being chased by the police for a murder he did not commit and he, in turn, trying to find the real culprit—a man with a twitching eye who is eventually discovered in true Hitchcock style with a 145-ft. tracking shot that starts in a hotel lounge and comes to rest finally on the blacked face of a musician playing in a dance band. Bernard Knowles, who photographed such early Hitchcock films as *The Thirty-Nine Steps, The Secret Agent* and *Sabotage,* was behind the camera and Charles Frend (later director of *Scott of the Antarctic* and *The Cruel Sea*) was the editor.

GAINSBOROUGH, GAUMONT–BRITISH PICTURES

Production—Edward Black
Direction—Alfred Hitchcock
Screenplay (from novel by Josephine Tey)—Charles Bennett & Alma Reville

Photography—Bernard Knowles
Art direction—Alfred Junge
Music—Louis Levy
Editing—Charles Frend

PLAYERS: Derrick de Marney, Nova Pilbeam, Percy Marmont, Edward Rigby, Mary Clare, John Longden, George Curzon, Basil Radford

YOUNG MR. LINCOLN   U.S.A. (1939)

Fictitious account of the early career of Abraham Lincoln built mainly around his life as a young lawyer in Springfield where he saves two farm boys from lynching and successfully defends them in court against a charge of murder. A likable, leisurely John Ford film which splendidly evokes the atmosphere of pioneer life in a small town in rural America. Contains perhaps Henry Fonda's best performance as the young Lincoln and an excellent supporting cameo from Donald Meek as prosecuting counsel. Lamar Trotti, one of Hollywood's most accomplished screenwriters of the 1930's and '40's, wrote the script. He later contributed to such distinguished movies as *The Ox-Bow Incident, Wilson* and *The Razor's Edge.*

TWENTIETH CENTURY–FOX

Executive producer—
   Darryl F. Zanuck
Production—Kenneth MacGowan
Direction—John Ford
Screenplay—Lamar Trotti

Photography—Bert Glennon
Art direction—Richard Day &
   Mark Lee Kirk
Music—Alfred Newman
Editing—Walter Thompson

PLAYERS: Henry Fonda, Alice Brady, Marjorie Weaver, Arleen Whelan, Eddie Collins, Pauline Moore, Richard Cromwell, Ward Bond, Donald Meek

Z   France/Algeria (1969)
Based on a novel about the 1963 assassination of a left-wing Greek
deputy, this political thriller (set in an unspecified Mediterranean
country) centers on a young district magistrate (Jean-Louis Trintignant) and his investigation into the death of an influential pacifist
leader (Yves Montand), a death that proves to have been engineered
by police officials and the country's military authorities. Fascist thug-
gery and political corruption have seldom been more savagely attacked
than in this film which proved to be the most honored production of
1969, winning the Jury Prize at Cannes, the New York Critics Award,
and the American Academy Award as best foreign picture of the
year. Music by Mikis (*Zorba the Greek*) Theodorakis.

REGGANE FILM (PARIS)/O.N.C.I.C. (ALGIERS)

Production—Jacques Perrin
Direction—Costa-Gavras
Screenplay (based on novel by
   Vassili Vassilikos)—
   Costa-Gavras & Jorge Semprun

Photography (Eastmancolor
   Print by Technicolor)—
   Raoul Coutard
Art direction—Jacques d'Ovidio
Music—Mikis Theodorakis
Editing—Francoise Bonnot

PLAYERS: Yves Montand, Jean-Louis Trintignant, Jacques Perrin,
Francois Périer, Irene Papas, Georges Géret, Charles Denner, Bernard
Fresson

ZAZIE DANS LE METRO   France (1960)
Inventive and quite ambitious film version of Raymond Queneau's
best-selling novel about a foul-mouthed little nine-year-old (Catherine
Demongeot) and the terrible havoc she causes when she comes to stay
for a weekend with her uncle in Paris. The film allows Louis Malle
to indulge in a whole series of cinematic tricks—the chaotic chase over
the Eiffel Tower is particularly brilliant—and also to make fun of a large
number of well-known film styles, e.g. Mack Sennett comedies, Alan
Resnais, the Marx Bros., etc. Not so successful as the novel, but funny,
fast and very refreshing.

N.E.F. (IRÉNÉE LERICHE)

Direction—Louis Malle
Screenplay, adaptation &
   dialogue—Louis Malle &
   Jean-Paul Rappeneau

Photography (Eastmancolor)—
   Henri Raichi
Art direction—Bernard Evein
Music—Fiorenzo Carpi
Editing—Kenout Peltier

Zazie Dans le Métro

PLAYERS: Catherine Demongeot, Philippe Noiret, Vittorio Caprioli, Yvonne Clech, Hubert Deschamps, Antoine Roblot, Annie Fratellini, Carla Marlier, Jacques Dufilho

ZERO DE CONDUITE (Zero for Conduct)   France (1933)
A 49-minute surrealist fantasy by Jean Vigo about life in a French boarding school and the boys' eventual revolt against the tyranny of their masters. The film looks at the school and the masters from the viewpoint of the boys themselves, e.g. the principal is played by a bearded dwarf and, like Lindsay Anderson's *If . . .* made some 35 years later and also set in a boarding school, is one of the most sustained attacks on authority that the cinema has produced. Jean Vigo died tragically at the age of 29 having made only one other feature (*L'Atalante*) and two shorts (*A propos de Nice* and *Jean Taris, Champion de Natation.*)

ARQUIS FILM

Direction & screenplay—
Jean Vigo
*Photography—*Boris Kaufman

*Assistants—*Albert Rière,
Henri Storck, Pierre Merle
*Music—*Maurice Jaubert
*Lyrics—*Charles Goldblatt

ZIEGFELD FOLLIES   U.S.A. (1945)
Lavish, beautifully colored Minnelli revue made up of a series of unrelated musical numbers and comedy sketches. Among the best numbers: Judy Garland's "A Great Lady Has an Interview," a burlesque
on Tallulah Bankhead; "The Babbit and the Bromide," a Kelly/Astaire
dance duet, and "Limehouse Blues," a dream ballet danced by Fred
Astaire and Lucille Bremer. Among the worst: Esther Williams' water
ballet; Kathryn Grayson's "There's Beauty Everywhere," and the "La
Traviata" sequence sung by James Melton and Marion Bell.

METRO–GOLDWYN–MAYER

Production—Arthur Freed	*Art direction*—Cedric Gibbons,
Direction—Vincente Minnelli	Merrill Pye, Jack M. Smith
Photography (Technicolor)—	*Dance direction*—Robert Alton
George Folsey &	*Musical direction*—
Charles Rosher	Lennie Hayton

PLAYERS: Fred Astaire, Lucille Ball, Lucille Bremer, Judy Garland,
Kathryn Grayson, Lena Horne, Gene Kelly, James Melton, Victor
Moore, Red Skelton, Esther Williams, William Powell, Edward Arnold,
Marion Bell, Cyd Charisse, Robert Lewis, Virginia O'Brien, Keenan
Wynn

ZIEGFELD GIRL   U.S.A. (1941)
Routine backstage Metro musical of the early 1940's. A standard vehicle
of its time although the passing of the years has given it a nostalgic
charm. The performances of an unrepeatable female cast (Lana
Turner, Judy Garland and Hedy Lamarr all appear as Ziegfeld girls)
are quite splendid. Top numbers include Judy Garland's "I'm Always
Chasing Rainbows" and "Minnie from Trinidad" and the duet "Mr.
Gallagher and Mr. Shean" performed by Charles Winninger and Al
Shean. Dance numbers by Busby Berkeley.

METRO–GOLDWYN–MAYER

Production—Pandro S. Berman	*Music & lyrics*—
Direction—Robert Z. Leonard	Nacio Herb Brown,
Screenplay (based on original	Gus Kahn, Roger Edens,
story by William Anthony	Harry Carroll, Joseph
McGuire)—Marguerite	McCarthy, Edward Gallagher,
Roberts & Sonya Levien	Al Shean

Photography—Ray June   *Dance direction*—
Editing—Blanche Sewell   Busby Berkeley
PLAYERS: James Stewart, Judy Garland, Hedy Lamarr, Lana Turner,
Tony Martin, Jackie Cooper, Ian Hunter, Charles Winninger, Edward
Everett Horton, Philip Dorn, Eve Arden, Al Shean

ZORBA THE GREEK   Greece/U.S.A. (1965)

Michael Cacoyannis film about the way the relationship between a
bighearted, grizzled old Greek (Anthony Quinn) and a quiet-spoken
young English writer (Alan Bates) matures during the latter's attempts
to reopen the Cretan mine he has inherited from his father. Long (140
minutes), slow, sometimes pretentious, but of interest for the memorable acting of Lila Kedrova who, as an aging French whore living
in a broken-down hotel with nothing but her memories to keep her
alive, gives one of the great acting performances of the modern cinema.
The film is more famous, however, for Mikis Theodorakis' music score
which became popular the world over.

ROCHLEY/CACOYANNIS

Production & direction—   *Photography*—Walter Lassally
  Michael Cacoyannis   *Art direction*—
Screenplay (based on novel by   Vassilis Photopoulos
  Nikos Kazantzakis)—   *Music*—Mikis Theodorakis
  Michael Cacoyannis   *Editing*—John Dwyre
PLAYERS: Anthony Quinn, Alan Bates, Irene Papas, Lila Kedrova, George
Foundas, Eleni Anousaki, Sotiris Moustakas